PUBLIC PURPOSE IN INTERNATIONAL LAW

Rethinking Regulatory Sovereignty in the Global Era

This text explores how the public purpose doctrine reconciles the often conflicting, but equally binding, obligations that states have to engage in regulatory sovereignty while honoring host-state obligations to protect foreign investment. The work examines the multiple permutations and iterations of the public purpose doctrine and concludes that this principle needs to be reconceptualized to meet the imperatives of economic globalization and of a new paradigm of sovereignty that is based on the interdependence, and not independence, of states. It contends that the historical expression of the public purpose doctrine in customary and conventional international law is fraught with fundamental flaws that, if not corrected, will give rise to disparities in the relationship between investors and states, asymmetries with respect to industrialized nations and developing states, and, ultimately, process legitimacy concerns.

Pedro J. Martinez-Fraga is a partner in Bryan Cave LLP's International Arbitration and Litigation Practice Group, where he is the firm's coleader and the cofounder of the Miami office. He has represented eight countries as lead counsel, and he has served as an arbitrator in ICSID (World Bank) proceedings. Martinez-Fraga graduated from St. John's College, Annapolis (BA, Institutional Awards); and Columbia University (J.D.), where he was Harlan Fiske Stone Scholar; and he holds a PhD (international law) (cum laude) from Universidad Complutense de Madrid. He has published more than fifty articles in fifteen countries, which have been translated into five languages, and he has written five books on public and private international law.

C. Ryan Reetz is a partner in Bryan Cave LLP's International Arbitration and Litigation Practice Group, where he is cofounder and office-managing partner of the firm's Miami office. In addition to serving as counsel and as arbitrator in a wide range of international arbitration matters, he teaches and lectures and publishes extensively on international dispute resolution topics. A member of the American Law Institute since 2005, he served as chair of the Florida Bar International Law Section from 2013 to 2014. Reetz is a graduate of Harvard College (A.B. magna cum laude) and of Boston University School of Law (J.D. summa cum laude).

Public Purpose in International Law

RETHINKING REGULATORY SOVEREIGNTY IN THE GLOBAL ERA

PEDRO J. MARTINEZ-FRAGA
C. RYAN REETZ

CAMBRIDGE
UNIVERSITY PRESS

CAMBRIDGE
UNIVERSITY PRESS

32 Avenue of the Americas, New York, NY 10013-2473, USA

Cambridge University Press is part of the University of Cambridge.

It furthers the University's mission by disseminating knowledge in the pursuit of education, learning, and research at the highest international levels of excellence.

www.cambridge.org
Information on this title: www.cambridge.org/9781107081741

First published 2015

A catalog record for this publication is available from the British Library.

Library of Congress Cataloging in Publication Data
Martinez-Fraga, Pedro J., author.
Public purpose in international law : rethinking regulatory sovereignty in the global era / Pedro J. Martinez-Fraga, Bryan Cave LLP; C. Ryan Reetz,
Bryan Cave LLP.
pages cm
1. Public policy (International law) I. Reetz, C. Ryan, author. II. Title.
KZ1256.M37 2014
341.5–dc23 2014034128

ISBN 978-1-107-08174-1 Hardback

To my mother, Anita Nuñez Aragón, my wife Liza, and my daughters Alejandra Sofía and Valentina Lucía, and in memoriam, *Andrés Fábian Sommerfeld:*

*"My hands are of your colour but I shame to wear a heart so white."**

– Pedro J. Martinez-Fraga

For my parents, Heather and Gene; my wife, Susanne; and our daughter, Samantha, from whom I have learned all that matters most.

– C. R. R

* William Shakespeare, *Macbeth* (Simon & Brown 2011).

Our concern here is not with philanthropy, but with right, and in this context *hospitality* (hospitableness) means the right of an alien not to be treated as an enemy upon his arrival in another's country. If it can be done without destroying him, he can be turned away; but as long as he behaves peaceably he cannot be treated as an enemy. He may request the *right* to be a *permanent visitor* (which would require a special, charitable agreement to make him a fellow inhabitant for a certain period), but the *right to visit*, to associate, belongs to all men by virtue of their common ownership of the earth's surface; for since the earth is a globe, they cannot scatter themselves infinitely, but must, finally, tolerate living in close proximity, because originally no one had a greater right to any region of the earth than anyone else. Uninhabitable parts of this surface – the sea and deserts – separate these communities, and yet ships and camels (the *ship* of the desert) make it possible to approach one another across these unowned regions, and the right to the *earth's surface* that belongs in common to the totality of men makes commerce possible. The inhospitableness that coastal dwellers (e.g., on the Barbary Coast) show by robbing ships in neighboring seas and by making slaves of stranded seafarers, or of desert dwellers (the Arabic Bedouins), who regard their proximity to nomadic peoples as giving them a right to plunder, is contrary to natural right, even though the latter extends to the right of hospitality, i.e., the privilege of aliens to enter, only so far as makes attempts at commerce with native inhabitants possible. In this way distant parts of the world can establish with one another peaceful relations that will eventually become matters of public law, and the human race can gradually be brought closer and closer to a cosmopolitan constitution.

Immanuel Kant, To Perpetual Peace: A Philosophical Sketch 1, 15–16
(Ted Humphrey trans., Hackett Publishing Co., Inc. 2003)

Contents

Foreword

Pedro J. Martinez-Fraga and Ryan Reetz open their very important study with two observations that frame and situate the question they address: What, under international law, may be understood to be State action for a public purpose? On the one hand, the authors observe that ancient Athens – existing in a time of distinct polities – would have no hesitation in concluding that the public purpose of Athens was, of course, what Athens concluded it to be: an approach "championing the polity's public purpose objectives often to the detriment of the rights of foreigners" and providing "an inward-looking public purpose that is understood as achieving the common good" of that particular polity. On the other hand, public purpose today – existing in a time of economic globalization – *must* have a meaning other than that given by a particular nation at a particular time. The first observation, the authors argue, fits a world of independence "where national interests were perceived to be segregated from the common concerns of the international community of states." The second observation, in the authors' view, fits a world of interdependence, one that results from economic globalization and where both Home and Host States have expectations about the fate of capital investment flows.

Observing that a shift from the first observation to the second is needed, the authors argue that the concept and content of "public purpose" in international law remains "elusive" and is "not rigorously defined." Even as globalization calls for clarity, the authors argue that the public purpose doctrine instead "reflects a substantively bankrupt doctrine that is nearly eviscerating itself."

In setting for themselves the task of taking a "modest step toward this now quite necessary undertaking," the authors give us a learned volume that is rich in its reference to practice, masterfully broad in its reach to associated fields, and unusually deep in its reflection on how a complex river of judicial decisions and international and national instruments is shaping the course of what we will come to know as public purpose. Their study nimbly goes from treaty to custom and back again. Their investigation starts with the rambling text of the North American Free Trade Agreement (NAFTA) and the jurisprudence it has spawned, and it treats with great care the relevance and significance of trade conceptions but then dives deeply into public purpose as a part of the jurisprudence of human rights courts. The study examines the subtle influence of the fact that investment protection is, for the most part, bilateral rather than multilateral – although this fact may yet shift. Finally, in a deft juxtaposition reframing their initial two observations, the authors revisit the principle of sovereignty over natural resources as an expression of a world of independent states and illuminate the modern national practice of foreign investment statutes that "may be used in concert among interested members of the international community to render the public purpose doctrine relevant to the needs of nations and to the struggle for transparency in the quest for process legitimacy."

Fifteen years into the twenty-first century, the investor-states arbitration system is, quite appropriately, held to a very high standard and, not surprisingly, is often found wanting in particular cases or in particular respects. This study is a part of the answer to the dilemma facing the investor-state arbitration system that will be with us for the foreseeable future. Tribunals necessarily rely on counsel to argue the facts and the law. But counsel, in presenting cases to tribunals, cannot for reasons of time and expense undertake to understand "public purpose" and other difficult terms as the authors do here. Even if counsel were to attempt this work, they would necessarily do it imperfectly, given that they look from the perspective of their client. It is for the academy and the international arbitration bar to together undertake works such as this. That the authors do so without apparent bias to the position of investor or State is to their great credit. To look consistently beyond the perspective of investors or States is an achievement; they do so by looking consistently to understand the definition of "public purpose." As the authors are the first to acknowledge, the process of defining the standard has only begun. But, with their work, Pedro J. Martinez-Fraga and Ryan Reetz have initiated a very important debate. In that debate, their guidelines will play no small part.

David D. Caron
Dean, The Dickson Poon School of Law
King's College London

Acknowledgments

Acknowledgments are compelled. The thoughts and contributions of the authors' students at NYU, Emory, and the University of Navarra, where the authors now teach, and of the University of Miami School of Law, where the authors taught for eight years, have played a decisive role in the writing of this text. They have taught us more than we ever will fully comprehend. Special gratitude is extended to John Berger, senior editor at Cambridge University Press, who supported and believed in this project and without whom this work would not have been possible. Tutor (ret.) Nicholas Maistrellis of St. John's College, Annapolis, helped the authors navigate the deliciously treacherous waters of the Attic Greek in the effort to find the earliest Western expression of public purpose in an interstate context. He was patient and generous with us.

David D. Caron, Dean of the Dickson Poon School of Law, King's College London, was sufficiently gracious to accept the authors' invitation to write a prologue. The Foreword alone justified the writing of the book. The authors appreciate his contribution and valuable insight. Michael H. Graham, professor of law and Dean's Distinguished Scholar for the Profession at the University of Miami School of Law, offered extremely valuable suggestions, particularly regarding the text's structural organization.

Professor Franco Ferrari, director of the Center for Transnational Litigation, Arbitration, and Commercial Law at New York University School of Law, demonstrated that there is such a thing as infinite patience residing within finite human beings. Professor Ferrari spent more weeks than anyone would care to admit focusing on the authors' use of the "decisional law of international investor-state arbitration." His input was central to this effort.

The authors wish to express their gratitude to Professor José E. Alvarez, Herbert and Rose Rubin Professor of International Law at New York University School of Law. Professor Alvarez was mercifully relentless in his review of text and critical analysis. He contributed mightily to every significant aspect of the text's conceptual coherence. Antonio Vasquez Alvarez, a distinguished member of the Ilustre Colegio de Abogados de Madrid, and likely the most versatile lawyer with whom the authors have had the privilege of working, was giving of his time and energy, particularly with respect to those portions of the text comparing and contrasting bilateral investment treaties. His rigor improved the work product. The late Sir Ian Brownlie was extremely generous in offering his thoughts on early formulations of the ideas here. Enrique de Marchena Kaluche, managing partner of Estudio Legal DMK Abogados, read and reread every iteration of the manuscript and offered helpful insights from a civil law perspective. Special acknowledgment is extended to Peter Pantaleo, a gifted New York practitioner who taught the authors that, more often than not, form and substance are one and the same. The authors wish to thank Christian Cameron and Hope Zelinger, who at the time of the initial idea for this book served as research assistants to the authors and were students at the University of Miami School of Law, as well as Kamal Sleiman, who provided further assistance and worked on the Appendices. Fernando Alvarez-Pérez, now an IDR associate at the Bryan Cave Miami office, provided the authors with valuable research during his third year at the University of Chicago School of Law.

It is important, however, to add a disclaimer. Whatsoever inconsistencies or ill-witted propositions may be present are all of the authors' doing and have nothing to do with the valuable contributions of those mentioned.

The principal typist, Alexandra Rincones, deserves this recognition and the honors of a Purple Heart. Regrettably, the authors can only provide her with the former. The authors' legal assistants, Ericka Garcia and Nivia Lascaibar, certainly deserve more recognition than we could ever provide to them by reason of this mention.

Introduction and Sketch of Historical Origins

Economic globalization and non-territorially based understandings of sovereignty have underscored a need to revisit – or perhaps just simply visit – the role of the public purpose doctrine in customary and conventional international law. The tension between a State's legitimate right to regulate and its equally genuine and binding obligations concerning foreign investment protection often rests on the scope and application of this doctrine. Unlike the orthodox territorially grounded principle of sovereignty, the public purpose doctrine has commanded little attention from jurists and scholars. Therefore, it has not developed to meet the multiple demands of capital-exporting and capital-importing countries in a global environment. The legacy public purpose doctrine[1] reflects a substantively bankrupt doctrine that is nearly eviscerating itself. Economic globalization has called for a qualification of public purpose in international law. This text seeks to contribute the mere suggestion of a first modest step toward this now quite necessary undertaking.

In order to contextualize the nature of the relevant issues that place in high relief the inadequacies of the legacy-orthodox application of the public purpose doctrine in an era of economic globalization and of an attendant conceptualization of sovereignty that prioritizes the needs of the international community over the perceived national interests of particular States, the

[1] The term "legacy public purpose doctrine" is used throughout the text. For purposes of this writing, the term "legacy public purpose doctrine" refers to the common juridical public purpose doctrine that arises from a governmental pronouncement pursuant to which the term is one applied by the States subjectively (self-judging) that purports to concern the general interests of citizens within a single State that overrides – because of its "public" nature – the interests of a particular citizen in favor of bestowing benefits for the collective members of a polity. It defies an objective standard and is conducive to "all-or-nothing" results because it does not embrace principles of proportionality. The legacy iteration of this principle also is understood to be based on traditional notions of territorially based sovereignty.

origins of the public purpose doctrine in international law, which the authors identify as resting in Classical Greece, need to be summarily reviewed.

The doctrine of public purpose in international law is not a self-evident truth. Its rich origins in Homeric and later Classical Greece, however, have contributed to a modern understanding of the doctrine as a concept that is intuitive, self-evident, and, therefore, one that would only be obscured by discursive reasoning seeking to reduce to syllogistic form its normative foundation. To explain a self-evident truth in order to submit to the light of reason its underpinnings, so the argument suggests, is to obscure the very object sought to be explained. The incomplete conception of the public purpose doctrine developed in Classical Greece as a principle of international law and justice provided very limited conceptual space for the consideration of "foreign" interests while championing the polity's public purpose objectives, often to the detriment of the rights of foreigners.

The Greece of Homer, Socrates, Plato, Aristotle, the great playwrights, and the elegant analytics of Euclidean geometry that gave birth to the founding tenets of Western philosophy, literature, and mathematics, simply did not recognize a common public purpose doctrine that enveloped multiple city-states, expanding beyond the geopolitical subdivisions of a single πολισ ("polis"). The original and legacy origins of public purpose as a principle of international law were sufficiently circumscribed to the political boundaries of the πολισ and to language so as to justify slavery and the taking of a slave's property for the public purpose of serving the common good. It provided for two takings, the first of which was the very act of enslaving (i.e., the taking of a slave as property, as further discussed later in the analysis of terms). Thus, the mere crossing of a political/territorial boundary of one πολισ to the next would transform a free citizen into a slave. The perceived public purpose and benefit to the πολισ was deemed sufficient to justify a dehumanized status of captives from person to commodity. This slave status is most eloquently explained by the actual words used for slaves first appearing in Homer (δμῶσ *f.* or δμοσ *m.*) and later in Attic-Classical Greek (ανδραπωδων), both of which not too loosely may be translated as "plunder with feet."[2] It thus follows that, under this

[2] Even Greece's keenest philosopher argued in favor of the commodification of human beings when concerning slave status. In *Politics*, Aristotle argues:

> Just as the phrase "an article of property" is used akin to the word "part," anything that is a part not only forms by definition part of something else, but also must necessarily belong to such other thing. It is no different as concerns an item of property. Therefore, while it is clear that a master is only the slave's master and cannot belong to the slave, a slave is not just the slave of the master, but also belongs to the master in its entirety.

rubric, the act of enslavement was considered to be little more than the taking of property, of plunder or chattel with feet.

Pursuant to application of international public purpose strictures, Classical Greece understood public purpose as a normative doctrine of international law that enshrined the inwardness of the parochial world of the πολισ. In this context, it makes sense that the Attic Greek word for foreigner, βᾰρβαροσ, originally meant "all who were not Greeks," especially the Medes and Persians. More indicative still of the inwardness that constituted the basis for public purpose and justified sacrificing the rights of "foreigners" is the verb βᾰρβαριζειν, meaning to "speak gibberish," or at best, to enunciate broken Greek; an onomatopoeic word that to the ears of Ancient Greeks resembled the guttural babble of languages other than their own.[3] The root of the English word *barbarian* certainly is related to a conceptual disdain for peoples not Greek, but this conceptualization by itself cannot stand as sufficient to explain public purpose in international law at the time.[4] It is also inextricably

> These propositions clearly establish the nature of slaves and of their fundamental quality. A slave is a human being that by nature is not autonomous and cannot be said to belong to himself, but rather belongs to another human being by dint of the very nature of a slave. Now a human being who belongs to another despite being a person also must be considered an article of property. In turn, an article of property is a chattel, item or instrument that is susceptible to being separated or severed from its owner.

Politics I. II. 6–8.

> A person is by nature a slave when that person is such that he can belong to another person, and indeed it is because of this capacity to belong to another person that he so belongs, and such a person is rational enough to understand belonging to another person but not being himself but a slave; for other than man animals are not subservient, animals do not follow reason, but instead are guided by feelings.

Politics, I. II. 13–14 (translation from the original Greek by the authors).

3 *See, e.g.*, An Intermediate Greek-English Lexicon: Founded upon the Seventh Edition of Liddell and Scott's Greek-English Lexicon, 146 (Oxford University Press, 7th ed., December 31, 1945) [hereinafter Liddell & Scotts Greek-English Lexicon].

4 Plato in his work *The Statesman* suggests that the origins of the word are not based on a theory premised on onomatopoeia. He specifically states:

> It appears as if in classifying peoples (citizens of other States) this classification were to have nearly two parts, a practice that is shared by popular culture among Greeks. On the one hand, one half of all peoples are Greek and the other half, which includes many other peoples unrelated to each other by blood or language, are all classified under the single name of "barbarian," under the thinking that they have identified a single and particular race.

The Statesman, Lines 262 D–E (translation by the authors).

According to Plato's account, the origin is based on an "otherness" that is unrelated to a perception of languages other than Greek.

connected to an inward-looking public purpose that is understood as serving the common good of the πολισ.

Significantly, whereas the intuitive nature of public purpose justified the commodification of free citizens now turned slave when wandering into a foreign jurisdiction, "and even the philosopher, who visited foreign countries to enrich his native land with the merchandise of science and art was exposed to be captured and sold as a slave to some barbarian master,"[5] the taking of "property" in the form of a slave based on a public purpose exercised for the common good of the πολισ was not absolute. A solitary but quite significant and now relevant exception was recognized in the form of a treaty that ostensibly bestowed nonforeigner status on peoples who otherwise would be deemed "barbarians." These original and embryonic precursors to the contemporary concept of *national treatment protection* contained in conventional international law were called σπονδαι in the plural. Even though the original source literature that would explain the normative foundation of an agreement preempting public purpose justification for the taking of property is scant, its meaning is settled. It is connected to "the wine poured out to the gods before drinking."[6] There is consensus, however, that the term for treaty, alliance, truce, or agreement is one and the same, with libations first offered to the gods because, upon signing a truce or treaty, "solemn drink-offerings were made on concluding them."[7]

Parties to the treaties were called εν-σπονδοσ, meaning a party to the treaty, or more literally, "included in a truce or treaty."[8] Similarly, persons or peoples outside of the treaty's ambit (i.e., nonparties or nonsignatories to the convention) were referred to as εκ-σπονδοσ (singular), more literally translated as "out of the treaty, [or] excluded from it."[9]

Conceptually, then, it appears reasonable that any exception to a public purpose-based taking or confiscation in furtherance of the common interests of the πολισ would be qualified by the "sanctity" of a treaty or convention and, in this sense, somewhat partaking in an underlying normative premise connected to the divine.

Except for a treaty or convention blessed by the gods, public purpose-based confiscations or takings for the benefit of the πολισ constituted a settled doctrine of international law well-established in Classical Greece. But for

5 *See* Henry Wheaton, Elements of International Law: With a Sketch of the History of the Science 1 (originally published 1836 by Carey, Lea & Blanchard, reprinted 3d ed. 2002).

6 Liddell & Scotts Greek-English Lexicon, *supra* note 3, at 740.

7 *Id.*

8 *Id.* at 265.

9 *Id.* at 244.

this qualification, public purpose was supreme, preempting all considerations and justifying disregard for foreigners for the benefit of the πολισ. Wheaton, in his venerable chestnut published in 1836, *Elements of International Law: With a Sketch of the History of the Science*,[10] observed that:

> Thucydides has correctly stated the leading political maxim of his countrymen, – "that to a king or commonwealth, nothing is unjust which is useful." The same idea is openly avowed by the Athenians, in their reply to the people of Melos. Aristides distinguished in this respect between public and private morality, holding that the rules of justice were to be sacredly observed between individuals, but as to public and political affairs, a very different conduct was to be followed. He accordingly scrupled not to invoke upon his own head the guilt and punishment of a breach of faith, which he advised the people to commit in order to promote their national interests.[11]

The self-evident and nearly absolute character of the public purpose doctrine as a protagonist in public international law keeps close to its origins and has persisted unchanged into the twenty-first century concerning its (i) attribution of the self-evident status and (ii) virtually unqualified standing and preempted only by *jus cogens*. Consequently, the public purpose doctrine when invoked as part of the exercise of regulatory sovereignty by a State in furtherance of its national interests is generally accepted as application of an intuitive, self-evident truth no different from, for example, fundamental human rights that are not subject to mitigation, exception, or qualification, such as the right to humane treatment,[12] freedom from slavery,[13] the right to a name,[14] and the right to not be subjected to torture or to inhuman or degrading treatment or punishment.[15]

The public purpose doctrine is practically ubiquitous in the form of a material doctrinal and conceptual principle in both customary and conventional international law. It is foremost present in tempering and regulating a State's legitimate right to regulate and in its equally genuine and binding obligation to protect foreign investors and investments. Illustrative in this regard is the conventional and customary international law on expropriation and the taking of property. As a general principle, it is universally accepted that

[10] *See* WHEATON, *supra* note 5.

[11] *Id.*

[12] *See, e.g.*, American Convention on Human Rights art. 5, November 22, 1969, 1144 U.N.T.S. 123 (entered into force on July 18, 1978) [hereinafter American Convention].

[13] *Id.* at art. 6.

[14] *Id.* at art. 18.

[15] *See, e.g.*, European Convention for the Protection of Human Rights and Fundamental Freedoms, as amended by Protocols Nos. 11 & 14, art. 3, November 4, 1950, 213 U.N.T.S. 222 [hereinafter European Convention].

a State has a right to expropriate or nationalize directly or indirectly or to undertake acts tantamount or equivalent to an expropriation or nationalization of property pertaining to a noncitizen so long as such a measure is taken (i) for a public purpose, (ii) in a nondiscriminatory manner, (iii) in accordance with due process of law, and (iv) on payment of compensation. In addition to being central to any analysis concerning the protection of foreign investor rights, defining the scope of a sovereign's regulatory space, and harmonizing conflicts between international trade law and domestic regulations, the doctrine is pivotal to the application of international human rights and to the workings of such public international law doctrines as permanent sovereignty over natural resources and numerous iterations of sustainable development (i.e., health, safety, environment, labor, and economic regulation).

Despite the public purpose doctrine's preeminence in public international law and its time-honored historical prominence, public purpose remains an elusive concept. It is not rigorously defined anywhere in customary or conventional law. What sparse pronouncements exist on "the jurisprudence of public purpose in international law" are mostly inconclusive and merely suggest that, although not without limits, States enjoy wide discretion in determining what constitutes public purpose. Such pronouncements are of little utility for use of the doctrine in the present and inspire little hope for greater understanding in the future.[16] Moreover, the treatment of the doctrine as encompassing "all things public," based on a subjective content that is self-judging on the part of States and therefore not susceptible to challenge, may have been viable in an

[16] Commenting on this issue Schrijver observes:

> In most relevant arbitral decisions, the view has been taken that a lawful nationalization or expropriation must serve a public purpose [citation omitted] but sometimes with qualifications. For example, in the *Liamco case* it was held:
>
> > As to the contention that the said measures were politically motivated and not in pursuance of a legitimate public purpose, it is the general opinion in international theory that public utility is not a necessary requirement for the legality of a nationalisation' [citation omitted]
>
> .... While many conclude that the demand of a "public interest" or "public purpose" should be maintained, there is recognition of the fact that ultimately it is the taking government which determines the public purpose or utility of a particular expropriation, and that in many cases, it can be taken as impossible that an international court or organization can form a reasonable judgment on the accuracy of a claim by a State that an action served a public purpose [citation omitted].
>
> In Summary, a State is not completely free to determine the justification and conditions for a nationalization but is bound by certain international law requirements. In practice, however, it has wide margins of discretion.

Nico Schrijver, Sovereignty over Natural Resources: Balancing Rights and Duties (Cambridge University Press, 1997) at pp. 291–92.

international law framework based on orthodox understandings of sovereignty, in turn premised on territoriality in an environment of pre-economic globalization. Such "practical or functional success" was possible where States asserted "*international-independence*" within a rubric where national interests were perceived to be segregated from the common concerns of the international community of States. This paradigm no longer exists.

The advent of economic globalization has introduced a paradigm of interdependence. Traditional notions of territorially based Westphalian sovereignty are no longer responsive to the common needs of nations. International human rights law serves as a model of a new sovereignty that is neither absolute nor any longer resting on geopolitical borders. In this new space and era that economic globalization delineates, a legacy public purpose doctrine that is self-judging (subjective), based on models of dependence, and conducive to "all-or-nothing" results will frustrate the expectations of both capital-exporting and capital-importing States, as well as the answers to fundamental questions of process legitimacy in the adjudication of investor-state disputes. Can this legacy public purpose doctrine be redefined so as to comport with paradigms of interdependence, the exigencies of economic globalization, and the expectations of Home and Host States? Are there nongovernmental organizations appropriately positioned and sufficiently credentialed to lead this effort? Is the legacy public purpose doctrine susceptible to substantive reconfiguration so as to account for international principles of *proportionality* and *bilateralism?* What would be the mechanics pursuant to which the content, scope, and application of the doctrine may be conditioned in order to satisfy an objective standard? Is the prevailing paradigm of global interdependence sufficiently developed so as to cause the international community of nations to set aside competing interests and reach a consensus on a neutral and objective-based understanding of public purpose in customary and conventional international law?

More fundamentally still, are the various iterations of public purpose, such as environmental concerns; human, animal, and plant life; national security; and exercise of police powers susceptible to being classified under the overarching umbrella nomenclature of "public purpose"? Is the doctrine of public purpose susceptible to hierarchical categorization, if indeed there are multiple subject-matter public purposes? Can a government by decree transform a governmental initiative and objective, such as the "institutionalization" and perpetuation of a political revolutionary agenda, into a public purpose within the purview of the public purpose doctrine? This latter inquiry is particularly applicable in the context of nationalizations or expropriations undertaken in furtherance of the alleged public purpose of promoting purported revolutionary and political ideological principles.

Although not seeking to provide conclusive answers to these inquiries and other equally relevant queries, this contribution does aspire to address these concerns within the framework of six chapters, each of which contains multiple subparts.

The first chapter uses the framework of the North American Free Trade Agreement (NAFTA) as a microcosm of customary and conventional international law to explore the public purpose doctrine as an exception – more precisely a reservation – to treaty obligations addressing investment protection provided to the NAFTA parties. Thus, emphasis is placed on Chapter Eleven of the NAFTA ("Investment Services and Related Matters"). As to methodology, the NAFTA Chapter Eleven first is analyzed strictly within the chapter's context and then more generally in select chapters where public purpose serves a foundational role in defining the scope, content, and application of specific provisions. The treatment of the public purpose doctrine in the NAFTA's text beyond the Chapter Eleven framework is used as a predicate to tracing the doctrine's contours in conventional international law. Foundational NAFTA arbitral opinions (i.e., the NAFTA's "decisional law") also is used as a tool for penetrating the orthodox view of the public purpose doctrine in customary international law. Thus, as Chapter Eleven is to the remainder of the NAFTA framework, so is the entirety of the NAFTA to conventional international law. It also draws a distinction between treaty-based reservation exceptions and public purpose exceptions.

This first chapter sets forth the analytical methodology used in subsequent chapters to identify the workings of the doctrine within the parameters of specific subject-matter treaties, such human rights conventions, but also within international law instruments concerning macroeconomics that have contributed to the formation and transformation of the public purpose doctrine in customary international law. Finally, Chapter 1 aspires to understand whether the cross-fertilization between public purpose-based exceptions imported from international trade law into international investment protection law may affect the relationship among the delicate and competing interests of capital-exporting States and their capital-importing counterparts. The chapter concludes with reflections on conventional international law's use of public purpose.

Chapter 2 aspires to identify both the role and status of the public purpose doctrine in customary international law. It does so, however, first by testing the quantity and content of the public purpose doctrine in customary international law and rejecting an a priori judgment even as to the doctrine's very existence. This chapter posits that common elements of public purpose compellingly argue in favor of a single public purpose doctrine that, even when embedded in instruments that limit a State's domestic regulatory space, the doctrine despite its multiple iterations broadens the regulatory authority of States. The chapter further advances the proposition that meaningful contributions to the content and scope of the public purpose doctrine arose from the tension between capital-exporting and capital-importing countries. Here, careful consideration is accorded to the World Trade Organization (WTO) Agreement on Trade-Related Aspects of Intellectual Property Rights (1994), the WTO General Agreement on Trade in Services (1994), and the WTO Doha Ministerial Declaration of November 14, 2001, all of which are used as analytical and synthetic instruments that help explain the existing shortcomings of the legacy public purpose doctrine and also are suggestive of detailed ways in which the doctrine can be developed to meet the demands of economic globalization, the interests of both industrialized and underdeveloped countries, and the often conflicting requirements of a paradigm of transnational political and economic interdependence. The recurring motif of the right to regulate and this right's relationship to a State's international obligations is viewed in the context of the United Nations Conference on Trade and Development (UNCTAD) World Investment Report 2012 and the Principle of Sustainable Development.

The public purpose doctrine's role in the law of international human rights is examined through the lenses of (i) the African Charter on Human and People's Rights, (ii) the European Convention on Human Rights, and (iii) the Inter-American Convention on Human Rights in Chapter 3. These three conventions are used to analyze the extent to which the public purpose doctrine has been influenced by regional historical developments as to scope and content. In this context, historicity is understood as a temporal and constraining element that need not form part of the public purpose doctrine of the twenty-first century. Chapter 3 also asserts that delineating the public purpose doctrine as it appears in international human rights law serves as a tenet that is fundamental in identifying a hierarchy of human rights precepts that enjoy a status akin to that of *jus cogens*. The analysis advanced in this chapter helps to facilitate an understanding of public purpose in international law as a doctrine that must be subjected to discursive reasoning and, therefore, cannot be treated as a self-evident truth the normative foundations of which are intuitively known and knowable.

Chapter 4 chronicles the effect of bilateral investment treaties (BITs) on the public purpose doctrine, as well as the doctrine's distortion of symmetry and bilateralism in the conventional international law of investment protection. Specifically, the virtually ad hoc and decentralized framework of BITs is considered from the perspective of the manner in which structural framework issues attendant to BITs have contributed to the contemporary understanding of the legacy public purpose doctrine.

Chapter 5 primarily advances the proposition that the principle of permanent sovereignty over natural resources (PSNR) constitutes an expression of the legacy public purpose doctrine. This chapter also attempts to identify formal and substantive connections between PSNR and the principle of sustainable development; the latter also is treated as an important iteration of the legacy public purpose doctrine. The status of the public purpose doctrine in customary international law is critically revisited in this chapter. The conceptual effects of PSNR on regulatory sovereignty and Host-State investor protection obligations are also reviewed.

Finally, Chapter 6 addresses domestic legislation purporting to protect foreign investors in order to attract foreign direct investment (FDI). This chapter compares and contrasts foreign investment protection statutes (FIPS) to BITs, focusing on structure, content, and the role of the public purpose doctrine. In addition, it is suggested that the FIPS' structural configuration may serve as a practical and effective instrument of reform that may contribute to the much needed remedial work that is required to redeem the public purpose doctrine's promise to harmonize the right to engage in regulatory sovereignty with the obligation to enforce juridically binding foreign investor protection obligations. This final chapter aspires to demonstrate the subtle and more immediate relationships between the preceding five chapters and eight very particular suggestions of ways in which FIPS may be used in concert among interested members of the international community to render the public purpose doctrine relevant to the needs of nations and to the struggle for transparency in the quest for process legitimacy.

1

Public Purpose in NAFTA

The North American Free Trade Agreement (NAFTA)[1] constitutes an ideal petri dish for any inquiry into the status of the public purpose doctrine in public international law. Featuring a comprehensive self-contained treaty structure that comprises eight parts, twenty-two chapters, and seven annexes, the NAFTA can serve as a microcosm of public international law, particularly concerning trade and investment. In addition, this treaty framework, most notably because of its Chapter Eleven ("Investment"), has spawned its own "jurisprudence" arising from contracting party arbitrations. This "decisional law," at least theoretically, in part serves to help define fundamental principles of international trade and investment law that are endemic to the NAFTA.

The seemingly all-encompassing breadth of the NAFTA treaty framework, ranging from national treatment and market access for goods to temporary entry for business persons, together with ambitious but practical objectives concerning (i) the elimination of barriers to trade, (ii) the promotion of conditions for fair competition in a free trade area, (iii) a commitment to increasing investment opportunities, (iv) the protection of intellectual property rights, (v) the provision of procedures for dispute resolution, and (vi) the establishment of a framework for further trilateral, regional, and multilateral cooperation to maximize the benefits of the treaty, provide an ideal configuration for understanding the role of the public purpose doctrine more broadly in customary and conventional international law beyond the scope of just a single treaty. Put simply, the NAFTA, with the benefit of the investor-state decisional law that it has spawned, much like Leibniz's monads – each said to have been imperceptibly small but reflecting the entire universe – can be said to embody in some sense the fundamental precepts of the public

[1] North American Free Trade Agreement, U.S.-Can-Mex., December 17, 1992, 32 I.L.M.639 (1993) (hereinafter NAFTA).

international law of trade and investment protection. Equally relevant for the purposes of this analysis is the NAFTA's application of the public purpose doctrine broadly throughout the whole of its treaty framework, but more particularly in its Chapter Eleven rubric. The NAFTA both references and relies on the public purpose doctrine directly in the most pristine form of its nomenclature as "public purpose" and less explicitly pursuant to the doctrine's multiple iterations, such as "public order," "public morals," and "social welfare." It develops a "public purpose standard" while also relying doctrinally on public purpose as a substantive principle explicitly having specific categorical or subject matter content, and thus it presents the compelling case of a principle that is more than a "boiler plate catchall" that conceivably concerns a sovereign's exercise of sovereignty under the banner of the public good. The NAFTA is ideally tailored to an exploration of the role, scope, and content of public purpose in conventional and customary international law. Accordingly, this first chapter serves to identify the fundamental workings of the public purpose doctrine in a treaty framework and includes analyses of the doctrine's iterations, subject matter content, application, and scope. In tracing the edges of public purpose within the NAFTA framework, an analytical "blueprint" will be developed that, in turn, will be applied more comprehensively in identifying the relationship between public purpose and the sphere of regulatory sovereignty in the context of divergent international law instruments forming part of customary international law. The challenge of identifying and understanding public purpose within the doctrine is one and the same, from a purely analytical perspective, as identifying and studying the doctrine's role and effect in customary international law. Challenges common to a single treaty analysis and consideration of numerous international law instruments pertaining to different fields of law and regions of the world promise to facilitate the exercise while preserving its virtually infinite and inviting challenges.

The NAFTA rubric has carved out a meaningful and substantive space for public purpose. Throughout the NAFTA Chapter Eleven scheme,[2] public

[2] Chapter Eleven of the North American Free Trade Agreement forms part of PART 5 entitled: INVESTMENT SERVICES AND RELATED MATTERS, Chapter 11, Investment. This chapter of the NAFTA is most unique because it comprises both international trade law and international investment law, at times indiscriminately intermingling both concepts. *Id.*

For example, Chapter Eleven incorporates the orthodox standards found in customary and conventional international investment law aimed at protecting foreign investors that also represent substantive claims for affirmative relief: Article 1102 ("National Treatment"), Article 1103 ("Most-Favored-Nation Treatment"), Article 1104 ("Standard of Treatment"), Article 1105 ("Minimum Standard of Treatment"), and Article 1106 ("Waiver of Performance Requirements"). *Id.*

purpose is explicitly referenced only once.[3] The doctrine of public purpose, however, is conceptually addressed without the identifying "public purpose" nomenclature on ten distinct occasions.[4] The most significant reference is found in Article 1101(4). This provision reflects well-conceived temperance on the part of the NAFTA parties in their treatment of public purpose. The Article merits citation in its entirety:

> 1. This Chapter applies to measures adopted or maintained by a Party relating to:
>   investors of another Party;
>   investments of investors of another Party in the territory of the Party; and

Significantly, however, Paragraph 6 of Article 1106 engages in the wholesale importation of recognized principles of international trade law that comprise the fundamental general exceptions found in Article XX of the General Agreement on Tariffs and Trade (GATT) relating to the protection of human, animal, or plant life and health:

> Provided that such measures are not applied in any arbitrary or unjustifiable manner, or do not constitute a disguised restriction on international trade or investment, nothing in paragraphs 1(b) or (c) or 3(a) or (b) shall be construed to prevent any Party from adopting or maintaining measures, including environmental measures:
> (a) necessary to secure compliance with laws and regulations that are not inconsistent with the provisions of this Agreement;
> (b) necessary to protect human, animal or plant life or health; or
> (c) necessary for the conservation of living or non-living exhaustible natural resources.

Id. art. 1106 ¶ 6; *cf.* General Agreement on Tariffs and Trade art. XX, October 20, 1947, 55 U.N.T.S. 188, 262 [hereinafter GATT]. The challenges that the co-mingling of international trade law and international investment law principles raise are significant with respect to the development of a public purpose doctrine that seeks legitimacy based on an objective standard, uniform application, and a configuration that comports with the effects of economic globalization on the concept of sovereignty in the twenty-first century, as more fully discussed in this text.

3 NAFTA Article 1110, entitled "Expropriation and Compensation," directly references "public purpose" as one of four predicates to a lawful *nationalization* or *expropriation* under international law. Article 1110 reads:

> **Expropriation and Compensation**
> 1. No Party may direct or indirectly nationalize or expropriate an investment of an investor of another Party in its territory or take a measure tantamount to nationalization or expropriation of such an investment "(expropriation"), except:
> (a) for a public purpose;
> (b) on a non-discriminatory basis;
> (c) in accordance with due process of law and Article 1105(1); and
> (d) on payment of compensation in accordance with paragraphs 2 through 6.

NAFTA, *supra* note 1, art. 1110 ¶ 1(a)–(d) (emphasis added).

4 *See, e.g., Id. art.* 1101 ¶ 4; art. 1105 ¶ 3; art. 1106 ¶¶ 2, 4, 6(a)–(c); art. 1108 in 1, 3; art. 1110 ¶ 8; art. 1114 IR 1, 2.

with respect to Articles 1106 and 1114, all investments in the territory of the Party.

2. A Party has the right to perform exclusively the economic activities set out in Annex III and to refuse to permit the establishment of investment in such activities.
3. This Chapter does not apply to measures adopted or maintained by a Party to the extent that they are covered by Chapter Fourteen (Financial Services).
4. Nothing in this Chapter shall be construed to prevent a Party from providing a service or performing a function *such as* law enforcement, correctional services, income security or insurance, social security or insurance, social welfare, public education, public training, health, and childcare, in a manner that is not inconsistent with this Chapter.[5]

The term "such as" in Paragraph 4 suggests that the NAFTA parties were aware that reducing the public purpose doctrine to a definition was not possible.[6] The eleven disciplines identified in Paragraph 4, ranging from law enforcement to childcare, are neither exclusive nor exhaustive. Instead, they are categorical but thematically consistent with each other based on having a "public character" as a common denominator.[7]

5 *Id.* art. 1101 (emphasis added).

6 *See, e.g.*, Alberto R. Salazar V., PhD, *NAFTA Chapter 11, Regulatory Expropriation, and Domestic Counter-Advertising Law*, 27 ARIZ. J. INT'L & COMP. L. 31, 44–45 (2010) (identifying Article 1101(4) as one of the provisions in Chapter Eleven that operates to "shed important light on a possible definition of public purpose," but noting that "while this NAFTA provision permits governments to provide essential public services, it largely limits or negates the public purpose exception to trade rules due to its NAFTA compatibility requirement"); Benjamin W. Jenkins, *The Next Generation of Chilling Uncertainty: Indirect Expropriation Under CAFTA and Its Potential Impact on Environmental Protection*, 12 OCEAN & COASTAL L.J. 269, 294 (2007) (arguing that Article 1101(4) "highlights the uncertainty surrounding when a legitimate public policy goal might be considered an expropriation" and that in some circumstances the services alluded to in the provision "could be provided in a way that is inconsistent with chapter 11"); L. Kinvin Wroth, *Lingle and Kelo: The Accidental Tourist in Canada and NAFTA-Land*, 7 VT. J. ENVTL. L. 62 (2006) (noting that Article 1101(4) recognizes "a Party's right to take domestic measures for certain police power purposes, expressly including environmental measures, though these measures must be consistent with Chapter 11").

7 In the June 15, 1992, draft of Article 1101(4), Mexico sought to broaden the scope of this paragraph by including all branches of government, a public purpose category entitled "Public Retirement Plans," and welfare services. Additionally, "services" identified in statutes pertaining to specific public purpose categories were included:

4. [MEX][Nothing in this Chapter prevents a Party through its executive, legislative and judicial bodies, from providing services or functions such as public welfare services and services forming part of a statutory system of social security, public health care, public education, and public retirement plans to its citizens.]

Article 1101(4) adjusts for the elusive status of public purpose in international law by fashioning a criterion or standard rather than a definition for the doctrine.[8] The final subordinate clause of the paragraph, "that is not inconsistent with this Chapter," is consonant with both a "proportionality" and an "effects test," as the plain language itself invites policy comparison and contrast.

Paragraph 4 of Article 1101 of the NAFTA, when construed as a *standard*, represents a meaningful contribution toward vesting the public purpose doctrine with uniformity while tacitly acknowledging the conceptual difficulties endemic to an international law doctrine characterized by uncertainty and want of predictability because of its subjective content and application.

Draft of June 15, 1992, OFFICE OF U.S. TRADE REP., EXEC. OFFICE OF THE PRESIDENT, NAFTA CH. 11 TRILATERAL NEGOTIATING DRAFT TEXTS [hereinafter NAFTA Negotiating Drafts]. All NAFTA negotiating documents are available for download at the Office of United States Trade Representative, http://www.ustr.gov/archive/assets/Trade_Agreements/Regional/NAFTA/NAFTA_Chapter_11_Trilateral_ Negotiating_Draft_Texts/.

8 The United States, in the August 4, 1992, draft pertaining to this paragraph, sought to place limits on "public purpose" and to limit its subjective content, but in so doing emphasized the circular reasoning that is so common to this undertaking. Specifically, the United States proposed that "[t]he term 'public purpose' does not include the *deliberate* disadvantaging of investors of another Party or country." *Id.* (Draft of August 4, 1992; emphasis added). Pursuant to this stricture, the proscribed conduct would entail an inquiry into the subjective motive ("deliberate") of the State in characterizing an act as within the ambit of public purpose. Consequently, the effort does not bring us closer to a narrowly defined public purpose construct that would limit overreaching by sovereigns. This proposed language formed part of a broader proposal qualifying a sovereign's ability to act through State enterprises:

> USA[1. This Chapter, and in particular the obligation to accord nondiscriminatory treatment to investments in the territory of a Party of investors of another Party, shall apply to the State enterprises of a Party. (n. 16: Mexico can agree to this provision if placed outside the Investment Chapter and only in respect of non-discriminatory treatment when buying and selling goods or services.)
>
> 2. Where a Party owns and controls, at the federal level, State enterprises that are not monopolies, it shall not by provision of subsidies or otherwise, take measures to support such State enterprises in conduct that results in serious prejudice to investors of another Party, contrary to such investors' reasonable expectations. This provision shall not apply where such conduct is authorized by law to fulfill a public purpose and is reasonably related thereto. The term "public purpose" does not include the deliberate disadvantaging of investors of another Party or country.]

Id. (emphasis in original). This proposed provision sought to narrow the scope of State action that may adversely compromise foreign investments on the part of the NAFTA parties. Because the United States and Canada are representative of capital-exporting countries, it is consonant with this status that a narrowing of sovereign action vis-à-vis foreign investment would be welcomed. Here, the United States sought to protect prospective investments in Mexico (it stands to reason primarily but not exclusively) from adverse effects in connection with State-owned entities at the federal level.

Moreover, the configuration of a standard inviting policy analysis as a predicate to application comports with the shifting legal landscape that economic globalization has spawned, a landscape demanding a public purpose doctrine characterized by greater flexibility and certainty. The "NAFTA approach" to public purpose contributes to moving the doctrine further toward an objective space and, in this narrow sense, limits or more literally defines the doctrine by circumscribing it to the categories making up Article 1101(4) or other categories that conform to these elements.[9]

After carefully engaging in a succinct etymological and discriminating survey of the meaning of *standard* in international law, in the context of consistency of fair and equitable treatment as a standard,[10] Tudor provides a composite picture of what is commonly understood by *standard*, reduced to five precepts:

[9] The Canadian Statement on Implementation supports a flexible, "standard-like" construction of Article 1101(4). Helpful language from that text reflects the "such as" approach to public purpose categories:

> The section does not apply to any measure to the extent it is covered by chapter fourteen relating to financial services. Article 1101 affirms the right of a Party to perform functions (such as law enforcement) and to provide services (such as social welfare and health). The article also affirms the right of Mexico to perform exclusively the economic activities set out in annex III, which lists those sectors reserved to the State in the Mexican Constitution. To the extent that Mexico permits foreign investment in these sectors (e.g., in the form of a service contract or joint production arrangement), the protections of the investment chapter apply to that investment.

Government of Canada, *Statement on Implementation of the North American Free Trade Agreement*, CANADA GAZ. PART 1C(1) 147 (January 1, 1994) [hereinafter Canadian Statement on Implementation].

[10] Ioana Tudor identifies various definitions of *standard* in international law that A. Sanhoury, S. Rials, and P. Julliard advance. Sanhoury asserts that a mutation occurs at the apogee of a specific developmental stage of a legal system pursuant to which rules and principles are no longer viable because of their inability to embrace the legal system's own "evolutionary development." He observes that at this stage the *standard* appears as "a more elaborated concept that leaves space for adaptation and evolving situations [which] is embraced in order to make the system function properly. This new concept is the standard. Its nature is more adapted because it is more general and more flexible than rules and principles, and therefore leaves space for interpretation while it can be applied to a broader number of situations." IOANA TUDOR, THE FAIR AND EQUITABLE TREATMENT STANDARD IN THE INTERNATIONAL LAW OF FOREIGN INVESTMENT, OXFORD UNIVERSITY PRESS at 112, 113 (Oxford University Press 2008) (citing A. SANHOURY, LES RESTRICTIONS CONTRACTUELLES A LA LIBERTE INDIVIDUELLE DETRAVAIL DANS LA JURISPRUDENCE ANGLAISE, CONTRIBUTIONS A L'ETUDE COMPARATIVE DE LA REGLE DE DROIT ET DU STANDARD JURIDIQUE (1925)).

Rials defines standard as an indefinite concept "which refers to the fundamental values of society and that analyzes the behaviors of the legal actors by reference to an average conduct." *Id.* at 114 (citing S. RIALS, LE JUGE ADMINISTRATIF FRANCAIS ET LA TECHNIQUE DU STANDARD, ESSAI SUR LE TRAITEMENT JURIDICTIONNEL DE L'IDEE DE NORMALITE 3–4 (1980)).

(i) the broad behavioral direction or an indeterminate concept;
(ii) a large margin of maneuver left to the arbitrator/judge and a very flexible character, which allows the decision maker to adapt to a variety of circumstances;
(iii) a link between law and society;
(iv) the reference point constituting an average social conduct; and
(v) a reference to the conformity between national and international law.[11]

A construction of Article 1101(4) as a standard for public purpose, together with the title of the Article ("Scope and Coverage"), compels an interpretation of the paragraph as one vesting the term "public purpose" within Article 1110(1)(a) with a standard that removes the doctrine from the realm of subjectivity and relativism as to expropriation *and* compensation. By ascribing to public purpose an objective definitional criteria in both theory and practice, the relationship between the competing interests – of (i) protecting foreign investments, (ii) safeguarding the right to regulate (regulatory sovereignty), and (iii) promoting the objectives of international trade law – is best harmonized. The importance of this latter concern is multiplied even further because of the commingling of public purpose categories of international trade law with public purpose concerns underlying fundamental precepts of international investment law. The seven "conceptual references" to public purpose in Chapter Eleven of the NAFTA, particularly in Article 1108,[12] best illustrate the cross-contamination of public purpose elements having their origins

[11] *Id.* at 115.
[12] Article 1108 reads:

Reservations and Exceptions
1. Articles 1102 ["National Treatment Standard"], 1103 ["Most-Favored Nation"], 1106 ["Performance Requirements"], and 1107 ["Senior Management and Boards of Directors"] do not apply to:
(a) any existing non-conforming measure that is maintained by
(i) a Party at the Federal level, as set out in its Schedule to Annex I or **III**,
(ii) a State or province for two (2) years after the date of entry into force of this Agreement, and thereafter as set out by a Party in its Schedule to Annex I in accordance with 2 or,
(iii) a local government;
(b) the continuation or prompt renewal of any non-conforming measure referred to in subparagraph (a); or

an amendment to any non-conforming measure referred to in subparagraph (a) to the extent that the amendment does not decrease the conformity of the measure, as it existed immediately before the amendment, with Articles 1102 ["National Treatment Standard"], 1103 ["Most-Favored Nation"], 1106 ["Performance Requirements"], and 1107 ["Senior Management, Boards of Directors"].

NAFTA, *supra* note 1, art. 1108 ¶ 1(a)–(c).

in international trade law and international investment law but contained within a single chapter of a statutory rubric that must account for the protection of foreign investments while preserving a State's exercise of regulatory sovereignty. The public purpose doctrine theoretically serves as a principle that reconciles these two competing rights and obligations.

Article 1105(3)[13] identifies a public purpose in the form of "subsidies or grants," a concept that amply comports with the NAFTA public purpose standard.[14] This paragraph establishes the preeminence of public purpose in the form of subsidies or grants pertaining to armed conflict or civil strife over the public purpose of protecting foreign investments or investors by according such investments or investors treatment no less favorable than that provided to citizens of the Host State. This pronouncement is quite significant, particularly within the narrow framework of Article 1105, because this article encompasses virtually all of the international investment law standards that, if satisfied, give rise to an affirmative claim for relief on the part of an investor in an international arbitration against a NAFTA party.[15] Thus, even though Article 1105 at first would appear to be an eminently international investment law provision providing for foreign investor protection, it in fact highlights *subsidies* and *grants*, albeit within the confines of armed conflict or civil strife, as a legitimate public purpose that overrides equitable and nondiscriminatory practices on the part of the State with respect to foreign investors and investments. The generic nature of the terms "armed conflict" and "civil strife" bespeak an intent to provide a Host State with considerable latitude and its "entitlement" to discriminate on this basis. It also demonstrates a manifestly

[13] Article 1105 in its entirety provides:

> **Article 1105: Minimum Standard of Treatment**
> Each Party shall accord to investments of investors of another Party treatment in accordance with international law, including fair and equitable treatment and full protection and security.
>
> Without prejudice to paragraph 1 and notwithstanding Article 1108(7)(b), each Party shall accord to investors of another Party, and to investments of investors of another Party, non-discriminatory treatment with respect to measures it adopts or maintains relating to losses suffered by investments in its territory owing to armed conflict or civil strife.
>
> Paragraph 2 does not apply to existing measures relating to subsidies or grants that would be inconsistent with Article 1102 but for Article 1108(7)(b).

Id. art. 1105.

[14] The "NAFTA public purpose standard" refers to Article 1101(4). *See Id. art.* 1101 ¶ 4.

[15] Article 1105(1)–(2) includes, *without limitation*, (i) fair and equitable treatment, (ii) full protection and security, (iii) nondiscriminatory treatment in keeping with international minimum standard, and (iv) nondiscriminatory treatment concerning losses suffered by investments in the Host State owing to armed conflict or civil strife. Accordingly, expropriation and denial of justice are the only standards absent from those included in Article 1105. *See Id*. art. 1105.

identifiable penchant favoring a public purpose that furthers no regulatory State interests over investment or investor protection.[16]

The public purpose categories that are enunciated in Article 1106(2), (4), and (6)(a)–(c), certainly meet the NAFTA public purpose standard.[17] The *health, safety*, or *environmental* exceptions contained in Article 1106(2) are indicative of the standard fare of international trade law exceptions that (i) meet the NAFTA public purpose standard and (ii) are derived from international trade law but now find themselves forming part of the NAFTA Chapter Eleven investment regime.[18] In contrast with Article 1105, the Article 1106(2)

[16] The inclusion of nonqualified or earmarked "subsidies" or "grants" in subsection 3 also suggests a heightened sense of priority favoring nonregulatory State-sanctioned discrimination over foreign investment or investor protection. *See Id.* art. 1105 ¶ 3.

[17] Article 1106 subsections 2, 4, and 6(a)–(c) state:

> **Article 1106: Performance Requirements**
>
> 2. A measure that requires an investment to use a technology to meet generally applicable health, safety or environmental requirements shall not be construed to be inconsistent with paragraph 1(f). For greater certainty, Articles 1102 ["National Treatment"] and 1103 ["Minimum Standard of Treatment"] apply to the measure.
> 4. Nothing in paragraph 3 shall be construed to prevent a Party from conditioning the receipt or continued receipt of an advantage, in connection with an investment in its territory of an investor of a Party or of a non-Party, on compliance with a requirement to locate production, provide a service, train or employ workers, construct or expand particular facilities, or carry out research and development, in its territory.
>
> ...
>
> 6. Provided that such measures are not applied in an arbitrary or unjustifiable manner, or do not constitute a disguised restriction on international trade or investment, nothing in paragraph 1(b) or (c) or 3(a) or (b) shall be construed to prevent any Party from adopting or maintaining measures, including environmental measures:
>   (a) necessary to secure compliance with laws and regulations that are not inconsistent with the provisions of this Agreement;
>   (b) necessary to protect human, animal or plant life or health; or
>   (c) necessary for the conservation of living or non-living exhaustible natural resources.

Id. art. 1106 ¶¶ 2, 4, 6(a)–(c).

[18] The "health, safety or environmental" public purpose exceptions that legitimately empower the State to exercise its authority in ways that may be inconsistent with a foreign investor's business or investment, although in some circumstances compensable, finds their genesis in international trade law. These exceptions, which shall be demonstrated in greater detail in this text, arise from the general exceptions contained in the GATT Article XX, which provides States with a normative foundation for encroaching on agreed trade principles where an exception may be deemed applicable. These exceptions have been incorporated into the NAFTA Chapter Eleven without qualification. The more relevant GATT Article XX exceptions include protection for acts:

> (*a*) necessary to protect public morals;
> (*b*) necessary to protect human, animal or plant life or health;
>
> ...
>
> (*d*) necessary to secure compliance with laws or regulations which are not

Public Purpose Exceptions do not preempt the investment law tenets of *national treatment* and *most-favored-nation (MFN) treatment* designed to protect foreign investors and investments. The paragraph, in an effort to underscore uniformity and predictability, provides that "[f]or greater certainty, Articles 1102 [National Treatment Standard] *and* 1103 [Most-Favored Nation] apply" to the health, safety, and environmental measures that are exempted from Article 1106(1)'s requirements.[19]

Therefore, pursuant to an Article 1106(2) analysis, the State's exercise of its regulatory fiat prescribing a measure requiring an investment to adopt specific technology to meet health, safety, or environmental requirements must be equally enforced among foreign investors and Host-State citizens. The State's use of its regulatory authority in this context is limited by investment law principles of nondiscriminatory practice and not left unbridled on the basis of regulatory subject matter. As with Article 1105(3), Article 1106(2) stands in sharp relief to the overriding standing of the public purpose categories provided in Article 1106(4) pertaining to (i) the location of production, (ii) the provision of services, (iii) the training of personnel, (iv) the employment of workers, (v) the construction or expansion of particular facilities, and (vi) research and development within the national territory.[20]

The Article 1106(4) public purpose categories are consistent with the NAFTA public purposes standard. This paragraph, however, vests the State with absolute authority to act in furtherance of the enumerated exceptions, irrespective of the consequences of these actions on foreign investment protection or international trade either at a practical or policy level.[21]

> inconsistent with the provisions of this Agreement, including those relating to customs enforcement, the enforcement of monopolies operated under paragraph 4 of Article II and Article XVII, the protection of patents, trademarks and copyrights, and the prevention of deceptive practices;
>
> . . .
>
> (*g*) relating to the conservation of exhaustible natural resources if such measures are made effective in conjunction with restrictions on domestic production or consumption.

GATT, *supra* note 2, art. XX ¶¶ *(a)–(b), (d), (g).*

19 *See* NAFTA, *supra* note 1, art. 1106 ¶ 2 (emphasis added).

20 Article 1106(4) states:

> Nothing in paragraph 3 shall be construed to prevent a Party from conditioning the receipt or continued receipt of an advantage, in connection with an investment in its territory of an investor of a Party or of a non-Party, on compliance with a requirement to locate production, provide a service, train or employ workers, construct or expand particular facilities, or carry out research and development, in its territory.

Id. art. 1106 ¶ 4.

21 The consequences of the exercise of the State's regulatory and nonregulatory authority on foreign investment represents the most significant deficit in the NAFTA's public purpose treaty

Article 1106(6)(a)–(c) in addition to meeting the NAFTA Standard, exemplifies a direct and verbatim incorporation of the General Agreement on Tariffs and Trade (GATT) Article XX "General Exceptions"[22] that materially amplify the State's regulatory space.[23] Paragraph 6 tempers the "international trade law exceptions" that favor the interest of traditional State sovereignty over investor protection by stating that any such measure is not to be applied "in an arbitrary or unjustifiable manner." It does, albeit tepidly, arguably incorporate international law providing that foreign investments and investors are not to be arbitrarily or unjustifiably discriminated against and, therefore, are entitled to national treatment and international minimum standard protection. This reading is bolstered by the use of the disjunctive "or," which in the second subordinate clause explicitly adds that any such measure must "not constitute a disguised restriction on *international trade or investment*."[24] The first subordinate clause addresses the *application* of measures (i.e., actions by the State in the implementation and execution of its regulatory sovereignty), whereas the second subordinate clause concerns "restriction[s]" on international trade or investment (i.e., the *effects* of the subject measures).[25]

construct. As discussed in considerable detail, *see infra* at Chapter 1.H(2). The "proportionality," "effects," and "sole effects" tests that the NAFTA "jurisprudence" has fashioned in determining the extent to which a particular measure that a State prescribes may give rise to detrimental consequences that far exceed the remedial or public benefit stemming from the measure in question in order to pass on its propriety are rife with conceptual and practical shortcomings that militate against uniformity, predictability, and transparency of standard.

22 *Compare* NAFTA, *supra* note 1, art. 1106 ¶¶ 6(a)–(c) *with* GATT, *supra* note 2, art. XX.

23 Article 1106(6)(a)–(c) provides:

> Provided that such measures are not applied in an arbitrary or unjustifiable manner, or do not constitute a disguised restriction on international trade or investment, nothing in paragraph 1(b) or (c) or 3(a) or (b) shall be construed to prevent any Party from adopting or maintaining measures, including ***environmental measures***:
> (a) necessary to secure compliance with laws and regulations that are not inconsistent with the provisions of this Agreement;
> *(b) necessary to protect human, animal or plant life or health*; or
> *(c) necessary for the conservation of living or non-living exhaustible natural resources.*

NAFTA, *supra* note 1, art. 1106 in 6(a)–(c) (emphasis added).

24 *Id.* art. 1106 ¶ 6 (emphasis added).

25 The absence of any plain language referencing "international law" certainly detracts from the proposition that the first part of this subsection aims at protecting foreign investors and investments. Yet the use of the words "arbitrary" and "unjustifiable," together with the overall construction of that subsection, certainly do not render the proposition at all implausible. The NAFTA Chapter Eleven drafters achieved the extremely challenging objective of simultaneously addressing international trade and investment law concepts and spheres of protection that are premised on different and often competing underlying principles that in turn are expressed in disparate terms of art.

Paragraph 6 further broadens the State's regulatory sovereignty for purposes of adopting "environmental measures," a broad and unqualified term far exceeding the scope of the term "environmental" within the meaning of Paragraph 2 of the same article.[26] Paragraph 6, subsection (b) explicitly references measures, "necessary to protect human, animal or plant life or health," which is identical language to the GATT Article XX(b).[27] Similarly, Paragraph 6, subsection (c), pertaining to measures "necessary for the conservation of living or non-living exhaustible natural resources," also draws heavily on the GATT General Exceptions.[28]

The categories of public purpose enunciated in Paragraph 6, perhaps with the notable exception of "non-living exhaustible natural resources," fall into five quite distinct categories: (i) human life or health, (ii) animal life or health, (iii) plant life or health, (iv) living exhaustible natural resources, and (v) environmental measures. These five categories, having as their subject matter life, health, environment, and exhaustible natural resources, likely represent a higher categorical status in the hierarchy of a State's priorities than the public purposes categories identified in Article 1105(3)[29] or in Article 1106(4).[30] The five categories contained in Article 1106(6), however, are treated no differently; that is, *in pari materia* with such public purpose categories as subsidies, grants, the procurement of services, or the training of workers, as set forth in Articles 1105(3) and 1106(4), respectively.

All of these categories, indiscriminately, at least prima facie provide a NAFTA party with a normative foundation for exercising its authority in ways that may be detrimental to investors or investments. This NAFTA

[26] Article 1106(2) limits the scope of "environmental" to measures requiring investments to use specific environmentally sensitive technologies:

> A measure that requires an investment to use a technology to meet generally applicable health, safety or environmental requirements shall not be construed to be inconsistent with paragraph 1(f). For greater certainty, Articles 1102 and 1103 apply to the measure.

NAFTA, *supra* note 1, art. 1106 ¶ 2.

[27] *See* GATT, *supra* note 2, art. XX ¶ (b).

[28] See *Id. art.* XX ¶ (g) ("[R]elating to the conservation of exhaustible natural resources if such measures are made effective in conjunction with restrictions on domestic production or consumption").

[29] Article 1105(3), read together with Article 1108(7)(b), exempts existing measures relating to subsidies or grants by a Party or State enterprise from the Article 1105(2) requirement of nondiscriminatory treatment during armed conflict and civil strife. NAFTA, *supra* note 1, art. 1105¶¶ 2–3; art. 1108 ¶ 7(b).

[30] Article 1106(4) provides that the prohibition on conditioned advantages in Article 1106(3) "shall not be construed to prevent a Party from conditioning the receipt or continued receipt of an advantage … on compliance with a requirement to locate production, provide a service, train or employ workers, construct or expand particular facilities, or carry out research and development, in its territory." *Id.* art. 1106 ¶¶ 3–4.

Chapter Eleven structural feature represents a policy that adopts a broad understanding of public purpose, one that does not categorically discern among public purpose constructs in connection with the extent that regulatory sovereignty based on such a public purpose category must be qualified. The general treatment of public purpose categories as equal in every regard, without a need to qualify a State's exercise of regulatory sovereignty based on *any* public purpose category, constitutes a material deficit in the NAFTA Chapter Eleven's rubric with respect to investor/investment protection.[31]

Article 1108, entitled "Reservations and Exceptions," perhaps best exemplifies the multifarious nature of public purpose within a single chapter of one treaty alone.[32] It is also illustrative of the indiscriminate cross-pollination

[31] This shortcoming, together with the uncertainty that the NAFTA "jurisprudence" has spawned, encompass the most significant public purpose deficits within the NAFTA investor protection system.

[32] Article 1108 reads:

Article 1108: Reservations and Exceptions

1. Articles 1102 ["National Treatment Standard"], 1103 ["Most-Favored Nation"], 1106 ["Performance Requirements"] and 1107 ["Senior Management, Boards of Directors"] do not apply to:
   (a) any existing non-conforming measure that is maintained by
      (i) a Party at the federal level, as set out in its Schedule to Annex I or **III**,
      (ii) a State or province, for two years after the date of entry into force of this Agreement, and thereafter as set out by a Party in its Schedule to Annex I in accordance with paragraph 2, or
      (iii) a local government;
   (b) the continuation or prompt renewal of any non-conforming measure referred to in subparagraph (a); or
   (c) an amendment to any non-conforming measure referred to in subparagraph
   (a) to the extent that the amendment does not decrease the conformity of the measure, as it existed immediately before the amendment, Articles 1102 ["National Treatment Standard"], 1103 ["Most-Favored Nation"], 1106 ["Performance Requirements"], and 1107 ["Senior Management, Board of Directors"].
2. Each Party may set out in its Schedule to Annex I, within two years of the date of entry into force of this Agreement, any existing nonconforming measure maintained by a State or province, not including a local government.
3. Articles 1102 ["National Treatment Standard"], 1103 ["Most-Favored Nation"], 1106 ["Performance Requirements"], and 1107 ["Senior Management, Board of Directors"] do not apply to any measure that a Party adopts or maintains with respect to sectors, subsectors or activities, as set out in its Schedule to Annex II.
4. No Party may, under any measure adopted after the date of entry into force of this Agreement and covered by its Schedule to Annex II, require an investor of another Party, by reason of its nationality, to sell or otherwise dispose of an investment existing at the time the measure becomes effective.
5. Articles 1102 ["National Treatment Standard"] and 1103 ["Most-Favored Nation"] do not apply to any measure that is an exception to, or derogation from, the obligations under Article 1703 ["Intellectual Property-National Treatment"] as specifically provided for in that Article.

between international investment law and international trade law. All but three of the paragraphs comprising this Article explicitly reference either national treatment standard *and* MFN treatment or one of these two treatment standards.[33] Because Article 1108 addresses both reservations and exceptions, it is the most complex of the Chapter Eleven NAFTA Articles.

A. PUBLIC PURPOSE IN THE CONTEXT OF RESERVATIONS

Reservations and *exceptions* represent two normatively related but distinct sets of public purpose precepts that often encompass overlapping categories. Reservations fall within the ambit of public purpose, at least within the context of this contribution, because by definition they are the product of the State's exercise of regulatory sovereignty. Their normative standing, and therefore their propriety as a juridically cognizable public purpose, is founded on the procedural adherence to a legitimate negotiation of a treaty forming part of international conventional law. Consequently, the structure of a treaty reservation has an objective grounding based on process, and, in this sense, it is universal and commonly shared by all members of the community of nations. The content of treaty reservations, however, is subjective. In contrast with its formal process-driven structure, its substantive subject matter is particular and, hence, subjective. The subject matter arises from the unique needs of States and is determined within a framework of orthodox Westphalian notions of sovereignty.[34] Because of this duality, "treaty reservation public purpose"

6. Article 1103 ["Most-Favored Nation"] does not apply to treatment accorded by a Party pursuant to agreements, or with respect to sectors, set out in its Schedule to Annex IV.
7. Articles 1102 ["National Treatment Standard"], 1103 ["Most-Favored Nation"] and 1107 ["Senior Management, Board of Directors"] do not apply to:
   (a) procurement by a Party or a State enterprise; or
   (b) subsidies or grants provided by a Party or a State enterprise, including government-supported loans, guarantees and insurance.
8. The provisions of:
   (a) Article 1106 ["Performance Requirements"](1)(a), (b) and (c), and (3)(a) and (b) do not apply to qualification requirements for goods or services with respect to export promotion and foreign aid programs;
   (b) Article 1106 ["Performance Requirements"](1)(b), (c), (f) and (g), and (3)(a) and (b) do not apply to procurement by a Party or a State enterprise; and
   (c) Article 1106 ["Performance Requirements"](3)(a) and (b) do not apply to requirements imposed by an importing Party relating to the content of goods necessary to qualify for preferential tariffs or preferential quotas.

NAFTA, *supra* note 1, art. 1108 (emphasis added).

33 *See, e.g., Id.* art. 1108 ¶¶ 2, 4, 8.

34 Westphalian sovereignty refers to the peace treaty between the Holy Roman Emperor and the King of France and their respective allies, October 24, 1648 (the "Treaty of Westphalia").

cannot be analyzed together with public purpose categories such as those constituting the NAFTA Standard.[35] Most of Article 1108 addresses the inapplicability of the national treatment and MFN standards to reservations.[36] Paragraph 7 does carve out public purpose exceptions consonant with the NAFTA public purpose standard that are not contained in the annexes to the agreement and thus fall beyond the ambit of reservations.[37] This paragraph renders inapplicable national treatment and MFN standards to State-sponsored (i) subsidies, (ii) grants, (iii) loans, (iv) guarantees, and (v) insurance. State procurement is also sanctioned as an exception.[38]

Although the Treaty of Westphalia indeed brought an end to the Thirty Years' War, its most enduring legacy has been the treaty's general discussion on the nature of sovereignty, which provided the foundations for a territorially based conception that accorded a virtual monopoly in international law to sovereign States. The writings of Grotius and Leibniz together with the treaty's text provided a framework for a rigid and dogmatic conception of sovereignty that prevailed throughout the twentieth century and is still accepted in some quarters today. Pedro J. Martinez-Fraga, *Juridical Convergence in International Dispute Resolution: Developing A Substantive Principle of Transparency and Transnational Evidence Gathering*, 10 Loy. U. Chi. Int'l L. Rev. 37, 38 n.3 (2012) (citing J. G. Starke, Introduction to International Law 7–14 (9th ed. 1984)).

35 What here has been identified as "treaty reservation public purpose" represents a right to State action that may infringe on the fundamental rights of a foreign investor or investment, which is substantively spawned by a State's perceived needs. The "public purpose" component of this right to act on the part of a State can be divorced completely from such public purpose categories as health, education, orthodox regulatory State prerogatives, child care, or income security and still enjoy binding juridical legitimacy. Its subjective content derives from the exercise of the State's political will, which may or may not coincide with the public purpose categories found in and suggested by the NAFTA Standard.

36 *See, e.g.*, NAFTA, *supra* note 1, art. 1108 in 1–6.

37 For example, Article 1108(7) provides:

> 7. Articles 1102, 1103 and 1107 do not apply to:
> (a) procurement by a Party or a State enterprise; or
> (b) subsidies or grants provided by a Party or a State enterprise, including government-supported loans, guarantees and insurance.

Id. art. 1108 ¶ 7.

38 The procurement exception is a common public purpose category traceable to the GATT Article XX, subsections (i) and (j):

> Subject to the requirement that such measures are not applied in a manner which would constitute a means of arbitrary or unjustifiable discrimination between countries where the same conditions prevail, or a disguised restriction on international trade, nothing in this Agreement shall be construed to prevent the adoption or enforcement by any contracting party of measures:
> (i) involving restrictions on exports of domestic materials necessary to ensure essential quantities of such materials to a domestic processing industry during periods when the domestic price of such materials is held below the world price as part of a governmental stabilization plan; *Provided that such restrictions shall not operate to increase the exports of or the protection afforded to such domestic industry, and shall not depart from the provisions of this Agreement relating to non-discrimination*;

The Article 1108 exceptions, construing Paragraphs (a) and (b) together, are more akin to public purpose exceptions deriving from the State's police powers because their direct relationship to a common good of the State is less clear than their parity with an activity of the State. The public purpose found in the exercise of orthodox administrative authority forming part of a State's police powers are distinct from the public purpose categories enunciated in Article 1106 Paragraphs 4 (concerning the training or employment of workers, construction or expansion of facilities, and research and development) and 6 (pertaining to human, animal, and plant life and health and exhaustible natural resources). The difference between the public purpose categories contained in Article 1108(7)(a)(b) and those mentioned in Article 1106(4) does not necessarily suggest a hierarchical difference between the two sets of categories. Yet both sets of exceptions (those of Article 1106(4) and Article 1108(7)) would appear to be subordinated to the public purpose category of Article 1106(6) concerning life, health, and the conservation of exhaustible resources. On the other hand, the Article 1108(7)(b) public purpose categories conceptually comport best with the limited and qualified public purpose categories of Article 1105(2).

The tension between exceptions and reservations that is present in any effort that aspires to analyze public purpose in international law finds fertile ground in Article 1108. The *drafts* of this article suggest that the NAFTA parties initially sought to categorize as "general exceptions" many of the international trade law categories of exceptions that are contained in the GATT's Article XX.[39] Most notably, Canada assumed a protagonistic role in promoting these general exceptions that ultimately were incorporated into the various

> (j) essential to the acquisition or distribution of products in general or local short supply; *Provided that any such measures shall be consistent with the principle that all contracting parties are entitled to an equitable share of the international supply of such products, and that any such measures, which are inconsistent with the other provisions of the Agreement shall be discontinued as soon as the conditions giving rise to them have ceased to exist ....*

GATT, *supra* note 2, art. XX ¶ (i), (j) (emphasis added).

[39] For example, in the January 16, 1992, NAFTA Chapter Eleven draft, Canada proposed:

> CDA [**Article 111: General Exceptions**
> Nothing in this Agreement shall be construed to prevent the adoption or enforcement by any Party of measures:
> (i) necessary to protect public order, safety or public morals;
> (ii) necessary to protect human, animal or plant life or health or the environment in its territory, or to enforce generally agreed international environmental or conservation rules or standards;
> (iii) relating to the products or services of prison labor;
> (iv) imposed for the protection of national treasures of artistic, historic or archaeological value;
> (v) necessary for fiduciary or consumer protection reasons;

annexes memorializing the reservations.[40] The proposed GATT-derived general exceptions amply meet the NAFTA public purpose standard, yet their expansive scope, ranging from measures "necessary to protect public order, safety or public morals" to decrees "imposed for the protection of national treasures of artistic, historic, or archaeological value," would overwhelm the public purpose doctrine, rendering it all too general and encompassing for practical and even analytical application. Here, the distinction between the public purpose categories consonant with the NAFTA Standard and "treaty reservation public purpose" indeed is helpful in obtaining a more comprehensive understanding of the public purpose doctrine and of its functional application in international law, particularly with respect to tempering foreign investor expectations, a State's exercise of its regulatory authority, meeting the aspirations of international investment law, and maximizing international trade law efficacy.

Because treaty reservation public purpose is too subjective in content and too general in scope, it serves the de facto function of limiting the conceptual universe of the NAFTA public purpose standard exceptions. This categorical segregation in turn renders plausible meaningful analysis concerning possible public purpose exceptions without creating an unworkable criteria that is weak on discriminating among practices falling within the public purpose doctrine. Despite Canada's laudable intent to have broad and all-encompassing public purpose exceptions pervade Chapter Eleven, the final iteration of Article 1108 – limiting public purpose to (i) procurement, (ii) subsidies, (iii) grants, (iv) government-supported loans, (v) government-supported guarantees, and (vi) government-supported insurance – actually furthers the plight of public purpose. In addition, narrowing the scope of public purpose exceptions helps serve the conceptual interests of international investment law without drawing on a doctrinal reservoir of public purpose constituted by terms and categories of both international trade and international investment law.[41]

(vi) necessary to secure compliance with laws or regulations which are not inconsistent with the provisions of this Agreement, including those relating to the avoidance of fraudulent or deceptive practices;

Provided that such measure is:

(vii) consistent with Article 106; and

(viii) is the least trade-restrictive necessary for securing the protection required.]

NAFTA Negotiating Drafts, *supra* note 7, draft of January 16, 1992.

40 *See, e.g.*, NAFTA, *supra* note 1, annex II ("Schedule of Canada").

41 The Article 111: General Exceptions draft is illustrative on this point. *Supra* note 39. That draft article included such public purpose categories as "the products or services of prison labor" and measures "necessary for fiduciary or consumer protection reasons." Even though the public purpose component to these categories is eminently clear, the categories do not have their origins in, nor do they form part of, international investment law. To the contrary, they are

The single reference to the nomenclature "public purpose" in Chapter Eleven is found in Article 1110(1)(a).[42] The term appears as one of four elements that give rise to a legal expropriation provided that all four tenets are met.[43] Although the NAFTA Standard engrafts conceptual and practical meaning to the term "public purpose," Article 1110 nowhere defines it. Moreover, the drafts of Chapter Eleven suggest that the NAFTA parties expressed no concern over defining public purpose within the confines of this article. Instead, the drafts reflect that the NAFTA parties at the time had divergent views on the issue of compensation, with the United States and Canada agreeing on a specific and discernible standard consonant with established principles of compensation found in public international law and with Mexico expressing a penchant for a domestic criteria.[44] The discrepancy among the NAFTA parties on the question of compensation perhaps

categories consistently associated with international trade law. Because their origin is disassociated from the law and principles governing the protection of aliens, the doctrinal development and application of these concepts suggest that their highest and best use is within a framework that pertains to macroeconomic regulation over significant time frames and not the short- to medium-term microeconomic issues more common to international investment law and treaty based arbitrations. *See generally*, Nicholas DiMascio & Joost Pauwelyn, *Nondiscrimination in Trade and Investment Treaties: Worlds Apart or Two Sides of the Same Coin?*, 102 A.J.I.L. 48 (January 2008).

42 NAFTA, *supra* note 1, art. 1110 ¶ 1(a).

43 The Article, which identifies public purpose as the first of four tenets that, if collectively met, legalize direct or indirect nationalization or expropriation, provides no guidance as to the meaning of public purpose or its hierarchical relationship as to the three remaining tenets found in subsections (b) through (d). *Id.* art. 1110¶ 1.

44 By way of example, the February 13, 1992, draft of Article 1110 concerning expropriation and compensation states:

> 1. No Party shall directly or indirectly nationalize or expropriate an investment of an investor of another Party in its territory or take any measure or series of measures tantamount to expropriation USA, CDA, *[or nationalization]* or such an investment USA CDA *[("expropriation")]*, except:
>   (a) for a public purpose;
>   (b) on a nondiscriminatory basis;
>   (c) in accordance with due process of law USA *[and the general principles of treatment provided for in Article —]*; and
>   (d) upon payment of USA, CDA *[prompt, adequate and effective]* compensation.
> 2. Compensation shall be MEX *[paid within a reasonable period of time]* USA CDA *[equivalent to the fair market value of the expropriated investment immediately before the expropriatory action was taken or became known, whichever is earlier; be paid without delay; include interest at a commercially reasonable rate from the date of expropriation; be fully realizable; and be freely transferable at the prevailing market rate of exchange on the date of* USA *[expropriation].* CDA *[transfer.]]*

NAFTA Negotiating Drafts, *supra* note 7, draft of February 13, 1992 (emphasis in original). The differences between the Parties on this issue become all the more stark, with Mexico underscoring its rejection of the United States' and Canada's adherence to public international law finds foundation in Mexico's status as the NAFTA party most likely to be classified as a "capital-importing State."

The extent to which the public purpose doctrine in its legacy form affects compensation in the context of direct or indirect expropriations or nationalizations should not be altogether severed from the often disparate treatment of public purpose between capital-exporting and capital-importing States.[45] Understandably, in the context of Chapter Eleven, the NAFTA parties elected to negotiate aggressively and comprehensively the question of compensation within the framework of Article 1110 instead of engaging in the more challenging and, from a pragmatic treaty negotiation perspective, less viable endeavor of "defining" (literally crafting limits on) the public purpose doctrine, which

principles with respect to compensation for indirect or direct nationalizations or expropriations of another Party's investment:

<u>**EXPROPRIATION AND COMPENSATION**</u>

1. No Party shall directly or indirectly nationalize or expropriate an investment of an investor of another Party in its territory or take any measure or series of measures tantamount to expropriation or nationalization of such an investment ("expropriation"), except:
   (a) for a public purpose;
   (b) on a nondiscriminatory basis;
   (c) in accordance with due process of law [USA] *[and the general principles of treatment provided for in Article —]*; and
   (d) upon payment of [USA CDA] *[prompt, adequate and effective]* compensation.
2. Compensation shall be equivalent to the fair market value of the expropriated investment immediately before the expropriatory action was taken or became known, whichever is earlier. Valuation criteria shall include going concern value, asset value (including declared tax value of tangible property), and other criteria, as appropriate to determine fair market value. Compensation shall be paid without delay; include interest at a commercially reasonable rate from the date of expropriation; be fully realizable; and be freely transferable at the prevailing market rate of exchange on the date of [USA] *[expropriation.]* [MEX CDA] *[transfer]*.

Mexican Note 2–Mexico considers that the concerns expressed by the U.S. and Canada delegations on compensation are covered by the new draft proposal on paragraph 2. On that basis Mexico will only accept this paragraph if the U.S. and Canada delegations drop the actual bracketed text in paragraph 1(c) and (d).

Id. (emphasis in original), draft of February 21, 1992.

45 *See, e.g.*, Professor Alan C. Swan, *NAFTA Chapter 11- "Direct Effect" and Interpretive Method: Lessons from Methanex v. United States*, 64 U. MIAMI L. REV. 21, 85 (2009) ("[C]apital-exporting countries promoted a strong legal tradition, both international and domestic, of requiring the government to pay full compensation to the owner. While the international version of that requirement was challenged particularly by the developing countries in the United Nations General Assembly, it nevertheless seemed to retain its vitality among the various tribunals that were from time to time called to pass on the issue. It was against this background that the developing countries increasingly found it in their interests to use regulatory intervention, rather than an outright 'taking,' to achieve their purposes").

already received considerable attention – albeit without being overtly saddled with the "public purpose" nomenclature – in Article 1101(4).[46]

Article 1114 addressing "environmental concerns" comports with the NAFTA Standard.[47] Although at first glance this public purpose "environmental exception" may appear to be, from a public purpose categorical classification perspective, duplicative of the general reference to "environmental measures" in Article 1106(6), the phrase "sensitive to environmental concerns" appears to suggest an even broader scope. This amplified categorical construction is further bolstered by the participles "adopting, maintaining or enforcing" any measure presumably deemed to be "sensitive to environmental concerns."[48] This observation notwithstanding, Paragraph 2 of Article 1114 does suggest a new environmental public purpose different from the general category contained in Article 1106(6).

Paragraph 2 of Article 1114 proscribes conduct that encourages investment "by relaxing domestic health, safety or environmental measures."[49] This provision constitutes a measure directed at foreclosing pollution havens. The *Canadian Statement of Implementation of Chapter Eleven* corroborates this interpretation of the public purpose category enunciated in Article 1114.[50]

46 The Article 1101 drafts do not contain any permutations of the term "public purpose," nor do they even mention public purpose.

47 This Article reads:

> 1. Nothing in this Chapter shall be construed to prevent a Party from adopting, maintaining or enforcing any measure otherwise consistent with this Chapter that it considers appropriate to ensure that investment activity in its territory is undertaken in a manner sensitive to environmental concerns.
> 2. The Parties recognize that it is inappropriate to encourage investment by relaxing domestic health, safety or environmental measures. Accordingly, a Party should not waive or otherwise derogate from, or offer to waive or otherwise derogate from, such measures as an encouragement for the establishment, acquisition, expansion or retention in its territory of an investment of an investor. If a Party considers that another Party has offered such an encouragement, it may request consultations with the other Party and the two Parties shall consult with a view to avoiding any such encouragement.

Id. art. 1114.

48 *Id*. art 1114 ¶ 1.

49 *Id*. art. 1114 ¶ 2.

50 For example, the Canadian Statement on Implementation in part provides:

> The first paragraph of article 1114 affirms each Party's right to adopt and enforce environmental measures, consistent with the chapter (e.g., environmental measures must be applied on a national treatment basis). The second paragraph, which addresses the pollution haven issue, requires that the Parties recognize that it is inappropriate to encourage investment by relaxing domestic health, safety or environmental measures, and that Parties should not waive or derogate from such environmental measures to

The NAFTA Chapter Eleven contribution to public purpose is significant. In addition to fashioning what is here regarded as a public purpose standard,[51] it also categorically enriched the public purpose doctrine by listing fifteen identifiable public purpose categories pursuant to which State action may adversely compromise a foreign investor or an investment without incurring liability:

(i) human life and health;[52]
(ii) animal life and health;[53]
(iii) plant life and health;[54]
(iv) living and non-living exhaustible resources;[55]
(v) general environmental;[56]
(vi) modification to technology to meet health requirements;[57]
(vii) modification to technology to meet safety requirements;[58]
(viii) modification to technology to meet environmental requirements;[59]
(ix) subsidies directed at investments affected by civil strife or armed conflict;[60]

attract investment. If one Party considers that another has done so, it may request consultations.

Canadian Statement on Implementation, *supra* note 9, at 152.

51 The Article 1101(4) construct that has been identified as a "public purpose standard" lists ten public purpose categories that are not exhaustive but rather are to be used as a paradigm against which actions on the part of the State that purport to be of a public purpose nature may be challenged and/or identified:

(i) law enforcement,
(ii) correctional services,
(iii) income security,
(iv) insurance,
(v) social security,
(vi) social welfare,
(vii) public education,
(viii) public training,
(ix) health care,
(x) child care.

NAFTA, *supra* note 1, art. 1101 ¶ 4.

52 *See, e.g., Id.* art. 1106 ¶ 6(b).

53 *Id.*

54 *Id.*

55 *Id.* art. 1106 ¶ 6(c).

56 *Id.* art. 1106 ¶ 6.

57 *Id.* art. 1106 ¶ 2.

58 *Id.*

59 *Id.*

60 *Id.* art. 1103 ¶ 2.

(x) grants directed to investments affected by armed conflict;[61]
(xi) government-supported loans;[62]
(xii) government-supported guarantees;[63]
(xiii) government-supported insurance;[64]
(xiv) government grants generally;[65] and
(xv) measures to proscribe the creation of future pollution havens.[66]

This contribution to the public purpose doctrine demonstrates a serious and sustained effort aspiring to develop a functioning public purpose standard. The NAFTA Chapter Eleven public purpose experiment is a successful one. The chapter studiously balances public purpose categories within the ambit of the NAFTA Standard and public purpose treaty reservations. Even more significantly, Article 1101(4) sets a tone that seeks to impose limits on the public purpose doctrine so that it may serve a practical function. This effort, however, hardly brings us closer to understanding the doctrine of public purpose in international law beyond merely a "catch-all" phrase attaching to all matters reasonably related to a sovereign's exercise of sovereignty (i.e., to all things public in a State).

B. CHAPTER ELEVEN OF THE NAFTA DOES NOT DEVELOP AN OBJECTIVE TEST

The orthodox conception and treatment of public purpose is not workable in large measure because it is grounded on a subjective normative framework.[67] This subjective configuration necessarily leads to uncertainty and lack of uniformity, and it lends itself to "justifiable abuse." The relative nature of the legacy public purpose doctrine in international law is particularly dysfunctional and conceptually at odds in the context of economic globalization and shifting

[61] *Id.*
[62] *Id.* art. 1108 ¶ 7(b).
[63] *Id.*
[64] *Id.*
[65] *Id.*
[66] *Id.* art. 1114.
[67] *See* RESTATEMENT (THIRD) OF FOREIGN RELATIONS LAW § 712 cmt. *e* (1987) ("The requirement that a taking be for a public purpose is reiterated in most formulations of the rules of international law on expropriation of foreign property. That limitation, however, has not figured prominently in international claims practice, perhaps because the concept of public purpose is broad and not subject to effective reexamination by other States"); *see also* Banco Nacional de Cuba v. Sabbatino, 376 U.S. 398, 458 (1964) ("Of course, there are many unsettled areas of international law, as there are of domestic law, and these areas present sensitive problems of accommodating the interests of nations that subscribe to divergent economic and political systems. It may be that certain nationalizations of property for a public purpose fall within this area").

paradigms concerning the related doctrine of sovereignty. Chapter Eleven of the NAFTA vests the doctrine with the requisite objective foundation. To be sure, although what here has been identified as the "NAFTA Standard" does *not* remove public purpose from the realm of absolute subjectivity and relativism, it does set forth subject matter-based categories that serve as a first step toward limiting the doctrine from a substantive content perspective. Still, however, when addressing complex issues (primarily in the regulatory sphere), the objective deficit and lack of doctrinal development necessarily surface. This difficulty is compounded by the unique status that the public purpose doctrine holds in determining the legality of expropriations and even nationalizations under public international law.[68] The challenge is equally exacerbated in the effort to harmonize the public purpose doctrine's regulatory sovereignty-enhancing features with the sovereignty-restricting effects of international human rights.

The drafts and working papers pertaining to Chapter Eleven are unavailing in the effort to develop a public purpose doctrine having an objectively discernable content. The NAFTA parties, although concerned with public purpose, soon realized that the proliferation of public purpose categories in the treaty's actual text would further dilute the protection to be accorded to investors and investments. A proliferation of public purpose categories, in addition to treaty reservations, would emphasize the lack of investor protection policies underlying the chapter and completely distort the measured temperance that is to characterize the relationship between investment protection and the State's regulatory authority or *regulatory sovereignty*.[69] Despite the development of the NAFTA Standard, Chapter Eleven does not remedy the subjective content ill that plagues the orthodox public purpose doctrine. It

[68] A functional public purpose doctrine should and must account for differences between expropriation and nationalization. The policies underlying expropriations are less dependent on "matters of State" and closer to identifiable concerns having a public character than are those policies framing sector-based nationalizations. *See, e.g.*, United Nations Conference on Trade & Development, Expropriation: UNCTAD Series on Issues in International Investment Agreements II, U.N. Doc. UNCTAD/DIAE/IA/2011/7, U.N. Sales No. E.12.II.D.7 (2011) ("Nationalization usually refers to massive or large-scale takings of private property in all economic sectors or on an industry- or sector-specific basis. Outright nationalizations in all economic sectors are generally motivated by policy considerations; the measures are intended to achieve complete State control of the economy and involve the takeover of all privately owned means of production").

[69] The Chapter Eleven drafts do not overtly state the reasons why public purpose categories first identified as general exceptions were later regarded as reservations contained in the annexes. Close scrutiny of the texts (drafts), particularly between December 1, 1991, and March 23, 1993, does support the proposition that the NAFTA policy seeking to maximize the effect of international trade law while providing for a comprehensive investor protection rubric was best furthered by the exceptions methodology that typifies Article 1101(4) and that avails itself of broad but limited public purpose categories.

also fails to cure the ills arising from the accepted practice of according deference in defining what is public purpose to the invoking State.

C. PUBLIC PURPOSE IN THE NAFTA LACKS HIERARCHICAL STRUCTURE

The NAFTA's Chapter Eleven framework is rich with emphasis on the fifteen public purpose categories identified. Assuming a "rule of reason" approach – the extent to which a State's regulatory measure is akin to or may derive from any of these categories – the evaluation of whether a particular measure constitutes a public purpose category within the NAFTA Standard would be considerably facilitated. This approach, however, assumes that the universe of public purpose categories that reasonably relate to the NAFTA Standard share an equal status or hierarchy for purposes of furthering the common good. This assumption is unreliable. Concerns pertaining to public health and safety likely outweigh administrative public purpose categories such as government-supported guarantees. Similarly, as discussed in the context of international human rights, not all rights are or can be considered to be equal from a regulatory perspective.[70] By way of example, can the human right to be free from slavery be considered the same from a regulatory perspective as the right to freedom of assembly?[71] Similarly, the human right to humane treatment or the rights of children cannot be deemed susceptible to the same degree, if any, of regulatory sovereignty as freedom of movement nationally and internationally. The presence of a hierarchy in international human rights principles and norms is evident and established. The same cannot be said for the multiple iterations of the public purpose doctrine.

Chapter Eleven does not at all emphasize some public purpose categories over others. A system that relies on a public purpose doctrine to determine the juridical standing of an expropriation or a nationalization cannot rest on a conception of public purpose that lacks objective content and categorical hierarchy.

D. THE CHAPTER ELEVEN FRAMEWORK INDISCRIMINATELY INCORPORATES AND COMMINGLES TERMS OF ART FROM THE GATT: AN UNWANTED CROSS-POLLENIZATION

Chapter Eleven of the NAFTA fashions public purpose categories drawn from international trade law even though this chapter fundamentally applies to

[70] *See infra* at Chapter 3.
[71] *See Id.*

"*investment*, services and related matters."[72] In broad strokes, the chapter's architecture speaks to three objectives.

First, it identifies treatment standards for investor and investment protection.[73] Second, exceptions in the form of public purpose categories and public purpose treaty reservations earmarked to protect regulatory sovereignty are carved out.[74] Third, Chapter Eleven sets forth an international dispute resolution methodology.[75] Accordingly, the chapter aspires to harmonize investment law with the underlying policies and objectives of international trade law even though it nowhere explicitly states so. In so doing, general exceptions pertaining to international trade law are introduced into Chapter Eleven and provided with "public purpose category status." As noted, verbatim subparagraphs from the GATT's Article XX General Exceptions are transposed into Chapter Eleven and presented as exceptions and not reservations.[76] This cross-fertilization does more than commingle terms of art that have different origins and that seek disparate objectives that are often in conflict.

The introduction of international trade law terms into investment protection instruments is not unique to the NAFTA's Chapter Eleven. A number of second-generation bilateral investment treaties (BITs), particularly those in which Canada is a party and generally acting as the capital exporting country to the treaty, have incorporated international trade law terms of art, mostly from the GATT's Article XX General Exceptions.[77] Several other States

[72] NAFTA, *supra* note 1, art. 1101 ¶ 1 (emphasis added).

[73] *Id.* art. 1102 (National Treatment); art. 1103 (Most-Favored-Nation Treatment); art. 1104 (Standard of Treatment); art. 1105 (Minimum Standard of Treatment); and art. 1110 ¶ 1 (Expropriation & Compensation).

[74] *Id.* art. 1101 ¶ 4; art. 1106 ¶¶ 2,4, 6(a)–(c); art. 1108; art. 1114.

[75] *See, e.g.*, *Id.* art. 1117–38.

[76] *See supra* note 18 and accompanying text.

[77] Among the Canadian BITs (called "Foreign Investment Promotion and Protection Agreements" or "FIPAs") that include such protections are those entered into with the following:

(i) Armenia (signed May 8, 1997; protection for "human, animal or plant life or health," "environmental" measures, and "the conservation of living or nonliving exhaustible natural resources if such measures are made effective in conjunction with restrictions on domestic production or consumption");

(ii) Barbados (signed May 29, 1997; including "environmental protection," the protection of "human, animal or plant life or health," and "the conservation of living or non-living exhaustible natural resources");

(iii) Costa Rica (signed May 18, 1998; including the protection of "human, animal or plant life or health," the "conservation of living or non-living exhaustible natural resources, if such measures are made effective in conjunction with restrictions on domestic production or consumption," "the protection of investors, depositors, financial market participants, policy holders, policy claimants, or persons to whom a fiduciary is owed by a financial institution," and the "maintenance of the safety, soundness, integrity or financial responsibility or financial institutions");

have also incorporated such provisions into their investment protection regimes.[78]

The effect of this doctrinal confluence has more than just theoretical consequences. Conditioning what at first may appear to be orthodox public

(iv) Croatia (signed January 30, 2001; including "any current or future foreign aid program to promote economic development, whether under a bilateral agreement or pursuant to a multilateral arrangement or agreement, such as the OECD Agreement on Export Credits," the protection of "human, animal or plant life or health," "the conservation of living or non-living exhaustible natural resources if such measures are made effective in conjunction with restrictions on domestic production or consumption," "the production, distribution, sale or exhibition of film or video recordings");
(v) Czech Republic (entered into force January 22, 2012; including the protection of "human, animal or plant life or health," "the conservation of living or nonliving exhaustible natural resources," "the protection of investors, depositors, financial market participants, policy holders, policy claimants, or persons to whom a fiduciary is owed by a financial institution," and "ensuring the integrity and stability of a Contracting Party's financial system");
(vi) Ecuador (signed April 29, 1996; including the protection of "human, animal or plant life or health," and measures concerning "the conservation of living or non-living exhaustible natural resources"); and
(vii) Egypt (signed November 13, 1996; including measures necessary to protect "human, animal or plant life or health," and acts "relating to the conservation of living or non-living exhaustible natural resources if such measures are made effective in conjunction with restrictions on domestic production or consumption").

[78] The role of the public purpose doctrine in BITs is explored in Chapter 4. For non-Canadian BITs including these protections, see the following nonexhaustive listing:

1. Bilateral Agreement for the Promotion and Protection of Investments Between the Government of the Republic of Colombia and the Government of the Republic of China, Colom.-Chi, November 22, 2008, investmentpolicyhub.unctad.org/Download/TreatyFile/720 (including the preservation of "public order") [hereinafter Colombia-China BIT];
2. Agreement for the Promotion and Protection of Investments Between the Republic of Colombia and the Republic of India, Colom.-Ind., November 10, 2009, http://investmentpolicyhub.unctad.org/Download/TreatyFile/796 (including "public order," "human, animal, plant life or health," "the protection of the environment or the conservation of exhaustible natural resources," and "pursuance of obligations under the United Nations Charter for the Maintenance of International Peace and Security") [hereinafter Colombia-India BIT].
3. United States-Colombia Trade Promotion Agreement, Chapter 10 (Investment), November 22, 2006, http://www.ustr.gov/trade-agreements/free-trade-agreements/colombia-fta/final-text (including "environmental measures," the protection of "human, animal, or plant life or health," and "conservation of living or non-living exhaustible natural resources") [hereinafter U.S.-Colombia TPA];
4. Republic of Korea-United States Free Trade Agreement, Chapter 11 (Investment), June 30, 2007, http://www.ustr.gov/trade-agreements/free-trade-agreements/korus-fta/final-text (including the protection of "human, animal, or plant life or health," and "the conservation of living or non-living exhaustible natural resources") [hereinafter U.S.-South Korea FTA];

policy categories on trade law principles such as "restrictions on domestic production or consumption" or "ensuring the integrity and soundness of financial institutions," which are far removed from the objectives of international investment protection law, unconditionally and unjustifiably amplifies the State's regulatory authority. To the extent that this broadening of the scope of the State's regulatory sovereignty takes place, investor and investment

5. Agreement between the Government of the Republic of Korea and the Government of Japan for the Liberalisation, Promotion and Protection of Investment, Kor.-Jap., entered into force January 1, 2003,
6. http://investmentpolicyhub.unctad.org/Download/TreatyFile/1727 (including the protection of "essential security interests," "pursuance of its obligations under the United Nations Charter for the Maintenance of International Peace and Security," the protection of "human, animal or plant life or health," and "the maintenance of public order") [hereinafter South Korea-Japan BIT];
7. Agreement Between Canada and the Republic of Peru for the Promotion and Protection of Investments, Can.-Peru, November 14, 2006, http://investmentpolicyhub.unctad.org/Download/TreatyFile/626 (including the protection of "human, animal or plant life or health," the protection of "public morals or to maintain public order," "the prevention of deceptive and fraudulent practices or to deal with the effects of a default on contract," "the protection of the privacy of the individual in relation to the processing and dissemination of personal data and the protection of confidentiality of personal records and accounts," the protection of "national treasures of artistic, historic or archaeological value," and the "pursuance of its obligations under the United Nations Charter for the Maintenance of International Peace and Security") [hereinafter Canada-Peru BIT];
8. Panama-United States Trade Promotion Agreement, June 28, 2007, http://www.ustr.gov/trade-agreements/free-trade-agreements/panama-tpa/final-text (including the protection of "environmental measures," the protection of "human, animal or plant life or health," and the conservation of "living or non-living exhaustible natural resources");
9. Free Trade Agreement between the Republic of China ("Taiwan") and the Republic of Panama, Tai.-Pan., March 26, 1992, http://www.sice.oas.org/Investment/BITSbyCountry/BITs/PAN_TW_s.pdf (including the protection of "environmental measures," the protection of "human, animal or plant life or health," and the conservation of "living or non-living exhaustible natural resources");
10. Australia-Thailand Free Trade Agreement, Aus.-Tha., entered into force January 1, 2005, http://www.dfat.gov.au/fta/tafta/aus-thai_FTA_text.pdf (including the following language: "1. For the purposes of Chapters 2–7, Article XX of GATT 1994 is incorporated into and made part of this Agreement, mutatis mutandis. 2. For purposes of Chapters 8–10, Article XIV of GATS is incorporated into and made part of this Agreement, mutatis mutandis. 3. Article XX (e)–(g) of GATT 1994 is incorporated into and made part of Chapter 9, mutatis mutandis"); and
11. Australia-Singapore Free Trade Agreement, Aus.-Sin., February 17, 2003, http://www.dfat.gov.au/fta/safta/index.html (including the protection of "public morals" and "public order," as well as "human, animal or plant life or health," "the prevention of deceptive and fraudulent practices or to deal with the effects of a default on a contract," "the protection of the privacy of individuals in relation to the processing and dissemination of personal data and the protection of confidentiality of individual records and accounts").

protection is significantly diminished. Furthermore, because of the quite tenuous connection between international trade law precepts and the fundamental protection principles of investment law, uncertainty, lack of predictive value, and considerable want of uniformity ensue. The consequence is to provide Host States with a virtually unbridled license to regulate foreign investments in ways that could not have been reasonably foreseeable.[79]

Chapter Eleven of the NAFTA is distinct from other chapters of the treaty in that its purpose is to attract "foreign investment" among the NAFTA parties primarily by ensuring the twin goals of (i) providing foreign investors with a supernational arbitral forum in which to resolve disputes and (ii) protecting "foreign investment" among the NAFTA parties. The challenge in executing these objectives within the matrix of a trade agreement is to fashion a public purpose rubric that harmonizes different and even inimical principles and objectives of international investment and trade law. This theoretical and functional aspiration is frustrated where States are granted, under the guise of a legitimate public purpose, a license to regulate and compromise foreign investment protection in ways that are detrimental both to the investments and to investors.[80] Indeed, in the event of any inconsistency between Chapter Eleven of the NAFTA – the single investment and investor protection chapter in the treaty that also provides for international dispute resolution – and any other NAFTA chapter, it is the latter (the *trade* and not the *investment* chapter) that is to prevail.[81] The NAFTA parties were acutely aware that Chapter Eleven and its investment protection rubric was to be subordinated to all other NAFTA trade-related articles.[82] In this sense, investment law policies

79 *See, e.g.*, Andrew Newcombe, *The Boundaries of Regulatory Expropriation in International Law*, 20:1 ICSID REV. 1, 23 (2005) ("Moreover, arbitral tribunals also share this view and have held that parties are 'not liable for economic injury that is the consequence of bona fide regulation within the accepted police powers of the State.' While this abstract principle is said to be 'indisputable' its application is anything but clear") (internal citations omitted).

80 Without purporting to draw a necessary and apodictic connection between this distortion of public purpose caused by the indiscriminate wholesale importation of international trade law principles into the positive law and consequently the "jurisprudence" of investment law, it still remains paramount to underscore that, as of this writing, a NAFTA Chapter Eleven claimant only has prevailed once in a NAFTA treaty-based arbitration. *See* Metalclad Corp. v. United Mexican States, ICSID Case No. ARB (AF)/97/1, Award (August 30, 2000), 5 ICSID Rep. 212 (2002) [hereinafter Metalclad].

81 *See* Article 1112(1): Relation to Other Chapters, which provides: "In the event of any inconsistency between this Chapter and another Chapter, the other Chapter shall prevail to the extent of the inconsistency." NAFTA, *supra* note 1, art. 1112 ¶ 1.

82 *See, e.g.*, Canadian Statement on Implementation, *supra* note 9, at 152 ("In the case of any inconsistency between the investment chapter and other chapters, article 1112 provides that the latter shall prevail to the extent of the inconsistency. This article ensures that the specific provisions of other chapters are not superseded by the general provisions of this chapter").

are but a stepchild to the overarching trade policies permeating the treaty's architecture.

E. THE NAFTA STANDARD PUBLIC PURPOSE EXCEPTIONS AND THE TREATY RESERVATION PUBLIC PURPOSE CATEGORY: HARMONIZING A DICHOTOMY

Even though public purpose reservations in international treaties are rightfully construed as singular or particular categories that result as a process of diplomatic negotiations,[83] the question lingers as to whether and to what extent they inevitably may constitute general categories of customary international law.[84] Often, conventional international law results from the codification of principles found in customary international law. The less common but still viable methodology of fashioning customary international law based on principles of international conventional law is a phenomenon that has been amply chronicled.[85] The customary practice of interpreting reservations as having an objective structure but a subjective content arising from the particular needs of States and the treaty negotiation process simply cannot be relied on to ensure that recurring reservations, often hidden under the banner of "public safety and protection," will not form part of a collective international law consciousness.[86]

[83] *See* RESTATEMENT (THIRD) OF FOREIGN RELATIONS LAW § 313 *cmt. d* (1987) ("A reservation, an express acceptance of a reservation, or an objection to a reservation, must be formulated in writing and communicated to the contracting states and other states entitled to become parties to the agreement").

[84] General reservations may result from a sovereign's explicit adoption of customary international law principles. This proposition, however, does not preclude the negotiation of reservations precisely because they do not appear in international customary law. It is this latter universe of general reservations that is disconcerting with respect to the likelihood of having such reservations eventually populate the realm of customary international law.

[85] *See* Gary L. Scott & Craig L. Can, *Multilateral Treaties and the Formation of Customary International Law*, 25 DENY. J. INT'L L. & POL'Y 71, 72 (1996) (Arguing that "those parts of multilateral treaties which are generalizable beyond the particulars of the treaty can serve as a source of customary international law provided three basic conditions are met: 1) The treaty is accepted by a sufficient number of states in the international system. 2) Among the parties to the treaty there are a significant number of those states whose interests are most affected by the treaty. 3) The treaty provisions are not subject to reservations by the accepting parties"); *see also* Lt. Colonel Vincent A. Jordan, *Creation of Customary International Law by Way of Treaty*, 9 A.F. L. REV. 38 (1967).

[86] For example, in Annexes I–III, each of the three NAFTA parties provided a Schedule pertaining to "Reservations for Existing Measures and Liberalization Commitments." NAFTA, *supra* note 1, annexes I–III. In these annexes, each Party delineated certain domestic legislation to be deemed inapplicable in evaluating the treatment to be accorded to investors of another NAFTA Party, including the duties placed on a Host State under Article 1102's National

Although the elements of customary international law[87] certainly do bestow normative legitimacy on the principles that constitute it – and to this extent serve to enhance substantive and process legitimacy, – the consequence necessarily leads to still a broader conception of public policy exceptions that distorts the workings of international investment law. Moreover, the orthodox legacy conceptualization of the public purpose doctrine is based on a subjective analysis rendered legitimate by dint of State pronouncement that enjoys minimum process.[88] Legitimacy is solely grounded on the authority of the State to negotiate a space for its political will to express itself irrespective of the effects that it may have on foreign investments. The ratification of the treaty provides for the requisite consent that engrafts the final imprimatur of juridical legitimacy and normative standing.[89] Transitioning from a treaty reservation public purpose to a commonly recognized general principle of public purpose is both plausible and virtually inevitable.[90] Content scrutiny

Treatment Standard. Notably, one of the reservation chapters, Annex III "Activities Reserved to the State," only includes a Schedule of Reservations for Mexico, in which Mexico specified certain industries – petroleum, electricity, nuclear power, etc. – that it reserved the right to perform exclusively and "to refuse to permit the establishment of investments." *Id.* annex III.

87 Arthur M. Weisburd, *Customary International Law: The Problem of Treaties*, 21 VAND. J. TRANSNAT'L L. 1, 6 (1988) ("The fact which one must constantly keep in mind with respect to rules of customary international law is that proving the existence of such rules requires proof of two elements: first, the general practice of states must reflect the rule (the generality requirement); and second, states must follow the rule in the belief that such a course is legally required (the *opinio juris sive necessitatis* requirement)") (citing IAN BROWNLIE, PRINCIPLES OF PUBLIC INTERNATIONAL LAW 7–9 (3d ed. 1979)).

88 Reservation exceptions constitute binding conventional law. They do not, however, arise from a political process akin to the enactment of domestic legislation. *See, e.g.*, Edward T. Swaine, *Reserving*, 31 YALE J. INT'L L. 307, 319 (2006) ("[I]f a non-reserving State accepts another State's reservation, it modifies the relevant treaty provisions for them both. If, on the other hand, a non-reserving State objects – without specifically denying the reserving party's status as a party – 'the provisions to which the reservation relates do not apply as between the two states to the extent of the reservation.'") (citing Vienna Convention on the Law of Treaties art. 21, May 23, 1969, 1155 U.N.T.S. 331 [hereinafter VCLT]).

89 *See* VCLT, *supra* note 88, art. 14 ¶ 1 ("The consent of a State to be bound by a treaty is expressed by ratification when: (a) the treaty provides for such consent to be expressed by means of ratification; (b) it is otherwise established that the negotiating states were agreed that ratification should be required; (c) the representative of the State has signed the treaty subject to ratification; or (d) the intention of the State to sign the treaty subject to ratification appears from the full powers of its representative or was expressed during the negotiation"); *see also* RESTATEMENT (THIRD) OF FOREIGN RELATIONS LAW § 312 cmt. *d* (1987) ("A State can be bound upon signature, but that has now become unusual as regards important formal agreements. For such agreements, signature is normally ad referendum, i.e., subject to later ratification, and has no binding effect but is deemed to represent political approval and at least a moral obligation to seek ratification").

90 An example of this process can be found in the development of the Hull Rule:

> Consider, for example, customary rules governing compensation for expropriation. In 1938, in response to Mexico's nationalization of oil and agrarian assets, U.S. Secretary of

would then be minimal because the validating normative predicate – in the first instance a State pronouncement and, in the second, a common State pronouncement that is recurring and consonant with customary international law process legitimacy – would prevail, particularly in connection with a doctrine that is almost exclusively based on subjective content.

The transposition of general reservations contained in international conventional law to principles of international customary law likely to be categorized as public purpose precepts indiscriminately applicable to international trade and investment law is more than a theoretical construct. It is an inevitable historical mandate. This cross-fertilization simply cannot be properly managed with reliance based solely on the legacy public purpose doctrine. The consequence of expanding the scope of the existing public purpose doctrine, in addition to amplifying the regulatory sphere of States to the detriment of investment protection, also destabilizes the preferred equipoise in the economic relationship between capital-exporting and capital-importing countries. The widening of this chasm in turn destabilizes public international law policies, as well as the juridical principles that are fundamental to international trade and investment law, such as the seminal question of whether a finding of public purpose discharges a State's obligation to compensate a foreign investor as a result of a direct or indirect expropriation or nationalization or conduct tantamount to a taking. This central concern has been obscured and polarized by competing interpretations that are directly related to the status of a State as capital-exporting or capital-importing.[91]

A corollary to the question of compensation[92] from a sovereign's perspective needs to be raised as well. Should the public purpose doctrine play any role,

> State Cordell Hull articulated the Hull Rule, which requires prompt, adequate, and effective compensation in the event of expropriation. The United States, as well as many developed countries, has long considered it to be the customary rule on compensation for expropriation. In the 1970s, developing countries sought to weaken the Hull Rule (along with the broader international investment regime) through a series of U.N. General Assembly resolutions. In response, developed countries, led by the United States, began employing BITs to shore up the existing regime.

Timothy Meyer, *Codifying Custom*, 160 U. PA. L. REV. 995, 1025–26 (2012) (internal citations omitted).

91 *See* Patrick M. Norton, *A Law of the Future or A Law of the Past? Modern Tribunals and the International Law of Expropriation*, 85 AM. J. INT'L L. 474, 505 (1991) ("[I]t was argued that the Hull formula could not continue to be valid law in the face of the opposition of a majority of states. At the same time, since the development of customary international law requires the consent of all significant interest groups of states, the persistent opposition of one group, i.e., the capital-exporting states, prevented the development of any alternative formula into new law" [internal citations omitted]).

92 A detailed consideration of the extent to which the public purpose doctrine effects compensation within the framework of direct or indirect expropriations or nationalizations is referenced

let alone a dispositive one, in determining whether a sovereign's tender of compensation in an *indirect* expropriation, where the legacy public purpose doctrine is applied, constitutes the imposition of a penalty on a State for merely exercising its obligations as a sovereign? In this connection, should the legacy public purpose doctrine constitute a material test, standard, or predicate consideration for determining whether a nationalization represents a justifiable expression of regulatory sovereignty in a specific economic sector or an abuse of that authority under the mantle of public purpose? These concerns relate not only to the workings of the existing legacy public purpose doctrine but, in particular, can be quite meaningfully traced to consequences derived from the amplification of the public purpose doctrine because of its subjective content.[93]

In addition to subordinating the investment chapter to all other chapters of the NAFTA "to the extent of [any] inconsistency" pursuant to Article 1112, Chapter Eleven's cornerstone investment protection provision[94] (Article 1110

in the context of BITs, *infra* Chapter 4, and Foreign Investment Protection Statutes, *infra* Chapter 6.

93 The September 2, 1992, draft iteration of Article 1101(4), at Canada's initiative, sought to include "monetary policy" as a public purpose category. This inclusion would have been tantamount to infusing into the public purpose subjective content national policies deemed to be necessary, and, therefore, also would have had the effect of suggesting that "necessity, without more" (i.e., lacking the predicate principles constituting the State Necessity Defense) would suffice as a public purpose. The text of this draft, however, suggests that Mexico opposed it:

> 4. Nothing in this Chapter shall be construed to prevent a Party from providing functions or services such as law enforcement, correctional services, [monetary policy,] [n.3 "Canada is considering this bracket. Mexico does not agree to subject the Mexican monetary policy to the dispositions on the Investment Chapter."] income security or insurance, social security or insurance, social welfare, public education, public training, public health and childcare, in a manner that is inconsistent with this Chapter.

NAFTA Negotiating Drafts, *supra* note 7, Draft of September 2, 1992.

94 The proscription against direct or indirect nationalization or expropriation of an investment of another NAFTA Party was first framed using the permissive "may," where the final version adopts the mandatory "shall." The paragraph in part reads:

> **Article 1110: Expropriation and Compensation**
> 1. No Party *[may]* directly or indirectly nationalize or expropriate an investment of an investor of another Party in its territory or take a measure tantamount to nationalization or expropriation of such an investment ....

Id. (emphasis added).

One commentator has argued that the NAFTA has the effect of weakening the sovereign's exercise of sovereignty in the regulatory sphere. Marisa Yee, *The Future of Environmental Regulation after Article 1110 of NAFTA: A Look at the Methanex and Metalclad Cases*, 9 Hastings W.-N.W. J. Env. L. & Pol'y 85 (Fall 2002). Like Jackson, *infra* note 132, she generally points to the NAFTA's international dispute resolution mechanism. More specifically, she contends that because the term "expropriation" within Article 1110 of the NAFTA "remains unclear," Host States are left "vulnerable to law suits by foreign companies that conduct business

entitled "Expropriation and Compensation") is made applicable to "taxation measures" but arguably qualified by the *jurisdictional* predicate of submitting a claim to arbitration pursuant to Article 1120 ("Submission of a Claim to Arbitration").[95] To the extent that the public purpose category of taxation[96] requires a prospective claimant first to submit the issue of whether a particular taxation measure constitutes an expropriation "to the appropriate competent authorities"[97] as a condition precedent to perfecting an arbitration claim

in the host country whenever the host country's action reduces the company's profits. This may jeopardize national regulations, including efforts to protect the environment." *Id.*

In a similar vein, it has been asserted that "[n]on-discriminatory, non-arbitrary regulations that are legitimate exercises of the police power should be exempted from Article 1110's scrutiny. That exclusion should include not only those police-power regulations exempted from arbitration under GATT, Article XX, but also human rights and labor standards, which are not covered by GATT Article XX due to their impermissible focus on production process methods rather than on criteria of products." Jessica C. Lawrence, *Chicken Little Revisited: NAFTA Regulatory Expropriations after Methanex*, 41 GA. L. REV. 261, 305 (2006). The author further asserts that "[b]ecause the burden of proof will remain on the claimants under the 'presumptions that respondent states act lawfully' such an alteration or interpretation of the NAFTA text would provide a significant check on the ability of investors to interfere with a State's right to enact regulations for the benefit of its citizens." *Id.* at 305–06.

Although helpful in contextualizing the disparate tensions between investors generally arising from income-exporting countries and Host States (typically income-importing sovereigns), Lawrence elects not to comment on the overbroad scope that is engrafted on the public purpose doctrine (in the form of "police powers") and its effect on FDI incentives. Under her formulation, an expansive construction of the public purpose doctrine is amply checked by the international dispute resolution burden of proof that a prevailing claimant first must meet.

95 Article 2103 ("Taxation") Paragraph 6 states:

> Article 1110 ["Expropriation and Compensation"] shall apply to taxation measures except that no investor may invoke that Article as the basis for a claim under Article 1116 ["Claim by an Investor of a Party on Its Own Behalf"] or 1117 ["Claim by an Investor of a Party on Behalf of an Enterprise"], where it has been determined pursuant to this paragraph that the measure is not an expropriation. The investor shall refer the issue of whether the measure is not an expropriation for a determination to the appropriate confident authorities set out in Annex 2103.6 at the time that it gives notice under Article 1119 ["Notice of Intent to Submit a Claim to Arbitration"]. If the competent authorities do not agree to consider the issue or, having agreed to consider it, fail to agree that the measure is not an expropriation with a period of six months of such referral, the investor may submit its claim to arbitration under Article 1120 ["Submission of a Claim to Arbitration"].

NAFTA, *supra* note 1, art. 2103 ¶ 6.

96 Taxation is not mentioned Article 1101(4), but amply meets the NAFTA Standard as defined in this text.

97 Annex 2103.6 defines competent authorities for purposes of Article 2103 ("Taxation") as follows:

> For purposes of this Chapter: competent authority means:
> a. in the case of Canada, the Assistant Deputy Minister for Tax Policy, Department of Finance;
> b. in the case of Mexico, the Deputy Minister of Revenue of the Ministry of Finance and Public Credit ("Secretaria de Hacienda y Credito Publico");

alleging expropriation, the NAFTA rubric accords expropriation a distinct status from that of other public purpose categories.[98]

F. BEYOND THE NAFTA CHAPTER ELEVEN FRAMEWORK: THE NAFTA'S ANATOMY PROVIDES FOR AN EXPANSIVE CONSTRUCTION OF THE PUBLIC PURPOSE DOCTRINE AND THE "LEGITIMATE OBJECTIVE" STANDARD

The term "public purpose" does not appear in the NAFTA beyond Chapter Eleven.[99] A permutation of the term, mostly in the form of "public interest," appears eight times.[100] The term appears once in the "public welfare" iteration.[101] Throughout the NAFTA, the public purpose doctrine serves as an organizing principle. The doctrine is fundamental in structuring, defining, and harmonizing the allocation of affirmative obligations and proscriptions concerning a substantively diverse gamut of public purpose categories.[102] From a macro point of view, the entire NAFTA significantly mirrors the public purpose doctrine structural organization of Chapter Eleven.

Central to the NAFTA's development and application of the public purpose doctrine are Articles 904, 915, and 1201, which are conceptually interrelated with respect to the public purpose doctrine and should be analyzed

c. in the case of the United States, the Assistant Secretary of the Treasury (Tax Policy), Department of the Treasury.

NAFTA, *supra* note 1, annex 2103.6.

98 The requirement to submit, for a determination the question of whether a taxation measure constitutes an expropriation, to competent authorities in the context of a six-month waiting period or determination period, whichever comes first, may constitute a jurisdictional condition precedent that can only be obviated either (i) upon penalty of triggering lack of consent in the event that an arbitral claimant's filing would provide a Host State with a jurisdictional defense to the claim or (ii) in situations where the competent authority structurally or politically is incapable of or unlikely to process the claim within the applicable time frame. Just as a provision calling for recourse to a competent authority of the Host State or a limited time frame at the expiration of which a claimant may initiate an arbitral proceeding imposes an obligation on the claimant, such obligation is bilateral and also places on the Host State the duty to make available competent authorities or tribunals within the meaning of the treaty that can meet the treaty obligation. Such provisions are bilateral and, therefore, equally applied to investors-claimants and Host State respondents. *See, e.g.*, Daimler Financial Services AG v. Argentine Republic, ICSID Case No. ARB/05/1, Award ¶¶ 179–204 (August 22, 2012), http://www.italaw.com/sites/default/files/case-documents/ita 1082.pdf.

99 *Supra* note 42 and accompanying text.

100 *See, e.g.*, NAFTA, *supra* note 1, art. 721 ¶ 2(b); art. 912 ¶ (b); art. 1015 ¶¶ 4(c), 8(a), 8(i); art. 1017 ¶ 1(j); art. 1019 ¶ 6; art. 1411 ¶ 5(b); art. 1804 ¶ (b).

101 *Id.* preamble (stating, in relevant part, the parties' aim to "*PRESERVE* their flexibility to safeguard the public welfare" [emphasis in original]).

102 *See, e.g.*, *Id.* art. 1015.

together.[103] Article 904, entitled "Basic Rights and Obligations," relies on the GATT Article XX's public purpose categories primarily grounded on (i) safety; (ii) the protection of human, animal, or plant life or health; (iii) environmental concerns; and (iv) consumer protection.[104] The international law trade exceptions contained in Article 904 comport with fundamental principles governing cross-border trade in goods and services; as noted, a subject matter that is materially distinct from investment or investor protection in international law. Therefore, but for the hierarchy established in Article 1112[105] subordinating the Chapter Eleven investor-investment protection strictures to all other chapters of the NAFTA, the unqualified GATT-based public purpose categories appear to be in keeping with furthering cross-border trade in goods and services. The Article 1112 mandate, however, contributes to a

[103] Even though these three articles are not sequentially in immediate order, they are conceptually inextricable when viewed in a public purpose doctrinal context.

[104] This Article provides:

> **Article 904: Basic Rights and Obligations**
> *Right to Take Standards – Related Measures*
> Each Party may, in accordance with this Agreement, adopt, maintain or apply any standards related measure, including any such measures relating to safety, *the protection of human, animal or plant life or health*, the environment or consumers, and any measure to ensure its enforcement or implementation. Such measures include those to prohibit the importation of a good or another Party, or the provision of a service by a service provider of another Party that fails to comply with the applicable requirements of those measures or to complete the Party's approval procedures.
>
> *Right to Establish Level of Protection*
> 2. Notwithstanding any other provision of this Chapter, each Party may, in pursuing its *legitimate objectives* of *safety* or the *protection of human, animal or plant life or health, the environment or consumers*, establish the levels of protection that it considers appropriate in accordance with Article 907 (2).
>
> *Non-Discriminatory Treatment*
> 3. Each Party shall, in respect of its standards-related measures, accord to goods and service providers of another Party:
>   (a) national treatment in accordance with Article 301 (Market Access) or Article 1202 (Cross-Border Trade in Service); and
>   (b) treatment no less favorable than that it accords to like goods, or in the circumstances to service providers, of any other country.
>
> *Unnecessary Obstacles*
> 4. No Party may prepare, adopt, maintain or apply any standards-related measure with a view or with the effect of creating an unnecessary obstacle to trade between the Parties. An unnecessary obstacle to trade shall not be deemed to be created where:
>   (a) the demonstrable purpose of the measure is to achieve a *legitimate objective*;
>   (b) the measure does not operate to exclude goods of another Party that meet that *legitimate objective* (emphasis added).

NAFTA, *supra* note 1, art. 904 (emphasis added).

[105] *Id.* art. 1112.

distortion of the tempered ratio that must be present between the trade and investor-investment protection objectives of the NAFTA.

Paragraph 4 of Article 904 does purport to limit party autonomy as to measures implemented in furtherance of the public purpose categories contained in this Article to the extent that any such measure may have "the effect of creating an unnecessary obstacle to trade between the Parties."[106] This qualification in turn is itself subject to a "legitimate objective" test that first appears in Paragraph 2 of Article 904 and is repeated in Paragraph 4 subsections (a) and (b). The "legitimate objective" standard serves to broaden the scope of the Host State's regulatory sovereignty.[107] Article 904 on three occasions relies on the "legitimate objective" standard, but nowhere in this article is the standard defined. The standard oddly is not defined until eleven articles later, in Article 915 entitled: "Definitions."[108] Because "legitimate objective" within the meaning of Chapter Nine ("Standards-Related Measures") of the NAFTA is defined as a *standard* and not as a "term," it is vested with latitude and flexibility in keeping with the use of standards in international law and as described in this text.[109] Consequently, the Article 904(4) "check" on the extent to which a NAFTA party may infringe on another party's goods or service providers is further broadened by the treatment of "legitimate objective" as a "standard" and not a "term."

[106] *Id.* art. 904 ¶ 4.

[107] This effect of the Host State's or host Parties' regulatory-legislative space is corroborated by the language contained in Paragraph 3 of Article 905, which provides:

> Nothing in paragraph 1 [relating to the NAFTA Party's use of relevant international standards or international standards] shall be construed to prevent a Party, in pursuing its *legitimate objective* from adopting, maintaining or applying any standards-related measure that results in a higher level of protection than would be achieved if the measure were based on the relevant international standard.

Id. art. 905 ¶ 3 (emphasis added).

[108] Article 915: Definitions, in pertinent part reads:

> 1. For purposes of this Chapter:
>
> **Legitimate objective** includes an objective such as:
>
> (a) safety,
>
> (b) protection of human, animal or plant life or health, the environment or consumers, including matters relating to quality and identifiability of goods or services, and
>
> (c) sustainable development,
>
> considering, among other things, where appropriate, fundamental climactic or other geographical factors, technological or infrastructural factors, or scientific justification but does not include the protection of domestic production.

Id. art. 915 ¶ 1.

[109] Accordingly, Article 915, although seeming to define the words "legitimate objective" taken together, instead reconfigures it with the matrix of a standard, as evinced by the words "such as" and the subordinate clause "considering, among other things, where appropriate, . . . " *Id.*

Even though strictly the term "public purpose" does not appear beyond its solitary reference in Chapter Eleven (in Article 1110(1)(a)), Article 1201(3)(b) is identical to the NAFTA Standard as set forth in Article 1101(4).[110] The unqualified incorporation of the NAFTA Standard in the chapter regulating cross-border trade to limit a Host State's exercise of regulatory sovereignty in ways that may be detrimental to another party's investment or trade interests further demonstrates a doctrinal conception of public purpose that commands refinement. Investment-investor protection and cross-border trade interests have different objectives and underlying policies.[111] The microeconomic model

[110] In governing the scope of and coverage of cross-border trade in services within the Chapter 12 framework in paragraphs, Article 1201, Paragraphs 1 and 3 provide:

> 1. This Chapter applies to measures adopted or maintained by Party relating to
>   (a) cross-border trade in services by service providers of another Party, including measures respecting:
>   (b) the production, distribution, marketing, sale, and delivery of a service;
>   (c) the purchase or use of, or payment for, a service;
>   (d) the access to and use of distribution and transportation systems in connection with the provision of a service;
>   (e) the presence in its territory of a service provider of another Party; and
>   (f) the provision of a bond or other form of financial security as a condition for the provision of a service.
>
> ...
>
> 3. Nothing in this Chapter shall be construed to:
>
> ...
>
>   (b) prevent a Party from providing a service or performing a function such as law enforcement, correctional services, income security, or insurance, social security or insurance, social welfare, public education, public training, health, and child-care, in a manner that is not inconsistent with this Chapter.

NAFTA, *supra* note 1, art. 1201 ¶¶ 1,3.

[111] "[I]nternational investment law is designed to support economic development by protecting the interests of foreign investors." Elizabeth A. Martinez, *Understanding the Debate over Necessity: Unanswered Questions and Future Implications of Annulments in the Argentine Gas Cases*, 23 DUKE J. COMP. & INT'L L. 149, 175 (2012); *see also* Stephan W. Schill, *Enhancing International Investment Law's Legitimacy: Conceptual and Methodological Foundations of A New Public Law Approach*, 52 VA. J. INT'L L. 57, 59 (2011) ("The public function of international investment law consists of establishing principles of investment protection under international law that provide for the protection of property and endorse rule of law standards for the treatment of foreign investors by states. These principles have the purpose of reducing the so-called 'political risk' inherent in any foreign investment situation").

By contrast, the "chief purpose" of international trade law is to promote free trade. Stephen McCaffrey, *Biotechnology: Some Issues of General International Law*, 14 TRANSNAT'L LAW. 91 (2001). *See also* O.A. Odiase-Alegimenlen, *Globalization, the World Trade Organization and Developing States; A View from the "South,"* CURRENTS: INT'L TRADE L.J., Winter 2003, at 24 ("The purpose of International trade as espoused today is the ultimate prosperity of the generality of humankind. This is supposed to occur through the increase in the volume of trade amongst countries of the world, which will stimulate demand and therefore production, thus opening up jobs and expanding opportunities in all spheres").

incident to international investment law generally consists of (i) a single-sector investment, (ii) by a private entity or natural person, (iii) for a limited time frame, and (iv) of an amount unlikely to affect materially a State's economy.[112] In high relief, the subject matter of international trade law generally consists of a (i) full sector or multiple sector economic event, (ii) taking place over an extended time frame and after a very measured contractual period of time, (iii) with revenue that materially affects a State's economy, and (iv) concerning treaties between nations or geopolitical subdivisions, but not private entities or natural persons.[113] The objectives and underlying economic policies pertaining to international trade law are grounded in a macroeconomic framework that generally seeks to remove or mitigate the effects of trade barriers and other forms of protectionism.[114]

Similarly, the international dispute resolution configuration for controversies arising from alleged noncompliance with investment protection and from violations pertaining to international trade law also differ. A breach of international investment law consists of an arbitration configuration having a private entity or natural person as a claimant and a State as a respondent.[115] Treaty-based investment arbitrations concern claims for damages. These damages principally are calculated based on analysis of past events giving rise to the alleged investment protection violation.[116] In contrast, the relief sought arising

[112] Generally, the harm to the investor stemming from a violation of international investment law "would be derived primarily from the conduct of the State, which has actively utilized its sovereign power to place the investor in a worse position than it had enjoyed before the State's action." Joshua Robbins, *The Emergence of Positive Obligations in Bilateral Investment Treaties*, 13 U. MIAMI INR'L & COMP. L. REV. 403, 419 (2006).

[113] For example, it has been argued that "the WTO system prioritizes, in terms of remedies, consistency and conformity with the WTO rules over compensation whose concept is deeply associated with such elements as injury, damages and nullification or impairment." Sungjoon Cho, *The Nature of Remedies in International Trade Law*, 65 U. PITT. L. REV. 763, 771 (2004).

[114] *See* Sara Dillon, A *Farewell to "Linkage": International Trade Law and Global Sustainability Indicators*, 55 RUTGERS L. REV. 87, 97 (2002) ("[T]he operation of the current global trading system, complete with its legal rules and dispute resolution mechanisms, must be examined for evidence of its larger effects").

[115] *See, e.g.*, Robbins, *supra* note 112, at 415 ("The modern investor-State dispute resolution system takes a dramatically different approach. Virtually every BIT contains a section allowing investors who feel their treaty-based rights have been violated to institute arbitration against the Host State. Such arbitrations are frequently to be administered by the International Center for the Settlement of Investment Disputes (ICSID), an institution within the World Bank Group formed in 1966 to conduct and promote investor-State dispute resolution" [internal footnotes omitted]).

[116] Christopher M. Ryan, *Discerning the Compliance Calculus: Why States Comply with International Investment Law*, 38 GA. J. INT'LZ & COMP. L. 63, 83 (2009) ("International investment law permits investors to bring claims directly against states. As such, a breach of international investment law carries with it the prospect of significant financial liability. A

from alleged violations of international trade law does not contemplate an award of pecuniary damages based on past violations, but rather issuance of appropriate modifications to trade regulations that would eviscerate the allegedly wrongful conduct on a prospective basis.[117] The affirmative relief sought in treaty-based investment arbitrations is premised on alleged violations of international investment law standards such as the fair and equitable treatment standard,[118] national treatment standard,[119] and international minimum standards.[120] Claims predicated on alleged violations of international trade law commonly concern principles that international investment law and international trade law have in common, such as MFN clauses, but contextualized within a radically different framework governing trade and tariffs.[121]

recent study shows that, as of 2006, the amount of quantified damages claimed in investment treaty arbitrations ranged from $155,314 to $9.4 billion, with an average claim of approximately $345 million") (citing Susan D. Franck, *Empirically Evaluating Claims about Investment Treaty Arbitration*, 86 N.C. L. REV. 1, 54–58 (2007)).

117 *See, e.g.*, Cho, *supra* note 113, at 771.

118 *See, generally*, ROLAND KLAGER, FAIR AND EQUITABLE TREATMENT IN INTERNATIONAL INVESTMENT LAW (Cambridge University Press 2011).

119 A. F. M. Maniruzzaman, *Expropriation of Alien Property and the Principle of Non-Discrimination in International Law of Foreign Investment: An Overview*, 8 J. TRANSNAT'L L. & POL'Y 57, 71 (1998) ("[N]ational treatment is the commitment by a country to treat enterprises operating on its territory, but controlled by the nationals of another country, no less favorably than domestic enterprises in like situations"). *See, generally*, ROLAND KLAGER, FAIR AND EQUITABLE TREATMENT IN INTERNATIONAL INVESTMENT LAW (Cambridge University Press 2011).

120 One NAFTA tribunal has described the Minimum Standard as follows:

> The minimum standard of treatment provision of the NAFTA is similar to clauses contained in BITs. The inclusion of a "minimum standard" provision is necessary to avoid what might otherwise be a gap. A government might treat an investor in a harsh, injurious and unjust manner, but do so in a way that is no different than the treatment inflicted on its own nationals. The "minimum standard" is a floor below which treatment of foreign investors must not fall, even if a government were not acting in a discriminatory manner.

S.D. Myers Inc. v. Government of Canada, First Partial Award on Liability ¶ 259 (November 13, 2000), 8 ICSID Rep. 18 (2005) [hereinafter S.D. Myers First Partial Award].

121 In the international trade context the *national treatment standard*, by way of example, has applied to the GATT, only concerns trade in goods, and, therefore, is not applicable to trade and services or technology. Similarly, the MFN clause, which pervades the GATT, seeks to affect economic categories that are wholly unrelated to investment law policies. The most notable MFN clause in the GATT, contained in Article I, Paragraph 1, is illustrative of this point:

> With respect to customs duties and charges of any kind imposed on or in connection with importation or exportation or imposed on the international transfer of payments for imports or exports, with respect to the method of levying such duties and charges, and with respect to all rules and formalities in connection with importation and exportation, and with respect to all matters referred to in paragraphs 2 and 4 of Article III, any

It soon becomes clear that the economics, subject matter, objectives, underlying policies, and even international dispute resolution configuration of international investment law and international trade law are disparate. The NAFTA's use of a single overarching public purpose standard in Chapter Eleven and with respect to the remaining NAFTA chapters on trade is as incongruous as the wholesale importation of GATT Article XX ("Exceptions") into Chapter Eleven of the NAFTA or into BITs.[122] A less malleable public purpose doctrine with objective content is necessary if the goals of both international trade and investment law are to be maximized and reconciled with the interests of all parties (i.e., foreign investors, capital-exporting countries, and capital-importing countries). The public purpose doctrine in the guise of "public interest" in the NAFTA chapters beyond Chapter Eleven plays a distinct role in relation to disclosure or access to information. Pursuant to Article 912(b), the NAFTA parties are not obligated to disclose any information deemed to be "contrary to the public interest."[123] Linking limitations on the provision of information to so general a standard as "contrary to the public interest," even where the NAFTA Standard vests "public interest" with substantive import, is no different from according the NAFTA parties unbridled discretion to limit the provision of information.[124] A similar stricture

> advantage, favor, privilege or immunity granted by any contracting party to any product originating in or destined for any other country shall be accorded immediately and unconditionally to the like product originating in or destined for the territories of all other contracting parties.

GATT, *supra* note 2, art. I ¶ 1. It is worth underscoring that the MFN clause in Article I, Paragraph 1 of the GATT only applies to the importation and exportation of products. It is also of an unconditional nature in that it proscribes that any concession granted by a contracting party to a product of another country "shall by accorded immediately and unconditionally to the like product originating in or destined for the territories of all other contracting parties."

122 *See infra* Chapter 4.

123 Article 912 "Limitations on the Provision of Information" reads: Nothing in this Chapter shall be construed to require a Party to:

> *(a)* communicate, publish texts, or provide particulars or copies of documents other than in an official language of the Party; or
> *(b)* *furnish any information the disclosure of which would impede law enforcement or otherwise be contrary to public interest, or would prejudice the legitimate commercial interests of particular enterprises.*

NAFTA, *supra* note 1, art. 912 (emphasis added).

124 Considerable ink has been spilled on the issue of transparency in the NAFTA. *See, e.g.*, Jack J. Coe, Jr., *Transparency in Investor-State Disputes – Adoption, Adaption, and NAFTA Leadership*, 54 U. Kan. L. Rev. 1339, 1379–80 (2006) (addressing a new generation of texts "consolidating, clarifying and promoting transparency practice"); Fulvio Fracassi, *Confidentiality and NAFTA Chapter Eleven Arbitrations*, 2 Chi. J. Int'l L. 213 (2001); *see, generally*, Carl-Sebastian Zoellner, *Transparency in Analysis of an Evolving Fundamental Principle of International Economic Law*, 27 Mich. J. Int'l L. 579, 580–81 (2006); Pedro

is found in Articles 1019 of Chapter Ten ("Government Procurement")[125] and Article 1411 of Chapter Fourteen ("Financial Services").[126] "Public interest" in the NAFTA may determine whether to award a procurement contract, withhold information pertaining to such an instrument, or withhold information in connection with the procurement of consulting services.[127]

J. Martinez-Fraga, *Juridical Convergence in International Dispute Resolution: Developing a Substantive Principle of Transparency and Transnational Evidence Gathering*, 10 LOY. U. CM. INT'L L. REV. 37 (2012).

Furthermore, the NAFTA Parties have interpreted the agreement as follows:

> Nothing in the NAFTA imposes a general duty of confidentiality under disputing Parties to a Chapter 11 Arbitration [or] precludes the Parties from providing public access to documents submitted to, or issued by, a Chapter 11 Tribunal.
>
> . . .
>
> Each Party agrees to make available to the public in a timely manner all documents submitted to, or issued by a Chapter 11 Tribunal, subject to redaction of:
>
> (a) confidential business information;
> (b) information which is privileged or is otherwise protected from disclosure under the Party's domestic law; and
> (c) information which the Party must withhold pursuant to the relevant arbitral rules, as applied.

Notes of Interpretation of Certain Chapter Eleven Provisions of the NAFTA Free Trade Commission (July 31, 2001), http://www.sice.oas.org/tpd/nafta/Commission/CH11understanding_e.asp

125 Article 1019 in part reads:

> 1. Further, to Article 1802(1) (Publication), each Party shall promptly publish any law, regulation, precedential judicial decision, administrative ruling of general application in any procedure, including standard contract clauses, regarding government procurement covered by this Chapter in the appropriate publications referred to in Annex 1010.1.
>
> . . .
>
> 6. Nothing in this Chapter shall be construed as requiring any Party to disclose confidential information the disclosure of which would impede law enforcement or otherwise be contrary to the public interest.

NAFTA, *supra* note 1, art. 1019 ¶ 1,6.

126 Article 1411 "Transparency," in relevant part states:

> 5. Nothing in this Chapter requires a Party to furnish or allow access to:
>
> (b) any confidential information, the disclosure of which would impede law enforcement or otherwise be contrary to the public interest or prejudice legitimate commercial interests of particular enterprises.

Id. art. 1411 ¶ 5(b).

127 Article 1015 "Submission Receipt and Opening of Tenders and Awarding of Contracts States," reads in relevant part:

> 4. An entity shall award contracts in accordance with the following:
>
> (c) unless the entity decides in the public interest not to award the contract, the entity shall make the award to the supplier that has been determined to be fully capable of undertaking the contract and whose tender is either the lowest-priced tender or

Finally, a reviewing authority investigating a BIT challenge "may delay the awarding of the proposed contract pending resolution of the challenge, except in cases of emergency or where the delay would be contrary to public interest."[128] Beyond Chapter Eleven of the NAFTA, the NAFTA rubric conceptually and structurally follows the organizational principles found in Chapter Eleven. The public purpose doctrine finds identical expression and is not at all modified. The doctrine's scope and content remained identical but for the seemingly expansive recourse to "public interest" principally in the context of disclosures.[129] The entire framework fundamentally adheres to the NAFTA Standard and therefore mirrors the virtues incident to Chapter Eleven, particularly as a result of the Article 1101(4) effort to fashion a public purpose standard. The NAFTA regime beyond Chapter Eleven does not contribute to a doctrinal *context* or *content* for the public purpose doctrine other than setting forth a more detailed iteration of the orthodox-legacy public purpose scheme. Put simply, the NAFTA chapters beyond Chapter Eleven do not contribute a satisfactory answer to the underlying inquiries: to what extent are governmental measures exercised for genuine and legitimate domestic objectives "legal" despite their detrimental effect on foreign investors or investments? Is there a limited and identifiable universe of substantive categories that, from a global legal perspective, rightfully fall under the umbrella of public purpose and therefore supersede obligations owed to foreign investor/investments despite the adverse consequences of their application? Is the public purpose doctrine as embedded in the NAFTA regime determinative in parceling legitimate State action from the discriminatory issuance of regulatory decrees? This dynamic upsets the very principles of bilateralism and symmetry between Home and Host States that, when present, give rise to the requisite transparency, uniformity, and predictability that

> the tender determined to be the most advantageous in terms of the specific evaluation criteria set out in the notices or tender documentation;
>
> 8. Notwithstanding paragraphs 1–7, an entity may withhold certain information on the award of a contract where disclosure of the information:
>   (a) would impede law enforcement or otherwise be contrary to public interest.

Id. art. 1015 ¶¶ 4(c), 8(a).

Additionally, Article 1016 "Limited Tendering Procedures," in pertinent part provides:

> 2. An entity may use limited tendering procedures in the following circumstances and subject to the following conditions, as applicable:
>   (i) where an entity needs to procure consulting services regarding matters of a confidential nature, the disclosure of which could reasonably be expected to compromise government confidences, cause economic disruption or similarly be contrary to the public interest.

[128] *Id.* art. 1016 ¶ 2(i).

[129] *See supra* notes 123–26 and accompanying text.

purport to be the hallmarks of BITs, as well as of treaty-based arbitral proceedings. International investment law and treaty-based international arbitration deserve more from the public purpose doctrine.

G. CONCLUSIONS AND OBSERVATIONS

The NAFTA regime ably crafts what may be construed as a public purpose doctrine standard in Article 1101(4), which is later replicated in Article 1106(6).[130] Certainly, this effort represents a notable landmark in seeking to bestow meaning on the doctrine, at least within the NAFTA framework. The broad and all-encompassing scope of the categories comprising what in this writing has been identified as the NAFTA Standard is problematic. The NAFTA *describes* the content of its version of public purpose but does not define it with any rigor in the classical etymological sense of that word (i.e., *definire*, as in rendering distinct because of its very limits or boundaries). Instead, the limitless and unqualified public purpose categories forming part of the NAFTA Standard by itself, let alone when coupled with the use of the term "public interest" throughout the NAFTA chapters beyond Chapter Eleven, divests the doctrine of all objective content. The doctrine is thus accorded an intuitive, self-evident status. Consequently, instead of serving as a standard capable of harmonizing the policies incident to investment protection with regulatory sovereignty, the public purpose doctrine of the NAFTA disproportionately favors the State's regulatory authority to the likely detriment of investment protection.[131] The practical result has problematic consequences that extend to investor-state arbitration well beyond the confines of the NAFTA.

The indiscriminate commingling of international trade law with international investment law exceptions under the public purpose banner is not conducive to yielding a functional public purpose doctrine beyond the legacy-orthodox paradigm. The wholesale importation into investment law of general exceptions from the GATT[132] is not conducive to yielding a public purpose doctrine capable of harmonizing the interests of "foreign investors" and "Host

[130] NAFTA, supra note 1, arts. 1104 ¶ 4; 1106 ¶ 6.

[131] The proposition that the public purpose doctrine within the NAFTA more favorably bolsters the regulatory authority of sovereigns is contrary to the orthodox understanding of the effects of trade agreements generally and of the NAFTA in particular. By way of example, Jackson has observed that, "[t]he North American Free Trade Agreement (NAFTA) in some respects went very far in its measures seeking national government changes arguably necessary to fulfill the NAFTA international obligations. This was true for the NAFTA investor protection rules, and also in relation to environment and labor standards." JOHN H. JACKSON, THE JURISPRUDENCE OF GATT AND THE WTO: INSIGHTS ON TREATY LAW AND ECONOMIC RELATIONS 1, 5 (Cambridge University Press 2000).

[132] *Compare* NAFTA, *supra* note 1, art. 1106 ¶¶ 6(a)–(c) *with* GATT, *supra* note 2, art. XX.

States." The general exceptions endemic to international trade law in theory and practice seek to further underlying policies that are radically distinct from those pertaining to international investment law. The Article XX General Exceptions of the GATT enjoying robust standing in the NAFTA framework, including Chapter Eleven, should be tepidly applied[133] in furtherance of the objectives of international investment law. The subject matter of international trade law principally concerns: (i) the protection of the value of tariff concessions;[134] (ii) distortions of trade flow; (iii) the effects of nontariff measures, including subsidies and countervailing duties; antidumping obligations, technical barriers to trade, government procurement;[135] (iv) trade regulation pertaining to agricultural goods so as to preserve its advantage in developing countries, primarily with respect to trade agreement clauses that distinguish between "industrialized" and "primary" goods;[136] (v) restrictions on imports that may injure domestic producers through "safeguards" techniques;[137] and

[133] The GATT Article XX, General Exceptions, are to be applied only *if* "necessary." Accordingly, in the matter of treaty construction, the exceptions are not to apply where their objectives can be served by a less restrictive alternative. This principle, however, is not triggered in the context of protection of foreign investments and investors under international investment law. To the contrary, because the "jurisprudence" that treaty-based international arbitral tribunals generate simply do not constitute binding legal precedent, the application and construction of General Exceptions are not governed by a set of binding principles capable of having predictive value. In addition, with respect to the international law of investment protection, there is no universally accepted or consistently applied "proportionality" or "effects" tests capable of mitigating the policy consequences arising from a lack of checks and balances in the application of General Exceptions. GATT, *supra* note 2, art. XX.

[134] For example, "tariffs are the 'preferred trade policy instrument' under GATT because the most-favored-nation and national treatment requirements reinforce negotiated tariff concessions; because tariffs are relatively open, predictable, pro-competitive, and domestically acceptable trade policy instruments; and because alternative trade policy instruments are restricted or prohibited." Robert J. Girouard, *Water Export Restrictions: A Case Study of WTO Dispute Settlement Strategies and Outcomes*, 15 GEO. INT'L ENVTL. L. REV. 247, 254 (2003).

[135] *See, e.g.*, David G. Forgue, *An Overview of an International Trade and Customs Practice*, CBA REC., February/March 2002, at 28 ("International Trade law issues include representing parties in antidumping duty cases involving foreign producers that allegedly sell their goods at unfairly low price in the U.S., countervailing duty cases involving subsidies to foreign companies by their governments, matters brought under Section 201 of the Trade Act of 1974, and similar matters").

[136] *See, e.g.*, Ari Afilalo, *Not in My Backyard: Power and Protectionism in U.S. Trade Policy*, 34 N.Y. U. J. INT'L L. & POL. 749, 782 (2002) ("The Uruguay Round of negotiations resulted in the reduction of protectionist policies in developed countries. The Agriculture Agreement that issued from these negotiations required the developed countries to convert nontariff barriers into tariffs, while preserving equivalent market-access opportunities").

[137] *See* Frank J. Garcia, *Three Takes on Global Justice*, 31 U. LA VERNE L. REV. 323, 332–33 (2010) ("The core commitment of contemporary trade law is that of free trade: international economic relations are to be free, or as free as possible, from governmental restrictions in the form of tariff and non-tariff barriers, and nondiscriminatory with respect to country of origin (the most-favored-nation rule) and domestic origin (the national treatment rule)" [citation omitted]).

(vi) rules seeking to minimize government intervention and also to enhance domestic government intervention in trade law both with respect to *type* and *amount* of trade.[138] The general exceptions found in international trade law are meant to comport with these (above-referenced) macroeconomic issues. Hence, such public purpose categories as "prison labor" are staples of the GATT General Exceptions but conceptually remain far afield from the issues pervading international investment law.[139] The precepts of international trade law used to enhance trade flow patterns simply are ill-suited to constitute the substantive content of a public purpose doctrine seeking to preserve this objective while protecting foreign investor/investments and attracting foreign direct investment (FDI).

The development of the Public Purpose Standard and the legitimate effort to engraft a subject matter "definitive" to the doctrine must be recognized as more than a first step toward developing public purpose beyond a self-evident truth pertaining to all things public and must remain self-judging by the invoking State. This contribution notwithstanding, the importance of public purpose as both an organizing principle and a source for legitimacy in the process of exercising regulatory sovereignty commands objective content and application. The public purpose doctrine within the NAFTA is accorded great weight but little specificity. The role of the doctrine within customary international law as simplified by the NAFTA is significant, but its workings all too often resemble a license granted to the Host States to engage in regulatory sovereignty at the expense of investor/investment protection.

H. THE JURISPRUDENCE OF PUBLIC PURPOSE IN THE NAFTA

Structurally, the jurisprudence of any statutory framework would serve to define principles and terms. One of the rudimentary promises that decisional law aspires to redeem is the development of statutory frameworks vested with predictive value, uniformity of standard, and transparency,[140] notwithstanding the lack of *stare decisis* of such awards.[141] The "jurisprudence" of public

[138] JOHN H. JACKSON, THE JURISPRUDENCE OF GATT AND THE WTO 1, 38–40 (Cambridge University Press 2000) (citing Subcommittee on International Trade of the Senate Committee on Finance, 96th Cong., 1st Sess., MTN Studies: MTN and the Legal Institutions of International Trade (Committee Print, 1979) Vol. IV. 4–5 (report prepared by J. Jackson at the request of the Subcommittee on International Trade)).

[139] GATT, *supra* note 2, art. XX ¶ *(e)*.

[140] *See generally* BENJAMIN CARDOZO, THE NATURE OF JUDICIAL PROCESS (1921).

[141] *See, e.g.*, Pedro J. Martinez-Fraga and Harout Jack Samra, *The Role of Precedent in Defining Res Judicata in Investor-State Arbitration*, 32 NW. J. INT'L L. & BUS. 419, 449 (2012) (noting "[t]he uncertain nature and application of the doctrine of precedent – stare decisis – in international arbitration").

purpose within the NAFTA does not meet this objective. To the contrary, the "decisional law" that the NAFTA has spawned emphasizes the shortcomings of the public purpose doctrine generally and within the NAFTA in particular.

The failings of the "NAFTA common law" in part arise from the very nature of treaty-based international arbitration.[142] The Chapter Eleven dispute resolution framework provides for ad hoc arbitration tribunals. The arbitrators are empaneled for the exclusive purpose of processing the single case over which they preside. Unlike judicial courts, investor-state arbitrations are not altogether part of a sovereign's exercise of sovereignty through the judicial branch of government. Treaty-based international arbitration formally takes place beyond the realm of a sovereign's exercise of sovereignty. Even though investor-state international arbitrations address issues of public policy and public international law, arbitral awards do not generate second-instance jurisprudence because they are not appealable.[143] Moreover, because of their ad hoc configuration and want of judicial status (a non-State administration of justice), arbitral awards do not constitute binding precedent.[144] These awards, at most, are deemed to constitute persuasive authority. Treaty-based arbitration proceedings, and particularly Chapter Eleven arbitrations, in contrast with judicial proceedings, have been widely criticized by commentators as suffering from a "transparency deficit."[145] In fact, both the party-appointed arbitrator system and the practice of dissent writing in treaty-based international arbitration have been identified as problematic features that tend to delegitimize the entire treaty-arbitral process because they are emblematic of lack of arbitrator impartiality and, in some instances, independence.[146] The lack of a mature NAFTA jurisprudence providing for a systematic development and refinement of the public purpose doctrine can, in part, be explained as the consequence of an overarching systemic debility arising from the very nature of decisional law in treaty-based international arbitration.

[142] It would be a mistake to represent that an arbitration based on consent arising from a treaty and concerning issues in dispute is of great public importance.

[143] *See, e.g.*, Convention on the Settlement of Investment Disputes between States and Nationals of Other States art. 53, March 18, 1965, 17 U.S.T. 1270, 575 U.N.T.S. 159 [hereinafter ICSID Convention].

[144] *See, e.g.*, Statute of the International Court of Justice art. 59, June 26, 1945, 59 Stat. 1055 (providing that a "decision of the Court has no binding force except between the parties and in respect of that particular case").

[145] As noted in prior writing, the "arbitral decision-making remains an impenetrable 'black box' process. Despite ably chronicled significant gains for transparency, deliberations remain obscured by design and practice in order to minimize the scope of judicial intervention at the enforcement stage." Martinez-Fraga, *supra* note 34, at 46.

[146] NAFTA, *supra* note 1, art. 1110 ("Expropriation and Compensation").

A second contributing factor that helps explain the impoverished and often conceptually contradictory status of the jurisprudence addressing the public purpose doctrine within the NAFTA must be attributed to the unduly broad scope and subjective content (State-oriented) of the legacy public purpose doctrine. The orthodox conception of the public purpose doctrine is based on the unworkable proposition that a State's subjective intent to use the property that has been the subject of a direct or indirect expropriation or nationalization for a public purpose renders the taking a legal act of State.[147] In fact, the proposition has been advanced that where the public purpose standard has been met, a State is exempt from the payment of *any* compensation because the failure to exempt a State would result in imposing a fine on a sovereign for merely undertaking its regulatory obligations.[148] After all, a sovereign has an obligation to regulate. Pursuant to this standard, however, virtually every act of State constitutes a public purpose. Hence, a very simple and legitimate question remains: What constitutes a public purpose? Three related but distinct inquiries also need to be raised. How is public purpose defined? When is public purpose met? What type of tribunals should sit in judgment of a public purpose issue?

The NAFTA jurisprudence of public purpose does not bring us any closer to answering these questions. In contrast, the conceptual categories discernible from the complex mosaic of ad hoc tribunals struggling with public purpose – either as a determinative standard by itself or as one of four elements to be considered in determining the legality of an expropriation or nationalization – are patently inconsistent in harmonizing the policies of international investment law with the underpinnings of international trade law.[149]

As shall be discussed, efforts to devise tests and standards for calibrating the delicate balance between the protection of foreign investment/investor and

[147] Article 1110 "Expropriation and Compensation" of the NAFTA is illustrative of the standard. It provides that a direct or indirect nationalization or expropriation of an investment of an investor of another Party in its territory constitutes a legal taking where "(a) [the property is used] for a public purpose; (b) [and has been taken] on a non-hyphen discriminatory basis; (c) in accordance with due process of law and Article 1105(1); and (d) on payment of compensation in accordance with paragraph 2 through 6." *Id.* art. 1110 ¶¶ 1(a)–(d).

[148] *See, e.g.*, Matthew C. Porterfield, *State Practice and the (Purported) Obligation Under Customary International Law to Provide Compensation for Regulatory Expropriations*, 37 N.C. J. Int'l L. & Com. Reg. 159, 164 (2011) (noting that there appears to be "some support for the position that there is a police power exception to the compensation requirement – i.e., that a nondiscriminatory regulatory measure cannot constitute an act of expropriation regardless of its adverse economic impact," but that only a minority of cases have found this to be so).

[149] As suggested in Article 1110 1(a)–(d), as part of both conventional and customary international law expropriation/nationalization analysis, public purpose often is considered together on equal footing with (i) nondiscriminatory basis, (ii) the presence of due process of law, and (iii) payment of compensation. NAFTA, *supra* note 1, art. 1110 ("Expropriation and Compensation").

the lawful exercise of sovereignty in furtherance of a public purpose only have served to obscure even further the public purpose doctrine. Much like the Ptolemaic effort directed at "saving the appearances" of the movement of celestial bodies by repeatedly engrafting an epicycle upon an epicycle in a near infinite effort to devise a theory that would bestow uniformity and predictive value on the movement of the heavenly bodies, "legal epicycles" began to appear in the firmaments of treaty-based arbitration awards. Legal gyrations such as the "proportionality test" first identified by the tribunal in the *Fireman's Fund* case[150] sought to discern the appropriate proportionality between the means employed by a State and the aim sought to be achieved, together with the good faith nature of the measure. The *Fireman's Fund* tribunal was silent with respect to any theoretical or practical definition of the proportionality principle that it created. Similarly, it failed to explain the principle's foundation in international law and also did not detail the application of proportionality to any fact pattern.

Other tribunals, such as in *TecMed*,[151] which was decided three years before *Fireman's Fund*, observed the need to use "proportionality" as a principle of public international law that would serve as a litmus test in harmonizing a State's exercise of its regulatory authority appropriately with investment/investor protection. The use of a concept such as "proportionality" bespeaks objectivity and compromise. *TecMed* mentions the proportionality principle, but, as with the tribunal in *Fireman's Fund*, did not voice any theoretical or practical definition of the principle or of the important role that the public purpose doctrine may enjoy if infused with greater substantive content and applied within the context of a proportionality rubric.

A proportionality standard addresses the State's objective in any alleged expropriation or nationalization against the effects that such a taking would have on the subject foreign investment/investor. These two elements – effects and a State's objective in exercising its authority – invariably led to a "sole effects" standard under which only the purportedly detrimental effects that a measure may have on an investment/investor need to be considered in assessing the viability of a claim arising from a direct or indirect nationalization or expropriation.[152]

[150] Fireman's Fund Insurance Co. v. United Mexican States, ICSID Case No. ARB (AF)/02/01, Award (July 17, 2006), 16 ICSID Rep. 523 (2012) [hereinafter *Fireman's Fund*].

[151] *See* Tecnicas Medioambientales Tecmed S.A. v. United Mexican States, ICSID Case No. ARB (AF)/00/2, Award (May 29, 2003), 10 ICSID Rep. 134 (2006) [hereinafter TecMed].

[152] *See, e.g.*, Saipem S.p.A. v. The People's Republic of Bangladesh, ICSID Case No. ARB/05/07, Award ¶ 133 (June 30, 2009) [hereinafter Saipem S.p.A.] ("[A]ccording to the so-called 'sole effects doctrine,' the most significant criterion to determine whether the dispute actions amount to indirect expropriation or are tantamount to expropriation is the impact of the measure").

This gamut ranging from *proportionality*, *effects*, and *sole effects*, all presumably aspiring to limit a State's use of its regulatory authority in the context of expropriations or nationalizations, only fosters greater confusion, inconsistency, and lack of uniformity.

The divergent positions that theoretically would vastly contribute to the definition of the public purpose doctrine within the NAFTA framework reach their apogee in the competing views expounded by the tribunals in *Metalclad*[153] and *Methanex*.[154]

1. *The* Metalclad *Legacy: One Extreme*

Metalclad, decided five years before the issuance of the final award on jurisdiction and merits in *Methanex*, was one of the pioneer cases in the NAFTA jurisprudence addressing environmental regulations and, therefore, directly falling within the ambit of the GATT's Article XX General Exceptions that were incorporated into the NAFTA's Chapter Eleven framework, as well as into the treaty's general structure.[155] The case presents a wealth of issues and a rich factual narrative ranging from (i) State responsibility; (ii) the failure to meet conditions precedent to contractual obligations; (iii) conflicting State/federal representations communicated to a foreign investor by the Host State; (iv) the closure of a hazardous waste transfer station by the federal government of Mexico prior to its acquisition; (v) a municipality's challenge to an operation agreement ("Convenio") entered into by the federal government of Mexico and the foreign investor; (vi) estoppel and ratification defenses arising from the continuous, open, and notorious construction of a hazardous land waste facility; and (vii) to the effect of an ecological decree banning operation of a hazardous land waste facility for the public purpose of protecting a species of cacti. The case also serves as an ideal case study for analysis of the public purpose doctrine within the NAFTA because it enjoys the added benefit of an opinion issued by the Supreme Court of British Columbia arising from the Host State's effort to vacate the award.[156]

[153] Metalclad, *supra* note 80.

[154] Methanex Corp. v. United States of America, NAFTA Ch. 11/UNCITRAL, Final Award on Jurisdiction and Merits (August 3, 2005), 16 ICSID Rep. 40 (2012) [hereinafter Methanex].

[155] *Metalclad* was decided in August 2000, and although the *Methanex* tribunal issued a partial award on jurisdiction and evidence-gathering in 2002, the final award on jurisdiction and merits was not entered until August, 2005.

[156] *See* United Mexican States v. Metalclad Corp., 2001 BCSC 664 (2001). This opinion is helpful because, among other considerations, it premises its analysis exclusively on uncontroverted facts.

The *Metalclad* tribunal virtually dispensed with any sustained analysis of the role of the public purpose doctrine in any of its permutations (i.e., public interest, police powers, or even in the form of a State's regulatory authority). It also refrained from any "proportionality" scrutiny pursuant to which the public purpose or benefit of the regulatory measure at issue would be weighed against its effect on the operative investment/investor. Instead, the tribunal selected as its organizing conceptual principle – ratio *decidendi* – three factors: (i) the detrimental effects that the regulatory measure had on the investment,[157] (ii) what the tribunal characterized as "lack of transparency" concerning the workings of the Mexican government,[158] and (iii) the thwarted investor expectations stemming from representations made by Mexican government officials.[159]

The emphasis placed on this triad wrests all predictive value from the public purpose doctrine or even the NAFTA Public Purpose Standard articulated in Article 1101(4). Revisiting the tribunal's analysis through the particular prism of the public purpose doctrine, however, is necessary if in fact its reasoning and decision are to be rescued from the "catch-all" quagmire of basing its analysis on the "particular nature" or "unique facts" underlying the case.[160]

The *Metalclad* case concerned a property site ("the site") in La Pedrera, a valley located within the municipality of Gualdalcazar ("the Municipality"), in the State of San Luis Potosi ("the State of SLP"), Mexico.[161] The site was owned by Confinamiento Técnico De Residuos Industriales, S.A. de C.V. ("COTERIN"), a Mexican corporation. Both the site and COTERIN were first owned by Mexican nationals.[162] In 1993, Metalclad Corporation ("Metalclad"), a U.S. corporation incorporated under the laws of Delaware, through its subsidiary, purchased COTERIN. Simultaneously with that transaction, the ownership of the site was transferred to COTERIN.[163]

Prior to Metalclad's acquisition of COTERIN, the federal government of Mexico ordered the closure of a hazardous waste transfer station that was located at the site and operated by COTERIN on the grounds that 20,000 tons of waste were not transferred from the site after having been deposited on

[157] Metalclad, *supra* note 80, at ¶ 104.
[158] *Id. at* ¶ 99.
[159] *Id. at* ¶¶ 107–08.
[160] Because of the nature of the decisional law that treaty-based arbitration generates, specifically its ad hoc character, the danger of ascribing selective consideration of international law principles to "a unique set of facts" (an observation applicable to virtually every dispute) looms large and must be obviated.
[161] Metalclad, *supra* note 80, at ¶ 28.
[162] *Id. at* ¶ 29.
[163] *Id. at* ¶ 30.

the site without treatment or separation. Moreover, the Municipality of Guadalcazar ("the Municipality") in 1991, prior to Metalclad's acquisition of COTERIN, had denied COTERIN an application for a permit to construct a hazardous waste landfill at the site.[164]

What follows are uncontroverted but conflicting statements of fact between federal and municipal authorities. Specifically, in January 1995, COTERIN received a third construction permit from federal authorities authorizing the construction of the final phases of the facility.[165] By that time, COTERIN already had commenced construction of the hazardous waste landfill facility.[166] The Municipality, however, never authorized the construction and, in fact, issued a stop order to the activity on the site based on the absence of a municipal permit.[167] Notwithstanding the Municipality's stop-work order, COTERIN continued with the construction of the hazardous waste landfill facility at the site for approximately five months until completion.[168]

The tribunal's award suggests that the conflicting dispositions between municipal and federal authorities were such that while the Municipality had issued a stop order and denied Metalclad's application for a construction permit for the facility on the site, the federal authorities negotiated with Metalclad and reached an agreement called the *Convenio*. Pursuant to this instrument, Metalclad would be allowed to operate the landfill facility for a five-year term, and, during the first three years of this term, to remediate the previous contamination on the site.[169]

[164] In 1993, COTERIN did receive three permits concerning the hazardous waste landfill at the site. These permits, however, were not issued by the Municipality. Two of the permits were issued by the National Institute of Ecology and Agency of Mexico's Secretariat of the Environment, National Resources and Fishing. These permits authorized the construction and operation of the landfill. The third permit was issued by the State of SLP and concerned land use. The receipt of these three permits and the nonissuance of a permit by the Municipality were material to the tribunal's analysis because Metalclad's agreement to purchase COTERIN provided that the payment of the purchase price was subject to, *inter alia*, the condition that *either* (i) a municipal permit was issued to COTERIN or (ii) COTERIN had received a final nonappealable judgment from Mexican tribunals that a municipal permit was not required for the construction of the landfill. *Id.* at ¶¶ 50–56, 77–87.

Factually, Metalclad closed its acquisition of COTERIN without either of these conditions having been met. *Id.* at ¶ 43.

[165] *Id.* at ¶ 39.

[166] *Id.* at ¶ 40.

[167] *Id.* at ¶ 50. Indeed, approximately two years after Metalclad applied for a municipal construction permit, the Municipality denied it.

[168] *Id.* at ¶¶ 41–45.

[169] *Id.* at ¶¶ 47–48. Subsequent to the execution of the *Convenio* federal authorities provided COTERIN with a permit allowing it to increase by tenfold the annual permitted capacity of the facility from 36,000 tons to 360,000 tons. *Id. at* ¶ 58.

The Municipality unsuccessfully challenged the *Convenio* by pursuing an administrative complaint with the Secretariat of the Environment and simultaneously pursued an injunction in federal court in Mexico seeking to enjoin the *Convenio*'s execution. Injunctive relief initially was issued but was subsequently dismissed.[170] After engaging in multiple appeals to a Mexican Federal Court and the Mexican Supreme Court, COTERIN decided to abandon the pursuit of judicial remedies as a gesture of good faith to the Municipality and as a predicate to negotiations. Upon reaching an impasse in the negotiations with the Municipality, Metalclad commenced arbitration under Article 1119 of the NAFTA.

Remarkably, the tribunal's award does not mention, let alone elaborate on, the environmental/ecological harm that the Municipality sought to mitigate or prevent. This aspect of the case is salient because of its omission. In addition to the obvious subject matter of the dispute (i.e., the operation of a *hazardous waste* landfill), a threat to the environment can be inferred from two factual assertions that are fleetingly stated and virtually lost in the body of the award (which comprises 131 paragraphs). First, in October 1991, prior to Metalclad's acquisition of COTERIN, the Municipality had denied COTERIN its application for the construction of the facility.[171] Second, the award reflects that demonstrators impeded the "open house" or "inauguration" of the facility by blocking major access arteries and thus preventing access to the facility to workers and guests (i.e., invited dignitaries from the United States and from Mexico's local, State, and federal governments).[172] This heightened level of concern bespeaks fear for health and safety, even though the award is bereft of

[170] *Id.* at ¶ 56.

[171] The reasons underlying this initial denial of the application are not continued in the award. In fact, that there was a denial at all *prior* to Metalclad's acquisition of COTERIN is scarcely referenced as part of a subordinate clause of a two-sentence paragraph. Accordingly, no weight was accorded to this fact, and the environmental considerations attendant to it cannot be gleaned with any degree of specificity:

> On December 5, 1995, thirteen months after Metalclad's application for the municipal construction permit was filed, the application was denied. *In doing this, the Municipality recalled its decision to deny a construction permit to COTERIN in October 1991 and January 1992 and noted the "impropriety" of Metalclad's construction of the landfill prior to receiving a municipal construction permit.*

Id. at ¶ 50 (emphasis added). We also learn from the tribunal's recitation of the terms of the *Convenio* that "Metalclad would also provide one day per week of free medical advice for the inhabitants of Guadalcazar through Metalclad's qualified medical personnel, employ manual labor from within Guadalcazar, and give preference to the inhabitants of Guadalcazar for technical training." *Id. at* ¶ 48. It is not clear, however, the extent to which Metalclad's provision of medical advice to the inhabitants of Guadalcazar is related to the possible effects of the hazardous waste facility.

[172] *Id.* at ¶¶ 45–46.

any such suggestion.[173] Other than these two scant references, the environmental effect that the landfill could have had and its consequences to health, safety, and fauna simply is not discussed.[174]

The substance of what otherwise likely would have been a deeper inquiry into the public safety, health, and environmental issues surrounding the landfill were ironically marred by the tribunal's discussion of transparency/jurisdictional conflicts. Using its understanding of the NAFTA's reference to "transparency" in Article 102(1) to extend to the workings of a Host State's government in relation to a particular investment, the tribunal reads the Article 102(1) ("Transparency Principle") "to include the idea that all relevant legal requirements for purposes of initiating, completing, and successfully operating investments made, or intended to be made, under the Agreement [the NAFTA] should be capable of being readily known to all affected investors of another Party. There should be no room for doubt or uncertainty on such matters."[175] Mexico, the tribunal found, "failed to ensure a transparent and predictable framework for Metalclad's business planning and investment."[176]

This want of transparency, in the tribunal's analysis, stemmed from diametrically conflicting jurisdictional statements and strictures concerning the extent to which the Municipality's permit for the construction of the landfill facility was a requirement in circumstances where such construction already had received federal approval.[177]

173 In fact, as to this point, the award limits itself to restating Metalclad's position "that the demonstration was organized *at least in part* by the Mexican State and local governments, and that State troopers assisted in blocking traffic into and out of the site. Metalclad was thenceforth effectively prevented from opening the landfill." *Id.* at ¶ 46.

174 There is minor discussion on whether the landfill site was geographically suitable for a hazardous waste landfill facility. This issue, however, was limited to a single paragraph reference because the concern appeared to have been allayed:

> In February 1995, the Autonomous University of SLP issued a study confirming earlier findings that, although the landfill site raised some concerns, with proper engineering, it was geographically suitable for a hazardous waste landfill. In March 1995, the Mexican Federal Attorney's Office for the Protection of the Environment [citation omitted], and independent sub-agency of SEMARNAP [Secretariat of the Mexican Environment, Natural Resources and Fishing], conducted an audit of the site and also concluded that, with proper engineering and operation, the landfill site was geographically suitable for hazardous waste landfill.

Id. at ¶ 44.

175 *Id.* at ¶ 76.

176 *Id.* at ¶ 99.

177 The tribunal observed that "[e]ven if Mexico is correct that a municipal construction permit was required, the evidence also shows that, as to hazardous waste evaluations and assessments, the federal authority's jurisdiction was controlling and the authority of the Municipality only extended to appropriate construction considerations. Consequently, the denial of the permit by the Municipality by reference to environmental impact considerations in the case of what was

The conflicts between Mexico's federal government and the Municipality were stark. Federal officials allegedly told Metalclad that if it submitted an application for a municipal construction permit "the Municipality would have no legal basis for denying the permit and that it would be issued as a matter of course."[178] The question of whether Metalclad as an investor rightfully harbored expectations that it was entitled to construct a facility and acted reasonably in reliance of federal officials manifestly diverted the analysis away from consideration of the health, safety, and environmental issues associated with the landfill and the manner in which such issues in turn would be affected by the Municipality's denial of a construction permit. Consequently, whether wittingly or by happenstance, the tribunal fashioned part of the test as a subjective inquiry premised on investor expectations. This conceptual approach placed considerable emphasis on (i) the licensing jurisdictional conflict between Mexico's federal government and the Municipality and (ii) the extent to which an investor may legitimately rely on the representations advanced by government officials, instead of formulating a more broad-based approach that would not fail to consider the Municipality's environmental concerns and how these issues could be addressed by denial of a construction permit.[179] Moreover, in addition to finding that the Municipality's jurisdiction was limited to denying construction permits only with respect to "construction aspects or flaws of the physical

basically a hazardous waste disposal landfill, was improper, as was the Municipality's denial of the permit for any reason other than those related to the physical construction or defects in the site." *Id.* at ¶ 86. The Municipality never alleged that there were physical construction or engineering defects in the site.

[178] *Id.* at ¶ 88. In fact, "[t]he absence of a clear rule as to the requirement or not of a municipal construction permit, as well as the absence of any established practice or procedure as to the manner of handling applications for a municipal construction permit, amounts to a failure on the part of Mexico to ensure the transparency required by NAFTA." *Id.*

[179] The award is rife with references to the issue of representations advanced by officials of Mexico's federal government to Metalclad:

85. Metalclad was led to believe, and did believe, that the federal and State permits allowed for the construction and operation of the landfill. Metalclad argues that in all hazardous waste matters, the Municipality has no authority. However, Mexico argues that constitutionally and lawfully the Municipality has the authority to issue construction permits.

87. Relying on the representations of the federal government, Metalclad started constructing the landfill, and did this openly and continuously, and with the full knowledge of the federal, State and municipal governments, until municipal "Stop Work Order" on October 26, 1994. The basis of this order was said to have been Metalclad's failure to obtain a Municipal construction permit.

88. In addition, Metalclad asserted that federal officials told it that if it submitted an application for a municipal construction permit, the Municipality would have no legal basis for denying the permit in that it would be issued as a matter of course ...

facility," the tribunal also underscored that, pursuant to Articles 26 and 27 of the Vienna Convention on the Law of Treaties, compliance with domestic law does not justify nonperformance of a treaty violation.[180] The local government's lack of authority for denying the construction permit and its connection to a finding of violation of fair and equitable treatment on Mexico's behalf, was not at any time juxtaposed to its logical countervailing consideration. If the investor has been denied fair and equitable treatment, is the State being penalized for lawfully exercising its sovereignty in the form of a permit denial and issuance of an Ecological Decree?[181]

Having concluded that the Municipality lacked authority to deny the permit and that the investor's expectations had been wrongfully and unjustifiably undermined, the tribunal fashioned an "effects test" that appears to have been crafted in a vacuum and not within the framework of a system that, in great measure, rests on the public purpose doctrine.

2. *An "Effects Test" Beyond the Purview of Public Purpose*

The *Metalclad* tribunal's "effects test" appears to derive from Article 1110 of the NAFTA.[182] The tribunal observed that:

> [E]xpropriation under NAFTA includes not only open, deliberate, and acknowledged takings of property, such as outright seizure or formal or obligatory transfer of title in favour of the Host State, but also covert or incidental interference with the use of property which has the effect of depriving the owner, in whole or in significant part, of the use or reasonably-to-be-expected economic benefit of property even if not necessarily to the obvious benefit of the Host State.[183]

> 89. Metalclad was entitled to rely on the representations of federal officials and believes that it was entitled to continue its construction of the landfill . . ..

Id. at ¶¶ 85–89.

[180] *Id.* at ¶ 100; *see also* VCLT, *supra* note 88, arts. 26–27.

[181] The Governor of SLP issued an Ecological Decree declaring a Natural Area for the protection of rare cactus. The area of the landfill is encompassed by the Decree's Natural Area. Even though Metalclad *also* relied on this Ecological Decree as an additional ground in furtherance of its claim of expropriation, *inter alia*, asserting that the Decree effectively and permanently precluded the operation of the landfill (Metalclad, *supra* note 80, at ¶¶ 59, 96), the tribunal did not rely on the Ecological Decree in its finding in favor of Metalclad on the expropriation claim. It did, however, add that "the implementation of the Ecological Decree would, in and of itself, constitute an act tantamount to expropriation." *Id.* at ¶ 111.

[182] Nowhere, however, in Article 1110 does the word "effect" or any permutation of the term appear. *See* NAFTA, *supra* note 1, art. 1110.

[183] Metalclad, *supra* note 80, at ¶ 103 (emphasis added).

This subordinate clause "or take a measure tantamount to ... expropriation" the *Metalclad* tribunal construed as appropriately having the corresponding standard of having "the effect of depriving" an owner of the use or economic benefit of property. The elements of the Article 1110 nationalization or expropriation exception – (i) public purpose, (ii) on a nondiscriminatory basis, (iii) in accordance with due process of law, and (iv) nonpayment of compensation consonant with Article 1110 – are not ostensibly incorporated into the test, except perhaps for the obscure phrase, "even if not necessarily to the obvious benefit of the Host State."[184]

The second source on which the tribunal relied in fashioning its "effects test" was the arbitral award issued in *Biloune, et al v. Ghana Investment Centre, et al.*[185] This authority is the only decisional law cited in the award forming part of the tribunal's *ratio decidendi*. It is also significant to note that the tribunal opined that *Biloune* materially resembled the case before it.[186] Consonant with its analysis of Article 1110, which strictly focused on the language pertaining to an indirect expropriation of an investment and completely excluded *any* public purpose consideration, the tribunal's treatment of *Biloune* centered on the connection between the denial of a permit and the effect of that the denial on the investment. Other factors, including the investor's "justified reliance on these government representations regarding the permit," were also considered.[187] A closer reading of *Biloune*, however, suggests that an "effects test" without consideration of a public purpose doctrine justifiably finds credible resonance in that dispute because the underlying facts simply did not give rise to a public purpose countervailing analysis.

[184] *Id.*

[185] Biloune and Marine Drive Complex Ltd. v. Ghana Investments Centre and the Government of Ghana, Award on Jurisdiction and Liability (27 October 1989), 95 I.L.R. 183 (1993) [hereinafter Biloune].

[186] The tribunal placed considerable weight on what it understood to be meaningful and material factual parallels between the two cases. It noted the following points in common:

> The present case resembles in a number of pertinent respects that of *Biloune, et al v Ghana Investment Centre, et al* [citation omitted]. In that case, a private investor was renovating and expanding a resort restaurant in Ghana. As with *Metalclad*, the investor, basing itself on the representations of a government affiliated entity, began construction before applying for a building permit. As with *Metalclad*, a Stop Work Order was issued after a substantial amount of work had been completed. The order was based on the absence of a building permit. An application was submitted, but although it was not expressly denied, a permit was never issued.
>
> Metalclad, *supra* note 80, at ¶ 108.

[187] *Id.*

Only very superficially does *Biloune* resemble the competing interests configuring *Metalclad*.[188]

Poles apart from the construction and operation of a hazardous waste landfill facility, the investment in *Biloune* concerned "renovating, expanding, and operating [a] restaurant/resort complex at Palm Court."[189] Public safety, health, and risk to the environment were not at issue. The "effects test" that the tribunal applied in *Biloune* correctly was limited to determining the extent to which Ghanaian governmental authorities exercised measures preventing the investor from pursuing the hospitality renovation effort.[190] The *Biloune* factual configuration, together with the tribunal's actual analysis, suggests that the dispute was framed as a contractual dispute only, having at issue whether the expropriation clause in the operative concession contract applied to an indirect expropriation.[191] This narrow framing of the issues meaningfully invited an "effects test" analysis that only warranted examination of two sets of issues. First, whether, as a matter of international law, a distinction may be drawn where a government may indirectly expropriate the subject matter of a contract with a foreign investor that cannot be directly expropriated pursuant to positive law.[192] Second, whether, when analyzed together, the stop-work order, the investor's reliance on representations,[193] the arrest, the detention,

[188] The only public purpose doctrine that would be relevant in *Biloune* would be along the lines of a State's legitimate and justifiable exercise of its police powers. Regulatory considerations touching upon health, safety, and public welfare were not at issue in that proceeding.

[189] Biloune, *supra* note 185, at 207.

[190] The *Biloune* tribunal found that "Given the central role of Mr. Biloune in promoting, financing and managing MDCL, his expulsion from the country effectively prevented MDCL from further pursuing the project. In the view of the tribunal, such prevention of MDCL from pursuing its approved project would constitute constructive expropriation of MDCL's contractual rights in the project and, accordingly, the expropriation of the value of Mr. Biloune's interest in MDCL unless the Respondents can establish by persuasive evidence sufficient justification for these events." *Id.* at 210.

The tribunal did not find the government's evidence concerning the arrest and deportation of Mr. Biloune to be credible. More importantly, the *Biloune* award does not reflect that the issue of the extent to which a State may legitimately and justifiably exercise its police powers to the detriment of a foreign investment-investor was ever raised or even considered. The term "a State's police power" does not appear anywhere in the *Biloune* award.

[191] *Id.* at 206.

[192] *Id.*

[193] In contrast with the representations on which the investor in *Metalclad* relied, in *Biloune*, the investor relied on representations of a "long-term leaseholder of the premises" as well as those advanced by "an experienced government-affiliated entity." Consequently, the much-vaunted estoppel argument that the tribunal underscores in *Metalclad* is not comparable to the factual configuration of the representations constituting the estoppel argument applied in *Biloune*. *Id.* at 208.

Also distinguishable from *Metalclad* is the legal status of the permit denial. In *Metalclad*, the denial was deemed to be of no moment because the Municipality had limited jurisdiction

and the deportation of the primary investor without possibility of reentry constitutes an indirect or regulatory expropriation.

A salient distinction between *Biloune* and *Metalclad* that directly influenced the tribunal's analysis concerns the absence of any underlying BIT.[194] The *Metalclad* tribunal's failure to consider this rudimentary issue will remain enigmatic.

Although Article 15 of the GIC Agreement that claimant signed was broad in providing for arbitration of "[a]ny dispute between the foreign investor and the government in respect of an approved enterprise," and contained language protecting against expropriation, the *Biloune* tribunal observed that its "competence is limited to commercial disputes arising under a contract entered into in the context of Ghana's Investment Code."[195] Indeed, unlike *Metalclad* – where public international law applied – in *Biloune*, the rights and obligations of the parties were governed by the laws of Ghana.[196] Moreover, the dispute was configured strictly within the framework of a private international law contract dispute. To the extent that the tribunal applied principles of customary international law, (i) these precepts were limited to a claim for expropriation only, and (ii) the tribunal studiously observed that "there is no indication that Ghanaian law diverges on the central issue of expropriation from customary principles of international law."[197]

The *Metalclad* tribunal's construction of the NAFTA's Article 1110 indirect expropriation language and its wholesale inclusion of the *Biloune* analysis based on presumptively "similar pertinent facts" leaves much to be desired.[198] The analysis of the NAFTA's Article 1110 failed to consider *any* fact or factual

concerning the content of a construction permit because it could only pass on physical defects or engineering flaws, neither of which were at issue. The *Biloune* tribunal in contrast, acknowledged that "[w]hile the letter of the law, as pleaded by the Respondents, supports the contention that extension works of the character contemplated cannot go forward without a permit – or, if they did, would be subject to fine or demolition – nevertheless, the practice with regard to this site indicates an exception to the rule." *Id.*

Biloune is distinguishable from *Metalclad* even on fundamental technical issues concerning estoppel and the legal status of the permit at issue.

[194] The claimant, Antoine Biloune, Syrian national, executed an agreement with the Ghana Investments Centre that included an arbitration clause and referred to the UNCITRAL arbitration rules. *Id.* at 202.

[195] *Id.* at 203.

[196] Article 24 of the GIC Agreement required the tribunal to "constru[e]" the Agreement "according to the laws of Ghana." The Parties, however, did not draw on the law of Ghana as to the construction of the Agreement and the tribunal relied on principles of customary international law in adjudicating the expropriation claim. *Id.* at 207.

[197] *Id.*

[198] The *Metalclad* tribunal did not observe that the *Biloune* analysis was undertaken within the context of a commercial contractual dispute pursuant to which the application of an "effects test," without more, along with reliance on the contractual defense of estoppel were sufficient

inference that would have triggered a public purpose exception as prescribed in Paragraph 1, Subsection (a). By omitting even reference to this pivotal element, the tribunal carved out of Article 1110(1) an important criteria for any indirect expropriation analysis. In so doing, it misapprehended the workings of Chapter Eleven generally and Article 1110 in particular. Disavowing the public purpose doctrine in its entirety in the context of an indirect expropriation analysis frustrates the workings of Article 1110 and unduly advantages a prospective claimant. Similarly, the failure to apprehend the commercial context in which *Biloune* was decided, with jurisdiction based on an Agreement between a private individual and a State and not between two sovereigns, and lacking countervailing public purpose considerations attendant to the protection of health, life, and the environment, is equally disconcerting.[199] The exclusion of these considerations is conducive to penalizing States for having legitimately and justifiably exercised their sovereignty. It swings the pendulum of symmetry and bilateralism too far in favor of

in order to harmonize competing interests arising between foreign investment protection and a Host State's exercise of its regulatory authority. Its unqualified adoption of the *Biloune's* tribunal's "effects test" and estoppel argument presents conceptual challenges because of the meaningful distinguishing elements that separate the cases, among the most significant of which is the nonapplication of international *conventional* law. The *Metalclad*'s tribunal recitation on this point merits citation in its entirety:

> The Tribunal found that an indirect expropriation had taken place because the *totality of the circumstances* had the *effect of causing* the irreparable cessation of work on the project. The Tribunal paid particular regard to the investor's justified reliance on the government's representations regarding the permit, the fact that the government authorities knew of the construction for more than one year before issuing the Stop Work Order, the fact that permits had not been required for other projects and the fact that no procedure was in place for dealing with building permit applications. Although the decision in *Biloune* does not bind this Tribunal, it is a persuasive authority and the Tribunal is in agreement with its analysis and its conclusion.

Metalclad, *supra* note 80, at ¶ 108 (emphasis added).

199 In the vacature proceeding that Mexico initiated before the Supreme Court of British Columbia, the Court found that the *Metalclad* tribunal had placed undue reliance on *Biloune*. Even though the Supreme Court of British Columbia did not raise the industry sector differences (operation of a hazardous waste landfill facility in contrast with renovation of a hotel and restaurant), it did note:

> There are substantial differences between the situation in the present case and the circumstances in *Biloune*. The main two distinctions are that in *Biloune* (i) the building was partially destroyed and then closed by government officials, and (ii) the investor was deported from the country and was not allowed to return. Apart from the Ecological Decree [which the arbitral tribunal did not rely on and only commented hypothetically with respect to it], the circumstances in the present case fall considerably short of those in *Biloune* and it would not logically follow that *Biloune* could be an independent basis for concluding that the actions in this case prior to the issuance of the Decree amounted to an expropriation.

capital-exporting States without contributing countervailing doctrinal tenets that could justify the occasionally asymmetrical analysis.

Metalclad's "effects test" hardly enriches the NAFTA's decisional law concerning direct or indirect nationalization or expropriation. Application of an "effects test" without reference to countervailing State interests has the consequence of rigidly halting a pendulum at an extreme far from equipoise. Conceptually, the approach fails to account for the underlying policies of the NAFTA that, at least aspirationally, seek to further the interests of both Home and Host States. A consequence of the *Metalclad* analysis is to introduce into the public purpose jurisprudence of the NAFTA a narrow and rigid methodology that is indistinguishable – as the Tribunal's reliance on *Biloune* demonstrates – and impervious to the legitimate interests of Host States while unduly enshrining a subjective standard in the form investor expectation. Analysis of an expropriation under public international law commands more than the application of basic commercial contract principles.

3. *Revisiting* Methanex *through the Prism of the Public Purpose Doctrine*

Conceptually, decisional law or the jurisprudence of the NAFTA with respect to the public purpose doctrine should be conducive to certainty, predictability, uniformity, and transparency. This expectation, at minimum from the point of departure of the NAFTA's doctrinal development, is further encouraged because tribunals are bound by official interpretive statements offered by the NAFTA[200] but are not subject to judicial review in the NAFTA parties' courts.[201] The jurisprudence should seek to harmonize likely conflicts between international investment law and the public policy trade objectives of the NAFTA. Decisional law would serve to reconcile the competing interests attendant to foreign investment protection and a sovereign's rightful

Metalclad Corp., 2001 BCSC 664, at ¶ 80 (2001). The Supreme Court of British Columbia additionally stated that it did not agree with the *Metalclad* tribunal's approach of considering the Ecological Decree but not relying on it. *Id.* at ¶ 81. The Court specifically concluded that the Metalclad tribunal "used an incorrect tense in the Award when it stated that it considered that the implementation of the Ecological Decree *would*, in and of itself, constitute an act tantamount to expropriation, it is clear from another passage of the Award that the Tribunal considered that the implementation of the Decree *did* constitute expropriation. In the second paragraph preceding the misuse of the future tense, the Tribunal stated that the Decree *had* the effect of barring forever the operation of the landfill." *Id.* at ¶ 83 (emphasis in original).

200 *See* NAFTA, *supra* note 1, art. 1131 ¶ 2.

201 See, e.g., Vicki Been & Joel C. Beauvais, *The Global Fifth Amendment? NAFTA's Investment Protections and the Misguided Quest for an International "Regulatory Takings" Doctrine*, 78 N.Y.U. L. Rev. 30 n.117 (2003) (stating that "the tribunals are not bound by stare decisis and are not subject to centralized appellate review").

use of its regulatory space. A recharacterization of this latter tension would be to suggest that, more generally, the decisional law of treaty-based international arbitration should serve to ameliorate the conflicting investor-state interests that distinctly separate Home and Host States. Regrettably, despite the many helpful public purpose features of the NAFTA, the NAFTA jurisprudence remains plagued by the dysfunctional contributions of a legacy public purpose doctrine. This decisional law is lacking in objective criteria, properly defined exceptions, applicable burdens of proof, and a holistic "proportionality" approach susceptible to consistent and transparent application.[202] *Metalclad* also represents the current juridical disarray that leads to "all-or-nothing" results. Effects tests must be applied in the context of a tempered public purpose doctrine that could lead to a reasonable and proportionality driven result.

I. THE METHANEX APPROACH AND A SWING OF THE PENDULUM

The *Metalclad* tribunal at best diminished the role of the public purpose doctrine as a defense or a mitigating factor in an indirect expropriation or regulatory taking and, at worse, stands for a pronouncement of the doctrine's irrelevancy when raised in specific factual scenarios. Put simply, the public purpose doctrine in *Metalclad* played no role in determining whether (i) a regulatory expropriation occurred and (ii) the issuance and extent of compensation.[203] Poles apart from an approach minimizing or altogether foreclosing consideration of the public purpose doctrine, the tribunal in *Methanex*[204] rejected claims premised on violations of Article 1102 ("National Treatment"),[205] Article 1105 ("Minimum Standard of Treatment"),[206] and Article 1110 ("Expropriation and Compensation")[207] in considerable measure based upon the scope of the legacy public purpose doctrine.

[202] As shall be examined, the current status of the "proportionality test" enunciated in the NAFTA jurisprudence is wanting in numerous respects, including uniformity in its application and rigor as to its most fundamental elements.

[203] *See* Alberto R. Salazar V, *NAFTA Chapter Eleven, Regulatory Expropriation, and Domestic Counter-Advertising Law*, 27 ARIZ. J. INR'L. & COMP. L. 31, 67 (2010) (observing that *Metalclad* "remains important in the context of the uncertainties associated with the inconsistencies in the current State of Chapter 11 jurisprudence, the public purpose was not a determinant factor in establishing a regulatory expropriation and the tribunal thus found the government liable for expropriation").

[204] Methanex, *supra* note 154.

[205] *Id.* at Part IV-B in 29, 38 (asserting that the legislation at issue was not discriminatory and therefore legitimately needing a public purpose).

[206] *Id.* at Part IV-C ¶ 27.

[207] *Id.* at Part IV-D ¶ 15.

Understandably, the *Methanex* case has given rise to considerable commentary.[208] At the time of its filing, the *Methanex* dispute was viewed as a possible landmark case with far-reaching policy implications in the realm of public safety, health, and environmental regulations.[209] For present purposes, the *Methanex* story need not be told anew, nor is a detailed recitation of its many procedural reincarnations during the course of its protracted life necessary.[210] Some background, however, is indispensable.

Methanex Corporation ("Methanex"), as a Canadian corporation and investor, brought an action against the United States of America (The United States or "The U.S.") pursuant to Article 716(1) of the NAFTA with claims fundamentally based on the alleged breach by the United States of two provisions in Section A of Chapter Eleven of the NAFTA: Article 1105(1) and Article 1110(1).[211] It premised its claims on the production and sale of a methanol-based source of octane and oxygenate for gasoline that is known as methyl-tertiary-butyl ether (MTBE). Specifically, Methanex averred that MTBE was a safe, effective, and economical component of gasoline and the oxygenate of choice "in markets where free and fair trade is allowed."[212] The

[208] *See, e.g.*, Salazar, *supra* note 203; Kara Dougherty, *Methanex v. United States: The Realignment of NAFTA Chapter Eleven with Environmental Regulation*, 27 NW. J. INT'L L. & BUS. 735 (2006); Jessica C. Lawrence, *Chicken Little Revisited: NAFTA Regulatory Expropriations after Methanex*, 41 GA. L. REV. 261 (2006); Vicki Been & Joel C. Beauvais, *The Global Fifth Amendment? NAFTA's Investment Protections and the Misguided Quest for an International "Regulatory Takings" Doctrine*, 78 N.Y.U. L. REV. 30 (2003); Marisa Yee, *The Future of Environmental Regulation after Article 1110 of NAFTA: A Look after the Methanex and Metalclad Cases*, 9 HASTINGS W.-NW. J. ENVT'L L. & POL'Y 85 (2002); Lucien J. Dhooge, *The Revenge of the Trail Smelter: Environmental Regulation as Expropriation Pursuant to the North American Free Trade Agreement*, 38 AM. BUS. L.J. 475 (2001); Frederick M. Abbott, *The Political Economy of NAFTA Chapter Eleven: Equality before the Law and the Boundaries of North American Integration*, 23 HASTINGS INT'L & COMP. L. REV. 303 (2000).

[209] *Methanex* rightfully has been distinguished as meaningfully contributing to a transparent dispute resolution regime. *See, e.g.*, Howard L. Mann, *The Final Decision in Methanex v. United States: Some New Wine in Some New Bottles*, 3 TRANSNAT'L DISP. MGMT. (December 2006). This recognition is well-justified. The manifold richness of the opinion in addressing trilateral parties, deftly adjudicating the extent to which domestic regulations concerning public health, safety, and the environment may affect international law protecting foreign investors; exploring the conceptual role of *amici curiae*; and finally, addressing the privacy/confidentiality dichotomy, is noteworthy.

[210] Methanex's claim was first advanced in its Statement of Claim dated December 3, 1999. The final award of the Tribunal on Jurisdiction and Merits was issued August 3, 2005. Emphasis of its general configuration, however, will help define the workings of the public purpose doctrine within the case and, more generally, the post-*Methanex* effect that the doctrine has within the NAFTA and its jurisprudence.

[211] Methanex, *supra* note 154, at Part I–Preface ¶ 2.

[212] See *Id.* at Part II–Ch. D ¶ 2.

claimant also alleged that MTBE generated environmental benefits and did not at all pose a risk to human health or the environment.[213] Methanex further claimed that it neither produced nor sold MTBE, but rather only engaged in the limited business of the production, transportation, and marketing of methanol,[214] a key ingredient for the production of MTBE. Central to Methanex's position was the contention that (i) no methanol production plants were located in California and (ii) during the period 1993–2001 only a fraction of the methanol directly consumed in California was produced anywhere in the United States (an average of 20.2 thousand metric tons out a total consumption figure of 185.5 thousand metric tons).[215] It advanced the contention that the State caused significant losses.[216]

Because the case was properly viewed as a seminal decision with far-reaching policy implications concerning whether California's ban on the sale and use of MTBE was a legitimate exercise of public safety, health, and environmental regulation, the International Institute for Sustainable Development ("the Institute") was the first of four nongovernmental organizations (NGOs) to file a petition for *amicus curiae* status asserting an argument in favor of a Host State's proper exercise of regulatory sovereignty in furtherance of the public welfare with respect to health, safety, and environmental objectives, applied on a nondiscriminatory basis.[217] The NGOs further advanced that under no analysis can such regulations be construed as violating international law and that they probably pertain to a Host State's prerogative

[213] *Id.*

[214] *Id.* at Part II–Ch. D ¶ 3.

[215] *Id.* at Part II–Ch. D ¶ 4. In the proceeding, it was uncontested that methanol is the essential oxygenating element of MTBE.

[216] *See id.* at Part I–Preface ¶ 2. Methanex ultimately challenged three legislative texts:

(i) the 1999 California Executive Order certifying that, "On balance, there is significant risk to the environment from using MTBE in gasoline in California";

(ii) California Code of Regulations Title Thirteen, §§2273 requiring gasoline pumps containing MTBE to be labeled in California as follows: "contains MTBE. The State of California has determined that use of this chemical presents a significant risk to the environment." §§2262.6 provided at sub-section (a)(1) that: starting December 31, 2002, no person shall sell, offer for sale, supply or offer for supply in California gasoline which has been produced with the use of methyl-tertiary-butyl ether (MTBE)"; and

(iii) Amended California Regulation of May 2003, expressly banning the use of methanol as an oxygenate in California.

Id. at Part II–Ch. D ¶¶ 14–23.

[217] Petitions eventually were filed by (i) the International Institute for Sustainable Development, (ii) Communities for a Better Environment, (iii) the Bluewater Network of Earth Island Institute and, (iv) the Center for International Environmental Law. *Id.* at Part II–Ch. C ¶ 26.

within its regulatory space.[218] Two additional precepts on which the Institute predicated its petition were (i) that the interpretation of Chapter Eleven of NAFTA should reflect legal principles underlying the concept of sustainable development[219] and (ii) "that participation of an *amicus* would allay public disquiet as to the closed nature of arbitration proceedings under Chapter Eleven of NAFTA."[220]

The *Methanex* tribunal's analysis of Claimant's Article 1110 ("Expropriation and Compensation") claim is most eloquent in emphasizing the normative and substantive differences between the *Metalclad* and *Methanex* tribunals with respect to the public purpose doctrine within the NAFTA. In sharp relief with *Metalclad*, the *Methanex* tribunal observed that the regulation at issue did not give rise to a case for a direct or indirect nationalization or expropriation within the framework of Article 1110. The tribunal specifically observed:

> In this case, there is no expropriation decree or creeping expropriation. Nor was there a "taking" in the sense of any property of Methanex being seized and transferred in a single or a series of actions, to California or its designees. Insofar as Methanex can make a claim under Article 1110(1) it is not a claim for nationalization or expropriation, simpliciter, but for "measures tantamount to expropriation." Thus, Methanex must establish that the California ban was tantamount to an expropriation within the meaning of Article 1110 in NAFTA.[221]

The tribunal's fundamental organizing principles can be found in both (i) its demonstration that the California ban was "tantamount to an expropriation" within the ambit of Article 1110 of the NAFTA and (ii) the element of public purpose within the operative legal standard.

[218] *See* Methanex v. United States of America, Petitioner's Final Submission Regarding the Petition of the International Institute for Sustainable Development to the Arbitral Tribunal for Amicus Curiae Status, 10–18 (October 16, 2000) *available at* http://www.iisd.org/pdf/methanex_petition_oct162000.pdf [hereinafter Methanex Amicus Curiae Submission]; *see also*, Methanex v United States, Decision of the Tribunal on Petition from Third Persons to Intervene as "Amici Curiae," ¶ 5 (January 15, 2001) *available at* http://www.iisd.org/pdf/methanex_tribunal_first_amicus_decision.pdf (The Institute's Petition sought leave "(i) to file an *amicus* brief preferably after reading the Parties' written pleadings, (ii) to make oral submissions, (iii) to observe status at oral hearings").

[219] The principle of sustainable development is explored at length *infra* Chapter 2 in the context of what collectively is referred to as "the UNCTAD documents," *infra* Chapter 3 in connection with the African Charter on Human and Peoples' Rights, and again *infra* Chapter 4 in the context of public purpose in BITs.

[220] *See* Methanex Amicus Curiae Submission, *supra* note 218.

[221] Methanex, *supra* note 154, at Part IV–Ch. D ¶ 6 (emphasis added).

Quite predictably, the *Methanex* claimants sought analytical and conceptual support in *Metalclad*'s definition of expropriation. Claimants reiterated that standard in the following terms:

> ... *expropriation under* NAFTA *includes not only open, deliberate, and acknowledged takings of property, such as outright seizure or formal or obligatory transfer of title in favor of the Host State, but also covert or incidental interference with the use of property which has the effect of depriving the owner, in whole, or in significant part, of the use of reasonably-to-be-expected economic benefit of property even if not necessarily to the obvious benefit of the Host State.*[222]

This definition of expropriation within Article 1110 is wholly bereft of the words "public purpose." It is *effects-based* and mostly invites a narrow analysis limited to scrutiny of the relationship between the claimant and the property at issue. Similarly, pursuant to the *Metalclad* tribunal's definition of expropriation within Article 1110, the subject matter of the taking, expropriation, or nationalization is not described in terms of *investment* nor was the claimant framed as an *investor.*[223]

Far from embracing whole cloth the *Metalclad* standard, the *Methanex* tribunal merely reduced the definition to a single element of a direct or indirect expropriation or nationalization. In this connection, it noted that "*Metalclad* is correct that an intentionally discriminatory regulation against a foreign investor fulfills a key requirement for establishing expropriation."[224] The tribunal, however, advanced a conceptually different corollary to *Metalclad*'s definition that is doctrinally closer to the NAFTA's Article 1110 ("Expropriation and Compensation") *and* premised on public purpose considerations:

> ... *as a matter of general international law, a non-discriminatory regulation for a public purpose, which is enacted in accordance with due process and, which affects, inter alios, a foreign investor or investment is not deemed expropriatory and compensable unless specific commitments had been given by the regulating government to the then putative foreign investor contemplating investment that the government would refrain from such regulation.*[225]

[222] *Id* at Part IV–Ch. D ¶ 4 (citing Metalclad, *supra* note 80, at ¶ 103) (emphasis in original).

[223] The absence of these terms of art (investment and investor), particularly within the context of Chapter 11, an investment chapter, emphasizes an expansive claimant-oriented approach and incident policy. *Investor* and *investment* status are significant jurisdictional predicates that must be met upon penalty of the claim's dismissal. As such, a definition of expropriation de-emphasizes central jurisdictional defenses and suggests a diminished role for the Host State.

[224] Methanex, *supra* note 154, at Part IV–Ch. D ¶ 7.

[225] *Id.* (emphasis added).

The "Methanex corollary" literally tracks the four elements to an indirect or direct nationalization or expropriation contained in Article 1110:[226] (i) public purpose, (ii) nondiscriminatory treatment, (iii) due process of law, and (iv) the payment of compensation. Moreover, the term of art "foreign investor or investment" is used to accentuate jurisdictional technical requirements.[227]

In addition, the *Methanex* tribunal further buttressed the standard for expropriation under Article 1110 by borrowing from the *Feldman v. Mexico* award:

> *The regulatory action has not deprived the Claimant of control of his company, ... interfered directly in the internal operations ... or displaced the Claimant as the controlling shareholder. The claimant is free to pursue other continuing lines of business activity .... Of course, he was effectively precluded from exporting cigarettes .... However, this does not amount to Claimant's deprivation of control of its company.*[228]

Consequently, under the *Methanex* public purpose rubric, a regulatory measure tantamount to an expropriation, let alone a direct or indirect expropriation or nationalization, in addition to an absence of (i) due process of law, (ii) public purpose, and (iii) nondiscriminatory practice, also must establish that the investor was deprived of shareholder controlling status or control of the investment at issue. This "control" test continues to wander the corridors of conceptual development of public international law without finding definitive doctrinal repose in any quarter.[229]

[226] *See* NAFTA, *supra* note 1, art. 1110.

[227] The treaty-based arbitration decisional law finding that a tribunal lacks jurisdiction based on failure to meet the *investor* or investment predicates. *See, e.g.*, Salini Costruttori SpA and Italstrade SpA v. Morocco, ICSID Case No. ARB/00/4, Decision on Jurisdiction, ¶ 52 (July 23, 2001), 14 ICSID Rep. 306 (2010) ("The doctrine generally considers that investment infers: contributions, a certain duration of performance of the contract and a participation in the risks of the transaction ... In reading the [ICSID] Convention's preamble, one may add the contribution to the economic development of the Host State of the investment as an additional condition").

[228] Methanex, *supra* note 154, at Part IV–Ch. D ¶ 16 (citing Feldman Insurance Co. v. Mexico, ICSID Case No. ARB (AF)/99/01, Award ¶ 152 (December 16, 2002)) (emphasis in original).

[229] *See* Steven R. Ratner, *Regulatory Takings in Institutional Context: Beyond the Fear of Fragmented International Law*, 102 AM. J. INT'L L. 475, 484 (2008) ("The control test is notably subject to multiple interpretations. Some have attempted to find the silver bullet that will reconcile the cases and serve as a guide for the future, including by emphasizing the intent of the State and the distinction between State takeover of property and mere regulation of its use. Others have eschewed a simple solution" [footnotes omitted]).

In holding that the California ban did not constitute a measure tantamount to an expropriation,[230] the public purpose doctrine was accorded a preeminent status in the award's architecture.[231] Indeed, although not expressly mentioned in the Article 1110(1) analysis, the tribunal's factual foundations concerning the

[230] The award as to this point, Article 1110(1), reads:

> For the reasons elaborated here and earlier in this Award, the Tribunal concludes that the California ban was made for a public purpose, was non-discriminatory and was accomplished with due process. Hence, Methanex's central claim under Article 1110(1) of expropriation under one of the three forms of action in that provision fails. From the standpoint of international law, the California ban was a lawful regulation and not an expropriation.

Methanex, *supra* note 154, at Part IV–Ch. D ¶ 15.

[231] Methanex framed its cornerstone expropriation claim on four premises that sought to meet the Article 1110 exceptions:

> 317. First, a substantial portion of Methanex's investments, including its share of the California and larger U.S. oxygenate market were taken by facially discriminatory measures and handed over to the domestic ethanol industry. Such a taking is at minimum "tantamount . . . to expropriation" under the plain language of Article 1110.
> 318. Second, these measures were not intended to serve a "public purpose" as is required by Article 1110(a), but rather were primarily a mechanism for seizing Methanex's U.S.'s and Methanex Fortier's share of the California oxygenate market and handing it directly to the domestic ethanol industry.
> 319. Third, the discriminatory nature of the measures fail to meet the requirement of Article 1110(c)that they comply with "due process of law and Article 1105(1)."
> 320. Finally, Methanex has not been compensated for the harms it has suffered as a result of these measures.

Id. at Part IV–Ch. D ¶ 3 (citing Second Am. Claim, ¶¶ 317–20). The tribunal fashioned five arguments that addressed Methanex's averments.

First, it asserted that the Respondent, the United States, never communicated false representations to Methanex upon which Methanex relied to its detriment. To the contrary, the tribunal emphasized that:

> Methanex entered a political economy in which it was widely known, if not notorious, that governmental, environmental and health protection institutions at the federal and State level, operating under the vigilant eyes of the media, interested corporations, nongovernmental organizations and a politically active electorate, continuously monitored the use and impact of chemical compounds and commonly prohibited or restricted the use of some of those compounds for environmental and/or health reasons.

Id. at Part IV–Ch. D ¶ 9. Second, because Methanex did not rely on any representations purporting to state that a ban would not issue, the tribunal distinguished its case from that of *Revere Copper & Brass, Incorporated v. Overseas Private Investment Corporation (OPIC)*, AM. ARB. ASS'N (August 24, 1978), 17 I.L.M. 1321 (1978). *See* Methanex, *supra* note 154, at Part IV–Ch. D ¶ 10.

Third, Methanex's averments that the process pursuant to which the California ban was enacted was corrupted by contributions to then Lieutenant Governor, later Governor Davis, were found devoid of any record evidence. *Id.* at Part IV–Ch. D ¶ 11.

The tribunal noted that California's governor "followed the protocol established in California Senate Bill 521 [and that] there is no indication in the record that he varied from

Host State's legitimate and appropriate exercise of its sovereignty pursuant to the issuance of a legislative enactment was directly related to its adoption of the University of California's Report.[232] The award's emphasis on the scientific evidence and detailed factual findings concerning the relationship between this evidence and health and the environment reflects considerable concern for the public purpose doctrine generally and, in particular, for the orthodox GATT Article XX international trade law exceptions. The *Methanex* tribunal, however, does not at all frame this penchant in the language of public international law principles. It notably does not undertake any sustained analysis that sets forth a standard or otherwise suggests the basis of the public purpose doctrine's primacy in relation to the countervailing foreign investor investment law protections. In this regard, the analysis deftly limits itself merely (i) to rephrasing three of the NAFTA's Article 1110 exceptions and (ii) emphasizing the want of representations concerning the California ban on which the claimant did not rely. The paucity of language on this point is profoundly disconcerting. It leaves the parties, future tribunals, and commentators without any sense of standard, doctrinal guidepost, or specific policy issues that may serve as either instructive precedent or a principle that meaningfully contextualizes competing interests, particularly in the wake of the *Metalclad* award.

A more subtle but equally eloquent indicator of the considerable weight that the tribunal accorded to a State's traditional police powers or public doctrine is found in its very analysis of the NAFTA's Article 1101(1),[233] which the tribunal indicates "is not assisted by [Methanex's] arguments under

it in any *way*." *Id.* at Part IV–Ch. D ¶ 12. Thus, the tribunal reasoned that "[t]he terms of Governor Davis's Executive Order and subsequent action by the State of California are inconsistent with Methanex's contention that the California ban was designed to transfer the gasoline oxygenate market to ethanol." *Id.*

Fifth and finally, the operative factual timeline before the tribunal led it to conclude that Methanex's factual submissions are inconclusive because they rely, as Methanex admitted, on inferences. The tribunal observed that "where the time-line of California Senate Legislation, scientific study, public hearing, executive order and initiative to secure an oxygenate waiver are all objectively confirmed, the argument for resorting to inference as a way of reaching a conclusion inconsistent with the objective evidence is untenable." *Id.* at Part IV–Ch. D ¶ 14.

[232] Part of California Senate Bill 521, enacting the MTBE Public Health and Environment Protection Act of 1997, directed the University of California to conduct research on the effects of MTBE. The University of California Report comprised five volumes, 600 pages that constituted seventeen separate papers compiled by more than sixty researchers. *Id.* at Part III–Ch. A ¶ 3.

Among other findings, the University of California Report recommended "a full environmental assessment of any alternatives to MTBE in Ca. RFG2, including the components of Ca. RFG2 itself, before any changes are made in California State law." *Id.* at Part III-Ch. A ¶ 14.

[233] NAFTA, *supra* note 1, art. 1101 ¶ (1).

Article 1110."[234] The sufficiency of Methanex's claim rested on the extent to which it could demonstrate the requisite legal connection between the 1999 California Executive Order, the 2000 California Regulations, and its investments, evincing California's intent to harm the specific class of foreign methanol producers, including Methanex.[235]

The *Methanex* tribunal construed the "relating to" predicate in Article 1101(1)[236] as consisting of an "effects plus" test that "signifies something more than the mere effect of a measure on an investor or an investment in that it requires a legally significant connection between them."[237] This construction of the "relating to" element of Article 1101(1) provides a Home State with considerable defenses in establishing that a particular regulatory measure could not have "related to" a particular investor or investment without placing the burden on a claimant to demonstrate intent or another iteration of *scienter*. From an evidentiary perspective, establishing specificity of this nature with respect to intent is just as daunting, if not altogether impossible in most circumstances, as demonstrating intent for purposes of establishing that a particular measure issued in furtherance of a public purpose. This unremarkable construction of "relating to" within the meaning of Article 1101(1) is a negative byproduct of the subjective standard incident to the legacy public purpose doctrine.[238] This stringent standard comports with an expansive view of a State's regulatory space. It is conceptually consistent with the standard to conclude that a measure does not *relate to* an investor or investment where its effect on public health or the environment is scientifically sound, as was the case in *Methanex*.[239]

The proposition that scientific evidence negates the legal requirement for meeting the "relating to" stricture in Article 1101(1) is fundamentally flawed. The scientific soundness of a measure cannot have the de facto effect of negating

[234] Methanex, *supra* note 154, at Part IV–Ch. D ¶ 18.

[235] The tribunal framed the jurisdictional issue as "whether the two U.S. measures 'relate' to Methanex as an investor or its investments within the meaning of Article 1101(1)(a) and (b) in NAFTA." *Id.* at Part IV–Ch. E ¶ 2.

[236] In relevant part, Article 1101(1) provides that Chapter 11 of NAFTA "applies to measures adopted or maintained by a party relating to: (a) investors of another Party; (b) investments of investors of another party in the territory of the Party . . . . " NAFTA, *supra* note 1, art. 1101 ¶ (1)(a)–(b).

[237] Methanex, *supra* note 154, at Part II–Ch. E ¶ 3.

[238] Indeed, Methanex failed to meet this standard to the tribunal's satisfaction. Despite the proliferation of partial awards and analysis in the final award on jurisdiction and merits consisting of 278 pages, this rudimentary tenet for purposes of Chapter 11 initially was not even properly averred and never met. Methanex Corp. v. United States of America, NAFTA Ch. 11/UNCITRAL, Partial Award, ¶ 147 (August 3, 2005), 7 ICSID Rep. 239 (2012) [hereinafter Methanex Partial Award].

[239] Methanex, *supra* note 154, at Part IV–Ch. E ¶ 20.

effects triggering Article 1101(1)'s "relating to" stricture. Consequently, the "effects plus test" that the *Methanex* tribunal affixed to Article 1101(1) gives rise to a corollary suggesting that the requisite "relating to" showing is not demonstrable where the measure at issue rests on legitimate scientific foundations. The consequence of this reading renders the Article 1101(1) standard insurmountable with respect to virtually any credible regulatory measure.

The use of the public purpose doctrine in *Methanex* is unbridled and detached from the more tempered statement of the doctrine throughout the NAFTA treaty framework. Devoid of standard as to application and equally lacking as to tempering regulatory sovereignty, the award links the public purpose doctrine with uncertainty and the lack of a functional standard having predictive value. It becomes clear and more than just a coincidence that, after the *Methanex* case – the award that stands as the antinomy to the *Metalclad* "effects test" – the public purpose doctrine appears as the determinative principle that tips the pendulum almost absolutely in favor of regulatory Host-State sovereignty. The "effects test" in all of its iterations has not redeemed the promise of tempering regulatory sovereignty.

J. BEYOND METALCLAD AND METHANEX: THE NAFTA JURISPRUDENCE

In addition to being conceptually and doctrinally diametrically opposed on the role of the public purpose doctrine, the *Metalclad* and *Methanex* awards raise many more questions than they could ever aspire to address satisfactorily. *Metalclad* and *Methanex* do not address the new challenge that the public purpose doctrine must meet. The advent of economic globalization has given rise to a paradigm of *interdependence* that shuns "winner-take-all" applications and definitions of the public purpose doctrine.[240] The paragon of *independence* of States has passed. Globalization underscores the shared approach of exploration, exploitation, and development of resources among States. Short from even suggesting the need to explore new methodologies in the application of the doctrine, the *Metalclad* and *Methanex* analyses remarkably do not at all reference, let alone rely upon, the NAFTA's public purpose standard contained in Article 1101(4).[241] The Article 1101(4) effort to fashion a public purpose standard or, alternatively, provide the doctrine with substantive content within the Chapter Eleven rubric simply is ignored. Along this same vein,

[240] One of the shortcomings of the NAFTA public purpose jurisprudence is the "all-or-nothing" results that it has generated. This shortcoming is not unique to NAFTA, but in fact pervades the entire public purpose doctrine. *See infra* Conclusion.

[241] NAFTA, *supra* note 1, art. 1101 ¶ 4.

neither tribunal (*Metalclad* nor *Methanex*) even purports to draw upon the rich and manifold references to public purpose throughout the NAFTA's framework beyond just Chapter Eleven.[242] The scant but helpful working papers and drafts prepared by the NAFTA parties relating to the public purpose standard or doctrine as well were not referenced in the awards. It necessarily follows that neither *Metalclad* nor *Methanex* at all enriched or otherwise assisted in clarifying the totality of the NAFTA's public purpose workings.

The command in *Methanex* is both succinct and clear but equally disconcerting. A conservative construction of the award suggests that a direct or indirect expropriation or nationalization is not compensable where the Article 1110 exceptions (the presence of due process, nondiscriminatory, and public purpose) are present so long as the investor did not rely on false representations on the part of the Host State. This proposition is neither an uncontroverted principle of public international law[243] nor conceptually comprehensive in scope. Specifically, it fails to address whether such a taking is compensable even where the operative bilateral or multilateral treaty, such as the very NAFTA itself, suggests otherwise.[244] The Article 1110 framework

[242] *See Id.* art. 721 ¶ 2(b); art. 912 ¶ (b); art. 1015 ¶¶ 4(c), 8(a), 8(i); art. 1017 ¶ 1(j); art. 1019 ¶ 6; art. 1411 ¶ 5(b); art. 1804 ¶ (b).

[243] In fact, steps have been taken post-*Methanex* and *Metalclad* to make the scope of such obligations clearer. For example, the 2004 U.S. Model BIT "clarifies that '[e]xcept in rare circumstances, nondiscriminatory regulatory actions by a Party that are designed and applied to protect legitimate public welfare objectives, such as public health, safety, and the environment, do not constitute indirect expropriations.'" Karen Halverson Cross, *Converging Trends in Investment Treaty Practice*, 38 N.C. J. INT'L L. & Com. REG. 151, 191 (2012). Such language should "make it significantly more difficult for investors such as Metalclad to convince an arbitral tribunal that a regulatory measure, particularly an environmental protection, health or safety measure, is expropriatory." *Id.* (internal footnotes omitted).

[244] Article 1110 in pertinent part provides:

> 1. No Party may directly or indirectly nationalize or expropriate an investment of an investor of another Party in its territory or take a measure tantamount to nationalization or expropriation of such an investment ("expropriation"), except:
>   (d) on payment of compensation in accordance with paragraph 2 through 6.
> 2. Compensation shall be equivalent to the fair market value of the expropriated investment immediately before the expropriation took place ("date of expropriation"), and shall not reflect any change in value occurring because the intended expropriation had become known earlier. Valuation criteria shall include going concern value, asset value including declared tax value of tangible property, and other criteria, as appropriate, to determine fair market value.
> 3. Compensation shall be paid without delay and be fully realizable.
> 4. If payment is made in a G7 currency, compensation shall include interest at a commercially reasonable rate for that currency from the date of expropriation until the date of actual payment.

contemplates that a Host State has an obligation to compensate a foreign investor, without more, as to any of the following six events: (i) a direct expropriation, (ii) an indirect expropriation, (iii) a direct nationalization, (iv) an indirect nationalization, (v) a measure tantamount to a nationalization, and (vi) a measure tantamount to an expropriation. Nowhere does Article 1110 or Chapter Eleven of the NAFTA assert that a Host State is relieved from any legal obligation to issue compensation for a direct or indirect expropriation or nationalization, or a measure tantamount to a nationalization or expropriation, so long as false misrepresentations with respect to an investment relied upon by an investor did not issue. This principle does find support in international law beyond the *Methanex* tribunal's pronouncement.[245] The *Methanex* tribunal, however, hardly explains the circumstances pursuant to which application of this general principle trumps the clear command in Article 1110(1). The absence of any analysis on this issue from a policy perspective mitigates against a very broad construction of the governing precept in *Methanex* as an illustration of the application of the NAFTA Article 1110 for a public purpose.

Because the *Methanex* tribunal neither defines what constitutes a public purpose nor explains the Article 1110(1)(d) "compensability issue," no conceptual residue remains that would have didactic value for purposes of illustrating the workings of the public purpose doctrine within the meaning of the NAFTA's Article 1110(1) subsections (a) through(d).[246] Once the *Methanex* tribunal accepted the scientific evidence proffered by the University of California Report, no attention was accorded to consideration of the benefits and detriments on both the investor/investment and the public welfare by dint of issuance of a legislative ban and the Executive Decree. To the contrary, the acceptance of this scientific evidence proved to be dispositive with respect to (i) legitimizing the effects of the measures on the subject investment and (ii) proscribing compensation.[247]

5. If a Party elects to pay in a currency other than a G7 currency, the amount paid on the date of payment, if converted into G7 currency at the market rate of exchange prevailing on that date, shall be no less than if the amount of compensation owed on the date of expropriation had been converted into that G7 currency at the market rate of exchange prevailing on that date, and interest had accrued at a commercially reasonable date for that G7 currency from the date of expropriation until the date of payment.
6. On payment, compensation shall be freely transferable as provided in Article 1109.

NAFTA, *supra* note 1, art. 1110.

[245] *See supra* note 243 and accompanying text.

[246] *See infra* Chapter J.1.

[247] From a technical perspective, the tribunal did not have to reach either of these issues because it ultimately held that the "relating to" jurisdictional predicate of Article 1101(1) was never met.

The inordinate weight that the *Methanex* tribunal ascribes to public purpose generally (not even the public purpose standard)[248] has the doctrinal and conceptual effect of marginalizing all other factors that merit consideration.[249] The pragmatic effect of vesting public purpose with dispositive status once the scientific legitimacy of the measure at issue has been legally established is to vest the Host State's regulatory sphere with juridically unbridled discretion as to foreign investor/investment protection. This approach in the context of the NAFTA eviscerates even the most rudimentary policy objective underlying Chapter Eleven. More universally, beyond the NAFTA, this misapprehension of the public purpose doctrine:

(i) wrests from foreign investors any reasonable hope of protecting their investments from takings and even from noncompensable expropriations/nationalizations;
(ii) delegitimizes treaty-based arbitrations as a genuine international dispute resolution methodology that protects investors/investments from the parochialism of Host-State judiciaries by providing for a supernational tribunal where public international law applies;
(iii) frustrates the policy tenets of international investment law that seek to foster enhanced foreign direct investments;
(iv) heightens the tensions between capital-exporting and capital-importing States by disrupting equipoise in favor of developing nations to the detriment of industrialized States;
(v) further deepens an "all-or-nothing" risk factor in treaty-based investment arbitrations that is contrary to pervading principles of economic globalization and "globalized sovereignty" that favor viability sharing frameworks;
(vi) does not contribute to a rubric that seeks to harmonize the disparate and often conflicting policy objectives of international investment law and international trade law, and;
(vii) furthers the distorting effects of treating all regulatory measures as equal in importance with respect to public purpose.[250]

[248] *See Supra* notes 230–31 and accompanying text.

[249] Even though it does not so state, the *Methanex* tribunal, based upon its very analysis, does not treat the elements of Article 1110 para. 1(a)–(d) ("Public Purpose, Non-Discriminatory Treatment, Due Process of Law, and Payment of Compensation") as having to be construed *in pari materia*.

[250] As is suggested in considerable detail in this text, *see infra* Chapter 4, health, life, safety, and measures concerning plant, animal, and human life vary in importance, as well as exigency. The same, so the argument here advanced says, holds true for environmental measures. Measures that seek to conserve and preserve are materially different concerning remediation

1. *The Public Purpose Legacy of* Metalclad *and* Methanex

Although *Metalclad* enshrined the effects on the investment to the detriment of the relevant regulatory measure, *Methanex* embraces the measure wholesale without inquiry into its bona fide nature or its effects on the investor/investment. The consequences of government regulations on the investor/investment are of little to no moment when viewed through the prism of a *Methanex* analysis.

Whether read together or separately, *Metalclad* and *Methanex* cast considerable doubt on the extent to which treaty or contract provisions proscribing regulatory expropriations have any practical effect. Neither case contributes to the decisional law on the narrow issue of the relationship between compensability and public purpose in the context of direct or indirect expropriations or nationalizations. Indeed, both *Metalclad* and *Methanex* cloud these issues.[251] Is there a defined standard of proof to which investor States, Host States, and arbitral tribunals must be sensitive and should apply concerning the assessment of a regulatory measure and its effects on foreign investors/investments?[252] Despite more moderate and balanced approaches, the

and mitigation issues, together with triggering exigency. It is therefore unclear why these exceptions would be treated the same and accorded identical normative standing.

[251] *See supra* Chapter 1.H and 1.I.

[252] Although the *Methanex* tribunal referenced, but did not define, "burden of proof," Methanex, *supra* note 154, at Part IV–Ch. B ¶ 9, neither the *Methanex* nor the *Metalclad* tribunals spoke to an applicable standard of proof in evaluating "effects" on investments or "the nature of a particular regulatory measure" characterized as an expropriation, nationalization, or a measure tantamount to an expropriation or nationalization. Here, too, a considerable lack of rigor is demonstrated by both the *Methanex* and *Metalclad* tribunals, and, as shall be established, it is a shortcoming that pervades the NAFTA jurisprudence and the decisional law of treaty-based investor-state arbitration.

Read together, *Metalclad* and *Methanex* certainly provide a normative foundation for the development of a "proportionality test," but neither tribunal examines the legal space of mitigation that suggests that "less intrusive measure" analysis is warranted in managing competing investor and Host State interests. The availability of less restricting measures is not wholly segregated from consideration of the extent to which a measure is bona fide or of whether the measure at issue is an effective one. Scrutiny of the efficacy of a government measure or of its effectiveness or place on a scale measuring least restrictive means presents considerable challenges. Most of these obstacles concern access to government data and premises for decision making. These obstacles, however, are being progressively shed. The confluence of access to scientific data and technology has made it possible for NGOs and other interested private sector participants to evaluate regulatory measures purporting to have a scientific foundation and to be able to analyze efficacy, cost efficiency, and the availability of less restrictive options. Also, although it is still work in progress, transparency with respect to access to government information has obtained the unprecedented status of a universal human right. *See* Case of *Claude-Reyes et al. v. Chile*, Merits, Reparations and Costs, Judgment, INTER-AM. CT. H.R. (ser. C) No. 151, ¶¶ 86–87 (September 19, 2006). Even though much of the

"NAFTA Jurisprudence" does not satisfactorily address these issues. They remain witnesses to an impoverished legacy public purpose doctrine that has been incorporated by ad hoc tribunals into different tests that fail to address the foundational queries that the public purpose doctrine comprehensively must be able to address if it is to reconcile the competing interests of investor States and Host States in an era of economic globalization.

2. *A Broader Examination of the NAFTA's Jurisprudence and Other Investor-State Decisional Law: In Search of a Viable Public Purpose Framework*

The NAFTA's decisional law addressing the public purpose doctrine primarily in the context of a direct or indirect expropriation or nationalization or regulatory measures tantamount to an expropriation is internally inconsistent and doctrinally in disarray.[253] The *Metalclad* and *Methanex* awards serve as prime examples.[254] The "foundational NAFTA cases" and other jurisprudence often analyzed together with NAFTA decisional law, such as *Tecmed*,[255] struggle to devise a standard that may best harmonize the competing investor-state interests, as well as reconcile international trade and investment law. These efforts fail, however, because the different "effects test" and "proportionality" standards apply a fundamentally flawed public purpose doctrine.

practical application of the principle of transparency as a right remains aspirational and embryonic, on a relative scale, transparency can point to notable objective accomplishments.

253 *See* Tecmed, *supra* note 151, at ¶ 115 and n.26 (citing Giorgio Sacerdoti, *Bilateral Treaties & Multilateral Instruments on Investment Protection*, in 269 RECUEIL DES COURS 255, 383, 385–86 (Académie de Droit International de la Haye ed., 1997)). There is a difference to be drawn between a creeping expropriation and a de facto expropriation, although both typically are classified as within the broader concept of "indirect expropriation." To be sure, both types of expropriations may be undertaken pursuant to a variety of acts that compel case by case examination. *Id.* at ¶ 116 & n. 27 (citing R. Dolzer & M. Stevens, BILATERAL INVESTMENT TREATIES 99–100 (Martinus Nijhoff 1995)).

254 The two different and contrasting expropriation compensability rules in *Methanex* and *Metalclad* rightfully deserve to be joined by yet a third paradigm that further contributes to obfuscate the dispositive standard. In *Compainia del Desarrollo de Santa Elena, S.A. v. Republic of Costa Rica*, the award on this issue provided:

> Expropriatory environmental measures – no matter how laudable and beneficial to society as a whole – are, in this respect, similar to any other expropriatory measures that a State may take in order to implement its policies: where property is expropriated, even for environmental purposes, whether domestic or international, the State's obligation to pay compensation remains.

Compañia del Desarrollo de Santa Elena, S.A. v. Republic of Costa Rica, ICSID Case No. ARB/96/1, Award ¶ 72 (February 17, 2000), 5 ICSID REV. 169, 192 (2000).

255 *See* Tecmed, *supra* note 151.

As shall be examined, it is the fundamental use of a legacy public purpose doctrine enjoying an embedded subjective standard that generates the inconsistencies. The various competing interests and policies pertaining to Home and Host States cannot be harmonized and reconciled merely as a byproduct of awards resulting from ad hoc tribunals applying an ill-defined doctrine. More is necessary if such awards indeed aspire to yield a jurisprudence that is uniform, transparent, and having predictive value. The shortcomings of this decisional law can be traced to an approach that "places the cart before the horse" by fashioning different tests that lead to inconsistent results. The preferred methodology is one that focuses on developing the very principles being applied in ways that address the competing interests identified. The emphasis on methodology rather than principle development inevitably will give rise to issues of process legitimacy and foster an unacceptable level of uncertainty.

The dissonance arising from emphasis on developing a workable methodology or standard becomes evident and perhaps reaches a pinnacle with the "proportionality test" enunciated in the *Tecmed* award.[256] Often analyzed within the framework of the NAFTA even though the claim is brought by an investor from a non-NAFTA party pursuant to the Spain and Mexico BIT,[257] the facts underlying *Tecmed* somewhat resemble *Metalclad*[258] but without the municipal, State, and federal dichotomy of positions concerning the purported need for a municipal permit as a predicate to constructing and operating a hazardous waste landfill facility.[259]

[256] *Id. at* ¶ 122.

[257] *Id. at* ¶ 4. The *Tecmed case* is often discussed in conjunction with cases brought pursuant to NAFTA. *See, e.g.*, Timothy Meyer, *Codifying Custom*, 160 U. PA. L. REV. 995, 1041 n.177 (2012); Allan Ingelson & Lincoln Mitchell, *NAFTA, the Mining Law of 1872, and Environmental Protection*, 51 NAT. RESOURCES J. 261, 283 (2011); Alberto R. Salazar V., PhD, *NAFTA Chapter 11, Regulatory Expropriation, and Domestic Counter-Advertising Law*, 27 ARIZ. J. INT'L & COMP. L. 31, 48 (2010); Vicki Been, *NAFTA's Investment Protections and the Division of Authority for Land Use and Environmental Controls*, 20 PACE ENVTL. L. REV. 19, 41 n.135 (2002).

[258] *See supra* Chapter 1.H.

[259] The claimant in *Tecmed* was the awardee in connection with a public auction held by Promotora Inmobiliaria del Ayuntamiento de Hermosillo ("Promotora"), a decentralized municipal agency of the Municipality of Hermosillo, located in the State of Sonora, Mexico. The auction concerned the sale of real and improved property in addition to facilities and assets concerning a controlled landfill of hazardous industrial waste. The facility was known as "Cytrar," which eventually became the holder of Tecmed's rights and obligations under the tender. Tecmed, *supra* note 151, at ¶ 35.

Although the land on which the landfill was built had been purchased by the Government of the State of Sonora, in the locality of Las Viboras, falling within the jurisdiction of the Municipality of Hermosillo, in the State of Sonora, the landfill operated pursuant to a renewable license issued by the Ministry of Urban Development and Ecology (SEDUE) of the

The *Tecmed* tribunal's analysis of the role of public purpose is less than lucid. Even though, for purposes of determining whether there has been a compensable expropriation, the tribunal acknowledges "[t]he principle that the State's exercise of its sovereign powers within the framework of its *police power* may cause economic damage to those subject to its powers as administrator without entitling them to any compensation whatsoever is undisputable,"[260] it struggles with the role that public purpose defined as "a legitimate aim 'in the public interest' plays in determining whether there is an expropriation or a compensable expropriation."[261] At the outset, the tribunal appears to articulate an "effects test" approach to determining whether there is an expropriation that is completely severed from any meaningful consideration of the connection that such effects arising from the government measure at issue may have with a State's police powers or legitimate public purpose.[262] It

federal government of Mexico. Initially, Parque Industrial de Hermosillo, a public agency of the State of Sonora, operated the facility. Upon a transfer of ownership of the landfill to a decentralized agency of the Municipality of Hermosillo, Confinamiento Controlado Parque Industrial de Hermosillo O.P.D., this agency was provided with authorization to operate for an indefinite period of time. Authorization was granted by the Hazardous Materials Waste and Activities Division of the National Ecology Institute of Mexico (INE), an agency of the federal government of the United Mexican States within the Ministry of the Environment, Natural Resources and Fisheries (SEMARNAP), which cancelled the initial authorization that SEDUE had issued. *Id. at* ¶¶ 36–37.

Eventually, INE rejected Tecmed's application for renewal of the authorization to operate the landfill and requested Cytrar to submit a program for the closure of the landfill. *Id.* at ¶ 39. Tecmed commenced the arbitration, alleging, among other things, that the failure to grant a new permit renewing authorization to operate the landfill constitutes an expropriation of its investments without compensation or justification, in addition to a violation of the operative agreement and of Mexican law. In this connection, Tecmed further averred that "such refusal would frustrate its justified expectations of the continuity and duration of the investment made and would impair recovery of the invested amount and the expected rate of return." *Id.* at 41.

260 *Id.* at ¶ 119.

261 *Id.* at ¶ 122 (citing Case of James & Others v. United Kingdom, 98 Eur. Ct. H.R. (ser. A) ¶ 50 (February 21, 1986)).

262 The tribunal underscores the "effects test" as a talisman that distinguishes between a State's legitimate exercise of its police powers (which we here construe as public purpose) and a de facto expropriation that wrests all value or ownership from the investor with respect to the investment. In so doing, however, the tribunal failed to explain or even attempt to elucidate whether a legitimate exercise of a State's police power constitutes a de facto expropriation that is or may not be compensable. The extent to which public purpose affects compensability is simply never stated. The tribunal's reasoning merits citation:

> To establish whether the Resolution is a measure equivalent to an expropriation under the terms of Section 5(1) of the Agreement, it must be first determined if the Claimant, due to the Resolution, was radically deprived of such economical use and enjoyment of its investments, as if the rights related thereto – such as the income or benefit related to the Landfill or its exploitation – had ceased to exist. In other words, if due to the actions of the Respondent, the assets involved have lost their value or economic use for the holder and the extent of the loss. This determination is important because it is one of the main

is observed that "[t]he government's intention is less important than the effects of the measures on the owner of the assets or on the benefits arising from such assets affected by the measures; and the form of the deprivation measure is less important than its actual effects."[263] This preliminary "effects test" also is segregated from the legal status of the domestic law purporting to provide a normative basis for the measure at issue.[264]

The objective analytical elegance of an "effects test" is wholly undermined by its inability to account for the interests of the Host State. The understanding of interests among States within an independent framework cannot be abandoned. *Metalclad* best exemplifies this debility. *Tecmed*'s incorporation of this analytical rubric from cases decided by the European Court of Human Rights only exacerbates the need for a doctrinally developed public purpose principle, without which the proportionality test flatly fails.[265] The tribunal's construction of the European Court of Human Rights' proportionality test

> elements to distinguish, from the point of view of an international tribunal, between a regulatory measure, which is an ordinary expression of the exercise of the State's police power that entails a decrease in assets or rights, and *a de facto* expropriation that deprives those assets and rights of any real substance. *Upon determining the degree to which the investor is deprived of its goods or rights, whether such deprivation should be compensated and whether it amounts or not to a de facto expropriation is also determined. Thus, the effects of the actions or behavior under analysis are not irrelevant to determine whether the action or behavior is an expropriation.*

Id. at ¶ 115 (emphasis added).

[263] *Id.* at ¶ 116 (citing Tippetts, Abbett, McCarthy, Stratton v. TAMS-AFFA Consulting Engineers of Iran, 6 Iran-U.S. Cl. Trib. Rep. 219, 225 (1984); Phelps Dodge Corp. et al. v. Iran, 10 Iran-U.S. Cl. Trib. Rep. 121, 130 (1986)).

[264] The tribunal noted, "[t]hat the actions of the Respondent are legitimate or lawful or in compliance with the law from the standpoint of the Respondent's domestic laws does not mean that they conform to the Agreement or to international law," *Id.* at ¶ 120, and provided:

> An Act of State must be characterized as internationally wrong if it constitutes a breach of an international obligation, even if the Act does not contravene the State's internal law – even if under that law, the State was actually bound to act that way.

Id. (citing James Crawford, The International Law Commission's Articles on State Responsibility 1, 84 (Cambridge University Press 2002)).

[265] The *Tecmed* award transitions from an "effects test" to a proportionality test by drawing analytical support from the European Court of Human Rights' jurisprudence. *Id.* at ¶ 122 (citing Case of Mellacher & Others v. Austria, 169 Eur. Ct. H.R. (ser. A) ¶ 24 (December 19, 1989); Case of Pressos Compañia Naviera & Others v. Belgium, 332 Eur. Ct. H.R. (ser. A) ¶ 19 (November 20, 1995)). Specifically, the tribunal provided:

> Not only must a measure depriving a person of his property pursue, on the facts as well as in principle, a legitimate aim "in the public interest," but there must also be a reasonable relationship of proportionality between the means employed and the aim sought to be realised . . . . The requisite balance will not be found if the person concerned has had to bear "an individual and excessive burden". . . . The Court considers that a measure must be both appropriate for achieving its aim and not disproportionate thereto.

results in a hybrid of international investment law and international trade law when articulated within the context of the proceeding before it:

> [T]he Arbitral Tribunal should consider whether community pressure and its consequences, which presumably gave rise to the government action qualified as expropriatory by the Claimant, were so great as to lead to a serious emergency situation, social crisis or public interest, in addition to the economic impact of such a government action, which in this case deprived the foreign investor of its investment with no compensation whatsoever. These factors must be weighed when trying to assess the *proportionality* of the action adopted with respect to the purpose pursued by such measure.[266]

Although the proportionality test introduced a public purpose balancing component, in applying the very test that it had reformulated for purposes of application in a treaty-based arbitration the tribunal denaturalized the public purpose element by specifically concluding that only where the regulatory measure at issue is in furtherance of the protection from imminent peril to the ecological balance or public health would such a measure constitute an exception where an investment's ownership is dislodged or its value fundamentally diminished.[267] Therefore, according to the *Tecmed* holding and

> . . .. Non-nationals are more vulnerable to domestic legislation: Unlike nationals, they will generally have played no part in the election or designation of its authors nor have been consulted on its adoption. Secondly, although a taking of property must always be effected in the *public interest*, different considerations may apply to nationals and non-nationals and there may well be legitimate reason for requiring nationals to bear a greater burden in the *public interest* than non-nationals.

Id. at ¶ 122 (citing Case of James & Others v. United Kingdom, 98 Eur. Ct. H.R. (ser. A) ¶¶ 50, 63 (February 21, 1986)) (emphasis added) (internal footnotes omitted).

[266] *Id.* at ¶ 133 (emphasis added). As to the meaning of "public interest" as referred to by the tribunal, had identified "the protection of the environment, ecological balance and public health", as additional factors comprising its understanding of "public interest." *Id.* at ¶ 129.

[267] As to this point, the tribunal's language could not be clearer:

> As expressed by the Respondent, the Landfill's proximity to Hermosillo's urban center, and not concrete evidence that the Landfill's operation is harmful for the environment or public health, is the issue that concentrates opposition of the groups that are against the Landfill.

Id. at ¶ 140.

The Award further states:

> In this case, there are no similar or comparable circumstances of emergency [similar or comparable to the situation in *Elettronica Sicula Sp.A.* No serious social situation, nor any urgency related to such situations, in addition to the fact that the Mexican Courts have not identified any crisis. The actions undertaken by the authorities to face these socio-political difficulties, where these difficulties do not have serious emergency or public hardship connotations, or wide-ranging and serious consequences, may not be

analysis, the element of the proportionality test relating to public purpose only concerns a very narrow segment of the State's regulatory space.

Tecmed's extrapolation of proportionality from the European Court of Human Rights' jurisprudence has the residual effect of serving primarily as an "effects test" based on three key analytical premises. First, the tribunal engaged exclusively in an "effects test" suggestive of an expropriation.[268] Second, the "effects test" was supplemented with a "private interest" element rendering possible a proportionality of the ratios between the burden of the measure on the investment and its relationship with the nature of the measure at issue and the objective that this measure seeks to redress. Third, the tribunal defines the measure to be redressed as posing an immediate threat to ecological balance, leading to a social crisis, or affecting health. This third level of the tribunal's construction substantially limits the scenarios in which a measure could meet the exception and, as a result, carves out of the proportionality test the public purpose component – leaving only an "effects" standard favoring claimants. In so doing, it undermines the equipoise sought between capital-exporting (likely claimants) and capital-importing countries (likely Host States). The extent to which the *Tecmed* tribunal intended to identify a category of public purpose commanding greater deference in the proportionality analysis and enjoying exception status with respect to the measure at issue is left wholly unclear. In undertaking this exercise, the tribunal remained silent and did not articulate *any* intent to create customary law by identifying a specific public purpose matrix.[269]

The identification of public purpose categories serving as exceptions justifying the legitimate and nondiscriminatory exercise of a State's regulatory

> considered from the standpoint of the Agreement or international law to be sufficient justification to deprive the foreign investor of its investment with no compensation, particularly if it has not been proved that Cytrar or Tecmed's behavior has been the determinant of the political pressure or the demonstrations that led to such deprivation, which underlie the Resolution and conclusively conditioned it.

Id. at ¶ 147 (citing Case Concerning Elettronica Sicula S.p.A. (ELSI) (U.S. v. Italy), 1989 I.C.J. 15 (July 20)).

[268] *Id.* at ¶ 115.

[269] The tribunal's reasoning on this issue is somewhat truncated. Although it is true that the evidence before it, as recited in the award, underscored the location of the site as not an immediate threat to health, ecological balance, or a social crisis, it would appear to follow that political pressure incident to the landfill's location as being too close to an urban center itself suggests a deeper state of apprehension arising from the increased risk of danger inversely proportional to the landfill's proximity to more densely populated areas. The duration and nature of the community reactions to the operation and transportation of hazardous waste from the facility gave rise to the filing of a complaint before Mexico's National Commission of Human Rights. *Id.* at ¶ 135.

authority to the detriment of a foreign investment, even beyond the State necessity exception,[270] finds support in the NAFTA and its jurisprudence.

3. *The* Tecmed *Contribution*

Chapter Fourteen of the NAFTA entitled "Financial Services" is a helpful example of a framework that reveals the *developmental potential* of the public purpose doctrine. It exemplifies ways in which public purpose may be enriched by creating special categories defined with particularity that are to be accorded extraordinary status in tempering the conflicting interests pertaining to the protection of foreign investments and the autonomy of Host-State regulatory space.[271] The development of a functional public purpose doctrine

[270] The customary international law doctrine of necessity is reflected succinctly in Article 25 of the International Law Commission's Draft Articles on State Responsibility for Wrongful Acts:

> 1. Necessity may not be invoked by a State as a ground for precluding the wrongfulness of an act not in conformity with an international obligation of that State unless the act:
>   (a) is the only way for the State to safeguard an essential interest against a grave and imminent peril; and
>   (b) does not seriously impair an essential interest of the state or states towards which the obligation exists, or of the international community as a whole.
> 2. In any case, necessity may not be invoked by a State as a ground for precluding wrongfulness if:
>   (a) the international obligation in question excludes the possibility of invoking necessity; or
>   (b) the State has contributed to the situation of necessity.

International Law Commission, *Articles on Responsibility of States for Internationally Wrongful Acts, With Commentaries*, UN Doc. A/56/10 (2001), p. 80, *available at* http://legal.un.org/ilc/texts/instruments/english/commentaries/9_6_2001.pdf (last accessed April 1, 2013) [hereinafter ILC Articles]. The commentary further provides that there is "substantial authority in support of the existence of necessity as a circumstance precluding wrongfulness. It has been invoked by states and has been dealt with by a number of international tribunals. In these cases the plea of necessity has been accepted in principle, or at least not rejected." *Id.* at 80–81.

[271] Article 1401: Scope and Coverage, identifies the parameters of this public purpose category:

> 1. This Chapter applies to measures adopted or maintained by a Party relating to:
>   (a) financial institutions of another Party;
>   (b) investors of another Party, and investments of such investors, in financial institutions in the Party's territory; and
>   (c) cross-border trade in financial services.
> 2. Articles 1109 through 1111, 1113, 1114 and 1211 are hereby incorporated into and made a part of this Chapter. Articles 1115 through 1138 are hereby incorporated into and made a part of this Chapter solely for breaches by a Party of Articles 1109 through 1111, 1113 and 1114, as incorporated into this Chapter.
> 3. Nothing in this Chapter shall be construed to prevent a Party, including its public entities, from exclusively conducting or providing in its territory:
>   (a) activities or services forming part of a public retirement plan or statutory system of social security; or

embracing an objective substantive content shall require paradigms of public purpose categories that refine and limit application of public purpose exceptions as a general principle that currently are broadly related to the welfare of a State. *Fireman's Fund Insurance Company (Fireman's Fund)*[272] was the first case, and, as of the date of this writing, remains the only case brought under the "Financial Services" chapter of the NAFTA. It thus provided the tribunal in that matter with a unique opportunity to interpret the "reasonable measures for prudential reasons" standard contained in the Article 1410(1) exceptions.[273] The case serves as a vast analytical source for any endeavor aspiring to redefine the public purpose doctrine for three principal reasons:

First, the Article 1410(1) exceptions represent a special class of public purpose category that exceed in importance other regulatory measures that a State may undertake as part of its normal exercise of sovereignty. Any tribunal addressing application of such a public purpose category must reconcile a normative basis of the category with the burdens that the regulatory measure at issue imposes on a foreign investment. In doing so, the tribunal credibly has to address reasons why a generic "public purpose" formula, pursuant to which public purpose is merely defined as an act undertaken by a State with the intent to serve the general welfare, is simply insufficient. This challenge is considerable. Indeed, to date, no decisional award has met it, in large measure because of the juridical cultural consensus that public purpose is a self-evident principle, which it is not.

In a very basic sense, application of a special public purpose category in the context of dispute resolution leads to an abandonment of the orthodox public purpose doctrine because of its emphasis on the *nature* and *character* of the special public purpose class rather than on the particular factual configuration

(b) activities or services for the account or with the guarantee or using the financial resources of the Party, including its public entities.

NAFTA, *supra* note 1, art. 1401 ¶¶ 1–3.

[272] *See* Fireman's Fund, *supra* note 150.

[273] NAFTA Article 1410(1) (Exceptions) states:

1. Nothing in this Part [5., i.e., "Investment, Services and Related Matters"] shall be construed to prevent a Party from adopting or maintaining *reasonable measures for prudential reasons*, such as:
   (a) the protection of investors, depositors, financial market participants, policyholders, policy-claimants or persons to whom a fiduciary duty is owed by a financial institution or cross-border financial service provider;
   (b) the maintenance of the safety, soundness, integrity or financial responsibility of financial institutions or cross-border financial service providers; and
   (c) insuring the integrity and stability of a Party's financial system.

NAFTA, *supra* note 1, art. 1410 ¶ 1(a)–(c) (emphasis added).

of the case. A public purpose doctrine that aspires to meet the needs of an economic globalization framework premised on the interdependence of States as an organizing principle must comprise special categories that are known a priori, in part, so that investor expectations can be met.

In addition, the focus on the application of a special public purpose category mitigates negative consequences from an "effects only test." Most notably, the chilling effect that an effects test may have on beneficial Host-State regulatory pronouncements is somewhat mitigated. Similarly, States negotiating bilateral or multilateral investment treaties shall enjoy greater transparency in understanding the extent to which prospective investments may be adversely compromised by regulatory measures. This bilateral transparency, in addition to harmonizing party expectations, may serve for more robust treaty negotiation and drafting concerning issues that touch and concern special public purpose categories.

Second, the "reasonable measures for prudential reasons" standard introduces much needed "objective criteria" into the public purpose doctrinal analysis. The orthodox public purpose doctrine is premised on a subjective intent standard that presents practically insurmountable evidentiary challenges. For this reason, the doctrine is often rendered inconsequential from a pragmatic standpoint or as a thinly veiled pretext presumably justifying an indirect expropriation that cannot be meaningfully assailed.[274] Even though the terms "reasonable" and "prudential" within the standard are broad and susceptible to flexible constructions, they still bespeak universality and vest the public purpose doctrine with workable parameters.

[274] The orthodox public purpose doctrine's subjective constitution has contributed to inconsistencies in the understanding and application of the doctrine as evinced by the diametrically opposite results in *Metalclad* and *Methanex*. For example, in *Feldman v. Mexico*, in discussing what it perceived to be the challenge of applying to specific cases the general language of the NAFTA's Article 1110(1)(a)–(d) the tribunal stated:

> The view that the conditions (other than the requirement for compensation) are not of major importance in determining expropriation is confirmed by the Restatement of the Law of Foreign Relations of the United States, a source relied on by many American and Canadian lawyers that has been discussed in the memorials of both the Claimant and the Respondent in this proceeding. For example, according to the Restatement, the *public purpose requirement* "has not figured prominently in international claims practice, *perhaps because the concept of public purpose is broad and not subject to effective reexamination by other states.*"

Feldman v. United Mexican States, ICSID Case No. ARB (AF)/99/1, Award, ¶ 99 (December 16, 2002), 7 ICSID Rep. 341 (2005) [hereinafter Feldman] (citing RESTATEMENT (THIRD) OF THE FOREIGN RELATIONS LAW OF THE UNITED STATES § 712, cmt. g. (1987)) (emphasis added).

Third, the Article 1410(1) exceptions raise the predicate question concerning the manner in which, if at all, the legacy orthodox public purpose element of expropriation in public international law is to be applied in cases where special public purpose categories are likely to be triggered. Even though the meaning of expropriation is less than monolithic as a matter of customary and conventional international law within the very NAFTA anatomy itself,[275] the public purpose doctrine or any of its permutations (i.e., police powers, public interest, public welfare, etc.) underlies the various definitions of expropriation. It is a constant common denominator in the doctrine of expropriation. Consequently, is public purpose as a doctrine to be taken seriously in determining whether a direct or indirect expropriation or nationalization has taken place? And, if so, whether or not such taking is compensable where a public purpose is present? Should public purpose within the meaning of Article 1110(1) of the NAFTA, and as articulated in the jurisprudence of

[275] The tribunal explained that

> NAFTA does not give a definition for the word "expropriation." In some ten cases in which Article 1110(1) of the NAFTA was considered to date, the definitions appear to vary. Considering those cases and customary international law in general, the present tribunal retains the following elements:
>
> (a) Expropriation requires a taking (which may include destruction) by a government-type authority of an investment by an investor covered by the NAFTA.
> (b) The covered investment may include intangible as well as tangible property.
> (c) The taking must be a substantially complete deprivation of the economic use and enjoyment of the rights to property, or of identifiable distinct parts thereof (i.e., it approaches total impairment).
> (d) The taking must be permanent and not ephemeral or temporary.
> (e) The taking usually involves a transfer of ownership to another person (frequently the government authority concerned), but that need not necessarily be so in certain cases (e.g., total destruction of an investment due to measures by a government authority without transfer of rights).
> (f) The effects of the Host State's measures are dispositive, not the underlying intent, for determining whether there is expropriation.
> (g) The taking must be de jure or de facto.
> (h) The taking may be "direct" or "indirect."
> (i) The taking may have the form of a single measure or a series of related or unrelated measures over a period of time (the so-called creeping expropriation).
> (i) To distinguish between a compensable expropriation and a non-compensable regulation by a Host-State, The following factors (usually in combination) may be taken into account: whether the measure is within the recognized *police powers of the Host State*; the *(public) purpose* effect of the measure; whether the measure is discriminatory; the proportionality between the means employed and the aim sought to be realized; and the bona fide nature of the measure.

Fireman's Fund, *supra* note 150, at ¶¶ 176(a)–(j) (internal footnotes omitted and emphasis added).

expropriation more generally, be accorded a distinctive deference from the other elements that suggest treatment in *pari materia?*

Fireman's Fund is helpful because it places in sharp relief two important "special public purpose category" issues that are of practical and theoretical significance. First, is the discriminatory "lack of effort by Host State to rescue an investment that has become virtually worthless" an expropriation or divestment of that investment?[276] Second, where a measure adopted by a Host State is neither "reasonable" nor "prudential" within the meaning of Article 1410(1) of the NAFTA, does it then automatically give rise to liability?

The Article 1410(1) exceptions foreclose actions that would constitute a violation under the NAFTA pursuant to Chapter Eleven. So long as the measure in question qualifies as a "reasonable measure taken for prudential reasons" from a methodological standpoint, a special public purpose category provides for discriminatory application without violating the national treatment standard. The tribunal in *Fireman's Fund* correctly rejected the claimant's contention that "if a measure adopted or maintained by [the Host State] is found not to be reasonable or taken for prudential reasons, it would give rise to liability, or at least to a presumption of liability, under Article 1110."[277]

Regrettably, the tribunal disturbingly clouded its reasoning by focusing on the methodology incident to an Article 1110 analysis instead of elaborating on the status of a special public purpose category contained in Article 1410.[278] A measure, for example, premised on a State's protection of the integrity and stability of its financial system – and therefore falling within the ambit of an Article 1410 exception – should not be evaluated based on an "effects test," which is what "an initial" or "tentative" Article 1110 analysis would require. The tribunal did in fact grasp this principle in analyzing the proscribed discrimination claim under Chapter Fourteen that the claimant sought to assert. It did observe that "the [discriminatory] exception applies to all provisions of Part Five ('Investments, Services and Related Matters') of the NAFTA applicable to Financial Services including the National Treatment Article (Article 1405)," and, therefore, "concludes that Article 1410(1) permits

[276] *Id.* at ¶ 207.

[277] *Id.* at ¶ 160.

[278] On this point, the tribunal reasoned:

> The Tribunal rejects this contention [that a measure adopted or maintained by a Host State found not to be reasonable or taken for prudential reasons would give rise to liability]. As the Tribunal understands Article 1410 within the anatomy of the NAFTA, a judgment as to whether the exception applies is called for only after an initial, at least tentative, conclusion that Article 1110 or another applicable provision of the NAFTA may have been violated.

Id.

reasonable measures of a prudential character even if their *effect* (as contrasted with their motive or intent) is discriminatory. The Tribunal rejects the contention that a measure discriminatory in effect is *eo ipso* unreasonable."[279] The citation to the writings of the principal negotiator of Chapter Fourteen on behalf of the United States is instructive in illustrating application of a special public purpose category beyond just national treatment:

> Article 1410(1)(a) . . . carves out of the national treatment and other obligations of the Financial Services chapter, a right to take reasonable measures even though discriminatory in application, to protect the safety and soundness of the financial system. This regulatory prerogative to protect the integrity of the financial system is accepted internationally.[280]

The proposition that the "condition preceding for invocation of the Prudential Measures Exception [is] a finding of expropriation," has the consequence of subordinating application of the exception to an "effects test" and of treating a special public purpose category no differently than the "standard exceptions" articulated in Article 1110(1)(a) through (d).[281]

The condition preceding the analysis here proposed both conceptually and analytically best comports with the tribunal's treatment of the two above-mentioned questions. Namely, is the discriminatory "lack of effort by a Host State to rescue an investment that has become virtually worthless" an expropriation or divestment of that investment?[282] Second, where a measure adopted by a Host State is neither "reasonable" nor "prudential" within the meaning of Article 1410(1) of the NAFTA, does it then automatically give rise to liability?[283]

[279] *Id.* at ¶ 162.

[280] *Id.* at. ¶ 163 (citing to Olin L. Wethington, Financial Market Liberalization § 5.07 (Sheppard's McGraw Hill 1994)).

[281] *Id.* at ¶ 165. It is not being suggested that an orthodox expropriation analysis is altogether obviated where a special public purpose category is alleged. To the contrary, the proposition asserted maintains that only by first determining as a precedent condition that, in fact, a special public purpose category (such as the Article 1410 Exceptions) applies can the elements of an expropriation under the NAFTA and international customary law find its most efficient and analytically consistent workings. This methodology is particularly suited and appropriate for the NAFTA because, as the tribunal in *Fireman's Fund* aptly noted, the NAFTA, much like the ICSID convention with "investment," deliberately does not define "expropriation." Therefore, a predicate analysis of the bona fide nature of the special public purpose category at issue would be required. The soundness of this approach is underscored even more because the single common denominator of the mosaic of "tests," each purporting to identify the dispositive expropriation cornerstone, is the public purpose element.

[282] *Id.* at ¶ 207.

[283] *Id.* at ¶ 162. The tribunal also reframed the issue as to the NAFTA's Article 1110:

> "The question before the Tribunal is whether it could also give rise to a claim under Article 1110 ('Expropriation and Compensation') of the NAFTA since the Tribunal lacks competence over claims under Article 1102, 1105 and 1405." *Id.* at ¶ 203. It responded

Both of these queries were decided in the negative. Critical to their determination is a preliminary assessment of the measure in question as rising to the level of a special public purpose category. A finding in the affirmative as to this predicate issue streamlines and fast-frames an expropriation or nationalization analysis.[284]

Decided six years after *Metalclad* and one year after *Methanex*, it becomes necessary to ask whether *Fireman's Fund* helped to narrow the conceptual and doctrinal chasm conceptually and doctrinally separating its two predecessors. Does *Fireman's Fund*, as the first case under the NAFTA's Chapter Fourteen, contribute to our understanding of the public purpose doctrine generally and within the NAFTA, and, if so, how? Is the meaning of "public purpose" any clearer after *Fireman's Fund*? Is the *Tecmed* proportionality test and its application rendered any more practical by the *Fireman's Fund* award? Indeed, does the status of the measure at issue in *Fireman's Fund* as falling within Article 1410 contribute to the finding that there was no direct or indirect expropriation or any actions tantamount to an expropriation of the property in question?

The *Fireman's Fund* award does not bring us any closer to a more comprehensive understanding of the application of an Article 1410 exception. The tribunal's analysis preempts consideration of the special public purpose category that the NAFTA's Chapter Fourteen offers. In this very narrow sense, the award does not call attention to any specific methodology or doctrinal construction applicable to a NAFTA Chapter Fourteen case that would not attach to a "standard" Chapter Eleven contention. The award manages to obviate a

in the negative: "The Tribunal concludes that it does not rise to a claim under Article 1110." *Id.*

[284] In *Fireman's Fund*, the tribunal ignored the status of the measure at issue as a special public purpose category clearly within Article 1410 when attempting to reconcile discriminatory treatment with nationalization or expropriation status. Rather than focusing on the conceptual link between the discriminatory treatment at issue as one arising from a measure falling with the province of Article 1410, the tribunal undertook an analysis that carved out the conceptual effects of a special public purpose category altogether. Instead, it focused on the relationship between *any* form of discrimination and the general customary international law standard for expropriation by emphasizing three propositions. First, the finding of a discriminatory measure, without more, does not necessarily lead to a conclusion that an expropriation is present. *Id.* at ¶ 205. Second, a finding of discriminatory treatment is but one of several factors used to distinguish between a compensable expropriation and a noncompensable expropriation by a Host State. *Id.* at ¶ 206. Third and finally, a "misrepresentation" and "investor expectation" analysis ensued pursuant to which the tribunal determined that "[n]or were there reasonable investor-backed expectations created by Mexico, even though Mexico should have pursued the conclusion of an agreement." *Id.* at ¶ 207. Only because the tribunal decided that the elements of an expropriation or nationalization were not met did it conclude that liability did not attach despite a factual finding of discrimination. "In the Tribunal's view, this is a clear case of discriminatory treatment of a foreign investor." *Id.* at ¶ 203.

special public purpose category Chapter Fourteen analysis because it only focused on the extent to which the claimant had established that an expropriation took place within the meaning of the NAFTA's Article 1110.[285] The *Fireman's Fund* award nearly segregates five principal grounds alleged for expropriation and rejects each pursuant to an Article 1110 analysis that nowhere references the effects or application of Article 1410 exceptions.[286]

[285] The award, in pertinent part, states:

> The Tribunal concludes with respect to prudential measures that Article 1410 of the NAFTA provides a defense to the State-Party if a tribunal has found a challenged measure to constitute an expropriation in violation of Article 1110 of the NAFTA. The validity of that defense, as necessary to decide a claim under Article 1110, is to be judged either by the Financial Services Committee, or if no request has been submitted for invoking the Committee procedure, by the arbitral tribunal. In the present case, the issue whether the challenged measures were reasonable or arbitrary is moot, because the Tribunal has not found these measures to constitute expropriation under the NAFTA.

Id. at ¶ 68.

[286] The tribunal found as follows with respect to the five specific averments identified and construed as not constituting an actionable taking of whatsoever ilk:

(i) "The *first* act alleged by *[Fireman's Fund]* cannot be considered by any standard a taking that deprived *[Fireman's Fund]* of the economic use and enjoyment of the Dollar Debentures." *Id.* at ¶ 186 (emphasis added).

> "Assuming that the Government of Mexico 'compelled' *[Fireman's Fund]* to participate in the Recapitalization Plan in early 1988, it was for the purpose of rescuing *[Fireman's Fund's]* investment, rather than taking it away from [them]." *Id.* at ¶ 189 (emphasis in original).

(ii) "The contentions regarding the *second act* as alleged by *[Fireman's Fund]* must also fail. It is based on a Recapitalization Program that never materialized. *[Fireman's Fund's]* Dollar Debentures were never redeemed and *[Fireman's Fund]* never made the additional US$50 million capital contribution. Nor was the participation by a foreign bank accomplished. Consequently, the Mexican authorities cannot have proceeded 'to thwart the Program' or 'destroyed' that Program." *Id.* at ¶ 192 (emphasis in original).

(iii) "The *third act* is more troubling but does not constitute a taking under Article 1110 of the NAFTA either." *Id.* at ¶ 200.

> "In the Tribunal's view, this is clear case of discriminatory treatment of a foreign investor .... Such treatment might have given rise to claim by an investor under Articles 1102 (National Treatment), Article 1105 (Minimum Standard of Treatment), or Article 1405 (National Treatment) of the NAFTA, or under two or all of them. The question before the Tribunal is whether it could also give rise to a claim under Article 1110 (Expropriation and Compensation) of the NAFTA since the Tribunal lacks competence over claims under Articles 1102, 1105 and 1405. The Tribunal concludes that it does not rise to a claim under Article 1110." Id. *at* ¶ 203 (emphasis in original).

(iv) "The *fourth act* is the return of the loan portfolio by FOBAPROA in November 1998 .... " *Id.* at ¶ 210 (emphasis in original).

The examination of all five premises on which *Fireman's Fund*'s claims rested was merely subjected to an "effects test" that hardly considered the *nature* and *character* of the measures at issue. Consequently, from both an analytical and doctrinal perspective, *Fireman's Fund* does not shed much light on the extent to which treatment of a NAFTA Chapter Fourteen case at all differs from a Chapter Eleven proceeding where Article 1410 defenses do not apply.

The case also fails to enhance the anatomy or application of the proportionality test first raised in *Tecmed*.[287] This omission is quizzical because an Article 1410 (or any other type of special public purpose category case) would be particularly amenable to a proportionality analysis. The omission is particularly odd because the tribunal references the proportionality test as constituting the penultimate element of its synopsis of the NAFTA decisional law on expropriation predating the *Fireman's Fund* award.[288] The proportionality test's aspiration of identifying, balancing, and analyzing two pivotal aspects of the regulatory measure at issue (means and ends) would be necessary to a Chapter Fourteen or special public purpose category case because of the need to provide for process legitimacy, among other considerations, in fleshing out a Host State's exercise of regulatory sovereignty causing harm to a foreign investment/investor where compensation for such harm does not ensue as a matter of law.[289] The policies underlying the NAFTA's Chapter Fourteen may best be expressed as an analysis purporting to explain "the aim

> "In any event, the effect of the return of the portfolio in November 1998 cannot be said to have taken away the value of *[Fireman's Fund]* investment. At that point in time, the financial position of BanCrecer was so bad, that it was *de facto* already in a State of insolvency. Moreover, the effect of the return of the portfolio appears to be included in BanCrecer's financial statements for 1999 only." *Id.* at ¶ 214.
>
> In addition, the Tribunal held that *Fireman's Fund* did not reasonably rely on FOBAPROA's commitments and, therefore, had no legitimate expectations that could have sustained a claim against Mexico. *Id.* at ¶¶ 214–15.

(v) "Finally, the *fifth act* is the taking of control by IPAB of BanCrecer in November 1999 . . . .

> It appears that the shareholders of BanCrecer, i.e., GFB voted in favour of a taking of control by IPAB over BanCrecer and a dissolution of liquidation of GFB. They did so in light of the hopeless financial position of BanCrecer and as a consequence of GFB. The facts do not demonstrate that the action by IPAB constituted a taking by IPAB in the sense of an expropriation on behalf of the State." *Id.* at ¶ 216 (emphasis in original).

[287] *See* Tecmed, *supra* note 151, at ¶ 122.

[288] *Fireman's Fund* identifies and attributes the proportionality test to *Tecmed*. Fireman's Fund, *supra* note 150, at ¶ 176(j) ("the proportionality between the means employed and the aim sought to be realized" [citing *Tecmed, supra* note 151, at ¶ 122]).

[289] *Fireman's Fund*'s request for an award compensating it for the full value of its investment was denied, and each Party was ordered to bear its own costs and to share in the tribunal's costs in equal shares corresponding to the Parties' cost advances. *See Id.* at ¶¶ 226(2)–(3).

sought to be realized" by the Host State's regulatory measure.[290] *Fireman's Fund*, however, altogether passes on application of proportionality without explanation.

A broad reading of *Fireman's Fund* supports the proposition that where a foreign investment is (i) significantly diminished in value,[291] (ii) pursuant to a discriminatory measure imposed by a Host State,[292] (iii) as a result of the regulatory measure at issue causing the investor significant losses,[293] then (iv) the taking is not compensable if the public purpose underlying it does not need a conventional expropriation analysis.[294] This reasonable and eminently plausible construction of the holding in *Fireman's Fund* is particularly troubling because of the manner in which the public purpose doctrine, from a purely conceptual standpoint, fashions the entirety of the legal reasoning. The tribunal's award invests virtually no ink on the status of the doctrine either within or beyond Chapter Fourteen.[295] Without explicitly acknowledging the relationship between a special public purpose category within the ambit of Article 1410 and its effect on the particular investment concerned, the tribunal does little more than to reduce its holding and reasoning to a mere "effects test" indistinguishable from *Metalclad* but lacking an equitable holding resulting in a compensable expropriation. *Fireman's Fund* fails to shed any additional light on how best to understand the relationship between the substantive content of a special public purpose category and an orthodox expropriation analysis.

Although *Fireman's Fund* does purport to have canvassed the ten previously decided NAFTA cases concerning expropriation in order to fashion a comprehensive test,[296] it refrains from noting the very different weight and application accorded to the doctrine, where relevant, in each of those matters.

[290] *Id.*

[291] *Id.* at ¶ 176(c).

[292] *Id.* at ¶ 176(j).

[293] *Id.* at ¶¶ 206, 218.

[294] *Id.* at ¶¶ 205–08.

[295] Nowhere in Paragraphs 186–210 or 216 of the award, where the five specific acts alleged are analyzed and contextualized, does the tribunal allocate a single sentence to explain the manner in which the legacy public purpose doctrine is being used, without any express reference, to support its findings. *Id.* at ¶¶ 186–202, 210, 216.

[296] *Id.* at ¶ 176. The ten cases to which the tribunal presumably was referring are:

1. Methanex Corp. v. United States of America, NAFTA Ch. 11/UNCITRAL, Final Award on Jurisdiction and Merits (August 3, 2005), 16 ICSID Rep. 40 (2012).
2. International Thunderbird Gaming Corp. v. United Mexican States, NAFTA Ch. 11/ UNCITRAL, Final Award (January 26, 2005), http://www.iisd.org/pdf/2006/itn_award.pdf.
3. Waste Management, Inc. v. United Mexican States, ICSID Case No. ARB (AF)/00/3, Award (April 30, 2004), 11 ICSID Rep. 361 (2007).

Moreover, the tribunal amassed its expansive ten-category expropriation standard without noting any need to apply those principles within the public policies unique to the NAFTA and its parties. Such contextualization necessarily would have entailed analysis of the various competing interests that the public purpose doctrine is saddled with reconciling. The award does not live up to its promise to meet the expectations attendant to its status as the first case to be decided under Chapter Fourteen of the NAFTA.

The tribunal's "reasoning" as to the actions or omissions on the part of the Host State are not doctrinally or analytically presented as part of a NAFTA Chapter Fourteen case and, therefore, appear to be without conceptual foundation and lacking in value as precedent or persuasive authority. These findings on the part of the Host State merely are advanced as just acts or omissions that do not rise to the level of an expropriation under the NAFTA's Article 1110.[297] The tribunal's findings with respect to the first three acts of expropriation attributable to the Host State's regulatory authority as claimant alleged are revealing.

The initial averment that the Host State somehow compelled *Fireman's Fund* to participate in a recapitalization plan[298] for purposes of bolstering a financial institution falls squarely within the purview of Article 1410(1)(a)–(c). Rather than emphasizing the very proximate connection between the Mexican government's actions and Article 1410 requirements, the tribunal

4. Técnicas Medioambientales Tecmed S.A. v. United Mexican States, ICSID Case No. ARB (AF)/00/2, Award (May 29, 2003), 10 ICSID Rep. 134 (2006).
5. Feldman v. United Mexican States, ICSID Case No. ARB (AF)/99/1, Award, ¶ 99 (December 16, 2002), 7 ICSID Rep. 341 (2005).
6. Mondev International Ltd. v. United States of America, ICSID Case No. ARB (AF)/99/2, Award (October 11, 2002), 6 ICSID Rep. 192 (2004).
7. S.D. Myers Inc. v. Government of Canada, First Partial Award on Liability (November 13, 2000), 8 ICSID Rep. 18 (2005).
8. Metalclad Corp. v. United Mexican States, ICSID Case No. ARB (AF)/97/1, Award (August 30, 2000), 5 ICSID Rep. 212 (2002).
9. Pope & Talbot Inc. v. Government of Canada, Interim Award (June 26, 2000), 7 ICSID Rep. 69 (2005) [hereinafter Pope & Talbot].
10. Robert Azinian et al. v. United Mexican States, ICSID Case No. ARB/AF/97/2, Award (November 1, 1999), 5 ICSID Rep. 272 (2002).

[297] Fireman's Fund, *supra* note 150, at ¶ 203. ("In the Tribunal's view, this is a clear case of discriminatory treatment of a foreign investor .... The question before the Tribunal is whether it could also give rise to a claim under Article 1110 (Expropriation and Compensation) of the NAFTA since the Tribunal lacks competence over claims under Articles 1102, 1105 and 1405. The Tribunal concludes that it does not rise to a claim under Article 1110"); *Id.* at ¶ 217 ("In conclusion, none of the acts and omissions alleged by *[Fireman's Fund]* constitutes individually, or taken together, an expropriation of *[Fireman's Fund's]* investment under Article 1110 of the NAFTA ").

[298] *Id.* at ¶ 186.

limits its analysis to a plain "effects test."[299] Similarly, the second contention that the claimant advanced in support of its expropriation claim was deemed to be of no moment in the tribunal's analysis because of either "a change in the political climate in Mexico at the time"[300] or "due to [the] fact that Mexico amended its legislation . . . to the effect that any rescue plan of a bank required that the existing capital be first applied to losses."[301] Here, the tribunal identifies two plausible causes for the detrimental effects that the Host State's actions had on the investment. The tribunal even notes that the Host State's actions are inappropriate.[302] Yet, instead of establishing the exculpatory nature of the measure because of its character as within the ambit of Article 1410, it settles for simply substituting its judgment in lieu of any Article 1410 analysis.

The tribunal specifically advances that "such a failure cannot be elevated to interference by a Host State in the rights of an investor in the sense that it constitutes a deprivation of the investor's rights in its investment within the meaning of Article 1110 of the NAFTA."[303]

Drawing a connection between Article 1410 and a Host State's obligations to salvage a foreign investment would have vested the award with greater conceptual rigor that equally would have the effect of limiting the claim, rather than the adoption of the tribunal's rather circular argument; "[a] failure to enter a binding agreement to improve that condition, and possibly [Fireman's Fund's] investment, does not deprive [Fireman's Fund's] investment of its economic use since there was virtually none at the time of the Government's failure."[304]

The third example drawn from claimant's expropriation allegations understandably identified the Mexican government's refusal to allow *Fireman's Fund* both directly and indirectly to purchase the dollar debentures at face value as part of a discriminatory taking.[305] Even the tribunal found itself impelled to state that this event "is more troubling"[306] and

[299] The tribunal reasons that "[a]ssuming that the Government of Mexico 'compelled' *[Fireman's Fund]* to participate in the Recapitalization Plan in early 1998, it was for the purposes of rescuing *[Fireman's Fund's]* investment, rather than taking it away from *[Fireman's Fund]*." *Id.* at ¶ 189.

[300] *Id.* at ¶ 198.

[301] *Id.*

[302] It is observed that "[o]n the basis of the record before it, the Tribunal is of the view that the Mexican Authorities *did not behave appropriately* in failing to pursue the conclusion of an agreement." *Id.* (emphasis added).

[303] *Id.* at ¶ 199.

[304] *Id.*

[305] *Id.* at ¶ 202.

[306] *Id.* at 200.

"*certainly discriminated* against *[Fireman's Fund]*,"[307] "but [still] does not constitute a taking under Article 1110 of the NAFTA either."[308] Again, the tribunal remains silent as to any relationship between the Mexican government's refusal to allow for a face value purchase of the instruments and the extent to which the nature of such a refusal comports with "the maintenance of the safety, solvency, integrity or financial responsibility of financial institutions or cross-border financial service providers," [or] "ensuring the integrity and stability of [Mexico's] financial system," as prescribed by Article 1410(b) and (c).[309]

Even within the context of Chapter Fourteen, the *Fireman's Fund* award does not vest *public purpose* with objective normative content. Yet it construes concrete actions on behalf of a sovereign as not constituting an expropriation despite (i) the discriminatory nature of the measures, (ii) their palpable adverse effects on a foreign investment/investor, and (iii) perhaps even the presence of bad faith conduct on the part of the sovereign concerning the application of the measure to the investment. The case provides for exculpatory conduct on behalf of a sovereign but cloaks it in terms of not meeting a conventional standard for expropriation within the NAFTA's jurisprudence.[310] As with the standard for expropriation, the proportionality test was mentioned *but never applied*, let alone developed or modified to meet the workings of a special public purpose category (such as the category enunciated in Article 1410).[311] The disproportionate weight accorded to the workings of the Host State's regulatory space and the lack of analysis as to public purpose from a doctrinal perspective generally and within the NAFTA severely limits *Fireman's Fund*'s standing as persuasive authority or even a helpful analytical rubric. To the contrary, it further nourishes uncertainty[312] and a "taking sides

[307] *See Id.* at ¶ 201 (emphasis added).

[308] *Id.* at ¶ 200.

[309] *See* NAFTA, *supra* note 1, art. 1410 ¶¶ (b)–(c).

[310] Even though a tribunal took considerable pains to ensure that it had canvassed the entire gamut of "expropriation standards" within the NAFTA's jurisprudence, *see Id.* at ¶ 176, it did not undertake a systematic application of law to fact pursuant to which each of the eleven elements identified was applied to the facts of the case. From an analytical perspective, this standard was simply mentioned but never applied.

[311] *See Id.* at ¶ 122 (mentioning the proportionality test).

[312] Essentially, as one commentator has suggested, the tribunal, "with the sparest of reasoning, both effectively adopts the proportionality test as stemming from earlier cases within NAFTA and points out the problems of *Tecmed's* incorporation of it ... It suggests that, rather than any kind of *stare decisis* across arbitrations, a sliding scale of respect for precedent is warranted depending on the regime context of the earlier decisions." Steven R. Ratner, *Regulatory Takings in Institutional Context: Beyond the Fear of Fragmented International Law*, 102 AM. J. INT'L L. 475, 527 (2008).

approach" that is conducive to "all-or-nothing" results.[313] Similarly, little was accomplished by way of illustrating the workings particular to a special public purpose category within the meaning of Chapter Fourteen. These unsatisfactory results are in large measure prompted by the subjective but malleable constitution of the legacy public purpose doctrine, which invites a mild "effects test" to be juxtaposed against an enshrined Host State's regulatory space.

The NAFTA jurisprudence has carved a particular space for "police powers" that, depending on the authority consulted, is different, but not altogether removed, from public purpose. Although the police powers NAFTA jurisprudence at first appears to contribute an organizing principle to an entire body of inconsistently applied precepts and definitions, it actually contributes to adding another layer of uncertainty to the meaning and role of the public purpose doctrine.

4. *The Police Power Dichotomy and* Feldman v. Mexico

Likely compelled by the need to distinguish between regulation that renders it possible for a sovereign to exercise its sovereignty in furtherance of more general public interest and an expropriation, the NAFTA jurisprudence distinctively has relied upon the police powers nomenclature.[314] These cases draw a distinction between public purpose and police powers but do not articulate any basis for the perceived doctrinal differences between the two.[315] *Feldman v. Mexico*[316] is just such a case. In that proceeding, the tribunal affirmatively diminished the public purpose doctrine while relying on a vague notion of police powers that it nowhere defines.[317] The *Feldman*

[313] The tribunal "neither strayed far from the consensus position under customary international law – rejecting most claims of regulatory takings – nor proved inconsistent even within the regime of NAFTA." *Id.* at 511.

[314] *See, e.g.*, Corn Products Int'l v. United Mexican States, ICSID Case No. ARB(AF)/04/01, Decision on Responsibility, ¶ 87 (January 15, 2008), http://italaw.com/sites/default/files/case-documents/ita0244.pdf; Fireman's Fund, *supra* note 150, at ¶ 176; Pope & Talbot, *supra* note 296, at ¶ 99; Feldman, *supra* note 274, at ¶¶ 105–06.

[315] *See, e.g.*, Fireman's Fund, *supra* note 150, at ¶ 176 (listing "whether the measure is within the recognized police powers of the Host State" and "the (public) purpose and effect of the measure" as distinct factors for "distinguish[ing] between a compensable expropriation and noncompensable regulation by a Host State").

[316] *Supra* note 274.

[317] One possible explanation of the tribunal's disavowance of public purpose in adoption of police powers may be attributable to its reliance on the Third Restatement of the Foreign Relations Law of the United States ("the Restatement") from which it draws analytical support for the proposition that (i) "the public purpose requirement 'has not figured prominently in

Tribunal virtually reduces public purpose to the status of a nonfactor even within the language of Article 1110:

> In the Tribunal's view, the essential determination is whether the actions of the Mexican Government [Host State] constitute an expropriation or nationalization, or are valid government activity. If there is no expropriatory action, factors (a)–(d) are of limited relevance,[318] except to the extent that they have helped to differentiate between governmental acts that are expropriation and those that are not, or are parallel to violations of NAFTA Articles 1102 and 1105. If there is a finding of expropriation, compensation is required, *even if* the taking is for a public purpose, nondiscriminatory and in accordance with due process of law and Article 1105(1).[319]

To the extent that the tribunal understands Article 1110 or customary international law to assert that compensation attaches even where an expropriation is undertaken for a public purpose, pursuant to due process and in a nondiscriminatory manner, this is indistinguishable from advancing that public purpose is irrelevant to compensability when an expropriation has been found.

international claims practice, perhaps because the concept of public purpose is broad and not subject to effective reexamination by other states,' and (ii) in distinguishing between a non-compensable government regulation and an expropriation." *Id.* at ¶¶ 99, 105. With respect to this latter point, the tribunal cites directly to the police power language of the Restatement, § 712, comment g, which reads:

> A State is responsible for an expropriation of property under Subsection (1) when it subjects alien property to taxation, regulation, or other action that is confiscatory, or that prevents, unreasonably interferes with, or unduly delays, effective enjoyment of an alien's property or its removal from the State's territory ... *a State is not responsible for loss of property or other economic disadvantage resulting from bona fide general taxation, regulation, forfeiture for a crime, or other action of the kind that is commonly accepted as within the police power of states, if it is not discriminatory.*

Id. at ¶ 105 (citing RESTATEMENT (THIRD) OF FOREIGN RELATIONS LAW § 712 cmt. g (1987)) (emphasis added).

318 The Award is referencing Chapter 11, Article 1110 subsections (a)–(d) which provide:

> 1. No Party may *directly* or *indirectly* nationalize or expropriate an investment of an investor of another Party in its territory *or take a measure tantamount to nationalization or expropriation* of such an investment ("expropriation"), except:
>   (a) for a public purpose;
>   (b) on a non-discriminatory basis;
>   (c) in accordance with due process of law and Article 1105(1); and
>   (d) on payment of compensation in accordance with paragraphs 2 through 6.5.

NAFTA, *supra* note 1, art. 1110 ¶ 1.

319 Feldman, *supra* note 274, at ¶ 98 (emphasis added).

Terms such as "bona fide,"[320] "reasonable governmental regulation[s],"[321] or "commonly accepted government regulations"[322] often are associated with the exercise of a "police power" regulatory measure that does not support a claim for expropriation. Although the tribunal in *Feldman* found it necessary to observe that "[n]o one can seriously question that in some circumstances government regulatory activity can be in violation of Article 1110,"[323] it failed to articulate the boundaries of public purpose so that a regulatory measure tantamount to an expropriation can be rendered readily discernible. Indeed, despite language bolstering the proposition that, in some circumstances, government regulatory activity may constitute an expropriation or an act or series of acts tantamount to an expropriation under Article 1110, the tribunal did not find a violation of Article 1110 in the case *sub judice* despite acknowledging that the claimant had "experienced great difficulties in dealing with [government] officials" and had been "treated in a less than reasonable manner."[324] As to unreasonable and disparate treatment suffered by the claimant at the hands of government tax officials, general platitudes concerning public policy underlying tax laws, predictive value, and consistency on the part of tax authorities executing the responsibilities were advanced:

> Unfortunately, tax authorities in most countries do not always act in a consistent and predictable way ... as in most tax regimes, the tax laws are used as instruments of public policy as well as fiscal policy, and certain taxpayers are inevitably favored, with others less favored or even disadvantaged.[325]

It is not a broad construction of the tribunal's analysis in *Feldman* to assert that it is common, and therefore acceptable, for the execution of a State's police powers by government officials to lead in some instances to disparate treatment that materially disadvantages a class of persons and for those actions seeking to implement regulatory measures to lack consistency, uniformity, and predictive value. The "police powers" construction of "public purpose" within the anatomy of international claims practices generally provides for an even broader veneer with which to cloak the exercise of actionable regulatory measures that are detrimental to the protection of foreign investment and investors. This legal fiction is little more than a pretext for the expansion of regulatory sovereignty. It is unfortunate and regrettable that the debilities of

[320] *Id.* at ¶ 106.
[321] *Id.* at ¶ 103.
[322] *Id.* at ¶ 105.
[323] *Id.* at ¶ 110.
[324] *Id.* at ¶ 113.
[325] *Id.*

governmental bureaucratic execution in connection with the implementation of regulatory measures are characterized as being an essential element of a State's police powers.

The expansive construction accorded to police powers has had the consequence of reducing an Article 1110 analysis to an intensive fact-driven undertaking that, in turn, is to be analyzed against a mercurial legal standard.[326] The expropriatory public purpose character ascribed to regulatory measures, and particularly to a sovereign's authority to tax, further compels vesting police powers (public purpose) with objective substantive content and brings into the fold the public purpose doctrine more generally.[327] Adding to the all-encompassing configuration of police powers within the NAFTA jurisprudence is the view that a State's prerogative in a post-market entry to change or modify existing regulatory schemes to the material detriment of a foreign investor may render an economic activity "less profitable or even uneconomic to continue" but not necessarily constitute an indirect or creeping expropriation under Article 1110.[328]

[326] As noted, *supra* note 275, in *Fireman's Fund*, the tribunal aptly observed that no single expropriation standard common to all cases had been enunciated in the ten arbitral proceedings that preceded it, thus inviting the *Fireman's Fund* tribunal to fashion a comprehensive, all-encompassing standard that it then failed to apply systematically to the facts of that case.

Following this very line of thought, the Feldman tribunal acknowledged that "[t]he Article 1110 language is of such generality as to be difficult to apply in specific cases." Feldman, *supra* note 274, at ¶ 98. Consonant with this vision, it further observed that "under NAFTA Article 1136(1), '[a]n award made by a tribunal shall have no binding force except between the disputing Parties and in respect of the particular case,' and that each determination under Article 1110 is necessarily fact-specific." *Id.* at ¶ 107.

[327] The expropriatory character ascribed to police power and to specific regulatory measures such as taxation should not be viewed as per se exculpatory, but rather as creating a rebuttable presumption that may be overcome depending on the specific public purpose sought to be served. The *Feldman* tribunal noted this "expropriatory penchant" of a sovereign's taxing authority, but did not link it to the exigency of analyzing it within the context of an objective public purpose framework:

> By their very nature, tax measures, even if they are designed to and have the effect of an expropriation, will be indirect, with an effect that may be tantamount to an expropriation. If the measures are implemented over a period of time, they could also be characterized as "creeping," which the tribunal believes is not distinct in nature from and is subsumed by the terms "indirect" expropriation or "tantamount to expropriation" in Article 1110(1).

Id. at ¶ 101.

[328] As to this point, the *Feldman* tribunal stated:

> [T]he Tribunal is aware that not every business problem experienced by a foreign investor is an indirect or creeping expropriation under Article 1110, or a denial of due process or fair and equitable treatment under Article 1110(1)(c). As the *Azinian* Tribunal observed, "it is a fact of life everywhere that individuals may be disappointed in their dealings with public authorities ... it may be safely assumed that many Mexican Parties can be found who had business dealings with governmental entities which were not to their

The character and scope that the NAFTA jurisprudence has engrafted on a State's police powers necessarily gives rise to an inherent presumption of correctness attaching to regulatory acts. This presumption itself needs to be questioned in the context of a proliferation of public purpose usages that can only lead to an understandable loss of confidence in the efficacy of investment protection. It also further provides rogue States with formal juridical justification for substantive inequities that rise to the level of illicit conduct. The tribunal in *S.D. Myers*, for example,[329] stated that "[t]he general body of precedent usually does not treat regulatory action as amounting to expropriation. Regulatory conduct by public authorities is unlikely to be the subject of legitimate complaint under Article 1110 of the NAFTA, although the Tribunal does not rule out that possibility."[330] This remarkable statement is disconcerting.

Treating regulatory measures as unlikely to constitute conduct tantamount to an expropriation, where the meaning of the word "tantamount" within Article 1110(1) only pertains to equivalent of an expropriation and not more,[331] can only generate greater uncertainty and further contribute to undermining process legitimacy. Consideration of a State's police powers should only serve to further principles of symmetry, bilateralism, and transparency in the relationship between capital-exporting and capital-importing States. Anointing regulatory measures with a presumption of correctness and legitimacy cannot at all contribute toward equipoise between Home and Host States. The use of nomenclature such as "police powers" should not serve as a means to circumvent the public purpose doctrine on the grounds that historical conceptual legacies loosely associate specific State functions (principally those that can only be undertaken by a sovereign and not an individual person or juridical

> satisfaction . . ." To paraphrase *Azinian*, not all government regulatory activity that makes it difficult or impossible for an investor to carry out a particular business, change in the law or change in the application of existing laws that make it uneconomical to continue a particular business, is an expropriation under Article 1110.

Id. at ¶ 112 (internal citations omitted).

329 S.D. Myers First Partial Award, *supra* note 120.

330 *Id.* at ¶ 281.

331 The NAFTA jurisprudence is of a single voice in agreeing that "tantamount to expropriation" within the meaning of Article 1110(1) does not extend beyond the customary scope of the term expropriation under international law and simply means "equivalent" to and not greater than an expropriation. *See, e.g., id.* at Ili 285–86; Fireman's Fund, *supra* note 150, at ¶ 176 n.159 ("According to certain case law, the expression 'a measure tantamount to nationalization or expropriation' in Article 1110 of the NAFTA means nothing more than 'a measure equivalent to nationalization or expropriation'" [citations omitted]); *see also* Cargill Inc. v. United Mexican States, ICSID Case No. ARB(AF)/05/2, Award, ¶ 335 (September 18, 2009), http://www.italaw.com/sites/default/files/case-documents/ita0133_0.pdf; Pope & Talbot, *supra* note 296, at ¶¶ 96, 104; Feldman, *supra* note 150, at ¶ 100.

entity) to legitimize a State's violation of its treaty obligations to foreign investors.[332] Both analytically and substantively, police powers and the public purpose should be considered as one and the same, each encompassing an identical scope.

In assessing whether a regulatory measure constitutes an expropriation or the equivalent to an expropriation, both burdens and presumptions must be inverted to favor a claimant where substantial prejudice to an investment/investor is established or conceded. At that time, scrutiny is to be equally placed on the effect that a measure has on the investment as concerning more than just a "mere diminution in value," as well as on the nature and extent to which the measure comports with a substantively objective public purpose category. The current NAFTA jurisprudence completely effaces consideration of this second component in favor of a nonrebuttable and virtually boundless public purpose category reconfigured with "police powers" nomenclature.

5. *Reflections on Conventional International Law's Use of Public Purpose*

Having analyzed the public purpose doctrine within the conventional international law framework of the NAFTA, it becomes readily apparent that the doctrine's morphology is both elusive and perhaps even ostensibly contradictory. Despite the merits of Article 1101(4)[333] (the NAFTA Public Purpose Standard), the workings of a public purpose category within Chapter Fourteen,[334] and the jurisprudence interpreting and applying public purpose within the meaning of Article 1110, the very elements of public purpose at rudimentary levels remain ill-defined. This problem is far-reaching. It suggests that the pivotal principle governing the effects of regulatory sovereignty on foreign investment protection remains underdeveloped and in pragmatic and theoretical terms reduced (or wrongfully elevated) to the status of a self-evident principle – a conceptual category that no longer can account for the burdens that regulatory sovereignty and economic globalization have placed on public purpose analysis.

[332] One reason for not providing unyielding deference to this broad exception is that the scope of the police powers exception has never been fully developed at international law. Jason L. Gudofsky, *Shedding Light on Article 1110 of the North American Free Trade Agreement (NAFTA) Concerning Expropriations: An Environmental Case Study*, 21 Nw. J. Int'l L. & Bus. 243, 295 (2000) ("The full scope of the police powers exception under international law has not yet been fully developed. More case law and attention must be devoted to the exception").

[333] *See supra* notes 5–8 and accompanying text.

[334] *See supra* Chapter 1.F.

The subjective content of public purpose in its historical legacy iteration purports to be broad – that is, as generally concerning the public welfare, such that any conflicting interest pertaining to the protection of a foreign investment/investor would be vastly outweighed by the purported public purpose in furtherance of the common good. A broad subjectively based conceptualization of the doctrine, even within the NAFTA's conventional international law context, cries for greater specificity, clarity, and definition.[335] This problem is meaningfully compounded because the broad public purpose category, "in furtherance of the general welfare," in turn is premised on a Host State's very particular understanding of public purpose. Therefore, this functional, all-encompassing public purpose framework, pursuant to which any reasonable relationship between a State's undertaking and a "public consequence" constitutes a "public purpose" within conventional international law, also includes a *restrictive* character arising from a State's subjective understanding of public purpose.[336] "Public purpose" thus is transformed and denaturalized into "political purpose," a purpose that does not necessarily further a State's common welfare but rather some (less likely all) of its administrative institutions.[337] This denaturalization of public purpose shall continue to become more destabilizing to the investment treaty and dispute resolution development of an integrated, interdependent paradigm of resources and economic coexistence. Indeed, public purpose has devolved into a substantively bankrupt doctrine that is nearly eviscerating itself.

Are the teachings of conventional international law (albeit through the lens of the NAFTA) with respect to the public purpose doctrine rendered more developed or clearer by customary international law? Are there competing definitions of public purpose in conventional international law and customary international law? If so, how may these differences be harmonized? Is the architecture of conventional international law more conducive to articulating a public purpose doctrine that may meaningfully serve to harmonize the competing underlying policies of international trade law and international investment law? Has, in fact, customary international law given rise to a public

[335] Kevin Banks, *NAFTA's Article 1110 – Can Regulation Be Expropriation?*, 5 NAFTA: L. & Bus. Rev. Am. 499, 510 (1999) (noting that "the range of public purposes included within the police power appears to be wide and relatively undefined").

[336] *Id.* at 510 (suggesting that "deference can be expected from international tribunals in the face of a State's assertion of a public purpose").

[337] *See, e.g.*, Jason Webb Yackee, *Do Bilateral Investment Treaties Promote Foreign Direct Investment? Some Hints from Alternative Evidence*, 51 Va. J. Int'l L. 397, 399–400 (2011) ("If investment treaties are important elements in the foreign investment decision-making process because they protect against the risk of adverse political actions (like expropriation), it might be expected that companies whose line of business is to gauge such risks will incorporate the presence or absence of treaties into their evaluations").

purpose doctrine capable of reconciling conflicting interests concerning the legitimate expectations of foreign investors and Host-State obligations to exercise their regulatory authority to protect or enhance the public welfare? Is there a public purpose doctrine that customary international law identifies, and, if so, is it vested with a content that leads to uniformity, predictability, and transparency of standard? Is the public purpose doctrine premised on a customary international law the same or similar to that codified in the NAFTA and presumably developed by the NAFTA's decisional law? Is the legacy public purpose doctrine found in customary international law suited to mitigating competing expectations between capital-exporting and capital-importing countries, or, as with its conventional international law counterpart, crafted as a doctrinal category that unduly promotes regulatory sovereignty to the detriment of foreign investments/investors?

Addressing all of these queries, let alone meaningfully purporting to answer them, is beyond this text's aspiration. Having canvassed the role of the public purpose within the framework of conventional international law as it appears in the NAFTA, the necessary question is whether customary international law reveals a different public purpose doctrine and the extent to which it separates itself from the NAFTA's conventional international law iteration, as well as the pronouncements and role of the doctrine in the NAFTA's decisional law. This inquiry does find space in this contribution. A related analysis addresses the grounds for the differences concerning scope in the doctrine as it appears in these two sources of international law. The nature of the source of law, so it shall be asserted, is material to the doctrine's morphology.

The anatomy of customary international law is particularly relevant. It will be advanced that the long-standing debilities endemic to the very structure of customary international law merely serve to compound the lack of predictive value and universal definition that now pervades the orthodox public purpose legacy doctrine. It also shall be demonstrated that the public purpose doctrine's status as represented in international instruments unduly amplifies regulatory sovereignty, thereby exacerbating the very challenge that the public purpose doctrine seeks to overcome. The historicity arising from the process of political and economic decolonization has given rise to such principles as (i) sustainable development and (ii) permanent sovereignty over natural resources, both of which aim to assist developing countries and economies in transition. These principles, themselves experiencing refining and doctrinal development, are emblematic of a broader, if not nearly all-encompassing, public purpose doctrine. Although contained in multiple public international law instruments, both principles are yet to be uniformly defined, let alone applied. It follows, so the argument says, that the customary international law iteration of the public purpose doctrine generally multiplies the vagueness and inadequacies with which its conventional international law counterpart struggles at a more limited scale. Because of customary international law's unique structural features, lacking in centralized legislating and decision making, and wanting in enforcement capacity, there is no basis from which to infer that it may be capable of at all addressing the doctrinal needs of the public purpose doctrine. A brief analysis of customary international law with emphasis on these framework features is necessary if public purpose is at all to be understood within this context. More specifically, it is necessary to identify the evidence of public purpose within the ambit of customary international law.

2

Identifying Public Purpose in Customary International Law

Select International Instruments

A. THE PLACE OF THE PUBLIC PURPOSE DOCTRINE IN CUSTOMARY INTERNATIONAL LAW

1. *Revisiting Fundamentals of Customary International Law*

The classical point of departure for any discussion on customary international law is Article 38 of the Statute of the International Court of Justice (ICJ), which identifies "'international custom' as evidence of a general practice accepted as law."[1] The "general practice" refers to the *practice of*

[1] The Statute of the ICJ forms an integral part of the Charter of the United Nations. The Statute's objective is to provide a framework for the ICJ's composition and general workings. Article 7 of the United Nations Charter, among other organs, provides for the International Court of Justice. Article 93 of the Charter of the United Nations provides that "all members of the United Nations are *ipso facto* parties to the Statute. Non-members . . . may become parties to the Statute on conditions to be determined in each case by the General Assembly upon the recommendation of the Security Council." The underlying assumption is that the world political organization, already possessed of organs with executive, deliberative, and administrative functions, would be incomplete unless it also had a fully integrated judicial organ of its own." SHABTAI ROSENNE, THE WORLD COURT: WHAT IT IS AND HOW IT WORKS 1, 26 (Martinus Nijhoff Publishers, 5th ed. 1994).

Article 38 of the ICJ Statute reads:

1. The Court whose function is to decide in accordance with international law such disputes as are submitted to it, shall apply:
   a. international conventions, where a general or a particular, establishing rules expressly recognized by the contesting states;
   b. *international custom, as evidence of a general practice accepted as law*;
   c. the general principles of law recognized by civilized nations;
   d. subject to the provisions of Article 59, judicial decisions and the teachings of the most highly qualified publicists of the various nations, as subsidiary means for the determination of rules of law.

States[2] and must in turn be undertaken by States (most but not all members of the international community)[3] as a binding legal obligation.[4] This normative binding character of customary international law does not require the explicit acceptance of it by a State compelled to follow it.[5] Brownlie observes that the terms "custom" and "usage," although "used interchangeably," also "are terms of art and have different meanings. A usage is a general practice [that] does not reflect a legal obligation, and examples are ceremonial salutes at sea and the practice of exempting diplomatic vehicles from parking prohibition."[6]

2. This provision shall not prejudice the power of the Court to decide a case *ex aequo et bono*, if the parties agree thereto.

I.C.J. Statute art. 38, paras. 1–2 (emphasis added).

2 North Sea Continental Shelf Cases, 1969 I.C.J. 3, 232 (Lachs, J., dissenting) (February 20) ("In sum, the general practice of states should be recognized as prima facie evidence that it is accepted as law.").

3 *Id.* at 43–44 (majority opinion); *see also* Kiobel v. Royal Dutch Petroleum Co., 621 F.3d 111, 137 (2d Cir. 2010) ("Although all treaties ratified by more than one State provide *some* evidence of the custom and practice of nations, 'a treaty will only constitute *sufficient proof* of a norm of *customary international law* if an overwhelming majority of states have ratified the treaty, *and* those states uniformly and consistently act in accordance with its principles'"; emphasis in original; citation omitted); Flores v. S. Peru Copper Corp., 414 F.3d 233, 248 (2d Cir. 2003) ("In short, customary international law is composed only of those rules that states universally abide by, or accede to, out of a sense of legal obligation and mutual concern. Of course, states need not be universally successful in implementing the principle in order for a rule of customary international law to arise. If that were the case, there would be no need for customary international law. But the principle must be more than merely professed or aspirational"; internal citations omitted).

4 Restatement (Third) of Foreign Relations Law § 102(2) (1987) ("Customary international law results from a general and consistent practice of states followed by them from a sense of legal obligation"); *see also North Sea Continental Shelf Cases*, 1969 I.C.J. at 44 ("Not only must the acts concerned amount to a settled practice, but they must also be . . . carried out in such a way as to be evidence of a belief that this practice is rendered obligatory by the existence of a rule of law requiring it"); *see also Flores*, 414 F.3d at 248 ("Furthermore, a principle is only incorporated into customary international law if states accede to it out of a sense of legal obligation").

5 Even though customary international law follows conventional international law as Article 38 enunciates them, both conventional international law and customary international law share in the same normative standing; i.e., they are both equally authoritative. *See, e.g.*, Phillip R. Trimble, *A Revisionist View of Customary International Law*, 33 UCLA L. Rev. 665, 669 (1986).

However, customary international law is not without its critics. J. Patrick Kelly, *The Twilight of Customary International Law*, 40 Va. J. Int'l L. 449, 452 (2000) (arguing that customary international law "should be eliminated as a source of international legal norms and replaced by consensual processes").

6 Ian Brownlie, Principles of International Law 1, 6 (Oxford University Press, 7th ed. 2008) (citing *Parking Privileges for Diplomats Case*, Federal Republic of Germany, Fed. Admin. Ct., 70 ILR 396 (January 22, 1971)).

The Restatement of the Law Third, The Foreign Relations Law of the United States draws a distinction between general and special custom. "Special" customary law arises from a "regional" or "special" grouping that in turn gives rise to regional customary law as binding on States of a particular region. Drawing on the *Asylum Cases*,[7] it notes that the State alleged to be bound must have "accepted or *acquiesced* in the custom as a matter of legal obligation, not merely for reasons of political expediency."[8]

Although the source for customary international law rests with Article 38 of the ICJ Statute, the material evidence from which *custom* and a consistent practice on the part of States may be gleaned is vast. Brownlie notes that it may include:

> [D]iplomatic correspondence, policy statements, press releases, the opinions of official legal advisors, official manuals on legal questions, e.g., manuals of military law, executive decisions and practices, orders to naval forces etc., comments by governments on drafts produced by the International Law Commission, State legislation, international and national judicial decisions, recitals in treaties and other international instruments, a pattern of treaties in the same form, the practice of international organs, and resolutions relating to legal questions in the United Nations General Assembly.[9]

The manner in which principles or rules become international law rising to the status of binding customary international law in turn defines normative standing or the weight to be accorded to such precepts. Thus, the means of establishing, from an evidentiary perspective, that a "customary rule" has developed into customary international law depends on primary evidence such as State practice as memorialized in official government documents and other indicia of government practice and secondary evidence mostly in the form of authoritative commentators and reporters.[10]

7 Asylum Case (Columbia v. Peru), 1950 I.C.J. 266 (November 20).

8 RESTATEMENT (THIRD) OF FOREIGN RELATIONS LAW § 102 *cmt. e* (1987). Section 102(2) defines customary law as by drawing on "consistency in the practice giving rise to a binding principle of law" and "a sense of legal obligation." *Id.* § 102(2) (1987) ("Customary international law results from a *general and consistent practice* of states followed by them from a *sense of legal obligation*"; emphasis added).

9 BROWNLIE, *supra* note 6, at 6–7.

10 Without purporting to establish hierarchy in the order of the clause, Section 103(2) of the Restatement references secondary evidence:

> (2) In determining whether a rule has become international law, substantial weight is accorded to:
> a. the judgments and opinions of international judicial and arbitral tribunals;
> b. the judgments and opinions of national judicial tribunals;
> c. the writings of scholars;

Even though these elements of custom are readily identifiable,[11] the premises comprising these elements are far from clear and are susceptible to interpretation.[12] The less than "bright-line standard" incident to the very elements that serve as a standard for determining whether a rule, principle,

> d. pronouncements by states that undertake to state a rule of international law, when such pronouncements are not seriously challenged by other states.

RESTATEMENT (THIRD) OF FOREIGN RELATIONS LAW § 103(2) (1987).

11 Commentators tend to agree that relevant factors include (i) duration of the practice at issue, (ii) uniformity and consistency of the practice, (iii) generality of the practice, (iv) *opinio juris*, and (v) protest and acquiescence. *See* BROWNLIE, *supra* note 6, at 7–10; MALCOLM N. SHAW, INTERNATIONAL LAW 1, 72–93 (Cambridge University Press, 6th ed. 2008); RESTATEMENT (THIRD) OF FOREIGN RELATIONS LAW § 103 *cmt. a–c* (1987).

12 By way of example, the required *duration* is wholly undetermined. Although a protracted amount of time is preferred and of obvious benefit, there is no specific time frame requirement. In fact, Shaw speaks of "instant" customary law pursuant to which normative standing is attained without any meaningfully long gestation period. SHAW, *supra* note 10, at 74.

For example, in holding that Article 6 of the Geneva Convention on the Continental Shelf of 1958, which provided for the equidistance-special circumstances principle, had not yet formed part of customary law and therefore, was not binding on West Germany, the ICJ observed:

> An indispensable requirement would be that within the period in question, short though it might be, State practice, including that of states whose interests are specially affected, should have been both extensive and virtually uniform in the sense of the provision invoked, and should moreover have occurred in such a way as to show a general recognition that a rule of law or legal obligation is involved.

North Sea Continental Shelf Cases, 1969 I.C.J. 3, 41 (February 20). The "uniformity, consistency of the practice" element is equally undetermined. Although most commentators agree that complete uniformity simply is not a predicate, the general consensus does require "substantial uniformity," a term that is hardly distinct or particular. Thus, in the *Fisheries Case*, concerning the question of whether the ten-mile rule for bays constitute custom international law, the Court stated:

> In these circumstances the Court deems it necessary to point out that although the ten-mile rule has been adopted by certain states both in their national law and in their treaties and conventions, and although certain arbitral decisions have applied as between these states, other states have adopted a different limit. Consequently, the ten-mile rule has not acquired the authority of a general rule of international law. In any event, the ten-mile rule would appear to be inapplicable as against Norway inasmuch as she has always opposed any attempt to apply it to the Norwegian coast.

Fisheries Case (U.K. v. Norway), 1951 I.C.J. 116, 131 (December 18; emphasis supplied). In that case, (i) the disparate adoption of the rule by the community of countries and (ii) Norway's long-standing objection to imposition or adoption of the rule with respect to its coastline negated application and, more importantly, mitigated against a finding that the ten-mile rule had met the customary international law threshold.

Opinio juris is perhaps the most elusive tenet of the customary practice elements because it is essentially subjective. Its cornerstone proposition is that a particular practice shall not attain customary international law status unless the country engaging in the practice believes that it is

or doctrine rises to the level of a custom and in turn evinces a "general State practice" thus acquires the requisite normative standing to constitute binding customary international law, which is a concern that affects the status of the public purpose doctrine within a customary international law framework. In

legally bound to adhere to the practice at issue. Shaw succinctly states it as "States will behave a certain way because they are convinced it is binding upon them to do so." SHAW, *supra* note 10, at 74. The manner in which a State views and understands its own conduct presents virtually insurmountable challenges. How is a State's conduct to be examined in order to determine whether the State deems a recurring practice legally obligatory and in this way transforms a usage into a binding custom? In the *Case of the S.S. Lotus*, the ICJ's predecessor, the Permanent Court of International Justice, rejected France's contention that customary international law recognizes a rule providing that in a maritime accident occurring in international waters the country of the flag State of the accused has exclusive jurisdiction over the national State of the victim. The French government premised its contention on States' abstention from criminal prosecutions arising from collision cases of this sort, which more frequently involved proceedings before civil courts. The French government went on to conclude that the paucity of such cases gives rise to an inference of State practice pursuant to which prosecutions only take place within the courts of the State whose flag is flown. It was on this factual predicate that France also relied to demonstrate tacit consent among the international community of states. Case of the S.S. Lotus, 1927 P.C.I.J. (ser. A) No. 10, at 18 (September 7). The Court noted that:

> [T]his conclusion is not warranted. Even if the rarity of the judicial decisions to be found among the reported cases were sufficient to prove in point of fact the circumstance alleged by the Agent for the French Government, it would merely show that states had often, in practice, abstained from instituting criminal proceedings, and *not that they recognized themselves as being obliged to do so;* for only *if such abstention were based under being conscious of having a duty to abstain would be possible to speak of an international custom.* The alleged fact does not allow one to infer that states have been conscious of having such a duty; on the other hand, as will presently be seen, there are other circumstances calculated to show that the contrary is true.

Id. at 28 (emphasis added).

In the *North Sea Continental Shelf Cases*, the Netherlands sought to impose on West Germany the "equi-distance-special circumstances principle" in conformance with Article 6 of the Geneva Convention on the Continental Shelf of 1958, as part of the general process of delimiting the Continental Shelf of the North Sea in furtherance of oil and gas exploration and exploitation. Because West Germany had neither signed nor ratified the 1958 Geneva Convention, it was not found by that instrument. Accordingly, the extent to which the delimiting principle in Article 6 of the Geneva convention constituted customary international law became the case dispositive issue. The ICJ ruled in favor of West Germany and rejected arguments that the principle formed part of customary international law, either before or after the execution of the Geneva Convention on the Continental Shelf. The Court's reasoning as to *opinio juris* and the requisite time frame for normative rule making is instructive:

> Insofar as this contention is based on the view that Art. 6 of the Convention has had the influence, and has produced the effect, described [normative standing of the principle as part of customary international law], it clearly involves treating that Article as a norm-creating provision which has constituted the foundation of, or has generated a rule which, while only conventional or contractual in its origin, has since passed into the general *corpus* of international law, and is now accepted as such by the *opinio juris*, so as to have

this regard, debilities pertaining to process legitimacy cannot be segregated from effects on the substantive rule at issue (here, the public purpose doctrine).

B. FOUNDATIONAL CONCERNS ENDEMIC TO CUSTOMARY INTERNATIONAL LAW CHALLENGING THE DEVELOPMENT OF A PUBLIC PURPOSE DOCTRINE

In any effort to sketch a profile of public purpose as a doctrine forming part of customary international law, it is necessary to identify features of customary international law that may contribute to obscuring the actual content, application, and development of the public purpose doctrine. It is central to any inquiry seeking to address public purpose within the context of customary international law to emphasize these unique elements of uncertainty that pervade customary international law in order to select a source for the conduct of nations that may best articulate the scope and content of the public purpose doctrine. Such an element of proof can be evaluated despite the structural ambiguities of this normative system. In commenting on the contrast between international law generally and the domestic law of States, Shaw rightfully observes:

> The contrast is very striking when one considers the situation in international law. The lack of a legislature, executive and structure of courts within international law has been noted and the effects of this will become clearer

> become binding even for countries which have never and do not become parties to the Convention. There is no doubt that this process is a perfectly possible one and does from time to time occur: It constitutes indeed, one of the recognized methods by which new rules of customary international law may be formed. *At the same time this result is not likely to be regarded as having been attained* . . ..

As regards the time element, the Court noted that it was more than ten years since the Convention was signed, but less than five since it came into force in June 1964, and that when the present proceedings were brought it was less than three years, while less than one year had elapsed at the time when the respective negotiations between the Federal Republic [the former West Germany] and the other two Parties for a complete delimitation broke down on the question of the application of the equidistance principle. "Although the passage of only a short period of time was not necessarily or of itself a bar to the formation of a new rule of customary international law on the basis of what was originally a purely conventional rule," an indisputable requirement will be that within the period in question, short though it may be, State practice, "including that of states whose interests were specially affected, should have been both extensive and virtually uniform in the sense of the provision invoked[and moreover] should have occurred in such a way as to show a general recognition that a rule of law or legal obligation is involved."

North Sea Continental Shelf Cases, 1969 I.C.J. at 41, 44 (February 20; emphasis added).

> as one proceeds. There is no single body able to create laws internationally binding upon everyone, nor a proper system of courts with comprehensive and compulsory jurisdiction to interpret and extend the law. One is therefore faced with the problem of discovering where the law is to be found and how one can tell whether a particular proposition amounts to a legal rule. This perplexity is reinforced because of the archaic nature of world affairs in the clash of competing sovereignties. Nevertheless, international law does exist and is ascertainable. There are "sources" available from which the rules may be extracted and analyzed.[13]

This lack of institutional centralization and policy making is amplified and ever apparent in the context of customary international law.

As a point of departure, whether a generally accepted State practice is discernible at all constitutes a legitimate question that cannot be readily and fully satisfied. What is the governing phenomenology? A State practice uniformly repeated by a sovereign over time may be causally connected to specific nonpermanent circumstances. Similarly, is a practice arising from the exercise of comity, by way of example, suggestive of a legal rule? It is unclear how and under what circumstances what ostensibly appears to be a general State practice actually becomes a legal principle, rule, or tenet. Inference from phenomenon alone cannot be deemed to be wholly conclusive.[14]

The discernibility of State action or conduct rising to the level of customary international law is further obscured because of the very nature of a State. The surface and unavailing analogy between a State and a biological self-sustained organism is not helpful. A sovereignty comprises thousands of binding agencies, instrumentalities, governmental departments, and officials through which States act. Moreover, political regimes and their policy agendas are but a passing phenomenon. The inevitable question is raised: Which acts or

[13] SHAW, *supra* note 10, at 70.

[14] *See* J. Patrick Kelly, *The Twilight of Customary International Law*, 40 VA. J. INT'L L. 449, 453 (2000) ("Customary law may be discerned through the inductive method. Norms may be inferred from repeated and consistent acts that are believed to be required by a community, but customary law is not State practice. It is the community-wide belief that a norm is legally required that provides customary law with authority and legitimacy. The asserted CIL norms of the literature, however, are declared without either general, consistent practice or clear evidence that the vast majority of states have accepted the norm as a legal obligation. In short, CIL norms are not customary"; footnotes omitted); Andrew T. Guzman, *Why LDCs Sign Treaties That Hurt Them: Explaining the Popularity of Bilateral Investment Treaties*, 38 VA. J. INT'L L. 639, 685–86 (1998) ("The states concerned must therefore feel that they are conforming to what amounts to a legal obligation. The frequency, or even habitual character of the acts is not in itself enough. Therefore, in the words of another scholar, 'the repetition of common clauses in bilateral treaties does not create or support an inference that those clauses express customary law .... To sustain such a claim of custom one would have to show that apart from the treaty itself, the rules in the clauses are considered obligatory'"; footnotes omitted).

omissions, and by whom within a State, unquestionably reflect the imprimatur of the State? Can this inquiry be meaningfully addressed despite the less-than-uniform configurations of State governments administering the interests of disparate cultures and stages of industrial and economic development? These concerns directly affect the public purpose doctrine.

In the context of competing interests, and contradictory acts by different government instrumentalities, agencies, departments, and officials, at what point does a discernible act of omission give rise to the emergence of a new norm of customary international law? The corollary to this query is equally intriguing. What is the talisman for determining that an existing tenet of customary international law has been modified or altogether disallowed?[15] Customary international law often is praised because of its flexibility and dynamic architecture. Yet, at what point is a precept in its original configuration no longer binding?[16]

In the creation of new customary international law, how may the workings of *opinio juris* be reconciled?[17] *Opinio juris* requires a State practice that conforms with established law. How, then, may a new customary international law principle develop if by definition it could not have formed part of a preexisting legal canon (i.e., a practice that was not *previously* regarded as constituting evidence of law?).[18]

Although international law generally suffers from lack of centralized authority at norm creation, application, and enforcement, this feature is minimized in the context of conventional international law and arguably maximized with respect to customary international law. Conventional international law makes up in structure what it lacks in radius coverage. Even within a rubric of a multinational agreement, conventional international law

[15] *See* Anthea Elizabeth Roberts, *Traditional and Modern Approaches to Customary International Law: A Reconciliation*, 95 AM. J. INT'L L. 757, 784 (2001) ("The formation and modification of custom is an uncertain process because international law lacks an authoritative guide as to the amount, duration, frequency, and repetition of State practice required to develop or change a custom").

[16] Jack L. Goldsmith & Eric A. Posner, A *Theory of Customary International Law*, 66 U. CHI. L. REV. 1113, 1114 (1999) ("CIL remains a puzzle. It lacks a centralized lawmaker, a centralized executive enforcer, and a centralized, authoritative decision maker. The content of CIL seems to track the interests of powerful nations. The origins of CIL rules are not understood. We do not know why nations comply with CIL, or even what it means for a nation to comply with CIL. And we lack an explanation for the many changes in CIL rules over time").

[17] "[F]or a new customary rule to be formed, not only must the acts concerned 'amount to a settled practice', but they must be accompanied by the *opinion juris sive necessitatis.*" Military & Paramilitary Activities in and against Nicaragua (Nicar. v. U.S.), Judgment, 1986 I.C.J. 14, 108–109 (June 27).

[18] SHAW, *supra* note 10, at 87–88.

in the Central America-United States Free Trade Agreement (CAFTA),[19] to draw on a widely consulted example, will contain dispute resolution provisions and well-defined frameworks purporting to memorialize the underlying policy and intent of the signatory parties with respect to technical execution. At least in theory, the decisional law arising from the international dispute mechanisms of treaty law further helps refine the interpretation of terms in conformance with the intent of the signatory parties. No such frameworks are available to customary international law. It lacks treaty negotiating history, structured terms, and dispute-enforcement mechanisms, all within the context of not enjoying the benefits of a decisional law that purports to have persuasive authority when refining the intent of the signatory parties.[20]

Some of the most fundamental questions pertaining to customary international law remain as opaque as when first raised by classical scholarship.[21] The very origins of customary international law remain unclear.[22] Equally bewildering is the basic question of why nations comply with customary international law or what State acts count as evidence of customary international law? Is there such a thing as a recurring State practice generally accepted by nations that does not rise to the level of customary international law?[23]

[19] Dominican Republic-Central America-United States Free Trade Agreement, August 5, 2004, http://www.ustr.gov/archive/Trade_Agreements/Regional/CAFTA/CAFTA-DR_Final_Texts/Section_Index.html [hereinafter DR-CAFTA].

[20] John A. Perkins, *The Changing Foundations of International Law: From State Consent to State Responsibility*, 15 B.U. INT'L L.J. 433, 472–73 (1997) ("Customary international law is not the instrument to which states now look in the development of purely consensual obligations, whatever the reality may have been at the time of the development of the sovereignty/consent thesis. A complex web of explicit contractual arrangements has developed a framework and rules for international trade, investment and finance. The occasion to invoke customary international law arises precisely where consensual arrangements are lacking or fall short and precisely because perceived unmet needs of the international community call for invoking a concept of binding law. This is evident in the familiar dynamic by which resort is made to 'soft law' declarations in an opinio juris building process looking to the development of binding customary international law.")

[21] "For Grotius, international law had two sources: (1) the law of nature and (2) mutual consent – or, in his terms, 'the law of nations.' These two sources, however, were deeply and inextricably intertwined. An observed custom could be evidence of either a principle derived from the law of nature or of mutual consent. Rules of international law could be derived from natural reason, but customary international law was also evidence of what natural reason required. Grotius's framework married custom and reason, imbuing the practice and opinio juris of states with great power and legitimacy." Harlan Grant Cohen, *Finding International Law: Rethinking the Doctrine of Sources*, 93 IOWA L. REV. 65, 80 (2007) (internal footnotes omitted).

[22] Jack L. Goldsmith & Eric A. Posner, *A Theory of Customary International Law*, 66 U. CHI. L. REV. 1113, 1114 (1999) (noting that the "origins of CIL rules are not understood").

[23] *Id.* ("CIL's standard definition raises perennial, and unanswered, questions. It is unclear which State acts count as evidence of a custom, or how broad or consistent State practice must be to satisfy the custom requirement. It is also unclear what it means for a nation to follow a custom from a sense of legal obligation, or how one determines whether such an obligation exists.")

These structural features represent uncertainties that themselves, in turn, create ambiguities in the theoretical and practical assessment of the normative standing of customary international law. Commentators appear to fall into three relatively distinct schools of thought as to foundational normative standing. A considerable number of scholars opine that customary international law's procedural shortcomings *inhibit* its ability to respond and adjust to rapid changes, for example, in the international law of human rights, trade, and investment.[24] A second representative class holds a diametrically opposite view. These commentators emphasize the decentralized configuration of

[24] For example, "[a]s recently as 1970, the International Court of Justice in the *Barcelona Traction* case found it 'surprising' that the evolution of international investment law had not gone further and that no generally accepted rules had yet crystallized in light of the growth of foreign investments and the expansion of international activities by corporations in the previous half-century." Jeswald W. Salacuse & Nicholas P. Sullivan, *Do BITS Really Work?: An Evaluation of Bilateral Investment Treaties and Their Grand Bargain*, 46 HARV. L.J. 67, 68 (2005) (citing Barcelona Traction Light & Power Co., Ltd. (Belg. v. Spain) 1970 I.C.J. 3, 46–47 (February 5)).

One primary reason for this deficiency was that "applicable international law failed to take account of contemporary investment practices and address important issues of concern to foreign investors." *Id.* (footnote omitted). Another issue was that "the principles that did exist were often vague and subject to varying interpretations. Thus, although there was strong evidence that customary international law required the payment of compensation upon nationalization of an investor's property, no principles had crystallized on how that compensation was to be calculated." *Id.* at 68–69 (footnote omitted). *See also* Karen Halverson Cross, *Converging Trends in Investment Treaty Practice*, 38 N.C. J. INT'L L. & COM. REG. 151, 157–58 (2012) ("Since customary international law was inadequate to provide meaningful protection to foreign investors, the United States and other capital-exporting countries concluded BITs with developing countries in order to create binding international commitments where customary international law standards were inconclusive or non-existent"; footnotes omitted); Eric Gottwald, *Leveling the Playing Field: Is It Time for a Legal Assistance Center for Developing Nations in Investment Treaty Arbitration?*, 22 AM. U. INT'L L. REV. 237, 242 (2007) ("Given the shortcomings of the customary international law, the United States and other capital-exporting nations turned to signing investment treaties to provide a source of clear and certain rules on foreign investment"); John K. Setear, *Treaties, Custom, Iteration, and Public Choice*, 5 CHI. J. INT'L L. 715, 721 (2005) ("Customary international law thus suffers from a lack of temporally distinct iterations and from ambiguous mechanisms for indicating formal consent . . . . Because practice figures so prominently in defining customary rules, any change in such rules can only be effectuated after a period during which neither the old nor the new rule clearly governs. While a new rule articulated in a treaty takes full effect when the treaty enters into force, a new customary international legal rule has no discrete activation date"); J. Steven Jarreau, *Anatomy of a BIT: The United States – Honduras Bilateral Investment Treaty*, 35 U. MIAMI INTER-AM. L. REV. 429 (2004) ("Foreign direct investment influences the world economy by promoting the transfer of capital, technology and managerial skills, improving economic efficiency through greater competition and enhancing market access. The United States and Honduras, appreciating the benefits of foreign direct investment (FDI) while mindful of the shortcomings of customary international law and the absence of a multilateral accord on FDI, entered into negotiations to promote and protect foreign investment in their respective countries"; footnotes omitted).

customary international law as a flexible and universally accommodating phenomenon capable of generating quick and efficient principles in response to changing circumstances.[25] Yet the "democratic character" of customary international law is viewed by a considerable number of voices as having an impromptu and much-desired character pursuant to which custom is generated in ways that reflect legitimate social interests. Despite enshrining custom as a welcomed tenet, it is recognized that custom's ability to provide uniformity and serve as a principle of integration of disparate and often competing social, political, economic, and cultural forces now experiencing unprecedented transformations is limited and restrictive.[26]

Galvanized by *custom* as its organizing principle, the configuration of customary international law can be seen as a daunting mosaic in progress. So long as a State's act, omission, publication, official statement, legislative decree, domestic political institutions, or international projection of whatsoever ilk contains even a modicum of probative value from which "customary State practice" may be gleaned, such evidence may serve as a normative foundation for a principle of customary international law. We have selected to limit our analysis of the status of public purpose in customary international law to a consideration of the role of public purpose (in all of its iterations) by analyzing (i) the status and meaning ascribed to public purpose international instruments, (ii) the status of the doctrine in bilateral investment treaties (BITs),[27] and (iii) domestic legislation concerning the protection of foreign investments/investors.[28] These three categories have been selected because of

[25] John O. McGinnis & Ilya Somin, *Should International Law Be Part of Our Law?*, 59 STAN. L. REV. 1175, 1221–22 (2007) ("Under certain conditions, customary law is likely to produce norms that increase efficiency. Customary norms under this theory evolve to create surpluses as interacting individuals or entities choose those norms that will provide them with the greatest possible increases in wealth. Accordingly, some have argued by analogy that customary international law is efficient"); Anthony D'Amato, *Modifying U.S. Acceptance of the Compulsory Jurisdiction of the World Court*, 79 AM. J. INT'L L. 385, 402 (1985) ("The rules of international law covering these subjects were not imposed on states from on high, but rather grew out of their interactions over centuries of practice and became established as customary international law. Thus the rules, almost by definition, are the most efficient possible rules for avoiding international friction and for accommodating the collective self-interest of all states"; footnotes omitted).

[26] McGinnis & Somin, *supra* note 25, at 1222 ("The first shortcoming of this argument lies again in the democracy deficit. Even if customs generated among states prove to be efficient, it only follows that they are efficient for State leaders, not for their subjects. Authoritarian and totalitarian states do not represent the preferences of their people. Thus, interactions among these states do not necessarily lead to rules that are efficient from the standpoint of the population as a whole").

[27] *See infra* Chapter 4.

[28] *See infra* Chapter 6.

the probative value that they have in *tending*[29] to demonstrate State practice with respect to the public purpose doctrine. The objective entails understanding the scope, content, and standard of the doctrine in customary international law. In doing so, it is legitimate to ask whether the public purpose doctrine articulated by customary international law differs from its conventional international law counterpart. How do customary international law's unique features affect the actual status of the public purpose doctrine, its content, and application? Does customary international law enrich the public purpose doctrine and help it bring into being the harmonization of investor/investment protection and regulatory sovereignty? Is it clear that the scope, content, and application of a public purpose doctrine as articulated in customary international law contributes to a fair interaction between capital-exporting and capital-importing countries in an environment of economic globalization? Finally, is customary international law a vehicle for a public purpose doctrine that focuses more on shared responsibility than on a winner-take-all dispute resolution approach?

C. DISCOVERING AND REVIVING THE PUBLIC PURPOSE DOCTRINE IN INTERNATIONAL INSTRUMENTS

International instruments impose limitations on the exercise of sovereignty. Treaties are structured, negotiated "sovereignty concessions" exchanged for perceived greater benefits arising from bilateral or multilateral agreements.[30] This traditional view of the relationship between international instruments and the plenary exercise of sovereignty is universally accepted. It is necessary, however, to observe that it is premised on a very orthodox Westphalian understanding of sovereignty, pursuant to which a sovereign may exercise its unbridled discretion, limited only by the physical boundaries of national territory, whereas sovereignty itself is understood as deeply related to territorial normative authority.[31] Although it is manifestly clear and somewhat obvious that international rules give rise to restrictions on the exercise of domestic regulatory autonomy or sovereignty, these very instruments (mostly treaties)

[29] We do not find that the applicable presumption should be one of prima facie conclusiveness as to enjoying customary international law status simply by meeting any of these criteria.

[30] Although "the conclusion of any Treaty by which a State undertakes to perform or refrain from performing a particular act" is not a complete abandonment of sovereignty, "any convention creating an obligation of this kind places a restriction upon the exercise of the sovereign rights of the State, in the sense that it requires them to be exercised in a certain way." S. S. Wimblendon (U.K. v. Japan), ¶ 35, P.C.I.J. (ser. A) No. 1 (August 17).

[31] *See supra* Chapter 1 note 33 and accompanying text.

also serve to vest States with "specific" or "particular" regulatory fiat that transforms a regulatory taking into an illegal fine imposed on a State merely for executing its obligations in furtherance of the greater public interest. It is in this context that the public purpose doctrine plays a dispositive role.

The extent to which existing international instruments appropriately restrict the domestic regulatory space of States while also allowing sovereigns to apply domestic regulations in ostensible derogation of international instruments, purportedly in the name of the common good, is governed by the public purpose doctrine. As shall be demonstrated, the rubric of *exceptions* and *reservations* to international instruments represents techniques that have been applied in efforts to strike this balance not only between a State's right to exercise its regulatory authority in the national/domestic realm and the expectations of foreign investors/investment, but also between national industries and the scope of domestic regulatory authority, including exceptions relating to the right to provide subsidies and to extend exceptions to taxation. Although the General Agreement on Tariffs and Trade (GATT), the North American Free Trade Agreement (NAFTA), and the Agreement on Technical Barriers to Trade (the TBT Agreement) certainly serve as valuable models illustrating resourceful approaches to these problems, as already suggested,[32] they are far from conclusive with respect to the development of a public purpose standard that contributes to uniformity because of its subjective substantive content.

The appearance of the public purpose doctrine in customary international law is accorded many names and asked to serve as a guiding principle in numerous contexts and disciplines, ranging from human rights,[33] permanent sovereignty over natural resources,[34] economic development,[35] harmonizing

[32] *See supra* Chapter 1.

[33] *E.g.*, Protocol to the Convention for the Protection of Human Rights and Fundamental Freedoms art. 1, March 20, 1952, Europ. T. S. No. 009 ("Every natural or legal person is entitled to the peaceful enjoyment of his possessions. No one shall be deprived of his possessions *except in the public interest* and subject to the conditions provided for by law and by the general principles of international law"; emphasis supplied; hereinafter Euro. Cony. Protocol 1). The entire Convention, as amended by Protocol 14, is *available at* http://www.echr.coe.int/documents/convention_eng.pdf

[34] *E.g.*, Permanent Sovereignty over Natural Resources, G.A. Res. 1803, U.N. GAOR, 17th Sess., Supp. No. 17, at 15, U.N. Doc. A/5217 (1962). ("Nationalization, expropriation or requisitioning shall be based on grounds or reasons of *public utility*, security or the national interest which are recognized as overriding purely individual or private interests, both domestic and foreign"; emphasis supplied; hereinafter G.A. Res. 1803).

[35] *E.g.*, ASEAN Comprehensive Investment Agreement, art. 14, February 26, 2009, *available at* http://www.boi.go.th/english/ASEAN/finalsign.pdf [hereinafter ACIA].

investment, and commercial law[36] to defining the domestic confines of a State's regulatory authority.[37] The public purpose doctrine's formal nomenclature and contextual references argue in favor of the development of a substantive principle governed by objective content or an altogether reevaluation of the doctrine that meaningfully diminishes its role as a controlling principle. The latter option is replete with challenges and troubling consequences.

D. THE MANY NAMES OF THE PUBLIC PURPOSE DOCTRINE: EXPLORING UNIFORMITY AND MULTIFARIOUS NOMENCLATURE

The initial challenge to discerning the actual existence of the public purpose doctrine within customary international law, let alone its content and scope, concerns fundamental nomenclature. "Public purpose," defined as a doctrine, does not find any space in international instruments. Despite this absence of any definition, the customary international law expression of the public purpose doctrine appears under many names. Some of the most notable and recurring names for the doctrine, as found in international instruments, are (i) *public purpose*,[38] (ii) *public interest*,[39] (iii) *public*

[36] E.g., GATT, *supra* Chapter 1 note 1, art. XX ¶ (a) ("Subject to the requirement that such measures are not applied in a manner which would constitute a means of arbitrary or unjustifiable discrimination between countries where the same conditions prevail, or a disguised restriction on international trade, nothing in this Agreement shall be construed to prevent the adoption or enforcement by any contracting party of measures ... necessary to protect public morals").

[37] E.g., Kelo v. City of New London, 545 U.S. 469, 480 (2005) ("The disposition of this case therefore turns on the question whether the City's development plan serves a 'public purpose.' Without exception, our cases have defined that concept broadly, reflecting our longstanding policy of deference to legislative judgments in this field").

[38] The literal "public purpose" term mostly appears in the context of an exception to a direct or indirect expropriation or nationalization, or of actions tantamount to an expropriation. *See, e.g.* U.N. GAOR, 62nd Sess., 121st plen. mtg. at 4, U.N. Doc. A/62/PV.121 (September 11, 2008); ACIA, *supra* note 35, art. 14 and annex 2; Future Government of Palestine, G.A. Res. 181 (II), U.N. Doc. A/RES/181(II) (November 29, 1947).

[39] The "public interest" nomenclature is the most recurring iteration of the public purpose doctrine in customary international law. *See, e.g.*, Euro. Cony. Protocol 1, *supra* note 33, art. 1; Org. for Econ. Cooperation & Dev. [OECD], The Multilateral Agreement on Investment: Draft Consolidated Text ¶¶ 56, 81, 143, DAFFE/MAI(98)7/REV1 (April 22, 1998), http://www1.oecd.org/daf/mai/pdf/ng/ng987r1e.pdf [hereinafter Draft MAI]; GATT, *supra* Chapter 1 note 1, art. X; General Agreement on Trade in Services arts. 3, 14, April 15, 1994, Marrakesh Agreement Establishing the World Trade Organization, Annex 1B, 33 I.L.M. 1167 (1994) [hereinafter GATS]; Agreement on Trade-Related Aspects of Intellectual Property Rights arts. 8, 63(d), April 15, 1994, Marrakesh Agreement Establishing the World Trade Organization, Annex 1C, 33 I.L.M. 1197 (1994) [hereinafter TRIPs]; Agreement on Government Procurement arts. 18–20, April 15, 1994, Marrakesh Agreement Establishing the

order,[40] (iv) *public utility*,[41] (v) *public morals*,[42] (vi) *common interest*,[43] (vii) *general or public welfare*,[44] (viii) *public need*,[45] (ix) *security* or *police powers*,[46] and (x) *permanent sovereignty over natural resources*.[47] This list is not exhaustive of terms that are used in lieu or otherwise equivalent to the

World Trade Organization, Annex 4, *available at* http://www.wto.org/english/docse/legal_e/gpr-94_e.pdf (last visited April 1, 2013) [hereinafter AGP]; World Trade Organization, Ministerial Declaration of 14 November 2001 ¶ 22, WT/MIN(01)/DEC/1, 41 I.L.M. 746 (2002) [hereinafter Doha Declaration]; United Nations Conference on Trade & Development, November 6–8, 2002, Geneva, Switz., *The Development Dimension of Foreign Direct Investment: Policies to Enhance the Role of FDI, in the National and International Context – Policy Issues to Consider* (Note by UNCTAD Secretariat) 1, 3, U.N. Doc. TD/B/COM.2/EM.12/2 (September 23, 2002) [hereinafter UNCTAD FDI Policy Note].

[40] *See, e.g.*, Protocol No. 4 to the Convention for the Protection of Human Rights and Fundamental Freedoms, securing certain rights and freedoms other than those already included in the Convention and in the first Protocol thereto: art. 2(3), September 16, 1963, Europ. T.S. No. 046 [hereinafter Euro. Cony. Protocol 4]; Protocol No. 7 to the Convention for the Protection of Human Rights and Fundamental Freedoms art. 1(2), November 22, 1984, Europ. T.S. No. 117 [hereinafter Euro. Cony. Protocol 7]; Treaty Establishing the European Economic Community arts. 36, 48, 56, 135, 25 March 1957, 298 U.N.T.S. 3. [hereinafter EEC]; ACIA, *supra* note 35, art. 17; American Convention, *supra* Introduction note 12; AGP, *supra* note 39, art. 23; GATS, *supra* note 39, art. 27; Report of the Economic & Social Council, *Alternative Approaches and Ways and Means Within the United Nations System for Improving the Effective Enjoyment of Human Rights and Fundamental Freedoms: Respect for the right of everyone to own property alone as well as in association with others and its contribution to the economic and social development of Member States*, October 27, 1988, U.N. Doc. A/43/739; GAOR, 43rd Sess. (1988) [hereinafter 43rd Sess. Report].

[41] *See, e.g.*, American Convention, *supra* Introduction note 12, art. 21; G.A. Res. 1803, *supra* note 34.

[42] *See, e.g.*, GATT, *supra* Chapter 1 note 1, art. XX; TRIPs, *supra* note 39, art. XVII.

[43] *See, e.g.*, Charter of Economic Rights & Duties of States preamble, G.A. Res. 3281, U.N. GAOR, 29th Sess., U.N. Doc. A/Res/29/3281 (1974) [hereinafter Charter of Economic Rights & Duties of States].

[44] *See, e.g.*, ACIA, *supra* note 35, annex II; 43rd Sess. Report, *supra* note 40.

[45] *See, e.g.*, African (Banjul) Charter on Human and People's Rights art. 14, June 27, 1981, 21 I.L.M. 58 (1982) (and entered into force October 21, 1986) [hereinafter African Charter]. Additionally, although domestic, the French *Declaration of the Rights of Man and Citizen*, decreed in 1789 and accepted by the King in 1789, merits citation as especially influential in this realm of public international law.

[46] *See, e.g.*, Euro. Cony. Protocol 7, *supra* note 40, art. 1(2); ACIA, *supra* note 35, art. 17 n.12, GATT, *supra* Chapter 1 note 1, art. XXI; GATS, *supra* note 39, art. XIV; TRIPs, *supra* note 39, art. 73; UNCTAD FDI Policy Note, *supra* note 39, at ¶ 45.

[47] The doctrine of permanent sovereignty over natural resources constitutes the most eloquent example of the public purpose doctrine amplifying the State's regulatory space at the expense of foreign investment. As will be explained in a section allocated to the permanent sovereignty over natural resources expression of the public purpose doctrine, this doctrinal expression of public purpose bolsters the need to reform the public purpose doctrine so that it may shed its historical legacy-driven elements in favor of a more balanced and inclusive framework that embraces the geopolitical consequences of economic globalization. It shall be asserted that the doctrine of permanent sovereignty over natural resources is but an application of the public

public purpose doctrine.[48] For purposes, however, of identifying and determining the scope, content, and standard of the public purpose doctrine as enunciated in customary international law, the nomenclature represented by these ten terms identified is sufficient. Moreover, the use of two or more of these terms in a single document is common.[49] Even where, however, multiple terms for the public purpose doctrine are used within a single international instrument, functional consistency is preserved, notwithstanding that greater rigor arising from uniformity is desired and proves to be ultimately necessary, as shall be more explicitly discussed.

The want of uniformity of nomenclature is a shortcoming endemic to the unique structural features of customary international law. It is also indicative of the taking for granted of the public purpose doctrine by ascribing to it the doctrinal status of a self-evident principle that rightly is left in the hands of the invoking State for scope and content. The lack of uniformity is also witness to the doctrine's fragmented content. Thus, the doctrine, in its different iterations, appears without being defined. It is applied without being analyzed. The appearance of a doctrine with different nomenclature within a single international instrument casts material uncertainty as to the doctrine's content and tends to bind the doctrine's scope to the specific subject matter contextualizing the term. This phenomenon regrettably leads to a fragmentation of the doctrine that is in turn accompanied by inevitably inconsistent constructions in its application.

A fragmented use of the doctrine within a single international instrument arising from varying nomenclature leads to normative problems attaching to the doctrine as pronounced in customary international law. In the context of these structural challenges, it is legitimate to inquire whether the iterations under different nomenclature of the public purpose doctrine are indeed references to *a* public purpose doctrine or different conceptual exceptions having a "public" common denominator but certainly not constituting a

purpose doctrine in institutional form and found to a specific subject matter category that was historically driven because of the process of decolonization. *See infra* Chapter 5.

For international instruments comprising customary international law evincing the permanent sovereignty over natural resources iteration of the public purpose doctrine, *see, e.g.*, G.A. Res. 1803, *supra* note 34; Permanent Sovereignty over Natural Resources, G.A. Res. 3171, U.N. GAOR, 28th Sess., Supp. No. 30, at 52, U.N. Doc. A/9030 (1973) [hereinafter G.A. Res. 3171]; Charter of Economic Rights & Duties of States preamble, *supra* note 43.

48 "Community interest," "social interest or welfare," and "common good," among others, also tend to appear.

49 *See, e.g.*, Euro. Conv. Protocol 4, *supra* note 40, art. 2(3) (referencing "public order"); Euro. Conv. Protocol 7, *supra* note 40, art. 1(2) (referencing "public order" and "national security"); American Convention, *supra* Introduction note 12, art. 21 (referencing "public utility"); and art. 22 ("public order"); ACIA, *supra* note 35, art. 14 (referencing "public purpose").

single public purpose doctrinal rubric. Are the various "public-based" exceptions found in international instruments independent grounds for expanding the regulatory sphere of States, or are they part of a single overarching principle? The answers to these queries appear to be in the affirmative.

A descriptive, content/normative, and practical analysis suggests that the somewhat distinct and fragmented terms rooted in conceptual and etymological formulations of what is *public* is suggestive of a single precept viewed through the shattered prism of customary international law's fractured and decentralized structure. The critical reading of texts helps.

E. EVIDENCE OF SCOPE AND SUBSTANCE OF THE PUBLIC PURPOSE DOCTRINE IN SELECT INTERNATIONAL INSTRUMENTS

1. *Identification, Scope, and Content of the Public Purpose Doctrine within International Instruments Concerning Transnational Trade and Investment: A Doctrine That Expands Sovereignty within Instruments That Limit State Authority*

The various iterations of the public purpose doctrine within customary international law share a very important common denominator. This common element bolsters support for the proposition that the various permutations of the public purpose doctrine all concern a simple principle, as here discussed. Despite forming part of instruments that, by their very nature, place constraints on signatory States as to regulatory sovereignty, the multiple manifestations of the public purpose doctrine have a diametrically contrary effect. Embedded in instruments that limit a State's domestic regulatory space, the public purpose doctrine in all of its manifestations has both the theoretical and practical consequence of indiscriminately broadening the regulatory authority of States. This salient feature argues compellingly in favor of the proposition that what has been identified as multiple iterations of a single doctrine are in fact so. Descriptive and contextual analyses only serve to further this understanding.

2. *Public Purpose in UN Conference on Trade and Development and World Trade Organization Instruments*

The tension between capital-exporting and capital-importing countries has contributed to the content and scope of the public purpose doctrine. Contextualizing this tension between developing and developed countries within the framework of efforts undertaken to fashion multilateral agreement on the international law of foreign investment, Sornarajah observes that:

> Several attempts have been made at bringing about a comprehensive code on foreign investment [citing to the Havana Charter of 1948 as the first attempt at crafting uniform foreign investment provisions that also entailed an international trade organization], but they have resulted in failure simply because of the ideological rifts and clashes of interests that attend this branch of international law. Most drafts have been made with the objective of providing as much protection as is possible for an investment. These have been rejected by capital-importing states.[50]

From a historical perspective, capital-importing countries have opposed prospective trade and investment agreements that seek to protect foreign investment, typically outbound from industrialized capital-exporting States, without at all subordinating the protection accorded to such investment/investors to concerns pertaining to human and animal health and life, national necessities, environmental concerns, and the financial institutional soundness of Host States.[51] Whereas capital-exporting countries steadfastly have maintained that the scope and substance of investment protection rules must be segregated from the traditionally domestic regulatory sphere of Host States, capital-importing countries view this aspiration as an unworkable proposition unduly detached from pragmatic realities.[52]

[50] M. Sornarajah, The International Law on Foreign Investment (Cambridge University Press, 3rd ed. 2010).

[51] The once pristine dichotomy between capital-exporting and capital-importing states itself is undergoing a historic transformation. A notable trend has emerged and continues to develop. Consonant with this new phenomenon, a third category of States has arisen that are neither strictly capital-exporting or capital-importing. Developed but not optimally industrialized nations such as Colombia, Brazil, India, Chile, South Korea, and, to some extent, even China, herald a new category of sovereignties. Economic development compels a reassessment of the relationship between these and other comparable States to international commercial law generally and particularly international investment law seeking to regulate contentions between foreign investment protection and a Host State's exercise of its regulatory authority. With the exception of Brazil, these States' evolving views on a relationship between the scope of domestic regulatory authority and protection to be accorded to foreign investment is to some extent contained in the more reasoned bilateral investment treaties that they most recently have executed as signatories.

[52] "Traditionally, the vested interests of states concluding BITs fell into two categories: those on the side of capital-exporting states, with an interest in adopting strong protections for foreign investors; and those on the side of capital-importing states, with an interest not only in attracting foreign investment but also in attempting to preserve host country sovereignty and authority to promote the public interest." Karen Halverson Cross, *Converging Trends in Investment Treaty Practice*, 38 N.C. J. Int'l L. & Com. Reg. 151, 154 (2012).

The processes of decolonization and economic globalization, together with the inclusion of human rights advocates and environmental activists into the discussion, have contributed to sharpening the debate concerning the extent to which investment treaties must be exclusively confined to investment protection. Despite the seductive appeal of this ongoing colloquy, this chapter does not seek to resolve the contention or articulate arguments in support of a proponent to the detriment of another. Instead, it focuses on the extent to which the public purpose doctrine, either by happenstance or design, has been called on to mitigate this friction if not to altogether eviscerate it. Therefore, international instruments concerning economic development, international investment law, and international trade law have served as battlegrounds where industrialized and developing States have debated the appropriate balance between investment protection and compliance with a State's obligation to exercise its regulatory authority. The malleable and evasive nature of the public purpose doctrine, which for the most part has been held to a subjective standard that virtually defies evidentiary challenge, has been sequestered by proponents of all sides. The net effect has favored those States that have benefited from the expansion of the domestic regulatory space. This asymmetry poses numerous risks to any investor protection.

3. *Public Purpose and the United Nations Conference on Trade and Development*

The United Nations Conference on Trade and Development (UNCTAD) on September 23, 2002, published the Commission on Investment, Technology and Related Financial Issues Note arising from its Sixth Session held earlier that year (January 21–25). The topic of that session and, therefore, of the Note, was framed as "An 'Expert Meeting' on the Development Dimension of FDI: Policies to Enhance the Role of FDI in Support of the Competitiveness of the Enterprise Sector and the Economic Performance of Host Countries, Taking into Account the Trade/Investment Interface, in the National and International Context."[53] The Commission sought to explore how best international investment agreements (IIAs) may help capital-importing countries (developing States and economies in transition) maximize their ability to attract foreign direct investments (FDI), as well as attain a thorough understanding of the limitations on domestic regulatory authority that IIAs impose on Host States. It is worth observing that the Committee understood its objective as helping developing countries. Consequently, it is to be expected that their efforts sought to preserve,

[53] UNCTAD FDI Policy Note, *supra* note 39, at 3.

if not altogether enhance, the regulatory space of developing countries despite constraints that IIAs likely impose. In this connection, understanding the terms of reference of the "Expert Meeting" is helpful:

> How can Host country policies encourage synergy between FDI and domestic enterprises to support the competitiveness of the latter in the national and international context?
>
> What measures can Home countries take to contribute to such outcome?
>
> How can the interests of Home and Host countries be balanced, taking into account the development policies and objectives of Host Governments as well their right to regulate in the public interest?
>
> How can safeguards be introduced to ensure that domestic enterprises are not adversely affected?[54]

Moreover, as part of an effort directed at assisting capital-importing countries and transition economies, the Commission also emphasized the difficulties that developing countries face in transitioning from "more interventionist policy approaches (at the point of FDI entry) to the regulation of markets [which] is difficult because of a lack of financial and human resources."[55]

The context and perspective of the Commission as represented in the UNCTAD Secretariat's Note is important to ascertain if indeed the public purpose doctrine is to be descriptively and contextually analyzed. The Committee's finding is indispensable to this task:

> In conclusion, while international rules obviously imply a measure of restriction on domestic regulatory autonomy, several techniques have been used to strike the right balance. The GATT, the Agreement on Technical Barriers to Trade (the TBT Agreement) and the GATS [General Agreement on Trade in

[54] *Id.* at 4 ¶ 8.

[55] *Id.* at 9 ¶ 21. Because of the challenges that this issue presents, the Committee encouraged consideration of the following questions:

(a) What host country government policies are particularly important for enhancing the ability of developing countries and economies in transition to *attract* and *benefit from* FDI in line with their development objectives?
(b) How do international agreements at the bilateral, regional and multilateral levels affect the ability of countries to use these policies?
(c) To what extent have various performance requirements help countries meet their development objectives?
(d) What "yellow light" [a category of host country operational measures – HCOMs – explicitly prohibited but not by multilateral agreements] have been particularly useful in this regard?
(e) How would developing countries benefit from making the use of such requirements more (or less) restrictive?

Id. at 6 ¶ 22.

> Services] all use different approaches and may provide useful reference models for any future rule-making in the area of investment. With regard to both regional and bilateral (international investment agreements), it is necessary to examine to what extent the right to regulate goes beyond "regulatory takings" and similar issues of investment protection to encompass the way other areas covered in the [international investment agreements] can be reconciled with the necessary preservation of policy space for development.[56]

Preservation of the domestic regulatory space of Host States is treated as a predicate to maximizing the effects that FDI can have on developing States. It is within the context of this policy position that the Secretariat's Note references the public purpose doctrine. It is of considerable importance to emphasize that the Note by the UNCTAD Secretariat does not purport to constitute a legal analysis, opinion, or position paper. Understandably, it does not engage in a sustained dissertation on the content, scope, or application of the public purpose doctrine. Instead, it merely references the term within the context of a policy perspective endeavoring to fashion techniques that will enhance the domestic regulatory authority of developing States with respect to foreign investments, notwithstanding the limitations imposed by BITs that are negotiated by only two nations, at an ad hoc basis, and that cannot be said to reflect a coherent approach arising from a broader community of nations.

The Secretariat's Note references the public purpose doctrine on six occasions.[57] All six references suggest that (i) "the right to regulate" is a central concern and (ii) public purpose is viewed as an exception that does not merit justification or explanation.

The Secretariat's Note's first mention of the public purpose doctrine references the Doha Ministerial Declaration.[58] The pronouncement is indicative of reliance on a doctrine to serve as an exception without a need to proffer any explanation. Again, the doctrine is accorded "self-evident" status:

> The Doha Ministerial Declaration, in the context of the relationship between trade and investment, stated in paragraph 22: "Any framework should reflect in a balanced manner the interests of Home and Host countries, and take due account of the development policies and objectives of the Host Governments, as well as their *right to regulate in the public interest*."[59]

The "right to regulate in the public interest" identifies "public interest" as the normative foundation for domestic regulation that may adversely affect "the

[56] *Id.* at 18 ¶ 48.
[57] *See Id.* at ¶¶ 31, 35, 39, 42, 45.
[58] *See infra* Chapter 2.G.
[59] UNCTAD FDI Policy Note, *supra* note 39, at 13 ¶ 31(emphasis added).

interests of Home [countries]." Stripped of any qualification, the term "public interest" is deemed to be sufficiently transparent and self-explanatory as to command freestanding status. The very grammatical construction also distinguishes the "right to regulate in the public interest" from (i) "development policies" and (ii) "objectives of Host Governments." It is the "public interest" component that purportedly both *limits* the "right to regulate" and also serves as that right's normative foundation. The paradox that the legacy public purpose doctrine presents when serving as a constraint on regulatory sovereignty is problematic.

Assuming that FDI triggers the issuance of new regulation in response both to pre- and post-entry FDI status within the context of a particular domestic industry sector, logic commands that, as a general proposition, such regulation would be narrow – that States would be doctrinally constrained in promulgating regulatory rubrics that may be adverse to FDI – particularly post-entry, when due process concerns are likely to arise. A narrow exercise of the right to regulate that touches or concerns FDI also comports with universally valued precepts of uniformity, transparency, and predictive value, which are central both to international trade and investment law. Yet, instead of serving as a temporary constraint on a sovereign's right to regulate post-entry FDI, iterations of the public purpose doctrine such as "public interest," as referenced in the Secretariat's Note, furthers a diametrically opposed interest that is expansive and not restrictive.

"Public interest," as referenced in the Secretariat's Note, through the prism of a plain and merely descriptive analysis refers to an inordinately broad category of "all things public." Contextually, within the writing at issue, "public interest" necessarily refers to an exception providing for what would be construed as legitimate encroachment on pre- and post-entry FDI arising from the "public" component to "public interest." The most comprehensive exegesis, however, commands reference to the public purpose doctrine as historically empowering a State to encroach on FDI at any juncture by dint of its regulatory authority so long as such regulation (i) concerned a public purpose, and (ii) the sovereign intended for the regulation to issue in furtherance of a public purpose. Under any analysis, premising the "right to regulate" on meeting a "public interest" standard so that the prejudicial effects of the regulation on FDI may be deemed to be legitimate and not actionable against a State is tantamount to providing Host States with an unbridled license to encroach on FDI. Regrettably, by virtue of mechanical boilerplate repetitions over time, "the right to regulate for a public purpose" superficially has been viewed as a *narrow* exercise of domestic regulatory fiat.

Because of the perception that any basis for encroachment on FDI would be "limited" by this "rule of law," the principles of transparency, uniformity, and predictive value were assumed in a sphere where nothing could be farther from the actual facts.[60] The friction between capital-exporting and capital-importing countries is only worsened by this application of the public purpose doctrine. The inevitable result shall continue to yield greater uncertainty and more transnational disputes. The lack of academic rigor, legacy weaknesses, and conflicting arbitral "decisional-law" touching on the public purpose doctrine all conspire to lessen the likelihood of maximizing the potential benefits of FDI for all concerned: developed, developing, and transitional economies.

The second reference to the public purpose doctrine in the Secretariat's Note is helpful to understanding the role that the doctrine plays in the effort to harmonize the tensions between Home and Host States. It also maximizes the potential gains of a robust FDI international culture. The text suggests that interpretive techniques, among others, may serve to secure rights for signatories to regulate the domestic economy where such regulation may adversely affect FDI. This effort to carve out regulatory rights in the context of international trade and investment law challenges is placed squarely on the shoulders of the public purpose doctrine. Significantly, despite reference to an emphasis on interpretive techniques, there is no suggestion that the foundational exception (i.e., *public purpose*) requires any such expansive treatment. Quite the contrary, the mere reference to the concept implies that doctrinal clarity already pervades the often-cited precept and is universally known:

> There are various ways to address the issue of the right to regulate. Some of these, with regard to both trade and investment agreements, are reviewed below. In all cases the ability of signatories to regulate the domestic economy is a governing concern. Insofar as this concept is restated in an agreement, for instance, in its preambular language – it also serves an interpretive function vis-à-vis the provisions of the agreement. Furthermore, whenever countries enter into standard-of-treatment obligations, such as fair and equitable

[60] As will be demonstrated *infra* Chapter 4, the debilities endemic to the legacy public purpose doctrine are multiplied and made worse where the public purpose doctrine appears as an exception in BITs negotiated only between two nations enjoying disparate marketing leverage, where the negotiations are pursuant to very idiosyncratic features unique to the relationship between the two States at issue. The resulting treaty embodies international principles and doctrines, such as the public purpose doctrine, but within the context of uniquely conceived, defined, and applied principles. The universe of BITs negotiated and conceived in this manner now represents more than 3,000 BITs that were independently negotiated, lack any centralized structure or organizing principle, and are both formally and substantively unrelated to each other. This configuration diminishes predictability, transparency, and uniformity. Perhaps the proliferation and negative consequences of this phenomenon may be averted were States to consent to executing multilateral agreements in the realm of international investment law. This lack of consensus, however, likely shall continue to spawn BITs and thus perpetuate this paradox.

> treatment, prohibition of arbitrary and discriminatory measures or most-favoured-nation treatment (MFN) and national treatment, various kinds of exceptions, reservations, derogations, waivers or transnational arrangements ensure that signatories retain the prerogative to apply non-conforming domestic regulations in certain areas. These can be general (e.g., for public order or national security), subject-specific (e.g., the so-called "cultural exception") or country-specific (e.g., as in the case of GATS schedules of commitments, with regard to commercial presence).[61]

Also noteworthy is the dichotomy between the characterization of "public order" as a *general exception* and the subjective standard governing the exception.

The UNCTAD Note restates the settled but untested principle of international law that Host States may discriminate against imports in favor of domestic products so long as that discrimination rests on a legitimate public purpose. According to UNCTAD, the GATT Article XX public purpose exceptions constitute legitimate grounds justifying foreign product discrimination by Host States.[62] Cloaked in its "public morals" iteration, Host country discrimination in favor of domestic commercial interests also extends to the regulation of services for presumably legitimate public claims. The Secretariat's Note suggests that exercise of its regulatory authority constitutes "the sovereign right of a country to regulate services for legitimate purposes," even though it also asserts that the GATT's "Article VI seeks to prevent the use of administrative decisions to disguise protectionist measures."[63]

[61] UNCTAD FDI Policy Note, *supra* note 38, at 13–14 ¶ 33.
[62] The Note on this issue in part provides:

> In the area of *trade*, the issue has been debated and litigated at length in the GATT/WTO system, where the dispute settlement process has been frequently used to police domestic regulatory measures that have an impact on trade. The main instrument for policing regulatory activities in the WTO comes from the 1947 GATT and is found in Article III's non-discrimination (national treatment) obligation as complemented by the exceptions contained in Article XX. *The general national treatment rule contained in Article III provides that internal taxes and regulations must not treat imports less favourably than domestic products. If a domestic regulatory measure is found to discriminate against imports, the regulating government may attempt to justify the discrimination by proving that it is necessary to achieve some legitimate purpose. Article XX of GATT defines these exceptions to include those necessary to protect public morals; to protect human, animal and plant life or health; and relating to the conservation of exhaustible resources. It should be noted that this list of policies that can justify measures otherwise considered in violation of national treatment is "closed" and thus provides limited scope for claiming an exception in many areas where countries may want to pursue regulatory action.*

Id. at 14 ¶ 35 (emphasis added).
[63] *Id.* at 15 ¶ 39.

The UNCTAD Note's concern for "protecting" the domestic regulatory space of Host States is explicit enough, but nowhere clearer than in its treatment of "the right to regulate" in the context of investment protection agreements. The committee sets forth an accurate narrative detailing the connection between issues relating to the right to regulate and regional and BIT language covering measures "tantamount" or "equivalent" to expropriation, as well as indirect and regulatory takings. The effects of "creeping expropriations," pursuant to which two or more legal regulatory acts carried out over a period of time have the effect of diminishing or substantially destroying the value of an investment, is deemed an actionable expropriation providing the Host State with the obligation to tender compensation for the consequences of its exercise of "legitimate" and arguably "obligatory" regulatory authority. The Secretariat's Note, however, somewhat implicitly suggests that the public purpose doctrine represents too narrow an exception for Host States, as this suggestion may appear to be when first considered:

> [BITs] *generally impose conditions on expropriations if it is to be considered lawful, by adopting some variation of the traditional rule of international law that a State may not expropriate the property of an alien except for public purpose, in a nondiscriminatory manner, in accordance with due process of law and upon payment of compensation.* Concerns have been expressed with regard to the impact that an expansive use of expropriation claims may have on sovereign governments' right to regulate.[64]

Although from a strict and literal perspective issues have been raised with respect to the expansive application of alleged breaches of direct or indirect nationalizations, expropriations, or actions tantamount to an expropriation,[65] the prevailing concern has focused more on attempting to address the need for transparent and predictive standards governing the law of expropriation in all of its incarnations to allay the fears of capital-exporting countries and thus maximize the benefits of FDI.[66] The view that somehow the efficiencies of

64 *Id.* at 16 ¶ 42 (emphasis added).

65 *See, e.g.*, Matthew C. Porterfield, *State Practice and the (Purported) Obligation under Customary International Law to Provide Compensation for Regulatory Expropriations*, 37 N.C. J. INT'L L. & COM. REG. 159, 165 (2011) ("The concept of indirect expropriation under investment agreements applies to a broad range of government actions, including not only regulatory measures but taxation as well."); Alberto R. Salazar V., Ph.D., *NAFTA Chapter 11, Regulatory Expropriation, and Domestic Counter-Advertising Law*, 27 ARIZ. J. INT'L & COMP. L. 31, 39 (2010) (citing *Metalclad as* an example of the how the "concept of regulatory expropriation, characterized by a focus on the *use* of property and the *expectations* of foreign investors, broadens the protection granted to the latter").

66 *See generally* Martinez-Fraga, *supra* note 34; *see also* Julie A. Maupin, *Transparency in International Investment Law: The Good, the Bad, and the Murky*, in TRANSPARENCY IN

international investment law were being compromised because of concerns pertaining to the expansive use of expropriation claims has not been chronicled as posing a material challenge to the law of international investment or to treaty-based arbitral proceedings premised on public international law.

The expansive scope of the public purpose doctrine under customary international law as memorialized in the UNCTAD Note also applies to "favourable tax treatment to investment by national companies without according the same treatment to investment by foreign companies," such as in Protocol No. 2 of the Indonesia-Switzerland BIT.[67] Therefore, the UNCTAD Note broadens and enriches the public purpose doctrine by according normative status to a State's economic development plight. Protocol No. 2 of the Indonesia-Switzerland BIT allowing for derogation from national treatment, in pertinent part provides:

> At the time of signing the Agreement concerning the Encouragement and the Reciprocal Protection of Investments concluded between the Swiss confederation and the Republic of Indonesia, the undersigned Plenipotentiaries have, in addition, agreed on the following provisions which shall be regarded as an integral part of the said Agreement:
>
> (2) In derogation of the national treatment provided for in article 4, paragraph 3, of the present agreement, the government of the Republic of Indonesia in view of the present stage of development of the Indonesian national economy reserves its position with regard to national treatment of Swiss investments in the territory of the Republic of Indonesia . . . :[68]

INTERNATIONAL LAW 14, n.81 (Andrea Bianchi & Anne Peters eds., 2013); Daniel Barstow Magraw Jr. & Niranjali Manel Amerasinghe, *Transparency and Public Participation in Investor-State Arbitration*, 15 ILSA J. INT'L & COMP. L. 337 (2009); Catherine A. Rogers, *Transparency in International Commercial Arbitration*, 54 U. KAN. L. REV. 1301 (2006); Statement by the OECD Investment Committee, Transparency and Third Party Participation in Investor-State Dispute Settlement Procedures, June 2005, *available at* http://dx.doi.org/10.1787/524613550768; Fulvio Fracassi, *Confidentiality and NAFTA Chapter 11 Arbitrations*, 2 CHI. J. INT'L L. 213 (2001).

67 UNCTAD FDI Policy Note, *supra* note 39, at 17 ¶ 45.

68 Agreement between the Swiss Confederation and the Republic of Indonesia Concerning the Reciprocal Protection of Investments, Switz. Indo., February, 6, 1974, http://investmentpolicyhub.unctad.org/Download/TreatyFile/1640.

> En signant la Convention concernant l'encouragement et la protection reciproque des investissements conclue entre le Gouvernement de la Confederation Suisse et le Gouvernement de la Republique Indonesienne, les plenipotentiaires soussignes sont en outre convenus des dispositions suivantes, qui font partie integrante de ladite Convention:
>
> (2) Par derogation au traitement national prevu a Particle 4, paragraphe 3, de la presente Convention, le Gouvernement de la Republique Indonesienne, vu le niveau de developpement actuel de Peconomie nationale indonesienne, reserve comme it suit sa position a Pegard du traitement national des investissements suisses sur le territoire de la Republique Indonesienne:

Both exceptions – (i) favorable tax treatment to investment by national companies to the detriment of investment by foreign companies and (ii) the abrogation of the national treatment standard on the ground of a State's economic development – materially contribute to amplifying the public purpose doctrine's scope and content, consonant with the Secretariat's Note where the public purpose doctrine is referenced. The abrogation of a national treatment standard in favor of a State's economic development and for tax purposes form part of customary international law as part of the public purpose doctrine, notwithstanding the sweeping reach and subjective standard accorded to the doctrine.

The UNCTAD Secretariat's Note explicitly references the public purpose doctrine. Any descriptive predicate for the identification of the doctrine in customary international law is amply met. This international instrument engrafts upon the doctrine the status of an exception that legitimizes a State's discriminatory use of its regulatory authority as to international investment, trade, or services so long as such regulation is in furtherance of a public purpose. The Secretariat's Note observes that a State's right to regulate is legitimate so long as it is in furtherance of a public purpose *notwithstanding* the effects that such regulation may have on foreign investment, trade, or services. Furthermore, the abrogation of the national treatment standard in favor of application of tax legislation favoring domestic interests over foreign trade or investment can be construed as the exercise of regulatory authority in furtherance of a public purpose and, therefore, constituting a legitimate act of sovereignty. Regulatory acts that arise from or are connected to a State's economic development policy have been identified as rising to the level of exceptions in several BITs and, therefore, arguably also form part of customary international law.

4. *UNCTAD World Investment Report 2012*

The UNCTAD World Investment Report 2012 heralds a "new generation" of investment policies that meaningfully broaden the regulatory space of income-importing countries with respect to FDI.[69] One construction of the 2012 Report leads to a seemingly paradoxical conclusion. Even though it acknowledges the ostensibly competing interests between the promotion and development of FDI through liberalization and constraining measures

[69] United Nations Conference on Trade & Development, World Investment Report 2012, U.N. Doc. UNCTAD/WIR/2012, U.N. Sales No. E.12.II.D.3 (2012) [hereinafter WIR 2012].The *UNCTAD World Investment Report 2012: Towards a New Generation of Investment Policies,* is also referred to as the *2012 Investment Report.*

pertaining to a Host State's regulatory imperatives that may take the form of protectionism, the UNCTAD Report represents a testament to an unmitigated broadening of the public purpose doctrine that finds no precedent. The drafters acknowledged:

> This new generation of investment policies has been in the making for some time, and is reflected in the dichotomy in policy directions over the last few years, with simultaneous moves to further liberalize investment regimes and promote foreign investment on the one hand, and to regulate investment *in pursuit of public policy objectives on the other.* It reflects the recognition that liberalization, if it is to generate sustainable development outcomes, has to be accompanied – if not preceded – *by the establishment of proper regulatory and institutional frameworks. The key policy change is to strike balance between regulation and openness.*[70]

What the drafters referred to as "the dichotomy in policy directions" permeates the UNCTAD Report.[71] The lack of clarity that hampers investment law and that arises from conflicting policy interests does violence to core principles of uniformity, transparency, and predictability. The absence of these basic tenets in turn fosters uncertainty and may explain in large measure the very stark decline of investment treaty making.

[70] *Id.* at 101 (from World Investment Report 2010 Epilogue; emphasis added).

[71] The tension between interests and expectations of capital-exporting states (foreign investor/investment) and the right to regulate as understood by Host States (mostly developing countries or transition economies) constitutes a recurring theme throughout the Report. By way of example, a key investment policy challenge is identified as the need "[t]o adjust the balance between the rights and obligations of states and investors, or making it more even." *Id.* at 103.

Harmonizing these competing interests is also noted in the Report as a condition precedent to negotiating sustainable development-friendly international investment agreements. The drafters observed:

> Ensuring an appropriate balance between protection commitments and regulatory space for development: IIAs [international investment agreements] protect foreign investment by committing host country governments to grant certain standards of treatment and protection to foreign investors; it is the very nature of an IIA's standards of protection, and the attendant stabilizing effect, to place limits on government regulatory freedom. . . . Countries can safeguard some policy space by carefully crafting the structure of IIAs, and by clarifying the scope and meaning of particularly vague treaty provisions such as the fair and equitable treatment standard and expropriation as well as by using specific flexibility mechanisms such as general or national security exceptions and reservations.

Id. at 136. Here, it is important to note that the treaty language that the drafters refer to as in need of further clarification for purposes of preserving party expectations concerns standards of treatment provided by the Host State to the foreign investor/investment. There is an equal and even greater need, however, to identify with specificity those principles, most notably the public purpose doctrine, that govern a State's exercise of sovereignty through its regulatory-making authority.

The decline in the momentum of traditional investment treaty making is undeniable. BITs and other types of international investment agreements (IIAs) reached maximum proliferation in 1995 and 1996, with notable spikes in 2001 and 2002.[72] In 2011, only forty-seven IIAs international investment agreements were signed (thirty-three BITs and fourteen other IIAs).[73] Equally significant is the decline of the economic significance of BITs. As of December 31, 2001, 3,164 international investment agreements were registered as in force. These included 2,833 BITs, and the remaining 331 were other types of IIAs.[74] The 2012 Report asserts that whereas "in quantitative terms, bilateral agreements still dominate international investment policy-making; however, in terms of economic significance, there has been a gradual shift towards regionalism."[75] The Trans-Pacific Partnership Agreement;[76] the 2012 Trilateral Investment Agreement between China, Japan, and the Republic of Korea;[77] and EEU measures arising from the EU Council's Directive to the EU Commission to Initiate Negotiations for a

[72] *Id.* at 84.

[73] *Id.*

[74] *Id.*

[75] *Id.*

[76] This agreement is in its twelfth round of negotiations and includes nine participating countries (Australia, Brunei Darussalam, Chile, Malaysia, New Zealand, Peru, Singapore, the United States, and Vietnam). Moreover, Canada and Mexico have been tendered formal invitations to participate in the negotiations. Japan has expressed interest in forming part of the effort. Should all twelve countries reach agreement, a free trade zone will be created comprising 35 percent of the global gross domestic product (GDP) and potentially replacing forty-seven IIAs in the form of eighteen BITs and twenty-nine other types of IIAs governing current international trade and investment relationships among these countries. *Id.* at 85.

[77] From an economic perspective, this agreement is comparable to the NAFTA. These three signatories account for one-fifth of the global GDP. The agreement accords foreign investment/investors with the panoply of protection standards common to most BITs and regional investment treaties, such as (i) promotion and protection of (Article 2); (ii) national treatment (Article 3); (iii) most-favored-nation treatment (Article 4), (iv) "fair and equitable treatment" and "full protection and security," which are defined as not requiring "treatment in addition to or beyond any reasonable and appropriate standard of treatment in accordance with generally accepted rules of international law" (Article 5); (v) prohibition of performance requirements (Article 7) and; (vi) expropriation and compensation (Article 11); thus, quite substantive regulatory space is carved out. Signatories reserve the right to implement measures that otherwise would violate provisions of the agreement, in the form of (i) security exceptions (Article 18), (ii) temporary safeguard measures (Article 19), (iii) prudential measures (Article 20), (iv) taxation (Article 21), and (v) environmental measures (Article 23). Moreover, Article 11 ("Expropriation and Compensation") virtually mirrors that of the NAFTA's Article 1110 paragraph 1(a)–(d) and, as with the NAFTA, provides for a "public purpose" exception. Also, similar to the NAFTA, measures "equivalent" to an expropriation or nationalization are recognized. The NAFTA speaks in terms of measures "tantamount" to a nationalization or expropriation. *See* Agreement among the Government of Japan, the Government of the Republic of Korea and the Government of the People's Republic of China for the Promotion, Facilitation and Protection of Investment, May 13, 2012, http://www.bilaterals.org/IMG/pdf/20120513001-3.pdf.

Free Trade Agreement with Canada, India, and Singapore are excellent examples. The material economic significance of such an agreement is highlighted by the financial strength of the member States, which comprise approximately 25 percent of the global GDP and 50 percent of global FDI.[78]

The UNCTAD Report advances two general propositions, among others, for the decline in traditional IIA treaty-making. First, it is asserted that the phenomenon may result from the "gradual shift towards regional treaty-making, where a single regional treaty takes the place of a multitude of bilateral pacts and where regional blocs (instead of their individual members) negotiate with third states."[79] Second, the Report cites IIAs as "becoming increasingly controversial and politically sensitive, primarily owing to the spread of IIA-based investor-state arbitrations."[80]

Both grounds in considerable measure are related to the shortcomings of the legacy public purpose doctrine. This proposition, however, is nowhere observed in the UNCTAD literature. Indeed, the Report is paradoxical because in identifying the flawed treaty management dichotomy between the capital-exporting countries and capital-importing countries, it not only overlooks problems related to the uncertainties arising from an ill-defined underlying public purpose doctrine, but it also actually argues in favor of an even more expansive legal construction of the doctrine based on the policy of "sustainable development."[81] In fact, the UNCTAD Report views an active regulatory course of conduct by States as favorable to FDI rather than as a source of concern for prospective investors from capital-exporting States.[82]

The trend toward regional or multilateral treaties in lieu of BITs is a testament to a global appetite for greater uniformity and certainty that would proscribe increasing and recurring frustration of expectations on the part of capital-exporting and capital-importing States. It is an untested assumption,

78 WIR 2012, *supra* note 69, at 85.

79 *Id.* at 84.

80 *Id.*

81 "Sustainable development" may be characterized as a "policy," but its practical application and theoretical underpinning suggest that, both doctrinally and conceptually, it is best treated as a principle. Standing as a "principle" instead of a "policy" best promotes uniformity and regulatory transparency. Moreover, policies are more properly associated with specific States and regimes in contrast with the delocalized and territorially detached nature of principle.

82 The 2012 UNCTAD Report views regulation as not only a State right, "but also a necessity. Without adequate regulatory framework, a country will not be attractive for foreign investors, because such investors seek clarity, stability, and predictability of investment conditions in the Host State." *Id.* at 109. In addition, the Report views an increased government role in investment policy as a plus that gives rise to "strategies [that] often contain elements of targeted investment promotion or restriction, increasing the importance of integrated and coherent development and investment policies." *Id.* at 100.

however, to posit that regional or multilateral agreements will eliminate the fundamental ills giving rise to these tensions where the scope of general or specific exceptions, most notably those based on public purpose, manifestly favor or empower Host States to infringe on foreign investments in ways that parties to the agreement could not have reasonably contemplated. Also, the success in achieving the objectives of international trade law do not necessarily imply that the goals incident to international investment law also are likely to be met. The NAFTA arguably stands as a faithful and representative example of the material disconnect that may characterize an IIA.[83]

The second ground identified as "a likely reason" for the decline of BIT making (e.g., increased controversy surrounding IIAs primarily resulting from treaty-based arbitrations that are expensive, time-consuming, politically polarizing, and often lacking predictive value while also yielding awards with pretensions of being universally executable but practically raising almost insurmountable enforcement challenges) constitutes a descriptive phenomenon and not a causal first principle. As with the proliferation of regional or multilateral international investment and trade agreements, general transparency and particular lucidity as to fundamental standards of care that attach to foreign investments/investors are predicates to fulfilling the expectations of treaty signatories and participants/beneficiaries. Policies pertaining to international investment or trade cannot be fashioned and implemented in the abstract. Such policies must heavily weigh a new global paradigm shift from *independence* to *interdependence* that most comprehensively and efficiently comports with an environment of economic globalization and a juridical historical juncture that has begun to understand orthodox conceptions of international law as unresponsive to shared global crises.[84] The shared

[83] The NAFTA's economic success is undisputed. *See, e.g.*, Jeffrey Turk, *Compensation for "Measures Tantamount to Expropriation" under NAFTA: What It Means and Why It Matters*, 1 INT'L L. & MGMT. REV. 41, 77 (2005) (stating "NAFTA is generally considered to be a great economic success"); David R. Haigh, Q.C., *Chapter 11 – Private Party vs. Governments, Investor-State Dispute Settlement: Frankenstein or Safety Valve?*, 26 CAN.-U.S. L.J. 115 (2000) ("Measured by the increase of trade and investment among the three North American economies, the NAFTA appears to have been an unparalleled success"); Daniel Griswold, *NAFTA at 10: An Economic and Foreign Policy Success*, FREE TRADE BULL. NO. 1 (December 2002), *available at* http://www.cato.org/publications/commentary/nafta-10-economic-foreign-policy-success (arguing that NAFTA "has spurred trade, investment, and integration between the United States and Mexico"); *see generally* OFFICE OF U.S. TRADE REP., EXEC. OFFICE OF THE PRESIDENT, *NAFTA: A Decade of Success* (July 2004), http://www.ustr.gov/about-us/press-office/fact-sheets/archives/2004/july/nafta-decade-success.

The NAFTA decisional law and textual analysis suggest that the lack of definition of special and general exceptions premised on the public purpose doctrine or any of its permutations cause considerable uncertainty and often spawn conflicting doctrinal analyses.

[84] *See supra* Chapter 2.B.

transnational problems facing the community of nations (environmental and climate challenges, poverty, institutionalized corruption, infant mortality, vertical and horizontal nuclear proliferation, and stark disparities globally in the distribution of natural resources, to name just a few) have contributed to the creation of a global consciousness of shared obligations and benefits.

The current IIA regimes, whether in the form of BITs or multilateral agreements, are conducive to a pattern of international dispute resolution that culminates in "all-or-nothing" arbitral awards, primarily with respect to direct or indirect expropriation or nationalizations, or averments *tantamount* to expropriation. Contemporary expectations of shared duties and benefits are inimical to orthodox doctrines providing for "zero-sum game" legal frameworks. The "increasingly controversial and politically sensitive" issues that the 2012 Report identifies as "primarily owing to the spread of IIA-based investor-state arbitrations" are not caused by the formal or substantive structure of BITs, but rather arise as a result of legacy orthodox legal concepts that obscure the boundaries between competing treaty interests and objectives, such as the public purpose doctrine. The ad hoc nature of treaty-based arbitration that gives rise to awards that do not and cannot constitute binding precedent and that reference protection standards common to most BITs as to nomenclature but not definition certainly does not help.

The 2012 Report explicitly and implicitly identifies the public purpose doctrine while adhering to the legacy practice it follows; the practice of assuming that public purpose in content, scope, and application is universally understood. The drafters amplified the doctrine's scope by linking it to policies of sustainable development.[85] It becomes necessary to inquire whether the

[85] Sustainable development or economic development policies are broadening the scope and enriching the content of the public purpose doctrine as part of what the UNCTAD World Investment Report 2012 identifies as "a new generation of investment policies." These international instruments may be viewed as part of an international customary law trend providing "economic development policies" with the status of a normative foundation that grants States a right to regulate that may have adverse consequences with respect to foreign economic interests. The following representative, and hardly exhaustive, list evinces this trend:

(i) The *2012 UN Guiding Principles on Business and Human Rights*. Although aspirational, the principles seek the implementation of the "Protect, Respect, and Remedy" rubric that was presented by UN Special Representative John Ruggie in 2006. These principles encourage the modification of international investment agreements to provide for a regulatory space allowing for the protection of human rights. They also call for business disclosure of the effects of their commercial activities on human rights to relevant stakeholders;

(ii) The *2012 Revision of the International Chamber of Commerce's Guidelines for International Investment* (1972). The 2012 revision promotes responsible investment that comports with the economic development of Host States and, in addition to underscoring the need for investors to obey municipal and international labor law, suggests that investors conduct environmental impact studies as a predicate to

legacy public purpose doctrine, broadened to include the principle of sustainable development primarily undertaken by capital-importing countries (presumably Host States), can reasonably limit the scope of sustainable development as a principle of both customary and conventional international law. Put differently, if sustainable development forms part of the public purpose doctrine and therefore is to constitute a universally recognized exception mostly favoring Host-State domestic regulatory activity, is the legacy public purpose doctrine in its current form sufficient to balance application of the exception without compromising Home-State expectations or Host-State obligation standards for the protection of foreign investment? Only by ascribing to sustainable development-based exceptions the status of a special public purpose category subject to qualifications will it be able to further the development objectives of most capital-importing countries without simply outright vesting them with a boundless license to regulate irrespective of treaty-based obligations to protect foreign investment/investors.

5. *The Public Purpose Doctrine and Sustainable Development*

The UNCTAD report identifies a shift in policy making, as a reaction to shared global crises, that in turn gives rise to four specific consequences bearing on the development and application of the public purpose doctrine. According to the argument, first, it is asserted that economic and market prices "[have] accentuated a longer-term shift in economic weight from developed countries to emerging markets."[86] This unsolicited protagonistic role has caused developing countries to have greater participation in global policy making.[87] It should be added that economic development in prospering nations, China in particular, also has contributed to providing developing nations and economies in transition with greater standing in addressing policies pertaining to current global issues.[88] Second, the global financial

investment development. The Guidelines emphasize the need for Home States to generate FDI that may contribute to the economic development of Host States;

(iii) The *Doha Mandate*, adopted at the *UNCTAD XIII Ministerial Conference 2012*. The Mandate synthesizes *UNCTAD*'s mission as primarily consisting in the (i) promotion of sustainable development and (ii) inclusive growth with respect to investment and enterprise; and

(iv) The 2012 *Rio Plus 20 Conference*, leading to the Outcome Document, "*The Future We Want.*" The *Future We Want* promotes investment in sustainable development frameworks that may contribute to reducing poverty.

86 WIR 2012, *supra* note 69, at 99.

87 *Id.*

88 China's sustained economic growth at an average rate of 10.41 percent during the past twenty years World Bank, World Development Indicators: GDP growth (annual%),

crisis has increased domestic government regulation in both capital-exporting and capital-importing States.[89] This increase in more vibrant and robust regulatory activity is a positive development, but, unlike the authors of the 2012 Report who opine that vibrant government intervention in promoting regulations leads to transparency and thereby encourages FDI, we believe that the foundation for this proposition remains unclear.[90] There is a paucity of empirical data supporting the proposition that a "developed" or "robust" regulatory rubric allays Home-State investor concerns. Only regulatory transparency can meet this concern. It is much more likely that objective and clearly delineated limits on the application of domestic regulation in ways that may affect international investment protection standards may best contribute to this objective. In this regard, a public purpose doctrine governed by objective criteria that serves both to regulate and to limit regulation in transparent ways that justify investor expectations would be an appropriate technique that may serve as an exception, as well as a principle conducive to legitimate Home- and Host-State expectations. It is the limits, not the complexity, of a regulatory framework that give rise to process legitimacy.

Third, the UNCTAD report observes that global challenges require global responses and solutions.[91] It is precisely this synergy between crisis and solution that best advocates for the development of transnational, and not just international, legal principles that serve more than mere regulation of relations between two specific States on a limited-agenda basis. Fourth, the primacy of social and environmental challenges has led "policy makers to reflect on an emerging new development paradigm that places inclusive and sustainable development goals on the same footing as economic growth and development objectives."[92]

As part of UNCTAD's effort to enhance the sustainable development dimension of international investment policies, thus placing sustainable development squarely within the purview of the public purpose doctrine, three self-contained frameworks that include meaningful references to the public purpose doctrine have been crafted: (i) core principles for investment

http://data.worldbank.org/indicator/NY.GDP.MKTP.KD.ZG?page=1 (last visited April 8, 2013). This growth has meaningfully contributed to the economies of resource-rich developing nations such as Brazil. Economic development in a global market and framework necessarily fosters greater interdependence that results in more meaningful policy standing for developing countries.

89 WIR 2012, *supra* note 69, at 99.

90 *See Id.* at 108.

91 The drafters specifically state that "the nature of the challenges, which no country can address in isolation, make better international coordination imperative." *Id.*, at 99.

92 *Id.*

policy making for substantial development,[93] (ii) national investment policy guidelines,[94] and (iii) Elements of International Investment Agreements: Policy Options.[95]

The core principles for investment policy making for sustainable development are particularly helpful to identifying the role of public purpose in customary international law, as well as in connection with the sustainable development public purpose category, because these central precepts are traceable to a substantial gamut of existing international law, international law instruments, treaties, and declarations.[96] Even though the public purpose doctrine arguably plays a role in all eleven Core Principles,[97] it is explicitly

[93] *Id.* at 107.
[94] *Id.* at 123.
[95] *Id.* at 143.
[96] The World Investment Report provides, in relevant part:

> Several other international instruments relate to individual Core Principles. They comprise, in particular, the Universal Declaration of Human Rights and the UN Guiding Principles on Business and Human Rights, the Convention on the Establishment of the Multilateral Investment Guarantee Agency, the World Bank Guidelines on the Treatment of Foreign Direct Investment, the UN Global Compact, the OECD Guidelines for Multinational Enterprises and the ILO Tripartite Declaration of Principles concerning Multinational Enterprises and Social Policy, and several WTO-related agreements, including the GATS, the TRIMs Agreement and the Agreement on Government Procurement.

Id. at 106.

[97] These Core Principles are (i) investment for sustainable development ("The overarching objective of investment policy making is to promote investment for inclusive growth and sustainable development"); (ii) policy coherence ("Investment policies should be grounded in a country's overall development strategy. All policies that impact on investment should be coherent and synergetic at both the national and international level"); (iii) public governance and institutions ("Investment policies should be developed involving all stakeholders, and embedded in an institutional framework based on the rule of law that adheres to high standards to public governance and ensures predictable, efficient and transparent procedures for investors"); (iv) dynamic policy making ("Investment policies should be regularly reviewed for effectiveness and relevance and adapted to changing development dynamics"); (v) balanced rights and obligations ("Investment policies should be bound in setting out rights and obligations of State's and investors in the interest of development for all"); (vi) right to regulate ("Each country has the sovereign right to establish entry and operational conditions for foreign investment, subject to international commitments, in the interest of the *public good* and to minimize potential negative effects"; emphasis added); (vii) openness to investment ("In line with each country's development strategy, investment policy should establish open, stable, and predictable entry conditions for investment"); (viii) investment protection and treatment ("Investment policies should provide adequate protection to established investors. The treatment of established investors should be nondiscriminatory"); (ix) investment promotion and facilitation ("Policies for investment promotion and facilitation should be aligned with sustainable development goals and designed to minimize the risk of harmful competition for investment"); (x) corporate governance responsibility ("Investment policies should promote and facilitate the adoption of a compliance with best international policies of corporate social

referred to in Principle Six (the right to regulate) in the form of "the interest of the public good."[98] According to the Notes on Principle Six, the right to regulate, from a sovereignty perspective, is expressed as generally being (i) an absolute right stemming from sovereignty; (ii) a necessary right encompassing legal, administrative frameworks and industry-specific rules; and (iii) a condition precedent without which prospective investors would be dissuaded from investing in Host States because of lack of regulatory framework development and transparency.[99] The operative presumption is that a developed regulatory rubric comports with a commitment to the rule of law.

The general *right to regulate* proposition is tempered by noting that its seemingly absolute fiat "can be subject to international obligations that countries undertake; with regard to the treatment of foreign investors this often takes place at the bilateral or regional level. International commitments thus reduce 'policy space'. *This principle advocates that countries maintain sufficient policy space to regulate for the public good.*"[100]

The UNCTAD Notes to Principle Six (the right to regulate) reference the public purpose doctrine, this time in the guise of "the public good," as the precept that allows countries to secure a regulatory space in the midst of treaty obligations, imposing upon its standards to protect foreign investment/investors and, presumably, Home-State investor expectations.

Two observations merit emphasis with respect to the Core Principles generally and Principle Six (the right to regulate) in particular. First, the public purpose doctrine ("the public good") is nowhere defined, despite its

responsibility and good corporate governance"); and (xi) international cooperation ("The international community should cooperate to address shared investment-for-development policy challenges, particularly in least developed countries. Collective efforts should also be made to avoid investment protectionism"). *Id.*

98 *Id.* at 106.

99 The Report describes this right as:

> [A]n expression of a country's sovereignty. Regulation includes both the general and legal and administrative framework of host countries as well as sector- or industry-specific rules. It also entails effective implementation of rules, including the enforcement of rights. Regulation is not only a State's right, but also a necessity. Without an adequate regulatory framework, a country will not be attractive for foreign investors, because such investors seek clarity, stability and predictability of investment conditions in the host country.

Id. at 109.

As has been observed, the "adequacy" of a regulatory framework that is material to foreign investment concerns clear and predictable limits to the regulatory structure at issue. A functional public purpose doctrine would foremost place such limits uniformly on a transnational basis.

100 *Id.* (emphasis added).

pivotal role.[101] Second, the doctrine is presented as a precept allowing countries (presumably mostly Host-State developing countries) to avail themselves of the public purpose doctrine in order to "maintain sufficient policy space" to exercise the right to regulate despite limitations imposed on that exercise of sovereignty by bilateral or regional investment treaties.[102] Viewed from this perspective, the concern would appear to be the likelihood of encroachment on the right to regulate arising from duly negotiated treaty-based obligations, thus transforming a right to regulate into an illicit action on behalf of the State, one warranting imposition of a fine in the form of liability in favor of foreign investors.

A different approach would be to understand the public purpose doctrine as a principle of international law that neither fosters nor proscribes regulatory activity, but rather harmonizes it as a reconciling principle pursuant to an objective criteria disengaged from a State's intent. Fashioning the doctrine in this manner most closely comports with more malleable principles of sovereignty, economic globalization, and paradigms of interdependence. It also is conceptually closer to a proportionality premised resolution of disputes that challenge the boundaries between investment protection and the right to regulate. Regrettably, the concept of public purpose, its standard, content, and practical application, all are assumed. The term "public good" within the meaning of Principle Six of the Core Principles is nowhere defined. "Self-evident status" again is accorded to the doctrine. Just as public purpose cannot be extended to all things that touch and concern the polity, the policy of sustainable development unrestricted by a public purpose construct would attach to all financial or economic endeavors undertaken by a developing nation under the welcoming banner of "economic development."

The National Investment Policy Guidelines[103] (NIPG) aspire to translate the Core Principles into practical and "implementation friendly" policy strategies that may help develop and frame rules and regulations amenable to sustainable development. Therefore, it is not surprising that the public

[101] Even though only Principle Six (right to regulate) explicitly references the public purpose doctrine expressed as the *public good*, the doctrine is central to most, if not to all, of the Core Principles. By way of example, Principle 5 (balance rights and obligations) seeking to harmonize the interests of Home and Host States, necessarily entails the workings of a public purpose doctrine. Similarly, Principle 8 (investment protection and treatment) proscribing discriminatory practice aimed at foreign investors and fostering "adequate protection to established investors" would lack all practical application were it to lack a public purpose doctrine organizing tenet providing for regulatory space while limiting the effects of regulatory pronouncements on the reasonable expectations of foreign investors.

[102] WIR 2012, *supra* note 69, at 109.

[103] *Id.* at 123.

purpose doctrine is both just as ephemeral and central to the NIPG as it is to the Core Principles. The public purpose doctrine is never defined or otherwise explained. Its presence, however, is obvious even in instances where neither the doctrine nor any of its iterations are explicitly referenced, as is the case with respect to Subsection 2.2–2.2.3.[104] The explicit reference to "not only the *right* but the *duty* to regulate,"[105] because of the conceptual relationship between the Core Principles and the NIPG, established that public purpose is the doctrinal governing principle with respect to this subsection. Within the framework of the UNCTAD Report, the right to regulate is subject to a legitimate and cognizable public purpose.[106] Accordingly, Subsection 2.2.3 of the NIPG must be viewed as directly and explicitly dependent on the public purpose doctrine.

Along the lines of Subsection 2.2.3, Subsection 2.2.7, "Investment Contract," also fails to identify the public purpose doctrine by any of its orthodox iterations. Instead, however, it references an abbreviated definition:

> States should honor their obligations deriving from investment contracts with investors, *unless they can invoke fundamental change of circumstances or other legitimate reasons in accordance with national and international law*.[107]

This subsection, however, is best understood when read together with Subsection 2.2.8, "Expropriation," which does in fact refers to the doctrine by explicit nomenclature. This subsection reads:

> When warranted for *legitimate public policy purposes*, expropriations or nationalizations should be undertaken in a non-discriminatory manner and conform to the principle of due process of law and compensation should be provided. Decisions should be open to recourse and reviews to avoid arbitrariness.[108]

Subsection 2.2.8 expands on the abbreviated "legitimate reasons" enunciated in Subsection 2.2.7 by linking *legitimate* with *public policy purposes*. This is a wholesale regurgitation of the public purpose doctrine in the context of expropriation or nationalization in the NIPG by repeating the general rule

[104] *Id.* at 124. Section 2 (Investment Regulation and Promotion), Subsection 2.2 (Treatment and Protection of Investors Treatment under the Rule of Law Core Standards of Treatment), Paragraph 2.2.3 reads: "While recognizing that countries have not only the *right* but the *duty* to regulate, regulatory changes should take into account the need to ensure stability and predictability of the investment climate." *Id.* (emphasis in original).

[105] *Id.* (emphasis in original).

[106] See *supra* note 100 and accompanying text.

[107] WIR 2012, *supra* note 69, at 125 (emphasis added).

[108] *Id.* (emphasis added).

of international law – providing that expropriations or nationalizations, whether direct, indirect, or comprising other actions tantamount to expropriation, are proscribed unless they are undertaken in furtherance of (i) a public purpose, (ii) in accordance with due process of law, (iii) on a nondiscriminatory basis, and (iv) for compensation.[109] It follows that the NIPG, although serving as compelling evidence that the public purpose doctrine is present and actually featured as a conceptually fundamental premise in international instruments and therefore by such measure part of customary international law, does not bring jurists, commentators, or practitioners any closer to a meaningfully functional understanding of the doctrine.

The third pillar of the sustainable development exception, here contextualized as falling within the ambit of the public purpose doctrine, is the Elements of International Investment Agreements: Policy Options ("International Policy Options")[110] Consonant with the Core Principles and the NIPG, the international policy guidelines seek to incorporate the Core Principles into the rule-making space of international law (i.e., the fashioning of treaties and other international agreements). As with the Core Principles and the NIPG, the public purpose doctrine occupies a special place that both identifies the central and determinative features of the legacy public purpose doctrine, as well as the nonworkable elements that are no longer responsive to the transnational needs of Home and Host States within a framework of interdependence and economic globalization. In fact, all three explicit references to the doctrine within the international policy guidelines merit detailed consideration.

Four explicit references to the public purpose doctrine are contained in the international policy options as viable alternatives that can be incorporated into international investment agreements. First, Section 2.3 ("Exclusions from the Scope") suggests the use of carve-out provisions in treaty language. Public purpose-related carve-outs are divided into (i) specific policy areas and (ii) specific sectors and industries.[111] Subsidies and grants, public procurement, and taxation are listed as examples of specific policy areas that can be excluded from treaty language.[112] Similarly, essential social services (such as health and education) and sensitive industries (cultural industries, fisheries, nuclear energy, defense, and natural resources) also are identified as counterpart-specific sectors and industries that can be removed from treaty jurisdiction.[113] The rationale underlying Section 2.3 quite lucidly identifies the basic

[109] *Cf.* NAFTA, *supra* Chapter 1 note 1, art. 1110.
[110] WIR 2012, *supra* note 69, at 143.
[111] *Id.* at 145.
[112] *Id.*
[113] *Id.*

mechanics between constraints placed on a Host State arising from a broader treaty scope as to the capital-importing country's policy space and possible liability to investor claims and the sustainable development (public purpose)-related Host State objectives.[114] The International Policy Options, however, are admittedly exploring ways in which international investment agreements may further sustainable development. Put differently, by preserving the substantive meaning of this objective, the International Policy Options seek to maximize the regulatory space in which the right to regulate is exercised while realistically considering the potential detrimental effect of such carve-outs on prospective FDI.[115]

The use of carve-out provisions in treaty language is a practical and transparent approach to preserving a State's regulatory space without frustrating the expectations of Home-State investors. A litany of carve-out provisions within a treaty may give rise to interpretive constructions that undermine the very goals that the carve-outs sought, in the first instance, to advance.[116] Section 4.5 on

[114] The drafter's annotations on the sustainable development implications of treaty carve-out or scope techniques aptly reflects a keen awareness of the dynamics between Home and Host States:

> The broader a treaty's scope, the wider its protective effect and its potential contribution to the attraction of foreign investment, however, a broad treaty also reduces a Host State's policy space and flexibility and ultimately heightens its exposure to investors' claims. States can tailor the scope of the agreement to meet the country's [sustainable development] agenda.

Id. Framing the relative concerns and expectations of Home and Host States in terms of claim exposure is not a comprehensive framing of the issue that the drafters themselves identified (i.e., rendering a Host State an attractive FDI target while preserving the Host State's right to regulate for a public purpose). A "claims analysis" approach, albeit practical, conceptually is too limited. *Id.*

[115] The International Policy Options' emphasis on Host States, without according due consideration to the expectations of foreign investors, may easily be gleaned from the annotations "By carving out specific policy areas and sectors/industries from treaty coverage, states preserve flexibility to implement national policies, such as industrial policies (e.g., to grant preferential treatment to domestic investors or to impose performance requirements), or to ensure access to essential/public services." *Id.*

[116] By way of example, Article 32 ("Supplementary Measures of Interpretation") of the Vienna Convention on the Law of Treaties provides for recourse "to supplementary means of interpretation." VCLT, *supra* Chapter 1 note 88, art. 32. The veritable chestnut *expressio unius est exclusio alterius* applied to an instrument that contains multiple carve-out provisions may lead to a restrictive construction of the public purpose doctrine under specific facts. For example, in applying the legal maxim *expressio unius est exclusio alterius*, the United States Supreme Court, citing Chancellor Kent, stated in *Tucker v. Alexandroff*:

> Treaties of every kind . . . are to receive a fair and liberal interpretation according to the intention of the contracting parties, and to be kept with the most scrupulous good faith. Their meaning is to be ascertained by the same rules of construction and course of reasoning which we apply to the interpretation of private contracts.

expropriation complies with the obligatory reference to public purpose as one of four conditions that must be met in the event of a dispossession of an investment by a Host State.[117] In fact, three of the four conditions – (i) public purpose, (ii) nondiscrimination, and (iii) due process – are expressed as "substantive conditions." Moreover, only by violating any of these three substantive conditions shall "full reparation" ensue.[118] Subsection 4.5.1 is particularly encouraging because it provides a foundational challenge to crafting a special public purpose category pertaining to sustainable development.[119] Despite the International Policy Options' developing country agenda focused on furthering sustainable development – in part through appropriate drafting of international investment agreements – the challenge of how best to balance the competing interests between FDI protection expectations and Home-State right to regulate concerns pertaining to critical sectors was clearly acknowledged.[120] The drafters sought to mitigate prospective liability against Host States arising from this issue by relying on drafting techniques rather than seeking to modify existing principles of international law:

183 U.S. 424, 437 (1902); *see also* Lozano v. Alvarez, 697 F.3d 41, 50 (2d Cir. 2012) ("General rules of statutory construction may be brought to bear on difficult or ambiguous passages, but we also look beyond the written words to the history of the treaty, the negotiations, and the practical construction adopted by the signatory parties in determining the meaning of a treaty provision"); Coplin v. United States, 6 Cl. Ct. 115, 127 (1984) ("[T]he enumeration of certain powers with respect to a particular subject matter is a negation of all other analogous powers with respect to the same subject matter . . .. The rule is curtly stated in the familiar legal maxim, *expressio unius est exclusio alterius*"; citing Tucker v. Alexandroff, 183 U.S. 424, 436 (1902)).

117 WIR 2012, *supra* note 69, at 148.

118 *Id.*

119 Subsection 4.5.1 reads:

> Limit protection in case of indirect expropriation (regulatory taking) by
> - establishing criteria that need to be met for indirect expropriation to be found,
> - defining in general terms what measures do not constitute indirect expropriation (non-discriminatory good faith regulations relating to public health and safety, protection of the environment, etc.),
> - clarifying that certain specific measures do not constitute an indirect expropriation (e.g., compulsory licensing in compliance with WTO rules).

Id.

120 The annotations to Section 4.5 ("Expropriation") of the International Policy Options provide, in relevant part:

> HA provisions typically cover "indirect" expropriation, which refers to regulatory takings, creeping expropriation and acts "tantamount to" or "equivalent to" expropriation. Such provisions have been used to challenge general regulations with an alleged negative effect on the value of an investment. This raises the question of the proper borderline between expropriation and legitimate public policymaking (e.g., environmental, social or health regulations).

Id.

> To avoid undue constraints on a State's prerogative to regulate in the *public interest*, an IIA may set out general criteria for State acts that may (or may not) be considered an indirect expropriation. While this does not exclude viability risks altogether, it allows for better balancing of investor and State interests.[121]

Treaty-drafting techniques may contribute to furthering process legitimacy and party expectation concerns, but they will not eviscerate the detrimental consequences stemming from a public purpose doctrine that adheres to a subjective standard and that is unduly expansive as to content. In addition, the balancing of interests between capital-exporting and capital-importing countries in the realm of international investment law should not be framed in terms of what may be necessary from the perspective of Host-State efforts "[to] exclude liability [and] risks altogether."[122] Instead, the objective should be to use or develop existing principles so that obligations running in favor of foreign investment protection may be duly balanced as to the exercise of domestic regulatory authority, all within a framework of interdependence and shared responsibility. Interdependence and shared responsibility, in turn, bespeak the need to re-examine the application of proportionality and to put an end to "winner-take-all" resolutions.

The third reference to public purpose within the International Policy Options is in Section 5, entitled: "Public Policy Exceptions."[123] In the same spirit as Section 4.5, which encourages the drafting of general criteria in order to identify indirect expropriations arising from regulatory fiat, Section 5 emphasizes the use of drafting techniques, both to "broaden" and to "limit" public purpose-based exceptions.[124]

The scope of the suggested public purpose exceptions, however, is problematic because it suffers from being overbroad and conceptually indistinguishable from "limiting" the public purpose doctrine as pertaining "only" to all things public. Even though Subsection 5.1.3 purports to be a provision that encourages limiting the exception, the suggested limitation is fundamentally boundless. It provides:

> 5.1.3 Limit the exception by specifying:
>
> – that the exception only relates to certain types of measures, e.g., those relating to trafficking in arms or nuclear nonproliferation; or taken in pursuance of State's obligations under the UN Charter for the Maintenance of International Peace and Security;

[121] *Id.* (emphasis added).
[122] *Id.*
[123] *Id.* at 151.
[124] *Id.*

– that it only applies in times of war or armed conflict or in emergency in international relations.[125]

Certainly, categorical specificity serves as a meaningful limitation on scope. Further qualification, as suggested, still remains a necessity. A general category can only function properly to the extent that additional specifications in the form of subcategories have a narrowing effect akin to concentric circles, such that very specific acts or omissions would trigger application of the exception. Section Five's objective is to broaden the regulatory space of Host States. Subsection 5.1.2, for example, encourages "[b]roaden[ing] the exception by clarifying that national security may encompass economic security."[126]

The expansive and all-encompassing definition of public purpose asserted in Section Five simply cannot be cured by enumerating a rosary of categories, as Subsection 5.1.4 suggests. That subsection invites IIA negotiators and drafters "[to]include exceptions for domestic regulatory measures that aim to pursue legitimate policy objectives" such as those aiming to:

- protect human rights,
- protect human health,
- preserve the environment (e.g., biodiversity, climate change),
- protect public morals or maintain public order,
- preserve cultural and/or linguistic diversity,
- ensure compliance with laws and regulations that are not inconsistent with the treaty,
- allow for potential measures (e.g., to preserve the integrity and stability of the financial system),
- allow for broader safeguards, including on development grounds (to address Host States' trade, financial and developmental needs),
- prevent tax evasion,
- protect natural resources of artistic, historic, or archeological value (or "cultural heritage").[127]

All of the suggested public purpose categories of exceptions asserted in Subsection 5.1.4 merely invite tautological reasoning. The protection of public morals or maintenance of public order is illustrative in this regard. Conceptually, virtually any State action or omission may reasonably fall within this category. As a matter of evidentiary proof, the all-encompassing scope of these two categories suggests that any particular act allegedly falling

[125] *Id.*
[126] *Id.*
[127] *Id.*

within their respective purviews would be asserted as part of a self-judging standard that would be difficult, if not altogether impossible, to challenge.

As to Section Five, "Public Policy Exceptions," the UNCTAD Report's drafters specifically contemplated amplifying Host States' regulatory space by suggesting that general exceptions be crafted as self-judging (i.e., pursuant to the subjective intent of the invoking State).[128] The UNCTAD Report's unvarnished admission that a self-judging standard is conducive to (i) reducing investor confidence and (ii) enhancing the likelihood the "possibilities for abuse"[129] (presumably on the part of Host States against the interests of foreign investors) quite starkly identifies the very problem that needs to be averted pursuant to the adaptation and adoption of a functional public purpose doctrine.

Vesting States with functionally limitless discretion under the banner of the "right to regulate" in furtherance of a public purpose represents the very conceptual deficit of the legacy public purpose doctrine that needs to be modified. In addition to the obvious deterrents to FDI endemic to such an approach, enhancing the likelihood of abuse and corruption undoubtedly shall continue to contribute to a crisis in process legitimacy at every critical juncture of international investment law.[130] A self-judging standard for public purpose is inimical to the international appetite for greater transparency and objective criteria concerning issues pertaining to international trade and investment law.[131] The self-judging criteria not only would generate a greater number of expensive and politically sensitive international disputes, primarily in the form of treaty-based arbitrations, but would also contribute to the

[128] The annotations to Section Five, Public Policy Exceptions, State:

> A number of features determine how easy or difficult it is for a State to use an exception. *To avoid review of the relevant measure by court or a tribunal, the general exception can be made self-judging (i.e., the necessity/appropriateness of the measure is judged only by the invoking State itself)*. This approach gives a wide margin of discretion to states, *reduces legal certainty for investors and potentially opens possibilities for abuse*. In contrast, exceptions designed as not self-judging imply that in case of a dispute, a court or tribunal will be able to determine whether the measure in question is allowed by the exception.

Id. (emphasis added).

[129] *Id.*

[130] "Corruption within procurement systems has been prevalent throughout the world and is not limited to developing countries." Anne Janet DeAses, *Developing Countries: Increasing Transparency and Other Methods of Eliminating Corruption in the Public Procurement Process*, 34 PUB. CONT. L.J. 553, 554 (2005). Efforts to curb such corruption have include the U.N. *Convention against Corruption*, the *Inter-American Convention against Corruption* and the OECD's *Convention on Combating Bribery of Foreign Officials in International Business Transactions (Anti-Bribery Convention)*. *Id.* at 561–68.

[131] *See supra* Chapter 1 note 123 and accompanying text.

development of doctrinally inconsistent arbitral "decisional law."[132] The legacy public purpose doctrine founded on a subjective standard cannot help but contribute to a body of persuasive precedent in the form of arbitral awards that lack uniformity, predictive value, and transparency of standard in seeking to strike the appropriate mean between an obligation in favor of protecting FDI and the right (actually duty) to regulate.

Finally, Section 6.2 is the fourth provision in the International Policy Options that most directly concerns or explicitly references the public purpose doctrine. This section also relies on specific treaty drafting rather than the development of appropriate legal precepts as a methodology for limiting the exposure of Host States to arbitral claims.[133] The emphasis on treaty negotiation and drafting suggested in Subsection 6.2.4 suffers from the identical shortcomings that also attach to the NIPG concerning the extent to which treaty drafting techniques may correct what is fundamentally a doctrinal and conceptual legal issue. Also, as with the NIPG, this suggestion gives rise to a new set of concerns spawned by the application of these very same treaty-drafting methodologies.[134] The strictures of Subsection 6.2.4 of the International Policy Options calling for the proliferation of carve-out provisions in treaties so as to limit the subject matter of international arbitration jurisdiction stands in considerable contrast with the annotations to Section 6.2 that generally identify the nature of the issues that most commonly give rise to treaty-based arbitral disputes. Embedded in the actual annotations are the very grounds that explain why treaty-drafting techniques may, at most, only serve to mitigate minimally challenges to abuse of regulatory authority in the context of FDI protection. The most relevant part of the annotation on this issue reads:

> As the number of ISDS [investor-state dispute settlement] cases increases, questions have arisen with regard to the effectiveness of the SD implications of ISDS. Many ISDS procedures are very expensive and often take several years to resolve. *ISDS cases increasingly challenge domestic regulatory*

[132] *See, e.g., supra* Chapter 1.H.

[133] Subsection 6.2.4 provides:

> Limit states' exposure to ISDS [investor-State dispute settlement], e.g.:
> - Clarify that certain treaty provisions and/or sensitive areas are excluded from ISDS, e.g., national security issues, including incoming investments; measures to protect the environment, health and human rights; prudential measures; measures relating to transfer of funds (or respective HA provisions); tax measures that do not amount to expropriation; HA provisions on transparency;
> - Specify only those issues/provisions to which ISDS should apply (e.g., only to the expropriation provision).

WIR 2012, *supra* note 69, at 152.

[134] See *supra* at Chapter 2.E(4).

> *measures implemented for public policy objectives*. Almost all ISDS cases lead to the breakdown of the relationship between the investor and the Host State. Due to the lack of a single, unified mechanism, different tribunals have issued divergent interpretations of similarly worded treaty provisions, resulting in contradictory outcomes of cases involving identical/similar facts and/or treaty language. Many ISDS proceedings are conducted confidentially, which has raised concerns when tribunals address matters of public policy.[135]

The annotation plainly emphasizes challenges to domestic regulatory measures as an important cause of disputes and the eventual collapse of relationships between investors and Host States. Quite remarkably, it very aptly draws a connection between the regulatory challenges and "contradictory outcomes"[136] generated by treaty-based arbitral tribunals. It also observes that "similarly worded treaty provisions"[137] lead to contradictory results. Accordingly, the fundamental problem is not one of formal uniformity (i.e., a common nomenclature) but rather a conceptual disparity pertaining to the actual scope and content of the principles at issue. The fundamental investor protection standards are uniform as to form (i.e., nomenclature but not substance). The content is typically the subject matter of negotiations under negotiating circumstances that rarely generate written evidence of "intent." Regrettably, BIT negotiations evolve from a practice based on "model" (euphemism for "form") treaties that scarcely were submitted to rigorous academic analysis. Even cornerstone terms such as *international minimum standard* (IMS) remain less than static as to content and thus in negotiating scenarios. The suggested drafting techniques asserted in Subsection 6.2.4, which detail little more than engaging in an exhaustive recitation of subject matters, is hardly adequate to address this problem. The issue is fundamentally of a normative and doctrinal nature.

6. *The Public Purpose Doctrine and Lessons from UNCTAD*

Both the UNCTAD Secretariat's Note Concerning the Development Dimension of Foreign Direct Investment: Policies to Enhance the Role of FDI in the National and International Context, as well as the 2012 World Investment Report explicitly and implicitly reference the public purpose doctrine. They contribute to the universe of evidence in the form of international instruments establishing that the public purpose doctrine constitutes part of customary international law. The UNCTAD pronouncements identify

[135] WIR 2012, *supra* note 69, at 152.
[136] *Id.*
[137] *Id.*

the public purpose doctrine as central to what is referred to as the right to regulate for the public interest (also expressed as a duty)[138] and as one of four principles that render an expropriation legal.

Even though the UNCTAD instruments identify an expansive domestic regulatory space harmful to FDI, the public purpose doctrine is used as an exception justifying a practically unbridled regulatory fiat on the part of Host States. Sustainable development, as contained in the UNCTAD documents, can be construed as a special public purpose category. Regrettably, sustainable development is, to the extent that it is "defined" at all, explained as encompassing practically all aspects of economics and finance that may reasonably be related to a State's *subjective* development need. Put simply, this special public purpose category is so broad that it cannot help but displace any tempered and harmonious relation between a State's obligation to protect foreign investments and its qualified right to regulate.

As expressed in the UNCTAD international instruments, the public purpose doctrine is contemplated as a self-judging category the appropriate application of which can only be determined by the invoking State, which is generally a Host State developing country or economy in transition. Substantial development (i.e., the public purpose doctrine) is accorded broad content and a subjective standard as to both content and application, even though the UNCTAD views that the amplification of the regulatory space through this methodology is conducive to protracted, expensive, and politically sensitive treaty-based arbitration disputes and that it also often leads to political corruption.

Although the UNCTAD concedes uncertainty and that international disputes are caused to proliferate because of conflicting constructions by tribunals of like or similar treaty (presumably protection standards) provisions and that these contentions in turn discourage FDI, the problem is not framed as a legal issue pursuant to which doctrinal and conceptual developments are warranted, but rather as a subject to cure through application of treaty-drafting techniques. The analysis is problematic. This lack of appreciation for the relationship between the need for doctrinal and conceptual development and a proposed solution in the form of treaty drafting and editing techniques is emblematic of the deeper crisis that the legacy public purpose doctrine in considerable measure has caused. The mechanical recitation of public purpose, in all of its incarnations, has created a culture of acceptance and

[138] Peter D. Szigeti, *Territorial Bias in International Law: Attribution in State and Corporate Responsibility*, 19 J. TRANSNAT'L L. & POL'Y 311, 332 (2010) (arguing that "the duty to regulate others' acts is inherent in sovereignty, indeed in all political power").

presumption that the meaning of public purpose is understood by all and in the same way. This fallacy in turn has led to the frustration of party expectations in the field of international investment law and caused capital-exporting States to question the efficacy of international arbitral tribunals that generate conflicting "decisional law" because of their adherence to an untested assumption configured by broad content and a subjective (self-judging) standard.

Although the UNCTAD pronouncements specify a type of public purpose doctrine believed to be required for the establishment of norms that presumably are to govern the relationship between FDI and Host States within a framework of substantial development, the effort appears to be too partial in favor of Host States and prescribes drafting techniques as a solution to a doctrinal and conceptual problem. The remedy does not fit the ill.

F. WHAT DOES IT ALL MEAN?

The Core Principles, NIGP, and the International Policy Options all purport to instruct States on domestic and international rule making. They thus must be accepted as probative evidence indicative of State practice for purposes of determining whether the public purpose doctrine, as presented in the various UNCTAD pronouncements, constitutes part of customary international law. Such an affirmative finding also entails acceptance of sustainable development as the broadest economics-based expression of the public purpose doctrine. The public purpose doctrine, embracing this principle of sustainable development of recent vintage, has started to find a space in BITs.

This new development certainly emphasizes the importance of the public purpose doctrine in both conventional and customary international law, but it also compounds the challenges endemic to a subjective standard and an arguably boundless realm of application. Engrafting a sustainable development content onto the public purpose doctrine, as is plainly established from the very embryonic development of this phenomenon in BITs, merely has the practical – and, at times, intentional – effect of transforming the *right to regulate* into an *absolute right to regulate irrespective of obligations to foreign investments/investors, so long as such regulation is reasonably related to a State's sustainable development*. Hence, the scope of the right to regulate in furtherance of sustainable development also may be rephrased: a State's right to regulate may infringe upon foreign investments/investors where such regulation relates to a financial or economic concern of the Host country. Although public purpose in the form of sustainable development is laudable, a sustainable development expression of the public purpose doctrine should not be used as a precept adopted by a developing State in order to cure what it perceives to be asymmetries between its obligation to protect foreign investments/investors and the right to regulate.

1. *The South African Development Community Model Bilateral Treaty Template*

The insertion of the sustainable development iteration of the public purpose doctrine into BITs arguably may have as much to do with correcting the perceived asymmetry between Home and Host States, as it does with technically providing for a special category public purpose exception. The South African Development Community (SADC) Model Bilateral Investment Treaty Template provides further evidence of the role of the public purpose doctrine in furthering sustainable development in BITs,[139] as well as of the use of this expression of the doctrine as a means to correct perceived inequitable asymmetries between capital-exporting and capital-importing States.[140] This approach to the public purpose doctrine and to BITs generally may have the negative collateral effect of placing broad economic burdens on investors who may be asked to subsidize, by way of relinquishing rights, Host-State domestic policies. The subsidization is a discernible trend that will require detailed analysis.

The SADC Model BIT Template encompasses eight sections[141] that most eloquently establish how the sustainable development expression of the public purpose doctrine is used to (i) correct perceived asymmetries between States, (ii) amplify the domestic regulatory space of Home States, (iii) reduce reasonable investor protection obligations on the part of Host States, and (iv) help shift the economic burden of Host States to foreign investors/investments.

The SADC Model BIT's anatomy contains eight specific references to the public purpose doctrine. Each of these references, however, help establish that the doctrine is being used to do more than just secure a reasonable space for the domestic exercise of regulatory authority by Host States. Each of these references commands close scrutiny.

First, the very preamble of the SADC Model BIT bespeaks an effort committed to interests of Host States, one that does not fully articulate

[139] The expression of the fundamental iterations of the public purpose doctrine in BITs is discussed *infra* at Chapter 4.

[140] South African Development Community, *SADC Model Bilateral Investment Treaty Template with Commentary*, July 2012, *available at* http://www.iisd.org/itn/wp-content/uploads/2012/10/sadc-model-bit-template-final.pdf [hereinafter SADC Model BIT Template].

[141] Such references appear in Articles 1, 6, 13, 20, 22, and 25, as well as in the preamble. *Id.*

countervailing Home-State concerns. Under the heading "Reaffirming," the Preamble in pertinent part reads:

> **Reaffirming** the right of the State Parties to regulate and to introduce new measures relating to investments in their territories in order to meet national policy objectives, and – taking into account any asymmetries with respect to the measures in place – the particular need of developing countries to exercise this right.[142]

The purported reaffirmation itself is less than clear because there is no evidence from which to infer or otherwise conclude that there existed any "asymmetries with respect to the measures in place," let alone specificity as to both "asymmetries" and "measures." Thus, the preamble purports to reaffirm a policy that is not at all identified with a similarly generic reference to a measure, presumably within the context of a general need pervading all "developing countries" (herein referred to as "developing countries or developing states") with respect to the exercise of a right. This reaffirmation in the SADC Model BIT calls into question the very propriety of the treaty's nomenclature itself. because it is far more than an *investment* treaty and purports to have *bilateral* rights. The reaffirmation only speaks to "developing countries" and references "national policy objectives" within the context of Host States.

The Commentary to the Preamble corroborates a reading of the Preamble as referencing a framework that goes beyond attracting greater investment and according such FDI additional levels of juridical protection so as to render the effort appetizing to capital-exporting States. Specifically, the Commentary asserts that a preamble to a bilateral investment treaty should be sufficiently broad so as to avert the immediate conclusion that presumptions favoring investor protection mostly or exclusively underlie a BIT. The most relevant language in this connection reads:

> In these circumstances [where an arbitral tribunal seeks interpretive help by consulting the preamble of a BIT], there have been several instances where arbitral tribunals have examined a preamble of a given treaty and found only references to the promotion of investment and the provision of investor rights under the treaty. As a result, the preamble has been held to establish a presumption that the sole purpose of the treaty is the protection of the investor in order, presumably, to attract higher levels of investment. This has led to several instances where arbitrators have specifically held that this creates a presumption in favour of broader over narrower rights for the investor, fewer and more limited rights for government regulatory activity in relation to an investment, and an overall presumption of investor-friendly interpretations.

[142] *Id.* at 5.

Although there are several arbitrations that have rejected this approach and it has been the subject of much academic and other professional criticism, it continues to be used in some instances. This includes in decisions made as recently as in 2010 and 2011. As a result, the preamble set out above is crafted to:

Reflect development goals of SADC Member States, both in general terms and specifically in relation to FDI.

Be balanced, as between development objectives and investor interests, so as to preclude unintended expansive interpretation of substantive provisions in favour of investors on the basis of the intent to protect investors expressed in the preamble, as seen in several arbitrations.

Be focused on key issues and not become a listing of all of the issues reflected in the final text.

The paragraph on the right to regulate and the recognition of asymmetry issues, with modification for the broader subject matter here, is drawn from the World Trade Organization's (WTO) General Agreement on Trade in Services (GATS), which of course has all developed countries as State Parties. This should enhance its acceptability in a north-south negotiating context. At least in some measure, asymmetry is part of the policy mix for developing states' development policy building. This preamble recognizes such asymmetries as part of this mix for international investment law purposes, which overlaps with Mode 3 of the GATS. Hence there is a strong correlation between the two, and the proposed text can be seen as derived from the already agreed upon GATS.[143]

Even though the Commentary references the aspiration of obtaining a balance "as between development objectives and investor interests,"[144] the objective is quite narrow and only addresses possible prejudice concerning Host States. Nowhere is there mention of the need to ensure that "the right to regulate" is confined to the promulgation of measures that comport with the expectation of both parties to a BIT. The Commentary travels on the presumption that frustrated expectations and asymmetrical issues only prejudice and concern capital-importing countries. Although it is true that there likely are instances where a developing country may have negotiated less than favorable terms in becoming a signatory to a treaty with a capital-exporting State, the assumption that all or most developing countries are disadvantaged and prejudiced because of asymmetrical issues and overly expansive foreign investment protection rights finds no foundation in theory or fact.[145]

[143] *Id.* at 5–6.

[144] *Id.*

[145] To the contrary, in 2011 and 2012, ICSID upheld investors claims either in whole or in part 46 percent and 63 percent of the time, respectively. https://icsid.worldbank.org/ICSID/Index.jsp (last visited April 28, 2013).

The derivation from the WTO-GATS of the paragraph addressing the right to regulate and the recognition of asymmetry issues, notwithstanding the qualifying clause, "with modification for the broader subject matter here,"[146] is of some concern. The scope and issues attendant to the WTO GATS pertaining to international trade law are materially distinct from those topics within the ambit of international investment law.[147]

Moreover, the SADC Model BIT also assumes that, to the extent that BITs do carry a "presumption of investor-friendly interpretations," such a presumption is not in a Host State's best interest.[148]

Article 1 of the SADC Model BIT qualifies the principal objective of the BIT as encouraging an increase in FDI that will "[support] the sustainable development of each Party."[149] The Commentary to Article 1 provides that part of the intent behind the provision is to emphasize the connection between FDI and the promotion of sustainable development. It specifically states that this connection "between foreign direct investment (FDI) and the promotion of sustainable development" is intended to stress that FDI is not "an end in itself."[150]

[146] SADC Model BIT Template, *supra* note 140, at 6.

[147] *Supra* Chapter 1 note 111 and accompanying text.

[148] The scholarship asserting the proposition that FDI is directly proportional to the presumption that foreign investment enjoys juridical protection, or that BITs are subject to a "presumption of investor-friendly interpretations," is vast. *See, e.g.*, Leon E. Trakman, *The ICSID under Siege*, 45 CORNELL INT'L L.J. 603, 608 (2012) ("The signing of bilateral investment agreements incorporating investor-State arbitration is therefore not simply about developed states imposing their will on developing states. Rather, these agreements are strategically important and states elect among them in a calculated manner according to the perceived benefits arising from prospective investment flows"; citation omitted).

[149] Article 1 states:

> The main objective of this Agreement is to encourage an increase investments [between investors of one State Party into the territory of the other State Party] that support the *sustainable development* of each Party, and in particular the Host State where an investment is to be located.

SADC Model BIT Template, *supra* note 140, at 8 (emphasis added).

[150] The Commentary states:

> Many treaties include an objective article to highlight, in a succinct manner within the substantive text, the treaty's main goal. This gives added weight to the objective as an interpretational guide, beyond that which is normally attributed to the preamble. The link between foreign direct investment (FDI) and the promotion of sustainable development is recognized in the Finance and Investment Protocol (FIP) and other SADC instruments. It is used here to support the key objective of the SADC Member States: for FDI to contribute to the development objectives of each State and the region as a whole, rather than simply being an end in itself.

Id.

The proposed objective, as drafted, raises exquisitely complex challenges. Is "sustainable development" much like the public purpose doctrine, a specifically defined principle of law? If so, where? Is sustainable development an absolute public purpose category, or one that is contingent on the development needs of particular States? If the latter, is a prospective investor charged with knowledge of a Host State's specific sustainable development needs as a matter of law? Assuming that an investor is charged with knowledge of the sustainable development content of the public purpose doctrine as expressed in Article 1 of the SADC BIT, is it conceptually or doctrinally possible then for the sustainable development expression of the public purpose doctrine to be self-judging (i.e., subjective) on the part of the invoking State?

Without pristine answers to these queries, it is unlikely that Article 1 of the SADC Model BIT will gain traction with the universe of sophisticated FDI prospective investors who are sensitive to the delicate balance between a State's exercise of sovereignty through regulatory enactments within its domestic space and the equally important and demanding obligation to protect foreign investor/investments.

The third material reference to the public purpose doctrine in the SADC Model BIT appears in Article 6, within the context of an expropriation provision that presents two options concerning the compensation obligation. In contrast with Article 1110 of the NAFTA, Article 6.1 of the SADC Model BIT omits any reference to nondiscriminatory treatment with respect to the four orthodox exception elements rendering the expropriation legal and charging the State only with an obligation to pay *some* form of compensation, depending on the applicable rubric.[151] Therefore, pursuant to this proposed expropriation exception, discriminatory regulation on the part of a Host State is countenanced where the taking is discriminatory but (i) in the public interest, (ii) in keeping with due process of law, and (iii) where fair and adequate compensation is tendered within a reasonable period of time.[152] This proposition places still greater reliance on the public purpose element of the

[151] Section 6.1 reads: "A State Party shall not directly or indirectly nationalize or expropriate investments in its territory except: (a) in the public interest; (b) in accordance with due process of law; and (c) on payment of fair and adequate compensation within a reasonable period of time." *Id.* at 24. *Cf.* NAFTA, *supra* Chapter 1 note 1, art. 1110.

[152] However, it should be noted that Subsection 6.7. of Article 6 does seem to suggest that a discriminatory indirect expropriation under the Model BIT may trigger a compensation standard more favorable to a foreign investor than the "fair and adequate" criteria, providing: "A [non-discriminatory] measure of a State Party that is designed and applied to protect or enhance legitimate public welfare objectives, such as public health, safety and the environment, does not constitute an indirect expropriation under this Agreement." SADC Model BIT Template, *supra* note 140, at 26 (brackets in original).

provision. The tolerance of a discriminatory nationalization or expropriation that is either direct or indirect evinces an expansive domestic regulatory space and arguably would command more than a reasonable showing of public purpose in connection with the taking. This model provision invariably prompts the question as to whether different showings of public purpose are necessary and warranted depending upon the number of elements required to constitute a legal and legitimate taking.

Section 6.1 is devoid of the "tantamount" or "equivalent to an expropriation" language present in Article 1110 of the NAFTA.[153] Thus, the provision arguably forecloses claims for expropriation arising from a series of regulatory enactments that, when taken together, render an investment only nominally valuable or altogether lacking in commercial purpose. This construction also materially amplifies the domestic regulatory space of Host States while weakening Host-State obligations to protect foreign investment.

This proposition is quite extraordinary. Viewed from this perspective, the workings of Section 6.1 would render juridically sound a series of regulatory acts undertaken within a fixed time frame that are discriminatory in nature and have the direct and proximate consequence of rendering a foreign investment commercially unviable so long as such acts comport with the three other delineated strictures. The proposition also invites the additional inquiry as to whether each such discrete discriminatory act must be in and of itself subject to a public interest requirement, or does such requirement attach only to the totality of the subject regulatory actions within the context of their cumulative effect? The answer to this inquiry, in turn, would presumably dictate the content of the public purpose doctrine against which any such alleged taking must be analyzed.

The commentary to Paragraph 6.7 suggests an intent on the part of the drafters to foreclose Home State investors from asserting that nondiscriminatory regulatory enactments constitute expropriations within the scope of the Model BIT:

> The exclusion for regulatory measures in paragraph 6.7 is specific and clear, rather than leaving open possibilities for investors to argue otherwise. This is the traditional customary international law approach, drawn from the notion that "police powers" measures are not, by definition, acts of expropriation. The text is inspired by the COMESA CCIA and ASEAN texts. The 1990s and early 2000s' texts did not include such provisions, but these types of clauses are becoming increasingly common and should be made clear and apparent in the treaty text. Indeed, it is likely that a failure to include such a provision now would lead to the assumption that such a clear exclusion was not meant to be included and create the risk that a tribunal will hold that by not excluding regulatory measures the parties meant to include them within the scope of the expropriation article.

Id.

[153] *See* NAFTA, *supra* Chapter 1 note 1, art. 1110

The meaningful reliance of the public purpose doctrine within the framework of the SADC Model BIT generally, and in particular the workings of Subsection 6.1 on expropriation, is emphasized because of the very unique relationship between the public purpose doctrine and the methodology for compensating foreign investors under this provision. Two options are articulated with respect to the valuation of a foreign investment that has been nationalized or expropriated within the meaning of Article 6. The first option places the public purpose doctrine at the very center of a valuation analysis that favors the interests of Host States, twice appealing to the doctrine. This single-sentence valuation tenet renders the term "fair market value" as only one of numerous factors to be considered:

> **6.2. Option 1:** The assessment of fair and adequate compensation shall be based on an equitable balance *between the public interest and interest of those affected*, having regard for all relevant circumstances and taking into account the current and past use of the property, the history of its acquisition, the fair market value of the property, *the purpose of the expropriation*, the extent of previous profit made by the foreign investor through the investment, and the duration of the investment.[154]

This first option fails to explain how it is that the public interest incident to the expropriation is to be weighed or balanced against the "interest of those affected." Similarly, it is less than clear how "the purpose of the expropriation" is to be weighed or considered with respect to the "fair market value of the property." Equally obscured is the relationship between profits that a foreign investor realized from the investment and the duration of the investment. What does stand out as clear, however, is that the public purpose component of the proposed assessment of value methodology enunciated in Option 1 is instrumental in diminishing "fair market value of the property" and transforming it into "fair and adequate compensation" pursuant to which fair market value is depreciated by considering the alleged public purpose component of the expropriation.

The second option actually suggests that the "fair market value" of the subject property immediately prior to the expropriation is to be used as the operative standard, except in cases where it is deemed more "appropriate" to assess *fair and adequate compensation* instead of *fair market value*. In such cases, the public purpose doctrine again is called upon to form part of a species of a proportionality test pursuant to which fair and adequate compensation is arrived at by balancing public interest against the interests of those prejudiced.

154 SADC Model BIT Template, *supra* note 140, at 24 (emphasis added).

This part of the proportionality test is consonant with the compensation analysis contained in Option 1.[155]

The importation of the public purpose doctrine into expropriation damages analysis creates uncertainty and expands the role of the doctrine beyond considerations only pertaining to liability.

The most balanced compensation proposal that would best appear to harmonize the interests of Home and Host States is Option 3. Partially equitable in nature, the provision is unique in its absence of any mention of the public purpose doctrine:

> **6.2. Option 3:** Fair and adequate compensation shall be assessed in relation to the fair market value of the expropriated investment immediately before the expropriation took place ("date of expropriation") and not reflect any change in value occurring because the intended expropriation had become known earlier.[156]

This compromise position retains the "fair and adequate" compensation element, which is meaningfully removed from *actual fair market value, fair market value*, or *actual value*, while still using fair market value as of a fixed date as a point of departure and standard. Moreover, by discarding consideration of the depreciation that the investment may have suffered (and in many cases indeed did experience) as a result of predicate acts to the expropriation or actions taken prior to the actual taking,[157] orthodox

[155] Subsection 6.2, Option 2 states:

> Fair and adequate compensation shall normally be assessed in relation to the fair market value of the expropriated investment immediately before the expropriation took place ("date of expropriation") and shall not reflect any change in value occurring because the intended expropriation had become known earlier. *However, where appropriate, the assessment of fair and adequate compensation shall be based on an equitable balance between public interest and interest of those affected, having regard for all relevant circumstances and taking account of the current and past use of the property, the history of its acquisition, the fair market value of the investment, the purpose of the expropriation, the extent of previous profit made by the foreign investor through the investment, and the duration of the investment.*

Id. (emphasis added).

[156] *Id.* at 25.

[157] It is common for investments to suffer material depreciation in value arising from the pre-expropriation process. Quite often, by way of example, public pronouncements precede actual regulatory enactments. These publications, usually industry-wide and available to the relevant universe of commercial interests, have the effect of diminishing investment value. In a nonexpropriation context, such depreciation naturally would be considered in any appraisal or valuation of an asset. In fact, one tribunal has awarded compensation for wrongful acts occurring prior to BIT coverage and noted that "the project was by then already severely damaged from earlier events for which the Respondent bears no liability under the BITs; and it

valuation methodologies[158] are being discarded to ensure that the valuation methodology comports with an expropriation framework that is somewhat severed from this sphere of commercial or juridical compensation paradigms.[159]

Yet another sustainable development expression of the public purpose doctrine within the SADC Model BIT is contained in Article 13, entitled "Environmental and Social Impact Assessment." This provision prescribes a two-pronged pre-entry requirement for investors. One requirement entails investor compliance with environmental "green" criteria and assessment processes relevant to the investment at issue in conformance with the laws of the Host and Home States, as well as with the International Finance Corporation's performance standards on Environmental and Social Impact Assessment, "whichever is more rigorous in relation to the investment in

remained subject to several commercial, legal and political risks." Gemplus, S.A., SLP, S.A. and Gemplus Industrial, S.A. de C.V. v. United Mexican States, ICSID Case No. ARB(AF)/04/3 & ARB(AF)/04/4, Award Part XIII ¶ 96 (June 16, 2010), http://www.italaw.com/sites/default/files/case-documents/ita0357.pdf.

[158] *See generally* Manuel A. Abdala & Pablo T. Spiller, *Damage Valuation of Indirect Expropriation in International Arbitration Cases*, 14 AM. REV. INT'L ARB. 447, 454 (2003) (delineating the orthodox valuation methods for assets damaged in an expropriation).

[159] Damage theories of restitution or that otherwise seek to render an aggrieved party whole (i.e. either placed in the same position that the party was in prior to the alleged prejudice or enjoying the status that the prejudiced party would have enjoyed had the noncompliant party performed the terms of a contract) find no place in the compensation scheme of public international law with respect to expropriation. There is no explanation for not awarding an injured party the depreciation caused by the acts or omissions of a Host State during a fixed and identifiable time frame leading up to the expropriation that constituted part of the subject of regulatory takings, other than the proposition that (i) the injured party assumed the risk of a lawful expropriation and therefore should not be made whole and (ii) obligating states to tender full "fair market value" rather than "fair and adequate compensation" would be tantamount to imposing a fine on the Host State merely for exercising its duty to regulate in furtherance of a public purpose. *See, e.g.*, LG&E Energy Corp., LG&E Capital Corp. and LG&E International Inc. v. Argentine Republic, ICSID Case No. ARB/02/1, Award ¶¶ 29–53 (July 25, 2007), http://www.italaw.com/sites/default/files/case-documents/ita0462.pdf (discussing the proper method for compensation, whether it be restitution, fair market value, or fair and adequate).

Article 1110(2) of the NAFTA excludes from the compensatory scheme of takings depreciation or damage occurring prior to the actual act depriving the owner of its investment, much like Option 3, but, in contrast with Option 3, it sets forth a "fair market value" standard:

> Art. 1110(2): Compensation shall be equivalent to the fair market value of the expropriated investment immediately before the expropriation took place ("date of expropriation"), and shall not reflect any change in value occurring because the intended expropriation had become known earlier. Valuation criteria shall include going concern value, asset value including declared tax value of tangible property, and other criteria, as appropriate, to determine fair market value.

NAFTA, *supra* Chapter 1 note 1, art. 1110 ¶ 2.

question."[160] The second part of the requirement concerns a social assessment subject to the same strictures as the environmental study.[161]

The scope of these impact assessments is to include both static and progressive analyses on the human rights "of the persons in the areas potentially impacted by the investment."[162] Article 13 charges investors with the obligation of rendering the environmental and social impact assessments public, including on the Internet,[163] and of making them available to local communities or other sectors that may be potentially affected by the investment "in an effective and sufficiently timely manner so as to allow comments to be made to the investor, investment, and/or government prior to the completion of the Host State processes for establishing an investment."[164] The rigors of transparency and lead time engraft material preconditions onto investors/investments subject to the SADC Model BIT's progenies. Even though this precondition technically applies both to Home and Host States, as per the substantive law on the relevant social and environmental issues that are the subject of the assessments pertaining to both jurisdictions, as a matter of practical implementation, the burden of the requirement will have its greatest effect on Home States. It will therefore increase foreign investors' participation in and financial contribution to the implementation of Host-State domestic policies, which has been identified as a salient feature of the sustainable development expression of the public purpose doctrine.[165] The Environmental Impact Assessment pursuant to Article 13 must be consonant with the *Precautionary Principle*.[166]

[160] SADC Model BIT Template, *supra* note 140, at 34.

[161] Article 13.1. provides:

> Investors or their Investments shall comply with environmental and social assessment screening criteria and assessment processes applicable to their proposed investments prior to their establishment, as required by the laws of the Host State for such an investment [[or the laws of the Home State for such an investment][or the International Finance Corporation's performance standards on Environmental and Social Impact Assessment], whichever is more rigorous in relation to the Investment in question.].

Id. at 34 (brackets in original).

[162] *Id.*

[163] *See Id.* (Art. 13.13).

[164] *Id.* at 34.

[165] *See supra* at Chapter 2.E(5).

[166] Principle 15 of the United Nations Rio Declaration on Environment and Development defines the precautionary principle, which is followed by the majority of states:

> In order to protect the environment, the precautionary approach shall be widely applied by states according to their capabilities. Where there are threats of serious irreversible damage, lack of full scientific certainty shall not be used as a reason for postponing cost-effective measures to prevent environmental degradation.

The sixth sustainable development expression of the public purpose doctrine in the SADC Model BIT appears under Article 20 ("Right of States to Regulate").[167] The drafters identify the right of States to regulate in conformance with (i) principles of sustainable development, (ii) legitimate social objectives, and (iii) economic policy goals as an obligation of Host States arising from customary international law.[168] In fact, the "right to regulate" as framed in Article 20 is further identified as falling "within a balance of the rights and obligations of Investors and Investments and Host States, as set out in [the Model BIT]."[169] Furthermore, nondiscriminatory acts undertaken by Host States in furtherance of compliance with other treaty obligations also are to be construed as part of a "right to regulate," notwithstanding the burdens that such compliance may place on foreign investment.[170]

Article 20 identifies a *right to regulate* as having a normative foundation in the sustainable development expression of the public purpose doctrine. In addition to requiring such measures to be "nondiscriminatory" and in accordance with "expressly stated . . .exception[s] to the obligations of this Agreement,"[171] the right to regulate is viewed as an expansive prerogative of Host States that appears to be unbridled in scope. Furthermore, it does not take into consideration any countervailing interests on the part of Home States and investors. The Commentary to Article 20.2 confirms this construction of

United Nations Conference on Environment & Development, Rio de Janeiro, Braz., June 3–14, 1992, *Rio Declaration on Environment & Development*, U.N. Doc.A/CONF.151/26/Rev. 1 (Vol. I), Annex I (August 12, 1992). Under such guidance, Paragraph 13.4 of Article 13 reads:

> Investors, their investments and the Host State authorities shall apply the precautionary principle to their environmental impact assessment and to decisions taken in relation to a proposed investment, including any necessary mitigating or alternative approaches to the investment, or precluding the investment if necessary. The application of the precautionary principle by investors and investments shall be described in the environment impact assessment.

SADC Model BIT Template, *supra* note 140, at 34 (internal citations omitted).

[167] *Id.* at 39.

[168] Paragraph 20.1 of Article 20 provides:

> In accordance with customary international law and other general principles of international law, the Host State has the right to take regulatory or other measures to ensure that development in its territory is consistent with the goals and principles of sustainable development, and with other legitimate social and economic policy objectives.

Id.

[169] *Id.* at 40.

[170] *Id.* (art. 20.3).

[171] *Id.* (art. 20.2).

the right to regulate principle. The drafters viewed the Article 20 "right to regulate" language as ensuring an understanding that the Model BIT's progeny are not construed as wresting from Host States any pretreaty rights[172] and as presenting the agreements based on the Model BIT as providing for more than only investor rights.[173] The right to regulate presented under Article 20 is not even contingent upon a "subjective necessity" requirement. It does subordinate all investor rights to nondiscriminatory regulatory measures that a Host State may undertake without consequence to the Host State, despite prejudice to the Home State's foreign investor.

Whether the right to development as described in Article 20 at all exists as part of customary international law is less than clear.[174] Embedded in the SADC Model BIT, this basic assumption, without more, is likely to work against the very policies that the BIT purports to protect and to promote. At some fundamental level, it is a challenge to conceive of a negotiated treaty that does not cause its signatories to assume burdens and obligations in the form of *conceded rights to regulate*. To the extent that the SADC Model BIT drafters understood that the effects of investor protections under BITs had a negative effect on Host States because parties and arbitrators "exploited ambiguities" in the standards of protection against the interests of Host States,[175] specifying the content and scope of standards of protection within the BIT is a more efficient course of conduct than a right to regulate that is boundless and, therefore, likely to discourage foreign investment.

[172] This intent is somewhat uncommon because it is fundamental that treaties are the means pursuant to which States yield sovereignty as a concession to the attainment of an international objective concerning one or more States.

[173] The commentary in its totality provides:

> This article confirms that the treaty does not alter the Host State's basic right to regulate, but without eliminating all the effects of the investor protections. [Here, "the effects of the investor protections" refers to effects with respect to the Host State, and not to the Investor or the Home State.] It should be read with more specific articles that enable performance requirements to be imposed, and carefully define the non-discrimination and expropriation rules, for example. All of these provisions are intended to work together.
>
> The broader goal is restated in paragraph 20.2, again ensuring that some of the predilections of arbitrators to view investment treaties purely as investor rights would be untenable under the present approach. In view of the broad obligations in BITs, it is useful to reaffirm the Host State's right to regulate investments in the public interest.

Id. at 40 (bracket language added).

[174] The right does appear in the African Charter of Human and Peoples' Rights, as discussed in Chapter 3. *See* African Charter, *supra* note 45, art. 21.

[175] SADC Model BIT Template, *supra* note 140, at 46–47 (providing rationale for detailed exceptions).

The final and seventh pronouncement of the public purpose doctrine is contained in Article 25, "Exceptions."[176] This article introduces no less than four standards in the application of seven expressions of the public purpose doctrine.[177] The proposed exceptions framework contemplates that, as a matter of post-entry investor rights, an investor shall have no rights where a regulatory measure is enacted pursuant to a nonarbitrary discriminatory measure or a justifiable regulatory act.[178] Such deliberate discrimination or "justifiable discrimination" in the way of regulatory measures shall be deemed to constitute an exception when purportedly taken in furtherance of the public purpose categories enunciated in Article 25.

[176] *Id.* at 46.

[177] Article 25 expressly addresses the following seven public purpose categories all within the context of sustainable development: (i) public morals; (ii) public safety; (iii) the protection of human, animal, or plant life or health; (iv) the conservation of living or non-living exhaustible natural resources; (v) protection of the environment; (vi) fiscal and monetary financial sums; and (vii) security. The relevant paragraphs in Article 25 provide:

> 25.1. [Subject to the requirement that such measures are not applied in a manner that would constitute a means of *arbitrary* or *unjustifiable discrimination* pursuant to Article [4]] Nothing in this Agreement shall be construed to oblige a State Party to pay compensation for adopting or enforcing measures taken in good faith and designed and applied:
> (a) to protect public morals and safety;
> (c) to protect human, animal or plant life or health;
> (d) for the conservation of living or non-living exhaustible natural resources; and
> (e) to protect the environment.
>
> 25.2. For greater certainty, nothing in this Agreement shall be construed to oblige a State Party to pay compensation if it adopts or maintains reasonable measures for prudential reasons, such as:
> (a) the protection of investors, depositors, financial market participants, policy-holders, policy-claimants, or persons to whom a fiduciary duty is owed by a financial institution;
> (b) the maintenance of the safety, soundness, integrity, or financial responsibility of financial institutions; and
> (c) ensuring the integrity and stability of a State Party's financial system.
>
> 25.5. Nothing in this Agreement shall apply to a State Party's measures that it considers necessary for the fulfillment of its obligations with respect to the maintenance or restoration of international peace or security, or the protection of its national security interests.
>
> 25.6 Nothing in this Agreement requires a State Party to furnish or allow access to any information, the disclosure of which it determines to be contrary to its national security interests.

Id. (emphasis added; brackets in original).

[178] *Id.* The first sentence of Paragraph 25.4 refers to "arbitrary or unjustifiable discrimination pursuant to Article 4."

Paragraph 25.1 exonerates a State from any obligation to tender compensation so long as such measures are "taken in good faith" and "designed and applied"[179] to the public categories enunciated in subparagraphs (a) through (d). This postulate, under the joint banner of *good faith* and the public purpose doctrine, amplifies the domestic regulatory space beyond what may be the reasonable expectations of investors from capital-exporting States. It can be synthesized as a subjective standard on the part of the State invoking the exception; this standard in turn rests upon a principle of *good faith* that is also self-judging (subjective) and thus lacking universal content.

As constructed, the limiting factors (i.e., the most closely objective elements contained in Paragraph 25.1(a)–(d)) are the public purpose categories identified in these subparagraphs. They, in turn, would need to be vested with some element of necessity if they are to serve any type of limiting, categorical function.

Two additional standards are introduced in Paragraph 25.2: (i) *reasonableness* and (ii) *prudential*.[180] That paragraph provides that a State party may enact or maintain regulatory measures without penalty of having to pay compensation so long as the measures are "reasonable" and used or intended "for prudential reasons."[181] Such "prudential reasons" include[182] the protection of fiscal and monetary policies (including investors, depositors, financial market participants, etc.), as well as measures relating to the State's financial system.[183] A "reasonableness" standard by which the adoption or maintenance of regulatory acts are to be measured is simply too broad and suffers from vagueness. Absent an aberrant conception, most, if not all, duly enacted regulatory measures will meet a *reasonableness* standard. Pursuant to this

[179] *Id.*

[180] *Id.* (art. 25.2).

[181] *Id.*

[182] The term "include" is here used because the paragraph indicates that the two categories given as examples are not exhaustive, relying on the term "such as." *Id.*

[183] Paragraph 25.2 states:

> For greater certainty, nothing in this Agreement shall be construed to oblige a State Party to pay compensation if it adopts or maintains *reasonable measures* for *prudential reasons*, such as:
>
> (a) the protection of investors, depositors, financial market participants, policy-holders, policy-claimants, or persons to whom a fiduciary duty is owed by a financial institution;
>
> (b) the maintenance of the safety, soundness, integrity, or financial responsibility of financial institutions; and
>
> (c) ensuring the integrity and stability of a State Party's financial system.

Id. (emphasis added).

criteria, the challenged measure would need to be irrational or otherwise unsustainable under any rational theory of equity, fact, or law.[184]

The term "prudential reasons" is also laced with vagueness and an over-inclusive scope. This term is also problematic because, despite its "term of art" status, as confirmed by the examples listed, the application and effects of these principles at a microeconomic level warrants more specific criteria or reference to an international NGO as an enabling check and balance.[185]

Under the SADC Model BIT, only measures that cannot be justified on rational grounds purportedly enacted for nonprudential reasons that do not at all touch or concern the categories enunciated in subparagraph (a)–(c) would give rise to an actionable claim against a State party. Article 25 precisely emphasizes the very subjective standard that has been identified as a lethal debility of the sustainable development expression of the public purpose doctrine and of the public purpose doctrine more generally. The commentary to Paragraph 25.1, however, emphasizes the exculpatory effects of the self-judging principle of good faith in Paragraph 25.1, the scope of which is also further unduly amplified because of the wholesale importation of international trade law exceptions drawn from Article XX of the GATT.[186]

The Article 25 "Exceptions" represent an amalgamation of investment law and trade law and the incorporation of the sustainable development

[184] Most enactments found to violate standards of treaty protection are rational in and of themselves and are frequently enacted by members of the international community. The reasonableness of a measure is qualitatively separate and distinct from the effect that it may have on a foreign investment/investor pursuant to a treaty protection obligation. Accordingly, the "reasonable measure" criteria asserted in the SADC Model BIT does not constitute a meaningful restriction or qualification as to the form or substance of the measure.

[185] SADC Model BIT Template, *supra* note 140, at 46.

[186] The commentary to Paragraph 25.1 in pertinent part provides:

> This article combines a number of exceptions, issues seen in various regional and bilateral agreements. Each is considered in order.
>
> Paragraph 25.1 is drawn from Article XX of the GATT, and is also reflected in the COMESA CCIA and other bilateral agreements. *However, it is more specifically drafted to make clear that no compensation is required to be paid to an investor for the types of measures set out therein as long as they are taken in good faith. This avoids a situation, for example, where a measure is "made legal" by virtue of paying compensation. Hence the test is not one being a breach of the treaty or not, but a more refined and specific statement that the covered measure simply does not require compensation when taken in a bona fide manner.*
>
> Paragraph 25.2 relates to measures to ensure the stability and integrity of the financial system. The notion of prudential measures in this text is intended to relate to the technical use of that term in relation to the financial sector only. It may be seen as complimentary to the provision on safeguards measures enabling certain limitations on the export of assets by an investor.

Id. at 46–47.

expression of the public purpose doctrine. It vastly amplifies the Host State's domestic regulatory space without according any concession to the Home State's interest in protecting investors by dint of obligations contained in treaty-based protection standards. To the contrary, the spirit of the SADC Model BIT is one that seeks to diminish investor protection in order to attract greater FDI as the principal objective of the treaty. This is accomplished by addressing treaty principles in ways that may enable Host States to remedy existing asymmetries. Thus, the very fundamental nature of the BIT is transformed into a more general and far-reaching instrument aimed at restructuring the anatomy of financial relationships between and among States. This overarching aspiration will also be encountered in analyzing the relationship between the public purpose doctrine and international human rights law.

The protagonistic role of the public purpose doctrine in the form of the principle of sustainable development throughout the BIT is laudable as a policy objective, but technically deficient as presented because of its lack of bilateralism and rudimentary symmetry. Based on the literal language of BIT provisions in the SADC Model BIT, Home-State investors are asked to give up protection rights on investments in order to help finance internal Host-State legislation described as "necessary" to the development of a particular State. The net effect of the Model BIT's workings is to render it unsignable because of its overwhelming penchant favoring Host States and its adherence to the proposition that the BIT does not at all represent any limited relinquishment of sovereignty on the part of Home States.[187] These challenges are further exacerbated by the incorporation of the legacy public purpose doctrine, together with an additional emphasis on Host-State self-judging criteria. Instead of furthering the sustainable development goals that the Model BIT quite laudably articulates and enhancing FDI, the BIT's framework offers little incentive to investors and protection transparency as to their investments. Many of these shortcomings, however, can be adjusted by using a public purpose doctrine that is vested with substantive content, limited by definition, applied through a proportionality principle, and rooted in objective standard.

[187] The authors acknowledge that the driving principle controlling how "signable" a BIT may be depends on the extent to which politically influential business sectors for prospective State parties to a BIT conclude that benefits may be reaped by having an executed treaty, despite clear and asymmetrical construction favoring a class of States generally over another. Here, professor José Alvarez has pointed to Norway's effort to craft a predominantly sovereign protective treaty may be referred to as an unsignable treaty, but one that Norway did not press to negotiate because of concerns that national economic interest groups expressed with the treaty.

2. *The Sustainable Development Expression of the Public Purpose Doctrine in BITs*

Notwithstanding the UNCTAD 2012 Report[188] and the SADC Model BIT,[189] the sustainable development expression of the public purpose doctrine remains as opaque as the legacy iteration of the public purpose doctrine itself. The sustainable development "principle" is nowhere defined conceptually and doctrinally in legislation, decisional law, academic writings, or international instruments.[190] It is thus legitimate to ask "what is sustainable development?" Even though this question may not be susceptible to a comprehensive answer, it does lead to a more modest and attainable inquiry. What is the relationship between the sustainable development doctrine as expressed in the SADC Model BIT and actual BITs in force? Are the broad policy objectives embodied in the UNCTAD 2012 Report and the SADC Model BIT discernible in actual, negotiated BITs that do not purport to be aspirational paragons? Has the sustainable development expression of the public purpose doctrine – as a principle to be applied in correcting asymmetries in the trade law and investment law relationship between States – found a voice in BITs? Last, is there a place for the sustainable development expression of the public purpose doctrine in BITs between industrialized States?

As part of the effort to identify and explore the contours of the public purpose doctrine in customary international law, a nonrandom sample of exactly 300 BITs[191] was selected (the "Sample BITs").[192] This set of BITs yielded only six BITs[193] that purported to incorporate sustainable development

[188] Discussed *supra at* Chapter 2.E(4).

[189] Discussed *supra at* Chapter 2.F(1).

[190] Here, a difference is being drawn between reference to our mention of *sustainable development* and authoritative writings that define sustainable development in such a way that references to the term trigger a succinct and uniform conceptual category that has been embraced by a significant number of States making up the international community.

[191] *See infra* Annex II.

[192] This terminology, "Sample BITs," is used throughout.

[193] The following six BITs from the Sample BITs contained reference to the sustainable development expression of the public purpose doctrine:

(i) Agreement between the Government of Canada and the Government of the People's Republic of China for the Promotion and Reciprocal Protection of Investments, Can.-China, September 9, 2012, http://investmentpolicyhub.unctad.org/Download/TreatyFile/600 [hereinafter Canada-China BIT];

(ii) Agreement between Canada and the Republic of Peru for the Promotion and Protection of Investments, Can.-Peru, November 14, 2006, http://investmentpolicyhub.unctad.org/Download/TreatyFile/626 [hereinafter Canada-Peru BIT];

(iii) Agreement between Japan and the Republic of Colombia for the Liberalization, Promotion and Protection of Investments, Jap.-Col., September 12, 2011,

as a principle pervading the treaty.[194] These six BITs, all executed between 2006 and 2012, suggest that the process of negotiation considerably curtails the scope of the sustainable development policy.[195] The rigors of the interstate treaty negotiating process notwithstanding, sustainable development contributes to yet a greater broadening of the legacy public purpose doctrine. Both the effects of the rigors of interstate treaty negotiation and the amplification of the legacy doctrine merit scrutiny as they manifest themselves in these five BITs.

a. The Canada-China BIT

The Agreement between Canada and China for the Promotion and Protection of Investments ("Canada-China BIT") mentions sustainable development in its very first sentence:

> ***recognizing*** the need to promote investment based on the principles of sustainable development.[196]

Other than this fleeting reference, the term "sustainable development" nowhere appears in the BIT. There is no definition or explanation of the term anywhere in the text. The BIT also is devoid of reference to external sources that may help define the term. Notably, the "Exceptions" Article of the BIT (Article 8) only

http://investmentpolicyhub.unctad.org/Download/TreatyFile/3116 [hereinafter Colombia-Japan BIT];

(iv) Agreement between the Government of Japan and the Government of the Independent State of Papua New Guinea for the Promotion and Protection of Investment, Jap.-Pap. New Guin., April 26, 2011, http://investmentpolicyhub.unctad.org/Download/TreatyFile/1732 [hereinafter Japan-Papua New Guinea BIT]; and

(v) Agreement between Government of the Republic of Croatia and the Government of the Republic of Azerbaijan on the Promotion and Reciprocal Protection of Investments, Cro.-Azer., November 2, 2007, http://investmentpolicyhub.unctad.org/Download/TreatyFile/229 [hereinafter Croatia-Azerbaijan BIT].

(vi) Agreement between the Government of Canada and the Hashemite Kingdom of Jordan for the Promotion and Protection of Investments, Can.-Jor., June 28, 2009, http://investmentpolicyhub.unctad.org/Download/TreatyFile/617 [hereinafter Canada-Jordan BIT].

[194] These six BITs referencing sustainable development are not being held out as the entire universe of BITs incorporating the principle or its nomenclature. They are, however, the only BITs at all referring to sustainable development that form part of the Sample BITs.

[195] It is here assumed that a near reference to the principles of sustainable development does not and cannot trigger an otherwise incorporation by reference of the sparse but broad precepts ascribed to the various narratives pertaining to sustainable development.

[196] Canada-China BIT, *supra* note 193, at 1.

extends conventional limits to foreign investment.[197] In fact, Article 10 ("Expropriation") materially differs from the expropriation provision that the SADC Model BIT promotes.[198] By way of example, the expropriation exception elements include "non-discriminatory manner." Similarly, and also in stark contrast with the SADC Model BIT, the expropriation compensation is to be valued at the "fair market value of the investment expropriated" and, unlike even the NAFTA, includes a valuation "before the expropriation, or before the impending expropriation became public knowledge, whichever is earlier."[199] Expropriation compensation also is to include "interest at a normal commercial rate until the date of payment."[200] Most significantly, the expropriation provision extends to "measures having an effect equivalent to expropriation or nationalization in the territory of the other Contracting Party."[201] This element also represents a material difference between the Canada-China BIT and the paradigmatic sustainable development SADC Model BIT.

[197] In addition to limiting the application the most-favored-nation treatment and national treatment to nonconforming measures, Paragraphs 4 and 5 read:

> 4. In respect of intellectual property rights, a Contracting Party may derogate from Articles 3 ["Promotion and Admission of Investment"], 5 ["Most Favoured Nation Treatment"] and 6 ["National Treatment"] in a manner that is consistent with international agreements regarding intellectual property rights to which both Contracting Parties are parties.
> 5. Articles 5, 6 and 7, do not apply to:
>   (a) procurement by a Contracting Party;
>   (b) subsidies or grants provided by a Contracting Party, including government-supported loans, guarantees and insurance.

Id. art. 8. ¶¶ 4–5.

[198] Article 10 (Expropriation) in relevant part reads:

> 1. Covered investments or returns of investors of either Contracting Party shall not be expropriated, nationalized *or subjected to measures having an effect equivalent to expropriation or nationalization* in the territory of the other Contracting Party (hereinafter referred to as "expropriation"), *except for a public purpose*, under domestic due procedures of law, in a non-discriminatory manner and against compensation. *Such compensation shall amount to the fair market value of the investment expropriated immediately before the expropriation, or before the impending expropriation became public knowledge, whichever is earlier, shall include interest at a normal commercial rate until the date of payment, and shall be effectively realizable, freely transferable, and made without delay.* The investor affected shall have a right, under the law of the Contracting Party making the expropriation, to prompt review, by a judicial or other independent authority of that Contracting Party, of his or its case and of the valuation of his or its investment in accordance with the principles set out in this paragraph.

Id. art. 10 ¶ 1 (emphasis added).

[199] *Id.*

[200] *Id.*

[201] *Id.*

The policies underlying the expropriation provision of the Canada-China BIT hardly bespeak any penchant favoring Host States. To the contrary, considerable deference in the form of compensation with interest based upon actual fair market value is accorded to the Home-State investor. It is safe to conclude that the sustainable development principle did not help shape the elements of the expropriation standard contained in this BIT. The scope and content of this standard of protection is more in keeping with the succinct but eloquent second sentence of the preamble that follows the reference to sustainable development. It reads: "*desiring* to intensify the economic cooperation of both States, based on equality and mutual benefit."[202] This statement of objectives is simply poles apart from the SADC Model BIT's preamble, which centered on explaining that investment protection for purposes of attracting greater FDI was not the primary objective of the BIT and would only be welcomed to the extent that such investment comported with the principle of sustainable development as articulated in the Model BIT.[203]

The sustainable development expression of the public purpose doctrine does find a space in two very important articles of the Canada-China BIT (Articles 12 and 33). Article 12 allows for regulation of transfers relating to a covered investment virtually on a limitless basis so long as the proscription is "equitable," "non-discriminatory," and meets with "good faith application" of the relevant law.[204] Most of the Article can be described as constituting an exception that provides the Host State with an unrestricted license to temper or altogether proscribe transfers pertaining to covered investments. The subject matters falling within this transfer exception range from criminal law and bankruptcy concerns to the soundness of a contracting party's balance of payment status.[205] The scope of the exception pursuant to Paragraph 4

[202] *Id.* preamble.

[203] *See supra* notes 140–42 and accompanying text for comparison with the preamble of the SADC Model BIT.

[204] Canada-China BIT, *supra* note 193, art. 12 ¶ 3.

[205] Article 12 in pertinent part provides:

> 3. Notwithstanding the provisions of paragraphs 1 and 2 of this Article, a Contracting Party may prevent a transfer through the equitable, non-discriminatory and good faith application of its laws relating to:
> (a) bankruptcy, insolvency or the protection of the rights of creditors;
> (b) issuing, trading or dealing in securities;
> (c) criminal or penal offenses;
> (d) reports of transfers of currency or other monetary instruments; or
> (e) ensuring the satisfaction of judgments in adjudicatory proceedings.
>
> 4. (a) Nothing in the Agreement shall be construed to prevent a Contracting Party from adopting or maintaining measures that restrict transfers when the Contracting Party

exclusively concerns financial effect at a macroeconomic level. Even though the global cross-industry consequences of fiscal policies pertaining to FDI may have a macroeconomic effect on Host States, individual FDI represents microeconomic events, typically limited to a single industry sector and structured to enjoy a limited or even abbreviated economic cycle or life span. Thus, BIT exceptions premised on macroeconomic concerns, but likely to apply indiscriminately to specific foreign private investment, command strict scrutiny.

The Article 33 "General Exceptions" of the Canada-China BIT are broad as to subject matter even though they invite classification into only three categories. The article represents a veritable confluence of dissimilar public purpose categories and attendant policies. The domestic regulatory space carved out in Paragraph 2 draws extensively from Article XX of the GATT.[206] Notably, the relationship between the need to regulate transfers arising from covered investments and that need's connection to

> experiences serious balance of payment difficulties, or the threat thereof, provided that such measures:
> (i) are of limited duration, applied on a good-faith basis, and should be phased out as the situation calling for imposition of such measures improves;
> (ii) do not constitute a dual or multiple exchange rate practice;
> (iii) do not otherwise interfere with an investor's ability to invest, in the territory of the Contracting Party, in the form chosen by the investor and, as relevant, in local currency, in any assets that are restricted from being transferred out of the territory of the Contracting Party;
> (iv) are applied on an equitable and non-discriminatory basis;
> (v) are promptly published by the government authorities responsible for financial services or central bank of the Contracting Party;
> (vi) are consistent with the Articles of Agreement of the International Monetary Fund done at Bretton Woods on 22 July 1944; and
> (vii) avoid unnecessary damage to the commercial, economic and financial interests of the other Contracting Party.

Id. art. 12 ¶¶ 4–5.

[206] Paragraph 2, Article 33 of the Canada-China BIT states:

> 2. Provided that such measures are not applied in an arbitrary or unjustifiable manner, or do not constitute a disguised restriction *on international trade or investment*, nothing in this Agreement shall be construed to prevent a Contracting Party from adopting or maintaining measures, including environmental measures:
> (a) necessary to ensure compliance with laws and regulations that are not inconsistent with the provisions of this Agreement;
> (b) *necessary to protect human, animal or plant life or health;* or
> (c) *relating to the conservation of living or non-living exhaustible natural resources if such measures are made effective in conjunction with restrictions on domestic production or consumption.*

Id. art. 33, ¶ 2 (emphasis added).

environmental measures and the protection of "human, animal or plant life or health"[207] is not at all clear.[208] Although the mechanical and boilerplate incorporation of international trade law principles into investment law exceptions certainly serves to broaden the public purpose doctrine and to impose constraints on investment protection obligations running from Host States in favor of foreign investors/investments, it does not advance the policies underlying international investment protection and the promotion of FDI.

Paragraph 3 of Article 33 adopts "prudential financial measures" that also are found in the UNCTAD 2012 Report[209] and in the SADC Model BIT.[210] This public purpose exception, as in the SADC Model BIT, relies on a "reasonable standard to determine 'measures for prudential reasons.'"[211] Even though "prudential reasons" in this context is a term of art, the "reasonable measures" standard broadens even further the scope of the exception beyond the already liberal industry sector subject matter.[212]

The third category of exceptions is much like those contained in Article XXI of the GATT, which pertains to State security. Even though this category finds a place within the seemingly all-embracing sustainable development principle as articulated by the UNCTAD 2012 Report and the SADC Model BIT, the exception traditionally finds its way into the public purpose doctrine by way of

[207] *Id.*

[208] *See infra* Chapter 5 discussing the wholesale importation of international commercial law principles into investment law instruments, particularly BITs.

[209] *See* discussion *supra at* Chapter 2.E(4).

[210] *See* discussion *supra* at Chapter 2.F(1).

[211] Canada-China BIT, *supra* note 193, art. 33 ¶ 3.

[212] Paragraph 3 of Article 33, states:

> 3. Nothing in this Agreement shall be construed to prevent a Contracting Party from *adopting or maintaining reasonable measures for prudential reasons*, such as:
> (a) the protection of depositors, financial market participants and investors, policy-holders, policy-claimants, or persons to whom a fiduciary duty is owed by a financial institution;
> (b) the maintenance of the safety, soundness, integrity or financial responsibility of financial institutions; and
> (c) ensuring the integrity and stability of a Contracting Party's financial system.

Id. (emphasis added).

Paragraph 4 further amplifies the prudential financial measures exception, providing:

> 4. Nothing in this Agreement shall apply to non-discriminatory measures of general application taken by any public entity – in pursuit of monetary and related credit policies or exchange rate policies. This paragraph shall not affect a Contracting Party's obligations under Article 12 [the transfer article].

Id. art. 33 ¶ 4.

what historically has been described as a State's "police powers."[213] The verbatim transposition of GATT Article XXI Exceptions into the general exceptions of the BIT emphasizes a dissonance between the policy objectives of the BIT and the broad macroeconomic and distinct character of the security exceptions. By way of example, it is a challenge to conceive the manner in which a Host State's investment protection obligations would justify being curtailed because of the Host State's actions arising from its "essential security interests relating to the implementation of national policies or international agreements respecting the nonproliferation of nuclear weapons or other nuclear explosive devices."[214] Notwithstanding this conceptual incompatibility, the unbridled vestiture of authority to implement "nondiscriminatory measures of general application" render it likely that a State may use seemingly unrelated subject matters under the guise of national security to limit its foreign investment protection obligations with respect to a specific FDI or industry sector.

[213] Paragraph 5 of Article 33 reads:

> 5. Nothing in this Agreement shall be construed:
> (a) to require a Contracting Party to furnish or allow access to any information if the Contracting Party determines that the disclosure of that information is contrary to its essential security interests;
> (b) to prevent a Contracting Party from taking any actions that it considers necessary for the protection of its essential security interests:
> (i) relating to the traffic in arms, ammunition and implements of war into such traffic and transactions in other goods, materials, services and technology undertaken directly or indirectly for the purpose of supplying a military order or other security establishment,
> (ii) in time of war or other emergency in international relations, or
> (iii) relating to the implementation of national policies or international agreements respecting the non-proliferation of nuclear weapons or other nuclear explosive devices; or
> (c) to prevent a Contracting Party from taking action in pursuance of its obligations under the United Nations Charter for the Maintenance of International Peace and Security.

Id. art. 32, ¶ 5. As one commentator has provided:

> But what are the police powers of a State? They are nothing more or less than the powers of government inherent in every sovereignty to the extent of its dominions. And whether a State passes a quarantine law, or a law to punish offences, or to establish courts of justice, or requiring certain instruments to be recorded, or to regulate commerce within its own limits, in every case it exercises the same powers; that is to say, the power of sovereignty, the power to govern men and things within the limits of its dominion.

In other words, the police power and State sovereignty are synonymous.

D. Benjamin Barros, *The Police Power and the Takings Clause*, 58 U. Miami L. Rev. 471, 477 (2004) (quoting Thurlow v. Com. of Mass., 46 U.S. 504, 583 (1847)).

[214] Canada-China BIT, *supra* note 193, art. 33 ¶ 5(b)(iii).

Generally, the sustainable development principle is present in the Canada-China BIT, but it is materially limited in scope. The direct reference to the principle in the preamble certainly may be construed to amplify the scope of existing exceptions. The confluence of general exceptions extracted from principles of international trade law, international investment law, and economic development policies – all falling under the umbrella of the public purpose doctrine – broadens the doctrine, contributes to ambiguity, and continues to cloud the predictive value and workings of the doctrine as a normative foundation for an expansive right to regulate on the part of Host States.

Despite a more limited scope as expressed in the Canada-China BIT, the sustainable development iteration of the public purpose doctrine, notwithstanding the effects of international treaty negotiation, demonstrates that treaty-drafting techniques alone are not enough to endow the principle with an objective standard and limited application. The technical challenge is conceptual and doctrinal, not simply one of lack of precision of expression – even though this latter issue does follow once there is an agreement on doctrine and concept. Specificity of subject matter, proportionality in application, and non-self-judging standard all are necessary predicates to the application of international treaty-drafting techniques that the doctrine must experience.

The Canada-China BIT, executed between the second and the eleventh largest economies in the world,[215] raises a most fundamental question: Is there a place for the sustainable development iteration of the public purpose doctrine in investment protection treaties where the co-signatories are developed industrialized States? Are the policies articulated in the UNCTAD 2012 Report and the commentaries to the SADC Model BIT – the correction of asymmetries and the nonyielding of rights that may be construed as reasonably related to economic development – at all relevant, let alone necessary, in the context of industrialized States? Is the invocation of the sustainable development principle in this context more helpful than harmful? When considering the problems endemic to the public purpose doctrine, the equally problematic iterations of the sustainable development principle, and the paucity of material purporting to ascribe a limited definition and content to public purpose and its sustainable development iteration, the answer to the queries ranges from *highly unlikely* to *no*. The economic status of industrialized States does not warrant the correction of historical asymmetries pursuant to principles embedded in investment treaties that favor Host States. The Canada-China BIT contributes to an empirical

[215] According to the World Bank, as of 2011, China had the second largest economy in terms of GDP and Canada ranked eleventh. World Bank, Gross domestic product 2011, http://databank.worldbank.org/databank/download/GDP.pdf (last visited April 8, 2013). As of this writing, the World Bank has yet to release the data for 2012.

understanding of the changes that the international arm's-length treaty negotiation process imposes on sustainable development as a normative ground for limiting Host-State investor protection obligations.[216]

The Agreement between Japan and the Republic of Colombia for the Liberalization, Promotion and Protection of Investment ("Colombia-Japan BIT"), signed in 2011, does provide greater recognition to the sustainable development principle than does the Canada-China BIT. It does so without merely referencing the principle while also acknowledging as paramount the need to promote investment:

> Recognizing the growing importance of the progressive liberalization of investment for stimulating initiative of investors and for promoting prosperity and mutually favorable business activity in the Contracting Parties;
>
> Recognizing that these objectives and the promotion of sustainable development can be achieved without relaxing health, safety and environmental measures of general application.[217]

b. The Colombia-Japan BIT

The Colombia-Japan BIT[218] does carve out broad exceptions to performance requirements in Article 5(6) subject to "unjustifiable" or "arbitrary" qualifications that are not particularly stringent and have proven to be amply flexible as a matter of scope.[219] This proposition needs to be qualified by observing that the public purpose categories constituting the subject matter of the public

[216] The agreement between Canada and the Republic of Peru for the Promotion and Protection of Investments was entered into on November 14, 2006, and very much resembles the Canada-China BIT in terms of the treaty's incorporation of the sustainable development iteration of the public purpose doctrine. Generally, it is materially indistinguishable from the Canada-China BIT. The Canada-Peru BIT, however, does contain an article on health, safety, and environmental measures, providing:

> The Parties recognize that it is inappropriate to encourage investment by relaxing domestic health, safety or environmental measures. Accordingly, a Party should not waive or otherwise derogate from, or offer to waive or otherwise derogate from, such measures as an encouragement for the establishment, acquisition, expansion or retention in its territory of an investment of an investor. If a Party considers that the other Party has offered such encouragement, it may request consultation with the other Party and the two Parties shall consult with a view to avoiding any such encouragement.

Canada-Peru BIT, *supra* note 193, art. 11.

[217] Colombia-Japan BIT, *supra* note 193, preamble.

[218] This BIT is analyzed in considerable detain in the Chapter 5 regarding public purpose in BITs.

[219] Paragraph 6 reads:

> 6. Provided that such measures are not applied in an arbitrary or unjustifiable manner and provided that such measures do not constitute a disguised restriction on international trade or investment activities, nothing in subparagraphs 1(b), (c) and (f) and 2(a)

purpose exception are significantly closer to the language in Article XX of the GATT than to the more generic development language that one may associate with the principle of sustainable development.

This BIT does contain a quite extraordinary provision in the expropriation and compensation Article 11 that quite clearly establishes the importance of the public purpose doctrine to Host States. Even though the BIT's expropriation article provides for Hull formula compensation ("payment of a prompt, adequate, and effective compensation")[220] and meaningfully deviates from the SADC Model BIT paradigm, such as in the inclusion of "any measure equivalent to expropriation or nationalization,"[221] these "pro-Home State" expropriation and compensation terms that broaden the application of the exception are tempered by the likely Host State's (here Colombia) emphasis on public purpose as more than just a boilerplate term of art mechanically included in expropriation provisions in BITs. The paragraph merits consultation:

> 1. Neither Contracting Party may expropriate or nationalize investments in its Area of investors of the other Contracting Party or take any measure equivalent to expropriation or nationalization (hereinafter referred to as "expropriation"), *except, for a public purpose,* in accordance with due process of law and Article 4, in a non-discriminatory manner, and upon payment of a prompt, adequate and effective compensation pursuant to paragraphs 2 through 4.
>
> *Note: In the case of the Republic of Colombia, the term "public purpose", being used in this paragraph, is a term used in international agreements and may be expressed in the domestic law of the Republic of Colombia using terms such as: "public purpose" or "social interest."*[222]

Quite significantly, Colombia, the likely Host State in this treaty relationship because of its status as an economy in transition,[223] caused the public purpose doctrine within the meaning of the BIT's expropriation provision to be defined jointly by (i) "international agreements" and (ii) "the domestic law of the

> and (b) shall be construed to prevent a Contracting Party from adopting or maintaining measures, including environmental measures:
> (a) necessary to secure compliance with laws and regulations that are not inconsistent with the provisions of this Agreement;
> (b) necessary to protect human, animal or plant life or health; or
> (c) related to the conservation of living or non-living exhaustible natural resources.

Colombia-Japan BIT, *supra* note 193, art. 5 ¶ 6(a)–(c).

220 *Id.* art. 11¶ 1.

221 *Id.*

222 *Id.* (emphasis added).

223 *See, e.g.*, Robert W. McGee, Corporate Governance in Transition and Developing Economies: A Case Study of Colombia (August 25, 2010), http://ssrn.com/abstract=1665056 or http://dx.doi.org/10.2139/ssrn.1665056 (last visited April 29, 2013) (evaluating Colombia as a transition economy under relevant OECD standards).

Republic of Colombia." This reference to international agreements also likely concerns the application of the customary international law of public purpose to the public purpose component of the BIT's Article 11 expropriation and compensation provision. The invocation of public purpose in international agreements or international customary law only is conducive to the legacy public purpose doctrine, which in turn would well serve both the expectations and needs of developing State signatories to BITs – here Colombia. A generic reference to international agreements further bolsters the proposition that what Colombia intended was to define public purpose as broadly as possible, as would inevitably ensue from a definition premised on international agreements that are multidisciplinary and ranging from human rights to international commercial law to international investment law.

The laws of Colombia provide for an expansive construction of the terms *public purpose, public interest,* and *social interest*. By way of example, Article 58 of the Colombian Constitution of 1991 is structured around the public purpose doctrine and emphasizes the deep connection between the doctrine, property rights, and a right to regulate based on public purpose:

Original	Translation
Art. 58. Se garantizan la propiedad privada y los demás derechos adquiridos con arreglo a las leyes civiles, los cuales no pueden ser desconocidos ni vulnerados por leyes posteriores. Cuando de la aplicación de una ley expedida por motivo de utilidad pública o interés social, resultaren en conflicto los derechos de los particulares con la necesidad por ella reconocida, *el interés privado deberá ceder al interés público o social.*	Art. 58. Private property is guaranteed together with all other rights arising from legislation, which rights cannot be disavowed or violated by subsequent legislation. Wherever emergency legislation arises from a matter of public or social interest, and such legislation results in a conflict with the rights of private parties, *private interest must yield to public or social interests.*
La propiedad es una función social que implica obligaciones. *Como tal, le es inherente una función ecológica.*	Property is a social function that entails obligations. *Accordingly, inherent in these obligations is an ecological responsibility.*
El Estado protegerá y promoverá las formas asociativas y solidarias de propiedad.	The State shall protect and promote all collective and private forms of property rights.
Por motivos de *utilidad pública* o de *interés social definidos por el legislador, podrá haber expropriación mediante sentencia judicial e indemnización previa. Esta se fijará consultando los intereses de la comunidad y del afectado.* En los casos que determine el legislador, dicha expropriación podrá adelantarse por vía administrativa,	*Based upon concerns pertaining to public utility or social interests as defined by the legislature, legal expropriations may take place pursuant to judicial judgment or prior indemnity. Any such expropriation shall balance community interests and those of the aggrieved party.* As set forth by the legislature, any such expropriation may be expedited

Original	Translation
sujeta a posterior acción contenciosa administrativa, incluso respecto del precio.	pursuant to an administrative proceeding subject to a subsequent administrative challenge that may also pertain to valuation.
Con todo, el legislador, por razones de equidad, podrá determinar los casos en que no haya lugar al pago de indemnización, mediante el voto favorable de la mayoría absoluta de los miembros de una y otra Cámara. *Las razones de equidad, así como los motivos de utilidad pública o de interés social, invocados por el legislador, no serán controvertibles judicialmente.*	*The legislature based upon equity consideration, may legislate instances where payment of indemnity pursuant to an expropriation shall not issue. These cases, however, shall be subject to a majority vote of all members of Congress at the time. The legislature's premises based on equity, public utility or social interest shall not be subject to judicial review.*[224]

The invocation of the domestic law of the Republic of Colombia as a basis for defining public purpose within the meaning of the Article 11 expropriation and compensation provision of the Colombia-Japan BIT also speaks to Colombia's intent as the presumed Host State to apply a public purpose doctrine that is self-judging (based on a subjective standard) and content expansive so as to defy a specific subject matter content that would limit its application.[225] The qualification in the note of the very text, "[i]n the case of the Republic of Colombia"[226] (i.e., not applicable to Japan) raises the issue as to whether the public purpose doctrine as embodied in customary international law should be construed by itself or also (i) within the context of the domestic law of the invoking State, (ii) the domestic law of all signatories to the treaty, or (iii) only the domestic law of the party to the treaty explicitly identified (if any) in the text. Although the annex referred to in Article 11 (Annex III) is silent on this issue, it does support a liberal construction of public purpose based on a self-judging subjective standard and thus argues for

[224] Constitution of 1991 of the Republic of Colombia (translation and emphasis supplied by author). *See also* Daniel Bonilla, *Liberalism and Property in Colombia: Property as a Right and Property as a Social Function*, 80 Fordham L. Rev. 1135 (2011).

[225] A note to Article 11 provides:

> Note: In the case of the Republic of Colombia, the term "public purpose," being used in this paragraph, is a term used in international agreements and may be expressed in the domestic law of the Republic of Colombia using terms such as "public purpose" or "social interest."

Colombia-Japan BIT, *supra* note 193, art. 11.

[226] *Id.*

a hybrid legacy-domestic law approach.[227] The comment to public purpose within the meaning of Article 11 explicitly refers to the exclusion of "measures [that are] so severe in the light of their purpose that they cannot reasonably [be] viewed as having been adopted and applied in good faith."[228] The purportedly explanatory Annex III to the article arguably creates greater uncertainty than the certainty it may otherwise ever aspire to redeem.

The Colombia-Japan BIT, in contrast with the expansive security exception approach of the SADC Model BIT and most of the Sample BITs, qualifies in a restrictive manner the public order element to the "general and security exceptions" contained in Article 15.[229] The Note contained in the text rests on four words – "genuine," "sufficiently serious," and "fundamental" – to qualify the exercise of a public order exception by providing:

> Note: The public order exception may be invoked only where a genuine and sufficiently serious threat is posed to one of the fundamental interests of society.[230]

Taken together, the use of public purpose within Article 11 ("Expropriation and Compensation") and public order within Article 15 ("General and Security Exceptions") notably evince the effects of the international treaty negotiation process. The Article 11 "Expropriation and Compensation" provision, arguably

[227] The Note in the text at the conclusion of Article 11 ("Expropriation and Compensation") reads: "Note: For greater certainty, Article 11 shall be interpreted in accordance with Annex III." *Id.* Paragraph 3 of Annex III provides:

> 3. Except in such circumstances as when a measure or a series of *measures is so severe in the light of their purpose* that they cannot be *reasonably* reviewed as having been adopted and applied in *good faith*, non-discriminatory measures of a Contracting Party that are designed and applied *to protect legitimate public welfare objectives* in accordance with paragraph 1 of Article 15, do not constitute indirect expropriation.

Colombia-Japan BIT, *supra* note 193, annex III ¶ 3.

[228] *Id.*

[229] The relevant provisions of Article 15 read:

> 1. Subject to the requirement that such measures are not applied by a Contracting Party in a manner which would constitute a means of arbitrary or unjustifiable discrimination against the other Contracting Party or a disguised restriction on investments of investors of that other Contracting Party in the Area of the former Contracting Party, nothing in this Agreement other than Article 12 shall be construed to prevent that former Contracting Party from adopting or enforcing measures, including those to protect the environment:
> (a) necessary to protect human, animal or plant life or health;
> (b) *necessary to protect public morals or to maintain public order.*

Id. at art. 15, ¶ 1 (a)–(b) (emphasis added).

[230] *Id.*

favoring the protection of Home-State investments, is substantively materially qualified by a very expansive construction of the public purpose exception that would tend to favor Host States. Similarly, but in reverse order, the broad Article 15 "General and Security Exceptions" that would typically favor Host States is tempered by a very narrow construction of the public order exception. Likely, the very severity of the international treaty negotiation process provided for a reference to sustainable development in the preamble[231] that exceeded the brief mention of the principle in the Canada-China BIT, but was not overtly implemented throughout the Colombia-Japan BIT. The more detailed reference in the BIT's preamble does facilitate any likely interpretive broadening of the application of the public purpose doctrine by a signatory.[232]

c. The Croatia-Azerbaijan BIT

Yet another BIT from the Sample BITs to reference sustainable development is the Agreement between the Government of the Republic of Croatia and the Government of the Republic of Azerbaijan on the Promotion and Reciprocal Protection of Investments ("Croatia-Azerbaijan BIT"), which was signed in 2007. Unlike the Canada-China BIT between two industrialized countries with leading economies and the Colombia-Japan BIT between an industrialized leading economy and an economy in transition, the Croatia-Azerbaijan BIT is between two developing countries or economies in transition.[233] It is likely that, whatever economic or developmental statistics may distinguish

[231] *See generally* ANTHONY AUST, MODERN TREATY LAW & PRACTICE (Cambridge University Press 2007).

[232] Even though the sustainable development iteration of the public purpose doctrine is not widely or very overtly implemented throughout the BIT, aspects of the principle are accorded considerable weight. By way of example, Article 21 ("Measures on Health, Safety, Environment, and Labor") is sufficiently broad so as to fall squarely within the sustainable development dialogue:

> 1. Each Contracting Party recognizes that it is inappropriate to encourage investment activities of investors of the other Contracting Party and of a non-Contracting Party by relaxing its domestic health, safety or environmental measures or by lowering its labor standards. Accordingly, each Contracting Party should not waive or otherwise derogate from such measures or standards as an encouragement for the establishment, acquisition or expansion in its Area of investments by investors of the other Contracting Party and of a non-Contracting Party.
> 2. Each Contracting Party may adopt, maintain or enforce any measure that it considers appropriate to ensure that investment activities in its Area are undertaken in a manner not incompatible with its environmental law, provided that such measure is consistent with this Agreement.

Colombia-Japan BIT, *supra* note 193, art. 21 ¶¶ 1–2.

[233] Even though Azerbaijan and Croatia have striking differences, they also enjoy material similarities pertaining to their respective economic development.

these countries from each other, they find themselves fundamentally at parity. It would likely follow that, absent the need to satisfy an exigent strategic resource need, neither State enjoyed a strategic or tactical negotiating posture over the other at the time of the signing of the BIT. These factors lend considerable interest to the Croatia-Azerbaijan BIT's treatment of the sustainable development iteration of the public purpose doctrine.

The term "sustainable development" appears only once in the treaty. The preamble, in a single sentence, mentions sustainable development in connection with the protection of health, safety, and the environment, even though the term is separated from these categories by a "conjunctive."[234] In contrast with the SADC Model BIT, Article 2 of the BIT identifies the promotion and protection of investments as the foundational policy underlying the Agreement, in part by detailing investment protection obligations extending from the Host State in favor of foreign investments/investors.[235]

Annual Data: 2011

	Azerbaijan	Croatia
Population (m)	9.1	4.4
GDP (US$ m; market exchange rate	57,773	62,493.4
GDP (US$ m; purchasing power parity)	119,560	78,620
GDP per head (US$; market exchange rate)	6,341	14,197
GDP per head (US$; purchasing power parity)	13,122	17,860
Exchange rate (av)	0.790 Manat:US$	5.34 HRK:US$

Historical Averages (%): 2007–2011

	Azerbaijan	Croatia
Population growth	1.3	−0.2
Real GDP growth	9.7	−0.3
Real domestic demand growth	6.3	−1.2
Inflation	10.3	2.9
Current-account balance (% of GDP)	28.5	−4.6
FDI inflows (% of GDP)	−1.9	5.1

Source: The Economist Intelligence Unit (most figures estimated).

[234] The reference reads: "Desiring to achieve these objectives in a manner consistent with the protection of health, safety, and the environment and the protection of sustainable development." Croatia-Azerbaijan BIT, *supra* note 193, preamble.

[235] Article II (Promotion and Protection of Investments) provides:

> 1. Each Contracting Party shall encourage and create favorable conditions in its State territory for investments by investors of the other Contracting Party and in exercise of powers conferred by its national legislation shall admit such investments.

Although Article 2 details orthodox investor protection standards in the form of (i) customary international law's minimum standard of treatment of aliens, (ii) fair and equitable treatment, (iii) full and constant protection and security, and (iv) the proscription of unreasonable, arbitrary, or discriminatory measures, the absence of sustainable development qualifying language is noticeable and, to some extent, at odds with the preamble's mention of sustainable development as a principle underlying the BIT. In this same vein, the general exceptions provision (Article 5) is remarkably narrow as to scope, omitting exceptions having their origins in the GATT, financial prudential measures, and even State security or those exceptions typically associated loosely with State police powers.[236] The BIT hardly carves out any meaningful or even orthodox exceptions that seek to broaden the domestic regulatory space of a presumably Host State.

Within the context of two developing States, at least pursuant to the Croatia-Azerbaijan BIT, the sustainable development iteration of the public purpose doctrine in fact finds no voice, a fact that cannot be altogether surprising. The BIT terms plainly state that its foremost objective is to foster foreign investment by according such investments the "orthodox standards of protection" without material qualifications or restrictions in the form of exceptions. In

> 2. Each Contracting Party shall at all times accord in its State territory to investments and returns of investors of the other Contracting Party treatment in accordance with the customary international law minimum standard of treatment of aliens, including fair and equitable treatment and full and constant protection and security.
> 3. Each Contracting Party shall not impair by unreasonable, arbitrary or discriminatory measures the management, maintenance, use, enjoyment, acquisition or disposal of investments in its State territory of investors of the other Contracting Party.
> 4. Each Contracting Party shall not impose mandatory measures on investments by investors of the other Contracting Party concerning purchase of materials, means of production, operation, transport, marketing of its products or similar orders having unreasonable or discriminatory effects.
> 5. Each Contracting Party shall, within the framework of its national legislation, consider in good faith all applications for necessary permits in connection with investments in its State territory, including authorizations for engaging executives, managers, specialists and technical personnel of the investor's choice.

Id. art. 2.

[236] A separate "security interests" provision is contained under Article 10 under the nomenclature "essential security interests." In addition to being brief, the single-sentence Article does limit its application to "essential security interests":

> Nothing in this Agreement shall be construed to prevent any Contracting Party from taking any action that it considers necessary for the protection of its essential security interests deriving from its membership in a customs, economic or monetary union, a common market or a free trade area.

Id. art. 10.

addition, the BIT is used neither as a methodology for addressing perceived or actual asymmetries in the relationship between States nor as a means to finance internal policies characterized as "development" efforts pursuant to the tenet limiting foreign investments only to the extent that they are compatible with the principle of "sustainable development." Countries of equal or comparable industrial development, economies, and spheres of political influence appear to be less likely to seek protection from a peer contracting party through adherence to the principle of sustainable development. Similarly, it is improbable that they would have sufficient negotiating gravitas to secure it.

d. The Japan–Independent State of Papua New Guinea BIT

The Agreement between the Government of Japan and the Government of the Independent State of Papua New Guinea for the Promotion and Protection of Investment ("Japan-Papua New Guinea BIT"), signed in 2011, also references sustainable development. In addition to a preamble that recognizes sustainable development as *in pari materia* with foreign investment,[237] transfer exceptions premised on national law and based on "good faith application" also constitute prominent elements of the BIT that enhance the Host State's regulatory space.[238]

[237] Because of the notably balanced approach that this BIT takes with respect to the promotion of foreign investment and the sustainable development iteration of the public purpose doctrine, the preamble merits citation in its entirety with emphasis placed on specific language:

> *Recognising the importance of foreign investment for national development, economic growth and general welfare* of the citizens in Japan and the Independent State of Papua New Guinea (hereinafter referred to as "the Contracting Parties");
>
> Desiring to promote investment in order to strengthen the economic relationship between the Contracting Parties;
>
> *Intending to create stable, equitable and favourable conditions for greater investment by investors of a Contracting Party in the Area of the other Contracting Party;*
>
> *Recognising that economic development, social development and environmental protection are interdependent and mutually reinforcing pillars of sustainable development and that cooperative efforts of the Contracting Parties to promote investment can play an important role in enhancing sustainable development;*
>
> *Recognising also that these objectives can be achieved without relaxing health, safety and environmental measures of general application;*
>
> *Acknowledging the importance of the cooperative relationship between labour and management in promoting investment between the Contracting Parties; and*
>
> *Convinced that this Agreement will contribute to the further development of the overall relationship between the Contracting Parties.*

Japan-Papua New Guinea BIT, *supra* note 193, preamble (emphasis supplied).

[238] The transfer of funds arising from covered investment exceptions pertains to laws or regulations found to be "relating to" a broad subject matter regulated by national law. Although seemingly

The Japan-Papua New Guinea BIT structurally resembles the Colombia-Japan BIT in that both agreements segregate exceptions arising from the GATT's Article XX, "Prudential Measures, and Health, Safety, and Environmental Measures and Labour Standards."[239] As to all three categories, however, the Colombia-Japan BIT accords the Host State with broader scope concerning these public purpose exceptions. The sustainable development principle in this treaty largely is limited to an expansive preamble and the fundamental exceptions contained in Articles 14, 17, 18, and 22. The tempered expression of the sustainable development principle throughout the BIT to some extent comports with the treatment accorded to sustainable development in the Colombia-Japan BIT, but within the context of Papua New Guinea (not Colombia) facing Japan, an industrialized State with considerably more resources and political influence than Papua New Guinea. This BIT helps to corroborate the proposition[240] that treaty-drafting techniques, without more, are insufficient in placing constraints on the public purpose doctrine or its sustainable development iteration. Also, notwithstanding the rigors of international treaty negotiations between an industrialized State and

national or parochial in nature, the "relating to" rubric is particularly broad. Article 14 ("Transfers") in pertinent part provides:

> 3. Notwithstanding paragraphs 1 and 2, a Contracting Party may delay or prevent a transfer through the equitable, non-discriminatory and *good-faith application of its laws* and regulations relating to:
>   (a) bankruptcy, insolvency or the protection of the rights of creditors;
>   (b) issuing, trading or dealing in securities;
>   (c) criminal or penal offences; or
>   (d) ensuring compliance with orders or judgments in adjudicatory proceedings.

Id. art. 14, ¶ 3 (a)–(d) (emphasis supplied). Measures tantamount to transfer exceptions in the international arena and under the heading of "temporary safeguard measures," are contained in Article 17, Paragraph 1, Subsections (a) and (b). This provision underscores the contrast between the multiple cross-industry sector foreign direct investments, which generally may only be characterized as microeconomic events and policies giving rise to exception fiat at a national level ostensibly premised on macroeconomic considerations:

> 1. A Contracting Party may adopt or maintain measures not conforming with its obligations under Article 2 relating to cross-border capital transactions and Article 14:
>   (a) in the event of serious balance-of-payments and external financial difficulties or threats thereof, or
>   (b) in cases where, in exceptional circumstances, movements of capital cause or threaten to cause serious difficulties for *macroeconomic management*, in particular, monetary and exchange rate policies.

Id. art. 17 ¶ 1(a)–(b) (emphasis added).

[239] *See Id.* art. 18 ("Prudential Measures"), art. 22 ("Health, Safety and Environmental Measures, and Labor Standards").

[240] *See supra* notes 133–37 and accompanying text.

a developing State, enough of the principle survives to accord both States considerable latitude in the exercise of their right to regulate. The "sustainable development BITs" further buttress the case for finding that the public purpose doctrine generally, and in its sustainable development configuration particularly, (i) forms part of customary international law and (ii) finds a materially broader expression under customary international law than within conventional international law, such as the NAFTA.

G. THE PUBLIC PURPOSE DOCTRINE IN WTO INTERNATIONAL INSTRUMENTS

The public purpose doctrine finds ample expression in WTO international instruments.[241] Throughout these instruments, the public purpose doctrine emerges as a central organizing principle that is fundamental in the creation of a hierarchy of constraints and premises that affect "regulatory sovereignty" and, under an orthodox paradigm, "the right to regulate." From an evidentiary perspective, the WTO international instruments, without more, well suffice to establish the existence of a vibrant public purpose doctrine within customary international law's normative sphere. These instruments demonstrate six fundamental propositions concerning the customary international law expression of the public purpose doctrine.

First, the international trade law exceptions broaden the subject matter content of the public purpose doctrine because of their macroeconomic policies. Second, the public purpose doctrine within the framework of WTO international instruments is expressed as a paramount precept to which principles of confidentiality, transparency, and compliance with legal authority are subordinated. Third, the public purpose doctrine, whether by design or happenstance, in part, is identified as necessary to the effort of harmonizing the policies and goals underlying international trade and international investment law. Fourth, the sustainable development expression of the public purpose doctrine that is so central to the UNCTAD 2012 Report and the SADC Model BIT, for example, has its genesis in WTO international instruments. Fifth, despite the reiteration of and conceptual reliance on the public purpose doctrine throughout the WTO international instruments, the

[241] By "WTO international instruments" a collective reference is intended to pertain to (i) the WTO General Agreement on Trade and Tariffs (1947), (ii) the WTO General Agreement on Trade and Tariffs (1994), (iii) the WTO Agreement on Government Procurement (1994), (iv) the WTO General Agreement on Trade and Services (1994), (v) the WTO Agreement on Trade-related Aspects of Intellectual Property Rights (1994), and (vi) the WTO Doha Ministerial Declaration (2001).

doctrine is nowhere defined, and self-judging (subjective) standards are implicitly referred to for the doctrine's application. Sixth, the WTO international instruments do not provide an actual or conceptual foundation for the proposition that "the right to regulate" remains one and the same irrespective of whether such regulatory exercise takes place within the context of foreign investment protection or the administration of international trade barriers.

The prominence of the public purpose doctrine in the WTO international instruments is testimony to the doctrine's importance. The absence, however, of substantive content and uniformity of nomenclature and application, as well as the dogmatic insistence on a self-judging methodology of application, all argue in favor of a meaningful reexamination of the doctrine through the lens of economic globalization and a paradigm of interdependence that commands transforming "the right to regulate" into "considerations of regulatory sovereignty" that are conducive to multilateral policy consequences.[242]

1. *WTO Doha Ministerial Declaration: November 14, 2001*

The WTO Doha Ministerial Declaration adopted on November 14, 2001 ("the Doha Declaration"), much like the UNCTAD international instruments,[243] references the public purpose doctrine in the context of a multilateral trading system. Thus, at first sight, public purpose within the context of the Doha Declaration would appear to be distinct from public purpose as a legal exception broadening the right to regulate to the detriment of an obligation to protect foreign investment. Careful consideration, however, demonstrates that the distinct iterations of the public purpose doctrine throughout the Doha Declaration are no different from the exceptions found in Articles XX and XXI of the GATT, as well as in the SADC Model BIT and other actual BITs in force in the form of the sustainable development principle. Consequently, the public purpose doctrine is, to a great extent, both a legal and economic principle. This dual character is markedly apparent in the Doha Declaration.

The preamble to the Doha Declaration is testament to the sustainable development expression of the public purpose doctrine and to sustainable development's dual configuration. Whereas the second and sixth paragraphs of the preamble quite significantly reference the preamble to the Marrakesh

[242] By "multilateral policy consequences" reference is made to the new use of public purpose as a principle that furthers the interests of both developing and developed States, by emphasizing interdependence and a policy of transnational cooperation wherein investor-State disputes find resolution in more than just "all-or-nothing" juridical rubrics.

[243] *See* discussion *supra* at Chapter 2.E.

Agreement,[244] Paragraph 6 explicitly mentions the "objective" and "promotion" of sustainable development.[245] This paragraph sets forth the premise that eventually would serve to bolster the public purpose doctrine found in international trade law and later incorporated into international investment law. By identifying exceptions, States are provided with the right to regulate for specific public purposes, "subject to the requirement that they are not applied in a manner which would constitute a means of arbitrary or unjustified discrimination between countries where the same conditions prevail, or a disguised restriction on international trade, and are otherwise in accordance with the provisions of the WTO Agreements."[246]

Identifying public purpose with the right to regulate within the framework of international trade law "at the levels [that a State] considers appropriate"[247]

[244] The Agreement establishing the World Trade Organization concluded on April 15, 1994 (a.k.a., the "Marrakesh Agreement") first identified the principle of sustainable development in connection with an international trade system and as a global objective. The principle is contained in embryonic form, and the preamble enjoys a neutral multilateral tone that does not express any particular penchant favoring industrialized or developing states. Instead, its emphasis is on the development of an integrated multilateral international trade framework that would maximize global efficiencies. It reads:

> The *Parties* to this Agreement,
>
> *Recognizing* that their relations in the field of trade and economic endeavour should be conducted with a view to raising standards of living, ensuring full employment and a large and steadily growing volume of real income and effective demand, and expanding the production of and trade in goods and services, while allowing for the optimal use of the world's resources in accordance with the objective of sustainable development, seeking both to protect and preserve the environment and to enhance the means for doing so in a manner consistent with their respective needs and concerns at different levels of economic development,
>
> *Recognizing* further that there is need for positive efforts designed to ensure that developing countries, and especially the least developed among them, secure a share in the growth in international trade commensurate with the needs of their economic development,
>
> *Being desirous* of contributing to these objectives by entering into reciprocal and mutually advantageous arrangements directed to the substantial reduction of tariffs and other barriers to trade and to the elimination of discriminatory treatment in international trade relations,
>
> *Resolved*, therefore, to develop an integrated, more viable and durable multilateral trading system encompassing the General Agreement on Tariffs and Trade, the results of past trade liberalization efforts, and all of the results of the Uruguay Round of Multilateral Trade Negotiations.

Marrakesh Agreement Establishing the World Trade Organization preamble, April 15, 1994, 1867 U.N.T.S. 154 [hereinafter Marrakesh Agreement].

[245] Doha Declaration, *supra* note 39, at ¶ 6.

[246] *Id.*

[247] *Id.*

also provides foundation for the subjective application of the doctrine, at least within the confines of international investment and trade law.[248] The public purpose doctrine, whether expressed in the form of the sustainable development principle or otherwise, requires a hybrid economic-law configuration. In this regard, the Marrakesh Agreement's preamble taken together with the Doha Declaration contribute mightily to the doctrine's multifaceted constitution. Indeed, the Doha Declaration further developed this duality by emphasizing the relationship between trade and investment. The public purpose doctrine must be able to contribute to harmonizing the underlying legal and economic policies pertaining to trade and investment while at the same time serving their respective efficiencies. Paragraphs 20 and 21 of the Doha Declaration directly speak to the need to meet the expectations of industrialized States in the arena of investment protection.[249]

[248] Paragraph 6 of the Preamble of the WTO Doha Ministerial Declaration provides:

> 6. We strongly reaffirm our commitment to the *objective of sustainable development*, as stated in the preamble to the Marrakesh Agreement. We are convinced that the aims of upholding and safeguarding an open and non-discriminatory multilateral trading system, and *acting for the protection of the environment and the promotion of sustainable development* can and must be mutually supportive. We take note of the efforts by members to conduct national environmental assessments of trade policies on a voluntary basis. We recognize that under WTO rules no country should be prevented from taking measures for the protection of human, animal or plant life or health, or of the environment at the levels it considers appropriate, subject to the requirement that they are not applied in a manner which would constitute a means of arbitrary or unjustifiable discrimination between countries where the same conditions prevail, or a disguised restriction on international trade, and are otherwise in accordance with the provisions of the WTO Agreements. We welcome the WTO's continued cooperation with UNEP and other inter-governmental environmental organizations. We encourage efforts to promote cooperation between the WTO and relevant international environmental and developmental organizations.

Id. preamble ¶ 6.

[249] Paragraphs 20 and 21 in pertinent part provide:

> 20. Recognizing the case for a multilateral framework to secure transparent, stable and predictable conditions for long-term cross-border investment, particularly foreign direct investment, that will contribute to the expansion of trade, and the need for enhanced technical assistance and capacity-building in this area as referred to in paragraph 21, we agree that negotiations will take place after the Fifth Session of the Ministerial Conference on the basis of a decision to be taken, by explicit consensus, at that Session on modalities of negotiations.
>
> 21. We recognize the needs of developing and least-developed countries for enhanced support for technical assistance and capacity building in this area, including policy analysis and development so that they may better evaluate the implications of closer multilateral cooperation for their development policies and objectives, and human and institutional development. To this end, we shall work in cooperation with

As part of reconciling incongruities between industrialized States by maximizing investment, but also requiring regulatory transparency within an investor-friendly and stable environment, the Doha Declaration addresses the need to reconcile Host States' developmental objectives and regulatory authority with Home-State expectations. It observed:

> Any framework should reflect in a balanced manner the interests of Home and Host countries, and take due account of the development policies and objectives of Home governments *as well as their right to regulate in the public interest.*[250]

The Doha Declaration is fair and reasonable on this issue inasmuch as it does not fashion a general imperative that irreversibly amplifies the regulatory sovereignty of least developed or developing countries, but rather aspirationally provides that the particular needs of States are to be considered as part of any framework that touches or concerns transnational trade and investment between capital-exporting and capital-importing States.[251]

The Doha Declaration argues for a tempered and balanced approach to public purpose that, at minimum, aspires to reconcile any conflict between policy and trade objectives pertaining to Home States and Host States. To be sure, the Doha Declaration expresses concern for the plight of developing and "least developed" States, but does not do so in a manner that may undermine the "transparency" and "stability" expectations of capital-exporting countries.[252] What language the Doha Declaration may have favoring capital-

> other relevant intergovernmental organisations, including UNCTAD, and through appropriate regional and bilateral channels, to provide strengthened and adequately resourced assistance to respond to these needs.

Id. ¶¶ 20–21.

250 *Id.* ¶ 22 (emphasis added).

251 As to this proposition, the Declaration provides:

> The special development, trade and financial needs of developing and least-developed countries should be taken into account as an integral part of any framework, which should enable Members to undertake obligations and commitments *commensurate with their individual needs and circumstances*. Due regard should be paid to other relevant WTO provisions. Accounts should be taken, as appropriate, of existing bilateral and regional arrangements on investment.

Id. (emphasis added).

252 For example, Paragraphs 49 and 50 provide:

49. The negotiations shall be conducted in a transparent manner among the participants, in order to facilitate the *effective of participation of all*. It shall be conducted with a view to *ensuring benefits to all participants and to achieving an overall balance in the outcome of the negotiations.*

importing States does not exceed a distinguished treatment based on consent that never abandons the need to have fundamental principles in place (e.g., transparency and stability) in order to maximize the likelihood of success and benefits redounding to all States. Consequently, the WTO Doha Ministerial Declaration conceptually comports with the adoption of a proportionality test in the application of the public purpose doctrine in order to determine the extent to which, if at all, the right to regulate may infringe on a State's obligation to protect foreign investments/investors. The broad content of the doctrine compels consideration of competing interests if, in fact, it is to further the aims of all parties and to contribute to the creation of a stable and transparent international investment community among industrialized States, developing States, and economies in transition.

2. *Public Purpose and the WTO Agreement on Trade-Related Aspects of Intellectual Property Rights (1994)*

Article 8 of the 1994 WTO Agreement on Trade-Related Aspects of Intellectual Property Rights (the "WTO Agreement on Intellectual Property Rights") identifies the public purpose doctrine (in the form of "public interest") as providing a normative basis for regulatory activity in a very distinct space identified as "sectors of vital importance to [States'] socio-economic and technological development."[253] The exercise of this right to regulate is stated as self-judging (subjective). Even though the term "necessary" generally is suggestive of some objective standard, contextually, the use of this adjective is more indicative of an internal criteria best rooted in the perceived needs of individual countries. Similarly, the term "vital importance" is not defined, and its relationship to such broad subject matters as "socio-economic and technological development" hardly narrows the

> 50. The negotiations and the other aspects of the Work Programme shall take fully into account the principle of special and differential treatment for developing and least-developed countries embodied in: Part IV of the GATT 1994; the Decision of 28 November 1979 on Differential and More Favourable Treatment, Reciprocity and Fuller Participation of Developing Countries; the Uruguay Round Decision on Measures in Favour of Least-Developed Countries; and all other relevant WTO provisions.

Id. ¶¶ 49–50 (emphasis added).

[253] Article 8, Paragraph 1, provides in full:

> Members may, in formulating or amending their laws and regulations, adopt measures necessary to protect public health and nutrition, and to promote the public interest in sectors of vital importance to their socio-economic and technological development, provided that such measures are consistent with the provisions of this Agreement.

TRIPs, *supra* note 39, art. 8 ¶ 1.

doctrine's substantive content. The first part of the conjunctive "and," pertaining to the protection of "public health and nutrition," most closely resembles the special category public purpose subject matter contained as exceptions in Article XX of the GATT. Paragraph 1 of Article 8 ("Principles"), read in its totality as a single-sentence paragraph, materially resembles the principle of sustainable development.

Pursuant to the guise of *ordre public* or public morality, signatories may proscribe the commercial exploitation of inventions within their territory.[254] Such public order or morality may serve as an exception to exclude from patentability certain inventions or their commercial exploitation based upon the GATT's Article XX Special Public Purpose Categories.[255]

This instrument also subordinates confidentiality to the public interest iteration of the public purpose doctrine[256] in the form of "security exceptions" that also find space in the WTO Agreement on Intellectual Property Rights, much in keeping with the subject matter spectrum enunciated in Article XXI of the GATS.[257] In keeping with most references to the public purpose

[254] *Id.* art. 27 ¶ 2 ("Patentable Subject Matter").

[255] Article 27, paragraph 2 ("Patentable Subject Matter"), states:

> Members may exclude from patentability inventions, the prevention within their territory of the commercial exploitation of which is necessary to protect *ordre public* or morality, including to protect **human, animal or plant life or health or to avoid serious prejudice to the environment**, provided that such exclusion is not made merely because the exploitation is prohibited by their law.

Id. (boldface emphasis added).

[256] Article 63, Paragraph 4, provides that: "[n]othing in paragraphs 1,2 and 3 shall require Members *to disclose confidential information* which would impede law enforcement *or otherwise be contrary to the public interest* or would prejudice the legitimate commercial interests of particular enterprises, public or private." *Id.* art. 63 ¶ 4 (emphasis added).

[257] Article 73 ("Security Exceptions") states:

> Nothing in this Agreement shall be construed:
> (a) to require a Member to furnish any information the disclosure of *which it considers contrary to its essential security interests*; or
> (b) to prevent a Member from taking any action *which it considers necessary for the protection of its essential security interests*;
> (i) relating to fissionable materials or the materials from which they are derived;
> (ii) relating to the traffic in arms, ammunition and implements of war and to such traffic in other goods and materials as is carried on directly or indirectly for the purpose of supplying a military establishment;
> (iii) taken in time of war or other emergency in international relations; or
> (c) to prevent a Member from taking any action in pursuance of its obligations under the United Nations Charter for the Maintenance of International Peace and Security.

Id. art. 73 (emphasis added).

doctrine, exercise of a security exception is based on a subjective standard, notwithstanding the use of the term "essential" as a presumably objective qualifying factor. Thus, within the confines of Article 73, confidentiality or nondisclosure obligations are subordinated to the security exception iteration of the public purpose doctrine. This exception is common to WTO international instruments.[258]

3. *The Public Purpose Doctrine in the WTO General Agreement on Trade in Services (1994)*

The subordination of the principle of confidentiality or obligations of nondisclosure to the public purpose doctrine is certainly not limited to security-centered iterations of the doctrine. The 1994 WTO GATS presents an illustrative example. Article III of that Agreement sets forth the following *transparency* imperative:

> Each Member shall publish promptly and, except in emergency situations, at the latest by the time of their entry into force, all relevant measures of general application which pertain to or affect the operation of this Agreement. International agreements pertaining to or affecting trade in services to which a Member is a signatory shall also be published.[259]

Article III bis, however, subordinates the obligation to provide transparency to "public interest."[260] In doing so, it places the public purpose doctrine on equal footing with a normative foundation to act that would arise from (i) impeding law enforcement or (ii) prejudicing legitimate commercial interests.[261]

Subject to general qualifications that are nowhere defined and are broad and malleable as to both meaning and scope, under the banner of the

[258] *See, e.g.*, GATS, *supra* note 39, art. XIV bis (containing identical security exceptions); AGP, *supra* note 39, art. XXIII ¶ 1; GATT, *supra* Chapter 1 note 2, art. XXI (containing identical language).

[259] GATS, *supra* note 39, art. III ¶ 1.

[260] *Id.* art. III bis.

[261] Article III bis *(Disclosure of Confidential Information)* reads:

> Nothing in this Agreement shall require any Member to provide confidential information, the disclosure of which would impede law enforcement, or otherwise be contrary to the public interest, or which would prejudice legitimate commercial interests of particular enterprises, public or private.

Id.

protection of "public morals" or the maintenance of "public order,"[262] signatories are authorized to implement whatever measure arguably may meet these broad public purpose categories.[263] The Agreement likewise enunciates the common international trade law public purpose exception that now has found space in BITs: "measures necessary to protect human, animal or plant life or health."[264]

The GATS further amplifies the public purpose category that the customary international law expression of the doctrine presents. Materially indistinguishable from the standard found in Paragraph 25.2 of Article 25 of the SADC Model BIT,[265] the Agreement carves out considerable regulatory space in the form of prudential measures as to finance and macroeconomics.[266] The all-encompassing scope of the prudential measures exception is purportedly limited "[w]here such measures do not conform with the provisions of the Agreement" or otherwise are "used as a means of avoiding the Member's commitments or obligations under the Agreement."[267] This language, however, is tantamount to asserting that, in cases where the measure undertaken for prudential reasons would give rise to a breach of the agreement, only then would it be deemed excessive. Consequently, the exception remains unfettered.

[262] Footnote 5 to Article XIV ("General Exceptions") of the WTO General Agreement on Trade in Services (1994) does restrict measures adopted for the purported maintenance of "public order" by asserting that "the public order exception may be invoked only where a genuine and sufficiently serious threat is posed to one of the fundamental interests of society." *Id. art.* XIV n.5. Despite a strict construction of this constraining factor, the relative meaning of such rudimentary elements of the qualifying sentence, such as "fundamental interests of society" and "genuine" and "sufficiently serious threat," limit its effectiveness.

[263] *Id.* art. XIV ¶ (a).

[264] *Id.* art. XIV ¶ (b).

[265] SADC Model BIT Template, *supra* note 140, at 46–47.

[266] The exception entitled "Domestic Regulation" reads:

> (a) Notwithstanding any other provisions of the Agreement, a Member shall not be prevented from taking measures for prudential reasons, including for the protection of investors, depositors, policyholders or persons to whom a fiduciary duty is owed by a financial service supplier, or to ensure the integrity or stability of the financial system. Where such measures do not conform with the provisions of the Agreement, they shall not be used as a means of avoiding the Member's commitments or obligations under the Agreement.
>
> (b) Nothing in the Agreement shall be construed to require a Member to disclose information relating to the affairs and accounts of individual customers or any confidential or proprietary information in the procession of public entities.

GATS, *supra* note 39, annex on financial services ¶ 2.

[267] *Id.*

Even though the WTO international instruments embrace the principle of sustainable development of the public purpose doctrine, they still aspire to fashion "a multilateral framework of principles and rules . . . aimed at promoting the interests of all participants on a mutually advantageous basis and that securing an overall balance of rights and obligations, while giving due respect to national policy objectives."[268] From a structural perspective, unlike the UNCTAD instruments[269] or the SADC Model BIT,[270] the interests of both industrialized States and developing countries are treated as being equally important.

This aspiration notwithstanding, the public purpose doctrine in its various iterations unduly broadens the domestic regulatory space of its members. The public purpose doctrine is used as an exception that supersedes (i) the right to confidentiality,[271] (ii) the right to transparency,[272] (iii) the right to patentability of inventions,[273] and (iv) rights arising from contractual commitments.[274] It also provides the State with a regulatory sovereignty that is practically unrestricted. States may enact measures of any kind in furtherance of (i) public order;[275] (ii) public morality;[276] (iii) the protection of human, animal, or plant life or health;[277] (iv) protection of the environment; (v) security;[278] and (vi) financial institutional or economic soundness,[279] among other interests. The customary international law profile of the public purpose doctrine that arises from these texts is one that shall inevitably lead to asymmetries between States. An unbridled right to regulate also is conducive to conflicts that are "resolved" pursuant to "all-or-nothing" arbitral adjudications. No principle of proportionality finds a voice in these international texts with respect to the public purpose doctrine. These complexities are made worse by the vast scope of special public purpose categories, such as the principle of sustainable development,

[268] *Id.* preamble.
[269] For the purpose of this writing, "UNCTAD Instruments" refers to (1) the UNCTAD FDI Policy Note, supra note 39 and (2) the 2012 World Investment Report, supra note 69.
[270] *See supra* Chapter 2.F(1).
[271] *See supra* notes 255–56 and accompanying text.
[272] *Id.*
[273] *See supra* notes 253–54 and accompanying text.
[274] *See, e.g.*, GATS, *supra* note 39, art. III.
[275] *See, e.g.*, ACIA, *supra* note 35, art. 17; American Convention, *supra* Introduction note 12; AGP, *supra* note 39, art. 23; GATS, *supra* note 39, art. 27.
[276] *See, e.g.*, TRIPs, *supra* note 39, art. 27 ¶ 2.
[277] *See, e.g.*, Doha Declaration, *supra* note 39, at ¶ 6.
[278] *See, e.g.*, TRIPs, *supra* note 39, art. 73.
[279] *See, e.g.*, GATS, *supra* note 39, annex on financial services ¶ 2.

which, in its pristine state within the context of the SADC Model BIT, would render any measure colorably related in any way to economic development a justifiable infringement on an obligation to protect foreign investment. The self-judging standard of most iterations of the public purpose doctrine also militates against uniformity, predictability, and process legitimacy. Finally, treaty-drafting techniques may alleviate – but certainly not cure – the ills arising from a legacy public purpose doctrine devoid of content that is subjective in application.

3

Defining the Profile of the Public Purpose Doctrine in Human Rights Conventions

The actual status of the public purpose doctrine in customary international law cannot be ascertained without reference to what is perhaps the most universal principle that prescriptively qualifies and constrains the exercise of sovereignty: human rights.[1] The relationship between the public purpose doctrine and human rights is both complex and inexhaustible. Because of these qualities, this effort is limited to contextualizing and analyzing the scant but ever-present references to the public purpose doctrine in only three international human rights instruments.[2] Several observations on the relationship between the public purpose doctrine and international human rights, as identified in the Universal Declaration of Human Rights proclaimed by the General Assembly of the United Nations on December 10, 1948, are necessary as a condition to understanding more comprehensively the scope and content of the public purpose doctrine in customary international law. The connection between these two precepts (public purpose and human rights) is both antagonistic and complementary.

1 For a discussion on the juxtaposition of international standards and national authority, *see* Bas De Gaay Fortman, *Beating the State at Its Own Game: An Inquiry into the Intricacies of Sovereignty and the Separation of Powers*, in CHANGING PERCEPTIONS OF SOVEREIGNTY AND HUMAN RIGHTS, ESSAYS IN HONOUR OF CEES FLINTERMAN 41 (Ineke Boerefijn & Jenny Goldschmidt, eds., Intersentia 2008). *See also* Fons Coomans, *Sovereignty Fading Away? Prioritising Domestic Health Needs Versus Promoting Free Trade*, in CHANGING PERCEPTIONS OF SOVEREIGNTY AND HUMAN RIGHTS, ESSAYS IN HONOUR OF CEES FLINTERMAN 123 (Ineke Boerefijn & Jenny Goldschmidt, eds., Intersentia 2008); JOSÉ E. ALVAREZ, INTERNATIONAL ORGANIZATIONS AS LAW MAKERS 156 (Oxford University Press 2005; discussing the relationship between human rights and what the author describes as "the shrinking concept of domestic jurisdiction").

2 The authors have selected (i) the European Convention, *supra* Introduction note 15; (ii) the American Convention, *supra* Introduction note 12; and (iii) the African Charter, *supra* Chapter 2 note 45.

The orthodox or legacy public purpose doctrine, since its meaningful origins in the writings of Plato,[3] Aristotle,[4] and Thucydides,[5] has had its normative foundations in a public interest and common welfare that overrides the interests of any single individual. The prescriptive foundation is in an overarching common welfare. The description of the doctrine, however, is one that assumes that the *polis* or State makes possible the execution and instantiation of this principle of public welfare. Such polis or State in turn has interests commensurate with its understanding of the broader public purpose that justifies placing decisions based on the public interests and the common good above the pursuits of any single individual or even any identifiable group or community within the very State. Therefore, in broad strokes, the legacy public purpose doctrine is an expression of the preeminence of the concerns of the public (i.e., presumably the State) over the individual – an expression of the normative standing of the general over the specific.

International human rights principles serve to safeguard the individual from the de jure or de facto deprivation of fundamental rights on the part of the State.[6] Whereas the invocation of public purpose is an exercise of regulatory sovereignty that broadens the State's regulatory space,[7] the principles of international human rights law seek, at least in part, to diminish the State's exercise of regulatory sovereignty where such exercise infringes on the rights of an individual, groups of individuals, or a people.[8] In fact, international human

3 *See generally* PLATO, THE REPUBLIC OF PLATO (Alan Bloom, trans., Basic Books, pub., 2nd ed.).

4 *See generally* ARISTOTLE, NICOMACHEAN ETHICS (Robert C. Bartlett & Susan D. Collins, trans., Univ. of Chicago Press 2011); ARISTOTLE, THE POLITICS (Carnes Lord, trans., Univ. of Chicago Press 2011, 1st ed.).

5 *See generally* THUCYDIDES, HISTORY OF THE PELOPONNESIAN WAR (M. I. Finley, ed., Rex Warner, trans., Penguin Classics 1954).

6 "The purpose of human rights is at root in harmony with the purpose of the rule of law, properly understood as establishing conditions under which human dignity, freedom, and equality will flourish." Kevin T. Jackson, *The Normative Logic of Global Economic Governance: In Pursuit of Non-Instrumental Justification for the Rule of Law and Human Rights*, 22 MINN. J. INT'L L. 71, 145 (2013). As such, when "in jeopardy, human rights must be entrenched not only in centralized and formal coercive systems of 'hard' rules of international law, but even more importantly in decentralized and informal systems of 'soft' norms of economic governance regimes. Regardless, the rule of law ideal which underwrites these respective normative systems demands that the norms be binding and overriding in their essential characters." *Id.* at 145–46.

7 *See supra* Chapter 1 note 34 and accompanying text (discussing the Westphalian concept of sovereignty).

8 *See, e.g.*, Eric Allen Engle, *The Transformation of the International Legal System: The Post-Westphalian Legal Order*, 23 QLR 23, 32 (2004) ("[T]he principles of national self-determination and human rights contradict the Westphalian concept of sovereignty. This contradiction cannot be harmonized because the competing poles tend toward mutually exclusive outcomes").

rights law attempts to place stark constraints on the State's exercise of regulatory fiat against an individual or a people, even in instances where such regulation purports to be justified by public purpose considerations.[9] Viewed from this perspective, international human rights champions a very specific and "narrow" universe of interests of an individual, individuals, or peoples over the imposition of competing measures by the State, or the "primacy" of the particular over the general. Analytically, pursuant to an international human rights normative framework, the prescriptive content of general human rights law is satisfied by the fundamental rights that provide the

[9] Although "[n]o strong historical basis exists for the protection of an individual's human rights from violations by his or her own government" as "[a] State's treatment of its nationals was tradition ally a matter of State sovereignty," Jo M. Pasqualucci, *The Inter-American Human Rights System: Establishing Precedents and Procedure in Human Rights Law*, 26 U. Miami Inter-Am. L. Rev. 297, 302 (1995), there has been a recent trend toward according international human rights a preeminent status on the hierarchal ladder of international law.

A strong indication of the super-priority given to human rights regulation can be gleaned from the judgment of the Court of First Instance of the European Union in the case of *Kadi v. Council*. Dinah Shelton, *Normative Hierarchy in International Law*, 100 Am. J. Int'l L. 291, 311 (2006) (citing Case T315/01, Kadi v. Council (Eur. Ct. Justice September 21, 2005)). In that case, "[t]he Court opined that from the standpoint of international law, the obligations of the UN member states 'clearly prevail' over every other obligation of domestic law or international treaty law, including, for those that are members of the Council of Europe, their obligations under the European Convention on the Protection of Human Rights and Fundamental Freedoms." *Id.* at 311 (footnote omitted). Ultimately, however, the Court left room for individual protections to prevail, as stated succinctly by Shelton:

> Thus, the Court's judicial review, in principle, did not extend to the lawfulness of Council measures. Lest this conclusion call into question the entire framework of human rights guarantees established in Europe since the end of World War II, the Court found an exception to the notion of unreviewable and unlimited Security Council power:
>
> > Nonetheless, the Court is empowered to check, indirectly, the lawfulness of the resolutions of the Security Council in question with regard to jus cogens, understood as a body of higher rules of public international law binding on all subjects of international law, including the bodies of the United Nations, and from which no derogation is possible.
>
> This astonishing conclusion was rationalized by the Court's statement that the UN Charter itself "presupposes the existence of mandatory principles of international law, in particular, the protection of the fundamental rights of the human person." The UN Charter also provides that the Security Council is to act in accordance with the purposes and principles of Charter Article 24(2). In effect, the Court claimed that the entire body of human rights law constitutes *jus cogens*, referring to "the mandatory provisions concerning the universal protection of human rights, from which neither the Member States nor the bodies of the United Nations may derogate because they constitute intransgressible principles of international customary law."

Id. at 311–12 (internal citations omitted).

individual with particular standing within the State concerning a person's right to action and omission within the organizational constraints of the State. Therefore, it follows that the prescriptive basis of this hierarchy in turn rests with principles that purport to be the most common and, therefore, universal and, for this reason, higher than any interest that a State may possibly justify based on mere invocation of public purpose.[10]

Conventional and customary international human rights law, however, is to find its perfect workings by supporting or supplementing domestic law.[11] International human rights law does not aspire to dislodge domestic law even though it serves as a "check and balance" on domestic law. To the extent that domestic law infringes on cognizable international human rights precepts, human rights law serves as a meta-State recourse for relief. It is within this framework that, in an era of informational and economic globalization, orthodox paradigms of Westphalian sovereignty yield to a more expansive, malleable, and flexible conception of sovereignty contemplating a juridical

[10] For example, as noted by Dinah Shelton:

> Apart from treaty provisions, claims of primacy may be made by those involved in promoting or ensuring respect for a particular body of international law. Some human rights institutions, for example, have asserted the priority of human rights guarantees in general over other international law, without necessarily claiming that the entire body of law constitutes *jus cogens*. The UN Committee on Economic, Social and Cultural Rights, in a 1998 statement on globalization and economic, social, and cultural rights, declared that the realms of trade, finance, and investment are in no way exempt from human rights obligations. The Committee's concerns were raised a second time in a statement urging members of the World Trade Organization (WTO) to adopt a human rights approach to trade matters, asserting that the "promotion and protection of human rights is the first responsibility of Governments."

Id. at 294 (internal footnotes omitted). However, as demonstrated by Shelton, this primacy has yet to run its course through a widespread State practice:

> The asserted primacy of all human rights law has not been reflected in State practice. If eventually accepted, it will reject the notion of *lex specialis* for trade or other fields where states can claim to be free from human rights obligations. It could also profoundly affect the work of all international organizations, which commonly claim to be governed only by their constituting legal instruments and the mandate therein conferred.

Id. at 294.

[11] "The purpose of international human rights treaties is not to limit a State's policy choices, but to ensure that the policy eventually chosen still allows the individual to enjoy his basic freedoms and rights." Jan Arno Hessbruegge, *Human Rights Violations Arising from Conduct of Non-State Actors*, 11 BUFF. HUM. RTS. L. REV. 21, 28 (2005). *See also* Dr. Anja Seibert-Fohr, *The Rise of Equality in International Law and Its Pitfalls: Learning from Comparative Constitutional Law*, 35 BROOK. J. INT'L L. 1, 38 (2010) ("The purpose of human rights norms is to set basic standards for the enjoyment of fundamental rights and freedoms, not to unduly limit legislative discretionary power by providing a judicially prescribed model for legislation").

hierarchy in which international law preempts domestic juridical authority.[12] Despite this presumed "hierarchy," international human rights law cannot be altogether severed from municipal law. Because international human rights law is to operate in tandem with municipal law, a robust, content-rich, and *objective* public purpose doctrine is not merely welcomed, but actually indispensable. The doctrine serves as a conceptual point of convergence where international human rights law, international investment law, and the interests of Home and Host States (particularly as concerns foreign investment) all find a meaningful space.

The European Convention on Human Rights ("European Convention"), the American Convention on Human Rights ("American Convention"), and the African Charter on Human Rights and Peoples' Rights ("African Charter") all have preambles that frame the particular historical context of their respective jurisdictions. Sensitivity to this historical framework is necessary. It points to the substantive role of historicity in the regional and global formation and transformation of international human rights, and, therefore, also of the public purpose doctrine. The content and scope of human rights conventional law is materially defined by the social and economic history of the signatory States.[13] In this sense, its aspiration to uniformity is challenged and must be questioned in analyzing its relation to the public purpose doctrine. Similarly, the subject matter and application of the public purpose doctrine also must be understood as differing accordingly.[14] The preamble of the European Convention on Human Rights, for example, *nowhere* explicitly mentions or alludes to economic or financial development. Economic development and human rights find no resonance in this preamble.[15] The preamble does not

[12] *See generally* Carlos M. Vazquez, *Customary International Law as U.S. Law: A Critique of the Revisionist and Intermediate Positions and a Defense of the Modern Position*, 86 NOTRE DAME L. REV. 1495 (2011); Curtis A. Bradley & Jack L. Goldsmith, *Customary International Law as Federal Common Law: A Critique of the Modern Position*, 110 HARV. L. REV. 815 (1997).

[13] *See* Myres S. McDougal, Harold D. Lasswell, & Lung-chu Chen, *Human Rights and World Public Order: A Framework for Policy-Oriented Inquiry*, 63 AM. J. INT'L L. 237, 242–43 (1969).

[14] The content, scope, and application of public purpose expressions such as the Principle of Sustainable Development, *supra* Chapter 2.E(5) and the Principle of Permanent Sovereignty over Natural Resources, *infra* Chapter 5, are illustrative examples of expressions of the public purpose doctrine that cannot be meaningfully understood or submitted to sustained analysis without first exploring their connection to developing states and the process and consequences of decolonization.

[15] The preamble to the European Convention on Human Rights, as amended by Protocols Nos. 11 and 14, is succinct and reads as follows:

> THE GOVERNMENTS SIGNATORY HERETO, being members of the Council of Europe, by the General Assembly of the United Nations on the 10th December 1948;
>
> Considering that this Declaration aims at securing the universal and effective recognition and observance of the Rights therein declared;

contain any etymological iteration of the words "economic" or "financial." The only connection between the European Convention's preamble and economic development as a foundational human right is through its *consideration* of the Universal Declaration of Human Rights. It is noteworthy that the European Convention does not incorporate by reference or otherwise explicitly embrace *all* of the principles enunciated as rights in that Declaration.[16]

> Considering that the aim of the Council of Europe is the achievement of greater unity between its members and that one of the methods by which that aim is to be pursued is the maintenance and further realization of human rights and fundamental freedoms;
>
> Reaffirming their profound belief in those fundamental freedoms which are the foundation of justice and peace in the world and are best maintained on the one hand by an effective political democracy and on the other by a common understanding and observance of the human rights upon which they depend;
>
> Being resolved, as the governments of European countries which are like-minded and have a common heritage of political traditions, ideals, freedom and the rule of law, to take the first steps for the collective enforcement of certain of the rights stated in the Universal Declaration, . . .

European Convention, *supra* Introduction note 15, preamble.

[16] The European Convention on Human Rights studiously uses the participle "considering" in connection with the Universal Declaration of Human Rights two of the three times that the Declaration is at all referenced in the preamble. The reference to the Declaration not containing the "considering" language also qualifies the wholesale incorporation of the Declaration by asserting that the signatories to the European Convention are taking "the first steps for the collective enforcement of *certain* of the rights stated in the Universal Declaration, . . ." *Id.* (emphasis added).

The United Nations Declaration on Human Rights directly or indirectly references economic development as a fundamental principle in the following six articles:

> Art. 17:
>
> (1) Everyone has the right to own property alone as well as in association with others.
>
> (2) No one shall be arbitrarily deprived of his property.
>
> Art. 22:
>
> Everyone, as a member of society, has the right to social security and is entitled to realization, through national effort and international co-operation and in accordance with the organization and resources of each State, of the economic, social and cultural rights indispensable for his dignity and the free development of his personality.
>
> Art. 23:
>
> (1) Everyone has the right to work, to free choice of employment, to just and favourable conditions of work and to protection against unemployment.
>
> (2) Everyone, without any discrimination, has the right to equal pay for equal work.
>
> (3) Everyone who works has the right to just and favourable remuneration ensuring for himself and his family an existence worthy of human dignity, and supplemented, if necessary, by other means of social protection.
>
> (4) Everyone has the right to form and to join trade unions for the protection of his interests.
>
> Art. 24:
>
> Everyone has the right to rest and leisure, including responsible limitation of working hours and periodic holidays with pay.

The preamble does affirmatively state that its paramount objective is "the achievement of greater unity between its members,"[17] which it asserts to be achievable through the addition of "realization of human rights and fundamental freedoms."[18] This preamble, in addition, asserts that it is through an "effective political democracy" and the observance of human rights that "fundamental freedoms which are the foundation of justice and peace in the world are best maintained."[19] The European Convention also invokes uniformity of thought and "heritage of political traditions"[20] as a foundation for "collective enforcement."[21]

In high relief, the preambles of the American Convention on Human Rights, and the African Charter on Human and Peoples' Rights both explicitly reference the very deep relationship between economic development and

> Art. 25:
> (1) Everyone has the right to a standard of living adequate for the health and wellbeing of himself and of his family, including food, clothing, housing and medical care and necessary social services, and the right to security in the event of unemployment, sickness, disability, widowhood, old age or other lack of livelihood in circumstances beyond his control.
> (2) Motherhood and childhood are entitled to special care and assistance. All children, whether born in or out of wedlock, shall enjoy the same social protection.
>
> Art. 26:
> (1) Everyone has the right to education. Education shall be free, at least in the elementary and fundamental stages. Elementary education shall be compulsory. Technical and professional education shall be made generally available and higher education shall be equally accessible to all on the basis of merit.
> (2) Education shall be directed to the full development of the human personality and to the strengthening of respect for human rights and fundamental freedoms. It shall promote understanding, tolerance and friendship among all nations, racial or religious groups, and shall further the activities of the United Nations for the maintenance of peace.
> (3) Parents have a prior right to choose the kind of education that shall be given to their children.

Universal Declaration of Human Rights, G.A. Res. 217 (III) A, U.N. Doc. A/RES/217(III) (December 10, 1948) [hereinafter UDHR].

[17] European Convention, *supra* Introduction note 15, preamble.

[18] *Id.*

[19] *Id.*

[20] *Id.*

[21] *Id.* Although the Convention's references to "like-minded" and "a common heritage of political traditions" may perhaps appear as too euphemistic a descriptive account of a "like-minded[ness]" that witnessed two world wars in the twentieth century, as well as a commonality as to a "heritage of political traditions" that more closely resembles a mosaic than a monolithic Euclidian plane, the *good faith* aspirational underpinnings of the Declaration command respect.

human rights.[22] Historicity, in the affirmative and in contrast with the European Convention, displays its hand in both of these Conventions, but especially with respect to the African Charter. The preamble to the African Charter further refers to the process of decolonization, in addition to economic rights and social rights, and construes this as rising to the level of human rights. It specifically reaffirms:

> [T]he pledge they [African member States] solemnly made in Article 2 of the said Charter to eradicate all forms of colonialism from Africa, to coordinate and intensify their cooperation and efforts to achieve a better life for the peoples of Africa and to promote international cooperation having due regard to the Charter of the United Nations and the Universal Declaration of Human Rights.[23]

[22] The Preamble to the American Convention on Human Rights in pertinent part states:

> Considering, that the Third Special Inter-American Conference (Buenos Aires, 1967) approved the incorporation into the Charter of the Organization itself [the Universal Declaration of Human Rights] of broader standards with respect to economic, social, and educational rights and resolved that an inter-American Convention on Human Rights should determine the structure, competence, and procedure of the organs responsible for these matters . . . .

American Convention, *supra* Introduction note 12, preamble.

[23] The preamble in its entirety states:

> The African states members of the Organization of African Unity, parties to the present convention entitled "African Charter on Human and Peoples' Rights,"
>
> Recalling Decision 115 (XVI) of the Assembly of Heads of State and Government at its Sixteenth Ordinary Session held in Monrovia, Liberia, from 17 to 20 July 1979 on the preparation of a "preliminary draft on an African Charter on Human and Peoples' Rights providing inter alia for the establishment of bodies to promote and protect human and peoples' rights";
>
> Considering the Charter of the Organization of African Unity, which stipulates that "freedom, equality, justice and dignity are essential objectives for the achievement of the legitimate aspirations of the African peoples";
>
> Reaffirming the pledge they solemnly made in Article 2 of the said Charter to eradicate all forms of colonialism from Africa, to coordinate and intensify their cooperation and efforts to achieve a better life for the peoples of Africa and to promote international cooperation having due regard to the Charter of the United Nations, and the Universal Declaration of Human Rights;
>
> Taking into consideration the virtues of their historical tradition and the values of African civilization which should inspire and characterize their reflection on the concept of human and peoples' rights;
>
> Recognizing on the one hand, that fundamental human rights stem from the attributes of human beings which justifies their national and international protection and on the other hand that the reality and respect of peoples' rights should necessarily guarantee human rights;
>
> Considering that the enjoyment of rights and freedoms also implies the performance of duties on the part of everyone; convinced that it is henceforth essential to pay a

Just as the European Convention on Human Rights must be read within the context of what is perceived as being one common European history with shared political values among European States, the African Charter on Human and Peoples' Rights needs to be contextualized within the framework of a history of colonialism, neocolonialism, and decolonialism. The sustainable development iteration of the public purpose doctrine, too, must be embraced as a human rights principle within the parameters of both the American Convention and the African Charter. Because the scope and content of the conventional international law of human rights varies based on the relevant history and region concerned, the interface between the public purpose doctrine and international human rights law also varies. The European Convention's silence on economic development cannot be altogether disassociated from the workings of the public purpose doctrine within the constraints of this Convention. Moreover, this omission is a testament to the expectations of, at a minimum, one group of industrialized States with respect to the scope and content of conventional international human rights law, as well as of the public purpose doctrine.[24]

Although the European Convention on Human Rights is selective in its adoption of principles from the United Nations Universal Declaration of Human Rights and does not engage in a verbatim incorporation by reference

> particular attention to the right to development and that civil and political rights cannot be disassociated from economic, social and cultural rights in their conception as well as universality and that the satisfaction of economic, social and cultural rights is a guarantee for the enjoyment of civil and political rights;
>
> Conscious of their duty to achieve the total liberation of Africa, the peoples of which are still struggling for their dignity and genuine independence, and undertaking to eliminate colonialism, neo-colonialism, apartheid, zionism and to dismantle aggressive foreign military bases and all forms of discrimination, particularly those based on race, ethnic group, color, sex, language, religion or political opinions;
>
> Reaffirming their adherence to the principles of human and peoples' rights and freedoms contained in the declarations, conventions and other instrument adopted by the Organization of African Unity, the Movement of Non-Aligned Countries and the United Nations;
>
> Firmly convinced of their duty to promote and protect human and peoples' rights and freedoms taking into account the importance traditionally attached to these rights and freedoms in Africa.

African Charter, *supra* Chapter 2 note 45, preamble.

[24] The disparate economic, social, and juridical histories of industrialized and developing states also give rise to materially differing opinions as to the scope and content of the public purpose doctrine. This dissonance is immediately translated into different expectations concerning the fundamental relationship between the right to accord standard protections to foreign investment and regulatory sovereignty or the right to regulate. The differences between the conventional international human rights law between industrialized and nonindustrialized States or economies in transition, it is here asserted, can be directly transposed to the different expectations between industrialized and developing states as to the public purpose doctrine.

of this Declaration,[25] both the American Convention on Human Rights[26] and the African Charter on Human and Peoples' Rights directly reaffirm and incorporate by reference the United Nations Universal Declaration of Human Rights.[27] These different perspectival approaches to international human rights law cannot be altogether severed from their corresponding understanding of the public purpose doctrine.

The three conventions also represent contrasting conceptions of the prescriptive foundation of human rights law that may serve to reconcile different expectations as to the scope and content of human rights and public purpose. The European Convention on Human Rights speaks of "fundamental freedoms" deemed to be "the foundation of justice and peace in the world [that] are best maintained ... by an effective political democracy."[28] In fact, it mentions "human rights and fundamental freedoms" in the conjunctive.[29] This Convention does not present human rights as being disassociated or completely separate and distinct from the State. The State, in turn, is an idiosyncratic historical experience. This "historicity" permeates the Convention's spirit and technical framework. It also disavows any pretense of "uniformity among Conventions" in this mercurial field. Terms such as "political traditions" and "political democracy" find prominent spaces in the preamble. The American Convention and the African Charter represent different fundamental conceptions of the prescriptive foundation of conventional international human rights.

The American Convention on Human Rights and the African Charter on Human and Peoples' Rights both understand the essential rights of man classified as "human rights" as not deriving from the State. The American Convention specifically provides that:

> [T]he essential rights of man are not derived from one's being a national of a certain State, but are based upon attributes of the human personality, and that they therefore justify international protection in the form of a convention reinforcing or complementing the protection provided by the domestic law of the American States.[30]

[25] *See* UDHR, *supra* note 16.

[26] *See* American Convention, *supra* Introduction note 12, preamble ¶¶ 3–4 (adopting the United Nations Universal Declaration of Human Rights).

[27] *See* African Charter, *supra* Chapter 2 note 45, preamble ¶¶ 3–4 (adopting the United Nations Universal Declaration of Human Rights).

[28] European Convention, *supra* Introduction note 15, preamble.

[29] *Id.*

[30] American Convention, *supra* Introduction note 12, preamble.

Similarly, the African Charter on Human and Peoples' Rights asserts that:

> [F]undamental human rights stem from the attributes of human beings which justifies their national and international protection and on the other hand that the reality and respect of peoples [sic] rights should necessarily guarantee human rights.[31]

This unique perspective of human rights as separate and distinct from any right associated with or deriving from the State – intrinsic to the *individual* and not the citizen – represents a considerable departure from the proposition of that "public purpose" or the "collective good" overrides the particular interests or well-being of a private individual or interest group. It is an understanding of rights that does not tend to broaden regulatory sovereignty. This reasoning comports with the very general proposition that a State's obligation to protect individual rights certainly may outweigh its right to regulate. Thus, it would follow that a public purpose doctrine that serves to diminish individual rights in furtherance of broadening the State's regulatory rights would do violence to a higher order of principles based on the individual person, separate and apart from the State. This prescriptive approach to rights and, therefore, to obligations, argues in favor of regulatory sovereignty exclusively predicated on general conceptions of public welfare; thus, to be applied in conjunction with a subjective (self-judging) standard, such application should be subordinated to a higher set of norms.

The public purpose doctrine should provide for a more tempered application accounting for instances in which private interests would prevail over *certain* matters of State. This conceptualization of the public purpose doctrine comports with a view of international human rights law as supporting and supplementing national law and not just serving as a parallel higher set of rules whose function it is to police the national law of States. This unique relationship between international human rights law and the domestic law of States requires a delicate balance. That balance, in turn, can only be attained where the public purpose doctrine adequately broadens and constrains the right to regulate, as is the case when State abuse of the public purpose doctrine may trigger application of international human rights law.

The European Convention on Human Rights references the public purpose doctrine three times. The first such mention is found in Article 1, in connection with "the peaceful enjoyment" of possessions and the proscription against the deprivation of a natural or legal person's possessions "except in the *public interest* and subject to the conditions provided for by law and by the

[31] African Charter, *supra* Chapter 2 note 45, preamble.

general principles of international law."[32] The unequivocal statement of this right is tempered by a recognition of orthodox regulatory sovereignty premised on the public purpose doctrine ("general interest") as the operative talisman. The article's second directive notably does not speak to direct or indirect expropriation or nationalization or actions equivalent to or tantamount to such taking. Instead, it relies on the word "control" in asserting that the right to peaceful enjoyment of possession and property "shall not, however, in any way impair the right of a State to enforce such laws as it deems necessary to control the use of property in accordance with the general interest or to secure the payment of taxes or other contributions or penalties."[33] Thus, "public interest" and "general interest" are identified as precepts that actually may serve to limit the application of international human rights law providing for the peaceful enjoyment of possessions and the fundamental right to property.

Critical to this framework is both a substantive and functional understanding of the public purpose doctrine. The deprivation of possessions referenced in the first provision of Article 1 and the control of the use of property enunciated in the second provision are genuine and lawful only to the extent that they comport with a *legitimate* understanding of the public purpose doctrine. Absent this assumption, Article 1 merely would be promoting a very general right to property, possession, and enjoyment of property and possession, subject to an arbitrary and subjective regime of public purpose to be indiscriminately applied by States, ostensibly pursuant to domestic law in furtherance of orthodox regulatory sovereignty. This conception, or misconception, of the workings and interface between the public purpose doctrine and conventional international human rights law is necessary if in fact the strictures of cognizable human rights law are ever to be at all applied in defense of individuals against the *illegal* and *unjustified* infringement and encumbrance of such rights by States.[34]

[32] European Convention, *supra* Introduction note 15, art. 1 (emphasis added). Article 1 ("Protection of Property") reads:

> Every natural or legal person is entitled to the peaceful enjoyment of his possessions. No one shall be deprived of his possessions except in the *public interest* and subject to the conditions provided for by law and by the general principles of international law.
>
> The preceding provisions shall not, however, in any way impair the right of a State to enforce such laws as it deems necessary to control the use of property in accordance with the *general interest* or to secure the payment of taxes or other contributions or penalties.

Id. (emphasis added).

[33] *Id.*

[34] Even though the first provision of Article 1 concerning an actual deprivation of possessions – in contrast with "control" of the use of property in the second provision of the Article – does not mention the right to compensation or the loss of property to the State, it may well do so as a matter of treaty construction by dint of referencing the qualifying clause, "subject to the

The second notable reference to the public purpose doctrine in the European Convention on Human Rights is contained in Article 2 ("Freedom of Movement"). Notwithstanding the four single-sentence succinct structure of the article, eight public purpose categories are referenced, including explicit mention of "*ordre public*" and "public interest."[35] Structurally, the first two paragraphs set forth an unqualified statement of the right to freedom of movement both within the territory of a State and to leave any country, including a citizen's own national State.[36] As with Article 1 ("Protection of Property"), the public purpose doctrine is central to the theoretical and practical viability of the right to freedom of movement. The only constraints on the right are the two iterations of the public purpose doctrine (*ordre public* and public interest) and the six public purpose categories otherwise making up the article. Without being contextualized as public purpose categories that may find substantive definition within the public purpose doctrine as expressed in conventional or customary international law, the broad scope and thematic content would render the unqualified right to freedom of movement enunciated in Paragraphs 1 and 2 meaningless. Specifically, the six public purpose categories – (i) "the interest of national security,"[37] (ii) "the interest of ... public safety,"[38] (iii) "for the prevention of crime,"[39] (iv) "for the protection of health,"[40] (v) "for the protection of ...

conditions provided for by law and by the general principles of international law." As a matter of general public international law, a taking of property directly or as a result of a series of regulatory measures cannot be lawfully effectuated without compensation. At issue in the juridical dialog on this question is the formula determining compensation; that is, prompt, adequate, and effective compensation (the Hull formula); fair and adequate compensation; or fair market value as the governing remedy.

35 Article 2 ("Freedom of Movement") states:

> 1. Everyone lawfully within the territory of a State shall, within that territory, have the right to liberty of movement and freedom to choose his residence.
> 2. Everyone shall be free to leave any country, including his own.
> 3. No restrictions shall be placed on the exercise of these rights other than such as are in accordance with law and are necessary in a democratic society in the interest of a national security or public safety, for the maintenance of *ordre public*, for the prevention of crime, for the protection of health or morals, or for the protection of the rights and freedoms of others.
> 4. The rights set forth in paragraph 1 may also be subject, to particular areas, to restrictions imposed in accordance with law and justified by the public interest in a democratic society.

European Convention, *supra* Introduction note 15, art. 2.

36 *Id.* art. 2 ¶¶ 1–2.

37 *Id.* art. 2 ¶ 3.

38 *Id.*

39 *Id.*

40 *Id.*

morals,"[41] and (vi) "for the protection of the rights and freedoms of others"[42] – are simply too expansive to engraft any meaningful constraints on these categories. Absent an objective standard for application and a substantive rubric pervaded by the tempering effects of proportionality, the public purpose categories would nearly invite abuse derived from the right to regulate. Moreover, as is the case with Article 1, the triggering of the right's protection becomes problematic where, as here, the governing standard (the six public purpose categories) turns out to be all-encompassing.

The conceptual problems stemming from a legacy public purpose approach to Article 2 is compounded because "the maintenance of "*ordre public*"[43] is also found in the very midst of the public purpose categories. The maintenance of the *ordre public* cannot be challenged, particularly within the anatomy of a self-judging framework. It would be eminently plausible to posit that any act that a State undertakes is susceptible to being characterized as representing a measure in furtherance of the maintenance of the *ordre public*, irrespective of subject matter consideration. Also, the six public purpose categories in Paragraph 3 can all be categorized as falling within the ambit of *ordre public*.

The last quarter of this symmetrically structured article, first advancing two pronouncements pertaining to one right followed by two sets of qualifications limiting application of that same right, explicitly invokes "public interest."[44] Here, the right to freedom of movement, in a grammatically efficient sentence authored by the conjunctive "and," asserts that this fundamental right "may also be subject, in particular areas, to restrictions imposed *in accordance with law* and *justified by the public interest* in a democratic society."[45] Arguably, the public interest qualification in Paragraph 4 both encompasses and exceeds conceptual

[41] *Id.*

[42] *Id.*

[43] *Id.*

[44] *Id.* art. 2 ¶ 4.

[45] *Id* (emphasis added). The term "democratic society" is nowhere defined. The collected edition of the *Travaux Preparatoires* of Protocol No. 4 to the Convention suggests that the term was imported from the United Nations International Convention on Civil and Political Rights. *See generally* International Covenant on Civil and Political Rights, G.A. Res. 2200, U.N. GAOR, 21st Sess., Supp. No. 16, at 56, U.N. Doc. A/6316 (1966). Furthermore, the work of Subcommittee No. 12 reflects that the first draft did not include the term "democratic society," providing:

> In this form Article 2 showed the following differences by comparison with the corresponding provision in the text finally adopted by the Assembly:
>
> a) Definition of the rights protected came after the statement of restrictions to their exercise;
>
> b) The restrictions were to be governed by "any general law" whereas the final text refers to "law";
>
> – The restrictions had to be "reasonable": this condition is not mentioned in the final text;

restraints on the right enunciated in Paragraph 3. Independent of this possible construction, but within the framework of the right to freedom of movement, it is the public purpose doctrine that serves as the single qualification to the exercise of this coveted right. The doctrine limits exercise of the right and empowers a right to regulate that may infringe or altogether eviscerate this right so long as the regulation also comports "with law."[46] Accordingly, the presence of the doctrine in the Article (and the Convention for that matter) only is dwarfed by the daunting task that it is asked to perform.

Article 2 raises additional complexities for the public purpose doctrine that merit reference but cannot be addressed within the scope of this effort, which is limited to understanding the nature of the evidence supporting the public purpose doctrine as part of customary international law and the scope of such a principle. In contrast with Article 1, Article 2 of the European Convention mentions the term "democratic society" and does so twice.[47] The public purpose categories, including the *ordre public*, are themselves qualified by the term "democratic society." It is thus suggested that, at least for purposes of Article 2 ("Freedom of Movement"), there is a public purpose endemic to a "democratic society" that rises to the level of a qualifying factor concerning a human rights norm. The "democratic society" realm within which the public purpose doctrine may rise to the level of engrafting constraints on the freedom of movement

- The restrictions were to be "necessary to protect" a number of interests listed, but the text did not define such necessity as that existing "in a democratic society."
- The following inherent necessities were not listed among the restrictions:
- The economic welfare of the country;
- The maintenance of law and order;
- The prevention of crime.

Council of Europe, Collected Edition of the "Travaux Preparatoires" of Protocol No. 4 to the Convention, Securing Certain Rights and Freedoms Other Than Those Already Included in the Convention and in the First Protocol Thereto, at 176 (Strasbourg 1976), *available at* http://www.echr.coe.int/LibraryDocs/Travaux/ECHRTravaux-P4-BIL2907919.pdf (emphasis added) [hereinafter Travaux Preparatoires to Protocol No. 4]. Moreover, the preparatory work follows with an explanatory memorandum, which reads, in pertinent part:

> Article 2 of the draft reproduces paragraph 1 of Article 12 of the Draft International Covenant on Civil and Political Human Rights, Apart from the Following Amendments:
> a) This Article has been re-worded to bring it into line with most of the Article's in Section I of the Convention on Human Rights. Thus the rights in question are defined in the first paragraph, while the second paragraph sets out the permitted restrictions to the application of those rights.
> c) *On the other hand, in the draft Protocol, the second paragraph stipulates that the restrictions permitted would be those which are "necessary in a democratic society."*

Id. at 178–79 (emphasis added).

46 *Id.*

47 European Convention, *supra* Introduction note 15, art ¶¶ 3–4.

human rights norm bespeaks a normative connection between a democratically organized geopolitical subdivision and the substantive content of the public purpose doctrine. It is only in conformance with this connection that the public purpose necessary within a democratically structured society may give rise to an application of the doctrine that may normatively justify curtailing so fundamental a right as freedom of movement. It is less clear why the "democratic society" term is found in Article 2 in relation to public purpose but not at all in Article 1, which qualifies the right to possession and enjoyment of property on "public interest," much as Paragraph 4 of Article 2 resorts to "public interest" in limiting the freedom of movement. The relationship between a "democratic society" and public purpose as a prescriptive foundation for limiting freedom of movement is perhaps an explicit acknowledgment that the legacy public purpose doctrine – itself enjoying only general content that is ill-defined and having its application based on a self-judging standard – can only function where the rule of law endemic to a democratic society pervades the very doctrine's content.

Limiting application of the public purpose doctrine as a principle of law that empowers States to limit the right of movement based on a higher norm in the form of regulatory sovereignty perhaps may only be entrusted to democratic societies in which peoples' right to move within the national territory and to leave the national territory can only be subordinated to a public purpose that finds expression within a democratically organized society. Even though the European Convention on Human Rights presumably comprises European States that are politically democratic, the drafters, negotiators, and signatories very implicitly proscribed nondemocratic signatories from restricting domestic or international travel.[48]

But for the use of the public purpose doctrine in Articles 1 and 2, the balance of the Convention only once references public purpose and fleetingly at that.[49]

The American Convention on Human Rights "PACT of San Jose, Costa Rica," like the European Convention, also uses the term "democratic society." The term appears only on three occasions.[50] These scant appearances throughout the

48 *See supra* note 47 and accompanying text.

49 Protocol No. 7 to the Convention for the Protection of Human Rights and Fundamental Freedoms in Article 1 ("Procedural Safeguards Relating to the Expulsion of Aliens"), paragraph 2, states:

> 2. An alien may be expelled before the exercise of his rights under paragraph 1.a, b and c of this Article, when such expulsion is necessary in the *interests of public order* or *is grounded on reasons of national security*.

Euro. Conv. Protocol 7, *supra* Chapter 2 note 40, art. 1 ¶ 2 (emphasis added).

50 *See* American Convention, *supra* Introduction note 12, Article 15 ("Right of Assembly"), Article 16 ("Freedom of Association"), and Article 22 ("Freedom of Movement and Residence").

eighty-two-article convention are connected to explicit references to the public purpose doctrine in a manner similar to that of the European Convention. The select use of the term in tandem with public purpose suggests an express intent by the drafters and signatories to limit a State's use of the doctrine in placing limits on fundamental freedoms of movement, assembly, and association only to those nations that have embraced democratic principles of governance.

The movement, residence, assembly, and association of citizens is fundamental to social conditions that may give rise to a democratic society and to the perpetuation of democratic rule. Studious "democratic society" limitation on the exercise of the public purpose doctrine, as evident from the European Convention and the American Convention, exists due to the need to fashion a public purpose doctrine that eliminates or may substantially mitigate the likelihood of "legitimate abuse" by States hiding behind a "right to regulate" that is only formally (not substantively) legitimate. This sporadic particular linking of the term "democratic society" with public purpose also supports the broader propositions that (i) application of the doctrine should be subject-matter specific (ii) specific circumstances warrant a limit on State application of the doctrine, and (iii) limits on a State's recourse to the doctrine to infringe on established and protected rights should be subject to an objective standard (such as, e.g., a "democratic society"). As to this latter premise, what constitutes a "democratic society" within the confines of the signatories to the American Convention becomes an inevitable query.[51]

[51] A number of Latin American countries – most notably Ecuador, Bolivia, and Venezuela – although formally purporting to subscribe to the rule of law and the majesty of the democratic process have instead substantively expanded the powers of the executive branch to the detriment of the judicial and legislative branches. In some instances, the executive branch has pronounced that the judiciary must subordinate juridical analysis and the rule of law to "revolutionary principles" or the "best interests of the revolution." Similarly, process legitimacy has been abused in furtherance of the promulgation of constitutional amendments that have the single purpose of perpetuating the head of State. In these "democracies," fundamental freedoms such as human rights and the right to assembly have been altogether eviscerated. *See generally* ALLAN R. BREWER-CARÍAS, DISMANTLING DEMOCRACY IN VENEZUELA: THE CHAVEZ AUTHORITARIAN EXPERIMENT (Cambridge University Press 2010). Brewer-Carias argues that the influence of the Venezuelan executive branch has trumped any checks and balances with respect to the judicial and legislative branches. Four fundamental propositions pervade the text. First, despite the ostensible semblance of democracy, Brewer-Carias argues that:

> The 1999 Constituent Assembly was, then, the instrument the President used to dissolve and interfere in all branches of government (particularly the judiciary) into dismissal, public officials *who had been elected just a few months earlier in November 1998*: namely, the representatives to the National Congress, the State legislative assemblies, and the municipal councils, as well as the State governors and municipal mayors. The sole exception to this interference was the President of the Republic itself, precisely the author of the constitutional fraud, whose tenure was not affected. In addition, the Constituent Assembly interfered in all other branches of government, particularly in the judiciary, whose autonomy and

The public purpose doctrine is fundamental to the American Convention's framework. It is the organizing principle of six of its

independence was progressively and systematically demolished. The result was tight executive control over the judiciary, particularly regarding the newly appointed Supreme Tribunal of Justice whose Constitutional Chamber has been the most the ominous instrument for consolidating authoritarianism in the country.

Id. at 13 (internal citations omitted). Second, Brewer-Carias further observes:

> Article 17 of the transitory regime decree also provided for the termination of the Supreme Court of Justice to give way to the Supreme Tribunal of Justice, even if the Constitution that created it was not still in force. (It was published on Dec. 30, 1999.) For such purpose, the three chambers of the former Supreme Court of Justice (political-administrative, criminal, and civil cassation) were extinguished and its magistrates dismissed.

Id. at 76. Third, as to the legislative branch, Brewer-Carias chronicles that the interior regulations of the Assembly were openly manipulated and reformed in 2003 and 2004 to allow the incorporation of deputies without formal requirement and to allow the Assembly to annul its own previous decisions by simple majority. Sessions of the Assembly were held outside the Parliament official headquarters, in public spaces, to prevent the participation of opposition representatives because of violent threats from the so-called Bolivarian circles. The provisions of the Constitution guaranteeing representatives the right to vote according to their conscience have never been enforced, and never during the past decade have representatives been accountable to their constituency, as provided for in the Constitution. *Id.* at 395.

Fourth, Brewer-Carias contends that essential elements of democratic elections set forth in the Inter-American Democratic Charter, such as "periodic, free and fair elections based on secret balloting and universal suffrage that expression of the sovereignty of the people," have never formed part of "Venezuelan democracy" under President Chavez's administration. *Id.* at 397. *See also* Frank M. Walsh, *The Legal Death of the Latin American Democracy: Bolivarian Populism's Model for Centralizing Power, Eliminating Political Opposition, and Undermining the Rule of Law*, 16 L. & Bus. Rev. Am. 241 (2010).

A strong argument regarding the substantive dissonance present between the appearance of democratic rule and the actual rule of law can be found in the Expert Report of Vladimiro Alvarez Grau recently filed in the Southern District of New York in *Chevron Corporation and Texaco Petroleum Company v. The Republic of Ecuador*, where Grau states that, in his opinion:

> Ecuador's problem is that since 2004 the Government has continually violated the rule of law. It is my conviction that under President Correa, the country is experiencing a severe institutional crisis. If the Government and certain politicians do not stop influencing the decisions of the Courts and Tribunals, the fact that today there is no independence in the administration of justice will not change. The judiciary can no longer act impartially and with integrity, and is instead subject to constant pressure and threats that influence its decision.

2010 WL 6380602, at ¶ 23 (S.D.N.Y. September 2, 2010) (Expert Report and Affidavit); *see also* International Bar Association, *Ecuador: Un Análisis Sobre la Independencia de la Funcion Judicial* (June 2005), http://www.ibanet.org/Document/Default.aspx?DocumentUid=6a00elfb-6974-41bc-a2bb-479f37b5f65c. As to Bolivia, *see* International Bar Association, *Justicia Denegada: La Apremiante Necesidad de Implementor una Reforma Significativa en el Sistema Judicial de Bolivia* (August 2006), http://www.ibanet.org/Document/Default.aspx?DocumentUid=DFCA 2074-046A-422C-94A2-68FF1AA49C3E. The IBA's report concludes that there is no separation between the legislative and the executive branches of power in Bolivia. Moreover, judicial process lacks transparency and independent authority in the administration of justice.

articles.[52] Article 12 ("Freedom of Conscience and Religion") is constituted by four single-sentence paragraphs. The first two paragraphs assert the right and its scope, whereas the symmetrical balance of the paragraphs deliberately articulate limitations on the right.[53] Aside from the right accorded to parents or guardians to impart "religious and moral education [to] their children or wards that is in accord with their own convictions,"[54] the single limitation to the right of freedom of conscience and religion is in the form of the public purpose. The doctrine, in the form of (i) "public safety," (ii) "public order," (iii) "public health," and (iv) "morals," is the single normative constraint on this fundamental freedom.[55] Similarly, the doctrine expressed in the form of (i) "national security," (ii) "public order," (iii) "public health," and (iv) "public morals," is identified as the principal possible limitation on the freedom of thought and expression together with "respect for the rights or reputation of others."[56] The application of the doctrine, however, pursuant to Article 13(2)(a)–(b) is limited to the imposition of liability and not censorship. This application of the doctrine is instructive because it does not

[52] *See* American Convention, *supra* Introduction note 12, art. 12 ("Freedom of Conscience and Religion"), art. 13 ("Freedom of Thought and Expression"), art. 15 ("Right of Assembly"), art. 16 ("Freedom of Association"), art. 21 ("Right to Property"), and art. 22 ("Freedom of Movement and Residence").

[53] *Id.* art. 12 ¶¶ 3, 4.

See American Convention, *supra* Introduction note 12, art. 12 ("Freedom of Conscience and Religion"), art. 13 ("Freedom of Thought and Expression"), art. 15 ("Right of Assembly"), art. 16 ("Freedom of Association"), art. 21 ("Right to Property"), and art. 22 ("Freedom of Movement and Residence").

Article 12 ("Freedom of Conscience and Religion") of the American Convention of Human Rights states:

1. Everyone has the right to freedom of conscience and of religion. This right includes freedom to maintain or to change one's religion or beliefs, and freedom to profess or disseminate one's religion or beliefs, either individually or together with others, in public or in private.
2. No one shall be subject to restrictions that might impair his freedom to maintain or to change his religion or beliefs.
3. Freedom to manifest one's religion and beliefs may be subject only to the limitations prescribed by law that are necessary to protect public safety, order, health, or morals, or the rights or freedoms of others.
4. Parents or guardians, as the case may be, have the right to provide for the religious and moral education of their children or wards that is in accord with their own convictions.

Id. art. 12.

[54] *Id.* art. 12 ¶ 4.

[55] *Id.* art. 12 ¶ 3.

[56] Article 13 ("Freedom of Thought and Expression") establishes this public purpose qualification on this right, providing in relevant part:

represent an absolute exception but rather one that is qualified and, in this limited regard, supports the broader principle that application of the public purpose doctrine may be such so as to avoid an "all-or-nothing" result. A compromising and qualified outcome bespeaks proportionality. Imposition of liability in lieu of absolute censorship comports with a "proportionality" approach to the otherwise *absolute* public purpose exception.[57] This contribution is an important one in identifying the existence and scope of a public purpose doctrine within the framework of customary international law.

The modified (proportional) approach to the application of the doctrine within the context of the fundamental human right of freedom of thought and expression is also evinced in Article 13(4). This provision provides that:

Notwithstanding the provisions of Paragraph 2 above, public entertainments may be subject by law to *prior* censorship for the sole purpose of regulating access to them *for the moral protection of childhood and adolescence*.[58]

The application of the doctrine to a "special class" represents yet another technique pursuant to which the principle may be applied in ways that are absolute but only where such rigor in turn is compelled and justified by the subject matter at issue, in this case "the moral protection of childhood and adolescence" within the narrow category of "public entertainments."

As previously discussed,[59] the American Convention readily avails itself of the public purpose doctrine, albeit within the context of States that may be described as having "a democratic society" with respect to the four essential rights that are migratory or of movement: (i) Article 15 ("Right of Assembly"), (ii) Article 16 ("Freedom of Association"), (iii) Article 22 ("Freedom of Movement"), and (iv) Article 22 ("Freedom of Residence"). In all four of these rights, the language expressed in the Convention is *materially* indistinguishable.[60]

> 2. The exercise of the right provided for in the foregoing paragraph shall not be subject to prior censorship but shall be subject to subsequent imposition of liability, which shall be expressly established by law to the extent necessary to ensure:
>   a. respect for the rights or reputations of others; or
>   b. the protection of national security, public order, or public health or morals.

Id. art. 13 ¶ 2(a)–(b).

57 The principle of proportionality finds ample support in the context of international human rights law. *See* discussion of the jurisprudence of the European Court of Human Rights *infra* Chapter 3.A(3).

58 American Convention, *supra* Introduction note 12, art. 13 ¶ 4 (emphasis added).

59 *See supra* note 47 and accompanying text.

60 As to Article 15 ("Right of Assembly"), the qualifying language provides that:

> No restrictions may be placed on the exercise of this right other than those imposed in conformity with the law and necessary in a democratic society in the interest of national

Much like Article 1 ("Protection of Property") of the European Convention on Human Rights, Article 21 ("Right to Property") of the American Convention on Human Rights also speaks to "enjoyment" of property but not to "ownership." As to "enjoyment," the second sentence of the first paragraph asserts that "[t]he law may subordinate such use and enjoyment to the *interest of society*."[61] Ownership is implicit in the qualification to the right to property in the negative (deprivation of a person's property) based on "payment of just compensation" and "for reasons of public utility or social interest."[62] A third amorphous qualification on the otherwise unbridled right to property appears in the form of language providing "in the cases and according to the forms established by law."[63]

The universality of the right to property in the American Convention is elevated to the status of a human right pertaining to all persons and, therefore, actually proscribes the uncompensated taking of property on the part of a nation of its own citizens. The citizenship status of a person is irrelevant for

> security, public safety or public order, or to protect public health or morals or the rights or freedom of others.

American Convention, *supra* Introduction note 12, art. 15. The qualification asserted in Article 16 ("Freedom of Association") states that:

> The exercise of this right shall be subject only to such restrictions established by law as may be necessary in a democratic society, in the interest of national security, public safety or public order, or to protect public health or morals or the rights and freedoms of others.

Id. art. 16. Finally, the Article 22 ("Freedom of Movement and Residence") restriction states that:

> The foregoing rights may be restricted only pursuant to a law to the extent necessary in a democratic society to prevent crime or to protect national security, public safety, public order, public morals, public health, or the rights or freedoms of others.

Id. art. 22.

61 *Id.* art. 21 ¶ 1 (emphasis added).

62 *Id.* art. 21 ¶ 2.

63 *Id.* As to compensation, this provision appears to codify a very general statement of the broad principle of customary international law providing that a nationalization or expropriation, a direct or indirect nationalization or expropriation, or an infringement on property that is tantamount or the equivalent to a direct or indirect expropriation or nationalization is contrary to law where compensation for the taking does not ensue.

Article 21 specifically references "payment of just compensation." *Id.* This element of the provision is less settled even in general terms as a matter of customary international law. There is considerable authority for compensation to be legally sufficient if payment is made in a form that is "prompt, adequate, and effective compensation" (the "Hull formula"). *See, e.g.*, Banco Nacional de Cuba v. Sabbatino, 376 U.S. 398, 429 (1963). Equally authoritative sources hold that compensation should reflect *fair market value. See, e.g.*, NAFTA, *supra* Introduction note 1, art. 1110 ¶ 2. A third line of authority suggests that "fair and just compensation" is sufficient. *See generally* United Nations Conference on Trade & Development, Taking of Property, U.N. Doc. UNCTAD/ITE/IIT/15, U.N. Sales No. E.00.II.D.4 (2000).

purposes of the human right to property under this Convention. Article 1, Paragraph 2 of the Convention explicitly states that "[f]or purposes of this convention, *person* means every human being" (emphasis added).

It follows that the American Convention carves out an exception to the *domestic takings rule* pursuant to which an uncompensated taking by a State of its citizens' property does not give rise to a violation of international law. By defining "person" as a "every human being," the American Convention negates application of the "*domestic takings rule*" in the context of domestic expropriations where the expropriating State is a signatory to this convention.

A. PUBLIC PURPOSE DOCTRINE AS A FULCRUM FOR A HIERARCHY OF HUMAN RIGHTS

The select application of the doctrine throughout the European Convention, as well as the American Convention on Human Rights, suggests that there exists an unstated hierarchy of human rights.[64] Thus, whether pursuant to the public purpose doctrine or a matter of "state emergency," certain rights cannot be suspended or otherwise modified without delegitimizing the particular human rights convention in its totality. It is certainly beyond man's wit to conceive of a public purpose, public danger, or a State of necessity that could justify infringement on the right to freedom from slavery, the right to humane treatment, or the right to life, to mention only three such rights that happen to be contained in the American Convention.[65] Conceptual and analytical support for the proposition that the public purpose doctrine, at least in its legacy iteration, must have subject matter limitations is also certainly provided for in the human rights context in Article 27 ("Suspension of Guarantees") of the American Convention. This provision is tasked with balancing the protection of fundamental human rights against the rights of States to regulate in times of crises; that is, the most extreme expression of the public purpose doctrine: State emergency. Article 27 in part states:

> In time of war, public danger, or other emergency that threatens the independence or security of a State Party, it may take measures derogating from its obligations under the present Convention to the extent and for the period of time strictly required by the exigencies of the situation, provided that such measures are not inconsistent with its other obligations under international

[64] *See generally* Tom Farer, *The Hierarchy of Human Rights*, 8 AM. U.J. INT'L L. & POL'Y 115 (1991).

[65] *See, e.g.*, American Convention, *supra* Introduction note 12, art. 4 ("Right to Life"), art. 5 ("Right to Humane Treatment"), and art. 6 ("Freedom from Slavery").

law and do not involve discrimination on the ground of race, color, sex, language, religion, or social origin.

The foregoing provision *does not authorize any suspension* of the following articles: Article 3 ("Right to Juridical Personality"), Article 4 ("Right to Life"), Article 5 ("Right to Humane Treatment"), Article 6 ("Freedom from Slavery"), Article 9 ("Freedom from *Ex Post Facto* Laws"), Article 12 ("Freedom of Conscience and Religion"), Article 17 ("Rights of the Family"), Article 18 ("Right to a Name"), Article 19 ("Rights of the Child"), Article 20 ("Right to Nationality"), and Article 23 ("Right to Participate in Government"), or of the judicial guarantees essential for the protection of such rights.[66]

Even a surface reading demonstrates that, in a very fundamental way, no general public good can outweigh any of the eleven enumerated rights: (i) the right to juridical personality, (ii) the right to life, (iii) the right to humane treatment, (iv) the right to freedom from slavery, (v) the right to freedom from ex post facto laws, (vi) the right to freedom of conscience and religion, (vii) the rights of the family, (viii) the right to a name, (ix) the rights of the child, (x) the right to nationality, and (xi) the right to participate in government. To the contrary, the public purpose doctrine, even amidst the most extreme expression of national necessity, exists for purposes of ensuring conditions so that fundamental rights of this nature may exist, develop, and prosper. Subject-matter limitation on the public purpose doctrine represents a meaningful contribution to international human rights law. It is equally a contribution to the customary international law development of a public purpose doctrine comparable in significance only to examples of instances in which the qualified application of the doctrine leads to more than just a mere semblance of proportionality between the public purpose asserted and the extent to which the right at issue is at all altered.

1. *The African Charter on Human and Peoples' Rights*

The African Charter on Human and Peoples' Rights, consonant with the European Convention on Human Rights and the American Convention on Human Rights, asserts fundamental human rights to assembly and movement within the national territory and to travel beyond the country, subject to law or restrictions arising from an expansive public purpose doctrine. As to the right of assembly, the African Charter on Human and Peoples' Rights ("the African Charter") provides that, although every individual has the right "to assemble freely with others," this right may be restricted "by law in particular those

[66] *Id* Ch. IV ("Suspension of Guarantees") art. 27.

enacted in the interest of national security, the safety, health, ethics and rights and freedoms of others."[67] The right to freedom of movement and residence within the borders of a State is qualified only by the imperative obligating individuals to abide by law. Here, the constraint on the human right to freedom of movement and residence is considerably broader, and certainly has greater predictive value, than the strictly public purpose doctrine qualification on the right contained in the European and American conventions on human rights.[68] The right to leave a country, including an individual's own nation, is subject to a much broader, less transparent, more predictable constraint in the form of a public purpose doctrine than the right to freedom of movement and residence also asserted in Article 12.[69] The inclusion of public purpose categories such as health, morality, order, and national security provides the "right to regulate" with considerable analytical premises with which to infringe on the human right to leave any country, including a person's own country.

In sharp contrast with the European and American Human Rights conventions, the African Charter does not distinguish between "democratic society" and a nondemocratic society in qualifying States that may restrict the fundamental freedoms of (i) movement, (ii) residence, and (iii) the right to leave any country, including an individual's own nation.

The African Charter also identifies the right to property, without reference to ownership, taking, deprivation of possessions, or compensation as an element incident or attendant to any type of taking of property.[70] The right to property also does not reference "use or enjoyment" and provides that such right "may only be encroached"[71] based on "interest of public need" or the "general interest of a community."

The importance of the public purpose doctrine within the meaning of Articles 11, 12, and 14 of the African Charter is considerable. Its select and

[67] African Charter, *supra* Chapter 2 note 45, art. 11.

[68] *Id.* art. 12 ¶ 1.

[69] Article 12 of the African Charter provides:

> 1. Every individual shall have the right to freedom of movement and residence within the borders of a State provided he abides by the law.
> 2. Every individual shall have the right to leave any country including his own, and to return to his country. This right may only be subject to restrictions, provided for by law for the protection of national security, law and order, public health or morality.

[70] Article 14 of the African Charter provides:

> The right to property shall be guaranteed. It may only be encroached upon in the interest of public need or in the general interest of the community and in accordance with the provisions of appropriate laws.

Id. art. 14.

[71] *Id.*

somewhat studious presence is testimony to the doctrine's central importance and not to a classification of its rule as a secondary precept in the Charter's mechanics. The doctrine is treated equally and in tandem with the obligation to follow the law as the only restrictions on any freedom contained in the Charter's entirety.[72]

The Charter recognizes a right that does resemble the sustainable development expression of the public purpose doctrine discussed in Chapter 2, Section E. The principle, however, is stated as a right and not as an exception to a right that justifies exercise of regulatory sovereignty to the detriment of obligations running from the State to individuals. Because, however, the Charter speaks of the "right to development" in individual and particular terms, a selective or "public" right to development conceptually provides normative support for its use as a constraint on protection obligations that a State may owe to private natural or juridical persons. Thus, broad as this "sustainable development" individual and collective human right may be, its public purpose doctrine counterpart in the form of an exception legitimizing the right to regulate would be broad and problematic, as we have found the sustainable development public purpose expression to be.[73] Reading "right to *economic* development" into the "right to development" is not too much of a conceptual indiscretion where a collective right to development also is at stake.

Just as Article 22(2) of the Charter suggests a relationship with the sustainable development expression of the public purpose doctrine exception to the right to regulate, Article 21(4)–(5) analogously expresses a *right* comparable to the permanent sovereignty over natural resources *exception* that is typically relied on by Host States to challenge long-term exploration and exploitation

[72] The only restrictions on human rights contained in the Charter are exceptions based on either the public purpose doctrine or in compliance with law. *See id.* art. 6; art. 9 ¶ 2; art. 10 ¶ 1 art. 11; art. 12 ¶¶ 1–2; art. 14. Notably, in contrast with the European Convention on Human Rights and the American Convention on Human Rights, the right of association prescribed in the Charter under Article 10(1) cannot be modified under the public purpose doctrine, but only on the ground of noncompliance with the law. *Id.* art. 10 ¶ 1.

[73] The collective and individual "sustainable development" iteration of a human right rather than an exception to the right to regulate, as set forth in Article 22(2). Paragraph 1 of this article, helps contextualize the "right to development." Article 22 reads:

> 1. All peoples shall have the right to their economic, social and cultural development with due regard to their freedom and identity and in the equal enjoyment of the common heritage of mankind.
> 2. States shall have the duty, individually or collectively, to ensure the exercise of the right to development.

Id. art. 22 ¶¶ 1–2.

contracts entered into with industrialized States.[74] The *human* right expressed in Paragraphs 4 and 5 of Article 21 has both an individual and a collective character, but the individuality and collectivity applies to State parties acting on behalf of their citizenries with respect to wealth and natural resources.[75]

The African Charter thus materially distinguishes itself from the anatomy and content of the European and the American conventions. The Charter's very name speaks to "human and 'peoples' rights." Paragraphs 4 and 5 of Article 21 of the African Charter specifically reference "[s]tates parties to the present Charter"; thus, this "human" right is one attaching to States (i) for the protection of its citizens, (ii) against other States, and (iii) only against the State of which individuals are citizens, to the extent that such a sovereign acts against its own right to explore, exploit, and dispose of its wealth and natural resources.[76] Consonant with Article 21 generally and Paragraphs 4 and 5 in particular, the public purpose doctrine of permanent sovereignty over natural resources – generally invoked as an exception-justifying exercise of a right to regulate in such a manner as to limit obligations extending to foreign investors – finds robust resonance in the African Charter. It is present as both an affirmative human right ultimately held by citizens and also by States in the form of both a *right* that presumably may be asserted by an individual against his own nation and as an *exception* raised by a State against infringement on the exploration, exploitation, and disposal of wealth and natural resources by a foreign State, presumably notwithstanding international contracts providing for foreign access to the resources falling within the purview of Article 21.

[74] The doctrine of permanent sovereignty over natural resources is addressed in Chapter 5 of this text.

[75] *See* African Charter, *supra* Chapter 2 note 45, art. 21 ¶ 4.

[76] Article 21 of the African Charter states:

> 1. All peoples shall freely dispose of their wealth and natural resources. This right shall be exercised in the exclusive interest of the people. In no case shall a people be deprived of it.
> 2. In case of spoliation the dispossessed people shall have the right to the lawful recovery of its property as well as to an adequate compensation.
> 3. The free disposal of wealth and natural resources shall be exercised without prejudice to the obligation of promoting international economic cooperation based on mutual respect, equitable exchange and the principles of international law.
> 4. States parties to the present Charter shall individually and collectively exercise the right to free disposal of their wealth and natural resources with a view to strengthening African unity and solidarity.
> 5. States parties to the present Charter shall undertake to eliminate all forms of foreign economic exploitation particularly that practiced by international monopolies so as to enable their peoples to fully benefit from the advantages derived from their national resources.

Id. art. 21.

Construed together, States and their citizens possess a human right to development that extends to exploration, exploitation, and disposition of wealth and natural resources. This right, presumably premised on the highest public interests of individuals and peoples, is intended to safeguard the use of wealth and natural resources of States. Pursuant to the most conventional paradigm, the Article 22 "right to development" and the Article 21 "wealth and natural resources" principles are used by States to justify the right to regulate in disavowance of rights arising from treaties and other international instruments, often to the detriment of foreign investors/investments. A second and less conventional paradigm would be recourse to these principles by individuals against their own governments for purposes of denouncing, in international super-State fora, unconstitutional or illicit disposition of resources by regimes that are impervious to the rule of law and the legitimate public interest of its own citizenry. This latter scenario most commonly takes place where States engage, for example, in the illicit privatization of strategic resources. Although this activity regrettably can hardly be characterized as rare or sporadic, the denouncement of such abuses by corrupt regimes on the part of private citizens most commonly is fraught with insurmountable challenges.[77]

The African Charter exemplifies perhaps the broadest expression of the use of the public purpose doctrine within the framework of the three human rights conventions analyzed. It shares with the European Convention and the American Convention the use of the doctrine in the context of property-related human rights. It also features the doctrine in the context of human rights concerning the right to assemble, the right to freedom of movement, and the right to leave any country (including one's own). *As to these specific rights*, however, in contrast with the European and American conventions, the African Charter does not distinguish between democratic and nondemocratic societies as a predicate to exercise of the doctrine by a State in ways that may infringe on or altogether eviscerate such rights. Also, the African Charter speaks to the rights of "peoples" and "State Parties" in connection with expressions of the public purpose doctrine that merges the doctrine into both affirmative human rights and regulatory exception categories in contrast with the European and American conventions. Specifically, the *sustainable development* and *permanent sovereignty over natural resources* expressions of the public purpose doctrine are codified by the African Charter as "human

[77] The entrenchment of those only formally purporting to subscribe (rather than actually subscribing) to rule of law in Latin America despite ongoing opposition is demonstrative of the difficulties inherent in denouncing such a regime. *See supra* note 51.

rights and peoples' rights." In this connection, it vastly amplifies the doctrine concerning entities in which the doctrine vests (States and private individuals) and the very doctrine's scope.

2. *The Findings and Effects of the European and American Human Rights Conventions and the African Charter on the Customary International Law Development of the Public Purpose Doctrine*

International human rights law applies to the public purpose doctrine even though it never defines it. Its contribution to public purpose in customary international law is quite meaningful. Based on the three conventions analyzed, it is evident that the public purpose doctrine is central to international human rights law despite the paucity of international instruments and writings purporting to establish the connection between the doctrine and the workings of international human rights customary and conventional law. Generally, the public purpose doctrine serves to amplify the scope of a State's right to regulate to the detriment of its legal obligation to protect foreign investors/investments. International human rights law represents a constraint on States' right to regulate and, in this sense, operates as a constraint on the exercise of orthodox sovereignty.[78] The public purpose doctrine bolsters additional sovereignty paradigms by enhancing regulatory sovereignty in its most traditional form.

Although seemingly at odds with respect to their respective relationship to conventional notions of regulatory sovereignty, as well as to the manner in which the doctrine and international human rights serve individuals and States, the two are inextricably interdependent. International human rights does not purport to displace or modify national or municipal law, which in turn rests on the public purpose doctrine as an organizing principle. To the contrary, as noted, international human rights law aspires to *supplement* and *work together with* domestic law.[79] Accordingly, there is an imperative need for international human rights to be able to rely on a robust iteration of the public purpose doctrine that is objective (and not self-judging) and content-rich (not driven by all things public, as characterized by a particular State). The teachings of the public purpose doctrine, as referenced in the European Convention, the American Convention, and the African Charter, identify public purpose as a central organizing principle in international human rights law that forms part of customary international law. Moreover, the doctrine plays a critical role in tempering application of international human rights. It

[78] *See supra* text accompanying notes 6–10.

[79] *See supra* text accompanying notes 11–12.

also plays a pivotal part in the organizational framework of international human rights. Seven distinct applications of the public purpose doctrine can be gleaned from the doctrine's role in the European and American conventions and the African Charter.

First, the scope and application of the public purpose doctrine is qualified as to the (i) subject matter, and (ii), at least in the European and American conventions, a State's right to apply the doctrine in order to curtail entitlement to human rights protection is predicated on a purportedly "objective" standard: specifically, the presence of a "democratic society."[80]

Second, the public purpose doctrine is indispensable to the actual formation of a hierarchy of international human rights norms that is not explicitly expressed or defined as such in these instruments. The mere presence of the doctrine in *some but not all* of the human rights contained in these conventions itself gives rise to a hierarchy of human rights. This proposition is supported, by way of example, by Article 27 of the American Convention ("Suspension of Guarantees").[81]

Third, the content, and therefore also the application, of the public purpose doctrine is materially different depending on the human rights convention at issue. Each convention analyzed is substantively influenced by the history and current economic status of the signatory States. Thus, the very human rights norms vary accordingly, as does the scope, content, and application of the public purpose doctrine contextualized by a specific convention. Therefore, the preambles of the three conventions analyzed considerably vary in content and in the signatory parties' understanding of the right to be applied in connection with a wrong to be avoided or corrected. Overarching these differences, however, is a proposition common to all three conventions: the public purpose doctrine is broader in scope than its iteration in the North American Free Trade Agreement (NAFTA), the General Agreement on Tariffs and Trade (GATT), or any of the United Nations Conference on Trade and Development (UNCTAD) instruments analyzed in this writing.[82]

Fourth, the conventions, specifically Article 13 of the American Convention, comport with a "proportionality" approach to the application of the doctrine that seeks avoidance of "all-or-nothing" outcomes. Qualifying certain freedoms of thought and expression on the ground of public purpose that lead to *liability* and not *censorship* is illustrative of this point. This application of the doctrine represents a meaningful contribution to the

[80] *See supra* notes 51, 60, and accompanying text.
[81] American Convention, *supra* note 13, art. 27.
[82] For a discussion of the NAFTA, *see supra* Chapter 1. Regarding the GATT and UNCTAD Instruments, *see supra* Chapter 2.

crafting of a public purpose rubric that, unlike its legacy iteration, best satisfies a global paradigm among nations of *interdependence* and not *independence*.[83]

Fifth, application of the public purpose doctrine as a complete bar to a human right is applicable only to a special-class category meriting extraordinary protection, as is the case with Article 13(4) of the American Convention concerning "the moral protection of childhood and adolescence."[84]

Sixth, depending on the human rights convention consulted, a particular expression of the public purpose doctrine may serve as an actual human right that, under some scenarios, rightfully limits State sovereignty or as an exception that amplifies regulatory sovereignty to the detriment of rights owed to individuals.[85]

Seventh, much like the public purpose doctrine of permanent sovereignty over natural resources,[86] the exploitation and disposition of wealth and resources may be characterized as a peoples' right that can serve both as an affirmative right and an exception triggering application of regulatory sovereignty.[87]

The American and European conventions, as well as the African Charter, serve as material evidence supporting the (i) existence of a public purpose doctrine, (ii) having the characteristics set forth in the preceding seven propositions, (iii) which are broader as to scope and application than the conventional international law iteration of the public purpose doctrine present in the NAFTA, in part because of the structural configuration of customary international law. Consequently, there is ample support for the proposition that the scope, content, and application of the public purpose doctrine find different expressions in customary international law and in conventional international law. This dichotomy further emphasizes the need to fashion a new public purpose doctrine vested with content and uniformity.

3. *The Jurisprudence of the European Court of Human Rights and Public Purpose Constraints on Regulatory Sovereignty*

The European Court of Human Rights has generated a jurisprudence that aids in understanding the relationship between international human rights and the domestic application of the public purpose doctrine as part of the exercise of regulatory sovereignty. Notably, the Court has adopted and applied

83 *See* discussion of proportionality *infra* Section 3.
84 American Convention, *supra* Introduction note 12, art. 13 ¶ 4.
85 *See, e.g.*, African Charter, *supra* Chapter 2 note 45, art. 21.
86 Addressed *infra* at Chapter 5.
87 *See, e.g.*, African Charter, *supra* Chapter 2 note 45, art. 21.

a proportionality test to claimants who allege denial of the fundamental human right to own, use, possess, or otherwise enjoy property. In an eloquently alleged wrongful expropriation action brought under Article 2 of the European Convention, the Court artfully applied the proportionality test in determining whether the public purpose doctrine had been wrongfully used in executing an expropriation where compensation ultimately was not tendered. The case is particularly relevant because it is an example of where an appropriate proportionality test was applied to the legacy public purpose doctrine articulated pursuant to an unduly broad statutory definition of public purpose consonant with a subjective (self-judging) standard.

a. *Farrugia v. Malta*

In the *Farrugia v. Malta* decision,[88] the applicants were deprived of property that they used for their livelihood as farmers. The taking followed receipt of a letter from the Ministry of Public Works and Construction of the Country of Malta. This letter requested the applicants' predecessor in interest to reach an agreement concerning the sale of the subject property to a private third party upon penalty of commencement of expropriation proceedings if an agreement was not reached.[89]

Having failed to reach an agreement for the sale-purchase of the property, the relevant third party seeking acquisition of the property petitioned the government to expropriate the land on the basis that it constituted the single access to its property. Contemporaneously with this petition, the third party applied for a permit to build residential apartments and garages on the property concerned.[90] In furtherance of the applicable statutory framework, Chapter 88 of the Laws of Malta – the Land Acquisition Public Purposes Ordinance (LAPPO) – the *Government Gazette* announced that the property concerned was being expropriated "for a public purpose."[91]

Applicants initiated a constitutional redress proceeding in observance of local law on the ground that the expropriation was illicit because no compensation was tendered, let alone "adequate compensation," and the taking was for the benefit of a *private party* and not the government. As such, the applicants argued that the taking did not meet the requisite public interest stricture.[92] Additionally, applicants averred that the proposed roadway would

88 Farrugia v. Malta, Fourth Section Decision, App. No. 67557/20 (March 6, 2012) [hereinafter Farrugia].
89 *Id.* at ¶¶ 3–4.
90 *Id.* at ¶ 5.
91 *Id.* at ¶ 6.
92 *Id.* at ¶ 7.

affect their farm and cultivated farmland in a manner that would materially diminish productivity. In this connection, applicants "noted that they had been cultivating and breeding animals on said land for forty years, long before the arrival of the present developer."[93] Furthermore, the applicants asserted that "they had not been informed of the expropriation until work on the construction of the road was commenced."[94]

The first instance tribunal denied applicants' claim based on want of public interest. The trial court provided that:

> [I]t considered that Article 2 of the LAPPO did not exclude that an expropriation could also serve the interests of third parties. Thus, while it was true that the expropriation in the present case had been triggered by third party's request, since the land had originally been earmarked as a road it could not be said that the taking had not been in the public interest.[95]

Further observing that the property constituted less than one-eighth of applicants' entire property, the trial court concluded that the burden to applicants was outweighed by the ingress/egress now made available for *public use*.[96]

In processing the applicants' application, the European Court of Human Rights ("the Court") noted that the rule contained in the second sentence of Article 1 – asserting that "[n]o one shall be deprived of his possessions except in the public interest and subject to the conditions provided for by law and by the general principles of international law" – requires satisfaction of the "proportionality" talisman in addition to the requisite "public interest" standard. In this connection, the Court asserted that:

> [A] fair balance must be struck between the demands of the general interest of the community and the requirements of the protection of the individual's fundamental rights, the search for such a fair balance being inherent in the whole of the Convention. The requisite balance will not be struck where the person concerned bears an individual and excessive burden.[97]

The Court thus summarized its task as having to determine whether application of the proportionality test yields "the requisite balance" in a way that comports with applicants' right of property.[98] Pursuant to its own

93 *Id.*
94 *Id.*
95 *Id.* at ¶ 9.
96 *Id.* Applicants also had asserted claims based on Article 1 ("Protection of Property"); Protocol No. 1, Article 3 ("Prohibition of Torture"); and Article 8 ("Right to Respect for Private and Family Life").
97 *Id.* at ¶ 20 (citing Sporrong and Lönnroth v. Sweden, 52 Eur. Ct. H.R. (ser. A) at ¶ 61 (1982)).
98 *Id.* at ¶ 20 (citing Abdilla v. Malta, First Section Decision, App. No. 38244/03 (November 3, 2005)).

precedent, the proportionality test fails where, for example, it is determined that a taking of property occurred without compensation or payment in an amount that is *not* reasonably related to its value.[99] Either scenario as a matter of law creates a "disproportionate inference" in the application of the proportionality test.[100]

Upon assuming "the lawfulness of the interference [with the subject property] which was confirmed by the domestic courts and of which the applicants have not complained,"[101] the Court engaged in a "public interest" analysis and reiterated the principle that:

> [T]he compulsory transfer of property from one individual to another, may, depending on the circumstances, constitute a legitimate means for promoting the public interest. In this regard, the taking of property effected in pursuance of legitimate social, economic or other policies may be "in the public interest" even if the community at large has no direct use or enjoyment of the property taken.[102]

As to the expropriation *sub judice*, while observing that "the system of expropriation initiated at the request of third parties in Maltese domestic law is novel," it held that the public purpose component of the inquiry had been amply met.[103]

Having established that the taking comported with the public purpose doctrine, it became clear to the Court that the single outstanding issue was whether lack of compensation triggered a violation of Article 2 of the European Convention. The finding in the negative was premised on a determination that the applicants, "through their own fault,"[104] failed to exhaust domestic remedies and, for this reason, did not allow for a finding on "the question of whether the compensation offered was sufficient to preserve a fair balance between the demands of the general interest and the requirements of the protection of the applicants' rights."[105] The Court's analysis as to the application of the proportionality prong raises considerably more questions than it can possibly address, in large measure because of the absence of any commentary as to why specifically the applicants were at "fault" such that absolute nonpayment of compensation for the taking does not affect

[99] *Id.* at ¶ 20.

[100] *See, e.g.*, Holy Monasteries v. Greece, 301-A Eur. Ct. H.R. (ser. A) at ¶ 71 (1994).

[101] Farrugia, *supra* note 88, at ¶ 21.

[102] *Id.* at ¶ 22 (internal citations omitted).

[103] *Id.*

[104] *Id.* at ¶ 25.

[105] *Id.* at ¶ 23 (citing J. Lautier Company Ltd. v. Malta, Decision, App. No. 37448/06 (December 2, 2008)).

proportionality.[106] The proposition that a taking took place without any compensation, without more, bespeaks more analysis from the Court than mere reliance on a technical procedural matter arising from domestic law. The burden of a taking without compensation must form part of any proportionality analysis. Ultimately, however, it is the public purpose analysis that causes the Court to dismiss the applicants' complaints.

Farrugia quite eloquently illustrates the relationship between international human rights and the public purpose doctrine. It also airs many of the reasons why the legacy public purpose doctrine is an obstacle to the efforts undertaken by international human rights law to redeem its promise to work together with and supplement domestic law. Beyond the technical and unremarkable inquiry concerning the extent to which a compulsory transfer of property to a private party may satisfy a taking's public purpose requirement and thus fail to trigger an Article 2 violation, the relevant public purpose inquiry concerns the relationship between the meaning of the doctrine within the relevant domestic law and the extent to which that definition comports with property rights as a fundamental human right under Article 2. Thus framed, the exigent need for a content-rich and objective public purpose doctrine that may functionally trigger human rights protection becomes much clearer. A broad and seemingly boundless definition of public purpose invites consistently reaching the wrong result for the right reason. *Farrugia* could not be more revealing concerning this broader point.

The operative definition of public purpose under the laws of Malta much resembles a codification of the legacy doctrine that simply is too broad and unqualified to be meaningful in identifying an abuse of the doctrine. Article 2 of the LAPPO, purporting to define "public purpose" within the meaning of the statute – a definition that the Court did not question or comment on – provides that:

[106] Irrespective of whether applicants wrongfully limited their first instance prosecution to the issue of lack of public purpose and as a result rendered the record bereft of any evidence of quantum as to compensation, it remains uncontroverted that no compensation *at all* issued. Extended to its logical consequence, the Court's treatment of compensation and the proportionality test leads to the conclusion that Malta was estopped from payment of compensation in connection with a taking because "the Constitutional Court considered that the applicants' appeal was solely related to the public interest requirement," even though a public interest analysis cannot be altogether severed from application of a proportionality test. Moreover, the inference or conclusion that a State is somehow estopped from meeting its obligation to tender payment in connection with an expropriation where the affected party, on technical grounds, failed to plead properly that the expropriation was legally defective because no payment at all was tendered represents but tautological reasoning that exhorts form over substance. The stark fact of record unequivocally establishes that the expropriation took place without any *compensation*.

> "Public purpose" means *any* purpose connected with exclusive Government use for general public use, or *connected with* or *ancillary to* the public interest or utility (whether the land is for use by the Government or otherwise), or for town planning or reconstruction or the generation of employment, the furtherance of tourism, the promotion of culture, the preservation of the national or historical identity, or the economic well-being of the State or any purpose connected with the defense of Malta or connected with or ancillary to naval, military or air operations; and *includes any other purpose specified as public by any enactment*; and for the purposes of this definition, where the purpose for the exercise of any right under this Ordinance is connected with the utilization of any land or any right in connection or in relation therewith for any purpose connected with the supply, storage or distribution of few or other sources of energy, or in connection with the provision of any utility or municipal services or infrastructural project shall be deemed to be connected with or ancillary to the public interest or utility.[107]

The definition of public purpose within LAPPO places little constraint on regulatory sovereignty based on a public purpose analysis. The Court is simply silent concerning this point. It fails to observe that practically any human undertaking in connection with organized society may be rightfully construed as within the ambit of or ancillary to a "public purpose" within the meaning of the statute. Instead of placing subject matter in parameters, Article 2 of the LAPPO appears only to be referenced for purposes of contextualizing public purpose and the direct or indirect connection to a public purpose that a compulsory transfer of property between *private* individuals is likely to have. Accordingly, as to the LAPPO legislation, it is virtually impossible conceptually for any activity concerning real property not to be interpreted as a public purpose, thus empowering a State to engage in regulatory sovereignty to the detriment of private persons, both foreign and domestic.

Even though the Court quite understandably lacks jurisdiction to sit in judgment of a Maltese legislative enactment, it certainly has jurisdiction to publish its understanding of the shortcomings of such an expansive and overbroad statutory framework that likely cannot be construed as in violation of any interest in property in derogation of Article 2, thus rendering a public purpose analysis under this statute as fundamentally meritless. The Court substitutes this challenging but necessary doctrinal scrutiny with merely announcing that the public purpose requirement is met because the Court "considers that the construction of a road which would give access to a housing complex, *even though private*, *may* be considered as being in the public

[107] Farrugia, *supra* note 88, at ¶ 13 (replicating Article 2 of the LAPPO – Malta's relevant domestic law; emphasis added).

interest."[108] Because the Court is charged with doing more than just participating in perfunctory affirmations of first-instance adjudications finding a legitimate public purpose exercised, it has authority to assert that the doctrine, even as defined by statute, must be narrower if it is to be reconciled with a specific human right at stake. The violation of the right to property would then be doctrinally linked to noncompliance with the public purpose requirement.

A legacy public purpose doctrine that subordinates international human rights law to domestic regulatory governance shall have the effect of minimizing the protection against State abuse that international human rights aspires to guard against. The European Court of Human Rights' acceptance of an unqualified expropriation, where it was uncontested that no compensation was tendered, leaves much to be desired.

b. *Leyla Sahin v. Turkey*

The need for a robust public purpose doctrine in the realm of international human rights law becomes all the more apparent in cases where the quality of domestic law restricting freedoms of expression and of religion are found to be "proportional" when weighed against the public order that such restrictions ostensibly are intended to secure. Only the broadest construction of a self-judging public purpose standard will yield a lack of disproportionate inference in the restriction of the fundamental human rights of expression and religion. A tempered public purpose analysis would serve as a necessary protection between individual human rights and the State's infringement of those rights under the banner of regulatory sovereignty exercised in furtherance of public order. The incongruity arising from application of an unbridled public purpose within the framework of regulatory sovereignty is compounded, made worse, and highlighted where fundamental human rights are restricted in contravention of the very domestic laws of the State issuing such restrictions and in defiance of the domestic laws of the majority of members of the community of nations addressing the identical issue. A paradigm example of the dysfunctional interface between international human rights law and the legacy public purpose doctrine is found in the European Court of Human Rights' analysis and adjudication in the case of *Leyla Şahin v. Turkey*.[109]

In *Şahin*, the applicant, then in her fifth year at the Faculty of Medicine at Bursa University, had enrolled in the Cerrahpasa Faculty of Medicine at Istanbul University. The Court's judgment reflects that "she wore the Islamic headscarf during the four years she spent studying medicine at the

[108] *Id.* at ¶ 22 (emphasis added).

[109] Şahin v. Turkey, 2005-XI Eur. Ct. H.R. 173 [hereinafter Şahin].

University of Bursa and continued to do so until February 1998."[110] On February 23, 1998, the vice-chancellor of Istanbul University issued a circular – allegedly based on the case law of the Supreme Administrative Court and the European Commission of Human Rights – proscribing admission to lectures and tutorials to students wearing the Islamic headscarf and also to students with beards.[111] On being denied access, the applicant filed for issuance of an order setting aside the circular, averring that it infringed her rights as guaranteed by Article 8 ("Right to Respect for Private and Family Life"), Article 9 ("Freedom of Thought, Conscience, and Religion"), Article 14 ("Prohibition of Discrimination"), and Article 2 of Protocol No. 1 ("Right to Education"). The applicant specifically stated that "there was no statutory basis for the circular and the Vice-Chancellor's Office had no regulatory power in that theater."[112]

The applicant exhausted her judicial remedies before domestic courts[113] but not before the entry into force of legislation granting students amnesty from penalties imposed for alleged disciplinary violations and "resulting disabilities."[114] Based on Article 9 ("Freedom of Thought, Conscience, and Religion") of the Convention, the applicant perfected an action before the European Court of Human Rights asserting that "the ban on wearing the Islamic headscarf in institutions of higher education constituted an

[110] *Id.* at 3 ¶ 15.

[111] *Id.* at 3 ¶ 16. The circular at issue in pertinent part provides:

> By virtue of the Constitution, the law and regulations, and in accordance with the case-law of the Supreme Administrative Court and the European Commission of Human Rights and the resolutions adopted by the university administrative boards, students whose "heads are covered" (who wear the Islamic headscarf) and students (including overseas students) with beards *must not be admitted to lectures, courses or tutorials.* Consequently, the name and number of any student with a beard or wearing the Islamic headscarf must not be added to the lists of registered students. However, students who insist on attending tutorials and entering lecture theatres although their names and numbers are not on the lists must be advised of the position and, should they refuse to leave, their names and numbers must be taken and they must be informed that they are not entitled to attend lectures. If they refuse to leave the lecture theatre, the teacher shall record the incident in a report explaining why it was not possible to give the lecture and shall bring the incident to the attention of the university authorities as a matter of urgency so that disciplinary measures can be taken.

Id. (emphasis added).

[112] *Id.* at 4 ¶ 18.

[113] The Istanbul Administrative Court dismissed the application on the very narrow ground that "a University Vice-Chancellor, as the executive organ of the university, had power to regulate students' dress *for the purposes of maintaining order.*" The Supreme Administrative Court dismissed a subsequent appeal. *Id.* at 4 ¶¶ 19–20 (emphasis added).

[114] *Id.* at 5 ¶ 26.

unjustified interference with her right to freedom of religion, specifically, her right to manifest her religion."[115] The application was denied by the Court's Chamber, which issued a judgment characterizing the restriction contained in the Istanbul University regulations proscribing the right to wear the Islamic headscarf as one of the legitimate objectives contained in the second paragraph in Article 9 of the Convention. Indeed, the restriction was viewed as "justified in principle and proportionate to the aims pursued and could therefore be regarded as having been 'necessary in a democratic society.'"[116]

On appeal to the Grand Chamber, the applicant narrowly challenged the specific grounds on which the Chamber had concluded that no violation of Article 9 of the Convention had taken place.[117] Moreover, in what appeared to be a keen and practical procedural adjustment, the applicant asserted that her redress was *not* one that sought a universal right of recognition for all women to wear the Islamic headscarf in all places and without qualification. She noted that "[i]mplicit in the section judgment is the notion that the right to wear the headscarf will not always be protected by freedom of religion. I do not contest that approach."[118]

The nuanced issue edited to apply only to the specific case before the Court did not at all advance applicant's cause. Notwithstanding the Court's penchant for formal, technical arguments – most notably whether transitional Section 17 of Law Number 2547 provided a legal basis for a regulatory provision proscribing use of the Islamic headscarf[119] – it ultimately premised

[115] *Id.* at 17–18 ¶ 70. Article 9 of the Convention reads:

> 1. Everyone has the right to freedom of thought, conscience and religion; this includes freedom to change his religion or belief and freedom, either alone or in community with others and in public or private, to manifest his religion or belief, in worship, teaching, practice and observance.
> 2. *Freedom to manifest one's religion or beliefs shall be subject only to such limitations as are prescribed by law a democratic society in the interests of national security or public safety, for the prevention of disorder or crime, for the protection of health or morals or for the protection of the rights and freedoms of others.*

European Convention, *supra* Introduction note 15, art. 9 ¶¶ 1–2 (emphasis added).

[116] Şahin, *supra* note 109, at 18 ¶ 71 (citing paragraphs 66–116 of the Fourth Section's Chamber Judgment of June 29, 2004, *available at* http://hudoc.echr.coe.int/sites/eng/pages/search.aspx?i=001-61863).

[117] *Id.* at 18 ¶ 72.

[118] *Id.* at 18 ¶ 73.

[119] The applicant had alleged that there was no legislative norm in existence capable of constituting a legal basis for the regulatory provision. Accordingly, she asserted that Circular 8 of February 23, 1998, upon which the ban on wearing the Islamic headscarf was based, simply could not be compatible with transitional section 17 of Law no. 2547, "as that section did not

its analysis and holding on deference to the workings of the public purpose doctrine within the sphere of regulatory sovereignty in a "democratic society." In ratifying the Chamber's reasoning, the Court reproduced the lower court judgment as follows:

> The Court . . . notes the emphasis placed in the Turkish constitutional system on the protection of the rights of women . . . Gender equality – recognized by the European Court as one of the key principles underlying the Convention and a goal to be achieved by member states of the Council of Europe was also found by the Turkish Constitutional Court to be a principle implicit in the values underlying the Constitution . . .
>
> . . . In addition, like the Constitutional Court . . ., the Court considers that, when examining the question of the Islamic headscarf in the Turkish context, it must be borne in mind the impact which wearing such a symbol, which is presented or perceived as a compulsory religious duty, may have on those who choose not to wear it. As has already been noted, the issues at stake include the protection of the "rights and freedoms of others" and the "*maintenance of public order*" in a country in which the majority of the population, while professing a strong attachment to the rights of women and a secular way of life, adhere to the Islamic faith. Imposing limitations on freedom in this sphere may, therefore, be regarded as meeting a pressing social need by seeking to achieve those two legitimate aims, especially since, as the Turkish courts stated . . ., this religious symbol has taken on political significance in Turkey in recent years.
>
> . . . The Court does not lose sight of the fact that there are extremist political movements in Turkey which seek to impose on society as a whole their religious symbols and conception of a society founded on religious precepts . . . It has previously said that each Contracting State may, in accordance with the Convention provisions, take a stance against such political movements, based on its historical experience The regulations concerned have to be viewed in that context and *constitute a measure*

proscribe the Islamic headscarf and there were no legislative norms in existence capable of constituting a legal basis for a regulatory provision." *Id.* at 21 ¶ 86.

Consequently, following this line of thought, the Court undertook extensive review of the meaning of such fundamental terms as "in accordance with the law" and "prescribed by law," as asserted in Articles 8–11 of the Convention, in an effort to canvass the extent to which the domestic legislature of the respondent State in fact had issued finding regulations relevant to wearing an Islamic headscarf. Because the terms "in accordance with the law" and "prescribed by law" within the meaning of Articles 8–11 of the Convention are accorded broad constructions as to the meaning of the word "law," the Court was able to find "that there was a legal basis for the interference in Turkish law, namely transitional section 17 of Law no. 2547 [when] read in light of the relevant case-law of the domestic courts." *Id.* at 23 ¶ 98.

Furthermore, the Court found that the legislation met both accessibility and foreseeability requirements.

> *intended to achieve the legitimate aims referred to above and thereby to preserve pluralism in the university.*[120]

In the name of *pluralism* and *public order*, the Court found that an inference of disproportionality existed between the constraints imposed on the Article 9 human right and the legitimate objective pursued by the subject interference.[121]

Thus, Article 9 was subordinated to the preservation of a "democratic society" within the meaning of the Convention.[122] In turn, the Court found "pluralism" to be "indissociable from a democratic society."[123] The public purpose doctrine serves as the theoretical fulcrum upon which the privacy of religious freedom as a matter of individual conscience may be balanced against the right to the freedom to manifest one's religion publicly within a community. Upon acknowledging that "Article 9 does not protect every act motivated or inspired by religion or belief,"[124] the Court asserted:

> In democratic societies, in which several religions coexist within one and the same population, it may be necessary to place restrictions on freedom to manifest one's religion or belief in order to reconcile the interests of the various groups and ensure that everyone's beliefs are respected.[125]

Public purpose, here in the form of "public order," is thus used as a precept justifying the curtailment of a freedom for the greater glory of "true religious pluralism, which is vital to the survival of a democratic society."[126] Indeed, analytic support was drawn from *Karaduman v. Turkey*,[127] where

[120] *Id.* at 28 ¶ 115 (citing paragraphs 107–109 of the Fourth Section's Chamber Judgment; emphasis added and internal citations omitted).

[121] As to proportionality, the Court observed that:

> Having found that the regulations pursued a legitimate aim, it is not open to the Court to apply the criterion of proportionality in a way that would make the notion of an institution's "internal rules" devoid of purpose. Article 9 does not always guarantee the right to behave in a manner governed by a religious belief and does not confer on people who do so the right to disregard rules that have proved to be justified. In light of the forgoing and having regard to Contracting states' margin of appreciation in this sphere, the Court finds that the interference and issue was justified in principle and proportionate to the aim pursued.

Consequently, there has been no breach of Article 9 of the Convention.
Id. at 30 ¶¶ 121–23 (internal citations omitted).

[122] *Id.* at 24 ¶ 104.

[123] *Id.*

[124] *Id.* at 24–25 ¶ 105 (citing Cha'are Shalom Ve Tsedek v. France [GC], App. No. 27417/95, 2000-VIII Eur. Ct. H.R. at ¶ 73).

[125] *Id.* at 25 ¶ 106.

[126] *Id.* at 27 ¶ 110 (citation omitted).

[127] Karaduman v. Turkey, App. No. 16278/90, 74 Eur. Comm'n H.R. Dec. & Rep. 93 (1993) [hereinafter Karaduman]; *see also* Dahlab v. Switzerland, 2001-V Eur. Ct. H.R. 447 [hereinafter Dahlab].

> [T]he Convention institutions found that in a democratic society the State was entitled to place restrictions on the wearing of the Islamic headscarf if it was incompatible with the pursued aim of protecting the rights and freedoms of others, *public order* and *public safety*.[128]

The Court's reliance on an unbridled understanding of public purpose, together with untested assumptions concerning the term "democratic society," are indeed disappointing and, even worse, conceptually unavailing. The record, consonant with the Court opinion's narrative, is lacking any facts from which it may be inferred that the regulation at issue was *necessary* upon penalty of endangering the public or otherwise assuming the risk of general disorder arising from the sight of a medical student sporting the Islamic headscarf. The analysis is problematic. Pluralism in the Court's analysis does not comport with diversity and multiculturalism. Also absent is any showing that "pluralism" in a democratic society within the meaning of the Convention would somehow be placed in jeopardy as a result of the applicant wearing the Islamic headscarf.

Rather than deferring to a tautological argument asserting a need to subordinate the Article 9 human right to the preservation of pluralism within a democratic society by dint of the public purpose doctrine, the Court should have questioned the brazen exercise of regulatory sovereignty in the pursuit of secularism and democratic values that led to the detriment of human rights. Both proportionality and public purpose, as standards governing the likelihood of infringement on a fundamental human right, were viewed strictly through the self-judging lens of the signatory State. Neither the public purpose doctrine nor the principle of proportionality were contextualized by the specific facts underlying the case.

The analysis, from a public purpose scope and content perspective, was defective on the additional ground that it did not at all accord any weight to the manner in which the specific issue before it had been treated by the majority of States in the relevant community of nations. Customary international law arising from the practice of States should serve as a source for substantive content that may be ascribed to principles such as the public purpose doctrine with respect to specific issues, such as the relationship between Article 9 human rights and domestic legislation. The Court's opinion demonstrates a diversity of treatment by the community of nations concerning the issue in question: regulating the wearing of religious symbols in educational institutions, generally, and in institutions of higher learning in particular.

[128] Şahin, *supra* note 109, at 27 ¶ 111 (emphasis added).

Article L. 141–5-1 of the Education Code of France, for example, provides:

> In State primary and secondary schools, the wearing of signs or dress by which pupils overtly manifest a religious affiliation is prohibited. The school rules shall state that the institution of disciplinary proceedings shall be preceded by dialogue with the pupil.[129]

This Act, however, does not apply to State universities. A circular issued on May 18, 2004, establishes that the act is only limited to "signs such as the Islamic headscarf, however named, the kippah, or a cross that is manifestly oversized, which make the wearer's religious affiliation immediately identifiable."[130] The policy underlying the interference is manifestly aimed at proscribing what may be perceived as undue influence among minors and for this reason should not extend to State universities. The wearing of the Islamic headscarf by adults in State universities constitutes a protected religious expression in France.

The Court's opinion also acknowledged that, in Belgium, "there is no general ban on wearing religious signs at school."[131] Indeed, a Belgian decree issued on March 13, 1994, in the French community "stipulates that education shall be neutral within the Community. Pupils are in principle allowed to wear religious signs."[132] This right to wear religious signs, however, is qualified by the public purpose doctrine.[133] In the Flemish community, religious or philosophical signs to be worn are not uniformly regulated. Here, too, restrictions on such vestments may attach based on "hygiene or safety."[134]

In Austria, Germany, the Netherlands, Spain, Sweden, Switzerland, and the United Kingdom, Muslim peoples and students are allowed to wear the Islamic headscarf.[135] The Court observed that:

> In Germany, where the debate focused on whether teachers should be allowed to wear the Islamic headscarf, the Constitutional Court stated on 24 September 2003 in a case between a teacher and the Land of Baden-Wurttemberg that the lack of any express statutory prohibition meant that

[129] *Id.* at 14 ¶ 56.
[130] *Id.*
[131] *Id.* at 15 ¶ 57.
[132] *Id.*
[133] The Court makes reference to the fact that, in Belgium, the right may be infringed upon "only if human rights, the reputation of others, national security, public order and public health and morals are protected and internal rules complied with. Further, teachers must not permit religious or philosophical proselytism under their authority or the organisation of political militancy by or on behalf of pupils." *Id.*
[134] *Id.*
[135] *Id.* at 15 ¶ 58.

> teachers were entitled to wear the headscarf. Consequently, it imposed a duty on the Lander to lay down rules on dress if they wished to prohibit the wearing of the Islamic headscarf in State schools.[136]

As in the Belgian Flemish community, Austria does not proscribe the wearing of the headscarf, turban, or kippah, but recognizes a right to regulate on the grounds of health or safety hazard for peoples.[137] Despite canvassing the status of the law with respect to the issue of wearing the Islamic headscarf as part of a fundamental human right in these countries, the Court also observed that in Russia, Romania, Hungary, Greece, the Czech Republic, Slovakia, and Poland this concern "does not yet appear to have given rise to any detailed legal debate."[138]

The dissenting opinion registered by Judge Tulkens focuses precisely on the Court's surface treatment of the majority view on this issue as expressed by the community of nations and principally the signatories to the Convention. Judge Tulkens asserts that the "margin of appreciation" methodology, pursuant to which deference is accorded to national authorities on the ground that they are "better placed" to determine their optimal compliance with Convention obligations, is fundamentally flawed because of the failure to incorporate meaningfully the positions taken by the majority of States on this issue:

> I would perhaps have been able to follow the margin-of-appreciation approach had two factors not drastically reduced its relevance in the instant case. The first concerns the argument the majority use to justify the width of the margin, namely the diversity of practice between the states on the issue of regulating the wearing of religious symbols in educational institutions and, thus, the lack of a European consensus in this sphere. The comparative-law materials do not allow of such a conclusion, as in none of the member states has the ban on wearing religious symbols extended to university education, which is intended for young adults, who are less amenable to pressure. The second factor concerns the European supervision that must accompany the margin of appreciation and which, even though less extensive than in cases in which the national authorities have no margin of appreciation, goes hand in hand with it. However, other than in connection with Turkey's specific historical background, European supervision seems quite simply to be absent from the judgment. However, the issue raised in the application, whose significance to the right to freedom of religion guaranteed by the Convention is evident, is not merely a "local" issue, but one of importance

[136] *Id* at 15 ¶ 59.
[137] *Id* at 15 ¶ 60.
[138] *Id* at 16 ¶ 65.

> to all the member states. European supervision cannot, therefore, be escaped simply by invoking the margin of appreciation.[139]

Judge Tulkens's observation requires context if it is to be analyzed within the framework of public purpose because the doctrine underlies this writing. The Court deferred to domestic law on the issue of whether Article 9 human rights were compromised by domestic law proscribing the wearing of the Islamic headscarf in institutions of higher learning. Foreclosing consideration of the European consensus on this fundamental human right comports with application of a public purpose doctrine that is self-judging by the invoking State – in this instance, Turkey – whose exercise of regulatory sovereignty was the subject matter of the application before the Court. The margin-of-appreciation approach is but an ancillary methodology that institutionalizes from a tactical perspective the proposition that only the invoking State is properly positioned to determine the extent to which regulatory sovereignty premised on public purpose may legitimately and genuinely infringe on individual rights and corresponding State obligations attendant to such rights. Although analytically sound and intuitively appealing, the Court's reliance on the *objective* standard that the European consensus represents would have signaled a major paradigm shift in the treatment of public purpose from a subjective criteria that is content-free to an objective rubric narrower in scope and substantively infused by the practice of the majority of European States.

Judge Tulkens's analysis properly acknowledges that European supervision based on an objective standard in relation to a fundamental human right cannot be viewed as simply a "local issue" subject to constraints pursuant to the application of a parochial public purpose talisman. The enshrining of secularism over religious freedom is in great measure based on and supported by the proposition that Article 9 rights relating to the manifestation of the person's religious beliefs in a secular university are appropriately restricted by the overriding public purpose obligation to protect adult students from "fundamentalist religious movements."[140] The Court's reading of the

[139] *Id* at 44 ¶ 3. (Tulkens, J., dissenting).

[140] *Id* at 27 ¶ 111 (majority opinion).

The Court misconstrues the legal principle that the Commission articulated in *Karaduman* as supporting the premise that:

> [M]easures taken in universities to prevent certain fundamentalist religious movements from exerting pressure on students who did not practise their religion or who belonged to another religion were not considered to constitute interference for the purposes of Article 9 of the Convention. Consequently, it is established that institutions of higher education may regulate the manifestation of the rites and symbols of a religion by imposing restrictions as to the place and manner of such manifestation with the aim of ensuring

Commission's procedural analysis in *Karaduman* is analytically more than a shade off because of both the legal issues addressed and the very unique factual configuration of that proceeding.

Reliance on the *Dahlab* decision is equally misplaced. In that proceeding, the applicant was a Swiss national employed as a primary school teacher and living in Geneva.[141] She had been asked by the Canton of Geneva Directorate for Primary Education to refrain from wearing a headscarf in the performance of her teaching duties because, so the argument alleged, such vestment was incompatible with Section 6 of the Public Education Act.[142] Upon unsuccessfully exhausting domestic remedies, the applicant perfected an appeal with the Court, alleging that Section 6 of the Public Education Act infringed her freedom to manifest her religion, consonant with Article 9 of the Convention. As part of her challenge, the applicant further averred that the Swiss courts committed judicial error in holding that the measure (i) enjoyed sufficient foundation in law and (2) in finding "that there was a threat to public safety and to the protection of public order" arising from her wearing of the Islamic scarf.[143] As to this latter proposition, the applicant asserted "that she [had] wor[n] an Islamic headscarf and had gone unnoticed for *four years* and did not appear to have caused any obvious disturbance within the school."[144]

Upon discarding applicant's challenge to the measure as not meeting the "prescribed by law" requirement of Paragraph 2 of Article 9,[145] the Court applied a proportionality test weighing the requirements of the protection of

> peaceful coexistence between students of various faiths and thus protecting public order and the beliefs of others.

Id. This interpretation of the *Karaduman* opinion simply finds no support based on the facts presented and the issues addressed in that case.

141 Dahlab, *supra* note 127, at 1.

142 *Id. at* 7. Section 6 of the Canton of Geneva Public Education Act, dated November 6, 1940 reads:

> The public education system shall ensure that the political and religious beliefs of pupils and parents are respected.

Section 120(2) of the Public Education Act states:

> Civil servants must be lay persons; derogations from this provision shall be permitted only in respect of university teaching staff.

Article 27, §3 of the Federal Constitution, May 29, 1874 reads:

> It shall be possible for members of all faiths to attend State schools without being affected in any way in their freedom of conscience or belief.

Id.

143 *Id.*

144 *Id.* (emphasis added).

145 *Id.* at 11.

the rights and liberties of others against the conduct at issue. In doing so, weight was accorded to the extent to which wearing such "a powerful external symbol" may affect the religious belief of her pupils.[146] Similarly, the Court noted that the domestic tribunal had placed emphasis on:

> [T]he very nature of the profession of State school teachers, who were both participants in the exercise of educational authority and representatives of the State, and in doing so weighed the protection of the legitimate aim of ensuring the neutrality of the State education system against the freedom to manifest one's religion.[147]

Upon conceding that it was "very difficult to assess the impact that a powerful external symbol such as the wearing of a headscarf may have on the freedom of conscience and religion of very young children,"[148] the Court stressed the young ages of the children who served as the applicant's students:

> The applicant's pupils were aged between four and eight, an age at which children wonder about many things and are also more easily influenced than older pupils. In those circumstances, it cannot be denied outright that the wearing of a headscarf might have some kind of proselytizing effect, seeing that it appears to be imposed on women by a precept which is laid down in the Koran and which, as the Federal Court noted, is hard to square with the principle of gender equality. It therefore appears difficult to reconcile the wearing of an Islamic headscarf with the message of tolerance, respect for others and, above all, equality and nondiscrimination that all teachers in a democratic society must convey to their pupils.[149]

The applicant's status as a teacher and the youth of her pupils are two facts that render the *Dahlab* decision inapposite to *Leyla Şahin v. Turkey*. Instead of grade school students, *Şahin* concerns a university setting and an interference arising from a circular promulgated pursuant to university rules. Moreover, although the applicant in *Dahlab* was in a role model capacity *and* serving as a government representative in a public post as a school teacher, in *Şahin*, the applicant was an adult student studying in a university and having no professional or other government ties. The remarkable misapprehension of the Court of its own "precedent" and wholesale importation of boilerplate recitations and concepts such as "democratic society," "public order," and "public safety" is testimony to the workings of a public purpose doctrine that cannot appropriately balance the objectives of international human rights law,

[146] *Id.* at 13.
[147] *Id.* at 12.
[148] *Id.* at 13.
[149] *Id.* at 13.

regulatory sovereignty, and the exercise of human rights by individual citizens. In fact, *Şahin*, *Karaduman*, and *Dahlab* all reach the identical conclusion based on the application of the same principles of law concerning a common human right (the Article 9 right to manifest religious belief) and notwithstanding materially disparate facts: (i) the Islamic scarf worn by a student in a secular university in defiance of university rules, (ii) a picture ID affixed to a diploma bearing the image of a person wearing an Islamic headscarf, and (iii) a teacher of grade-school-aged children employed by the government wearing an Islamic headscarf in defiance of federal legislation.

The tendency to defer to domestic law that, in turn, is premised on a content-impoverished self-judging public purpose doctrine shall more than likely disfavor the interests of the invoking State over those of the private individual whose rights are being infringed based on political agendas and social prejudices that are disguised under the "public purpose" cloak of legitimacy. Development of a new paradigm must include consideration of the teachings of the case studies examined as representatives of the jurisprudence of the European Court of Human Rights where the public purpose doctrine (i) appears as an organizing principle tempering the brittle relationships among customary and conventional human rights law, (ii) is pivotal to the exercise of regulatory sovereignty, and (iii) is necessary in providing access to the Court's supervisory powers on the part of individuals whose rights have been violated. Public purpose serves a central role regarding the development and application of the European international human rights rubric. Here, public purpose plays a decisive role.

Despite this prominence, the public purpose doctrine is never defined, even though its content and substantive effect always appear to be assumed. The unchallenged treatment of public purpose as a content-neutral precept encompassing all things public and deemed to be best understood and applied by invoking States necessarily tends to favor the interests of States over those of individuals whose rights have been compromised. Because international human rights law purports to supplement and work together with domestic law, it tends to yield to domestic legislative acts and decisional law that, in turn, purport to find normative standing based on its conceptual compatibility with such vague notions as "a democratic society" and "public interest" or "public safety."[150] Drawing on the practice of nations, the European consensus in the case of the European Court of Human Rights represents a substantive source that may serve to provide the public purpose doctrine with concrete content. It is only one of a number of possible methodologies

150 The frailties of the term "democratic society" have been singled out *supra* at Chapter 3.A(2).

available for re-engineering a public purpose doctrine that may best serve the many exacting demands that international human rights law imposes on it. Additionally, it also serves to help wrest from States the monopoly of the doctrine as a tool with which to expand regulatory sovereignty in specific fields to the detriment of State compliance with obligations owed to individuals or even to other nations.

4

The Complex Interaction between the Public Purpose Doctrine and BITs: Discerning Order and Structure

A. AN ANALYSIS OF THE RELATIONSHIP BETWEEN STRUCTURE AND CONTENT: A FRAGMENTED FRAMEWORK WITHIN A DECENTRALIZED BODY OF INTERNATIONAL LAW AND A LEGACY PUBLIC PURPOSE DOCTRINE

1. *Unsettled Structural Issues in the Framework of Bilateral Investment Treaties*

The structural status of bilateral investment treaties (BITs) contributes to the perpetuation of a dysfunctional legacy public purpose doctrine. The public purpose doctrine constitutes an integral part of BITs. It is one of the cornerstone exceptions common to all BITs.[1] The fragmented configuration of BITs, however, much like the decentralized framework of customary international law generally, wrests from the public purpose doctrine found in BITs any semblance of formal or substantive uniformity.[2] Because the BIT framework is substantively laced with a want of a uniform framework, this fractured structure impedes orthodox recourse to statutory interpretations that would otherwise mitigate the challenges incident to discerning the substantive content and scope of the doctrine within the BIT network.

[1] Even though not all extant bilateral investment treaties have been canvassed to confirm this proposition, it would be conceptually at odds with the very foundation of "bilateralism" in public international law generally and the construct of a bilateral investment treaty purporting to attract foreign investment while preserving strategic regulatory sovereignty to lack this exception. Moreover, none of the sample 300 BITs studied for purposes of this writing lacked some fundamental iteration of the doctrine that was accorded a prominent conceptual role in preserving regulatory sovereignty, potentially at material detriment to the expectation of compliance with a Host State's obligations to protect foreign investment.

[2] The lack of uniform terminology and attendant context within the universe of BITs does not altogether obscure discernible patterns of iterations of the doctrine throughout the BIT "system."

The universe of BITs is constituted by a fragmented system of approximately 3,000 treaties that are not at all interconnected, conceptually organized, or sharing monolithic substantive standards.[3] The universe of multilateral, regional, and bilateral investment treaties is completely devoid of structure, hierarchy, or of any comparable organizing principle.[4] This lack of structural-formal uniformity is present at substantive levels. By way of example, rudimentary protection standards contained in BITs remain materially unsettled. Perhaps the cornerstone standard contained in BITs is the fair and equitable treatment (FET) standard of protection provided to foreign investors.[5]

Significant questions surrounding this basic standard linger and arouse considerable polemic as to such fundamental issues as whether FET is a "principle" or a "standard."[6] In this same vein, FET's relationship to the international minimum standard (IMS) also has galvanized a number of competing theories of practical consequences to international dispute resolution.[7] Is IMS the same

3 One commentator creatively analogized the rubric as "a 'spaghetti bowl' of around 3,000 overlapping bilateral and regional treaties, tens of thousands of transnational contracts, and an unknown number of domestic statutes whose purported aim is to stimulate economic development by attracting and protecting foreign investments within the sovereign territories of individual Host States." Maupin, *supra* Chapter 2 note 66, at 14 n.81.

4 In this regard, international investment law stands in high relief with its international trade law counterpart, which has been duly endowed with a framework and multi-institutional standing, such as the WTO.

5 The fair and equitable treatment standard is perhaps the most malleable and, therefore, susceptible even to unintentional overuse by claimants seeking to assert multiple claims arising from the same or overlapping infractions. Commentators have criticized the standard as conducive to abuse by claimants seeking to engraft it on violations that, according to these writings, are substantively distinct from the fair and equitable treatment claim. Olivia Chung, *The Lopsided International Investment Law Regime and Its Effect on the Future of Investor-State Arbitration*, 47 VA. J. INT'L L. 953, 961 (2007) (quoting CMS Gas Transmission Co. v. Argentine Republic, ICSID Case No. ARB/01/8, Award of the Tribunal, ¶ 274 (May 12, 2005), http://www.worldbank.org/icsid/cases/CMS_Award.pdf) (citing Carlos G. Garcia, *All the Other Dirty Little Secrets: Investment Treaties, Latin America, and the Necessary Evil of Investor-State Arbitration*, 16 FLA. J. INT'L L. 301, 306 (2004)) ("Fair and equitable treatment clauses . . . have become 'black holes of investment treaties' that invite a flood of litigation not originally contemplated by developing countries").

6 *See generally* ROLAND KLAGER, FAIR AND EQUITABLE TREATMENT IN INTERNATIONAL INVESTMENT LAW (Cambridge University Press 2011).

7 *See, e.g.*, IOANA TUDOR, THE FAIR AND EQUITABLE TREATMENT STANDARD IN THE INTERNATIONAL LAW OF FOREIGN INVESTMENT (2011). The author cogently asserts that FET is separate and distinct from IMS and points to, *inter alia*, the aberrant development of the standard as being one that first was codified and only subsequently forming part of customary international law, in contrast with the converse conceptual development pursuant to which customary international law principles are later codified, as part of the grounds that give rise to this confusion. Yet, Klager in turn observes:

or different from FET? If substantively different, what is the difference? Could the difference have any effect on damages/*quantum*?[8]

Numerous other rudimentary issues concerning the standards of protection accorded to foreign investor/investment plague BITs and, in considerable measure, result from the ad hoc interrelationship among the approximately 3,000 BITs, which were not entered into as part of a centralized process and were not negotiated pursuant to consensus or a coordinated format-protocol. The invariable consequences of this want of rigor and structure is that it tends to weaken Host States by exposing them to unforeseen causes of action lacking predictive value and that never were contemplated by the BIT parties.

Ironically, as to the public purpose doctrine, this lack of structural soundness and conceptual and doctrinal consistency has empowered Host States by amplifying the space of their regulatory sovereignty.

2. *The Findings of Empirical Analysis of Public Purpose in BIT Clauses*

The methodology used in this writing to ascertain the status of the various iterations of the public purpose doctrine contained in BITs was limited to the selection of 319 BITs ("the Sample BITs") from different parts of the world so

> It might well be that in some circumstances in which the international minimum standard is sufficiently elaborate and clear, the standard of fair and equitable treatment might be equated with it. But in other cases, it might as well be the opposite, so that the fair and equitable treatment standard will be more precise than its customary international law forefathers.

Klager, *supra* note 6 at 81. Here, Klager suggests that the evolutionary development of the standard is one from customary international law to conventional international law. In material contrast to Tudor, Klager further asserts:

> On many occasions, the issue will not even be whether the fair and equitable treatment standard is different or more demanding than the customary standard, but only whether it is more specific, less generic and spelled out in a contemporary fashion so that its application is more appropriate to the case under consideration. This does not exclude the possibility that the fair and equitable treatment standard imposed under a treaty can also eventually require a treatment additional to or beyond that of customary law. Such does not appear to be the case with the present dispute, however. The very fact that recent interpretations of investment treaties have purported to change the meaning or extent of the standard only confirms that, those instruments aside, the standard is or might be a broader one.

Id.

8 *See generally* Martinez-Fraga, *supra* Chapter 1 note 34, at 61 (discussing the "uncertainty pervading in basic clauses contained in BITs because of the fractured and fragmented BITs framework").

as to ensure a juridically broad-based representative sample.[9] Discernible BIT categories were identified as part of this empirical exercise. Some appeared with greater regularity than others. Consideration was accorded to incidents of recurrence in trying to understand whether a corresponding conceptualization attached to the universality of the category. In total, eight public purpose doctrinal categories were identified.[10] A ninth public purpose doctrine exception appeared with considerable regularity in the preamble of certain BITs concerning the principle of sustainable development.[11] All nine require analysis.

Within the universe of the nine BIT public purpose doctrine iterations and clauses identified, five categories of the public purpose doctrine were most recurrent: (i) the principle of sustainable development alone or in conjunction with health, safety and environment, or labor;[12] (ii) environment and labor;[13] (iii) limited public purpose exceptions;[14] (iv) no relaxation for health, safety, or environment;[15] and (v) clarification of indirect expropriation.[16]

9 These treaties have been identified and listed in alphabetical order in a chart format forming part of Appendix II, entitled "An Empirical Review of the Preeminence of the Public Purpose Doctrine throughout the Ever-Expanding Universe of Bilateral Investment Treaties."

10 The eight exceptions in the form of public purpose doctrine iterations were (i) environmental and labor, (ii) limited specific public purpose exceptions, (iii) no relaxation of existing public purpose measures, (iv) general exceptions, (v) security exceptions (vi) exceptions for transfers, (vii) prudential financial measures exceptions, and (viii) clarification of indirect expropriation exceptions. Each exception is analyzed and exemplified in at least one form in Appendix II.

11 The Agreement between Canada and Jordan for the Promotion and Protection of Investments, by way of example, in the preamble states:

> RECOGNIZING that the promotion and the protection of investments of investors of one Party in the territory of the other Party will be conducive to the simulation of mutually beneficial business activity, to the development of economic cooperation between them and to the promotion of sustainable development.

Canada-Jordan BIT, *supra* Chapter 2 note 193, preamble.

12 Appendix II at 2. *See, e.g.*, Canada-China BIT, *supra* Chapter 2 note 193, preamble.

13 Appendix II at 3. *See, e.g.*, Agreement between the Government of Canada and the Government of the Republic of Armenia for the Promotion and Protection of Investments art. XVII ¶ 2, Can.-Arm., May 8, 1997, http://investmentpolicyhub.unctad.org/Download/TreatyFile/131 [hereinafter Canada-Armenia BIT].

14 Appendix II at 3. *See, e.g.*, Canada-Jordan BIT, *supra* Chapter 2 note 193, art. VII ¶ 2.

15 Appendix II at 4. *See, e.g.*, Canada-Jordan BIT, *supra* Chapter 2 note 193, art. XI; Agreement between the Belgium-Luxembourg Economic Union and the Republic of Colombia on the Reciprocal Promotion and Protection of Investments art. VII, Bel.-Col., February 4, 2009, http://investmentpolicyhub.unctad.org/Download/TreatyFile/342 [hereinafter Belgium-Colombia BIT].

16 Appendix II at 8. *See, e.g.*, Canada-China BIT, *supra* chapter 2 note 193, annex B.10 ("Expropriation"); Agreement for the Promotion and Protection of Investments between the Republic of Colombia and the Republic of India art. 6 ¶ 2 (iv), Colom.-Ind., November 10, 2009, http://investmentpolicyhub.unctad.org/Download/TreatyFile/796 [hereinafter Colombia-India BIT].

Analysis of the Sample BITs' treatment of the public purpose doctrine demonstrates that the BIT network *tends* to favor the interests of Host States because of their respective reliance on the public purpose doctrine as an organizing principle regulating the exercise of regulatory sovereignty. Although a number of the Sample BITs did not contain any public purpose doctrine language or provision,[17] it was hardly uncommon for most BITs containing public purpose-based exceptions to contain different iterations of the doctrine.[18] Analyses of each of the representative public purpose doctrine exceptions contained in BITs, as well as paradigmatic BITs asserting multiple iterations of the public purpose doctrine, are worth reviewing because they demonstrate a trend toward (i) broadening regulatory sovereignty and (ii) promoting a legacy public purpose doctrine containing exceptions that touch and concern "all things public" while preserving the right to a self-judging standard on the part of the invoking State. It is significant to observe that most of the Sample BITs containing representative public purpose-based exceptions are of recent vintage.[19]

B. PUBLIC PURPOSE IN THE FORM OF SUSTAINABLE DEVELOPMENT LANGUAGE IN BITS AND COMBINATIONS OF SUSTAINABLE DEVELOPMENT; HEALTH, SAFETY, AND ENVIRONMENT; AND LABOR

The Colombia-Japan BIT[20] is particularly helpful in analyzing the scope and content of the public purpose doctrine within BITs, as well as the multiple iterations of the doctrine within a single treaty. The public purpose doctrine pervades this BIT. It is an illustrative paradigm because all of the eight referenced public purpose categories[21] are contained in the treaty; additionally, language referencing the public purpose category of sustainable development, as well as health, safety, and environment, and labor can be found in the preamble.

[17] The lack of reference is aside from the standard recitation of the elements of a valid expropriation that is present in almost every BIT, which, due to its standardized form and prevalence, was not included in the empirical analysis. For an example of this standard, *see, e.g.*, Agreement between the Government of Australia and the Government of the Argentine Republic on the Promotion and Protection of Investments, and Protocol art. 7, Aus.-Arg., August 23, 1995, *available at* http://investmentpolicyhub.unctad.org/Download/TreatyFile/72

[18] Appendix II at 5–6. *See, e.g.*, Canada-Jordan BIT, *supra* Chapter 2 note 193; Colombia-Japan BIT, *supra* Chapter 2 note 193.

[19] Especially those evincing the sustainable development expression in Appendix II at 2.

[20] Colombia-Japan BIT, *supra* Chapter 2 note 193.

[21] *See supra* note 10 and accompanying text.

The prominence of the public purpose doctrine in this BIT also is conceptually helpful because the treaty concerns an unqualified industrialized nation (i.e., Japan) and an economy in transition that no longer can be classified in economic terms as a "developing country" (Colombia).[22] Signed on September 12, 2011, the treaty is rather recent and fairly can be said to be prototypical of a second-generation BIT. It is also indicative of contemporary trends concerning the use of the public purpose doctrine in recent second-generation BITs.

1. *A Rich Preamble: Sustainable Development, Health, Safety, and Environment; and Labor*

The preamble to the Colombia-Japan BIT reflects that the parties intended for the treaty to form part of customary international law.[23] This aspiration, best contextualized by the BIT's own language, is helpful to the construction of the legal principles that it embodies. Because the parties viewed this BIT as hopefully "contribut[ing] to the strengthening of international cooperation with respect to the development of international rules on foreign investment,"[24] it is reasonably certain to assume that recent developments in customary international law concerning foreign investment were consulted when the respective delegations were negotiating the BIT.[25] This sensitivity to the

[22] *See, e.g.*, Robert W. McGee, Corporate Governance in Transition and Developing Economies: A Case Study of Colombia (August 25, 2010), http://ssrn.com/abstract=1665056 or http://dx.doi.org/10.2139/ssrn.1665056 (last visited April 29, 2013; evaluating Colombia as a transition economy under relevant Organization for Economic Cooperation and Development [OECD] standards).

[23] The preamble provides:

> Wishing that this Agreement will contribute to the strengthening of international cooperation with respect to the development of international rules on foreign investment.

Colombia-Japan BIT, *supra* Chapter 2 note 193, preamble. This language suggests that the signatories viewed the Agreement as having consequences in the international arena beyond just the parties to the BIT.

[24] *Id.*

[25] These types of clauses that overtly state that the parties aspire for the treaty to contribute to the development of international rules on foreign investment are rare but not entirely uncommon, and Japan seems to be sensitive to them. By way of example, the Agreement between Japan and the Republic of Peru for the Promotion, Protection and Liberalization of Investment, signed on November 22, 2008, contains the identical clause:

> Wishing that this Agreement will contribute to the strengthening of international cooperation with respect to the development of international rules on foreign investment.

Agreement between Japan and the Republic of Peru for the Promotion, Protection and Liberalisation of Investment, Per.-Jap., November 22, 2008, http://investmentpolicyhub.unctad.org/Download/TreatyFile/1733 [hereinafter Japan-Peru BIT].

current status of international rules on foreign investment as "works in progress" is helpful because it causes doctrine to be embodied in rules and principles and not just the particular negotiating issues unique to the parties. There is value to a clause that may remind both parties to the BIT and nonparty readers that the juridical elements of the BIT serve a much broader and even nobler function than simply that of stimulating microeconomic transfers of wealth between signatories.

The view of BITs as contributing "to the development of international rules on foreign investment" comports with the Colombia-Japan BIT's inclusion, if only by mention in its preamble, of the doctrine of sustainable development.[26] The seemingly all-encompassing broad scope of the sustainable development expression of the public purpose doctrine in this clause is studiously accompanied by explicit reference to maintenance of status quo regulatory sovereignty as to "health, safety and environmental measures of general application."[27] Consequently, the all-encompassing breadth of the doctrine of sustainable development, which, as suggested, has been construed as justifying regulatory sovereignty in all spheres so long as such regulation can be said to be reasonably related to any aspect of economic development, is here materially narrowed. The qualification "without relaxing health, safety and environmental measures of general application," which draws on the public purpose exceptions in Article XX of the General Agreement on Tariffs and Trade (GATT) concerning international trade law, provides the principle of sustainable development with considerable analytical support. But for the public purpose categories of security (which arguably may be said to be contained in "safety and financial soundness"), the general gamut of exceptions fall under health, safety, and environment. The reference to sustainable development in the preamble is a quite meaningful negotiation accomplishment for the likely Host State: Colombia. It is possible, and even likely, that the Japanese and Colombian delegations negotiating the BIT reached an accommodation pursuant to which the gains secured by the inclusion in the BIT of the principle of sustainable development were not undermined by relaxing the imported GATT Article XX exceptions.

This creative preservation of the effects of the scope and content of the sustainable development iteration of the public purpose doctrine may result in

[26] The preamble in pertinent part provides:

> RECOGNIZING that these objectives and *the promotion of sustainable development* can be achieved without relaxing health, safety and environmental measures of general application.

Colombia-Japan BIT, *supra* Chapter 2 note 193, preamble.

[27] *Id.*

having practical implications that redound in favor of both Home and Host States, depending on the nature of the majority of the investments contemplated. In this particular case, the sustainable development exception, with the qualification of not relaxing health, safety, and environmental measures of general application, perfectly comports with the foreign direct investment (FDI) expectations of Japan and Colombia, which primarily (if not exclusively) concern resource development pertaining to oil and gas, mining, and forestry. According to the Vale Columbia University Center on Sustainable International Investment, Colombia received a total of $13.2 billion in FDI in 2011.[28] Approximately $7.835 billion of that total was allocated to primary resource development (oil and gas, forestry, and mining).[29] Only $987 million was earmarked for construction and manufacturing, while $4.46 billion was reserved for financial services, and $3.7 billion was invested in the hospitality and infrastructure sectors.[30] Assuming that, for purposes of this BIT, Japan contemplates being positioned as the Home State with Colombia serving as the Host State, it would logically follow that the stronger capital-exporting Japanese economy would have negotiated in effect for a freeze on the exercise of regulatory sovereignty concerning health, safety, and environmental measures of general application that are most likely to touch and concern FDI destined for resource development. Support for the sustainable development doctrine in a form restricted by security and general financial welfare, in exchange for status quo regulatory sovereignty as to resource development public purpose subject matters, makes eminent sense. The very opposite, however, turned out to be the case.

The Colombia-Japan BIT illustrates the evolution of a negotiation dynamic pursuant to which developing countries and economies in transition enjoy greater negotiating standing. Developing resource-rich States, although still far less influential than their industrialized counterparts, have benefitted from a more integrated global economy that favors and requires interdependence over independence. This healthy shift is conducive to greater balance and less disparity between industrialized States and developing countries. As such, it requires appreciation separate and apart from the need to reform public purpose so as to curtail abuses and corruption perpetuated under the cloak of a greater common good.

[28] Miguel Posada Betancourt, *Inward FDI in Colombia and Its Policy Context 2012*, Vale-Columbia University Center on Sustainable Investment, *available at* http://ccsi.columbia.edu/files/2014/03/Colombia_IFDI_-_FINAL_-_13_June_2012.pdf (last visited September 10, 2014).

[29] *Id.*

[30] *Id.*

As a second-generation BIT with signatories who have expressed a sensitivity for the development of international rules governing the liberalization, promotion, and protection of foreign investment, the use of the public purpose doctrine in different iterations ranging from international trade law principles garnered from the GATT's Article XX to the principle of sustainable development or of permanent sovereignty over natural resources comports with a trend that witnesses a vast expansion of the public purpose doctrine nourished by principles not only extracted from international investment law, but also having their origins in international trade law and human rights law. The international juridical culture of investment law now must face the challenges of a broader but equally ill-defined and self-judging public purpose doctrine that forms part of customary international law and that has pervaded international investment law purportedly concerning itself with the promotion and protection of foreign investment. Here, Japan and Colombia, in some sense, have attempted to meet this challenge so as to render the public purpose doctrine workable by skillfully providing a succinct but effective check on two different manifestations of the public purpose doctrine, presumably based on the subject matter of the likely FDI between these countries. Although the result may point to an imbalance between Home- and Host-State FDI protection, the tendency favoring greater interdependence merits acknowledgment as a sign of concrete gains in this field.

A second-generation BIT should be illustrative of a new generation of Host States enjoying greater bargaining standing with respect to industrialized States. Many States that historically were accurately termed "developing countries" have outgrown this nomenclature. A number of "developing countries" have, in effect, shed that status to become "economies in transition" or countries approximating industrial-developed nations. Colombia, Peru, and Brazil serve as helpful examples of such development in Latin America.[31] For example, between 2007 and 2011 Japan experienced a −0.136 percent growth

[31] Average Gross Domestic Product (GDP) Growth Rates

	2011	2010	2009	2008	2007	
China	9.3	10.4	9.2	9.6	14.2	10.54
India	6.86	9.55	8.24	3.89	9.8	7.668
Peru	6.81	8.78	0.84	9.8	8.91	7.028
Turkey	8.5	9.16	4.83	0.66	4.67	5.564
Colombia	5.91	4	1.65	3.55	6.9	4.402
Brazil	2.73	7.53	0.33	5.17	6.1	4.372
Chile	5.99	6.1	−1.04	3.66	4.6	3.862
Japan	−0.7	4.4	−5.53	−1.04	2.19	−0.136

Source: World Bank, World Development Indicators, *available at*: data.worldbank.org

rate; in stark contrast, Colombia posted a 4.402 percent figure.[32] Similarly, other resource-rich countries such as India, Mexico, Peru, Turkey, and Brazil, to name just a few, are transitioning from developing country status to the more economically equipoised posture of being both capital-exporting and capital-importing States.[33] This enhanced standing would, in part, explain greater bargaining power on the part of States such as Colombia that, in turn, would lead to the inclusion of broad public purpose exceptions into BITs. This negotiating posture was not contemplated in the preceding generation of BITs.

The preamble to the Colombia-Japan BIT, in addition to raising the (i) sustainable development public purpose exception and (ii) the international trade law GATT exceptions, also references (iii) "labor and management."[34] The "labor" public purpose exception is tempered by the conjunctive "and" that both grammatically and substantively combines labor with management "in promoting investment between the Contracting Parties."[35] Even though the preamble speaks of the BIT as "the beginning of a new economic partnership between the Contracting Parties," but for the sustainable development iteration of the public purpose doctrine referenced in the fifth paragraph of the preamble, the totality of the preamble is framed by the unqualified and predominant objective of promoting and protecting foreign investment by investors of the contracting parties.

Notwithstanding the explicit reference to the principle of sustainable development, the purpose of the BIT, as suggested by the title and preamble, is far removed from seeking to correct historical asymmetries between the parties. The language "[r]ecognizing the growing importance of the progressive liberalization of investment for stimulating initiative of investors and for promoting prosperity and mutually favorable business activity in the Contracting Parties" is not susceptible to being construed as setting forth objectives for the general growth of developing countries, correcting historical inequities, or in any way fostering the promotion of social justice, as suggested by the African Charter on Human and Peoples' Rights.[36] Thus, the Colombia-Japan BIT, a representative second-generation BIT, incorporates sustainable development but does so in a qualified manner and always within the context of the overarching objective of promoting the liberalization and protection of foreign investment.

32 *Id.*

33 The "capital-exporting" and "capital-importing" terminology is helpful but not descriptively precise for this reason. There are now many States that may fall under both categories. The United States is a prime example. The referenced economics in transition represent yet another category of States that now arguably have claims to both categories.

34 Colombia-Japan BIT, *supra* Chapter 2 note 193, preamble.

35 *Id.*

36 *See supra* Chapter 3 notes 67–77 and accompanying text.

It does so within a manifest consciousness of having the BIT contribute to the "development of international rules on foreign investment."[37]

2. *The GATT Article XX Exceptions in BITs*

The GATT international trade law public purpose exceptions now form part of standard exceptions in BITs.[38] As discussed,[39] the wholesale importation of the GATT Article XX international *trade law* exceptions into second-generation BITs materially expands the scope and application of the public purpose doctrine even though the policy objectives of international trade law materially differ from the goals of international investment law.[40] Vesting the public purpose exceptions in BITs with these trade law principles contributes to the lack of transparency and the uncertainty that pervades the legacy public purpose doctrine.[41]

The Colombia-Japan BIT incorporates the GATT Article XX exceptions in Article 5 ("Performance Requirements") of the BIT.[42] The explicit reference to the international trade law public purpose exceptions, within the context of the Colombia-Japan BIT, is particularly problematic because of the preamble's explicit reference to these exceptions as status quo categories that are not to be relaxed or altered. The preamble specifically states:

> Recognizing that these objectives and the promotion of sustainable development can be achieved without relaxing health, safety and environmental measures of general application.[43]

[37] Colombia-Japan BIT, *supra* Chapter 2 note 193, preamble.

[38] Appendix II at 5. *See, e.g.*, Agreement between the Government of Canada and the Government of the Kingdom of Thailand for the Promotion and Protection of Investments art. XVII ¶ 3, Can.-Thai., January 17, 1997, http://investmentpolicyhub.unctad.org/Download/TreatyFile/637 [hereinafter Canada-Thailand BIT].

[39] *See* discussion *supra* at Chapter 1.F.

[40] *See* note 128 and accompanying text.

[41] Appendix II, *infra*, reflects the number of representative Sample BITs that have adopted language substantially similar to the GATT Article XX exceptions: no less than nineteen BITs.

[42] Article 5, Paragraph 6 reads:

> 6. Provided that such measures are not applied in an arbitrary or unjustifiable manner and provided that such measures do not constitute a disguised restriction on international trade or investment activities, nothing in subparagraphs 1(b), (c) and (f) and 2(a) and (b) shall be construed to prevent a Contracting Party from adopting or maintaining measures, including environmental measures:
> (a) necessary to secure compliance with laws and regulations that are not inconsistent with the provisions of this Agreement;
> (b) necessary to protect human, animal or plant life or health; or
> (c) related to the conservation of living or non-living exhaustible natural resources.

Colombia-Japan BIT, *supra* Chapter 2 note 193, art. 5 ¶ 6.

[43] *Id* preamble.

An interpretation of the term "without relaxing" as meaning "without compromising or diminishing," but not including a limit on enhancing or increasing regulatory activity as to health, safety, and environmental measures, is the most reasonable and universal interpretation.[44] Pursuant to this understanding of the text, a Host State would be privileged to increase and not just maintain at status quo regulatory measures that pertain to health, safety, and the environment. This reading would comport with an expanded and proactive view of the public purpose doctrine as set forth in Article 5(6)(a)(b) of the BIT vesting the Host State with plenary regulatory sovereignty to regulate human, animal, or plant life or health to the likely detriment of the Host State's obligation to protect foreign investment/investor and other incident interests pertaining to the Home State. The enhancement of regulatory sovereignty could most efficiently be tempered to protect foreign investments/investors by developing a substantive public purpose doctrine that is not self-judging and is applied pursuant to a proportionality test. The gamut of Article XX GATT exceptions also would have to be viewed as applying in the context of macroeconomic scenarios and not just to the microeconomic events that typically characterize foreign investments that fall within the ambit of a BIT.

A second methodology that would limit the exercise of regulatory sovereignty pertaining to human, animal, or plant life or health would arise from an exhaustive disclosure on the part of contracting States of their regulatory framework. Here, transparency is paramount. Such disclosure or transparency, however, is hardly achievable even at a theoretical level. Regime change, among many other political factors, would render the most pristine rendition of a regulatory rubric materially less than fully predictable or certain not to infringe on foreign investments/investors. Attaining the highest possible level of transparency, despite the likelihood of securing absolute certainty arising from complete transparency, still should play a greater role in key BIT clauses where the public purpose doctrine is likely to be relied on as a source for expanding regulatory sovereignty.[45]

[44] The last paragraph of the Colombia-Japan BIT contained in Article 44 provides that all texts in the Japanese, Spanish, and English languages are "equally authentic," but that "in case of any divergency, the English text shall prevail." *Id.* art. 44. The Spanish language exemplar refers to "without relaxing" as "*disminucion*," meaning diminishing or reducing.

[45] Although a sensitivity for transparency with respect to regulatory sovereignty has appeared in BITs, the principle of transparency is yet to realize its full potential in this regard. The Colombia-Japan BIT, for example, references a need for transparency in the preamble:

> Intending to further create stable, equitable, favorable and *transparent conditions* for greater investment by investors of one Contracting Party in the Area of the other Contracting Party.

Id. preamble (emphasis added). This cursory reference in the preamble is still a far cry from a comprehensive disclosure requirement.

A third approach to placing reasonable constraints on regulatory sovereignty as to human, animal, or plant life or health in connection with transparency in regulatory rubric disclosure would be to substitute the term "without relaxing," as it appears in the fifth paragraph of the Colombia-Japan BIT, with the term "without altering existing status quo .... " Placing "a ceiling" on the quality and nature of regulatory measures concerning specific subject matter (i.e., health, safety, and environmental measures) by referencing a particular and known status quo certainly would contribute to a reasonable restraint on the use of this public purpose regulatory principle and its relation to obligations in favor of foreign investors/investments protection.

The environment and labor exceptions are very much discernible in second-generation BITs.[46] The two most common clauses containing the

[46] *See, e.g.*, Agreement between Japan and the Laos People's Democratic Republic for the Liberalisation, Promotion and Protection of Investment art. 24, Jap.-Laos, January 16, 2008, http://investmentpolicyhub.unctad.org/Download/TreatyFile/1729 [hereinafter Japan-Laos BIT]:

> The Contracting Parties recognise that it is inappropriate to encourage investment by investors of the other Contracting Party by relaxing environmental measures. To this effect each Contracting Party should not waive or otherwise derogate from such environmental measures as an encouragement for the establishment, acquisition or expansion in its Area of investments by investors of the other Contracting Party.

See also Treaty between the Government of the United States of America and the Government of the Republic of Rwanda Concerning the Encouragement and Reciprocal Protection of Investment art. 12 ¶ 2, USA-Rwa., February 19, 2008, http://investmentpolicyhub.unctad.org/Download/TreatyFile/2241 [hereinafter USA-Rwanda BIT] ("Nothing in this Treaty shall be construed to Prevent a party from adopting, maintaining, or enforcing any measure otherwise consistent with this Treaty that it considers appropriate to ensure that investment activity in its territory is undertaken in a manner sensitive to environmental concerns"); Agreement between the Government of the United Arab Emirates and the Government of the Republic of Azerbaijan on the Promotion and Reciprocal Protection of Investments art. 16, UAE-Aze., November 20, 2006, http://investmentpolicyhub.unctad.org/Download/TreatyFile/243 [hereinafter UAE-Azerbaijan] ("Nothing in this Agreement shall prevent a Contracting Party from applying measures according to its laws and regulations in order to protect ... environment"); Agreement between the Government of Canada and the Government of the Republic of Costa Rica for the Promotion and Protection of Investments annex I.III ¶ 1, Can.-C.R., March 18, 1998, http://investmentpolicyhub.unctad.org/Download/TreatyFile/601 [hereinafter Canada-Costa Rica BIT] ("Nothing in this Agreement shall be construed to prevent a Contracting Party from adopting, maintaining or enforcing any measure otherwise consistent with this Agreement that it considers appropriate to ensure that investment activity in its territory is undertaken in a manner sensitive to environmental concerns"); Agreement between the Government of Canada and the Government of Barbados for the Reciprocal Promotion and Protection of Investment art. XVII ¶ 2, Can.-Bar., May 29, 1996, http://investmentpolicyhub.unctad.org/Download/TreatyFile/280 [hereinafter Canada-Barbados BIT] (same); Agreement between the Government of the Republic of Hungary and the Government of the Russian

environmental exception can be found in the Canada-Armenia BIT[47] and the Colombia-UK BIT.[48] The Canada-Armenia BIT provides:

> Nothing in this Agreement shall be construed to prevent a Contracting Party from adopting, maintaining or enforcing any measure otherwise consistent with this Agreement that it considers appropriate to ensure that investment activity is undertaken in a manner sensitive to environmental concerns.[49]

The Colombia-UK BIT reads:

> Nothing in this Agreement shall be construed to prevent a Party from adopting, maintaining or enforcing any measure that it considers appropriate to ensure that an investment activity in its territory is undertaken in a manner sensitive to environmental concerns, provided that such measures are non-discriminatory and proportionate to the objectives sought.[50]

The Colombia-UK BIT represents the more stringent, and, therefore, balanced approach to the exception. It provides for two fundamental qualifying elements that must be met by the Host State. First, the measure must be nondiscriminatory. Second, it must be "proportionate to the objectives sought."[51] Those qualifications are helpful and conducive to a balanced approached that takes into consideration the interests of both Home and Host States. The nondiscriminatory and proportionality strictures bespeak an objective methodology that wrests presumptions of correctness from the invoking State based on the assumption that States are better placed to evaluate public purpose needs. Also, proportionality represents an important contribution toward mitigating the "all-or-nothing" approach that historically has categorized the unilateral application of public purpose exceptions on the part of Home States.

This approach to the environmental iteration of the public purpose doctrine is laudable but far from representative of a mainstream approach, despite its clearly discernible recurrence among the Sample BITs (albeit in the

Federation for the Promotion and Reciprocal Protection of Investments art. 2 ¶ 3, Hun.-Rus., March 6, 1995, http://investmentpolicyhub.unctad.org/Download/TreatyFile/1544 [hereinafter Russia-Hungary BIT] ("This Agreement shall not preclude the application of either Contracting Party of measures, necessary for … protection of the environment").

47 Canada-Armenia BIT, *supra* note 13, art. XVII ¶ 2.

48 Bilateral Agreement for the Promotion and Protection of Investments between the Government of the United Kingdom of Great Britain & Northern Ireland and the Republic of Colombia art. VIII, U.K.-Col., March 17, 2010, http://investmentpolicyhub.unctad.org/Download/TreatyFile/805 [hereinafter UK-Colombia BIT].

49 Canada-Armenia BIT, *supra* note 13, art. XVII ¶ 2.

50 UK-Colombia BIT, *supra* note 48, art. VIII.

51 *Id.*

context of clarifications or annexes.[52] The paradigmatic second-generation Colombia-Japan BIT, for example, dispenses with the very valuable "proportionality" restriction but qualifies exercise of regulatory sovereignty by proscribing (i) arbitrariness, (ii) lack of foundation as to manner, and (iii) an indirect or "disguised" constraint on international trade or investment:

> Provided that such measures are not applied in an arbitrary or unjustifiable manner and provided that such measures do not constitute a disguised restriction on international trade or investment activities, nothing in subparagraphs 1(b), (c) and (f) and 2(a) and (b) shall be construed to prevent a Contracting Party from adopting or maintaining measures, including environmental measures:
>
> (a) necessary to secure compliance with laws and regulations that are not inconsistent with the provisions of this Agreement;
> (b) necessary to protect human, animal or plant life or health; or
> (c) related to the conservation of living or non-living exhaustible natural resources.[53]

The three qualifying requirements need to be balanced against a considerable subject matter gamut ranging from enforcement of laws and regulations consistent with the BIT to "the conservation of living and non-living exhaustible natural resources."[54] The use of the GATT Article XX language to define the scope of contemplated regulatory measures is not suggestive of balanced symmetrical allocation of rights between Home and Host States.

Conceptually, it is not clear what general environmental measures may reasonably pertain to performance requirements, which is the centerpiece subject matter of Article V of the BIT. The Article V "Performance Requirements" concern international commercial trade issues such as (i) level or percentage of goods or services to be exported;[55] (ii) level or percentage of domestic content to be achieved;[56] (iii) requirements to purchase, use, or accord a preference to goods produced in a strategic area;[57] (iv) requirements pertaining to the volume or value of imports and exports;[58] (v) restrictions on sales of goods

[52] *See, e.g.*, Canada-Peru BIT, *supra* Chapter 2 note 193, annex IV ¶ (c); Treaty between the United States of America and the Republic of Mozambique Concerning the Encouragement and Reciprocal Protection of Investment Protocol ¶ 1, USA-Moz., December 1, 1998, http://investmentpolicyhub.unctad.org/Download/TreatyFile/2058 [hereinafter USA-Mozambique BIT].

[53] Colombia-Japan BIT, *supra* Chapter 2 note 193, art. V ¶ 6.

[54] *Id.* art. V ¶ 6(a)–(c).

[55] *Id.* art. V ¶ 1(a).

[56] *Id.* art. V ¶ 1(b).

[57] *Id.* art. V ¶ 1(c).

[58] *Id.* art. V ¶ 1(d).

or services in a particular Home-State geographic market that investments of the investor produce or in any way relating to the volume or value of foreign exchange earnings;[59] and (vi) the transfer of proprietary knowledge within the subject area save for specifically excepted requirements.[60] These categories of limits on performance requirements are not directly, or conceptually, at all related to issuance of environmental measures. The mention of the environmental exception expression of the public purpose doctrine in this context merely serves to broaden Home-State regulatory sovereignty. The very generic and conventional reference to "environmental measures," coupled with the shortcomings of the legacy public purpose doctrine all serve to multiply the disproportionate effect of the exception.

The Sample BITs identify a third category of "limited public purpose exceptions."[61] At a discernible level, this category of limited public purpose exceptions nicely fits into two narrow categories: (i) exceptions from performance requirements[62] and (ii) exceptions from national

[59] *Id.* art. V ¶ 1(e).

[60] *Id.* art. V ¶ 1(f). Performance requirements concerning the transfer of technology are qualified as follows:

> … except when the requirement:
> (i) is imposed or enforced by a court, administrative tribunal or competent authority to remedy an alleged violation of competition laws; or
> (ii) concerns the transfer or use of intellectual property rights or disclosure of proprietary information which is undertaken in a manner not inconsistent with the TRIPS Agreement.

Id.

[61] Appendix II at 3.

[62] *See, e.g.*, Canada-Jordan BIT, *supra* Chapter 2 note 193, art. 7 ¶ 2; Canada-Peru BIT, *supra* Chapter 2 note 193, art. 7 ¶ 2; Treaty between the Federal Republic of Germany and Antigua & Barbuda Concerning the Encouragement and Reciprocal Protection of Investments Protocol ad, art. 3 ¶ (a), Ger.-Ant., November 5, 1998, http://investmentpolicyhub.unctad.org/Download/TreatyFile/68 [hereinafter Germany-Antigua & Barbuda BIT]; Agreement between the Federal Republic of Germany and the People's Republic of Bangladesh Concerning the Promotion and Reciprocal Protection of Investments Protocol, ad art. 2 ¶ (a), Ger.-Ban., May 8, 1981, http://investmentpolicyhub.unctad.org/Download/TreatyFile/264 [hereinafter Germany-Bangladesh BIT]; Agreement between Barbados and the Federal Republic of Germany Protocol ad art. 3 ¶ (a), Ger.-Bar., December 2, 1994, *available at* http://investmentpolicyhub.unctad.org/Download/TreatyFile/283 [hereinafter Germany-Barbados BIT]; Agreement between the Federal Republic of Germany and Benin Concerning the Promotion and Reciprocal Protection of Capital Investment Protocol ad art. 2 ¶ *(a)*, Ger.-Ben., June 28, 1978, http://investmentpolicyhub.unctad.org/Download/TreatyFile/441 [hereinafter Germany-Benin BIT]; Treaty between the Federal Republic of Germany and the Federal Democratic Republic of Ethiopia Concerning the Encouragement and Reciprocal Protection of Investments art. 3 ¶ 3, Ger.-Eth., January 19, 2004, http://investmentpolicyhub.unctad.org/Download/TreatyFile/1164 [hereinafter Germany-Ethiopia BIT]; Treaty between the Federal Republic of Germany and the Co-operative Republic of Guyana Concerning the Encouragement and Reciprocal Protection of

treatment.[63] The Canada-Jordan BIT[64] in Article 7(2) is illustrative of the core language of the performance requirements exceptions. It reads:

> A measure that requires an investment to use a technology to meet generally applicable health, safety or environmental requirements shall not be construed to be inconsistent with subparagraph 1(f) [Performance Requirements].[65]

The totality of the performance requirements exception articulated in Article 7 of the Canada-Jordan BIT is quite extensive and mirrors that of the Colombia-Japan BIT as to key material terms.[66] The Canada-Jordan BIT, executed in 2009, approximately two years prior to the signing of the Colombia-Japan BIT, also is a paradigmatic second-generation BIT. Accordingly, even within the presumably narrow subject matter constraints of the very technical performance requirements public purpose exception, "health, safety or environmental requirements"[67] of GATT origin are

Investments Protocol ad art. 3 ¶ (a)(3), Ger.-Guy., December 6, 1989, http://investmentpolicyhub.unctad.org/Download/TreatyFile/1335 [hereinafter Germany-Guyana BIT]; Agreement between the Lebanese Republic and the Federal Republic of Germany on the Promotion and Reciprocal Protection of Investments Protocol ad art. 3 ¶ (a)(3), Ger.-Leb., March 18, 1997, http://investmentpolicyhub.unctad.org/Download/TreatyFile/1358 [hereinafter Germany-Lebanon BIT]; Agreement between the United Mexican States and the Federal Republic of Germany on the Promotion and Reciprocal Protection of Investments Protocol ad art. 3 ¶ *(a)*, Ger.-Mex., August 25, 1998, http://investmentpolicyhub.unctad.org/Download/TreatyFile/1371 [hereinafter Germany-Mexico BIT]; Agreement between the Federal Republic of Germany and the Republic of the Philippines for the Promotion and Reciprocal Protection of Investments Protocol ad art. 3 ¶ *(a)*, Ger.-Phi., April 18, 1997, http://investmentpolicyhub.unctad.org/Download/TreatyFile/1392 [hereinafter Germany-Philippines BIT]; Agreement between Japan and the People's Republic of China Concerning the Encouragement and Reciprocal Protection of Investment Protocol ¶ 3, Jap.-Chi., August 27, 1988, http://investmentpolicyhub.unctad.org/Download/TreatyFile/747 [hereinafter Japan-China BIT].

63 *See, e.g.*, Agreement on the Reciprocal Promotion and Protection of Investments between the Kingdom of Spain and the Federal Republic of Nigeria art. 5 ¶ 4, Spa.-Nig., July 9, 2002, http://investmentpolicyhub.unctad.org/Download/TreatyFile/2107 [hereinafter Spain-Nigeria BIT]; Treaty between the Federal Republic of Germany and the Federal Republic of Nigeria Concerning the Encouragement and Reciprocal Protection of Investments Protocol ad art. 4 ¶ (a), Nig.-Ger., March 28, 2000, http://investmentpolicyhub.unctad.org/Download/TreatyFile/1382 [hereinafter Nigeria-Germany BIT]; Agreement between the Government of the Kingdom of Thailand and the Government of the Russian Federation on the Promotion and Reciprocal Protection of Investments art. 3 ¶ 3, Rus.-Tha., October 17, 2002, http://investmentpolicyhub.unctad.org/Download/TreatyFile/2230 [hereinafter Thailand-Russia BIT].

64 Canada-Jordan BIT, *supra* Chapter 2 note 193, art. 7 ¶ 2.

65 *Id.*

66 *See infra* Appendix I for a comparison of the Performance Requirements provision in the Canada-Jordan BIT with the corresponding provision in the Colombia-Japan BIT.

67 Canada-Jordan BIT, *supra* Chapter 2 note 193, art. 7 ¶ 2.

commingled with a broad spectrum of performance requirements subject matter exceptions, much like the Article 5(6) performance requirements of the Colombia-Japan BIT.[68]

The second limited public purpose exception is found as tempering the National Treatment standard. The Sample BITs do vary considerably concerning the role of public purpose in connection with national treatment. Whereas, for example, second-generation BITs such as the Canada-Jordan BIT and the Colombia-Japan BIT are silent in referencing any iteration of the public purpose doctrine as a qualifying factor as to national treatment,[69] the UK-Colombia BIT and the Germany-Antigua and Barbuda BIT explicitly temper the national treatment obligation pursuant to the relatively broad construction of the public purpose doctrine. The UK-Colombia provides:

> The provision of this Agreement relative to the grant of treatment not less favourable than that accorded to investors of either Contracting Party or of any third State shall not be construed so as to preclude the adoption or enforcement by a Contracting Party of measures which are necessary to protect national security, public security or public order.[70]

[68] Colombia-Japan BIT, *supra* Chapter 2 note 193, art. 5 ¶ 6.

[69] In both of these BITs (Colombia-Japan and Canada-Jordan), the substantive obligation of National Treatment does not contain nor is it followed by qualifying public purpose exceptions. The same holds true for the closely related substantive obligation of Most-Favored-Nation Treatment. Article 3 ("Most-Favored-Nation Treatment") of the Colombia-Japan BIT nearly qualifies Most-Favored-Nation Treatment by noting that the treatment applies only to substantive and not to procedural obligations by asserting the following "Note":

> It is understood that the treatment referred to in paragraph 1 does not include treatment accorded to investors of a non-Contracting Party and their investments by provisions concerning the settlement of investment disputes such as the mechanisms set out in Chapter III and Chapter IV that are provided for in other international agreements between a Contracting Party and a non-Contracting Party.

Colombia-Japan BIT, *supra* Chapter 2 note 193, art. 3 *bis*.

[70] UK-Colombia BIT, *supra* note 48, art. IV ¶ 1. Article IV ("Exceptions") is immediately preceded by the Article III recitation of the substantive Most-Favoured-Nation provision stating:

> 1. Each Contracting Party shall grant to the investments of investors of the other Contracting Party made in its territory, a treatment not less favourable than that accorded, in like circumstances, to investments of its own investors or to investments of investors of another third State, whichever is more favourable to the investor.
> 2. The most favourable treatment to be granted in like circumstances referred to in this Agreement does not encompass mechanisms for the settlement of investment disputes, such as those contained in Articles IX and X of this Agreement, which are provided for in treaties or international investment agreements.

Id. art. IIII.

Similarly, the older Germany-Antigua and Barbuda BIT, originally signed in 1998 and amended by protocol in 2000, notably amends Article III by asserting:

> The following shall more particularly, though not exclusively, be deemed "activity" within the meaning of Article III (2): The Management, Maintenance, Use, Enjoyment and Disposal of an Investment. The following shall, and particularly, be deemed "treatment thus favourable" within the meaning of Article III: Unequal Treatment in the Case of Restrictions on the Purchase of Raw or Auxiliary Materials, of Energy or Fuel or of Means of Production or of Operation of Any Kind, unequal treatment in the case of impeding in the marketing of products inside or outside the country, as well as any other measures having similar effects. *Measures that have to be taken for reasons of public security or order, public health or morality shall not be deemed "treatment less favorable" within* the meaning of Article 111.[71]

Both the UK-Colombia BIT and the Germany-Antigua and Barbuda BIT suggest that "treatment not less favorable than that accorded to investors of either Contracting Party" is warranted, and, therefore, it does not constitute treatment any less favorable where the public purpose doctrine must be resorted to on a compulsory or mandatory basis. Neither BIT uses the words "compulsory" or "mandatory," but the same construction can be placed with respect to the word "necessary" in the case of the UK-Colombia BIT and the phrase "have to be taken" as to the Germany-Antigua and Barbuda BIT. This "mandatory" predicate to some extent does remove recourse to the public purpose doctrine from the ambit of self-judgment. Even though a sovereign itself is best placed to assess national exigencies, the compulsory nature of a necessity indeed engrafts meaningful objective criteria onto the process.

The broad conceptual categories of public purpose qualifying national treatment in both BITs merit emphasis. The potential use of (i) public security, (ii) public health, (iii) public morality, (iv) national security, (v) public security, and (vi) public order enable a rich set of possibilities on which to premise the exercise of regulatory sovereignty in ways that may invade treaty obligations to protect foreign investment.[72] Even the notably omitted categories – such as environment, and human and animal life and health – arguably may fall within the ambit of the public purpose iterations listed. Taken together, the exceptions of performance requirements and national treatment pervading many of the second-generation BITs give rise

[71] Germany-Antigua & Barbuda BIT, *supra* note 62, Protocol ad art. 3 ¶ (a).

[72] Compare UK-Colombia BIT, *supra* note 48, art. IV ¶ 1 with Germany-Antigua & Barbuda BIT, *supra* note 62, Protocol ad art. 3 ¶ (a).

to three fundamental propositions underlying this writing. First, the public purpose doctrine materially dilutes treaty obligation protections running in favor of investors (i) because of the debilities endemic to the legacy public purpose doctrine and (ii) the actual incorporation of the doctrine to qualify or limit protection standards within the very language of the substantive protection obligations. Second, the new paradigm of economic *interdependence* and the sustained growth enjoyed by a significant number of resource-rich jurisdictions that formerly were classified as "developing countries" and that now stand as "economies in transition" likely to attain industrialized-country economic status has led to greater bargaining power on the part of prospective Host States that previously were unable to negotiate in *pari materia* with their industrialized counterparts. Third, Home-State investor expectations have been, and are likely to continue to be, frustrated because of the predictive value that the public purpose doctrine in this context wrests from the substantive standards of investor protection. The consequence of these three propositions is simple enough. As concerns regulatory sovereignty, the symmetrical structure that *bilateral* investment treaties, at least in principle, contemplate is materially distorted in favor of Host States.

Lack of relaxation of standard with respect to health, safety, or environment as one collective category, and for labor as a distinct subject matter for categorical classification, is well represented in the Sample BITs.[73] In some

[73] *See, e.g.*, Belgium-Colombia BIT, *supra* note 15, art. VII ("Environment"), art. VIII ("Labour"); Canada-Jordan BIT, *supra* Chapter 2 note 193, art. 11 ("Health, Safety and Environmental Measures"); Canada-Peru BIT, *supra* Chapter 2 note 193, art. 11 ("Health, Safety and Environmental Measures"); Agreement between the Japan and the Republic of Iraq for the Promotion and Protection of Investment art. 22, Jap.-Iraq, June 7, 2012, http://investmentpolicyhub.unctad.org/Download/TreatyFile/1663 [hereinafter Japan-Iraq BIT] ("Health, Safety and Environmental Measures and Labour Standards"); Japan-Papau New Guinea BIT, *supra* Chapter 2 note 193, art. 22 ("Health, Safety and Environmental Measures and Labour Standards"); Japan-Laos BIT, *supra* note 46, art. 24 ("Environmental Measures"); Japan-Peru BIT, *supra* note 25, art. 26 ("Health, Safety and Environmental Measures and Labour Standards"); Agreement between Japan and the Socialist Republic of Vietnam for the Liberalization, Promotion and Protection of Investment art. 21 ("Environment"), Jap.-Viet., November 14, 2003, http://investmentpolicyhub.unctad.org/Download/TreatyFile/1738 [hereinafter Japan-Vietnam BIT]; Agreement between the Swiss Confederation and the United Mexican States on the Promotion and Reciprocal Protection of Investments Protocol ad. art. 3 ("Health, Safety and Environment"), Mex.-Swi., July 10, 1995, http://investmentpolicyhub.unctad.org/Download/TreatyFile/2006 [hereinafter Mexico-Switzerland BIT]; Agreement between the Government of the Republic of Turkey and the Government of the United Republic of Tanzania Concerning the Reciprocal Promotion and Protection of Investments art. 4 ("Health, Safety and Environmental Measures"), Turk.-Tanz., March 11, 2011, http://investmentpolicyhub.unctad.org/Download/TreatyFile/2342 [hereinafter Turkey-Tanzania BIT]; USA-Rwanda BIT, *supra* note 46, art. 12 ("Investment and Environment"), art. 13 ("Investment and Labour"); Treaty between the United States of America and the Oriental

instances, both categories appear together in BITs.[74] The Colombia-Japan BIT is representative of a treaty embracing both categories:

1. Each Contracting Party recognizes that it is inappropriate to encourage investment activities of investors of the other Contracting Party and of a non-Contracting Party *by relaxing its domestic health, safety or environmental measures or by lowering its labor standards. Accordingly, each Contracting Party should not waive or otherwise derogate from such measures or standards as an encouragement for the establishment, acquisition or expansion of its Area of investments by investors of the other Contracting Party of a non-Contracting Party.*
2. Each Contracting Party may adopt, maintain or enforce any measure that it considers appropriate to ensure that investment activities in its Area are undertaken in a manner not incompatible with its *environmental law*, provided that such measure is consistent with this Agreement.[75]

The measures on health, safety, environment, and labor contained in the first paragraph of Article 21 speak only of a State "relaxing its domestic" standards concerning the referenced public purpose categories, but they do not speak to enhancing or rendering more stringent any existing standards in these areas or otherwise introducing new ones. This interpretation is important, in part because it illustrates the possibly determinative role that regulatory transparency and attendant diligence by Home-State investors may play in the relationship between capital-exporting and capital-importing States such as Japan and Colombia.

The commitment to status quo with respect to regulatory measures concerning the referenced public purpose categories is significantly less clear in the case Paragraph 2 of Article 21. This paragraph, in addition to using the phrase "maintain or enforce" also explicitly references measures that a Contracting Party "may adopt." The two operative standards for issuance of measures along these lines are the measure's (i) compatibility with the State's environmental law and (ii) consistency with the Agreement (i.e., the Colombia-Japan BIT). Despite a surface semblance of objective criteria, what may be considered as consistent with the BIT agreement or compatible

Republic of Uruguay Concerning the Encouragement and Reciprocal Protection of Investment art. 12 ("Investment and Environment") and art. 13 ("Investment and Labour"), USA-Uru., November 5, 2005, http://investmentpolicyhub.unctad.org/Download/TreatyFile/2380 [hereinafter USA-Uruguay BIT].

74 *See, e.g.*, Japan-Iraq BIT, *supra* note 73, art. 22; USA-Rwanda BIT, *supra* note 46, art. 12 and art. 13.

75 Colombia-Japan BIT, *supra* Chapter 2 note 193, art. 21 ¶¶ 1–2 (emphasis added).

with a State's environmental law is hardly objectively demonstrable. In most cases, compatibility with a State's environmental law presents considerable challenges – not the least of which is acquiring an understanding of the compatibility between the measure at issue and the policies underlying "black letter" environmental law as they concern consistency with the BIT. A comprehensive analysis may not be possible without securing the intent of the Agreement's drafter, which in turn may not even be possible. Consistency, at least beyond the scope of physics and mathematics, is a relative term.

Variations on the prescription to relaxation for health, safety, or environment are well-illustrated in Article 11 of the Canada-Jordan BIT[76] and Article VII of the Belgium-Colombia BIT.[77] The nonrelaxing of domestic health, safety, or environmental measures provision contained in Article 11 of the Canada-Jordan BIT does not reference any language suggesting the expansion of regulatory sovereignty, much like Article 21(1) of the Colombia-Japan BIT.

[76] Article 11 of the Canada-Jordan BIT provides:

> The Parties recognize that it is inappropriate to encourage investment by relaxing domestic health, safety or environmental measures. Accordingly, a Party may not waive or otherwise derogate from, or offer to waive or otherwise derogate from, such measures as an encouragement for the establishment, acquisition, expansion or retention in its territory of an investment of an investor. If a Party considers that the other Party has offered such an encouragement, it may request consultations with the other Party and the two Parties shall consult with a view to avoiding any such encouragement.

Canada-Jordan BIT, *supra* Chapter 2 note 193, art. 11.

[77] Article VII of the Belgium-Colombia BIT provides:

> 1. Recognising the right of each Contracting Party to establish its own levels of domestic environmental protection and environmental development policies and priorities, and to adopt or modify accordingly its environmental legislation, each Contracting Party shall strive to ensure that its legislation provides for high levels of environmental protection and shall strive to continue improving this legislation.
> 2. The Contracting Parties recognise that it is inappropriate to encourage investment by relaxing domestic environmental legislation. Accordingly, each Contracting Party shall ensure that it does not waive or otherwise derogate from, or offer to waive or otherwise derogate from, such legislation as an encouragement for the establishment, maintenance or expansion in its territory of an investment.
> 3. The Contracting Parties recognize that co-operation between them provides enhanced opportunities to improve environmental protection standards.
> 4. Nothing in this Agreement shall be construed as to prevent a Contracting Party from adopting, maintaining or enforcing any measure that it considers appropriate to ensure that an investment activity in its territory is undertaken in accordance with the environmental law of the Party.
> 5. The dispute settlement mechanisms under Articles XII and XIII of this Agreement shall not apply to any obligation undertaken in accordance with this Article.

Belgium-Colombia BIT, *supra* note 15, art. VII.

In fact, the language of the two provisions are materially indistinguishable but for a reference to labor standards in Article 21(1).[78]

The public purpose doctrine is a centerpiece of "general exceptions" contained in the Sample BITs.[79] In the context of general exceptions, the public purpose doctrine suggests itself in three discernible modalities: (i) a *de minimus* expression pursuant to which regulatory sovereignty is encouraged and justified based simply on a basic unqualified reference to security interests, public health, animal and plant life;[80] (ii) a more global iteration of the public purpose doctrine akin to Article XX of the GATT;[81] and (iii) public purpose in the form of "public order" language.[82] Even though these three exceptions typically appear under an article entitled "General

[78] The no-relaxation provisions in BITs attaching to different iterations of the public purpose doctrine vest the Host State with considerable discretion to adopt labor policies, laws, and regulations that may adversely affect investment/investor protection obligations. A comprehensive example is provided in Article VIII of the Belgium-Colombia BIT:

> 1. The Contracting Parties recognize:
>   a. the right of each Contracting Party to establish its own domestic labour standards, and to adopt or modify accordingly its labour legislation;
>   b. that each Contracting Party shall endeavour to ensure that the principles set forth in paragraph 6 of Article I [Internationally Recognized Labour Standards] be recognized and maintained by its national legislation; and
>   c. that it is inappropriate to encourage the establishment, maintenance or expansion in its territory of an investment *by relaxing domestic labour legislation*.
> 2. The Contracting Parties recognize that co-operation between them provides enhanced opportunities to improve labour standards.
> 3. Nothing in this Agreement shall be construed as to prevent a Contracting Party from adopting, maintaining, or enforcing any measure that it considers appropriate to ensure that an investment activity in its territory is undertaken in accordance with the labour law of the Party.
> 4. The dispute settlement mechanisms under Articles XII and *XIII* of this Agreement shall not apply to any obligation undertaken in accordance with this Article.

Id. art. VIII (emphasis added).

[79] *See, e.g.*, Canada-Armenia, *supra* note 13, art. XVII ¶ 3; Canada-Barbados BIT, *supra* note 46, art. XVII ¶ 3; Canada-China, *supra* Chapter 2 note 193, art. 33 ¶ 2; Canada-Costa Rica BIT, *supra* note 46, annex I.III ¶ 3; Colombia-India BIT, *supra* note 16, art. 13 ¶ 5; Japan-Vietnam BIT, *supra* note 73, art. 15 ¶ 1

[80] *See, e.g.*, Agreement between the Government of New Zealand and the Government of the People's Republic of China on the Promotion and Protection of Investments art. 11, NZ-Chi., November 22, 1988, http://investmentpolicyhub.unctad.org/Download/TreatyFile/764 [hereinafter New Zealand-China BIT].

[81] *See, e.g.*, Agreement between the Government of Canada and the Government of the Kingdom of Thailand for the Promotion and Protection of Investments Art. XVIII ¶ 3, Can.-Thai., January 17, 1997, http://investmentpolicyhub.unctad.org/Download/TreatyFile/637 [hereinafter Canada-Thailand BIT].

[82] *See, e.g.*, Colombia-Japan BIT, *supra* Chapter 2 note 193, art. 15 ¶ 1; Hungary-Russia BIT, *supra* note 46, art. 2 ¶ 3.

Exceptions,"[83] they are also common to "catchall" clauses that serve as the functional equivalent to general exceptions articles in treaties.[84]

The New Zealand-China BIT, signed November 22, 1988, is clearly a first-generation BIT; therefore, it is illustrative of negotiation efforts concerning BITs between industrialized and nonindustrialized States at a time when economic globalization was far from apogee, and economic models were largely based on foundational premises of financial independence rather than interdependence. The New Zealand-China BIT presents a helpful example of this economic construction that reflected a negotiation dynamic that ultimately favored Home States (capital-exporting countries). That BIT's equivalent to a "General Exceptions" article is found in Article 11, entitled "Prohibitions and Restrictions," which reads:

> The provisions of this Agreement shall not in any way limit the rights of either Contracting Party to apply prohibitions or restrictions of any kind or take any other action directed to the protection of its essential security interests, or to the protection of public health or the prevention of disease and tests in animals or plants.[85]

It is not surprising that Host States generally were limited in their ability to negotiate successfully fundamental premises that amplified the scope of regulatory sovereignty. Even the title of Article 11 ("Prohibitions and Restrictions") could find less customary international law interpretive recourse than the term "General Exceptions" would be able to garner. Put simply, it is not altogether disconcerting that in 1988 nonindustrialized States would not have as much standing to negotiate general exceptions as they would at the height of economic globalization and the adoption of financial models that stressed economic interdependence as a material governing principle.[86] Despite the arguably expansive language contained in Article 11, only three public purpose categories are identified. Of the three, one,

[83] *See, e.g.*, Colombia-Japan BIT, *supra* Chapter 2 note 193, art. 15 ¶ 1; Canada-Thailand BIT, *supra* note 81, art. XVIII.

[84] *See, e.g.*, New Zealand-China BIT, *supra* note 80, art. 11 ("Prohibitions and Restrictions"); Hungary-Russia BIT, *supra* note 46, art. 2 ("Promotion and Reciprocal Protection of Investments").

[85] New Zealand-China BIT, *supra* note 80, art. 11.

[86] As noted by the United Nations Conference on Trade & Development, "[i]n 2011, FDI inflows increased in all major economic groups – developed, developing and transition economies." WIR 2012, *supra* Chapter 2 note 69, at 38. However, despite the fact that "[g]lobal foreign direct investment (FDI) flows exceeded the pre-crisis average in 2011, reaching $1.5 trillion despite turmoil in the global economy," such levels were still about 23 percent lower than the FDI flows at the peak of economic globalization in 2007. *Id.* at xi.

addressing animal and plant life, is fairly circumscribed. Even the remaining two (protection of essential security interests and protection of public health) by themselves do not stand out as unbridled licenses to regulate to the detriment of substantive investment/investor protection obligations.

The use of the public purpose doctrine as a pivotal premise of treaty-based general exceptions is well-chronicled in Article XVII of the Canada-Thailand BIT. The broad scope and clear influence of the GATT expressed in Article XVII commands analysis.[87] The general exceptions contained in Article XVII of the Canada-Thailand BIT are quite expansive and arguably all-encompassing. Paragraphs 2 and 3 of Article XVII do purport to set some kind of limitation on regulatory sovereignty. Consonant with Paragraph 2, Contracting Parties are proscribed from adopting or enforcing measures inconsistent with the BIT. Similarly, Paragraph 3 proscribes the adoption of the enforcement of measures that are either *arbitrary* or unjustifiable, as well as measures disguised to restrict international trade or investment. But for these two sets of constraints, the public purpose doctrine is asserted in

[87] Article XVII ("Application and General Exceptions") states:

> (1) This Agreement shall apply to any investment made by an investor of one Contracting Party in the territory of the other Contracting Party before or after the entry into force of this Agreement.
> (2) Nothing in this Agreement shall be construed to prevent a Contracting Party from adopting, maintaining or enforcing any measure otherwise *consistent with* this Agreement that it considers appropriate to ensure that investment activity in its territory is undertake in a manner sensitive to environmental concerns.
> (3) Provided that such measures are not applied in an *arbitrary* or *unjustifiable manner* or do not constitute a disguised restriction on international trade or investment, nothing in this Agreement shall be construed to prevent a Contracting Party from adopting or maintaining measures, including environmental measures:
> (a) necessary to ensure compliance with laws and regulations that are not inconsistent with the provisions of this Agreement;
> (b) necessary to protect human, animal or plant life or health; or
> (c) relating to the conservation of living or non-living exhaustible natural resources if such measures are made effective in conjunction with restrictions on the domestic production or consumption;
> (d) imposed for the protection of national treasures of artistic, historic or archeological value;
> (e) essential to the acquisition or distribution of products in general or local short supply provided that any such measures shall be consistent with the principle that all investors are entitled to an equitable share of the international supply of such products, in that any such measures which are inconsistent with the other provisions of this Agreement shall be discontinued as soon as the conditions giving rise to them have ceased to exist.

Canada-Thailand BIT, *supra* note 81, art. XVII (emphasis added).

the form of a verbatim recitation adoption of five fundamental general exceptions from the GATT's Article XX.[88]

The incorporation of the GATT Article XX General Exceptions represents an expansive spectrum of public purpose categories that, in turn, may justify regulatory sovereignty to the detriment of substantive treaty-based protection standards. Moreover, the qualifying standard in the double negative, "not inconsistent with the provisions of this Agreement,"[89] does not meaningfully temper the otherwise boundless public purpose subject matter exceptions listed in Subsections (3)(b)–(e). In contrast with the base public purpose exception contained in Article 11 of the China-New Zealand BIT, public purpose in the form of the GATT's Article XX General Exceptions vests both States (as capital-importing countries) with considerable advantages over foreign investors/investments. This normative foundation for the exercise of regulatory sovereignty undermines any legitimate aspiration to "bilateralism" that contracting parties to a BIT may hope to enjoy. Public purpose, as expressed through the GATT's General Exceptions cannot be tempered by even absolute regulatory transparency (if such a thing in fact existed) and, similarly, is incapable of being checked by mere treaty drafting techniques. It does remain unassailable that the role of public purpose in the form of GATT Article XX General Exceptions incorporated into a BIT represents a practically infinite capacity to disappoint investor/investment expectations and dangerously favors Host-State regulatory sovereignty to the detriment of substantive foreign investment/investor protection that theoretically represents the broader goal of a BIT in the first instance.

The third variation of the public purpose doctrine appearing in the form of general exceptions take the form of "public order" language. The maintenance of public order and the need to protect public morals are perhaps the potentially most dangerous public purpose expressions because of their inherently subjective content. At what point does *public order* mutate into the repression of the public? What public order exactly *is* remains as a classical query that perhaps is incapable of being satisfactorily at all addressed. Likewise, what is morality? Equally fundamental, can morality be contracted or legislated in the name of public purpose? Much like Xeno's paradoxes, inquiries concerning the nature of public order or public morality can be

88 The wholesale incorporation of the GATT's General Exceptions into Article XVII ("Application and General Exceptions") of the Canada-Thailand BIT is nothing short of remarkable. Compare Canada-Thailand BIT, *supra* note 81, art. XVIII ¶ 3(a)–(e) with GATT, *supra* Chapter 1 note 1, art. XX*(b)*, *(d)*, *(f)*, *(g)*, and *(j)*.

89 Canada-Thailand BIT, *supra* note 81, art. XVII(a).

posed ad infinitum without bringing the examiner any closer to a satisfactory resolution.

Public order language appears in the Sample BITs as having two contextual variants. In the first, exemplified in Article 15(1) of the Colombia-Japan BIT, public morals and public order are listed as only two public purpose general exceptions in a long list of public purpose categories.[90] The second variation of the public order exception forming part of general exceptions found in BITs is evidenced by Article 2(3) of the Russia-Hungary BIT. That provision states that the treaty:

> [S]hall not preclude the application of either Contracting Party of measures, necessary for the maintenance of defense, national security and public order, protection of the environment, morality, and public health.[91]

[90] Article 15(1) of the Colombia-Japan BIT reads:

> Subject to the requirement that such measures are not applied by a Contracting Party in a manner which would constitute a means of arbitrary or unjustifiable discrimination against another Contracting Party, or a disguised restriction on investments of investors of that other Contracting Party in the Area of the former Contracting Party, nothing in this Agreement other than Article 12 ["Treatment in Case of Strife"] shall be construed to prevent that former Contracting Party from adopting or enforcing measures, including those to protect the environment:
>
> (a) necessary to protect human, animal, or plant life or health;
> (b) *necessary to protect public morals or to maintain public order*;
>
> *Note: The public order exception may be invoked only where a genuine and sufficiently serious threat is posed to one of the fundamental interests of society.*
>
> (c) necessary to secure compliance with the laws or regulations which are not inconsistent with the provisions of this Agreement including those relating to:
> (i) the prevention of deceptive and fraudulent practices or to deal with the effects of a default on contracts;
> (ii) the protection of privacy of the individual in relation to the processing and dissemination of personal data and the protection of confidentiality of personal records and accounts; or
> (iii) safety; or
> (d) imposed for the protection of national treasures of artistic, historic, archeological or cultural value.

Colombia-Japan BIT, *supra* Chapter 2 note 193, art. 15 ¶ 1. (emphasis added).

[91] Hungary-Russia BIT, *supra* note 46, art. 2 ¶ 3. This exception is contained in Article 2 ("Promotion and Reciprocal Protection of Investments"), which provides, in full:

> 1. Each Contracting Party shall encourage and create favourable conditions for investors of the other Contracting Party to make investments in its territory and shall admit such investments in accordance with its laws and regulations.
> 2. Investments of investors of one Contracting Party shall at all times be accorded fair and equitable treatment and shall enjoy full protection and security in the territory of the other Contracting Party.

Public order, as part of general exceptions, finds resonance in the Sample BITs and, to some extent, can be viewed as a species of a "catchall" clause that vests States, most likely Host States, with a quite meaningful license to exercise regulatory sovereignty to the detriment of substantive investor protection obligations. The broad theoretical expanse of public order is evinced by the somewhat recurring practice of qualifying this exception by noting that its application is limited to instances of extreme emergencies affecting the State or even its national security. The Colombia-Japan BIT, by way of example, qualifies its single-sentence reference to public order (i.e., "necessary to protect public morals or to maintain public order") by a most distinctive observation:

> Note: The public order exception may be invoked only where a genuine and sufficiently serious threat is posed to one of the fundamental interests of society.[92]

This qualification is testament to the virtually unbridled foundation for exercise of regulatory sovereignty that a mere reference to "public order," as is the case in most BITs, may cause and thus unsettle expectations and any aspiration to symmetry and bilateralism to the Contracting Parties. In this connection, the Colombia-Japan BIT is helpful in illustrating how treaty drafting techniques may *help* mitigate the ills of the legacy public purpose doctrine.[93]

The three variants of the public purpose doctrine contained in the General Exceptions category illustrate the pivotal role that the public purpose doctrine plays across expansive subject matter even within one category. Yet, as with the reference to the doctrine in (i) preambles, (ii) environment and labor, and

> 3. *This Agreement shall not preclude the application of either Contracting Party of measures, necessary for the maintenance of defence, national security and public order, protection of the environment, morality and public health.*

Id. art. 2 (emphasis added).

92 Colombia-Japan BIT, *supra* Chapter 2 note 193, art. 15 ¶ 1 *bis*.

93 The role of treaty-drafting techniques as a partial solution to the disparities that the legacy public purpose doctrine creates is discussed in the context of the principle of sustainable development. *Supra* Chapter 2, Subsection E. There, it was suggested that treaty-drafting techniques are, at best, a partial solution to the technical and policy challenges that the legacy public purpose doctrine poses. Here, in the "public order" context, already a particular expression of the public purpose doctrine, the contributions of treaty-drafting techniques can be appreciated, but so too are their limitations revealed. Whereas terms such as "genuine," "sufficiently," "serious," and "fundamental interests of society" certainly engraft a quasi-objective standard against which to determine juridical legitimacy, they are far from conclusive. The virtues, however, of first steps in the direction of objectivity cannot be sufficiently praised.

(iii) no-relaxation clauses, nowhere in the general exception clauses canvassed among Sample BIT exemplars was public purpose, in any of its iterations, defined. Similarly, no standard was referenced as to its application, and very limited linkage to proportionality was observed.

The fifth public purpose exception notably contained in the Sample BITs is the *security* category.[94] The security exceptions expression of the public purpose doctrine comprises five variants: (i) restriction on the dispute settlement section of the BIT only,[95] (ii) a plain statement exception,[96] (iii) security exceptions

[94] *See, e.g.*, Canada-China BIT, *supra* Chapter 2 note 193, art. 33 ¶ 5; Canada-Jordan BIT, *supra* Chapter 2 note 193, art. 10 ¶ 4; Canada-Peru, *supra* Chapter 2 note 193, art. 10 ¶ 4; New Zealand-China BIT, *supra* note 80, art. 11; Agreement between the Government of the People's Republic of China and the Government of the Republic of Singapore on the Promotion and Protection of Investments art. 11, Chi.-Sing., November 21, 1985, http://investmentpolicyhub.unctad.org/Download/TreatyFile/776http://investmentpolicyhub.unctad.org/Download/TreatyFile/1794 [hereinafter China-Singapore BIT]; Belgium-Colombia BIT, *supra* note 15, art. II ¶ 3; Colombia-India BIT, *supra* note 16, art. 13 ¶ 5(d); Colombia-Japan BIT, *supra* Chapter 2 note 193, art. 15 ¶ 2; Croatia-Azerbaijan BIT, *supra* Chapter 2 note 193, art. 10; Agreement between the Government of the Slovak Republic and the Government of the Republic of Kenya for the Promotion and Reciprocal Protection of Investments art. 14 ¶ 1, Slo.-Ken., December 14, 2011, http://investmentpolicyhub.unctad.org/Download/TreatyFile/1794 [hereinafter Slovakia-Kenya BIT].

[95] For example, the Germany-Mexico BIT provides:

> The dispute settlement provisions of this Section shall not apply to the resolutions adopted by a Contracting State, which for National Security reasons, prohibit or restrict the acquisition of an investment in its territory, owned or controlled by its nationals, by nationals or companies of the other Contracting State, according to the legislation of the relevant Contracting State.

Germany-Mexico BIT, *supra* note 62, art. 20.

[96] The New Zealand-China BIT provides:

> The provisions of this Agreement shall not in any way limit the right of either Contracting Party to apply prohibitions or restrictions of any kind or take any other action direct to the protection of its essential security interests, or to the protection of public health, or to the prevention of disease and pests in animals or plants.

New Zealand-China BIT, *supra* note 80, art. 11. A second form of this variant is exemplified by the Austria-India BIT:

> Nothing in this Agreement precludes the host Contracting Party from taking necessary action in abnormal circumstances for the protection of its essential security interests or in circumstances of extreme emergency in accordance with its laws applied on a non-discriminatory basis.

Agreement between the Government of the Republic of Austria and the Government of the Republic of India for the Promotion and Protection of Investments art. 12 ¶ 2, Ind.-Aust., December 18, 2000, http://investmentpolicyhub.unctad.org/Download/TreatyFile/192 [hereinafter Austria-India BIT].

premised on the GATT Article XXI,[97] (iv) security exceptions that include *public order* language,[98] and (v) a qualification that national security interests are self-judging.[99] The security exceptions expression of the public purpose doctrine theoretically harbors the same fundamental concerns identified as pervading an orthodox understanding of the doctrine. In practice, however, with few notable exceptions (such as the use of public order as a premise for adversely compromising a standard of investment protection and commercial transactions alleged to be indirectly for the purpose of supplying a military or other security

[97] The Canada-China BIT, for example, provides:

> Nothing in this Agreement shall be construed:
> (a) to require a Contracting Party to furnish or allow access to information if the Contracting Party determines that the disclosure of that information is contrary to its essential security interests;
> (b) to prevent a Contracting Party from taking any actions that it considers necessary for the protection of its essential security interests:
> (i) relating to the traffic in arms, ammunition and implements of war and to such traffic and transactions in other goods, materials, services, and technology undertaken directly or indirectly for the purpose of supplying a military or other security establishment;
> (ii) in time of war or other emergency, in international relations; or,
> (iii) relating to the implementation of national policies or other nuclear explosive devices; or
> (c) to prevent a Contracting Party from taking action in pursuance of its obligations under the United Nations Charter for the maintenance of international peace and security.

Canada-China BIT, *supra* Chapter 2 note 193, art. 33 ¶ 5. Notably, with the exception of Article 35(5)(b)(iii), the remaining five subsections comprising the totality of Article 33(5) are based, in most instances verbatim, on the Article XXI ("Security Exceptions") of the GATT.

[98] The Belgium-Colombia BIT provides, in relevant part:

> Nothing contained in this Agreement shall bind either Contracting Party to protect investments made with capital or assets derived from illegal activities, and it shall not be construed so as to prevent a Party from adopting or maintaining measures intended to preserve *public order*, the fulfillment of its duties for the keeping or restoration of international peace and security; or the protection of its own essential security interests.

Belgium-Colombia BIT, *supra* note 15, art. II ¶ 3 (emphasis added). Similarly, the Hungary-Russia BIT states:

> This Agreement shall not preclude the application of either Contracting Party of measures, necessary for the maintenance of defence, national security and *public order*, protection of the environment, morality and public health.

Hungary-Russia BIT, *supra* note 46, art. II ¶ 3 (emphasis added).

[99] *See, e.g.*, Treaty between the Government of the United States of America and the Government of the Republic of Nicaragua Concerning the Encouragement and Reciprocal Protection of Investment Protocol 1, USA-Nic., July 1, 1995, http://investmentpolicyhub.unctad.org/Download/TreatyFile/2106 [hereinafter USA-Nicaragua BIT] ("With respect to Art. XIV, paragraph 1, the parties confirm their mutual understanding that whether a measure is undertaken by a party to protect its national security interests is self-judging").

establishment), noneconomic security exceptions are readily discernible and historically have proven to be statistically inconsequential in treaty-based international arbitrations.[100] Public purpose in the context of security exceptions have no pretense but to be self-judging; that is, far-removed from objective criteria.[101]

The Colombia-Japan BIT is premised on the GATT Article XXI model. As previously noted, this BIT organizationally treats security exceptions together with general exceptions in Article 15. Article 15 is substantially similar to Article XX[102] and Article XXI[103] of the GATT but for a notice provision that, significantly, is triggered after the undertaking of a measure inconsistent with Paragraph 1 of Article 15:

> 3. In cases where a Contracting Party takes any measure, pursuant to paragraph 1, that does not conform with the obligations under this Agreement other than Article 12, that Contracting Party shall endeavor to, as soon as possible, notify the measure to the other Contracting Party.[104]

The Article 15(3) notification provision *only* applies to the regulatory sovereignty premised on the GATT's Article XX exceptions and not to the security exceptions expression of the public purpose doctrine. Both the general exceptions and security exceptions, however, appear to be self-judging. The fundamental inference to be drawn from the plain language of Article 15 forecloses consideration of premeasure notice or consultation.

Although the unique character of noneconomic security interests conceptually and practically lends considerable support to an expansive content that is self-judging and wanting in proportionality of application, it remains critical to note that the fundamental principle underlying normative claims to unilateral and nonproportional regulatory sovereignty is based on a public purpose, albeit one that theoretically may entail the preservation of actual sovereignty.

Exceptions for transfers comprise the sixth category of public purpose exceptions contained in the Sample BITs.[105] The exceptions for transfers

[100] However, such issues have still drawn substantial attention from both domestic and multinational legislative bodies. *See generally* James K. Jackson, *Foreign Investment and National Security: Economic Considerations*, Congressional Research Service Report for Congress, April 4, 2013, *available at* http://fas.org/sgp/crs/natsec/RL34561.pdf (last visited July 8, 2013).

[101] *See, e.g.*, USA-Rwanda BIT, *supra* note 46, art. 18 ¶ 1 ("Nothing in this Treaty shall be construed ... to preclude a Party from applying measures that *it considers necessary* for ... protection of its own essential security interests"; emphasis added).

[102] Compare Colombia-Japan BIT, *supra* Chapter 2 note 193, art. 15 ¶ 1 with GATT, *supra* Chapter 1 note 1, art. XX.

[103] Compare Colombia-Japan BIT, *supra* Chapter 2 note 193, art. 15 ¶ 2 with GATT, *supra* Chapter 1 note 1, art. XXI.

[104] Colombia-Japan BIT, *supra* Chapter 2 note 193, art. 15 ¶ 3.

[105] *See, e.g.*, Canada-Armenia BIT, *supra* note 13, art. IX TT 3, 5; Canada-Barbados BIT, *supra* note 46, art. IX ¶¶ 3, 5; Agreement between the Government of the People's Republic of China

consist of two categories: (i) restrictions on transfers permitted for specific application of national laws[106] and (ii) exceptions for balance-of-payment difficulties.[107] These two categories of exceptions for transfers in turn have their own quite discernible variations.

Restrictions on transfers based on specific application of national laws is subject-matter-based and subject to (i) equitable, (ii) nondiscriminatory, and (iii) good faith application of law.[108] Restrictions on transfers permitted for specific application of national laws do not reflect any mandatory principle

and the Government of the State of Kuwait for the Promotion and Protection of Investments art. 6 ¶ 4, Chi.-Kuw., November 23, 1985, http://investmentpolicyhub.unctad.org/Download/TreatyFile/752 [hereinafter China-Kuwait BIT]; Colombia-India BIT, *supra* note 16, art. 5 ¶¶ 3–4; Agreement between the Government of the Republic of France and the Government of the United Mexican States on the Reciprocal Promotion and Protection of Investments art. 7, Fra.-Mex., November 12, 1998, http://investmentpolicyhub.unctad.org/Download/TreatyFile/1253 [hereinafter France-Mexico BIT]; Agreement between Japan and the Democratic Socialist Republic of Sri Lanka Concerning the Promotion and Protection of Investment art. 8 ¶ 2, Jap.-Sri., March 1, 1982, http://investmentpolicyhub.unctad.org/Download/TreatyFile/1735 [hereinafter Japan-Sri Lanka BIT].

106 *See, e.g.*, Agreement between the Government of Canada and the Government of Ukraine for the Promotion and Protection of Investments art. IX ("Transfer of Funds"), Can.-Ukr., October 24, 1994, http://investmentpolicyhub.unctad.org/Download/TreatyFile/640 [hereinafter Canada-Ukraine BIT].

107 *See, e.g.*, Agreement between the Kingdom of Spain and the Republic of Venezuela for the Promotion and Protection of Investments art. VII ¶ 4, Spa.-Ven., November 2, 1995, http://investmentpolicyhub.unctad.org/Download/TreatyFile/2289 [hereinafter Spain-Venezuela BIT].

108 The Canada-Armenia BIT, for example, provides:

> Notwithstanding paragraphs 1 and 2, a Contracting Party may prevent a transfer through the *equitable, non-discriminatory* and *good faith* application of its laws relating to:
> (a) bankruptcy, insolvency or the protection of rights of predators;
> (b) issuing, trading or dealing in securities;
> (c) criminal or penal offenses;
> (d) reports of transfers of currency or other monetary instruments;
> (e) ensuring the satisfaction of judgments in adjudicatory proceedings.

Canada-Armenia BIT, *supra* note 13, art. IX ¶¶ 3(emphasis added). A broader scope for restrictions on transfers based on the safety, soundness, integrity, or financial responsibility of financial institutions – yet, also subject to equitable, nondiscriminatory, and good faith application of measures – is further identified in Article XI(2) of the Canada-Armenia BIT, notwithstanding the provisions of Article IX(3). Article XI(2) of the Canada-Armenia BIT reads:

> Notwithstanding paragraphs (1), (2) and (4) of Article IX, and without limiting the applicability of paragraph (3) of Article IX, a Contracting Party may prevent or limit transfers by a financial institution to, or for the benefit of, an affiliate of or person related to such institution or provider, through the *equitable, non-discriminatory* and *good faith* application of measures relating to maintenance of the *safety, soundness, integrity* or *financial responsibility* of financial institutions.

Id. art. XI ¶ 2 (emphasis added).

qualifying such restrictions for a specific time frame; in fact, the exercise of regulatory sovereignty pursuant to issuance of a measure restricting transfers that comports with national law is not required to lift or modify the transfers restrictions at the earliest possible time. Likewise, such restrictions do not require "serious" or "exceptional" need.

Restrictions on transfers may issue in the form of regulatory sovereignty when a contracting party experiences "serious balance of payment difficulties, or the threat thereof."[109] In addition to the "seriousness" requirement imposed by the Canada-Slovakia BIT variant, such measures must comport with six material qualifications. The measure(s) (i) must be equitable, (ii) cannot be arbitrary, (iii) cannot be "unjustifiably discriminatory," (iv) must meet a "good faith" requirement, (v) must be of limited duration, and (vi) must be a specially tailored remedy for the particular balance of payments problem at issue.[110]

The exception for balance-of-payment difficulties clause contained in the Colombia-India BIT at Article 5(4) is indicative of a more streamlined approach premised on the hierarchy of placing macroeconomic management concerns over and above the microeconomic issues endemic to particular cases of foreign investment protection. This clause provides:

> Notwithstanding the provisions of paragraphs 1 and 2 of this Article, the Contracting Parties may temporarily restrict the transfers in the event of a serious balance-of-payments or threat thereof; or in cases where, in exceptional circumstances, movements of capital cause or threaten to cause serious difficulties for macroeconomic management, in particular, monetary and exchange rate policies, provided such restrictions are compatible or are issued in conformity with the agreements of the IMF or are applied upon request of the latter and are equitable, non-discriminatory and in good faith.[111]

This iteration of the clause, in addition to introducing macroeconomic necessity as a justifiable public purpose, also preserves the requirements that measures be equitable, nondiscriminatory, in good faith, and in response to serious balance-of-payments difficulties contained in the Canada-Slovakia BIT.[112]

[109] *See, e.g.*, Agreement between Canada and the Slovak Republic for the Promotion and Protection of Investment art. IX ¶ 3(a), Can.-Slo., July 20, 2010, http://investmentpolicyhub.unctad.org/Download/TreatyFile/634 [hereinafter Canada-Slovakia BIT].

[110] *Id.* art. IX ¶ 3*(b)*.

[111] Colombia-India BIT, *supra* note 16, art. 5 ¶ 4.

[112] It is important to note that, although the Canada-Slovakia BIT does not reference "conformity with the agreements of the IMF" as does the Colombia-India BIT, it does explicitly allude to "accordance" with "the WTO Agreement and the *Articles of Agreement of the International Monetary Fund.*" Compare Colombia-India BIT, *supra* note 16, art. 5 ¶ 4, with Canada-Slovakia BIT, *supra* note 109, art. IX¶ 3(b) (emphasis added).

The temporal qualifications such as "limited duration" and "a time schedule for [the] removal" of the measures restricting funding identified in the Canada-Slovakia BIT are altogether omitted from the Colombia-India BIT, including the stricture commanding that the measure be narrowly tailored to the problem that it seeks to address.[113]

The least qualified and, therefore, broadest expression of the exceptions for transfers iteration of the public purpose doctrine is exemplified by the Japan-Pakistan BIT. In that instrument, the single limiting qualification to the doctrine is the adjective "exceptional" modifying "financial or economic circumstances."[114]

The Colombia-Japan BIT covers exceptions for transfers under the banner of "temporary safeguard measures." It addresses exceptions for transfers akin to the clause used in the Japan-Pakistan BIT, but, unlike that treaty, the Colombia-Japan BIT does not mention the International Monetary Fund (IMF); instead, it limits its qualification to "serious difficulties for macroeconomic management."[115]

Notwithstanding carefully crafted variations of exceptions for transfers evinced in the Sample BITs under (i) restrictions on transfers permitted for specific application of national laws and (ii) exceptions for balance-of-payment difficulties, this public purpose-based exception intermingles macroeconomic standards pertaining to the WTO Agreement and the Articles of the IMF with protection standards that are best framed in a microeconomic

[113] Canada-Slovakia BIT, *supra* note 109, art. IX ¶ 3(b).

[114] The Japan-Pakistan BIT provides, in relevant part:

> Notwithstanding the provisions of paragraph 1 of the present Article, either Contracting Party may, in exceptional financial or economic circumstances, impose such exchange restrictions in accordance with its laws and regulations and in conformity with the Articles of Agreement of the International Monetary Fund so long as each Contracting Party is a party to the said Articles of Agreement.

Agreement between Japan and the Islamic Republic of Pakistan Concerning the Promotion and Protection of Investment art. 8 ¶ 2, Jap.-Pak., March 10, 1998, http://investmentpolicyhub.unctad.org/Download/TreatyFile/1731 [hereinafter Japan-Pakistan BIT].

[115] The Colombia-Japan BIT provides:

> 1. A Contracting Party may adopt or maintain measures not conforming with its obligations under paragraph 1 of Article 2 relating to cross-border capital transactions and Article 14:
>   (a) in the event of serious balance-of payments and external financial difficulties or threat thereof; or
>   (b) in cases where, in exceptional circumstances, movements of capital cause or threaten to cause serious difficulties for macroeconomic management, in particular, monetary and exchange rate policies.

Colombia-Japan BIT, *supra* Chapter 2 note 193, art. 16 ¶ *1(a)–(b)*.

context. The exceptions also are self-judging and rife with elements that ostensibly appear to be particular but, in fact, are less than uniform and are not actually defined within the ambit of public international law, such as "good faith."

An orthodox approach would suggest that macroeconomic standards are universal and, therefore, less susceptible to arbitrariness or manipulation. In this same vein, macroeconomic exigencies may be said to embrace objective criteria such that "exceptional financial or economic circumstances" that affect an entire nation itself points to a problem the solution of which inherently entails an expansive expression of public purpose that can be gauged. Absent from the exceptions is any reference to proportionality or causation beyond "movements of capital [that may] cause or threaten to cause serious difficulties for macroeconomic management,"[116] such as "actual cause" or "direct and proximate cause." Instead, vague terms such as "serious difficulties" that point to subjective self-judging criteria pervade the exceptions for transfers.

Prudential financial measures constitute the seventh expression of the public purpose doctrine contained as an exception in the Sample BITs.[117] Two variations of the prudential financial measures exceptions clause are discernible from the Sample BITs. The broadest exemplar is represented by a brief single-sentence clause that vests Host States with virtually unbridled regulatory sovereignty as to this subject matter. Accordingly, the scope of the clause is inversely proportional to its length. The Belgium-Colombia BIT contains such a clause, which provides:

> Nothing contained in this Agreement shall apply to measures adopted by any Contracting Party, in accordance with its law, with respect to the financial sector for prudential reasons, including those measures aimed at protecting investors, depositors, insurance takers or trustees, or to safeguard the integrity and stability of the financial system.[118]

Notably, the only limitation placed on a Host State exercising regulatory sovereignty pursuant to this provision is the qualifying language "in accordance with its law, with respect to the financial sector for prudential reasons."[119] In fact, even the objectives of the measures taken are not limited to protecting specific classes of individuals but extend more broadly to protecting the

[116] Colombia-India BIT, *supra* note 16, art. 5 ¶ 4.
[117] *See, e.g.*, Belgium-Colombia BIT, *supra* note 15, art. 2 ¶ 5; Canada-Costa Rica BIT, *supra* note 46, annex I.III ¶ 3; Japan-Vietnam BIT, *supra* note 73, art. 17.
[118] Belgium-Colombia BIT, *supra* note 15, art. 2 ¶ 5.
[119] *Id.*

financial system itself, as evinced by the word "including." The clause's ample scope, lacking reference to any "objective" standard, bespeaks an anatomy favoring a self-judging rubric that enhances Host-State regulatory sovereignty.

The Canada-Armenia BIT exemplifies the second variation of prudential financial measures exceptions contained in BIT clauses. This type of clause reads:

> Nothing in this Agreement shall be construed to prevent a Contracting Party from adopting or maintaining *reasonable measures* for prudential reasons, such as: the protection of investors, depositors, financial market participants, policy-holders, policy-claimants, or persons to whom a fiduciary duty is owed by financial institutions; the maintenance of the safety, soundness, integrity or financial responsibility of financial institutions; and ensuring the integrity and stability of a Contracting Party's financial system.[120]

The reference to "reasonable measures"[121] represents a compelling call for objective analysis. Moreover, the term "such as," in contrast with "including those measures" (this latter qualification contained in the Belgium-Colombia BIT) seeks to identify qualifying paradigms rather than general subject matter inclusion.

The Colombia-Japan BIT, paradigmatic of new-generation BITs, contains a hybrid of the two most notable variations of the prudential measures public purpose exception but limits the exception's application by subordinating it to the BIT's "obligations":

> Notwithstanding any other provisions of this Agreement, a Contracting Party shall not be prevented from taking measures relating to financial services sector for prudential reasons, including measures for the protection of investors, depositors, policy holders or persons to whom a fiduciary duty is owed by an enterprise supplying financial services, or measures to ensure the integrity and stability of its financial system.
>
> In cases where a Contracting Party takes any measure, pursuant to paragraph 1, that does not conform with the obligations under this Agreement, that Contracting Party shall not use such measure as a means of avoiding its obligations under this Agreement.[122]

The first paragraph of this clause limits measures for the protection of third parties by referencing "persons to whom a *fiduciary duty* is owed."[123]

[120] Canada-Armenia BIT, *supra* note 13, art. XI ¶ 1 (emphasis added).
[121] *Id.*
[122] Colombia-Japan BIT, *supra* Chapter 2 note 193, art. 17 (emphasis added).
[123] *Id.* (emphasis added).

The second paragraph of the clause speaks of not conforming with the "obligations under this Agreement."[124] Subordinating this ambit of regulatory sovereignty to the BIT's imperatives certainly illustrates the virtues of using treaty-drafting techniques to rein in what otherwise would be an unbridled license for the exercise of regulatory sovereignty with respect to a particular exception. Furthermore, the use of the word "conform" materially weakens application of the exception because of the term's expansive and general character. Alternative limiting language – standard qualifying clauses such as "not in compliance with the laws of the Contracting Party enforcing the measure" or "in conflict with the obligations under this Agreement" – provides Host States seeking to circumvent investor protection obligations with greater flexibility in construing limits to the exception.

Unlike other iterations of the public purpose doctrine, prudential measures and their appropriate application are inextricably related to the State necessity doctrine in ways that can be analyzed based on "objective" economic analysis. By way of example, the need to undertake specific macroeconomic measures to stabilize currency in a macroeconomic crisis or to render investors or depositors whole in the wake of an institutional financial collapse present tangible scenarios that command exercise of prudential measures that may adversely affect orthodox Host-State obligations in favor of foreign investors. The "jurisprudence" arising from investor-state arbitrations concerning application of this defense and/or prudential measures, provides the universe of investors in capital-exporting countries with considerable expectation guidelines in this field.[125]

C. COMPREHENSIVE CONCLUSIONS

Empirical analysis is affirmatively conclusive as to the presence, scope, and content of the public purpose doctrine in BITs. The fragmented configuration of BITs generally, together with particulars that are unique to private

[124] *Id.*

[125] *See generally* EDF International S.A v. Argentine Republic, ICSID Case No. ARB/03/23, Award (June 11, 2012) *available at* http://www.italaw.com/sites/default/files/case-documents/ita1069.pdf; Sempra Energy International v. Argentine Republic, ICSID Case No. ARB/02/16, Decision on the Argentine Republic's Application for Annulment of the Award (June 29, 2010), *available at* http://www.italaw.com/sites/default/files/case-documents/ita0776.pdf; Continental Casualty Company v. Argentine Republic, ICSID Case No. ARB/03/9, Award (September 5, 2008), *available at* http://www.italaw.com/sites/default/files/case-documents/ita0228.pdf.

and generally nontransparent negotiations between States, considerably cloud content and, therefore, any aspiration for substantive uniformity with respect to content. Although analysis of the 319 BITs comprising the "Sample BITs" certainly establishes that multiple iterations of the public purpose doctrine comprise customary international law, there is little evidence on how the public purpose exception is to be applied, let alone of any objective or uniform standard governing application of the doctrine's multiple iterations.

Based on analysis of the Sample BITs, the doctrine remains self-judging in application by Host States. Additionally, with few exceptions, the public purpose doctrine as embodied in the Sample BITs generally remains expansive and, therefore, favoring Host States over Home States. This asymmetry contributes to uncertainty and is eroding investor expectations with respect to process legitimacy. Put simply, the fragmented structure of the approximately 3,000 BITs constituting this decentralized network of treaties fosters asymmetrical treatment and not bilateralism in the relationship between investor and Host State. This problem is further exacerbated with respect to expressions of the public purpose doctrine such as "sustainable development," which themselves are the byproduct of multiple interpretations depending on the historically contingent development of the doctrine in different regions of the globe.[126]

The discernible appearance of the public purpose doctrine in a rather limited set of subject matter categories and an equally restricted number of variations of clauses does render an aspiration for uniformity as to scope, content, and application realistic. Also, the patent lack of symmetry, made worse by the wholesale[127] importation of macroeconomic principles from Article XX of the GATT, contributes to expanding disproportionately the fear of Host-State regulatory sovereignty. Second-generation BITs, such as the emblematic Colombia-Japan BIT, demonstrate a meaningful paradigm shift that favors developing nations and economies in transition. These newer

[126] In the case of sustainable development in particular, we have seen how the treatment of the doctrine differs because of the manner in which decolonization occurred in different regions of the world. No single definition of the principle is anywhere articulated or adopted. In the context of BITs, sustainable development is mentioned but never defined. *See* discussion *supra* Chapter 2, Subsection E.

[127] The term "wholesale importation" has been used because of the lack of empirical evidence suggesting otherwise. A nonconceptual approach to the introduction of these trade law principles into investment law is evinced by the lack of congruity internally among the principles introduced and externally in relation to the investment law context surrounding them.

BITs suggest that in an environment of economic globalization, traditionally weaker capital-importing States now have greater negotiating leverage in crafting BITs. The byproduct of this development, however, has contributed to causing the proverbial pendulum to swing in an extreme direction, fueling regulatory sovereignty.[128]

[128] The new-generation BITs do not altogether disavow the interests of Home States. A number of the BITs that Canada has executed, for example, contain clarification of indirect expropriation clauses that further Home State interests. The Canada-China BIT is illustrative:

The Contracting Parties confirm their shared understanding that:

1. Indirect expropriation results from a measure or series of measures of a Contracting Party that has an effect equivalent to direct expropriation without formal transfer of title or outright seizure.
2. The determination of whether a measure or series of measures of a Contracting Party constitutes an indirect expropriation requires a case-by-case, fact-based inquiry that considers, among other factors:
   a) the economic impact of the measure or series of measures, although the sole fact that a measure or series of measures of a Contracting Party has an adverse effect on the economic value of an investment does not establish that an indirect expropriation has occurred;
   b) the extent to which the measure or series of measures interferes with distinct, reasonable, investment-backed expectations; and
   c) the character of the measure or series of measures.
3. Except in rare circumstances, such as if a measure or series of measures is so severe in light of its purpose that it cannot be reasonably viewed as having been adopted and applied in good faith, a non-discriminatory measure or series of measures of a Contracting Party that is designed and applied to protect the legitimate public objectives for the well-being of citizens, such as health, safety and the environment, does not constitute indirect expropriation.

Canada-China BIT, *supra* Chapter 2 note 193, annex. B.10 ("Expropriation"). Many such clauses also contain the inclusion of government intent as a factor to be considered. *See, e.g.*, Canada-Slovakia BIT, *supra* note 109, annex A ¶ (b)(iii) ("... the character of the measure or series of measures, including their purpose and rationale ..."); Colombia-India BIT, *supra* note 16, art. 6 ¶ 2(iv) ("... the character and intent of the measures or series of measures, whether they are for bona fide public interest purposes or not and whether there is a reasonable nexus between them and the intention to expropriate").

5

Permanent Sovereignty over Natural Resources

Perhaps the most emblematic expression of the public purpose doctrine that manifests a commitment to bolstering regulatory sovereignty is found in the doctrine of permanent sovereignty over natural resources (PSNR). Much like fundamental principles of sustainable development and self-determination, the principle of PSNR has its genesis in the historical process of decolonization.[1] The historical phenomenon of decolonization witnessed a stark shift in domestic and international economic policy that prioritized the development and "repatriation" of natural and economic resources pertaining to former colonies.[2] Along the same vein as the *sustainable development* expression of the public purpose doctrine, the principle of PSNR is premised on the proposition that colonization gave rise to policies that disadvantaged colonial States in favor of the colonizing sovereignties.[3] PSNR, much like sustainable development,[4] varies both doctrinally and conceptually depending on its regional historic origins and development.

[1] Lillian Aponte Miranda, *The Role of International Law in IntraState Natural Resource Allocation: Sovereignty, Human Rights, and Peoples-Based Development*, 45 VANDERBILT J. TRANSNAT'L L. 785, 789 (2010) ("In the last century alone, international law has played a significant role in global debates regarding ownership, use, control, and development of land and natural resources. More specifically, in the period of colonial dissolution, the international doctrine of permanent sovereignty over natural resources was developed and applied to interstate disputes between colonizing states and newly independent colonies").

[2] *See Id.* at 789–90.

[3] *Id.* at 790 (noting that the "doctrine emerged with the aim of protecting newly independent states from economic recolonization resulting from the appropriation of their natural resource base by foreign actors").

[4] As noted, although there exists a general understanding of sustainable development with essential elements that are shared by the community of nations, the doctrine's expression, in considerable measure, is related to its historicity. Thus, for example, the doctrine's expression in the European Convention on Human Rights is materially different from the scope and subject matter of the doctrine as expressed in the Inter-American Convention on Human Rights. Moreover, the iteration of the doctrine in both of these conventions is materially

By way of example, Schrijver observes this phenomenon, but expresses it in terms of the doctrinal ambiguity present when identifying a homogeneous treaty-based objective:

> Treaties which implicitly or explicitly formulate the right of permanent sovereignty hardly ever spell out its objectives. The Human Rights Covenants of 1966 provide that: "Peoples may *for their own ends* dispose of their natural wealth and resources and that they should *enjoy and utilize* these fully and freely." The African Charter on Human and Peoples' Rights' of 1981 is slightly less general: "This right shall be exercised in the exclusive interest of the people." It is further provided that states shall exercise this right "with a view to strengthening African unity and solidarity."[5]

A review of international instruments distinctly identifies PSNR as a principle of customary and conventional international law.[6] Its content and scope, however, remain less clear. Both appear to be grounded on two propositions: (i) a construction of history that finds it necessary to redress resource and economic inequities arising from the colonizer/colony relationship and (ii) a narrow and "self-evident" approach to public purpose that provides a normative foundation for the self-determination of natural resources by States with little qualification regarding broader obligations attendant to the right of PSNR that a State may have with respect to the community of nations.[7]

distinct from the doctrine as found in the African Charter on Human and Peoples' Rights. *See* discussion *supra* Chapter 3.

5 Nico Schrijver, Sovereignty over Natural Resources: Balancing Rights and Duties 21 (Cambridge University Press 2008).

6 *See, e.g.*, Integrated Economic Development and Commercial Agreements, G.A. Res. 523, U.N. GAOR, 6th Sess., Supp. No. 20, at 20, U.N. Doc. A/2119 (1952) [hereinafter G.A. Res. 523]; Right to Exploit Freely Natural Wealth and Resources, G.A. Res. 626, U.N. GAOR, 7th Sess., Supp. No. 20, at 18, U.N. Doc. A/2361 (1952) [hereinafter G.A. Res. 626]; Permanent Sovereignty Over Natural Resources, G.A. Res. 1803, U.N. GAOR, 17th Sess., Supp. No. 17, at 15, U.N. Doc. A/5217 (1962) [hereinafter G.A. Res. 1803]; Permanent Sovereignty over Natural Resources, G.A. Res. 2158, UN GAOR, 21st Sess., Supp. No. 16, at 29, U.N. Doc. A/6518 (1966) [hereinafter G.A. Res. 2158]; Permanent Sovereignty over Natural Resources of Developing Countries, G.A. Res. 3016, U.N. GAOR, 27th Sess., Supp. No. 30, at 48, U.N. Doc. A/8963 (1972) [hereinafter G.A. Res. 3016]; Permanent Sovereignty over Natural Resources, G.A. Res. 3171, U.N. GAOR, 28th Sess., Supp. No. 30, at 52, U.N. Doc. A/9030 (1973) [hereinafter G.A. Res. 3171].

7 Schrijver compellingly argues that:

> The challenge of the next two or three decades will be how to balance permanent sovereignty over natural resources with other basic principles and emerging norms of international law – including the duty to observe international agreements, grant fair treatment to foreign investors, pursue sustainable development at national and international levels and to respect human and peoples' rights – and in this way to serve best the interests of present and future generations.

Schrijver, *supra* note 5, at 380.

Both of these premises command review of the foundation of international instruments giving rise to PSNR.

A. PSNR: THE STRUCTURAL FOUNDATIONS OF A DOCTRINE

1. *General Assembly Resolutions 523 and 626*

The pre-economic globalization United Nations resolutions giving rise to the principle of PSNR contain the seeds for what eventually would become conflicting paradigms of sovereignty. This fundamental dissonance – between traditional Westphalian conceptions of sovereignty[8] and a contemporary understanding viewed through the lens of transnational interdependence and shared global responsibilities[9] – can be gleaned by the not-too-delicate balance that the foundational resolutions sought to accomplish in harmonizing the interests between developed (Home States) and developing nations (Host States). The remedial nature of these resolutions emphasize a policy favoring developing States that would vest Host States with virtually unchecked regulatory sovereignty in the interest of an overtly nationalistic public purpose.

General Assembly Resolution 523, entitled "Integrated Economic Development and Commercial Agreements," for the first time asserts that as a matter of "right" – in conjunction with principles of self-determination – "under-developed countries" are empowered to use their "natural resources" in the interests of economic national development.[10] This foundational resolution on the principle of PSNR does not define any of its essential terms, but in fact affirmatively advances a stark contrast between developed and developing States and, in so doing, articulates the resolution's remedial nature.

The resolution not too indirectly suggests that the use and stockpiling of raw materials on the part of developed States has caused or increased "the

[8] *See supra* Chapter 1 note 34 and accompanying text.

[9] *See* discussion *supra* Chapter 4, Section B.

[10] General Assembly Resolution 523, provides in pertinent part:

> *The General Assembly,*
>
> *Considering* that the under-developed countries have the right to determine freely the use of their natural resources in that they must utilize such resources in order to be in a better position to further the realization of their plans of economic development in accordance with their national interests, and to further the expansion of the world economy[.]

G.A. Res. 523, *supra* note 6.

economic difficulties in many of the under-developed countries."[11] Even though the resolution does not address a remedial purpose incident to historical advantages that industrialized countries secured from developing States, it does express a causal relationship in the present originating in industrialized countries and having an effect on developing States. By so doing, the resolution expressed its conceptual commitment primarily to (i) orthodox Westphalian notions of sovereignty and (ii) the development of developing countries.

The principles of (i) self-determination, (ii) sustainable development, and (iii) PSNR (the last two understandably in very embryonic form) are explicitly referred to in the resolution interdependently, each providing analytical support for the other. The resolution in relevant part reads:

> *Bearing in mind* that one way of obtaining the means necessary for carrying out economic development plans in developing countries is the creation of conditions under which these countries could more readily acquire machinery, equipment and industrial raw materials for the goods and services exported by them,
>
> 1. *Recommends* that members of the United Nations within the framework of their general economic policy, should:
>   (a). Continue to make every possible effort to carry out the recommendations contained in paragraphs, 1, 2, 3, and 4 of Economic and Social Council Resolution 341 (XII), Section A of 20 March, 1951;
>   (b). Consider the possibility of facilitating through commercial agreements:
>
> . . .
>
> (ii). The development of natural resources which can be utilized for the domestic needs of the developing countries and also for the needs of international trade,

[11] General Assembly Resolution 523 does not explicitly identify developed or industrialized States as culprits in relation to the economic challenges that developing States face. The text of this section of the resolution, however, leaves little doubt that only by imputing these economic challenges to developed countries can the provision be reasonably construed. The pertinent language reads:

> *Considering*, that the existing sharp increase in the demand for raw materials, including the demand for stock-piling has resulted in an increase in the prices of a number of raw materials and in fluctuations in the price of others; has in many cases been accompanied by increased prices and reduced availability of important items of machinery, equipment, consumer goods and industrial raw materials necessary for the development of developing countries; *has created inflationary pressures and brought about the regulation of prices at different relative levels for different products and has thereby caused or increased the economic difficulties in many of the under-developed countries[.]*

Id.

> provided that such commercial agreements shall not contain economic or political conditions violating the sovereign rights of the under-developed countries, including the right to determine their own plans for economic development.[12]

The emphasis placed on national economic development pursuant to an ostensibly unbridled right on the part of developing countries[13] is inimical to post-economic globalization paradigms based on interdependence and broad exceptions to the exercise of regulatory sovereignty largely based on the more global concerns of the community of nations.

Resolution 523 is not altogether silent on the right of developing countries "to determine freely the use of their natural resources."[14] In three notable passages, Resolution 523 indeed references underlying policies that concern the community of nations and not just what would be in the national interest of particular States. The very first paragraph alludes to the connection between the right to determine freely the use of their natural resources by developing countries and the equally important task of seeking "to further the expansion of the world economy."[15] Second, the resolution recognizes the necessity of "[c]ontinu[ing] to make every possible effort to carry out the recommendations contained in Paragraphs 1, 2, 3 and 4 of Economic and Social Council resolution 341 (XII), Section A, of 20 March 1951."[16] But for a single reference

[12] *Id.* (emphasis added).

[13] The Resolution is silent as to *all* countries or industrialized countries having this unfettered "right to determine freely the use of their natural resources." *Id.* Analytically, within the framework of the resolution, the right logically would extend to all States because it is premised on the universal principle of self-determination. Because the resolution only mentions developing countries, the exclusion of industrialized and even of developing States is best construed as a point of emphasis and purpose only.

[14] *Id.* at ¶ 1.

[15] *Id.* It is noteworthy that the objective of expanding the world economy is treated *in pari materia* with the economic development of the national interests of developing States.

[16] As noted in Resolution 523, Paragraphs 1, 2, 3 and 4 of Economic and Social Council Resolution 341 (XII), Section A, set forth:

> 1. *Recommends* that all Members of the United Nations during the period of general shortage of goods, take special measures to bring about adequate production and equitable international distribution of capital goods, essential consumers' goods and raw materials especially needed for the maintenance of international peace and security, the preservation of standards of living and the furthering of economic development;
> 2. *Recommends* that all members of the United Nations during the period of general inflationary pressure, take measures, direct or indirect, to regulate at equitable levels and relationships, the prices of essential goods moving in international trade, including capital goods, essential consumers' goods and raw materials;
> 3. *Recommends* that the equitable regulation of distribution prices referred to in recommendations 1 and 2 above be maintained as long as strong inflationary pressures

to the purchasing power of the "poorer sections of the population,"[17] the resolution mostly aims to address macroeconomic measures at an international level that purport to benefit all members of the international community. Accordingly, the measures do not seek to redress past wrongs or to correct specific problems only confronting developed States as a result of economic and political measures that may be ascribed to developed or industrialized countries. Finally, Resolution 523 speaks to "the needs of international trade." Properly contextualized, this provision of the resolution concerns the use of commercial agreements to assist developing nations in developing their natural resources in order to meet their domestic needs. This proposition is then extended with a conjunctive to include "the needs of international trade."[18]

Notwithstanding these three surface references to issues that touch and concern all members of the international community, Resolution 523 is fundamentally a resolution premised on specific needs for particular nations; such needs in turn are unique to each nation and the set of developing countries. Those very particular needs – the economic wants of specific countries that are developing – are territorially based. Moreover, the resolution's emphasis on the freedom accorded to each country to utilize its natural resources freely suggests a subjective (self-judging) standard based on each country's understanding of the manner and the resource to be developed, as well as the domestic economic wants to be addressed. This subjective self-judging criteria comports with the precept of self-determination that pervades the resolution and the principle of PSNR. It also embodies an analytical methodology that constitutes the orthodox application, scope, and substantive content of the public purpose doctrine. The reliance on a subjective standard, together with the use of critical terms such as "natural resources," "rights," "developing countries," and "national interests," bereft of any proportionality, cannot help but bring to mind the self-judging, content-free, nonproportional, and territorially based public purpose doctrine. The resolution's reliance on

> persist, in order to minimize changes in the purchasing power, in terms of imports, of current earnings from exports as well as of monetary assets;
>
> 4. *Recommends* further that all Members of the United Nations take all steps in their power to prevent the development of inflationary pressures, thereby preventing speculative profits and maintaining the purchasing power of the poorer sections of the population.

Id. at n.l.

[17] *See Id.*

[18] Subsection 1(b)(ii) provides:

> The development of natural resources which can be utilized for the domestic needs of the developing countries and *also for the needs of international trade.*

Id. (emphasis added).

conventional sovereignty and its pre-dating of economic globalization by half a century, in itself, helps explain the normative foundations of the orthodox public purpose doctrine more generally and also identifies the very seeds of change that were embedded in the principle of PSNR since its very inception in this embryonic pronouncement.

Issued on December 21, 1952, scarcely twelve months after Resolution 523, General Assembly Resolution 626 entitled "Right to Exploit Freely Natural Wealth and Resources" further bolstered the legitimacy of PSNR. Consonant with Resolution 523, Resolution 626 emphasizes the existence of a right of States to use and exploit freely their natural resources.[19] Unlike its predecessor, however, Resolution 626 stresses that, in addition to aiding developing nations with their "progress" and "economic development," the right to exploit freely natural wealth and resources is conducive to "universal peace."[20] Second, Resolution 626 also distinguishes itself from Resolution 523 by proscribing "direct or indirect" acts aimed at interfering with "the sovereignty of any State over its natural resources."[21] Read together, General Assembly Resolutions 523 and 626 assert four continuing goals, ostensibly under the banner of furthering the interests of the international community: (i) fueling the expansion of the world economy,[22] (ii) regulating international production and equitable

[19] As noted in the third paragraph of Resolution 626:

> *Remembering* that the right of peoples freely to use and exploit their natural wealth and resources is inherent in their sovereignty and is in accordance with the Purposes and Principles of the Charter of the United Nations.

G.A. Res. 626, *supra* note 6, at ¶ 3.

[20] Two provisions in Resolution 626 bridge the right to exploit freely natural resources to peace. The first is found in the second paragraph of the resolution:

> *Bearing in mind* the need for encouraging the developing countries in the proper use and exploitation of their natural wealth and resources,
>
> *Considering* that the economic development of the under-developed countries is one of the fundamental requisites for the strengthening of universal peace.

Id. (underlined emphasis added). Less explicitly, Paragraph 1 of the resolution also draws attention to the relationship between the right to exploit freely natural resources and peace in the form of "security, mutual confidence and economic cooperation among nations." That paragraph reads:

> *Recommends* all Member States, and the exercise of their right freely to use and exploit their natural wealth and resources wherever deemed desirable by them for their own progress and economic development, to have due regard, consistently with their sovereignty, to the need for maintaining the flow of capital in conditions of security, mutual confidence and economic cooperation among nations.

Id. (underlined emphasis added).

[21] *Id.* at ¶ 2.

[22] G.A. Res. 523, *supra* note 6, at ¶ 1.

distribution of capital goods needed for the maintenance of peace and security,[23] (iii) curtailing international inflation,[24] and (iv) meeting the needs of international trade.[25]

Within the rubric of Resolutions 523 and 626, these four global objectives are best pursued by ensuring that States freely utilize their natural resources in order to meet particular economic needs. The regulations' argument for a State's right to develop its own natural resources freely is premised on the right of self-determination and perceived national interest. Therefore, both resolutions establish a direct relationship between enhanced regulatory sovereignty premised on a territorial conception of sovereignty and the desire to increase international trade, expand the global economy, and maintain world peace. The term "national interests" within the context of these two foundational PSNR General Assembly resolutions represents the public purpose normative foundation of the PSNR principle. Pursuant to this conceptual construction of public purpose, regulatory sovereignty in furtherance of the ostensible public purpose of freely utilizing natural resources would trump suspending the "free exercise of this right" based on overriding transnational concerns. To the contrary, the workings of the resolutions dictate that the unassailable and uncompromising principles of self-determination and national interests underlying "the right to determine freely the use of natural resources" by individual States are not at all juxtaposed to the global concerns of international trade, expansion of the global economy, or peace. According to the doctrinal configuration of the resolutions, absolute regulatory sovereignty in furtherance of the "free" use of natural resources serves as a requisite predicate to shared international economic concerns and development.

The conceptual and doctrinal origins of the PSNR expression of the public purpose doctrine rest on a paradigm of independence and an orthodox understanding of sovereignty that predates economic globalization. This pre-economic globalization Westphalian construct of sovereignty holds that public purpose based on precepts of self-determination and natural interests is both absolute and best understood pursuant to a State's own self-judging criteria. It disallows any conceptual space that would invite an exception to regulatory sovereignty arising from transnational needs, such as investment protection obligations running from a Host to Home States.[26]

[23] *Id.* at ¶ 1(a).

[24] *Id.*

[25] *Id.* at ¶ 1 (b)(ii).

[26] It is important to place these resolutions in their appropriate historical context. In 1951, the year in which G.A. Resolutions 341 (XII) and 523 (VI) were issued, international human rights law, by way of example, commanding that orthodox territorial sovereignty must be subordinated to transnational norms that seek the protection of persons irrespective of citizen status, also was in

B. THE DEVELOPMENT OF THE NOMENCLATURE "PERMANENT SOVEREIGNTY OVER NATURAL RESOURCES" AND THE CREATION OF A COMMISSION

Neither Resolution 523 nor Resolution 626 actually mention the term "permanent sovereignty over natural resources." Although both of these provisions do express a right to the development of natural resources that is based on the twin principles of self-determination and public purpose,[27] the concept of a permanent sovereignty over natural wealth is far from being fully developed, let alone reduced to its now familiar nomenclature of "*permanent sovereignty over natural resources*." The public purpose component of both resolutions, however, cannot at all be conceptually severed from pre-economic globalization notions of territorial sovereignty and regulatory paradigms based on economic models of independence. It would not be too much of a conceptual leap to conclude that the process of decolonization that spawned a need to issue United Nations resolutions – resolutions that identified a virtually unqualified right of States to develop their natural resources and wealth in furtherance of national interests and pursuant to the principle of self-determination – also materially influenced the development of a public purpose doctrine in public international law that is self-judging by the invoking State, does not provide for proportionality, and is treated as intuitively self-evident, much like the precept of self-determination.

The right to determine freely a State's use of its natural resources as set forth in Resolutions 523 and 626 first received its current nomenclature of PSNR in the two draft covenants on human rights that the United Nations Commission on Human Rights published during its tenth session (February 23–April 16, 1954).[28] It is in Part 1, Article 1 of the Draft International Covenants on Human Rights that the doctrine of permanent sovereignty over natural wealth and resources is first found. The historical context in which it surfaces, at the apogee of the Cold War when nationalistic fervor and decolonization also were at a pinnacle, is important. Also central to understanding the normative

an embryonic development phase. Thus, exceptions to regulatory sovereignty based on non-domestic or non-national issues found little precedent. In fact, the Universal Declaration of Human Rights, widely considered the first step in the international human rights movement, was not adopted until December 10, 1945. *See* UDHR, *supra* Chapter 3 note 16.

27 Resolution 523 expresses public purpose in terms of "national interests." G.A. Res. 523, *supra* note 6. Resolution 626 expresses the public purpose doctrine as "consistently with their sovereignty," in referring to the basis for the use and exploitation of natural resources. G.A. Res. 626, *supra* note 6.

28 *Official Records of the Economic and Social Council*, Eighteenth Session, Supplement No. 7 (E/2573), Annexes I–III (February 23–April 16, 1954) [hereinafter Draft International Covenant on Human Rights].

anatomy of this expression of public purpose, and more generally of the development of the orthodox conception of the public purpose doctrine as defined in this writing, is the textual context in which PSNR is mentioned.

PSNR appears early in the draft covenants, both in terms of nomenclature and as a right substantively, in Part 1, Article 1, Paragraph 3. The two-paragraph steps preceding it, however, are helpful to the understanding of PSNR's scope and content as originally conceived:

> All peoples and all nations shall have the right of self-determination, mainly, the right freely to determine their political economic, social and cultural status.
>
> All States, including those having responsibility for the administration of Non-Self-Governing and Trust Territories and those controlling in whatsoever manner the exercise of that right by another people, shall promote the realization of that right in all their territories and shall respect the maintenance of that right in other States, in conformity with provisions of the United Nations Charter.[29]

The principle of self-determination also is underscored as endemic to regulatory sovereignty in the context of economic development. Thus, the first historical mention of the principle of PSNR in an international instrument is preceded by two paragraphs that highlight the importance of the principle of self-determination and its connection to economic status or development. This context is suggestive of the proposition that the exercise of regulatory sovereignty in furtherance of political, economic, social, and cultural status is but an expression of self-determination that need only consider national interest or public purpose within an orthodox territorial framework. It is within this conceptual structure that PSNR is explicitly referenced as to nomenclature and hierarchy as an inalienable or absolute precept of public international law:

> 3. The right of peoples to self-determination shall also include *permanent sovereignty over their natural wealth and resources. In no case* may a people be deprived of its own means of subsistence on the grounds of any rights that may be claimed by other states.[30]

This first and historically significant reference to PSNR has two very distinct consequences that directly have influenced the character and application of the public purpose doctrine in international law. First, because PSNR is conceptualized and presented as drawing its normative foundation from the

[29] *Id.* at Part 1, art. 1 ¶¶ 1.

[30] *Id.* at ¶ 3 (emphasis added).

precept of "self-determination," the PSNR expression of the public purpose doctrine is accorded self-evident or *intuitive* status. Indeed, the very language of the draft international covenants on human rights states that PSNR actually forms part of and is subsumed by the precept of self-determination.[31]

Therefore, the customary treatment of public purpose as a self-evident principle concerning all things public, as understood through the prism of the State, was significantly bolstered by treating the PSNR expression of the doctrine as included in the principle of self-determination. The latter is held out to be a paradigmatic example of an intuitive and a self-evident principle that defies the need for conceptual understanding beyond intuition or doctrinal justification for its application as part of the exercise of regulatory sovereignty.

Second, the orthodox conceptualization and understanding of the public purpose doctrine is suggestive of a hierarchical status pursuant to which actions undertaken in furtherance of a purported public purpose preempt other legally binding obligations on the part of States. This normative standing certainly may be explained in part by the weight and standing historically accorded to "first principles" generally in philosophical discourses[32] and in public international law in particular.[33] More than this historical legacy, however, accounts for the primacy bestowed on public purpose and the public purpose expression of PSNR. The draft international covenants on human

[31] *Id.* (stating that "[t]he right of peoples to self-determination *shall also include* permanent sovereignty over their natural wealth and resources"; emphasis added).

[32] *See generally* Aristotle, Prior Analytics (Robin Smith, ed., Hackett Pub. Co. 1989); Thomas Aquinas, The Summa Theologica of St. Thomas Aquinas (Fathers of the English Dominican Province, ed., Christian Classics 1981).

[33] In the realm of public international law, those norms accorded hierarchical status are referred to as *jus cogens*. One scholar has attempted to summarize the application and relevance *of jus cogens* as follows:

> [R]ules of jus cogens can be defined in general terms as being non-derogable rules of international "public policy." Given their overriding importance and indeed because often they involve matters of international public order it can be stated that each and every State has a legal interest therein. As a result, one can state that peremptory obligations are owed all States (and other subjects of international law) to the international community of States as a whole. One can recall the well-known dictum of the ICJ in the Barcelona Traction Case:
>
> > [A]n essential distinction should be drawn between the obligations of a State towards the international community as a whole, and those arising vis-à-vis another State .... By their nature the former are the concern of all States. In view of the importance of the rights involved, all States can be held to have a legal interest in their protection; they are obligations erga omnes .... Such obligations derive, for example, in contemporary international law, from the outlawing of acts of aggression, and of genocide ... as also from the principles and rules concerning the basic rights of the human person, including protection from slavery and racial discrimination.

rights at minimum contributed to the "absolute" or "pre-eminent" treatment of PSNR. Here, too, the plain language of the text is eloquent because it provides that "*[i]n no case* may a people be deprived of its own means of subsistence on the grounds of any rights that may be claimed by other States."[34] The proposition is clear and arresting. The unequivocal nature of the phrase "in no case" supports the proposition that even pursuant to its lawful negotiations and treaties with other States or foreign, non-national, private entities (i.e., foreign investors), a State may not foreclose its citizens from control of or access to the wealth and resources of a nation, as may be argued to be the case in every instance where States contract with foreign private entities for the exploration, exploitation, and refinement of their natural resources.[35] Read together, public purpose is understood as a fundamental element of both the principle of self-determination *and* PSNR. In the latter case, the public purpose doctrine represents a State's "means of subsistence" and, in this sense, preempts the exercise of rights by other States or foreign private individuals. The public purpose doctrine is depicted as one that *cannot* be subordinated to the greater

> These erga omnes obligations have been defined as obligations of a State towards the international community as a whole, in the vindication of which all states have legal interest. They are rules which accord a right to all states to make claims. Such rules are "[o]pposable to, valid against, 'all the world' i.e., all other legal persons, irrespective of consent on the part of those thus affected.: It should be noted, however that although all norms of jus cogens are enforceable erga omnes not all erga omnes obligations are jus cogens.

Rafael Nieto-Navia, *International Peremptory Norms Gus Cogens and International Humanitarian Law*, in MAN'S INHUMANITY TO MAN, ESSAYS IN HONOUR OF ANTONIO CASSESE 595 *et seq.*, *at* 14 (The Hague 2003; internal citations omitted). There is no rigid definition of jus cogens or exhaustive, definitive, and immutable list detailing every category of jus cogens. Article 53 of the Vienna Convention on the Law, entitled "Treaties conflicting with a peremptory norm of general international law ('jus cogens')," recognizes the existence and peremptory nature of jus cogens:

> A treaty is void if, at the time of its conclusion, it conflicts with a peremptory norm of general international law. For the purposes of the present Convention, a peremptory norm of general international law is a norm accepted and recognized by the international community of states as a whole as a norm from which no derogation is permitted and which can be modified only by subsequent norm of general international law having the same character.

VCLT, *supra* Chapter 1 note 88, art. 53.

34 Draft International Covenant on Human Rights, *supra* note 28 (emphasis added).

35 Pursuant to the PSNR doctrine, exploitation and development agreements between States and private foreign entities that vest in foreign entities the control, disposition, or economic benefit of a State's natural resources may be susceptible to challenge and characterization as an illicit privatization. Similarly, even where such rights are vested in foreign private entities by legislative enactments, such legislation may still be vulnerable to constitutional challenges. The legality and legitimacy is further susceptible to attack where even narrow and restricted rights are accorded in perpetuity or for periods of time that compromise the potential benefits of such rights that one or more generations of a State's citizens may claim.

good of the community of nations (arguably a higher public purpose) because of legacy constructions of sovereignty, territoriality, and the political independence of States based on nineteenth-century economic globalization models.[36]

United Nations General Assembly Resolution 1803 corroborates PSNR's status as a fundamental principle because of its relationship to the right of self-determination and as a universally held, inalienable right.[37] Similarly, Resolution 1803 alludes to regulatory sovereignty and self-judging public purpose by identifying "national interests" as the talisman pursuant to which States are to utilize their natural wealth and resources.[38]

Entitled "Permanent Sovereignty over Natural Resources," Resolution 1803 is the first United Nations General Assembly Resolution to coin the nomenclature. In addition to the standing that this historical fact accords to the resolution, Resolution 1803 is also significant because of its role in aiding its predecessors: Resolution 523 (adopted January 12, 1952), Resolution 626 (adopted December 21, 1952), and Resolution 1314 (adopted December 12, 1958).[39] Although these three predecessor resolutions integrated economic development and commercial agreements along with the right to exploit freely natural wealth and resources, as well as the right to self-determination,[40] they do not explicitly and concisely adopt the nomenclature "permanent sovereignty over natural resources" nor do they distinguish PSNR from sustainable development or the promotion of economic development and economic independence with respect to nonindustrialized States. Because it explicitly references its predecessor resolutions, Resolution 1803 imparts conceptual coherence and uniformity to PSNR by appropriately chronicling its development.

Without abandoning the goals of economic development of developing countries,[41] reliance on the principle and the right of nations to self-

36 *See supra* Chapter 4 notes 125–28 and accompanying text.

37 Resolution 1803 specifically identifies PSNR "as a basic constituent of the right to self-determination." G.A. Res. 1803, *supra* note 6. Moreover, as to the "inalienable" status of PSNR, the resolution states:

> Any measure in this respect must be based on the recognition of the inalienable right of all states freely to dispose of their natural wealth and resources in accordance with their national interests, and on other respect for the economic independence of states.

Id.

38 *Id.*

39 *Id.*

40 *See supra* note 27 and accompanying text.

41 In this regard, Resolution 1803 provides:

> That it is desirable to promote international cooperation for the economic development of developing countries, and that economic and financial agreements between the

determination,[42] and provision of assistance to developing countries free of conditionality,[43] Resolution 1803 underscores PSNR as a free-standing principle. The resolution demonstrates that PSNR, although tangentially related to the general right of States to pursue and promote their economic development, is a distinct principle in and of itself. It reads:

> *Noting* that the creation and strengthening of the inalienable sovereignty of states over their natural wealth and resources reinforces their economic independence,
>
> *Desiring*, that there should be further consideration by the United Nations of the subject of permanent sovereignty over natural resources in the spirit of international co-operation in the field of economic development, particularly that of the developing countries.[44]

Here, PSNR's normative standing as an absolute principle of international law from which there can be no derogation and, in this sense, conceivably, a nascent *jus cogens*, is notable.[45] The resolution's ostensible but unspoken aspiration to accord *jus cogens* status to PSNR may be gleaned from the effort to "internationalize" the principle within the framework of economic development.[46]

Resolution 1803's commitment to the development of PSNR as a public purpose-based principle of international law that, although forming part of

> developed and the developing countries must be based on principles of equality and the right of peoples and nations to self-determination, ...

G.A. Res. 1803, *supra* note 6.

42 *Id.*

43 The resolution provides, in relevant part:

> That the provision of economic and technical assistance, loans and increased foreign investment must not be subject to conditions which conflict with the interests of the recipient State, ...

Id.

44 *Id.*

45 *See supra* note 34 and accompanying text.

46 *See Id.* Most commentators are of a single voice in recognizing that *jus cogens* as a category of international law contains the following essential elements: (i) it is a norm that is accepted and recognized by the international community of States; (ii) it cannot be derogated or otherwise altered by agreement or contract; (iii) a norm of *jus cogens* status may only be modified by a binding norm of equal hierarchies; (iv) the norm pertains to international law generally and, therefore, applies to all states making up the international community; and (v) the violation of a norm by one State affects or is of consequence to all other States and deemed an international crime. Additionally, enactments contrary to *jus cogens* are null, void, or voidable. *See* Fabian Novak Talavera & Luis Garcia-Corrochano Moyano, Derecho Internacional Publico, Introduccion y Fuentes (tomo I), Pontificia Universidad Catolica del Peru, Instituto de Estudios Internacionales, FONDO EDITORIAL 2003, at pp. 426–30, for a concise discussion of these elements.

the right to self-determination, is also independent and free-standing is exemplified by the resolution's own declaration. Seven of the eight paragraphs constituting this declaration explicitly reference and define PSNR.[47] Paragraph 4 of the resolution's declaration does not literally reference PSNR. However, the reasonable and arguably necessary construction of this paragraph leaves little room for a conclusion other than the understanding that a Host State's taking of both foreign and domestic property based on PSNR preempts any such ownership interest. Within the meaning of Paragraph 4, PSNR constitutes a public purpose (a "reason of public utility, security or the national interest") sufficient to override any foreign or domestic private

[47] Set forth here are the paragraphs in the resolution's declaration referencing and defining the content, scope, and application of PSNR. Paragraph 4 of the declaration concerning nationalization, expropriation, or requisitioning has been omitted:

Declares that:

1. The right of peoples and nations to *permanent sovereignty over their natural wealth and resources* must be exercised in the interest of their national development and of the well-being of the State concerned.
2. The exploration, development and disposition of such resources, as well as the import of the foreign capital required for these purposes, should be in conformity with the rules and conditions *which the peoples and nations freely consider to be necessary or desirable with regard to the authorization, restriction or prohibition of such activities.*
3. In cases where authorization is granted, the capital imported and the earnings on that capital shall be governed by the terms thereof, by the national legislation in force, and by international law. The profits derived must be shared in the proportions freely agreed upon, in each case, between the investors and the recipient State, *due care being taken to ensure that there is no impairment, for any reason, of that State's sovereignty over its natural wealth and resources.*
4. [omitted]
5. The free and beneficial exercise of the sovereignty of peoples and nations must be furthered by the mutual respect of States based on their sovereign equality.
6. International co-operation for the economic development of developing countries, whether in the form of public or private capital investments, exchange of goods and services, technical assistance, or exchange of scientific information, *shall be such, as to further their independent national development and shall be based upon respect for their sovereignty over their natural wealth and resources.*
7. *Violation of the rights of peoples and nations to sovereignty over their natural wealth and resources is contrary to the spirit and principles of the Charter of the United Nations and hinders the development of international co-operation and maintenance of peace.*
8. Foreign investment agreements freely entered into by or between sovereign states shall be observed in good faith; states and international organizations shall strictly and conscientiously respect the *sovereignty of peoples and nations their natural wealth and resources* in accordance with the Charter and principles set forth in the present resolution.

G.A. Res. 1803, *supra* note 6 (emphasis added).

interest in furtherance of a taking pursuant to the exercise of regulatory sovereignty.[48]

Read together, Paragraphs 2, 3, 6, 7, and 8 of the resolution's declaration emphasize the primacy of PSNR over Host-State obligations in favor of Home-State investors/investments.[49] These paragraphs attempt to preempt tensions arising from the expectations of investment protection held by investors from capital-exporting States and the diminution in value or taking of such investments pursuant to the exercise of regulatory sovereignty on the part of capital-importing states. By way of example, Paragraph 2 of the resolution's declaration speaks to harmonizing the interests of foreign capital invested in furtherance of the exploration, exploitation, and development of Host-State natural resources with Host-State exercise of regulatory sovereignty in the context of PSNR:

> The exploration, development and disposition of such resources [the natural wealth and resources of states], as well as the import of the foreign capital required for these purposes, should be in conformity with the rules and conditions which the peoples and nations freely consider to be necessary or desirable with regard to the authorization, restriction or prohibition of such activities.[50]

In addition to asserting that Host States and foreign investors are to honor agreements controlling the proportional distribution of income that foreign investments generate, Paragraph 3 adds that there is also a need for "due care being taken to ensure that there is no impairment, for any reason, of that State's sovereignty over its natural wealth and resources."[51] Similarly, Paragraph 8

[48] Paragraph 4 of Resolution 1803's declaration reads:

> 4. Nationalization, expropriation or requisitioning shall be based on grounds or reasons of *public utility, security* or *the national interest* which are recognized as overriding purely individual or private interests, *both domestic and foreign*. In such cases, the owner shall be paid appropriate compensation, in accordance with the rules in force in the State *taking such measures in the exercise of its sovereignty and accordance with international law*. In any case where the question of compensation gives rise to a controversy, the national jurisdiction of the State taking such measures shall be exhausted. However, upon agreement by Sovereign States and other parties concerned, settlement of disputes should be made through arbitration or international adjudication.

Id. (emphasis added).

[49] *See supra* note 47. These paragraphs predate the 1965 Washington Convention (also known as the ICSID Convention) by thirteen years. Accordingly, it does not contain "Home State," "Host State," or other "investor protection obligation" nomenclature. In this same vein, treaty-based standards and their scope and content are equally absent from the declaration's eight-paragraph text.

[50] G.A. Res. 1803, *supra* note 6.

[51] *Id.*

attempts to reconcile a bilateral good faith requirement between Host States and foreign investors and the seemingly unbridled preemptive scope of the PSNR expression of the public purpose doctrine:

> Foreign investment agreements freely entered into by or between sovereign states shall be observed in good faith; states and international organizations shall strictly and conscientiously respect the sovereignty of peoples and nations over their natural wealth and resources in accordance with the Charter and the principles set forth in the present resolution.[52]

The parameters of the principle of PSNR as set forth in Resolution 1803 are self-judging, based on a State's understanding of its own national interests and the scope of the exercise of its sovereignty. Moreover, the resolution enshrines PSNR as a principle of international law that, because of its grounding in an orthodox conception of the public purpose doctrine and traditional notions of sovereignty, overrides legitimately vested investor protection obligations on the part of Host States in favor of foreign investors.

Thus, the resolution demonstrates a historical understanding of public purpose pursuant to which interests grounded in the doctrine preempt "private" microeconomic interests, both foreign and domestic. This draconian approach to public purpose in the form of PSNR was of considerable utility during the historical juncture when decolonization required a strong and compelling sense of nationalism and the repatriation of national assets, most notably control over natural resources that would become ever more precious with the demands of the Cold War. This historical connection and economic utility are no longer relevant and have become a notable impediment to foreign direct investment (FDI) and to the relationship between developed countries and economies in transition. *Globalization has called for qualifications on all expressions of public purpose in international law.*

The legacy public purpose doctrine and, therefore, the PSNR expression of the doctrine reflect an asymmetrical content and application that favors Host-State interests over those of Home-State capital-exporting countries.[53] This understanding of public purpose arguably threatens the very bilateralism endemic to bilateral investment treaties (BITs) and, in so doing, gives rise to frustrated expectations between foreign investors and Host States. The international instruments demonstrating the early development of PSNR embody this lack of symmetry or penchant favoring economies in transition and developing countries.

[52] *Id.*

[53] *See supra* Chapter 4, Section B, where this phenomenon is discussed in the context of BITs.

United Nations General Assembly Resolution 2158 is instructive.[54] Issued only four years after its PSNR predecessor, Resolution 1803 treats PSNR as an established principle of public international law. Indeed, Resolution 2158 goes beyond establishing a nomenclature and content for PSNR and speaks to safeguarding the principle and ensuring that developing States benefit from their efficient and strategic application of resources.[55] This effort to safeguard the use and application of PSNR, particularly with respect to "foreign capital," is fundamentally predicated on supervision of foreign investment on the part of Host-State governments and the interests of developing countries. Although explicit reference is made to the need to provide "government supervision over the activity of foreign capital to ensure that it is used in the interests of national development," no reference is made to Host-State obligations to protect and "to safeguard" foreign investments.[56] To the contrary, Paragraph 4 of the resolution "*[c]onfirms* that the exploitation of natural resources in each country *shall always* be conducted in accordance with its national laws and regulations."[57] The application of PSNR as a paradigmatic public purpose tenet is absolutist and asymmetrical in favor of Host States (i.e., generally, developing countries). The international instruments giving rise to PSNR as a principle of public international law do not impose obligations on Host States beyond fleeting reference to bilateral good faith in adhering to contractual obligations.[58]

Instead of seeking bilateralism in the relationship between developing countries and industrialized States, Resolution 2158 actually extracts commitments from and imposes obligations on both Home States (developed countries)

[54] Resolution 2158, entitled "Permanent sovereignty over natural resources," was passed at the 1478th plenary meeting on November 25, 1966. G.A. Res. 2158, *supra* note 6.

[55] Resolution 2158, in pertinent part, provides:

> *Considering* that in order to *safeguard* the exercise of *permanent sovereignty over natural resources, it is essential that their exploitation and marketing should be aimed at securing the highest possible rate of growth of the developing countries,*
>
> *Considering further* that this aim can better be achieved if the developing countries are in a position to undertake themselves the exploitation and marketing of their natural resources so that they may exercise their freedom of choice in the various fields related to the utilisation of natural resources under the most favourable conditions,
>
> *Taking into account* the fact that foreign capital whether public or private, forthcoming at the request of the developing countries, can play an important role inasmuch as it supplements the efforts undertaken by them in the expectation and development of their natural resources, provided that there is government supervision over the activity of foreign capital to ensure that it is used in the interests of national development, ...

Id. (emphasis added).

[56] *Id.*

[57] *Id.* at ¶ 4 (emphasis added).

[58] *See, e.g.*, G.A. Res. 1803, *supra* note 6 ("Foreign investment agreements freely entered into by or between sovereign states shall be observed in good faith").

and the United Nations in favor of Host States (developing States).[59] The resolution actually calls for the Secretary-General to expedite the inclusion of programs addressing the exploration and exploitation of natural resources in order to accelerate economic development and to provide for appropriate progress reports.[60] Subsequent resolutions concerning PSNR, most notably Resolutions 2626 and 3171, emphasize the need for affirmative contributions from industrialized States based on *historical* economic dominance or colonization on the part of developed countries.[61] Both of these resolutions, to be

59 In this regard, Resolution 2158:

> 3. *States* that such an effort should help in achieving the maximum possible development of the natural resources of the developing countries and in strengthening their ability to undertake this development themselves, so that they might effectively exercise their choice in deciding the manner in which the exploitation and marketing of their natural resources should be carried out;
> 6. *Considers* that, when natural resources of the developing countries are exploited by foreign investors, the latter should undertake proper and accelerated training of national personnel at all levels and in all fields connected with such exploitation;
> 7. *Calls upon* the developed countries to make available to the developing countries, at their request, assistance, including capital goods and know-how, for the exploitation and marketing of their natural resources in order to accelerate their economic development, and to refrain from placing on the world market non-commercial reserves of primary commodities which may have an adverse effect on the foreign exchange earnings of the developing countries.

G.A. Res. 2158, *supra* note 6, at ¶¶ 3, 6–7 (underlined emphasis added).

60 The resolution calls on considerable international resources in furtherance of economic growth pursuant to PSNR:

> *Requests* the Secretary-General:
> (a) To co-ordinate the activities of the Secretariat in the field of natural resources with those of other United Nations organs and programmes, including the United Nations Conference on Trade and Development, the United Nations Development Programme, the regional economic commissions, the United Nations Economic and Social Office in Beirut, the specialized agencies and the International Atomic Energy Agency, and in particular with those of the United Nations industrial development organization;
> (b) To take the necessary steps to facilitate, through the work of the Centre for Development Planning, Projections and Policies, the United Nations Conference on Trade and Development, the United Nations Development Organization and the Advisory Committee on the Application of Signs and Technology to Development, the inclusion of the exploitation of the natural resources of the developing countries in programmes for their accelerated economic growth;
> (c) To submit to the General Assembly at its twenty-third session a progress report on the implementation of the present resolution.

Id.

61 International Development Strategy for the Second United Nations Development Decade, G.A. Res. 2626, U.N. GAOR 25th Sess., Supp. No. 30, at 39, U.N. Doc. A/8124 (1970) [hereinafter G.A. Res. 2626]; G.A. Res. 3171, *supra* note 6.

sure, stress the need for developing countries to exercise their best efforts in furtherance of economic development.[62] Notwithstanding resolution language emphasizing that developing countries have the primary responsibility of contributing to their own economic development, the resolution is far from prescribing that PSNR imposes duties on developing countries with respect to foreign investors or Home States (industrialized countries). In fact, these foundational resolutions continue to reference the primacy and absolute character of PSNR. Resolution 3171, by way of example, provides:

> [A]n intrinsic condition of the exercise of the sovereignty of every State is that it be exercised fully and effectively over all the natural resources of the State, whether found on land or in sea, . . .[63]

As such, Resolution 3171 specifically refers to regulatory sovereignty pertaining to economic development in the context of PSNR as an "inviolable principle" and adds that the full exercise by each State or sovereignty over its natural resources is an essential condition for achieving the objectives and targets of the Second United Nations Developmental Decade.[64] The resolution further provides that such "exercise requires that action by States aimed at achieving a better utilization and use of those resources must cover all stages, from exploration to marketing."[65]

Further, in stark contrast with the identification of obligations that PSNR engrafts on developing States, Resolution 2626 speaks to the obligations of

[62] In this regard, Resolution 2626 provides:

> (11) The primary responsibility for the development of developing countries rests upon themselves, as stressed in the Charter of Algiers, but however great their own efforts, these will not be sufficient to enable them to achieve the desired development goals as expeditiously as they must unless they are assisted through increased financial resources and more favorable economic and commercial policies on the part of developed countries.
>
> (73) Developing countries will take specific steps to augment production and improve productivity in order to provide goods and services necessary for raising levels of living and improving economic viability. While this will be primarily their own responsibility, . . .

G.A. Res. 2626, *supra* note 61 (internal citations omitted).

[63] G.A. Res. 3171, *supra* note 6.

[64] *Id.*

[65] Additionally, Paragraph 1 of Resolution 3171:

> *Strongly* reaffirms *all* the inalienable rights of states to permanent sovereignty over all their natural resources, on land within their international boundaries as well as those in the C-bed and the subsoil thereof within their national jurisdiction and in superjacent waters.

Id.

industrialized States in support of the efforts of developing countries in maximizing PSNR.[66]

The progressive interdependence among States delineated by both Resolution 2626 and Resolution 3171 is framed within the immediate post-colonization historical context. For this reason, the regulations stress both (i) reorganization on the part of developing States of their natural resources and (ii) an ever-increasing gap between industrialized and developing nations resulting from the ills of colonization and the systemic violation of sovereignty on the part of those industrialized States that implemented such conduct with respect to developing countries as a matter of national policy.[67]

Although global poverty and the development of natural resources in ways that maximize the needs of all nations remain as paramount challenges, the terms of this transnational dialogue must be recontextualized and defined anew, certainly as concerns PSNR. Economic globalization has caused "interdependence" to give rise to public purpose paradigms that transcend territorially based sovereignty models. The post-economic globalization world must

[66] Resolution 2626, Subparagraph 73, provides:

> While this [PSNR and the development of natural wealth and resources] will be primarily their [developing countries] own responsibility, production policies will be carried out in a global context designed to achieve optimum utilization of world resources, benefitting both developed and developing countries. Further research will be undertaken, by the international organizations concerned, in the field of optimal international division of labor to assist individual countries or groups of countries in their choice of production and trading structures. Depending on the social and economic structure and particular characteristics of individual countries, consideration will be given to the role which the public sector and co-operatives might play in augmenting production.

G.A. Res. 2626, *supra* note 61, at ¶ 73. Additionally, Paragraph 76 in part provides that, "[d]eveloped countries and international organizations will assist in the industrialization of developing countries through appropriate means." *Id.* at ¶ 76. Along this same vein, Paragraph 77 asserts that "[i]nternational financial and technical assistance will be extended in support of their [that of developing countries] endeavor." *Id.* at ¶ 77.

[67] Resolution 3171 speaks to the resolute support of "the efforts of the developing countries and of the peoples of the territories under colonial and racial domination in foreign occupation and their usage to regain effective control over their natural resources." G.A. Res. 3171, *supra* note 6. Resolution 2626 in turn points to disparities in allocation of wealth among States as the primary cause of international tensions:

> (3) However, the level of living of countless millions of people in the developing part of the world is still pitifully low. These people are often still undernourished, uneducated, unemployed and wanting in many other basic amenities of life. While a part of the world lives in great comfort and even affluence, much of the larger part suffers from abject poverty, and in fact the disparity is continuing to widen. This lamentable situation has contributed to the aggravation of world tensions.

G.A. Res. 2626, *supra* note 61, at ¶ 3.

rely on expressions of the public purpose doctrine, such as PSNR, premised on expectations of bilateralism beyond absolutist precepts suggesting that, without exception, States' treaty-based obligations, as well as duties arising under customary international law, a priori and under all circumstances, must be subordinated to regulatory sovereignty in furtherance of PSNR.

Without challenging the proposition that the consequences of colonialism have left economic scars that are yet to be fully healed and that therefore command redress by affluent nations, the advent of global and regional markets, together with the horizontal and virtually ubiquitous proliferation of global centers of processing and manufacturing within the rubric of a global economy, require a more comprehensive understanding of public purpose. Proportionality, bilateralism, and an understanding of interdependence beyond one rooted in the reparation of historical inequities must replace a legacy approach that fosters insecurity and want of predictive value concerning the very economic relationships on which *all* nations depend in order to maximize the efficient use and allocation of global resources. PSNR needs to be doctrinally revisited and perhaps modified as a rebuttable presumption that also creates obligations and duties in Host States in favor of foreign investors. In the era of economic globalization, FDI cannot be viewed as merely a "private" matter that must be subordinated to regulatory sovereignty under all circumstances.

C. SEMINAL DECISIONAL LAW ON PSNR

The "decisional law"[68] on PSNR is scant and not instructive. Despite PSNR's practical and theoretical reach, this expression of the public purpose doctrine has not surfaced as a contentious principle forming part of the arbitral culture arising from investor-state disputes. This paucity of "authority" in the form of awards is particularly quizzical because of the precept's amenability to construction as a Host-State defense and also in light of the prevalence of resource-based investor-state arbitration.[69] Additionally, PSNR's preeminence in international instruments would suggest greater prominence in the field. Sornarajah, for example, has maintained that PSNR is a principle of *jus cogens*.[70]

[68] The term "decisional law" refers to arbitral awards arising from treaty-based arbitration.

[69] As of June 30, 2013, 25 percent of all ICSID administered cases have pertained to "oil, gas, and mining," whereas another 12 percent have dealt with "electric power and other energy." ICSID CASELOAD-STATISTICS, Issue 2013-2, http://icsid.worldbank.org (last visited August 13, 2013).

[70] Specifically, Sornarajah reports in one writing that "some authorities regard as an *ius cogens* principle [permanent sovereignty over natural resources]." M. SORNARAJAH, THE INTERNATIONAL LAW ON FOREIGN INVESTMENT 193 (Cambridge University Press, 3rd ed.

PSNR's normative standing is based on three fundamental propositions that have, in turn, contributed to the orthodox understanding of public purpose in public international law. First, by treating PSNR as an element of the principle of self-determination, the tenet is thus derivatively classified *as* a *jus cogens*. Elevated to the status of a first principle, by definition, this expression of public purpose can no longer admit of discursive reasoning as a means for justifying its doctrinal preeminence. Conceptually, the validity and legitimacy of first principles must be assumed and explanation or discourse may only serve to obfuscate or derail.[71] Underlying PSNR is the principle that it serves a public purpose that is absolute and not subject to limitation by qualification or other conditionality. Because of its public purpose foundation forming part of the principle of self-determination, PSNR is not susceptible to discursive reasoning. It is in the pantheon of the "self-evident" and "intuitive" truths.

Second, the practical workings of PSNR are inextricably intertwined with the doctrine of sustainable development.[72] Also enshrined as a precept of universal regard and application, the doctrine of sustainable development is deemed to be an unassailable and absolute principle that also does not allow

2010). The tribunal in *El Paso Energy International Company v. The Argentine Republic* identified Professor Sornarajah as *himself* adopting the position that PSNR is a principle *of jus cogens*, citing the expert report that he filed in that case. The award in relevant part reads:

> 168. Professor Sornarajah finally turns to the permanent sovereignty over natural resources, which he considers to be a principle of *jus cogens*. This means that, with the fluctuations of what can be considered as being the public interest, an element of paramount importance in this matter, the rights granted to operators and investors may fluctuate as well; entrants to the field cannot but be aware of that possibility. Pursuant to the *jus cogens* argument, what may have been possible at a given time under the angle of the *jus cogens* principle of permanent sovereignty over natural resources will no longer be at another point in time. In technical terms, this means that a supervening impossibility of performance may occur under Article 61 of the Vienna Convention on the Law of Treaties. In such situations, the Respondent's expert concludes, "a recovery of sovereignty is permissible." According to the Respondent's expert, all BITs are subject to that limitation.

El Paso Energy International Co. v. Argentine Republic, ICSID Case No. ARB/03/15, Award ¶ 168 (October 31, 2011), http://www.italaw.com/sites/default/files/case-documents/ita0270.pdf [hereinafter El Paso Energy].

71 *Jus cogens* present prime examples of the intuitive and nondiscursive foundation of a first principle's normative status. The right not to be enslaved and the proscription of genocide are illustrative. Discourse aspiring to justify either of these tenets would not be necessary and actually is likely to detract from the immediacy of the normative foundation that underlies them. Bona fide first principles that are self-justifying, without more, preempt other tenets that may weaken their application and are not susceptible to less than absolute treatment. Thus, it would be irrational, or even inconceivable, to posit a qualification or partial application to the right to be free from slavery or the norm proscribing genocide.

72 *See supra* Chapter 4, Section B, for a discussion of the role of sustainable development within the public purpose doctrine.

for discursive argument or consideration. The, at times, inseparable references to economic development (the principle of sustainable development) and PSNR often confusingly appear as two aspects of a single doctrine.[73] Irrespective of this proximate and, at times, deceptive relationship between the doctrines, it remains uncontroverted that they are separate and distinct, although sharing a common historical origin founded on the process of decolonization. Furthermore, PSNR is widely regarded as a predicate to economic development. In turn, economic development is viewed as a universal, self-evident right shared by all peoples that is not subject to compromise or subordination pursuant to legal fiat. PSNR's close relationship with the precept of sustainable development and their common historicity contribute to the treatment of PSNR as an absolute, intuitive, and self-evident legal norm that cannot be compromised. This absolutist configuration and elite normative status itself is premised on public purpose, further nurturing a symbiotic relationship between public purpose and its multiple expressions that removes the doctrine from the realm of rational justification.

Third, PSNR, as a right has been described in international instruments as "inalienable."[74] The a priori configuration of a norm that is inalienable does not admit challenge even at a theoretical level. As with self-determination and sustainable development, the precept's inalienability stems from a public purpose that is framed by historical grounding. This historical foundation is important but cannot be construed as determinative. Inalienability further entrenches a legacy interpretation, understanding, and application of the public purpose doctrine in all of its expressions.

Fourth and finally, because PSNR is defined through the prism of first principles, its application is absolute and does not permit compromise. Therefore, it is conducive to "all-or-nothing" determinations. A global paradigm of integration, however, bespeaks proportionality and not resolutions that are absolute and detached in this regard from the practice of the community of nations.

Ascribing a *jus cogens* status to PSNR because of its alleged conceptual relationship with the (i) principle of self-determination, (ii) principle of economic development, and its characterization as (iii) inalienable and (iv) absolute or nonproportional contributes to a construction of public purpose that justifies exercise of regulatory sovereignty without regard to any countervailing or even mitigating proposition. For example, such elevated status could be used in connection with a public purpose that is not linked to

[73] *See, e.g.*, G.A. Res. 1803, *supra* note 6; G.A. Res. 2158, *supra* note 6; G.A. Res. 2626, *supra* note 42.

[74] *See supra* text accompanying note 44.

regulatory sovereignty but rather to an overarching concern for furthering a public purpose rooted in the common good of the community of nations.

PSNR exemplifies the manner in which public purpose has been infused with a subjective content framed within a historically based policy that is presented as beyond discursive reasoning (akin to a first principle or *jus cogens*), the application of which disavows proportionality. The practical consequence of this legacy construction is to arm regulatory sovereignty with a doctrinal and normative foundation that does not permit scrutiny or transparency and that, in the name of a higher principle, empowers States to undermine the very rule of law under which they purport to be organized.

Whereas the first decades of decolonization in a pre-economic globalization international community masked and actually rewarded these debilities, the exigent demands of a global economy has emphasized them without embracing a pendular shift that turns its back on the collective responsibility to assist developing nations and economies in transition.

6

The Role of Public Purpose in Foreign Investment Protection Statutes: Can FIPS Rehabilitate the Doctrine?

Most States have enacted domestic legislation that is characterized as intended to promote foreign investment pursuant to investor protection.[1] Much like their treaty counterparts – the network of more than 3,000 bilateral investment treaties (BITs) – the foreign investor protection statutes (FIPS) are not at all the product of a centralized legislative system.[2] Consequently, the FIPS are lacking in uniformity as to (i) structure, (ii) terms, (iii) common nomenclature, (v) substance, and even (vi) comprehensively shared aspirations or underlying policies. This want of uniformity bespeaks a structural debility that certainly commands concern. Fundamental principles of comity and reciprocity may legitimately be called into question, whereas here, disparate and at times even contradictory policies are memorialized pursuant to statutory frameworks that ostensibly purport to advance a shared objective: Host-State investor/investment protection. This absence of a coordinated effort by States at an international level with respect to legislating FIPS also has given rise to conflicting constructions and applications of the public purpose doctrine.

Generally, most FIPS apply public purpose normative standing in furtherance of Host-State investment protection obligations in favor of foreign investors. Put simply, an analytical sampling of FIPS conducted abstractly and *without* reference to BITs would suggest that Host States primarily are concerned with exercising their regulatory sovereignty and legislative fiat in furtherance of maximizing foreign investor protection even to the detriment of adherence to postinvestment enacted legislation.[3] The role of the

[1] *See generally* DENNIS CAMPBELL, INTERNATIONAL PROTECTION OF FOREIGN INVESTMENT VOL. I & II (Lulu.com, pubs., 2008).

[2] *See* discussion on the structural framework of BITs *supra* Chapter 4.

[3] The Socialist Republic of Vietnam's Law on Investment No. 59-2005-QH11, enacted by the National Assembly on November 29, 2005, is particularly instructive and revealing concerning

public purpose doctrine in FIPS provides public international law with an existing analytical framework and construct in which the very public purpose principles that are used to engraft unbridled regulatory authority on a State grants foreign investors investment protection premised on an application of the public purpose doctrine that preempts the public purpose justification for the exercise of regulatory sovereignty. This use of the public purpose doctrine is unique to FIPS. It starkly contrasts with Host-State friendly constructions of the doctrine more generally in customary and conventional international law.

Because of the proliferation of FIPS, this study traces the contours of the public purpose doctrine in these instruments by drawing from a set of seventeen FIPS gathered from (i) Eastern Europe,[4] (ii) Southeast Asia,[5]

this point. By way of example, under Chapter 2 ("Investment Guarantees"), Article 11 ("Investment Guarantees in the Event of Change in Law or Policies"), the law provides:

1. If a newly promulgated law or policy contains higher benefits and incentives than those to which the investor was previously entitled, then the investor shall be entitled to the benefits and incentives in accordance with the new law as from the date the new law or policy takes effect.
2. If a newly promulgated law or policy *adversely affects* the lawful benefits enjoyed by an investor *prior to the date of effectiveness of such law or policy*, the investor shall be guaranteed to enjoy incentives the same as the investment certificate or there shall be resolution by one, a number or all of the following methods:
   (a) Continuation of enjoyment of benefits and incentives;
   (b) There shall be deduction of the loss from taxable income;
   (c) There shall be a change of the operational objective of the project;
   (d) Consideration shall be given to paying compensation in necessary circumstances.
3. Based on the provisions of the laws and commitments in international treaties of which the Socialist Republic of Vietnam is a member, the Government shall make specific provisions on guarantee for interests of investors in the case where a change in laws or policies affects adversely the interests of the investors.]

Law on Investment (November 29, 2005), http://bit.ly/1uwQYsM (translation by Phillips Fox; emphasis added).

4 Law No. 7764 ("For Foreign Investments"; February 11, 1999), http://www.slas.info/legislazione_albanese/law%20_7764_1993_foreign_investments.php (Albania) [hereinafter Albania Law No. 7764]; Law of Georgia on the Investment Activity Promotion & Guarantees (November 12, 1999), http://www.wipo.int/wipolex/en/text.jsp?file_id=243072 [hereinafter Georgia Law on Investment]; Law of the Republic of Kazakhstan on Investments (January 8, 2003), http://www.kazembassy.org.uk/img/001%20Law%20of%20the%20Republic%20of%20Kazakhstan%20on%20Investments(1).doc.pdf [Kazakhstan Law on Investments]; Federal Law on Foreign Investment in the Russian Federation (July 9, 1999), 39 ILM 894 (2000) [Russian Law on Foreign Investment].

5 Law of the People's Republic of China on Foreign-capital Enterprises (October 31, 2000), http://www.china.org.cn/english/features/investment/36754.htm [China Foreign-capital Enterprise Law]; Law on Investment Promotion (July 8, 2009), http://thailand.nlambassade.org/binaries/content/assets/postenweb/t/thailand/nederlandse-ambassade-in-bangkok/import/

(iii) the Middle East,[6] (iv) Africa,[7] (v) Latin America,[8] (vi) understandings between the European Union and the United States,[9] and (vii) North America.[10] It is suggested that the FIPS represent an existing framework through which the public purpose doctrine may be further developed and institutionalized so as to temper the ill effects of a legacy doctrine. Although far from constituting a doctrinal solution to the consequences of a public purpose doctrine that is self-judging and absolute in application, FIPS may help to further the quest for application of the doctrine in ways that comport with the exigencies of a global era.

Viewed collectively, FIPS can be described as providing a confluence of premises in the name of foreign investor/investment protection. Indeed, often foreign investment protection is sought to be furthered by FIPS that merely

producten_en_diensten/handel_en_investeren/zakendoen_in_laos/laotiaanse-investeringswet-2009 (Lao PDR) [hereinafter Lao PDR Law on Investment Promotion]; Law on Investment (November 29, 2005), http://bit.ly/1uwQYsM (translation by Phillips Fox) (Vietnam) [hereinafter Vietnam Law on Investment].

6 Law No. 8/2001 Regulating Direct Foreign Capital Investment in the State of Kuwait (April 17, 2001), http://www.kuwaitemb-australia.com/files/direct_investment.pdf [hereinafter Kuwait Direct Foreign Capital Investment Law]; the Foreign Capital Investment Law for the Organization and Encouragement of Industry (October 16, 1994), http://om.mofcom.gov.cn/table/wgtz.pdf (Oman) [hereinafter Oman Foreign Capital Investment Law]; Law of Investment Guarantees and Incentives & Its Executive Regulations: Investment Law No. 8 (1997), http://www.egypt-law.com/Investments_law.pdf (Egypt) [hereinafter Egypt Investment Law No. 8].

7 Proclamation No. 280/2002 Re-Enactment of the Investment Proclamation (July 2, 2002), http://www.wipo.int/edocs/lexdocs/laws/en/et/et013en.pdf (Ethiopia) [Ethiopia Investment Proclamation No. 280/2002]; Act 478: Ghana Investment Promotion Centre Act (August 29, 1994), http://www.intax-info.com/pdf/law_by_country/Ghana/Ghana%20Investment%20Promotion%20Centre%20Act%201994.pdf [hereinafter Ghana Investment Promotion Centre Act].

8 Foreign Investment Law (March 3, 1998), http://www.lexadin.nl/wlg/legis/nofr/oeur/arch/gua/investment_law.pdf (Guatemala) [hereinafter Guatemala Foreign Investment Law]; Legislative Decree No. 662 – Approving the Juridical Stability System for Foreign Investment (September 2, 1991), http://www.lexadin.nl/wlg/legis/nofr/oeur/arch/per/D.L.%2520662tradrev.pdf (Peru) [hereinafter Peru Legislative Decree No. 662]; Overview of Law for the Promotion of Foreign Investment (Law No. 344) (May 24, 2000), http://www.PROnicaragua.org (Nicaragua) [hereinafter Overview of Nicaragua's Law for the Promotion of Foreign Investment].

9 1997 European Union-United States Summit, *11 April 1997 Understanding between the European Union and the United States on US extraterritorial legislation* (April 11, 1997); 1998 European Union-United States Summit, *Understanding with Respect to Disciplines for the Strengthening of Investment Protection* (London, May 18, 1998) [hereinafter 1998 E.U.–U.S. Understanding].

10 U.S. Dept. of State: Bureau of Economic & Business Affairs, *2012 Investment Climate Statements, available at* http://www.State.gov/e/eb/rls/othr/ics/2012/index.htm (last visited September 3, 2013).

provide for foreign investor/investment incentives and that offer little, if any, foreign investor protection beyond what may already be available by way of BITs.[11] Other FIPS provide investor protection – guarantees – as the cornerstone investment incentive.[12] A third set of FIPS emphasize neither economic-

[11] *See, e.g.*, Lao PDR Law on Investment Promotion, *supra* note 5. This legislation provides for no less than six different zones for purposes of facilitating foreign investment, i.e.: (i) industrial zones, (ii) export processing zones, (iii) duty-free zones, (iv) information and technology development zones, (v) ordered trade zones, and (vi) urbanized trade zones. Moreover, Article 1 of the Law on Investment Promotion duly emphasizes foreign investor incentives from a national systemic perspective:

> The Law on Investment Promotion stipulates principles, regulations and measures regarding the promotion and management of domestic and foreign investments aiming at ensuring investment with convenience; speediness; accuracy; being protected by the Government; and ensuring the rights and benefits of investors, of the State and of the people. The law aims to enhance the roles and benefits of investments contributed to the national socio-economic growth in a continuous and sustainable manner; and significantly to the national protection and development." *(art. 1)*

Id. art. 1. But for fleeting reference to "being protected by the Government," investment protection is only superficially mentioned in Article 61 "Forms of Investment Protection," and Article 62 "Protection of Intellectual Property." Neither provision, however, sets forth a compelling protection regime that would realistically incentivize foreign investment. Article 61 speaks to protection of investors against "seizure, confiscation or nationalization by administration processes" but omits such key elements as due process and nondiscriminatory practice as investor safeguards. *Id.* art. 61. The reference to "actual value" in the article is encouraging but of little practical consequence when contextualized within the framework of a dispute resolution clause (Article 78) that circumscribes the administration of justice to national institutions that hardly can be characterized as independent of the State's exercise of its own sovereignty.

Article 62 is but a single-sentence declaration providing that intellectual property will be protected consonant with "the Lao PDR or [disjunctive in original] international treaties to which Lao PDR is a contracting party." *Id.* Article 62. In contrast, the clear majority of the 99 articles comprising the Law on Investment Promotion concern economic or subject matter investor incentives.

[12] For example, the Albanian FIPS comprises a total of 12 articles with reference only to investment protection and no mention of economic incentives. *See* Albania Law No. 7764, *supra* note 4. Similarly, the Georgian FIPS states that "[t]he purpose of the law is to establish the investment-promotional regime" and comprises sixteen articles that emphasize investment protection or guarantee. *See* Georgia Law on Investment, *supra* note 4. Indeed, Article 16 providing for dispute resolution – in contrast, for example, with Article 9 of the Republic of Kazakhstan's FIPS omitting specific arbitral agreements – explicitly references any international arbitration body that has been set up by UNCITRAL (United Nations Commission on International Trade Law) and ICSID.

Ethiopia's Proclamation No. 280/2002 Re-enactment of the Investment Proclamation, for example, in Part 2 ("Investment Objectives, Areas and Incentives") consists of nine numbered paragraphs and eleven subparagraphs. Despite this elaborate narrative detailing investment objectives and incentives, special legislation and regulations concerning the protection of foreign investors/investments are nowhere mentioned. The investment objectives do underscore "the realization of sustainable economic and social development" as paramount to the legislation:

based incentives nor incentives premised on special legislative enactments protecting or guaranteeing foreign investment. This third category of FIPS, which is well-exemplified by the People's Republic of China's FIPS,

PART TWO: Investment Objectives, Areas and Incentives

4. Investment Objectives of the Federal Democratic Republic of Ethiopia

   The Objectives of the investment policy of the Federal Democratic Republic of Ethiopia are designed to improve the living standards of the peoples of Ethiopia through the realization of sustainable economic and social development, the particulars of which are the following:

   1) to accelerate the country's economic development;
   2) to exploit and develop the immense natural resources of the country;
   3) to develop the domestic market through the growth of production, productivity, and services;
   4) to increase foreign exchange earnings by encouraging expansion in volume and variety of the county's export products and services and the improvement of their quality as well as to save foreign exchange through production of import substituting products;
   5) to encourage balanced development and integrate economic activity among the Regions and to strengthen the inter-sectoral linkages of the economy;
   6) to enhance the role of the private sector in the acceleration of the development of the country's economy;
   7) to render foreign investment [able to] play its proper role in the country's economic development;
   8) to create wide employment opportunities for Ethiopians and to foster the transfer of technical know-how, of managerial skills, and of technology required for the progress of the country.

5. Areas of Investment Reserved for the Government or Joint Investment with the Government

   1) The following investment areas are exclusively reserved for the Government:
      (a) Transmission and supply of electrical energy through the Integrated National Grid System and
      (b) Postal services with the exception of courier services.
   2) Investors shall be allowed to invest in the following areas only in joint venture with the Government:
      a) Manufacturing of weapons and ammunition and
      b) Telecommunication services.

6. Areas of Investment Reserved for Domestic Investors

   Areas of investment exclusively reserved for Ethiopian nationals and other domestic investors shall be specified by regulations to be issued by the Council of Ministers.

7. Regarding investments to be undertaken in Joint Venture with the Government

   The Supervising Authority of Public Enterprises shall receive investment proposals submitted by any private investor intending to invest in joint venture with the government; it shall submit same to the Ministry of Trade and Industry for decision and, upon approval, designate a public enterprise to invest as partner in the joint investment.

8. Areas of Investment Open for Foreign Investors

   All areas of investment, other than those exclusively reserved, under this Proclamation, for the Government or joint venture with the Government or for

highlights the importance of Host-State development and investor obligation to adhere to domestic law.[13]

Viewed holistically, the FIPS represent a confluence of economic incentives, investment protection or guarantees, incentives, investor obligations, privileges, rights, and dispute resolution recourse. The public purpose doctrine pervades the FIPS framework – often, as discussed later, in ways that are contradictory even within the anatomy of a single FIPS.

A. THE PUBLIC PURPOSE OF FIPS INVESTOR PROTECTION

FIPS that are committed to investor protection as a fundamental tenet applied to incentivize foreign direct investment (FDI) attempt to legislate against the exercise of regulatory sovereignty. Where such regulatory activity infringes on investor protection obligations implicitly, if not altogether explicitly, such FIPS point to a different and higher form of public purpose, one that accounts for the aligned interests of both Home and Host States. The Socialist Republic

> Ethiopian nationals or other domestic investors, which shall be specified by regulations to be issued by the Council of Ministers, shall be open for foreign investors.
>
> 9. Investment Incentives
>   1) Areas of investment specified by regulations to be issued by the Council of Ministers pursuant to the investment objectives stated under Article 4 of this Proclamation shall be eligible for investment incentives.
>   2) The regulations to be issued pursuant to Sub Article (1) of this Article shall determine the type and extent of entitlement to incentives.

Ethiopia Investment Proclamation No. 280/2002, *supra* note 7, Part Two.

[13] The very first article (art. 1) of the Law of the People's Republic of China on Foreign-Capital Enterprises ("Order of the President of the People's Republic of China No. 41") is instructive concerning this point. Quite notably, the article fundamentally speaks to Host-State development and the national economy:

> With a view to expanding economic cooperation and technological exchange with foreign countries and promoting the development of China's national economy, the People's Republic of China permits foreign enterprises, other foreign economic organizations and individuals (hereinafter collectively referred to as "foreign investors") to set up enterprises with foreign capital in China and protects the lawful rights and interests of such enterprises.

China Foreign-capital Enterprise Law, *supra* note 5, art. 1. Most of the 24 articles comprising the People's Republic of China's FIPS are bereft of economic or protection incentives regarding foreign investments. The China FIPS mostly sets forth the foreign investment application format and the obligation of investors to abide by the laws and regulations of the People's Republic of China.

For completeness sake, it should be observed that the sum total of foreign investment protection strictures within the China FIPS is contained in a single sentence in Article 4 providing that: "[t]he investments of a foreign investor in China, the profits it earns and its other lawful rights and interests are protect by Chinese law." *Id.* Art 4. This general and scant recitation cannot be construed as aspiring to incentivize foreign investors, without more.

of Vietnam's FIPS, by way of example, provide that "lawful assets and invested capital of investors shall not be nationalized or confiscated by administrative measures."[14] This succinct and unqualified statement is presented as a self-standing proposition. It is tempered only by a subsequent paragraph that itself merits analysis because of its own limitations in restricting the blanket protection against nationalization or confiscation pursuant to legacy regulatory sovereignty. Absolute foreign investor protection against nationalization or confiscation is *only* subordinated to national defense and security:

> 2. In case *of real necessity for purpose of national defense and security* and *in the national interest*, if the State acquires compulsorily or requisitions an asset of an investor, such investor shall be compensated or paid damages at the market price *at the time of announcement* of such compulsory acquisition or requisition.[15]

In addition to limiting any exception to absolute protection accorded to investors from regulatory sovereignty to concerns pertaining to "national defen[s]e and security," the need identified must be a "real necessity." Moreover, the use of the conjunctive "and" stresses that a genuine national defense or security need must be present, thus materially narrowing application of the exception. Use of the "market price" compensation standard, as opposed to the common "adequate" or "fair" metric, comports with a protection regime that purports to grant to foreign investors virtually absolute protection. Linking *market prices* to "the time of announcement of such compulsory acquisition or requisition" conduct provides an additional layer of investor protection at the compensation phase because most non-FIPS (i.e., BITs or regional trade agreements) favor Host States by measuring damages as of the date of the actual taking and not the earlier time frame fixed by public notice of a prospective confiscation.[16]

[14] Vietnam Law on Investment, *supra* note 5, art. 6 ¶ 1.

[15] *Id*. art. 6 ¶ 2 (emphasis added).

[16] For example, Article 1110 of the NAFTA ("Expropriation & Compensation") provides, in relevant part:

> 2. Compensation shall be equivalent to the fair market value of the expropriated investment immediately before the expropriation took place ("date of expropriation"), and shall not reflect any change in value occurring because the intended expropriation had become known earlier. Valuation criteria shall include going concern value, asset value including declared tax value of tangible property, and other criteria, as appropriate, to determine fair market value.
> 3. Compensation shall be paid without delay and be fully realizable.

North American Free Trade Agreement art. 1110 ¶¶ 2–3, US-Can-Mex., December 17, 1992, 32 I.L.M.639 (1993).

Egypt's FIPS is similarly categorical in its commitment to foreign investor protection.[17] The provisions under part two of the Egyptian FIPS entitled "Investment Guarantees" specifically address four areas where the exercise of regulatory sovereignty premised on public purpose historically has raised risks for FDI: (i) nationalization or confiscation, (ii) encumbrance of assets, (iii) administrative intervention in pricing and profits, and (iv) regulatory authority governing licensing and land use. The first of these safeguards on its face provides an absolute commitment to protect foreign investment from nationalization or confiscation. In a crisp and concise sentence, the FIPS provides that "[c]ompanies and establishments may not be nationalized or confiscated."[18] Unlike the Vietnam FIPS, nowhere does the Egyptian FIPS qualify this statement, even with respect to national defense and security or national interest. The investor protection obligation is without exception and, in this sense, absolute. The absence of an indirect nationalization or expropriation, or actions tantamount to nationalizations or expropriations in the context of this FIPS, is not at all disconcerting because the omission is mitigated by subsequent articles in Part 2.

Investor protection against risks attendant to asset encumbrance also is forcefully presented. The single-sentence article states that "[c]ompanies and establishments may neither be sequestered nor may their assets be subject to administrative attachment, seized, restrained, frozen, or expropriated."[19] Article 9 contains the first reference to the term "administrative" in any form. Although its presence opens the door to the possibility of lawful *judicial* attachment, seizure, restraining orders, freezes on assets, or expropriations, it is the exercise of regulatory sovereignty through administrative agencies that historically has challenged foreign investment protection. Also, the absence of any qualifying language in this context is investor and Home-State friendly. Even though the term "assets" is not defined in the FIPS, the use of this generic term would suggest that tangible and intangible property is covered.[20]

[17] *See* Egypt Investment Law No. 8, *supra* note 6.

[18] *Id.* at art. 8.

[19] *Id.* at art. 9.

[20] Most FIPS contain a section defining terms deemed material. In this regard, the Egyptian FIPS is an exception. For example, Article 3 of the Law of Georgia on the Investment Activity Promotion & Guarantees defines "assets" as:

a) any contribution to the capital of an object established with the foreign investments;
b) any profit and dividend as well as the assets remaining after the whole or partial sale of the foreign investment;
c) levies associated with contractual (including debt) liabilities;
d) the right to use property tax to be preliminarily fixed as the income interest gained by using other person's property, including natural resources, copyright, patents (royalty) as well as payment of administrative and other charges.

The limitations on administrative authority with respect to intervening in prices and profits also is unqualified. The investment guarantees on this issue state that "[n]o administrative authority may intervene in pricing the products of companies and establishments knowingly determining their profits."[21] The provision of subsidies to domestic companies in competition with foreign investors in a particular sector has spawned considerable treaty-based arbitral disputes.[22] Indirect takings, actions tantamount to a taking, or administrative equivalent to a taking often present themselves in the form of competitive advantages that a Host State provides to key domestic players who in turn underprice foreign competitors. Frequently, such administrative gyrations are implemented post-entry and after foreign investor know-how has been acquired by key Host-State technocrats. Accordingly, a provision of this ilk may in fact serve as a material incentive to foreign investors.

The fourth pillar of the Egyptian investment guarantees goes far in allaying investor fears of an indirect taking or of exercise of regulatory sovereignty *tantamount* or *equivalent to* a taking pertaining to licensing and environmental concerns. This provision reserves termination or cancellation of a license to the prime minister and only upon referral by a competent administrative authority:

> No Administrative Authority may cancel or suspend, in whole or in part a license for usufruct of real estate, which the company or establishment is licensed to utilize, except in case of breach of the conditions of the license.
>
> A decree terminating or canceling a license shall be issued by the Prime Minister upon a proposal of the Administrative Authority. The involved party may challenge such decree before the Administrative Courts within thirty (30) days from the date of notification or acknowledgment thereof.[23]

Relegating licensing and environmental matters that touch or concern foreign investors to the prime minister with recourse to challenge such a decree to administrative courts underscores the severity of Host-State commitment to legal obligations favoring foreign investors. This unique and somewhat extraordinary provision may well serve as a paradigm for tempering

Georgia Law on Investment, *supra* note 4, art. 3. *See also* Russian Law on Foreign Investment, *supra* note 4, art. 2 ("Basic Terminology Used in This Federal Law"); Albania Law No. 7764, *supra* note 4, art. 1 ("General Provisions"); Lao PDR Law on Investment Promotion, *supra* note 5, art. 3; Vietnam Law on Investment, *supra* note 5, art. 3; Ethiopia Investment Proclamation No. 280/2002, *supra* note 7, art. 2 ("Definitions"); Guatemala Foreign Investment Law, *supra* note 8, art. 1; 1998 E.U.-U.S. Understanding, supra note 991, ¶ d ("Definitions").

21 Egypt Investment Law No. 8, *supra* note 6, art. 10.

22 *See, e.g.*, United Parcel Service of America Inc. v. Government of Canada, UNCITRAL, Award on the Merits, May 24, 2007, http://italaw.com/sites/default/files/case-documents/ita0885.pdf.

23 Egypt Investment Law No. 8, *supra* note 6, art. 11.

regulatory sovereignty in favor of Host States on an unqualified basis founded on application of the legacy public purpose doctrine.

Unlike the Vietnamese and the Egyptian FIPS, the FIPS enacted by the Lao People's Democratic Republic is representative of a weaker but more conventional protection standard that bears a closer resemblance to the takings regimes contained in most BITs.[24] The Laos statute's provisions on investment protection read:

> The Government fully acknowledges and protects the investment of investors against seizure, confiscation or nationalization by administration processes.
>
> In the case that the Government has the need for *public interests;* the investors shall be compensated with an actual value based on market price *at the time of transferring money* and the payment method is agreed by both parties.
>
> The Government acknowledges and protects the intellectual property of registered investors in accordance with the Law on Intellectual Property in the Lao PDR or international treaties to which Lao PDR is a contracting Party.[25]

The Lao foreign investment protection strictures contained in its FIPS are not indicative of a protection standard greater than that which is contained in most FIPS, and, arguably, perhaps even less so.[26] Despite mention of "an actual value based on market price"[27] that at first review appears to favor

[24] *Compare* Lao PDR Law on Investment Promotion, *supra* note 5, art. 61 ("Forms of Investment Protection") *with* Agreement between Japan and the Laos People's Democratic Republic for the Liberalisation, Promotion and Protection of Investment art. 11 ("Expropriation and Compensation"), Jap.-Laos, January 16, 2008, http://investmentpolicyhub.unctad.org/Download/TreatyFile/1729. The Japan-Lao PDR BIT tracks the traditional customary international law requirements for an expropriation:

> 1. Neither Contracting Party shall expropriate or nationalise investments in its Area of investors of the other Contracting Party or take any measure equivalent to expropriation or nationalisation (hereinafter referred to as "expropriation") except: *(a) for a public purpose; (b) in a non-discriminatory manner; (c) upon payment of prompt, adequate and effective compensation pursuant to paragraphs 2, 3 and 4; and (d) in accordance with due process of law and Article 5.*

Id. art. 11 (emphasis added); *see also* U.S. Const. amend. V ("[N]or shall private property be taken for public use, without just compensation").

[25] Lao PDR Law on Investment Promotion, *supra* note 5, art. 61 & art. 62 (emphasis added).

[26] The great majority of BITs proscribe expropriations or nationalizations direct or indirect, or acts tantamount to a direct or indirect nationalization or expropriation except for instances where the confiscation takes place (i) in accordance with due process, (ii) in a nondiscriminatory manner, (iii) in furtherance of a public purpose, and (iv) where compensation issued. Three of these four predicates for a legal taking are missing from the Lao PDR Article 61 investment protection rubric.

[27] *Id.*

foreign investment protection, the vesting period for calculating compensatory damages is placed at "the time of transferring money." The late damage calculation trigger point militates in favor of Host-State interests. Here, too, recourse to a legacy public purpose normative foundation for the exercise and legal justification of the exercise of regulatory sovereignty to the detriment of purportedly binding investor protection obligations introduces the panoply of concerns endemic to application of a subjective nonproportionality-based doctrine devoid of substantive content and commensurable standard.

The Kuwait FIPS is structured so as to proscribe in a succinct and compelling statement confiscation or nationalization of licenses provided to foreign investors.[28] The stricture plainly reads that: "[f]oreign enterprises licensed under the provision of this law may not be confiscated or nationalized."[29]

Despite the seemingly unqualified nature of the pronouncement, the ostensibly absolute protection tenet is actually subject to a legacy public purpose limitation. The second paragraph wrests away what the first paragraph granted:

> Expropriation may only be made for public interest in accordance with the laws applicable and against a compensation equivalent to the enterprise's *real economic value at the time of the expropriation*. Such value shall be assessed according to the economic situation prior to any threat of expropriation. Further the due compensation shall be paid without delay.[30]

Notwithstanding the vulnerabilities presented by an orthodox public purpose analysis in supplying a normative foundation for an expropriation, prospective victimized investors are accorded the most liberal and rewarding compensation calculus because the timeframe for computing compensatory damages commences "prior to any threat of expropriation."[31] As with the Vietnamese FIPS, this trigger date for computing compensation is more favorable to investors than the rubric contained in most BITs.[32]

[28] *See* Kuwait Direct Foreign Capital Investment Law, *supra* note 6, art. 8 ("Secured Guarantees for Foreign Investments").

[29] *Id.*

[30] *Id.* (emphasis added).

[31] *Id.*

[32] The Japan-Peru BIT is representative of the traditional standard for measuring the date at which compensation for an expropriation attaches:

> The compensation shall be equivalent to the fair market value of the expropriated investments *at the time when the expropriation was publicly announced or when the expropriation occurred, whichever is earlier*. The fair market value shall not reflect any change in value occurring because the expropriation had become publicly known earlier.

The Vietnam and Egypt FIPS are representative of a public purpose that overrides the normative command of the doctrine in its legacy form when underlying regulatory sovereignty. It therefore is indicative of a broader public purpose capable of subordinating orthodox regulatory sovereignty in pursuit of a common but national goal to a higher and more encompassing obligation that is specific in nature, narrow as to subject matter, objective in application, and more consonant with an environment of globalization. In addition, overriding exercise of regulatory sovereignty in furtherance of incentivizing FDI has the additional benefit of advancing the best interests of the very principles that regulatory sovereignty aspires to promote through the obligation of the legacy public purpose doctrine. The existence of a legal structure in place in Host States to protect and support foreign investors is most helpful to the extent to which the international community may extrapolate general principles of international law from FIPS, particularly those principles that may contribute to enriching the public purpose doctrine.

Mere enactment of FIPS, even where properly drafted and as part of coordinated uniform effort on the part of the international community, however, would only represent a very embryonic and partial solution. The U.S. Department of State has identified three shortcomings that would vitiate the effects of even model legislation. At the outset, FIPS may be enacted but are not always enforced in practice.[33] Corruption also plays a materially negative role in the application of investor protection obligations.[34] Moreover, in the case of former Soviet bloc countries, confiscations effectuated during the communist regime have created insurmountable title problems that may redound to the detriment of foreign investor protection.[35]

A fourth limitation on the efficacy of FIPS (discussed in greater detail in the next subsection) are carve-out provisions that limit foreign investor

Agreement between Japan and the Republic of Peru for the Promotion, Protection and Liberalisation of Investment art. 13 ¶ 2, Per.-Jap., November 22, 2008, *available at* http://investmentpolicyhub.unctad.org/Download/TreatyFile/1733.

[33] *See* U.S. Dept. of State: Bureau of Economic & Business Affairs, 2012 *Investment Climate Statement: Russia*, *available at* http://www.State.gov/e/eb/rls/othr/ics/2012/191223.htm (last visited September 3, 2013) ("A legal structure is in place to support foreign investors, although the laws are not always enforced in practice") [hereinafter Russia Investment Climate Statement].

[34] U.S. Dept. of State: Bureau of Economic & Business Affairs, 2012 *Investment Climate Statement: Albania*, *available at* http://www.State.gov/e/eb/rls/othr/ics/2012/191094.htm (last visited September 11, 2014) ("Despite progress in these reforms, major challenges remain with investors citing widespread corruption, weak law enforcement, insufficiently defined property rights, government bureaucracy, lack of developed infrastructure, and frequent changes in the legal framework") [hereinafter Albania Investment Climate Statement].

[35] *See* Russia Investment Climate Statement, *supra* note 33 and Albania Investment Climate Statement, *supra* note 34.

ownership in specifically designated properties and industry sectors. Fifth, in addition to these considerations, as of the date of this writing, the treaty-based arbitration decisional law does not suggest that FIPS have played any meaningful role in the doctrinal or conceptual adjudication of disputes. In this same vein, on the question of investor protection or of the role of public purpose in harmonizing principles of investor protection with the exercise of regulatory sovereignty, FIPS have generated scant, if any, authority.[36] Corruption, carve-outs, nonenforcement, and less than even a perfunctory presence in the decisional law of treaty-based international arbitration may indeed explain the limited role that FIPS have played in the doctrinal development of customary international law as to the relationship between investor protection and regulatory sovereignty, let alone in the development of the public purpose doctrine. Indeed, with respect to nonenforcement, corruption, and carve-outs, the U.S. Department of State's observations on Russia's FIPS are helpful:

> The 1991 Investment Code guarantees that foreign investors will enjoy rights equal to those of Russian investors, although *some industries have limits on foreign ownership* .... The 1999 Law on Foreign Investment [citation omitted; emphasis in original] also affirms this principle of equal treatment. Unfortunately, corruption plays a sizable role in the Judicial System.... Moreover, Russia has sought to enhance consultation mechanisms with international businesses, including through the Foreign Investment Advisory Council, regarding the impact of the country's legislation, regulations, and dispute mechanisms on the business and investment climate. Still, the country's investment dispute mechanisms *remain a work in progress and at present can result in a non-transparent, unpredictable process*.
>
> The 1991 Investment Code prohibits the nationalization of foreign investments, except following legislative action and where deemed to be in the *national interest*. Such nationalizations may be appealed to the courts of the Russian Federation, and the investor must be adequately compensated. At the sub-federal level, *expropriation has occasionally been a problem, as has local government interference and a lack of enforcement of court rulings protecting investors*.[37]

In connection with title encumbrances, the State Department's recent analysis with respect to Albania's FIPS is equally availing:

[36] In fact, as of the date of this writing, it appears that no decisional law regarding FIPS has been generated in the investor-state dispute context.

[37] Russia Investment Climate Statement, *supra* note 33 (emphasis added).

The Albanian Constitution guarantees the right of private property. According to Article 41 of the Albanian Constitution, expropriation or limitation in the exercise of a property right can be done only in the *public interest* and with *fair compensation*. In the post-communist period, expropriation has been limited to land needed for *projects in the public interest*, mainly infrastructure projects, including, but not limited to roads, energy infrastructure, waterworks, airports, etc. *However, compensation has generally been below market value and some owners have complained publicly about the compensation process being slow and unfair.*

There are many ongoing disputes concerning properties confiscated during the communist regime. The restitution compensation process started in 1993 has been slow and marred by corruption. The process still ongoing and many U.S. citizens of Albanian origin have long-running disputes with the government regarding restitution of property.[38]

B. FIPS CARVE-OUTS AND PUBLIC PURPOSE

The anatomy of FIPS is rife with "carve-out" provisions in which public purpose generally serves as an organizing principle and a qualifying doctrine.[39] These provisions suffer from the ills that orthodox public purpose workings generally engraft on rights and limitations, but they are generally helpful because they introduce transparency to the FIPS framework and thus shape and allay Home-State/investor expectations. These carve-outs typically concern (i) investor rights and guarantees,[40] (ii) investor obligations,[41] (iii) industry sectors where foreign investment is proscribed,[42]

[38] Albania Investment Climate Statement, *supra* note 34 (emphasis added).

[39] *See, e.g.*, Albania Law No. 7764, *supra* note 4, art. 4, art. 10; Kazakhstan Law on Investments, *supra* note 4, art. 4 ¶ 3(2); Russian Law on Foreign Investment, *supra* note 4, art. 4 ¶ 2; China Foreign-capital Enterprise Law, *supra* note 5, art. 4, art. 5; Lao PDR Law on Investment Promotion, *supra* note 5, art. 4; Kuwait Direct Foreign Capital Investment Law, *supra* note 6, art. 8; Oman Foreign Capital Investment Law, *supra* note 6, art. 12; Ethiopia Investment Proclamation No. 280/2002, *supra* note 7, art. 21.

[40] *See, e.g.*, Kazakhstan Law on Investments, *supra* note 4, art. 4 ¶ 3(2) ("These guarantees shall not cover amendments introduced to legislative acts of the Republic of Kazakhstan to ensure national and ecological security, public health and morality"); Lao PDR Law on Investment Promotion, *supra* note 5, art. 4 ("The Government promotes the investment in all sectors and business and all areas throughout the country, except areas and business operations which are related to national security; seriously harmful to environment either in short run or long term; negative effects to public health; and the national culture").

[41] *See, e.g.*, China Foreign-capital Enterprise Law, *supra* note 5, art. 4 ("Enterprises with foreign capital shall abide by Chinese laws and regulations and may not engage in any activities detrimental to China's *public interests*"; emphasis added).

[42] For example, Article 14 of the Ghana Investment Promotion Centre Act provides that "[t]he enterprises specified in the Schedule are reserved for citizens and shall not be undertaken by a

and (iv) formulas for the compensation of takings of foreign investments.[43]

In some instances, the cumulative effect of the carve-outs provide prospective investors with some insight into the regulatory sphere of the target Host State.[44] The Georgia FIPS is rich in carve-out provisions, specifically addressing investor rights, duties of investors, qualifications attendant to investment activity, and investment inviolability. Among the more practical investor rights is the guarantee to engage in business and in the conduct of the investment while having the rights and guarantees enjoyed by Georgian citizens. Investors also are granted the right to full bank accounts, secure loans, and purchase stocks. Upon satisfying domestic fiscal obligations, such as taxes, as a matter of right, investors are vested with "unlimited" transfer rights. Along these same lines, investors enjoy the right to export property.[45]

person who is not a citizen." Ghana Investment Promotion Centre Act, *supra* note 7, art. 14. The Schedule to the Act specifies the following:

Enterprises Wholly Reserved for Citizens

1. The sale of anything whatsoever in a market, petty trading, hawking or selling from a kiosk.
2. Operation of taxi service and car hire service. (A non-Ghanaian may undertake this service where there is a minimum fleet of ten new vehicles.)
3. All aspects of pool betting business and lotteries, except football pools.
4. Operation of beauty salons and barber shops.

Id. Schedule [Section 18].

43 *See, e.g.*, Albania Law No. 7764, *supra* note 4, art. 4 ("Foreign investments will not be expropriated or nationalized directly or indirectly, they will not be the subject of any measure equal to these measures, except in special cases, in the *interest of the public use*, defined by law, without any discrimination, with immediate, appropriate and effective compensation, in accordance with legal procedures"; emphasis added).

44 As may be expected, the connection between the quantity of carve-outs, the quality of the carve-outs, and the extent to which both of these first two factors yield transparency is particular to each FIPS.

45 For example, the Law of Georgia on the Investment Activity Promotion and Guarantees, Article 3 ("Rights of Investors"), provides:

1. In conducting the investment and entrepreneurial activity a foreign investor's rights and guarantees shall not be less [than] the rights and guarantees enjoyed by Georgian natural and legal person.
2. An investor shall be entitled to open current and other accounts in any currency with banking institutions located on the territory of Georgia.
3. An investor shall be entitled to take loans in banking and financial institutions located in Georgia or from natural or legal persons.
4. An investor shall be entitled to acquire stocks, bonds, and other securities and property both in Georgia and abroad.
5. A foreign investor shall, upon payment of taxes and necessary levies, have the right to convert the profit (income) gained from investments at the market rate of exchange of Georgian banking institutions and in the right of unlimited repatriation abroad.

The Article prescribing investor rights does not at all place such rights in jeopardy based on potential application of an overriding State interest in the form of the public purpose doctrine. Structurally, the Georgian FIPS artfully expresses the scope and depth of regulatory sovereignty premised on public purpose in a carefully crafted sentence that certainly hides much more than it may ever wish to reveal. Immediately following the narrative of investor rights, investor duties are collapsed into a formally plain twenty-five-word sentence that reads:

> An investor shall be liable to conduct activities in accordance with the effective Georgian legislation *as well as legislation concerning the environment and health protection.*[46]

Close analysis of this seemingly simple provision would suggest that regulation allegedly premised on environmental and health concerns may preempt Host-State foreign investment protection obligations.[47]

In a formal and perhaps even substantive effort to enhance transparency and legitimacy, proscribed investments in specific industry sectors are made subject to approval where presented by the president of Georgia to the parliament.[48] Moreover, special industry sectors regulated by permit or license issued by regulatory agencies are identified with specificity. These industry sectors, ranging from the manufacture and sale of weapons and explosives to the issuance of securities for public circulation, manifestly touch or concern strategic industries that in turn may affect the general population.[49] In

> Such assets may be:
> a) any contribution to the capital of an object established with the foreign investments;
> b) any profit and dividend as well as the assets remaining after the whole or partial sale of the foreign investment;
> c) levies associated with contractual (including debt) liabilities;
> d) the right to use property tax to be preliminarily fixed as the income interest gained by using other person's property, including natural resources, copyrights, patents (royalty) as well as payment of administrative and other charges.
> 6. A foreign investor shall be entitled to export the property being in his possession.
> 7. The right as per paragraph five of this Article may be subject to restriction under law by court's decision in connection with bankruptcy, committing an offense, or non-performance of a civil obligation.

Georgia Law on Investment, *supra* note 4, art. 3.

46 *Id.* art. 4 (emphasis added).

47 Notably, however, the Georgian FIPS does not specifically address the soundness of financial institutions as a public purpose consideration that may override investor protection obligations. The term "health protection" contained in Article 4, however, is sufficiently vague as to encompass perceived risks to the health and soundness of Georgian financial institutions.

48 *Id.* art. 9.

49 Article 9 ("Prohibition and Restriction in the Sphere of Investment Activity") reads:

> 1. A list of branches where the investment realization is prohibited shall be subject to approval of Parliament of Georgia on presentation by President of Georgia.

addition to rational corollaries arising from these strictures, the expectation of legacy public purpose regulatory sovereignty undoubtedly looms large. Although Article 9 in itself certainly represents a meaningful carve-out that serves notice and transparency policies concerning FDI, the provision itself is devoid of reference to legislative enactments or other authority earmarked to protect foreign investment or otherwise fashioned so as to incentivize foreign investors on the grounds of investment guarantee and security.

These shortcomings notwithstanding, it is worth emphasizing that the Georgian FIPS is emblematic of legislation that mitigates the hardships of regulatory sovereignty premised on public purpose to the detriment of Host-State investor protection obligations. Two salient strictures of the FIPS command particular attention because they illustrate the underlying policy favoring investor protection by mitigating the technical application of regulatory sovereignty with respect to issues as material as the conditions precedent to triggering the Host State's investor protection obligations: (i) juridical structure or form of ownership and (ii) citizenship status.

Pursuant to Chapter 1, Article 2., Investment Activity Subject (Investor) and Object, "[a] foreign investor shall be deemed to be ... [a] Georgian citizen permanently residing abroad." This seemingly innocuous provision is illustrative, at minimum, of a political willingness to shed technical jurisdictional defenses that Host States generally raise when challenging treaty-based claims asserted by a foreign citizen alleging to be a "foreign investor." Casting an expansive net that includes a Georgian citizen permanently residing beyond the national territory of Georgia as a "foreign investor" under any analysis represents a broad and liberal manifestation of a policy favoring foreign investors/investments. Even more meaningful is the adoption of a methodology for statutory construction of the actual FIPS that places substance over

2. An investor shall not be entitled without a permit or license issued by an appropriate agency to engage in the following activity:
   a) manufacture and sale of weapons and explosives;
   b) preparation and sale of medicines and substances that are subject to special control;
   c) use of forest resources and entrails;
   d) setting up of casinos and other gambling houses which provide for arranging games and lotteries;
   e) banking activity;
   f) insurance activity;
   g) issue of securities for public circulation;
   h) wireless communication service and TV and radio channels' creation;
   i) other activities defined by the effective Georgian legislation.

Id.

form. This overarching principle is a commendable contribution to the drafting of FIPS.

Along the very same lines as the broad definition of "foreign investor," the Georgian FIPS protects foreign investors against exercise of regulatory sovereignty based on a nearly formal definition of ownership in an investment within the territory of Georgia by adopting an all-inclusive understanding of the term limited only by Articles 9 and 12 of the FIPS.[50] The Georgian FIPS also emphasizes substance over form on the gateway issue of *ownership*:

> Investments on the territory of Georgia may be realized in an object with *any form of ownership* [in] which investment is not prohibited as per paragraph one of Article 9 of this law. Investments in the objects listed in Articles 9 and 12 of this law may be realized only on the basis of an appropriate special permit or license.[51]

The identification of agency-regulated licensing and permitting in the context of foreign investment, coupled with identified restrictions, provide both Home and Host States with a fundamental premise from which both may draw in formulating specific investor protection obligations and expectations. Although the "duties of investors" set forth in Article 4 of the Georgian FIPS are somewhat disappointing, they still represent a meaningful step in the right direction when appropriately contextualized.

Structurally similar to the Georgian FIPS, the Lao FIPS dedicates the entirety of Part V ("Rights and Obligations of Investors") of its FIPS, comprising eight articles, to setting forth affirmative investor rights.[52] Two

[50] As to Article 9, *see supra* note 48–49]and accompanying text. Article 12 ("Acquisition of Property Right to Land and Other Natural Resources") states:

> Acquisition of the Property Right to Land and Other Natural Resources as well as the right to develop natural resources shall be regulated under laws of Georgia 'On Property of Agricultural Land,' On Lease of Agricultural Land,' On the Procedure for Granting Concessions to Foreign Countries and Companies,' On Entails and other legislative acts.

Id. art. 12.

[51] *Id.* art. 2.

[52] Part V of the Lao PDR Law on Investment Promotion vests foreign investors with the fundamental rights necessary to conduct business, providing:

> Article 63 ("Rights of Investors"):
> Investors have the following basic rights:
> 1. Right to invest;
> 2. Rights to govern and manage business operations;
> 3. Rights to hire labor forces;
> 4. Rights to reside in the Lao PDR in case of foreign investors;
> 5. Rights to transfer capitals, assets, and incomes from Lao PDR to abroad in case of foreign investors.
>
> Article 64 ("Right to Invest"):

qualifications, however, are necessary for purposes of contextualizing the narrative of purported rights. First, Part V does not appear or purport to provide investors with rights greater than or different from those accorded to domestic investors. Nowhere in Part V does the carve-out enumerating investor rights contain premises specially tailored to meet concerns particular to foreign investors. Whereas the Lao FIPS does assert that foreign investors shall be treated no differently from domestic investors,[53] in bestowing rights to foreign investors, no right or privilege is extended beyond the qualified guarantee contained in Article 60 ("Protection of Investment"). Second, none of the enumerated investor rights is exempted from exercise of regulatory

Rights to invest are defined as follows:

1. To invest in all business sectors and zones which are not prohibited to invest under the laws of the Lao PDR;
2. To invest according to the types and forms of enterprises in accordance with laws and regulations;
3. To apply for project concession from the Government or local authorities on the case-by-case basis to develop a project;
4. To apply for a concession to establish a Special Economic Zone and Specific Economic Zone from the Government;
5. To establish a representative office or a branch in Lao PDR;
6. To apply for the changing of the investment objectives or activities in the case that the business operations are not effective due to the changes of the Government's policies, regulations and laws;
7. To own assets;
8. To receive protection from the Government in relation to rights and legitimate benefits from the investment;
9. To receive any facilitations provided by the Government to the investment;
10. To receive benefits from the lease or concession such as the right to use and to use this right as a collateral with another person or financial institutions or to allow the joint-venture, to sublease, to sell and to transfer the Land use rights in accordance with the terms of the lease or concession in the contract and other condition according to the laws;
11. A right holder of the land use or concession has the right to use land in accordance to the terms leasing contract or concession agreement; and [to own] property such as buildings or any constructions on that piece of land and to transfer the rights to local people or foreigners;
12. To open a Kip account or foreign currency account with banks located in Lao PDR;
13. To lodge complaints with the relevant authorities in the case of impairment of the investment;
14. To receive other rights and benefits as provided in the laws and regulations.

Lao PDR Law on Investment Promotion, *supra* note 4, arts. 63 and 64. *See also* art. 65 ("Rights to Administrate and Manage Business"); art. 66 ("Rights to Hire Labor Forces"); art. 67 ("Rights to Reside in Case Foreign Investors"); art. 68 ("Rights to Transfer Capitals, Assets and Income from the Lao PDR in Case of Foreign Investors"); and art. 70 ("Obligations to Protect the Environment").

[53] *See Id.*

sovereignty premised on public purpose. Indeed, much like Article 4 ("Duties of Investors") of the Georgian FIPS,[54] Article 70 of the Lao FIPS ("Obligations to Protect the Environment") raises ominous concerns:

> The investors are obliged to protect [the] environment; investors must ensure that their business activities [have no significant negative impacts] to the public, national security, public order or health of employees. In the event of causing any environmental problems, the investors have to undertake necessary measures to address these problems in a timely manner and in accordance with laws.[55]

Even though the "obligations" are worded in the affirmative and fashioned so as to require an affirmative violation on the part of the foreign investor to trigger the causal connections that would give rise to a violation, one cannot help but notice that the provision is replete with references to classical expressions of the legacy public purpose doctrine: (i) "the public [generally]," (ii) "national security," (iii) "public order," and (iv) "health of employees."[56]

In addition to the plain language requiring a causal connection to the investment/investor as a predicate to any liability – likely in the form of regulatory enactments – concerns based on the belief that the provision will be used ostensibly and affirmatively to justify an exercise of regulatory sovereignty to the detriment of investor protection is perhaps somewhat further allayed because, in light of any of the enumerated "problems," the initial burden first appears to be placed on the investor in order to mitigate or cure any damage.[57] Relegating these remedial tasks to foreign investors in the very plain language of the provision, so the argument says, does more than merely reiterate a preexisting obligation to mitigate. This carve-out language is helpful, in large measure, because it constitutes a paradigm for the future drafting of FIPS and BITs so as to harmonize the perceived exigencies of the exercise of regulatory sovereignty with Host-State obligations to protect foreign investments as a matter of both domestic positive law and public international law.

From a public purpose analysis perspective, Part VI ("Prohibited Actions") of the Lao FIPS prescribes three sets of prohibitions: (i) general, (ii) prohibited

[54] *See* Georgia Law on Investment, *supra* note 4, art. 4 ("An investor shall be liable to conduct activities in accordance with the effective Georgian legislation as well as legislation concerning the environment and health protection").

[55] Lao PDR Law on Investment Promotion, *supra* note 4, art. 70 [syntax and diction mistakes in original].

[56] *Id.*

[57] The plain meaning of the final subordinate clause of the provision is helpful in this sense: "the investors have to undertake necessary measures to address these problems in a timely manner and in accordance with laws." *Id.*

actions for government officials, and (iii) prohibited actions for investors.[58] Quite notably, the carve-outs for proscribed activity and actions studiously omit government reference. Indeed, two of the three provisions (Articles 71 and 73) are directed to investors, even though Article 71 does so by omitting reference to "government officials" or to the government. Instead, the prefacing sentence explicitly targets "[i]ndividuals" and "organizations." Article 72 is directed at "government officials," but it omits any reference to the actual government, State, geopolitical subdivisions, State agencies, or State instrumentalities. The Part VI "Prohibited Actions" simply do not qualify the Host State's regulatory fiat, although it indeed emphasizes potential investor liability when investor actions are deemed to fall within the ambit of "prohibited acts as described in the laws and regulations."[59] Certainly, it may be argued that these carve-outs, which do not bestow any exemptions from regulatory decrees to investors and that do not qualify at all the exercise of regulatory sovereignty, serve as clear warnings to prospective investors and, to this extent, foster transparency. The prohibited actions, more realistically, serve to buttress application of public purpose as set forth within Article 70 of the FIPS. Also, the prohibited action carve-outs would support a construction of Article 60 ("Protection of Investment") as not granting foreign investors any additional

[58] Part VI ("Prohibited Actions") of the Lao PDR Law on Investment Promotion provides, in relevant part:

> **Article 71: General prohibition**
> Individuals and organizations are prohibited to perform the following actions:
> 1. Authorize to conduct the prohibited or illegal business operations;
> 2. Take any forms of impediments to the investment promotion in Lao PDR;
> 3. Perform other prohibited acts as described in the laws and regulations.
>
> **Article 72: Prohibited actions for the government officials**
> Government officials are prohibited to perform the following actions:
> 1. Abuse the power, duties and position for the purpose of acquiring personal benefits;
> 2. Receive bribes from investors or persons who will receive the prospective benefits from investment;
> 3. Disclose confidential documents of the nation, Government and investors;
> 4. Create an unreasonable delay for the consideration of documents or retain investors' documents;
> 5. Perform other prohibited actions as described in the laws and regulations.
>
> **Article 73: Prohibited actions for investors**
> Investors are prohibited to perform the following actions:
> 1. Give bribes to officers and government officials who have responsibilities for concerned tasks;
> 2. Fail to fulfill obligations, conceal income and profit including duty and tax figures;
> 3. Slander or discredit organizations and government officials;
> 4. Perform other prohibited actions as described in the laws and regulations.

Lao PDR Law on Investment Promotion, *supra* note 4, arts. 71–73.

[59] *Id.* art. 71 ¶ 3.

protection beyond that already contained in international treaties to which Lao PDR is a signatory. This issue, however, remains wholly inconclusive.

C. DISPUTE RESOLUTION CLAUSES IN FIPS AND PUBLIC PURPOSE

The lack of centralization and coordinated administration in the enactment of FIPS globally has led to a material lack of uniformity in the dispute resolution clauses that form part of FIPS. Lack of uniformity is present both inter- and intranationally. Even among signatories to the Convention on the Settlement of Investment Disputes between States and Nationals of Other States (ICSID Convention), we find that the dispute resolution clauses contained in the FIPS of signatory countries vary considerably.[60] Additionally, material omissions or discrepancies also abound when analyzing the connection between specific country BITs and FIPS. Specifically, although a specific State may have signed a BIT that is expansive and rich (i) in investor protection obligations and (ii) containing an elaborate dispute resolution clause providing for domestic judicial and international arbitral recourse pursuant to specific predicate jurisdictional requirements, that same State's corresponding FIPS may be devoid of a dispute resolution provision that at all mirrors the analogous provision in a BIT to which it is a signatory.[61] These contradictions

[60] Compare Albania Law No. 7764, *supra* note 4, art. 8 with Russian Law on Foreign Investment, *supra* note 4, art. 10. These clauses, as well as the dispute resolution clauses of the other FIPS analyzed, are reproduced in Appendix III, which provides a means for comparing FIPS and BITs both intra- and internationally.

[61] Although this phenomenon is exposed more fully *infra* at Appendix III, an extreme example of this disparity may be presented by the State of Kuwait. In the Kuwaiti FIPS, the dispute resolution clause provides:

> Article 16. The Kuwaiti Courts alone shall be competent to consider whatever disputes arising between foreign investment enterprises and third parties. However, the parties may agree to refer such dispute to arbitration.

Kuwait Direct Foreign Capital Investment Law, *supra* note 6, art. 16. In stark contrast, the Lithuania-Kuwait BIT provides, in relevant part:

> Article 9. Settlement of Disputes between a Contracting State and an Investor
> (1) Disputes between a Contracting State and an investor of the other Contracting State relating to an investment of the latter in the territory of the former shall, if possible, be settled amicably.
> (2) If such disputes cannot be settled according to the provisions of paragraph (1) within a period of three months from the date at which either party to the dispute requested amicable settlement, the dispute shall, subject to paragraph (3) below, at the written request of the investor concerned be submitted to international arbitration in accordance with paragraph (4).

contribute to process legitimacy concerns in the areas of regulatory sovereignty and investor protection.

These ad hoc "corelationships" notwithstanding, a meaningful discernible pattern emerges between the public purpose-based investor protection obligations contained in FIPS and the efficacy of the corresponding dispute resolution clause set forth in a particular FIPS. The extent of investor protection obligation enunciated is directly proportional to the efficacy of the dispute resolution clause contained in thatsame FIPS, where efficacy is defined as the ability of an investor to prosecute a claim against the Host State (State enacting the FIPS) in the form of an international arbitration based on a bilateral or multilateral investment treaty.[62]

(3) An investor may choose to submit the dispute for resolution:
(a) before the courts or administrative tribunals of the Contracting State that is a party to the dispute; or
(b) in accordance with any applicable, previously agreed dispute-settlement procedures; or
(c) in accordance with paragraph (4), provided that the investor has consented in writing to the settlement by arbitration in accordance with the appropriate rules, thereunder.

(4) Unless within the periods of 3 months provided in paragraph (2) above, the parties to the dispute have agreed to an alternative dispute settlement procedure, the dispute may, at the election in writing of the investor concerned, be submitted for settlement by arbitration to:
(a) The International Centre for Settlement of Investment Disputes ("the Centre"), established pursuant to the Convention on the Settlement of Investment Disputes between States and Nationals of Other States, opened for signature at Washington 18 March 1965 ("the Washington Convention"), provided that the Washington Convention is applicable to the dispute; or
(b) an arbitral tribunal established under the Arbitration Rules of the United Nations Commission on International Trade Law (UNCITRAL), as those Rules may be modified by the parties to the dispute (the Appointing Authority referred to in Article 7 of the Rules shall be the Secretary General of the Centre); or
(c) an arbitral tribunal constituted pursuant to the arbitration rules of any arbitral institution mutually agreed between the parties to the dispute.

(5) Each Contracting State hereby gives its unconditional consent to the submission of an investment dispute for settlement by binding arbitration in accordance with the provisions of this Article.

(6) (a) The consent given in paragraph (5), together with the consent given under paragraph (3), shall satisfy the requirement for written agreement of the parties to a dispute for purposes of each of Chapter II of the Washington Convention, Article II of the United Nations Convention on the Recognition and Enforcement of Foreign Arbitral Awards, done at New York, June 10, 1958 ("New York Convention"), and Article I of the UNCITRAL Arbitration Rules.

Agreement between the Republic of Lithuania and the State of Kuwait for the Encouragement and Reciprocal Protection of Investments, art. 9, January 15, 2003, Lit.-Kuw., http://investmentpolicyhub.unctad.org/Download/TreatyFile/1849

[62] Efficacy here is not understood as efficiency, but rather as the ability to air disputes in a neutral international fora pursuant to a nonjudicial dispute resolution arbitral proceeding through

States that enshrine investor-protection obligations based on an understanding of public purpose that preempts the legacy doctrine extend this construction of the doctrine to the FIPS dispute resolution clause. Thus, they provide investors with a final layer of protection in the form of a nonparochial and neutral international fora where public international law applies in conjunction with FIPS protection obligations. As earlier noted, the Georgian FIPS stands out as particularly exemplary.[63] Article 7 of that FIPS views the public purpose of foreign investment protection as generally preempting the exercise of regulatory sovereignty based on the public purpose doctrine in furtherance of national objectives but for quite few and specially qualified circumstances requiring a showing of "urgent necessity established by organic law" and "only" when accompanied by "appropriate compensation."[64]

It is critical to note that "appropriate compensation" within the meaning of the Georgian FIPS represents "actual value" and *not* prompt, adequate, and effective compensation; fair compensation; or "just compensation."[65] Consonant with this commitment to foreign investor protection at the "expense" of regulatory sovereignty, the Georgian dispute resolution clause is compellingly fair and therefore in keeping with an investor protection rubric in which public purpose is not a priori subordinated to the exercise of regulatory sovereignty to the detriment of foreign investments/investors. The dispute resolution clause eviscerates parochial adjudication methodologies and renders viable treaty-based arbitral proceedings. It merits reading and re-reading.

1. A dispute between a foreign investor and an enterprise registered in Georgia shall be subject to resolution under the agreement of the parties or in courts of Georgia.
2. A dispute between a foreign investor and a State agency shall, unless the procedure for its resolution is not defined by way of their agreement, be subject to resolution in courts of Georgia or in the International Center for the Resolution Investment Disputes. Unless the dispute is considered in the International Center for the Resolution of Investment Disputes, a foreign investor shall be entitled to apply to *any* international arbitration body which has been set up by the Commission of the

which the claimant's causes of actions may be based upon violations of treaty-based investor protection obligations, as well as additional claims contained in the relevant FIPS.

63 *See supra* notes 45–46 and accompanying text.

64 Georgia Law on Investment, *supra* note 4, art. 7.

65 *See supra* Chapter 2 notes 156–59 and accompanying text for discussion on the distinction between actual value and prompt, adequate, and effective compensation, or "just compensation."

United Nations for International Trade Law (UNCITRAL) to resolve the dispute in accordance with the rules established under the arbitration and international agreement.

3. Any award of the international arbitration bodies as indicated in paragraph 2 of this Article shall be final and not subject to appeal. Its observance shall be secured by the State.[66]

The courts of Georgia are referred to in Paragraph 1 of Article 16 in the disjunctive and only after emphasizing resolution by agreement of the parties. Moreover, the clause mentions both ICSID and United Nations Commission on International Trade Law (UNCITRAL) investor-State arbitration as a mandatory ("shall") dispute resolution methodology subject only to an agreement by the parties concerning contentions arising from investments. Finally, the commitment to recognize the finality of an international arbitral award arising from Paragraph 2 of the clause and to reduce to writing the State's commitment to observing such an award represents an intent to adhere to ICSID or UNCITRAL arbitral awards that is rarely found even in dispute resolution clauses contained in BITs or anywhere else.

A similar directly proportional relationship between the investor protection obligations contained in a FIPS and the terms embodied in its dispute resolution clause is present in the Vietnamese FIPS. As is the case with the Georgian FIPS, the Vietnamese FIPS does not subordinate the public purpose of investor protection to the exercise of regulatory sovereignty in pursuit of domestic objectives.[67] Although less rich and not as aptly drafted as its Georgian counterpart, the Vietnamese FIPS dispute resolution provision protects investors against the asymmetries of Host-State adjudication of investment-driven contentions. Even though the provision also is replete with references to Vietnamese tribunals (both courts and arbitration bodies), it still provides prospective claimants with access to the benefits of an international treaty-based arbitration premised on application of public international law and of the FIPS's investor protection standards:

Article 12 Dispute resolution

1. Any dispute relating to investment activities in Vietnam shall be resolved through negotiation and conciliation, or shall be referred to arbitration or to a court in accordance with law.
2. Any dispute as between domestic investors or as between a domestic investor and a State administrative body of Vietnam relating to

[66] *See* Georgia Law on Investment, *supra* note 4, art. 16 ("Procedure for Dispute Resolution") (emphasis added).

[67] *See supra* notes 14–15 and accompanying text.

investment activities in the territory of Vietnam shall be resolved at a Vietnamese court or arbitration body.

3. Any dispute to which one disputing party is *a foreign investor or an enterprise with foreign owned capital*, or any dispute as between foreign investors shall be resolved by one of the following tribunals and organizations:
   (a) A Vietnamese court;
   (b) A Vietnamese arbitration body;
   (c) A foreign arbitration body;
   (d) An *international arbitration body*;
   (dd) An arbitration tribunal established in accordance with the agreement of the disputing parties.
4. Any dispute between a *foreign investor* and State administrative body of Vietnam relating to investment activities in the territory of Vietnam shall be resolved by a Vietnamese court or arbitration body, *unless otherwise provided in a contract signed between a representative of a competent State body of Vietnam with the foreign investor or in an international treaty of which the Socialist Republic of Vietnam is a member.*[68]

In keeping with the very meaningful and investor-oriented protection strictures of the Vietnam FIPS, the dispute resolution provision of the FIPS itself constitutes a recognizable investor-protection-based incentive. Access to the delocalized international arbitral fora, whether contract- or treaty-based, is accorded to claimants in any dispute in which a party is a foreign investor.

Perhaps the direct proportionality between investor protection obligations in FIPS and the efficacy of the dispute resolution provision contained in those very FIPS is best exemplified by the Investment Law of the People's Republic of China on Foreign-Capital Enterprises.[69]

Quite remarkably, that legislation provides virtually no foreign investment protection and heavily relies on a legacy public purpose framework. It merely asserts that "[t]he State does not nationalize or requisition any enterprise with foreign capital."[70] It immediately adds "[h]owever, [that] under special circumstances when *public interests* require, enterprises with foreign capital may be requisitioned through legal procedures and appropriate compensation shall be made."[71]

[68] Vietnam Law on Investment, *supra* note 5 art. 12 ("Dispute Resolution"; emphasis added).
[69] China Foreign-capital Enterprise Law, *supra* note 5.
[70] *Id.* Art 5.
[71] *Id.* (emphasis added).

Accordingly, application of the nomenclature "FIPS" to this legislation is arguably a misnomer. The China FIPS provides for less investor protection than any of the recent BITs to which China is a signatory.[72]

The term "dispute resolution" does not at all appear in the China FIPS. Likewise, the legislation is bereft of any reference to the term "arbitration," let alone "international arbitration." The paucity of any mention of foreign investment protection standards or strictures is met only by the outright omission of a dispute resolution provision. The substantive connection between investor protection obligations and standards, and dispute resolution provisions in FIPS can be readily established empirically.

D. THE TEACHINGS OF FIPS PUBLIC PURPOSE ANALYSIS AND THE USE OF FIPS AS REMEDIAL DOCTRINAL INSTRUMENTS

As a general principle, FIPS have not materially contributed to efforts aimed at defining with greater precision principles of customary international law. The history of contemporary customary international law – the international law of the past fifty years – does not abound in examples of instances where domestic statutes addressing issues of public purpose international law have had the effect (de jure or de facto) of having a causal influence on the development of an existing principle of customary international law so as to render such principle substantively meaningful in light of historical developments. FIPS are uniquely positioned to make such a contribution possible with respect to the legacy public purpose doctrine. From a practical perspective, the use of FIPS is by itself insufficient to rehabilitate so critical a doctrine that has been prolifically applied in multiple areas of customary and conventional

[72] *See, e.g.*, Agreement between the Government of Canada and the Government of the People's Republic of China for the Promotion and Reciprocal Protection of Investments, Can.-China, September 9, 2012, http://investmentpolicyhub.unctad.org/Download/TreatyFile/600 (referencing the Full Protection & Security, Fair & Equitable Treatment, National Treatment, Most-Favoured-Nation, and International Minimum Standards, and providing protection against Expropriation and Nationalization); Bilateral Agreement for the Promotion and Protection of Investments between the Government of the Republic of Colombia and the Government of the Republic of China, Colom.-Chi, November 22, 2008, http://investmentpolicyhub.unctad.org/Download/TreatyFile/720 (same); Agreement between the Government of New Zealand and the Government of the People's Republic of China on the Promotion and Protection of Investments, NZ-Chi., November 22, 1988, http://investmentpolicyhub.unctad.org/Download/TreatyFile/764 (referencing the Fair & Equitable Treatment and Most-Favoured-Nation Standards and providing protection against Expropriation and Nationalization); Agreement between the Government of the People's Republic of China and the Government of the Republic of Singapore on the Promotion and Protection of Investments, Chi.-Sing., November 21, 1985, http://investmentpolicyhub.unctad.org/Download/TreatyFile/776 (same).

international law ranging from human rights and investor protection to the exploitation of strategic natural resources and questions pertaining to national and regional sustainable economic development. The FIPS analysis of the public purpose doctrine, however, suggests that, in the realm of investor protection, there are six separate and distinct related areas in which FIPS may play a very significant role in helping to vest the doctrine with substantive attributes that may best help its application in an environment of economic globalization.

First, the most material contribution that FIPS may generate is fashioning investor protection standards based on a public purpose analysis that preempts the exercise of regulatory sovereignty in furtherance of national interests on a legacy understanding of the doctrine. As discussed,[73] a number of FIPS already have applied the public purpose doctrine in favor of investor protection so as to preempt exercise of regulatory sovereignty based on the doctrine to the detriment of foreign investors. This contribution is extraordinary, but it must be recognized as such and appropriately contextualized. These FIPS demonstrate the existence of a conceptual and doctrinal foundation for applying the public purpose doctrine in ways that preempt the exercise of regulatory sovereignty to the harm of foreign investors, as well as a political will to understand the public purpose doctrine as a normative rubric that may be exercised beyond the legacy framework in support of regulatory sovereignty and national interests. This existing "first step" is paramount in transcending the legacy public purpose doctrinal construct and at arriving at a substantive, objective, proportionality-driven, and bilateral conception of this principle. Much work remains.

A second contribution of FIPS, one that highlights the preeminence of a public purpose doctrine embodied in a domestic legislative enactment but used in furtherance of foreign investor protection so as to further the broader interests of an international community, concerns the issue of *intent*. The issue of signatory intent as to the meaning of public purpose in BITs, for example, in some sense is addressed or can be addressed through FIPS. Host States whose very legislative rubric creates a public purpose hierarchy in support of investor protection should be estopped and altogether proscribed from asserting in the context of investor-state arbitrations a public purpose-based right to invade the realm of investor protection in the name of regulatory sovereignty. As previously noted,[74] to date, the use of FIPS as foundational evidentiary proof of intent has been omitted from the analysis contained in

[73] *See supra* Chapter 6.B "FIPS Carve-Outs and Public Purpose."

[74] *See supra* note 36 and accompanying text.

arbitral awards. There is no justification for having such compelling evidence lie fallow. Moreover, as a matter of fundamental fairness, Host States should not be able to engage in a systematic "bait and switch" policy with respect to investor protection.

The practice is ethically and doctrinally unsound. It makes little sense for States to seek to entice foreign investors to invest in their economy by holding out a statutory framework that provides for material investor protection obligations, only then to have the same Host State assert that an expropriation or nationalization is justified based on public purpose, without at all being bound by the very plain language of its own FIPS. Structural integrity in holding States to one consistent position concerning investor protection in turn shall contribute to the systemic legitimacy of investor-state arbitration and to the promotion of FDI.

A third potential contribution that FIPS may offer to the role of the public purpose doctrine is to serve as an instrument that harmonizes the scope and content of BITs and domestic sustainable development. As demonstrated in Appendix III,[75] regrettably, in most instances, the FIPS pertaining to signatory countries of BITs contain investor-protection obligations that materially differ from those contained in BITs. Certainly, some part of this dissonance may be attributable to the differences between negotiations between representatives of two different countries (typically with Home- and Host-State interests) and the negotiation dynamic attendant to the enactment of domestic legislation that fundamentally seeks to incentivize foreign investors. Aside from the potential disparities between these two negotiating processes, an important reason explaining this lack of coherence, as well as the frequently attendant internal contradictions,[76] is that little or no weight is generally accorded to FIPS. Prospective Host States should be made accountable for ensuring that where FIPS proscribe exercise of regulatory sovereignty to the detriment of foreign investment protection, BITs to which such countries are signatories also should reflect this level of commitment to foreign investment protection obligations. States also should be encouraged to use FIPS as a paradigm for the crafting of public purpose BIT language that does not provide for the use of the public purpose doctrine to support investor protection policies and objectives in situations where regulatory sovereignty challenges such aspirations.

Fourth, FIPS constitute evidence of State practice consonant with Article 38 of the Statute of the International Court of Justice.[77] Thus, there already exists a

75 *See infra* Appendix III.

76 The comparisons within Appendix III amply demonstrate this contradiction.

77 *See supra* Chapter 2 note 1 and accompanying text for discussion on Article 38 of the ICJ and what constitutes evidence of State practice.

conceptual foundation for the development of a customary international law pursuant to which the public purpose doctrine would not be relegated to serving exclusively the interests of domestic regulatory sovereignty to the detriment of foreign investor protection. To the contrary, FIPS may serve as a foundation for the development of a customary international law that renders public purpose as a doctrine relevant to the exigencies of an economically globalized environment and to a world now configured by post-Westphalian sovereignty. This crevice may lead to a greater aperture for the fashioning of a public purpose doctrine that meets the demands of an international community that is increasingly interdependent and where the substantive distinction between Host State and Home States progressively is becoming less clear.

A fifth contribution of FIPS to the development of a meaningful doctrine is the potential of using FIPS as a legislative framework capable of establishing as a matter of law that the principle of public purpose (i) must be objective and susceptible to application in support of the exercise of national regulatory sovereignty only where clear and convincing industry-based standards are met, suggesting that a bona fide public purpose is present; (ii) shall be content-rich, meaning that public purpose must be defined with greater specificity than simply an understanding that the doctrine applies "to all things public"; and (iii) shall be removed from furthering the interests of political ideologies of whatsoever ilk.

A sixth and final contribution here mentioned on the part of FIPS toward a viable public purpose doctrine is the use of the FIPS structure to set forth a test based on *futility*. Application of a *futility* standard concerning the fundamental question of whether a particular measure alleged to be based on public purpose in fact comports with the doctrine's requirement helps foster objectivity. The self-judging rationale adduced by a State that merely characterizes a regulatory enactment as implemented "for a public purpose," without any other factual foundation for this legal finding, should be deemed insufficient.

In instances where it is demonstrated that a particular regulatory measure does not contribute in an objective manner – for example, in the case of a financial institution with respect to the rehabilitation of that entity or in instances of revoked licenses and the manner in which the revocation materially redounds to the best interests of a specific community – the measure will be deemed futile. Similarly, regulatory acts that are implemented in furtherance of political ideology but ostensibly premised on fiscal public purpose considerations shall be deemed futile if, in fact, economic benefit is either incommensurable or not material. The "futility element" of a public purpose analysis helps test the evidentiary foundations of a regulatory measure averred to have been grounded on the public purpose doctrine. Measures that prove to be futile when viewed through the lenses of pragmatism and utilitarianism will likely prove to be unworthy of public purpose justification.

The coordinated and concerted use of FIPS is a possibility but not a likely probability. Fundamental questions concerning this approach remain unresolved. How are FIPS to be drafted by individual countries for purposes of offering *sui generis* investor incentives in the form of protection guarantees to be harmonized internationally in order to present a uniform standard for public purpose requirements? Are there nongovernmental organizations appropriately positioned to facilitate such an undertaking? Can the international community set aside parochial interests and pursue the goal of adopting, implementing, and enforcing public purpose strictures along the lines of the six propositions here referenced? Even assuming that a collective political will can be summoned in furtherance of this aspiration, what measures can be secured to ensure implementation? Even with the decentralized and ad hoc network that characterizes the current standing of FIPS, the U.S. Department of State has identified corruption as a principal cause of the nonenforcement of FIPS. If FIPS that were enacted as part of a domestic legislative process and in keeping with a domestic agenda are not enforced because of corruption, the greater challenges incident to FIPS that adopt international standards more remote from a national political agenda are likely to be compounded by such legal irregularities. National legislation in the form of FIPS, however, do provide for an existing theoretical and practical construct through which the public purpose doctrine may be dislodged from the realm of self-serving national manipulation. Whether by happenstance or by design, more than an initial first step in this direction already has been taken by the very enactment of FIPS.

Conclusion

The public purpose doctrine is the conceptual arbiter between competing and equally legitimate legal obligations, each of which is binding on States. Whether a State's obligation to regulate in furtherance of its perceived or even actual national interests preempts its equally legal and binding obligations to protect foreign investment often depends on the nature of the public purpose on which the exercise of regulatory sovereignty is said to be premised. The self-judging configuration of the legacy public purpose doctrine provides States with unbridled discretion, tantamount to a license to exercise this regulatory authority systematically to the detriment of its obligations to protect foreign investment. Moreover, the subjective standard of the doctrine, in addition to fostering abuse, also places into question process legitimacy and militates against much-needed transparency. The scant academic and juridical pronouncements on public purpose, however, have led some voices to conclude that public purpose is to be ignored because of the doctrine's vulnerabilities to self-serving application on the part of States. Therefore, these despondent cries argue, in instances of expropriation, nationalization, or the taking of property on the part of States, only the presence of compensation, due process, and nondiscriminatory treatment actually matter because public purpose is bereft of content and little more than a pretext for State encroachment on what should be sacrosanct investor protection obligations.

Pretending that an established principle of international law does not exist because historical conditions and juridical strictures have rendered its orthodox content of little relevance and susceptible to abuse is hardly a productive and inspiring pragmatic posture. It is an equally hapless theoretical position. Even from simply a plain utilitarian standpoint, the international community cannot afford to turn a blind eye to public purpose. If for no other reason, the doctrine's challenges must be confronted precisely because it exists, it is ubiquitous within the framework of both customary and conventional international law, and, more importantly, there is the ground that the doctrine is being used as an aider and abettor to States that seek to renege on commitments to foreign investors after having extracted strategic value from foreign direct investments (FDIs).

Even though the public purpose doctrine is an integral part of conventional international law, there has been no systematic, nor perhaps even an ad hoc, effort to define it, notwithstanding the laudable efforts of the North American Free Trade Agreement (NAFTA)'s drafters and a few others who have expressed concern for its workings. To the contrary, the doctrine is used indiscriminately, with virtually no care being placed on its normative application based on content or subject matter (i.e., police powers, human health, animal life and environment, national security, resource licensing, or economic policy). Similarly, conventional international law does not discriminate with respect to application of the public purpose doctrine, irrespective of whether the public purpose exception at issue has its origins in international trade law or international investment law. Within the context of human rights conventions, the public purpose doctrine serves an important role, but it is one that is yet to find a powerful voice. The three human rights conventions here analyzed (the European Convention, the Inter-American Convention, and the African Charter) all avail themselves of the doctrine in order to craft qualifications applicable to many, but not all, human rights enunciated within each convention, thus implicitly, and all too quietly, suggesting that the doctrine is absolutely pivotal in helping to construct a hierarchy among human rights. Clearly, those rights that cannot be mitigated or conditioned on public purpose, such as the right to have a name or the rights of children, are not susceptible to State intervention without immediately prompting the outcry of the entire community of nations committed to protecting fundamental human rights. Other rights, such as the right to property, are open to public purpose doctrine qualification and State interdiction on that basis. Therefore, the public purpose doctrine also serves as a standard against which the inalienability of a human right can be measured. This important conceptual role is nowhere articulated within the framework of any of the referenced human rights conventions. Yet it should be. Indeed, it here has been argued that it must be mentioned and developed. Consciousness of the fundamental role of public purpose, be it in the context of human rights conventions, regional trade agreements, bilateral investment treaties (BITs), or commercial law conventions, is necessary if the doctrine is to be relied on as a talisman for exceptions to State intervention that provide States with the right to disavow the rights of others.

The public purpose doctrine also finds a voice in customary international law. International law instruments and resolutions issued by credible, legitimate nongovernmental organizations (NGOs) amply establish the existence of the public purpose doctrine as forming part of customary international law. Here, too, however, the doctrine is not vested with subject matter content, objective criteria for application, and a place in the hierarchy of customary international law principles, nor is it otherwise defined. These insufficiencies are arresting because, as with conventional international law, customary international law is rife with reliance on the public purpose doctrine, and the doctrine is pivotal to the very State practices that evince its existence in this realm of international juridical precepts.

The way in which the legacy public purpose doctrine must be modified certainly presents practical challenges, but it has the virtue of being clear. Eleven propositions that certainly have no pretense of exhausting the subject appear to be central to the meaningful rehabilitation of the doctrine. First, public purpose cannot be construed as a self-evident proposition. The doctrine must be understood necessarily as subject to discursive reasoning.

Second, all things public need not fall within the ambit of the public purpose doctrine. Put simply, a public act is not a priori legitimate as an exception to an obligation merely because of its public nature and therefore said to fall within the doctrine's purview. It is in the "purpose" component of the doctrine that content can best reside.

Third, as with all propositions susceptible to discursive reasoning, the subjective perception, origins, or justification of an act does not render it legal or normatively viable on the basis of the public purpose doctrine. The act itself must be subject to commensurable criteria based on its adduced objectives.

Fourth, economic globalization and its attendant paradigm of interdependence command that States compromise and jointly address transnational concerns within the framework of a paradigm that does not tolerate "zero-sum game" results when alternative scenarios are reasonably viable. In the context of investment protection as concerns the relationship between capital-exporting and capital-importing States, for example, "all-or-nothing" consequences from the doctrine's application need to be materially modified or altogether eliminated. The "effects test," for example, found in the NAFTA "decisional law" must yield to a test to be applied in the context of a tempered public purpose doctrine that may lead to a reasonable and proportionality-driven result. Principles of *international proportionality* and *bilateralism* can go far in curing this ill.

Fifth, there must be a concerted effort on the part of the international community of nations to fashion new criteria for public purpose when used as a normative foundation for the disavowance of binding obligations on States purportedly based on the doctrine. The transformation of a doctrine so deeply vested in public international law cannot be the product of unilateral initiatives. The structure of the doctrine's reform must be the product of collaborative efforts on the part of both capital-exporting and capital-importing States. Interdependence is an essential element of this reform. By definition it requires compromise.

Sixth, a hierarchy of public purposes, all falling within the ambit of a *single* public purpose doctrine, needs to be identified. The stratification of principles is not foreign to customary or conventional international law. Matters affecting the application of principles of *jus cogens* or touching on strategic areas that concern human life must be accorded preeminence over domestic policy making that may readily fall under the auspices of medium- to long-term (by way of example) economic planning. In this connection, principles such as permanent sovereignty over natural resources and sustainable development cannot be treated as general articles of faith justifying any and all measures rationally related to the elements of either stricture.

Seventh, public purpose cannot be confused with State action in furtherance of regime perpetuation or the "historical obligation" of ideological dissemination. Here, the "futility test" referenced in this writing can serve as an important standard that would help address this abuse of process. The current status of the doctrine, however, is so great as to imbue this issue with uncertainty and turn its consequences into little more than mere speculation. Comment *e* to Section 712 of the ALI Restatement (Third) of Foreign Relations Law (1987) is certainly helpful in demonstrating this State of affairs:

> *e. Taking for public purpose*. The requirement that a taking be for a public purpose is reiterated in most formulations of the rules of international law on expropriation of foreign property. That limitation, however, has not figured prominently in international claims practice, perhaps because the concept of *public purpose is broad* and not subject to effective reexamination by other states. Presumably, a seizure by a dictator or oligarchy for private use could be challenged under this rule. (emphasis in original, underlining added)

Eighth, harmonizing public purpose in foreign investment protection statutes (FIPS) and BITs so that the quantum and quality of investor protection obligations binding on States can lead to the fulfillment and not the frustration of expectations between Home and Host States is central to the doctrine's rehabilitation. Conflicting or disparate obligation standards in these instruments merely lend themselves to arbitrariness and lack of transparency and serve as the facilitators for irregularities and corruption.

Ninth, one practical partial solution that may be immediately implemented is to have signatories to international agreements agree on a definition of public purpose within the meaning of a particular instrument. Quite remarkably, there is little evidence in draft regional trade agreements that this approach has been explored, let alone exhausted.

Tenth, States applying public purpose in furtherance of the exercise of regulatory sovereignty should bear the burden by a standard akin to "clear and convincing" of demonstrating the objective foundations and commensurable underpinnings of the doctrine's application. In this connection, Home-State investors should enjoy a rebuttable presumption that public purpose is not sufficient to justify encroachment on an international obligation to protect foreign investment. Agreement on the allocation of burdens, presumptions, and rebuttability shall meaningfully contribute to the legacy doctrine's reform at a very practical level.

Eleventh, and last, there must be a recognition that NGOs and national policy-making instruments such as FIPS represent pragmatic vehicles for tempering, forming, transforming, and defining a new public purpose doctrine that may serve the interests of the *entire* community of nations consonant with the demands of economic globalization, an understanding of sovereignty that embraces principles of bilateralism and proportionality, and the exigency of harmonizing conflicting economic interests among States in different junctures of economic, social, and political development.

The development and implementation of these eleven propositions is daunting. The task is even more intimidating upon reflection, suggesting that the eleven elements are but just a small representative sample of necessary reform. Equally disconcerting are the pragmatic challenges endemic to any effort to bring into being a doctrine that touches so many different aspects of international law. Some comfort, nonetheless, perhaps can be found in realizing that consciousness of the problem in and of itself may serve as a mitigating factor. States can be called to task when applying the doctrine. Academics can be challenged to contribute to the development of public purpose within a rubric that meets some or all of the concerns that this contribution has identified. Similarly, legislators can be moved and legislation developed to address these issues pursuant to legislative drafting techniques. National treaty-negotiating teams also may facilitate bringing about short- to medium-term mitigation of the problems inherited from the legacy public purpose doctrine.

The practical, doctrinal, and conceptual road that must be traveled before a comprehensive doctrine is actually developed and accepted by the community of nations remains a difficult one, even where short- and medium-term pragmatic mitigation techniques are successfully applied. Indeed, it remains less than clear the extent to which these temporary measures may actually cause material improvement. It is with reference to Ovid's challenging maxim in the *Metamorphoses*, "*est nulla via invia virtuti*" ("for virtue no path is impossible") that perseverance in the face of the virtually insurmountable must be pursued.[1] Resolve for pursuing the seemingly impossible in and of itself is part of the objective sought.

[1] *See* OVID IV: METAMORPHOSES, BOOKS IX–XV, Book 14, Line 113 (Frank Justus Miller, Trans., G. P. Goold, ed., Loeb Classical Library 1916). Here, Aeneas asks a sibyl for a clear path through Avernus's realm so that he may visit his deceased father living in the realm of the shades:

> Great things do you ask, you man of mighty deeds, whose hand, by sword, whose piety, by fire, has been well tried. But have no fear, Trojan; you shall have your wish, with my guidance you shall see the dwellings of Elysium and the latest Kingdom of the universe; and you shall see your dear father's shade. *There is no way denied to virtue* (emphasis added).

APPENDIX I

A Comparison between the Performance Requirements Articles of the Canada-Jordan and the Colombia-Japan Bilateral Investment Treaties

Article 7 (Performance Requirements) Canada-Jordan BIT	Article 5 (Performance Requirements) Colombia-Japan BIT:
1. Neither Party may impose or enforce any of the following requirements, or enforce any commitment or undertaking, in connection with the establishment, acquisition, expansion, management, conduct or operation of an investment of an investor of a Party in its territory: (a) to export a given level or percentage of goods; (b) to achieve a given level or percentage of domestic content; (c) to purchase, use or accord a preference to goods produced or services provided in its territory, or to purchase goods or services from persons in its territory; (d) to relate in any way the volume or value of imports to the volume or value of exports or to the amount of foreign exchange inflows associated with such investment; (e) to restrict sales of goods or services in its territory that such investment produces or provides by relating such sales in any way to the volume or value of its exports or foreign exchange earnings;	1. Neither Contracting Party shall impose or enforce, in connection with investment activities in its Area of an investor of the other Contracting Party or of a non-Contracting Party, any of the following requirements: (a) to export a given level or percentage of goods or services; (b) to achieve a given level or percentage of domestic content; (c) to purchase, use or accord a preference to goods produced in its Area, or to purchase goods from natural or legal persons or any other entity in its Area; (d) to relate in any way the volume or value of imports to the volume or value of exports or to the amount of foreign exchange inflows associated with investments of that investor; (e) to restrict sales of goods or services in its Area that investments of that investor produce or provide by relating such sales in any way to the volume or value of its exports or foreign exchange earnings;

Article 7 (Performance Requirements) Canada-Jordan BIT	Article 5 (Performance Requirements) Colombia-Japan BIT:
(f) to transfer technology, a production process or other proprietary knowledge to a person in its territory, except when the requirement is imposed or the commitment or undertaking is enforced by a court, administrative tribunal or competition authorities to remedy an alleged violation of competition laws or to act in a manner not inconsistent with other provisions of this Agreement; or (g) to supply exclusively from the territory of the Party the goods it produces or the services it provides to a specific regional market or to the world market. 2. A measure that requires an investment to use technology to meet generally applicable health, safety or environmental requirements shall not be inconsistent with subparagraph 1(f). 3. Neither Party may condition the receipt or continued receipt of an advantage, in connection with an investment in its territory of an investor of a Party, on compliance with any of the following requirements: (a) to achieve a given level or percentage of domestic content; (b) to purchase, use or accord a preference to goods produced in its territory, or to purchase goods from producers in its territory; (c) to relate in any way the volume or value of imports to the volume or value of exports or to the amount of foreign exchange inflows associated with such investment; or (d) to restrict sales of goods or services in its territory that such investment produces or provides by relating such sales in any way to the volume or value of its exports or foreign exchange earnings.	(f) to transfer technology, a production process or other proprietary knowledge to a natural or legal person or any other entity in its Area, except when the requirement: (i) is imposed or enforced by a court, administrative tribunal or competent authority to remedy an alleged violation of competition laws; or (ii) concerns the transfer or use of intellectual property rights or disclosure of proprietary information which is undertaken in a manner not inconsistent with the TRIPS Agreement; (g) to locate the headquarters of that investor for a specific region or the world market in its Area; or (h) to supply one or more of the goods that the investor produces or the services that the investor provides to a specific region or the world market, exclusively from its Area. 2. Neither Contracting Party may condition the receipt or continued receipt of an advantage, in connection with the investment activities in its Area of an investor of the other Contracting Party or of a non-Contracting Party, on the compliance with any of the following requirements: (a) to achieve a given level or percentage of domestic content; (b) to purchase, use or accord a preference to goods produced in its Area, or to purchase goods from natural or legal persons or any other entity in its Area; (c) to relate in any way the volume or value of imports to the volume or value of exports or to the amount of

Article 7 (Performance Requirements) Canada-Jordan BIT	Article 5 (Performance Requirements) Colombia-Japan BIT:
4. Nothing in paragraph 3 shall be construed to prevent a Party from conditioning the receipt or continued receipt of an advantage, in connection with an investment in its territory of an investor of a Party, on compliance with a requirement to locate production, provide a service, train or employ workers, construct or expand particular facilities, or carry out research and development, in its territory. 5. Paragraphs 1 and 3 shall not apply to any requirement other than the requirements set out in those paragraphs. 6. The provisions of: (a) subparagraphs 1(a), (b) and (c), and 3(a) and (b) shall not apply to qualification requirements for goods or services with respect to export promotion and foreign aid programs; (b) subparagraphs 1(b), (c), (f) and (g), and 3(a) and (b) shall not apply to procurement by a Party or a State enterprise; and (c) subparagraphs 3(a) and (b) shall not apply to requirements imposed by an importing Party relating to the content of goods necessary to qualify for preferential tariffs or preferential quotas.	foreign exchange inflows associated with investments of that investor; or (d) to restrict sales of goods or services in its Area that investments of that investor produce or provide by relating such sales in any way to the volume or value of its exports or foreign earnings. 3. Nothing in paragraph 2 shall be construed to prevent a Contracting Party from conditioning the receipt or continued receipt of an advantage, in connection with investment activities in its Area of an investor of the other Contracting Party or of a non-Contracting Party, on compliance with a requirement to locate production, supply a service, train or employ workers, construct or expand particular facilities or carry out research and development, in its Area. 4. Paragraphs 1 and 2 shall not apply to any requirement other than those requirements set out in those paragraphs. 5. The provisions of: (a) subparagraphs 1(a), (b) and (c) and 2(a) and (b) shall not apply to qualification requirements for goods or services with respect to export promotion programs and foreign aid programs; and (b) subparagraphs 2(a) and (b) shall not apply to the requirements imposed by an importing Contracting Party relating to the content of goods necessary to qualify for preferential tariffs or preferential quotas. 6. Provided that such measures are not applied in an arbitrary or unjustifiable manner and provided that such measures do not constitute a disguised restriction on international trade or investment activities, nothing in

Article 7 (Performance Requirements) Canada-Jordan BIT	Article 5 (Performance Requirements) Colombia-Japan BIT:
	subparagraphs 1(b), (c) and (f) and 2(a) and (b) shall be construed to prevent a Contracting Party from adopting or maintaining measures, including environmental measures: (a) necessary to secure compliance with laws and regulations that are not inconsistent with the provisions of this Agreement; (b) necessary to protect human, animal or plant life or health; or (c) related to the conservation of living or non-living exhaustible natural resources.

APPENDIX II

An Empirical Review of the Preeminence of the Public Purpose Doctrine throughout the Ever-Expanding Universe of Bilateral Investment Treaties

PART I: THE KEY

Preamble

Key	Variations
S *Sustainable Development Reference*	**Canada-China** RECOGNIZING the need to promote investment based on the principles of sustainable development; **Canada-Jordan** RECOGNIZING that the promotion and the protection of investments of investors of one Party in the territory of the other Party will be conducive to the stimulation of mutually beneficial business activity, to the development of economic cooperation between them and to the promotion of sustainable development;
P *Health, Safety, & Environment Reference*	**China-Guyana** AGREEING that these objectives can be achieved without relaxing health, safety and environmental measures of general application;
L *Labor Reference*	**Kenya-Slovakia** RECOGNIZING that the development of economic and business ties can promote respect for internationally recognized labour rights; **USA-Poland** RECOGNIZING that the development of business and economic ties can contribute to the well-being of workers in both countries and promote respect for fundamental worker rights;

Key	Variations
PS, PL, PLS, LS *Some Combination of the Above*	**Colombia-Japan** RECOGNIZING that these objectives and the promotion of sustainable development can be achieved without relaxing health, safety and environmental measures of general application; RECOGNIZING the importance of the cooperative relationship between labor and management in promoting investment between the Contracting Parties; **Croatia-Azerbaijan** DESIRING to achieve these objectives in a manner consistent with the protection of health, safety, and the environment and the promotion of sustainable development, **Japan-Papua New Guinea** RECOGNISING that economic development, social development and environmental protection *are* interdependent and mutually reinforcing pillars of sustainable development and that cooperative efforts of the Contracting Parties to promote investment can play an important role in enhancing sustainable development; RECOGNISING also that these objectives can be achieved without relaxing health, safety and environmental measures of general application; ACKNOWLEDGING the importance of the cooperative relationship between labour and management in promoting investment between the Contracting Parties; **Turkey-Gabon** CONVINCED that these objectives can be achieved without relaxing health, safety and environmental measures of general application as well as internationally recognized labor rights;

Environment and Labor

Key	Variations
E *Environmental Exception*	**Canada-Armenia, Art. XVII(2)** Nothing in this Agreement shall be construed to prevent a Contracting Party from adopting, maintaining or enforcing any measure otherwise consistent with this Agreement that it

Key	Variations
	considers appropriate to ensure that investment activity is undertaken in a manner sensitive to environmental concerns.
	Colombia-UK, Art. VIII Nothing in this Agreement shall be construed to prevent a Party from adopting, maintaining, or enforcing any measure that it considers appropriate to ensure that an investment activity in its territory is undertaken in a manner sensitive to environmental concerns, provided that such measures are non-discriminatory and proportionate to the objectives sought.
L *Labor Exception*	**Colombia-Belgium, Art. VIII(3)** Nothing in this Agreement shall be construed as to prevent a Contracting Party from adopting, maintaining, or enforcing any measure that it considers appropriate to ensure that an investment activity in its territory is undertaken in accordance with the labour law of the Party.

Limited Public Purpose Exceptions

Key	Variations
P *Exception Performance Requirements*	**Canada-Jordan, Art. 7(2)** A measure that requires an investment to use a technology to meet generally applicable health, safety or environmental requirements shall not be construed to be inconsistent with subparagraph 1(f) [Performance Requirements].
N *Exception National Treatment*	**Colombia-UK, Art. IV(1)** The provisions of this Agreement relative to the grant of treatment not less favourable than that accorded to investors of either Contracting Party shall not be construed so as to preclude the adoption or enforcement by a Contracting Party of measures which are necessary to protect national security, public security, or public order.
	Germany-Antigua & Barbuda, Protocol Ad Art. 3 Measures that have to be taken for reasons of public security and order, public health or morality shall not be deemed "treatment less favourable" within the meaning of Article 3.

No Relaxation

Key	Variations
P *No Relaxation for Health, Safety, or Environment*	**Canada-Jordan, Art. 11** The Parties recognize that it is inappropriate to encourage investment by relaxing domestic health, safety or environmental measures. Accordingly, a Party should not waive or otherwise derogate from, or offer to waive or otherwise derogate from, such measures as an encouragement for the establishment, acquisition, expansion or retention in its territory of an investment of an investor. If a Party considers that the other Party has offered such an encouragement, it may request consultations with the other Party and the two Parties shall consult with a view to avoiding any such encouragement. **Colombia-Belgium, Art. VII** 1. Recognizing the right of each Contracting Party to establish its own levels of domestic environmental protection and environmental development policies and priorities, and to adopt or modify accordingly its environmental legislation, each Contracting Party shall strive to ensure that its legislation provides for high levels of environmental protection and shall strive to continue improving this legislation. 2. The Contracting Parties recognize that it is inappropriate to encourage investment by relaxing domestic environmental legislation. Accordingly, each Contracting Party shall ensure that it does not waive or otherwise derogate from, or offer to waive or otherwise derogate from, such legislation as an encouragement for the establishment, maintenance or expansion in its territory of an investment. 3. The Contracting Parties recognize that co-operation between them provides enhanced opportunities to improve environmental protection standards. 4. Nothing in this Agreement shall be construed as to prevent a Contracting Party from adopting, maintaining, or enforcing any measure that it considers appropriate to ensure that an investment activity in its territory is undertaken in accordance with the environmental law of the Party.

Key	Variations
	5. The dispute settlement mechanisms under Articles XII and XIII of this Agreement shall not apply to any obligation undertaken in accordance with this Article.
L *No Relaxation for Labor*	**Colombia-Belgium, Art. VIII** 1. The Contracting Parties recognize: a. the right of each Contracting Party to establish its own domestic labour standards, and to adopt or modify accordingly its labour legislation; b. that each Contracting party shall endeavor to ensure that the principles set forth in paragraph 6 of Article I [internationally recognized labor standards] be recognized and maintained by its national legislation; and c. that it is inappropriate to encourage the establishment, maintenance or expansion in its territory of an investment by relaxing domestic labour legislation. 2. The Contracting Parties recognize that co-operation between them provides enhanced opportunities to improve labour standards. 3. Nothing in this Agreement shall be construed as to prevent a Contracting Party from adopting, maintaining, or enforcing any measure that it considers appropriate to ensure that an investment activity in its territory is undertaken in accordance with the labour law of the Party. 4. The dispute settlement mechanisms under Articles XII and XIII of this Agreement shall not apply to any obligation undertaken in accordance with this Article.
PL *Provision for Both – Either Separate or Together*	**Colombia-Japan, Art. 21(1)** Each Contracting Party recognizes that it is inappropriate to encourage investment activities of investors of the other Contracting party and of a non-Contracting party by relaxing its domestic health, safety or environmental measures or by lowering its labor standards. Accordingly, each contracting Party should not waive or otherwise derogate from such measures or standards as an encouragement for the establishment, acquisition, or expansion in its Area of investments by investors of the other Contracting Party and of a non-Contracting Party.

General Exceptions

Key	Variations
B *Stripped-Down Exception*	**China-New Zealand, Art. 11** The provisions of this Agreement shall not in any way limit the right of either Contracting Party to apply prohibitions or restrictions of any kind or take any other action direct to the protection of its essential security interests, or to the protection of public health, or the prevention of disease and pests in animals or plants.
X *Similar to GATT Art. XX*	**Canada-Thailand, Art. XVII(3)** Provided that such measures are not applied in an arbitrary or unjustifiable manner, or do not constitute a disguised restriction on international trade or investment, nothing in this Agreement shall be construed to prevent a Contracting Party from adopting or maintaining measures, including environmental measures: (a) necessary to ensure compliance with laws and regulations that are not inconsistent with the provisions of this Agreement; (b) necessary to protect human, animal, or plant life or health; or (c) relating to the conservation of living or non-living exhaustible natural resources if such measures are made effective in conjunction with restrictions on domestic production or consumption. (d) imposed for the protection of national treasures of artistic, historic, or archaeological value; (e) essential to the acquisition or distribution of products in general or local short supply, provided that any such measures shall be consistent with the principle that all investors are entitled to an equitable share of the international supply of such products, and that any such measures, which are inconsistent with the other provisions of this Agreement shall be discontinued as soon as the conditions giving rise to them have ceased to exist.
O *Includes Public Order Language*	**Colombia-Japan, Art. 15(1)** Subject to the requirement that such measures are not applied by a Contracting Party in a manner which would constitute a means of arbitrary or unjustifiable discrimination against the other Contracting Party, or a disguised restriction on investments of investors of that other Contracting Party in the Area of the former Contracting Party, nothing in this Agreement other than Article 12 [**Treatment in Case of Strife**] shall be construed to prevent that former

Key	Variations
	Contracting Party from adopting or enforcing measures, including those to protect the environment: (a) necessary to protect human, animal, or plant life or health; (b) necessary to protect public morals or to maintain public order; Note: The public order exception may be invoked only where a genuine and sufficiently serious threat is posed to one of the fundamental interests of society. (c) necessary to secure compliance with the laws or regulations which are not inconsistent with the provisions of this Agreement including those relating to: (i) the prevention of deceptive and fraudulent practices or to deal with the effects of a default on contract; (ii) the protection of privacy of the individual in relation to the processing and dissemination of personal data and the protection of confidentiality of personal records and accounts; or (iii) safety; or (d) imposed for the protection of national treasures of artistic, historic, archaeological or cultural value. **Russia-Hungary, Art. 2(3)** This Agreement shall not preclude the application of either Contracting Party of measures, necessary for the maintenance of defence, national security and public order, protection of the environment, morality and public health.

Security Exceptions

Key	Variations
D *Dispute Settlement Only*	**Germany-Mexico, Art. 20** The dispute settlement provisions of this Section shall not apply to the resolutions adopted by a Contracting State, which for national security reasons, prohibit or restrict the acquisition of an investment in its territory, owned or controlled by its nationals, by nationals or companies of the other Contracting State, according to the legislation of the relevant Contracting State.
B *Stripped-Down Exception*	**China-New Zealand, Art. 11** The provisions of this Agreement shall not in any way limit the right of either Contracting Party to apply prohibitions or

Key	Variations
	restrictions of any kind or take any other action direct to the protection of its essential security interests, or to the protection of public health, or the prevention of disease and pests in animals or plants. **India-Austria, Art. 12(2)** Nothing in this Agreement precludes the Host Contracting Party from taking necessary action in abnormal circumstances for the protection of its essential security interests or in circumstances of extreme emergency in accordance with its laws applied on a non-discriminatory basis.
X *Similar to GATT Art. XXI*	**Canada-China, Art. 33(5)** Nothing in this Agreement shall be construed: (a) to require a Contracting Party to furnish or allow access to information if the Contracting Party determines that the disclosure of that information is contrary to its essential security interests; (b) to prevent a Contracting Party from taking any actions that it considers necessary for the protection of its essential security interests: (i) relating to the traffic in arms, ammunition and implements of war and to such traffic and transactions in other goods, materials, services, and technology undertaken directly or indirectly for the purpose of supplying a military or other security establishment; (ii) in time of war or other emergency in international relations; or (iii) relating to the implementation of national policies or other nuclear explosive devices; or (c) to prevent a Contracting Party from taking action in pursuance of its obligations under the United Nations Charter for the maintenance of international peace and security.
O *Includes Public Order Language*	**Colombia-Belgium, Art. II(3)** Nothing contained in this Agreement shall bind either Contracting Party to protect investments made with capital or assets derived from illegal activities, and it shall not be construed so as to prevent a Party from adopting or maintaining measures intended to preserve public order, the fulfillment of its duties for the keeping or restoration of international peace and security; or the protection of its own essential security interests.

Key	Variations
	Russia-Hungary, Art. 2(3) This Agreement shall not preclude the application of either Contracting Party of measures, necessary for the maintenance of defence, national security and public order, protection of the environment, morality and public health.
S *Self-Judging*	**USA-Nicaragua, Protocol 1** With respect to Article XIV, paragraph 1, the parties confirm their mutual understanding that whether a measure is undertaken by a party to protect its national security interests is self judging.

Exceptions for Transfers

Key	Variations
N *Restrictions On Transfers Permitted for Specific Application of National Laws*	**Canada-Armenia, Art. IX(3)** Notwithstanding paragraphs 1 & 2, a Contracting Party may prevent a transfer through the equitable, non-discriminatory and good faith application of its laws relating to: (a) bankruptcy, insolvency or the protection of rights of creditors; (b) issuing, trading or dealing in securities; (c) criminal or penal offenses; (d) reports of transfers of currency or other monetary instruments; or (e) ensuring the satisfaction of judgments in adjudicatory proceedings. **Canada-Armenia, Art. XI(2)** Notwithstanding paragraphs (1), (2), and (4) of Article IX, and without limiting the applicability of paragraph (3) of Article IX, a Contracting Party may prevent or limit transfers by a financial institution to, or for the benefit of, an affiliate of or person related to such institution or provider, through the equitable, non-discriminatory and good faith application of measures relating to maintenance of the safety, soundness, integrity or financial responsibility of financial institutions.
B *Exception for Balance of Payment Difficulties*	**Canada-Slovakia, Art. IX(3)** (a) Nothing in this Agreement shall be construed to prevent a Contracting Party from adopting or

Key	Variations
	maintaining measures that restrict transfers where the Contracting Party experiences serious balance of payments difficulties, or the threat thereof, and such restrictions are consistent with paragraph (b). (b) Measures referred to in subparagraph (a) shall be equitable, neither arbitrary nor unjustifiably discriminatory, in good faith, of limited duration and may not go beyond what is necessary to remedy the balance of payments situation. A Contracting Party that imposes measures under this Article shall inform the other Contracting party forthwith and present as soon as possible a time schedule for their removal. Such measures shall be taken in accordance with other international obligations of the Contracting Party concerned, including those under the WTO Agreement and the *Articles of Agreement of the International Monetary Fund.* **Colombia-India, Art. (5)4** Notwithstanding the provisions of paragraphs 1 and 2 of this Article, the Contracting Parties may temporarily restrict the transfers in the event of serious balance-of-payments or threat thereof; or in cases where in exceptional circumstances, movements, of capital cause or threaten to cause serious difficulties for macroeconomic management, in particular, monetary and exchange rate policies, provided such restrictions are compatible or are issued in conformity with the agreements of the IMF or are applied upon request of the latter and are equitable, non-discriminatory and in good faith. **Japan-Pakistan, Art. 8(2)** Notwithstanding the provisions of paragraph 1 of the present Article, either Contracting Party may, in exceptional financial or economic circumstances, impose such exchange restrictions in accordance with its laws and regulations and in conformity with the Articles of Agreement of the International Monetary Fund so long as each Contracting Party is a party to the said Articles of Agreement.

Prudential Financial Measures Exceptions

Key	Variations
P *Exception for Prudential Financial Measures*	**Canada-Armenia, Art. XI(1)** Nothing in this Agreement shall be construed to prevent a Contracting Party from adopting or maintaining reasonable measures for prudential reasons, such as: (a) the protection of investors, depositors, financial market participants, policy-holders, policy-claimants, or persons to whom a fiduciary duty is owed by a financial institution; (b) the maintenance of the safety, soundness, integrity or financial responsibility of financial institutions; and (c) ensuring the integrity and stability of a Contracting Party's financial system. **Colombia-Belgium, Art. 11(5)** Nothing contained in this Agreement shall apply to measures adopted by any Contracting Party, in accordance with its law, with respect to the financial sector for prudential reasons, including those measures aimed at protecting investors, depositors, insurance takers or trustees, or to safeguard the integrity and stability of the financial system.

Clarification of Indirect Expropriation

Key	Variations
C *Clarification of What Constitutes Indirect Expropriation*	**Canada-China, Annex B.10 ("Expropriation")** The Contracting Parties confirm their shared understanding that: 1. Indirect expropriation results from a measure or series of measures of a Contracting Party that has an effect equivalent to direct expropriation without formal transfer of title or outright seizure. 2. The determination of whether a measure or series of measures of a Contracting Party constitutes an indirect expropriation requires a case-by-case, fact-based inquiry that considers, among other factors:

Key	Variations
	(a) the economic impact of the measure or series of measures, although the sole fact that a measure or series of measures of a Contracting Party has an adverse effect on the economic value of an investment does not establish that an indirect expropriation has occurred; (b) the extent to which the measure or series of measures interferes with distinct, reasonable, investment-backed expectations; and (c) the character of the measure or series of measures. 3. Except in rare circumstances, such as if a measure or series of measures is so severe in light of its purpose that it cannot be reasonably viewed as having been adopted and applied in good faith, a non-discriminatory measure or series of measures of a Contracting Party that is designed and applied to protect the legitimate public objectives for the well-being of citizens, such as health, safety and the environment, does not constitute indirect expropriation.
I *Inclusion of Government Intent as a Factor*	**Canada-Romania, Annex B.** . . . .the character of the measure or series of measures, including their purpose and rationale. **Colombia-India, Art. 6(2)(iv)** . . .the character and intent of the measures or series of measures, whether they are for bona fide public interest purposes or not and whether there is a reasonable nexus between them and the intention to expropriate.

	Preamble	Environment & Labor	Limited Public Purpose Exceptions	No Relaxation	General Exceptions	Security Exceptions	Exceptions for Transfers	Prudential Financial Measures	Clarification of Indirect Expropriation
Argentina-Bolivia	–	–	–	–	–	–	–	–	
Argentina-Chile	–	–	–	–	–	–	–	–	
Argentina-China	–	–	–	–	–	–	–	–	
Argentina-Finland	–	–	–	–	–	–	–	–	
Argentina-Guatemala	–	–	–	–	–	–	–	–	
Argentina-Greece	–	–	–	–	–	–	–	–	
Argentina-Jamaica	–	–	–	–	–	–	–	–	
Argentina-Netherlands	–	–	–	–	–	–	–	–	
Argentina-Peru	–	–	–	–	–	–	–	–	
Argentina-Sweden	–	–	–	–	–	–	–	–	
Australia-Argentina	–	–	–	–	–	–	–	–	
Australia-Czech Republic	–	–	–	–	–	–	–	–	
Australia-Egypt	–	–	–	–	–	–	–	–	
	–	–	–	–	–	–	–	–	

	Preamble	Environment & Labor	Limited Public Purpose Exceptions	No Relaxation	General Exceptions	Security Exceptions	Exceptions for Transfers	Prudential Financial Measures	Clarification of Indirect Expropriation
Australia-Indonesia									
Australia-Lithuania	–	–	–	–	–	–	–	–	
Australia-Pakistan	–	–	–	–	–	–	–	–	
Australia-Papua New Guinea	–	–	–	–	–	–	–	–	
Australia-Romania	–	–	–	–	–	–	–	–	
Australia-Uruguay	–	–	–	–	–	–	–	–	
Australia-Vietnam	–	–	–	–	–	–	–	–	
Brazil-Chile	–	–	–	–	–	–	–	–	
Brazil-Finland	–	–	–	–	–	–	–	–	
Brazil-Netherlands	–	–	–	–	–	–	–	–	
Brazil-Venezuela	–	–	–	–	–	–	–	–	
Canada-Armenia	–	E	–	–	X	–	N	P	
Canada-Barbados	–	E	–	–	X	–	N	P	
Canada-China	S	E	–	–	X	DX	NB	P	C
Canada-Costa Rica	–	E	–	–	X	–	N	P	
Canada-Croatia	–	E	–	–	X	–	N	P	
Canada-Ecuador	–	E	–	–	X	–	N	P	

Canada-Egypt	–	E	–	–	X	–	N	P	
Canada-Jordan	S	–	P	P	X	X	N	P	C
Canada-Lebanon	–	E	–	–	X	–	N	P	
Canada-Panama	–	E	–	–	X	–	N	P	
Canada-Peru	S	–	P	P	X	DX	N	P	C
Canada-Poland	–	–	–	–	–	–	B	–	
Canada-Romania	–	E	–	P	X	X	NB	P	I
Canada-South Africa	–	E	–	–	X	–	N	P	
Canada-Slovakia	–	–	–	P	X	X	NB	P	I
Canada-Thailand	–	E	–		X	–	N	P	
Canada-Ukraine	–	E	–		X	–	N	P	
Canada-Venezuela	–	E	–		X	–	NB	P	
China-Albania	–	–	–		–	–	–	–	
China-Australia	–	–	–		–	–	–	–	
China-Bahrain	–	–	–		–	–	–	–	
China-Belgium	–	–	–		–	–	–	–	
China-Bolivia	–	–	–		–	–	–	–	
China-Bosnia Herzegovina	–	–	–		–	–	–	–	
China-Botswana	–	–	–		–	–	–	–	
China-Bulgaria	–	–	–		–	–	–	–	
China-Cote D'Ivorie	–	–	–		–	–	–	–	
China-Estonia	–	–	–		–	–	–	–	
China-Guyana	P	–	–		–	–	–	–	

	Preamble	Environment & Labor	Limited Public Purpose Exceptions	No Relaxation	General Exceptions	Security Exceptions	Exceptions for Transfers	Prudential Financial Measures	Clarification of Indirect Expropriation
China-Kuwait	–	–	–		–	–	B	–	
China-Netherlands	–	–	–		–	–	–	–	
China-New Zealand	–	–	–		B	B	–	–	
China-Pakistan	–	–	–		–	–	–	–	
China-Singapore	–	–	–		B	B	–	–	
China-Sweden	–	–	–		–	–	–	–	
China-Uganda	–	–	–		–	–	B	–	
Colombia-Belgium	–	EL	–	PL	–	O	NB	P	C
Colombia-China	–	–	–		–	O	N	P	C
Colombia-India	–	E	–		O	B	NB	P	I
Colombia-Japan	PLS	E	P	PL	O	X	NB	P	C
Colombia-UK	–	E	N		–		NB	P	C
Croatia-Azerbaijan	PS	–	–		–	B	N	–	–
Egypt-Albania		–	–		–	–	–	–	
Egypt-Argentina		–	–		–	–	–	–	
Egypt-Austria	–	–	–		–	–	–	–	
Egypt-Belarus		–	–		–	–	–	–	–
Egypt-China	–	–	–		–	–	–	–	
Egypt-Finland		–	–		–	–	–	–	

Egypt-Jordan		–	–	–	–	–	–	–
Egypt-Latvia		–	–	–	–	–	–	
Egypt-Netherlands		–	–	–	–	–	–	
Egypt-Portugal		–	–	–	–	–	–	–
Egypt-Thailand		–	–	–	–	–	–	–
Egypt-UK		–	–	–	–	–	–	
France-Malta		–	–	–	–	–	–	
France-Mexico	–	–	–	–	–	B	–	
France-Peru		–	–	–	–	–	–	
France-Uganda	–	–	–	–	–	B	–	
France-Uruguay		–	–	–	–	–	–	
Germany-Antigua & Barbuda		–	P	–	–	B	–	
Germany-Argentina	–	–	P	–	–	–	–	
Germany-Bangladesh		–	**P**	–	–	–	–	
Germany-Barbados		–	**P**	–	–	–	–	
Germany-Benin		–	**P**	–	–	**B**	–	
Germany-Ethiopia	–	–	**P**	–	–	–	–	
Germany-Guyana		–	**P**	–	–	–	–	
Germany-India	–	–	**P**	–	**B**	–	–	
Germany-Kuwait		–	–	–	–	–	–	

	Preamble	Environment & Labor	Limited Public Purpose Exceptions	No Relaxation	General Exceptions	Security Exceptions	Exceptions for Transfers	Prudential Financial Measures	Clarification of Indirect Expropriation
Germany-Lebanon	–	–	**P**		–	–	–	–	
Germany-Mexico	–	–	**P**		–	**D**	NB	–	
Germany-Philippines	–	–	**P**		–	–	–	–	
Germany-Poland	–	–	**P**		–	–	**B**	–	
Germany-Republic of Korea	–	–	**P**		–	–	**B**	–	
Germany-Syria	–	–	**P**		–	–	–	–	
Hungary-Australia	–	–	–		–	–	–	–	
Hungary-Canada	–	–	–		–	–	B	–	
Hungary-Chile	–	–	–		–	–	–	–	
Hungary-China	–	–	–		–	–	–	–	
Hungary-Croatia	–	–	–		–	–	–	–	
Hungary-Cuba	–	–	–		–	–	–	–	
Hungary-Greece	–	–	–		–	–	–	–	
Hungary-Israel	–	–	–		–	–	–	–	
Hungary-Lebanon	–	–	–		–	–	–	–	
Hungary-Netherlands	–	–	–		–	–	–	–	

Hungary-Singapore	–	–	–	–	–	–	–
Hungary-Sweden	–	–	–	–	–	–	–
Hungary-Thailand	–	–	–	–	–	–	–
India-Australia	–	–	–	–	B	–	–
India-Austria	–	–	–	–	B	–	–
India-Croatia	–	–	–	–	B	–	–
India-Czech Republic	–	–	–	–	B	–	–
India-Denmark	–	–	–	–	Pests Only	–	–
India-Egypt	–	–	–	–	B	–	–
India-Ghana	–	–	–	–	B	–	–
India-Indonesia	–	–	–	–	B	–	–
India-Morocco	–	–	–	–	O	–	–
India-Netherlands	–	–	–	–	B	–	–
India-Oman	–	–	–	–	B	–	–
India-Republic of Korea	–	–	–	–	–	–	–
India-Sri Lanka	–	–	–	–	B	–	–
India-Sweden	–	–	–	–	B	–	–
India-Switzerland	–	–	–	–	B	–	–
India-Turkey	–	–	–	–	B	–	–
India-UK	–	–	–	–	B	–	–
Italy-Bangladesh	–	–	–	–	–	–	–
Italy-Bosnia Herzegovina	–	–	–	–	–	–	–

	Preamble	Environment & Labor	Limited Public Purpose Exceptions	No Relaxation	General Exceptions	Security Exceptions	Exceptions for Transfers	Prudential Financial Measures	Clarification of Indirect Expropriation
Italy-Egypt	–	–	–		–	–	–	–	
Italy-Jordan	–	–	–		–	–	–	–	
Italy-Lebanon	–	–	–		–	–	N	–	
Italy-Malta	–	–	–		–	–	–	–	
Italy-Mexico	–	–	–		–	**D**	**NB**	–	
Italy-Mongolia	–	–	–		–	–	–	–	
Italy-Pakistan	–	–	–		–	–	–	–	
Italy-Philippines	–	–	–		–	–	–	–	
Italy-Republic of Korea	–	–	–		–	–	–	–	
Italy-Tanzania	–	–	–		–	–	–	–	
Japan-Bangladesh	–	–	–		–	–	–	–	
Japan-China	–	–	**P**		–	–	–	–	
Japan-Egypt	–	–	–		–	–	–	–	
Japan-Iraq	**PL**	–	–	**PL**	–	–	**NB**	**P**	
Japan-Laos	**PL**	**E**	–	**P**	**O**	**X**	**NB**	**P**	
Japan-Mongolia	–	–	–		–	–	**B**	–	
Japan-Pakistan	–	–	–		–	–	**B**	–	
Japan-Papua New Guinea	**PLS**	–	–	**PL**	–	–	**NB**	**P**	
Japan-Peru	**PL**	–	–	**PL**	**O**	**X**	**NB**	**P**	C
Japan-Sri Lanka	–	–	–		–	–	**B**	–	
Japan-Vietnam	**P**	–	–	**P**	**O**	**X**	**NB**	**P**	

Kenya-Slovakia	**PL**	–	–		–	**O**	**NB**	–
Mexico-Australia	–	–	–		–	–	**NB**	–
Mexico-Austria	–	–	–		–	**D**	**NB**	–
Mexico-China	–	–	–		–	–	**NB**	–
Mexico-Cuba	–	–	**P**		–	**D**	**NB**	–
Mexico-Czech Republic	–	–	–		–	–	**NB**	–
Mexico-Denmark	–	–	–		–	–	**NB**	–
Mexico-Greece	–	–	–		–	–	**NB**	–
Mexico-Iceland	–	–	–		–	**D**	**NB**	–
Mexico-India	–	–	–		–	**B**	**NB**	–
Mexico-Netherlands	–	–	–		–	**D**	**NB**	–
Mexico-Portugal	–	–	–		–	–	**B**	–
Mexico-Republic of Korea	–	–	–		–	–	**NB**	–
Mexico-Sweden	–	–	–		–	**D**	**NB**	–
Mexico-Switzerland	–	–	–	**P**	–	**D**	–	–
Mexico-UK	–	–	–		–	–	**NB**	–
Nigeria-Finland	**PL**	–	–		–	**O**	–	–
Nigeria-Germany	–	–	N		–	–	–	–
Nigeria-Netherlands	–	–	–		–	–	–	–
Nigeria-Republic of Korea	–	–	–		–	–	–	–
Nigeria-Spain	–	–	N		–	–	–	–

	Preamble	Environment & Labor	Limited Public Purpose Exceptions	No Relaxation	General Exceptions	Security Exceptions	Exceptions for Transfers	Prudential Financial Measures	Clarification of Indirect Expropriation
Nigeria-Turkey	–	–	–		–	–	–	–	
Nigeria-UK	–	–	–		–	–	–	–	
Peru-Belgium	–	–	**P**	**PL**	–	–	**N**	–	
Peru-Republic of Korea	–	–	–		–	–	–	–	
Peru-Singapore	–	–	–		–	B	N	–	
Republic of Korea-Algeria	–	–	–		–	–	–	–	
Republic of Korea-Austria	–	–	–		–	–	–	–	
Republic of Korea-Bangladesh	–	–	–		–	–	–	–	
Republic of Korea-Bolivia	–	–	–		–	–	–	–	
Republic of Korea-Chile	–	–	–		–	–	–	–	
Republic of Korea-El Salvador	–	–	–		–	–	–	–	
Republic of Korea-Finland	–	–	–		–	–	–	–	

Republic of Korea-Laos	–	–	–	–	–	–	–
Republic of Korea-Lithuania	–	–	–	–	–	–	–
Republic of Korea-Netherlands	–	–	–	–	–	–	–
Republic of Korea-Portugal	–	–	–	–	–	–	–
Republic of Korea-Qatar	–	–	–	–	–	–	–
Republic of Korea-Ukraine	–	–	–	–	–	–	–
Russia-Canada	–	–	–	–	–	B	–
Russia-Cyprus	–	–	–	–	–	–	–
Russia-Egypt	–	–	–	–	–	–	–
Russia-Ethiopia	–	–	–	–	–	–	–
Russia-Greece	–	–	–	–	–	–	–
Russia-Hungary	–	E	–	O	O	–	–
Russia-Japan	–	–	–	–	B	B	–
Russia-Lithuania	–	–	–	–	–	–	–
Russia-Netherlands	–	–	–	–	–	–	–
Russia-Norway	–	–	–	–	–	–	–
Russia-Thailand	–	–	N	–	–	–	–
Russia-Ukraine	–	–	–	–	–	–	–

	Preamble	Environment & Labor	Limited Public Purpose Exceptions	No Relaxation	General Exceptions	Security Exceptions	Exceptions for Transfers	Prudential Financial Measures	Clarification of Indirect Expropriation
Russia-UK	–	–	–		–	–	–	–	
Saudi Arabia-Austria	–	–	–		–	–	–	–	
Saudi Arabia-BeloLux	–	–	–		–	–	–	–	
Saudi Arabia-Czech Republic	–	–	–		–	O	N	–	
Saudi Arabia-Malaysia	–	–	–		–	–	–	–	
Saudi Arabia-Republic of Korea	–	–	–		–	–	–	–	
South Africa-Chile	–	–	–		–	–	–	–	
South Africa-Czech Republic	–	–	–		–	–	–	–	
South Africa-Finland	–	–	–		–	–	–	–	
South Africa-Iran	–	–	–		–	–	–	–	
South Africa-Mauritius	–	–	–		–	–	–	–	

South Africa-Turkey	–	–	–		–	–	–	–	
South Africa-Zimbabwe	–	–	–		–	–	–	–	
Spain-Croatia	–	–	–		–	–	–	–	
Spain-Cuba	–	–	–		–	–	–	–	
Spain-Czech Republic	–	–	–		–	–	–	–	
Spain-Hungary	–	–	–		–	–	–	–	
Spain-Lebanon	–	–	–		–	–	–	–	
Spain-Morocco	–	–	–		–	–	–	–	
Spain-Republic of Korea	–	–	–		–	–	–	–	
Turkey-Gabon	**PL**	–	–		X	X	**B**	–	**C**
Turkey-Italy	–	–	–		–	–	–	–	
Turkey-Japan	–	–	–		–	–	**B**	–	
Turkey-Tanzania	–	–	–	**P**	X	X	**B**	–	**C**
Turkey-UAE	–	–	–		–	–	–	–	
UAE-Austria	–	–	–		–	–	**B**	–	
UAE-Azerbaijan	–	E	–		O	O	–	–	
UAE-China	–	–	–		–	–	–	–	
UAE-Czech Republic	–	–	–		–	–	–	–	
UAE-Finland	–	–	–		–	–	–	–	
UAE-Malaysia	–	–	–		–	–	–	–	
UAE-Republic of Korea	–	–	–		–	–	–	–	

	Preamble	Environment & Labor	Limited Public Purpose Exceptions	No Relaxation	General Exceptions	Security Exceptions	Exceptions for Transfers	Prudential Financial Measures	Clarification of Indirect Expropriation
UAE-Turkmenistan	–	–	–		–	–	–	–	
UAE-Vietnam	–	–	–		–	–	–	–	
UK-Albania	–	–	–		–	–	–	–	
UK-Bulgaria	–	–	–		–	–	–	–	
UK-Burundi	–	–	–		–	–	–	–	
UK-Chile	–	–	–		–	–	–	–	
UK-China	–	–	–		–	–	**B**	–	
UK-Jamaica	–	–	–		–	–	**B**	–	
UK-Mongolia	–	–	–		–	–	–	–	
UK-Nicaragua	–	–	–		–	–	–	–	
UK-Oman	–	–	–		–	–	–	–	
UK-Singapore	–	–	–		–	–	**B**	–	
UK-Swaziland	–	–	–		–	–	–	–	
UK-Vanuatu	–	–	–		–	–	–	–	
USA-Albania	**PL**	–	–		–	**B**	N	–	
USA-Argentina	**L**	–	–		–	**O**	N	–	
USA-Armenia	**L**	–	–		–	**O**	N	–	
USA-Azerbaijan	**PL**	–	–		–	**B**	N	–	
USA-Bolivia	**PL**	–	–		–	**B**	N	–	
USA-Bulgaria	**L**	–	–		–	**O**	N	–	
USA-Cameroon	–	–	–		–	**O**	N	–	
USA-Croatia	**PL**	–	–		–	**B**	N	–	

USA-Czech Republic	L	–	–		–	O	N	–	
USA-Ecuador	L	–	–		–	O	N	–	
USA-El Salvador	PL	–	–		–	B	N	–	
USA-Georgia	PL	–	–		–	B	N	–	
USA-Haiti	–	–	–		–	O	N	–	
USA-Jordan	PL	–	–		–	B	N	–	
USA-Kyrgyzstan	L	–	–		–	O	N	–	
USA-Latvia	L	–	–		–	O	N	–	
USA-Lithuania	L	–	–		–	O	N	–	
USA-Mongolia	L	–	–		–	O	N	–	
USA-Morocco	–	–	–		–	O	N	–	
USA-Mozambique	PL	–	–		–	B	N	–	
USA-Nicaragua	PL	–	–		–	BS	N	–	
USA-Poland	L	–	–		–	O	N	–	
USA-Romania	L	–	–		–	O	N	–	
USA-Russia	L	–	–		–	O	N	–	
USA-Rwanda	PL	E	P	PL	–	X	N	P	C
USA-Senegal	–	–	–		–	O	N	–	
USA-Sri Lanka	L	–	–		–	O	NB	–	
USA-Trinidad &Tobago	PL	–	–		–	B	N	–	
USA-Tunisia	–	–	–		–	O	NB	–	
USA-Turkey	–	–	–		–	O	NB	–	
USA-Ukraine	L	–	–		–	O	N	–	
USA-Uruguay	PL	EL	–	PL	P	X	N	P	C

	Preamble	Environment & Labor	Limited Public Purpose Exceptions	No Relaxation	General Exceptions	Security Exceptions	Exceptions for Transfers	Prudential Financial Measures	Clarification of Indirect Expropriation
USA-Uzbekistan	PL	–	–		–	B	N	–	
Venezuela-Argentina	–	–	–		–	–	–	–	
Venezuela-Barbados	–	–	–		–	–	–	–	
Venezuela-Bolivia	–	–	–		–	–	B	–	
Venezuela-Brazil	–	–	–		–	–	–	–	
Venezuela-Chile	–	–	–		–	–	–	–	
Venezuela-Costa Rica	–	–	–		–	–	NB	–	
Venezuela-Czech Republic	–	–	–		–	–	–	–	
Venezuela-Denmark	–	–	–		–	–	–	–	
Venezuela-Ecuador	–	–	–		–	–	–	–	
Venezuela-Germany	–	–	N		–	–	–	–	
Venezuela-Lithuania	–	–	–		–	–	–	–	
Venezuela-Netherlands	–	–	–		–	–	–	–	

Venezuela-Paraguay	–	–	–	–	–	–	–
Venezuela-Peru	–	–	–	–	O	–	–
Venezuela-Spain	–	–	–	–	–	B	–
Venezuela-Sweden	–	–	–	–	–	–	–
Venezuela-UK	–	–	–	–	–	–	–

APPENDIX III

A Spatial Comparison of Provisions Relating to Investment Protection, Incentives, and Dispute Resolution in Foreign Investment Promotion Statutes and Bilateral Investment Treaties

	Protection and Incentives Provided under FIP	Dispute Resolution Procedure under FIP	Protection Provided under BIT	Dispute Resolution Procedure under BIT
Russia	1999 Law on Foreign Investment (July 9, 1999) *Article 4(1)* – National Treatment Standard *Articles 5, 6, & 7* – Guarantees of Legal Protection for and Availability of Foreign Investors/Investments in the Russian Federation *Article 8* – Protection against Expropriation & Nationalization *Article 9* – Guarantees to Foreign Investors against Unfavorable Changes in the Legislation of the Russian Federation *Articles 12–17* – Specific Investment-Related Incentives and Rights Provided for Foreign Investors, Such as the Right to Export *Article 23* – Governmental Policy in the Sphere of Foreign Investment	1999 Law on Foreign Investment (July 9, 1999) ***Article 10. Guarantee of Proper Settlement of Disputes Related to Investment and Business Activities of Foreign Investors in the Russian Federation*** Any dispute involving a foreign investor and related to the investment and business activities of such investor in the Russian Federation shall be settled in compliance with the international treaties of the Russian Federation and federal laws in a court, an arbitration court or international arbitration (arbitration tribunal).	Agreement between the Government of the Republic of Hungary and the Government of the Russian Federation for the Promotion and Reciprocal Protection of Investments *Article 2(1)* – Promotion of Investments *Article 2(2)* – Fair & Equitable Treatment Standard and Full Protection & Security *Article 3* – National Treatment Standard *Article 3* – Most-Favoured-Nation Treatment Standard *Article 5* – Protection against Expropriation & Nationalization	Agreement between the Government of the Republic of Hungary and the Government of the Russian Federation for the Promotion and Reciprocal Protection of Investments ***Article 8. Disputes between an Investor of one Contracting Party and the Other Contracting Party*** 1. Any dispute which may arise between an investor of one Contracting Party and the other Contracting Party in connection with an investment in its territory shall, as far as possible, be settled through negotiations. 2. If the dispute between an investor of one Contracting Party and the other Contracting Party can not be thus settled within a period of six months from the date it arose, the investor shall be entitled to submit the case either to: a) a competent court or arbitration tribunal of the Contracting Party in the territory of which the investment has been made; b) the Arbitration Institution of the Stockholm Chamber of Commerce; c) an ad hoc arbitration tribunal set up in accordance with the Arbitration Rules of the United Nations Commission on International Trade Law (UNCITRAL).

	Protection and Incentives Provided under FIP	Dispute Resolution Procedure under FIP	Protection Provided under BIT	Dispute Resolution Procedure under BIT
Albania	Law No. 7764 (February 11, 1999) *Article 2(1)* – Promotion of Investments *Article 2(2)* – Fair & Equitable Treatment Standard and Full Protection & Security *Article 2(3)* – International Minimum Standard of Treatment *Article 3* – Right to Employ Foreign Citizens *Articles 4 & 5* – Protection against Expropriation & Nationalization *Article 11* – Transparency	Law No. 7764 (February 11, 1999) *Article 8. Dispute Settlement* 1. If a dispute arises between a foreign investor and an Albanian private party or an Albanian State enterprise or company, which has not been settled through an agreement, the foreign Investor may choose to settle the dispute according to any kind of previously agreed upon and applied procedures. If there is no procedure foreseen for the settlement of disputes, then the foreign investor has the right to submit the dispute for resolution to a competent court or arbitrator of the Republic of Albania, according to its laws. 2. If a dispute arises between a foreign investor and the Albanian public administration, which has not been settled through an agreement, the foreign investor may submit the dispute for resolution to a competent court or arbitrator of the Republic of Albania, according to its laws. If the dispute relates to expropriation, Compensation for expropriation or discrimination, as well as to transfers as provided in article 7 of this law, the foreign investor may submit the dispute for resolution to the International Center for Settlement of Investment Disputes ("Center"),	Agreement on Encouragement and Reciprocal Protection of Investments between the Kingdom of the Netherlands and the Republic of Albania *Article 2* – Promotion of Investments *Article 3(1)* – Fair & Equitable Treatment Standard and Full Protection & Security *Article 3(2)* – National Treatment Standard *Article 3(3)* – Most-Favoured Nation Treatment Standard *Article 6* – Protection against Expropriation & Nationalization	Agreement on Encouragement and Reciprocal Protection of Investments between the Kingdom of the Netherlands and the Republic of Albania *Article 9.* (1) Any dispute between either Contracting Party and a national of the other Contracting Party concerning an investment of that national in the territory of the former Party shall as far as possible be settled by the parties to the dispute in amicable way. (2) If such a dispute can not be settled within a period of three months from the date at which either party to the dispute requested amicable settlement, the dispute shall at the request of the national concerned be submitted to an international arbitral tribunal established under the Arbitration Rules of the United Nation Commission on International Trade Law. (3) In case both Contracting parties have become members of the Convention of 18 March 1965 on the Settlement of Investment Disputes between States and Nationals of Other States, disputes between either Contracting party and nationals of the other contracting

		established by the Convention on the Settlement of Investment Disputes between States and Nationals of Other States, approved in Washington, on 18 March 1965. 3. Every decision of international arbitration according to this article is final and irrevocable for the parties in dispute. The Republic of Albania undertakes to apply without delay the provisions of these decisions and assure their implementation within its territory.		party under the first paragraph of the present Article shall be submitted for settlement by conciliation or arbitration to the International Centre for the Settlement of Investment Disputes. (4) A legal person which has the nationality of the Contracting party and which before such a dispute arises is controlled by nationals of another Contracting party shall for the purpose of Article 25 (2)(b) of the Convention referred to in paragraph 3 above be treated as a national of that other Contracting party. (5) Each Contracting party hereby gives its unconditional consent to the submission of disputes to international arbitration in accordance with the provisions of this Article. (6) The awards of arbitration shall be final and binding and shall be enforced in accordance with domestic law.
Georgia	**Law of Georgia on the Investment Activity Promotion 7 Guarantees (November 12, 1999)** *Article 3(1)* – National Treatment Standard *Article 3(2 –5)* – Financial & Monetary-Related Rights Accorded to Foreign Investors *Article 3(6)* – Right to Export *Article 5* – Promotion of Investment *Articles 7 & 8* – Guarantee of Investment Inviolability, i.e.,	**Law of Georgia on the Investment Activity promotion & Guarantees (November 12, 1999)** ***Article 16. Procedure for Dispute Resolution*** 1. A dispute between a foreign investor and an enterprise registered in Georgia shall be subject to resolution under the agreement of the parties or in courts of Georgia.	**Agreement between the Republic of Austria and Georgia for the Promotion and Protection of Investments** *Article 2* – Promotion of Investments *Article 3(1)* – Fair & Equitable Treatment Standard and Full Protection & Security *Article 3(2)* – Assurance of Non-Interference with Foreign Investment *Article 3(3)* – National Treatment Standard	**Agreement between the Republic of Austria and Georgia for the Promotion and Protection of Investments** ***Article 12. Means of Settlement, Time Periods*** (1) A dispute between a Contracting Party and an investor of the other Contracting Party shall, if possible, be settled by negotiation or consultation. If it is not so

Protection and Incentives Provided under FIP	Dispute Resolution Procedure under FIP	Protection Provided under BIT	Dispute Resolution Procedure under BIT
Protection against Expropriation & Nationalization *Article 10* – Right to Employ Foreigners; Right of Foreign Employees to Export Income; Exception from Taxation of Foreign Employees Not Residing Permanently in Georgia *Article 15* – Guarantees during Amendment of Legislation	2. A dispute between a foreign investor and a State agency shall unless the procedure for its resolution is not defined by way of their agreement, be subject to resolution in courts of Georgia or in the International Center for the Resolution Investment Disputes. Unless the dispute is considered in the International Center for the Resolution of Investment Disputes, a foreign investor shall be entitled to apply to any international arbitration body which has been set up by the Commission of the United Nations for International Trade law – UNCITRAL to resolve the dispute in accordance with the rules established under the arbitration and international agreement. 3. Any award of international arbitration bodies as indicated in paragraph 2 of this Article shall be final and not subject to appeal. Its observance shall be secured by the State.	*Article 3(3)* – Most-Favoured-Nation Treatment Standard *Article 4* – Transparency *Article 5* – Protection against Expropriation & Nationalization	settled, the investor may choose to submit it for resolution: (a) to the competent courts or administrative tribunals of the Contracting party, party to the dispute; (b) in accordance with any applicable previously agreed dispute settlement procedure; (c) in accordance with this Article to: (i) the International Centre for Settlement of Investment Disputes ("the Centre"), established pursuant to the Convention on the Settlement of Investment Disputes between States and Nationals of Other States ("the ICSID Convention"), if the Contracting Party of the investor and the Contracting Party, party to the dispute are both parties to the ICSID Convention; (ii) the Centre under the rules governing the Additional Facility for the Administration of Proceeding by the

				Secretariat of the Centre, if the Contracting Party of the investor or the Contracting Party, party to the dispute, but not both, is a party to the ICSID Convention; (iii) a sole arbitrator or an ad hoc arbitration tribunal established under the Arbitration Rules of the United Nations Commission on International Trade law ("UNCITRAL"); (iv) the International Chamber of Commerce, by a sole arbitrator or an ad hoc tribunal under its rules of arbitration. (2) A dispute may be submitted for resolution pursuant to paragraph 1(c) of this Article after 50 days from the date notice of intent to do so was provided to the contracting Party, party to the dispute, but not later than five years from the date the investor first acquired or should have acquired knowledge of the events which gave rise to the dispute.
Kazakhstan	**Law of the Republic of Kazakhstan on Investments (January 8, 2003)** *Article 4* – Guarantees of Legal Assistance for Investors, Including Right to Compensation for Illegal Activities of Republic of Kazakhstan	**Law of the Republic of Kazakhstan on Investments (January 8, 2003)** *Article 9. Settlement of Disputes* 1. Investment disputes can be settled either by negotiations, including involving experts, or in	**Treaty between the United States of America and the Republic of Kazakhstan Concerning the Encouragement and Reciprocal Protection of Investment**	**Treaty between the United States of America and the Republic of Kazakhstan Concerning the Encouragement and Reciprocal Protection of Investment** *Article VI*.

Protection and Incentives Provided under FIP	Dispute Resolution Procedure under FIP	Protection Provided under BIT	Dispute Resolution Procedure under BIT
***Article** 5* – Guarantees of Right to Use Revenues at Investor's Discretion ***Article** 6* – Transparency ***Article** 8* – Protection against Expropriation & Nationalization ***Articles** 11–22* – Public Support to Investments, Which Includes a Vast Array of Investment Incentives and Procedures for Obtaining Investment Preferences ***Article** 23* – Stability of Contracts	compliance with the procedure for disputes settlement agreed in advance. 2. If investment disputes cannot be settled in compliance with provisions of paragraph 1 of this Article disputes shall be settled in compliance with international agreements and legislative acts of the Republic of Kazakhstan in courts of the Republic of Kazakhstan as well as in international arbitrations identified upon agreement of parties. 3. Disputes which are not related to investments shall be settled in compliance with the legislation of the Republic of Kazakhstan.	***Article** II(1)* – National Treatment Standard ***Article** II(1)* – Most-Favoured-Nation Treatment Standard ***Article** II(2)(a)* – Fair & Equitable Treatment Standard and Full Protection & Security ***Article** II(2)(a)* – International Minimum Standard of Treatment ***Article** II(2)(b)* – Assurance of Non-Interference with Foreign Investment ***Article** II(7)* – Transparency ***Article** III* – Protection against Expropriation & Nationalization	2. In the event of an investment dispute, the parties to the dispute should initially seek a resolution through consultation and negotiation. If the dispute cannot be settled amicably, the national or company concerned may choose to submit the dispute for resolution. (a) To the courts or administrative tribunals of the Party that is a Party to the dispute; or (b) In accordance with any applicable, previously agreed dispute-settlement procedures; (c) In accordance with the terms of paragraph 3; 3. (a) Provided that the national or company concerned has not submitted the dispute for resolution under paragraph 2 (2) or (b) and that six months have elapsed from the date on which the dispute arose, the national or company concerned may choose to consent in writing to the submission of the dispute for settlement by binding arbitration: (i) to the International Centre for the Settlement of Investment Disputes

("Centre") established by the Convention on the Settlement of Investment Disputes between States and Nationals of Other States, done at Washington, March 18, 1965 ("ICSID Convention"), provided that the Party is a Party to such Convention; or

(ii) to the Additional Facility of the Centre, if the Centre is not available; or

(iii) in accordance with the Arbitration Rules of the United Nations Commission on International Trade law (UNCITRAL); or

(iv) to any other arbitration institution, or in accordance with any other arbitration rules as may be mutually agreed between the parties to the dispute.

(b) Once the national or company concerned has so consented, either Party to the dispute may initiate arbitration in accordance with the choice so specified in the consent.

4. Each Party hereby consents to the submission of any investment disputes for settlement by binding arbitration in accordance with the choice specified in the written consent of the national or company under paragraph 3. Such consent, together with the

	Protection and Incentives Provided under FIP	Dispute Resolution Procedure under FIP	Protection Provided under BIT	Dispute Resolution Procedure under BIT
				written consent of the national or company when given under paragraph 3 shall satisfy the requirement for: (a) written consent of the parties to the dispute for purposes of Chapter 11 of the ICSID Convention (Jurisdiction of the Centre) and for purposes of the Additional Facility Rules; and (b) an "agreement in writing," for purposes of Article II of the United Nations Convention on the Recognition and Enforcement of Foreign Arbitral Awards, done at New York, June 10, 1958 ("New York Convention"). 5. Any arbitration under paragraph 3 (a)(ii), (iii) or (iv) of this Article shall be held in a State that is a Party to the new York convention. 6. Any arbitral award rendered pursuant to this Article shall be final and binding on the parties to the dispute. Each Party undertakes to carry out without delay the provisions of any such award and to provide its territory for its enforcement.

China	**<u>Law of the People's Republic of China on Foreign-Capital Enterprises (October 31, 2000)</u>** ***Article 1*** – Permission and Protection for Foreign Investments ***Article 3*** – Special Promotion for Export-Oriented or Technologically Advanced Foreign-Capital Enterprises ***Article 4*** – General Protection for Investments ***Article 5*** – Protection against Expropriation & Nationalization ***Article 12*** – Right of Foreign Employees to Form Unions ***Article 15*** – Right to Import Materials from the World Market ***Article 19*** – Right to Remit Profits Abroad		**<u>Agreement between the People's Republic of China and Bosnia and Herzegovina on the Promotion and Protection of Investments</u>** ***Article 2(1)*** – Promotion of Investments ***Article 2(1)*** – Transparency ***Article 2(2)*** – Fair & Equitable Treatment Standard and Full Protection & Security ***Article 3(1)*** – National Treatment Standard ***Article 3(1)*** – Most-Favoured-Nation Treatment Standard ***Article 4*** – Protection against Expropriation & Nationalization	**<u>Agreement between the People's Republic of China and Bosnia and Herzegovina on the Promotion and Protection of Investments</u>** ***Article 8. Settlement of Disputes between an Investor and a Contracting Party*** 1. Any dispute between a Contracting Party and an investor of the other contracting Party, related to an investment, shall be as far as possible settled amicably through negotiations. 2. If the dispute cannot be settled amicably through negotiations within six months from the date it has been raised by either party to the dispute, it shall be submitted: – to the competent court of the Contracting Party that is a party to the dispute; or – to the International Center for Settlement of Investment Disputes ("the Centre") under the Convention on the Settlement of Investment Disputes between States and Nationals of Other States, done at Washington on March 18, 1965 provided that the Contracting Party involved in the disputes may require the investor concerned to go through the domestic administrative review procedures specified by the laws and regulations of that Contracting Party before the submission to the Centre. Once

	Protection and Incentives Provided under FIP	Dispute Resolution Procedure under FIP	Protection Provided under BIT	Dispute Resolution Procedure under BIT
				the investor has submitted the dispute to the jurisdiction of the concerned Contracting Party or to the Centre, the choice of one of the two procedures shall be final. 3. The arbitration award shall be based on: – the provisions of this Agreement; – the laws of the Contracting Party in whose territory the investment has been made including the rules relative to conflict of laws; and – the rules and universally accepted principles of international law. 4. The arbitration award shall be final and binding on both parties to the dispute and shall be executed by the Contracting Party concerned.
Laos	**Law on Investment Promotion (July 8, 2009)** *Articles* 2, 4, & 5 – Promotion of Investments; Governmental Policy on Investment Promotion; Principles of Investment Promotion *Article* 7 – Promotion of International Cooperation and Integration in Investment Promotion	**Law on Investment Promotion (July 8, 2009)** *Article* 78. *Forms of Dispute Resolution* The dispute resolution related to investment can be performed in the following forms: 1. Mediation; 2. Administrative dispute resolution; 3. Dispute resolution by the Committee for Economic Dispute Resolution.	**Agreement between Japan and the Lao People's Democratic Republic for the Liberalization, Promotion and Protection of Investment** *Article* 2 – National Treatment Standard *Article* 3 – Most-Favoured-Nation Treatment Standard *Article* 4 – Promotion of Investment	**Agreement between Japan and the Lao People's Democratic Republic for the Liberalization, Promotion, and Protection of Investment** *Article* 17. ***Settlement of Investment Disputes between a Contracting Party and an Investor of the Other Contracting Party***

Articles 44–46 – One-Stop-Service for Investment; Principles & Procedures

Articles 49 & 50 – Promoted Sectors and Promoted Zones for Foreign Investment

Articles 51–54 – Incentives Related to Taxes, Financing & Customs Duties; Specific Promotion Incentives for Public Investments, i.e., Hospitals, Schools, etc.

Articles 56–59 – Promotion of Investment via Transparency and Land Use Rights

Articles 60–62 – Protection of Investment, Including Protection against Expropriation & Nationalization

Articles 63–68 – General Rights of Investors, Including Right to Invest, Right to Govern & Manage Business Operations, Right to Hire Labor Forces, Right to Reside, Right to Transfer

Article 72 – Prohibited Actions for Govern Officials

Article 96 – Incentives for Outstanding Performance

Article 79. Mediation

In the case of conflict related to investment, the parties should make all efforts to solve the conflict by consultation and mediation to reach mutual benefits.

Article 80. Administrative Dispute Resolution

In the case of conflict that cannot be amicably settled or mediated the parties have the right to require the Planning and Investment authority or the Industry and Commerce authority or other relevant sectors to address the conflict as an administrative dispute resolution in accordance with their roles and duties.

Article 81. Dispute Resolution by the Committee for Economic Dispute Resolution

In case that the conflict cannot be amicably settled or remedied in the administrative dispute resolution process, the parties have the right to request the Committee for Economic Dispute Resolution for resolution in accordance with the laws and consent of both parties.

Article 82. Filing of Litigation

In case that a party finds that the conflict resolution from concerned authorities is not fair or the investment is damaged, the party has the right to file a complaint to the People's Court for settlement the conflict according to

Article 5 – International Minimum Standard of Treatment

Article 5 – Fair & Equitable Treatment Standard and Full Protection & Security

Article 6 – Access to Courts of Justice

Article 9 – Transparency

Article 12 – Protection against Expropriation & Nationalization

1. For the purposes of this Article, an investment dispute is a dispute between a Contracting Party and an investor of the other Contracting Party that has incurred loss or damage by reason of, or arising out of, an alleged breach of any right conferred by this Agreement with respect to investors of that other Contracting Party.
2. Nothing in this Article shall be construed so as to prevent an investor who is a party to an investment dispute (hereinafter referred to in this Article as "disputing investor") from seeking administrative or judicial settlement within the Area of the Contracting Party that is a party to the investment dispute (hereinafter referred to in this Article as "disputing Party").
3. An investment dispute shall, as far as possible, be settled amicably through consultation or negotiation between the disputing investor and the disputing Party (hereinafter referred to in this Article as "the disputing Party").
4. If the investment dispute cannot be settled through such consultation or negotiations within three months from the date on which the disputing investor requested the consultation or negation in writing

Protection and Incentives Provided under FIP	Dispute Resolution Procedure under FIP	Protection Provided under BIT	Dispute Resolution Procedure under BIT
	the laws and regulations. With regard to conflicts related to the investment contracting with the Government, the settlement of such conflicts shall follow the procedures stipulated in the Contract.		and if the disputing investor has not submitted the investment dispute for resolution under courts of justice or administrative tribunals or agencies, the disputing investor may submit the investment dispute to one of the following international conciliations or arbitrations: (a) conciliation or arbitration in accordance with the Convention on the Settlement of Investment Disputes between States and Nationals of Other States, done at Washington, March 18, 1965, as may be amended (hereinafter referred to in this Article as "ICSID Convention"), so long as the ICSID Convention is in force between the Contracting parties; (b) conciliation or arbitration under the Additional Facility Rules of the International Centre for Settlement of Investment Disputes, as may be amended, so long as the ICSID Convention is not in force between the Contracting Parties;

				(c) arbitration under the Arbitration Rules of the United Nations commission on International Trade Law, as may be amended; and (d) if agreed with the disputing Party, any arbitration in accordance with other arbitration rules. (5) The applicable arbitration rules shall govern the arbitration set forth in paragraph 4 except to the extent modified in this Article.
Vietnam	**Law on Investment (December 25, 2001)** *Article 4* – Policies on Investment, including Equal Treatment, Recognition of Ownership, and Policy of Incentives *Articles 6–11* – Investment Guarantees to Foreign Investors, including Guarantees Related to Capital & Assets, Protection of Intellectual Property Rights, Open Markets, Right to Remit Capital and Assets Abroad, Guarantee of Uniform Prices/Fees/ Charges, and Guarantees in Event of Changes in Law *Articles 12–19* – Rights of Investors, Including Right to Autonomy in Investment, Right to Access and Use Investment Resources, Right to Import & Export, Right to Purchase Foreign Currencies, Right to Assign, and Right to Mortgage	**Law on Investment (December 25, 2001)** *Article 12. Dispute Resolution* 1. Any dispute relating to investment activities in Vietnam shall be resolved through negotiation and conciliation, or shall be referred to arbitration or to a court in accordance with law. 2. Any dispute as between domestic investors or as between a domestic investor and a State administrative body of Vietnam relating to investment activities in the territory of Vietnam shall be resolved at a Vietnamese court or arbitration body. 3. Any dispute to which one disputing party is a foreign investor or an enterprise with foreign owned capital, or any dispute as between foreign	**Agreement between Australia and the Socialist Republic of Vietnam on the Reciprocal Promotion and Protection of Investments** *Article 3(1)* – Promotion of Investments *Article 3(2)* – Fair & Equitable Treatment *Article 3(3)* – Assurance of Non-Interference with Foreign Investment *Article 4* – Most-Favoured-Nation Treatment Standard *Article 6* – Transparency *Article 7* – Protection against Expropriation	**Agreement between Australia and the Socialist Republic of Vietnam on the Reciprocal Promotion and Protection of Investments** ***Article 12. Settlement of disputes between a Contracting Party and a National of the Other Contracting Party*** (1) In the event of a dispute between a Contracting Party and a national of the other Contracting Party relating to an investment, the parties to the dispute shall initially seek to resolve the dispute by consultations and negotiations. (2) If the dispute in question cannot be resolved through consultations and negotiations, either party to the dispute may: (a) in accordance with the law of the Contracting Party which

Protection and Incentives Provided under FIP	Dispute Resolution Procedure under FIP	Protection Provided under BIT	Dispute Resolution Procedure under BIT
Articles 32–39 – Investment Incentives, Including Taxes and Land Use Rights *Articles 40–44* – Various Promises of Support for Foreign Investments	investors shall be resolved by one of the following tribunals and organizations: (a) A Vietnamese court; (b) A Vietnamese arbitration body; (c) A foreign arbitration body; (d) An international arbitration body; (dd) An arbitration tribunal established in accordance with the agreement of the disputing parties. 4. Any dispute between a foreign investor and State administrative body of Vietnam relating to investment activities in the territory of Vietnam shall be resolved by a Vietnamese court or arbitration body, unless otherwise provided in a contract signed between a representative of a competent State body of Vietnam with the foreign investor or in an international treaty of which the Socialist Republic of Vietnam is a member.		has admitted the investment, initiate proceedings before that contracting Party's competent judicial or administrative bodies; (b) if both Contracting Parties are at that time party to the 1965 Convention on the Settlement of Investment Disputes between States and Nationals of Other States ("the Convention"), [1] refer the dispute to the International Centre for the Settlement of Investment Disputes ("the Centre") for conciliation or arbitration pursuant to Articles 28 or 36 of the Convention; (c) if both Contracting Parties are not at that time party to the Convention, or one party to the dispute has not consented to referring the dispute to the Centre, refer the dispute to an Arbitral Tribunal constituted in accordance with Annex B of this Agreement, or by agreement, to any other arbitral authority.

				(3) Once an action referred to in paragraph (2) of this Article has been taken, neither Contracting party shall pursue the dispute through diplomatic channels unless. (4) the relevant judicial or administrative body, the Secretary-General of the Centre, the arbitral authority or tribunal or the conciliation commission, as the case may be, has decided that it has no jurisdiction in relation to the dispute in question; or (5) the other Contracting Party has failed to abide by or comply with any judgment, award, or other determination made by the body in question. (6) In any proceeding involving a dispute relating to an investment, a Contracting Party shall not assert, as a defense, counter-claim, right of set-off or otherwise, that the national concerned has received or will receive, pursuant to an insurance or guarantee contract, indemnification or other compensation for all or part of any alleged loss.
Oman	**The Foreign Capital Investment Law (October 16, 1994)** *Article 8.1* – Exemption from Income Tax for Companies Conducting Activities in Specific Sectors	**The Foreign Capital Investment Law (October 16, 1994)** *Article 14*. It may be agreed to refer any dispute between the foreign investment	**Agreement between the Government of the Sultanate of Oman and the Government of the Republic of India for the Promotion and Protection of Investments**.	**Agreement between the Government of the Sultanate of Oman and the Government of the Republic of India for the Promotion and Protection of Investments**

Protection and Incentives Provided under FIP	Dispute Resolution Procedure under FIP	Protection Provided under BIT	Dispute Resolution Procedure under BIT
Article 9.1 – Exemption from Custom Duties on Plant & Machinery ***Article 11*** – Right to Transfer Profits Abroad ***Article 12*** – Protection against Expropriation & Nationalization	projects and third parties to a local or international arbitration tribunal.	***Article*** 3(1) – Promotion of Investments ***Article*** 3(2) – Fair & Equitable Treatment Standard ***Article 4*** – National Treatment Standard ***Article 4*** – Most-Favoured-Nation Treatment Standard ***Article*** 5 – Protection against Expropriation & Nationalization	***Article*** 9. ***Settlement of Disputes between an Investor and a Contracting Party*** (1) any dispute between an investor of one contracting Party and the other Contracting Party in relation to an investment of the former under this Agreement shall, as far as possible, be settled amicably through negotiations between the parties to the dispute. (2) Any such dispute which has not been amicably settled within a period of six months may, if both Parties agree, be submitted (a) to resolution, in accordance with the law of the Contracting party which has admitted the investment to that Contracting party's competent juridical or administrative bodies; or (b) to international conciliation under the Conciliation rules of the United nations Commission on International Trade law. (3) Should the Parties fail to agree on a dispute settlement procedure provided under in paragraph 2 of this Article or where a dispute is referred to

conciliation but conciliation proceedings are terminated other than by signing of a settlement agreement, the dispute may be referred to arbitration. The arbitration procedure shall be as follows:

(a) If the Contracting Party of the investors and the other Contracting Party are both parties to the Convention on the Settlement of Investment Disputes between States and Nationals of Other States, 1965 and the investor consents in writing to submit the dispute to the International Centre for the Settlement of Investment Disputes such as a dispute shall be referred to the Centre; or
(b) If both parties to the dispute so agree, under the Additional Facility for the Administration of Conciliation, Arbitration and Fact-Finding Proceedings; or
(c) To an ad hoc arbitral tribunal by either party to the dispute in accordance with the Arbitration Rules of the United Nations Commission on International Trade law, 1976 subject to the following modifications:

Protection and Incentives Provided under FIP	Dispute Resolution Procedure under FIP	Protection Provided under BIT	Dispute Resolution Procedure under BIT
			(1) The appointing authority under Article 7 of the Rules shall be the President, the Vice-President or the next senior Judge of the International court or Justice, who is not a national of either Contracting Party. The third arbitrator shall not be a national of either Contracting Party. (i) The parties shall appoint their respective arbitrators within two months. (ii) The arbitral award shall be made in accordance with the provisions of this agreement. (iii) The arbitral tribunal shall state the basis of its decision and give reasons upon the request of either party.

Kuwait	**Law No. 8/2001 Regulating Direct Foreign Capital Investment (April 17, 2001)** *Article 8* – Protection against Expropriation & Nationalization *Article 10* – Protection against Unfavorable Changes in Legislation *Article 11* – Right to Assign *Article 12* – Right to Transfer Profits Abroad *Article 13* – Exemptions & Privileges for Foreign Investors, Including Income Tax, Custom Duties, and Recruitment of Foreign Labor	**Law No. 8/2001 Regulating Direct Foreign Capital Investment (April 17, 2001)** *Article 16.* The Kuwaiti Courts alone shall be competent to consider whatever disputes arising between foreign investment enterprises and third parties. However, the parties may agree to refer such disputes to arbitration.	**Agreement between the Republic of Lithuania and the State of Kuwait for the Encouragement and Reciprocal Protection of Investments** *Article 2* – Promotion of Investments *Article 3(1)* – International Minimum Standard of Treatment *Article 3(1)* – Assurance of Non-Interference with Foreign Investment *Article 3(2)* – Transparency *Article 3(4)* – Access to Courts of Justice *Article 4(1)* – Fair & Equitable Treatment Standard *Article 4(2)* – National Treatment Standard *Article 4(2)* – Most-Favoured-Nation Treatment Standard *Article 6* – Protection against Expropriation & Nationalization	**Agreement between the Republic of Lithuania and the State of Kuwait for the Encouragement and Reciprocal Protection of Investments** *Article 9. **Settlement of Disputes between a Contracting State and an Investor*** (2) Disputes between a Contracting State and an Investor of the other Contracting State relating to an investment of the latter in the territory of the former shall, if possible, be settled amicably. (3) If such disputes cannot be settled according to the provisions of paragraph (1) within a period of three months from the date at which either party to the dispute requested amicable settlement, the dispute shall, subject to paragraph (3) below, at the written request of the investor concerned be submitted to international arbitration in accordance with paragraph (4). (4) An investor may choose to submit the dispute for resolution: (a) the courts or administrative tribunals of the Contracting State that is a party to the dispute; (b) in accordance with any applicable, previously agreed

dispute-settlement procedures;

(c) in accordance with paragraph (4), provided that the investor has consented in writing to the settlement by arbitration in accordance with the appropriate rules, thereunder.

(5) Unless within the periods of 3 months provided in paragraph (2) above, the parties to the dispute have agreed an alternative dispute settlement procedure, the dispute may, at the election in writing of the investor concerned, be submitted for settlement by arbitration to:

(a) The International Centre for Settlement of Investment Disputes ("the Centre"), established pursuant to the Convention on the Settlement of Investment Disputes between States and Nationals of Other States, opened for signature at Washington 18 March 1965 ("the Washington Convention"), provided that the Washington Convention is applicable to the dispute; or

(b) an arbitral tribunal established under the Arbitration Rules of the United Nations Commission on International Trade Law (UNCITRAL), as those Rules may be modified by the parties to the dispute (the Appointing Authority referred to in Article 7 of the Rules shall be Secretary General of the Centre); or

(c) an arbitral tribunal constituted pursuant to the arbitration rules of any arbitral institution mutually agreed between the parties to the dispute.

(6) Each Contracting State hereby gives its unconditional consent to the submission of an investment dispute for settlement by binding arbitration in accordance with the provisions of this Article.

(7) (a) The consent given in paragraph (5), together with the consent given under paragraph (s), shall satisfy the requirements for written agreement of the parties to a dispute for purposes of each of Chapter II of the Washington Convention, Article II of the United Nations Convention on the Recognition

				and Enforcement of Foreign Arbitral Awards, done at new York, June 10, 1958 ("New York Convention"), and Article 1 of the UNCITRAL Arbitration Rules.
Egypt	**Investment Law No. 8 (1997)** ***Overview Provided by Egyptian Investment Authority*** Companies may not be confiscated, nationalized, sequestered, seized or expropriated by administrative order. No administrative body can interfere in setting prices or profit margins. Projects are allowed to repatriate their capital and profits. Projects may be entirely owned by foreigners. Furthermore, their boards of directors may be wholly composed of foreigners. Companies have the right to own building, lands, and develop real estate as needed for implementing and expanding their activities, regardless of the nationality or place of residence of partners and shareholders or the percentage of their participation. (Except for Sinai, as foreign ownership is only allowed in the case of partnership with an Egyptian partner who has to own 51 percent of the land). Projects are exempted from certain labor requirements of the Egyptian Companies' Law and the Labor Law.	**Investment Law No. 8 (1997)** ***Overview Provided by Egyptian Investment Authority*** Law No. 8 stipulates that settling investment disputes in connection with the implementation of its provisions may be carried out in accordance with the convention or agreement of the investor's choice. Settlement of such disputes may be reached using the provisions of any one of the following: – Conventions in force between the Arab Republic of Egypt and the country of the investor. – Agreement on Settlement of Disputes which Arise in Respect of Investments between the Countries and the Nationals of Other Countries (a.k.a. the Washington Convention of March 18, 1965), which Egypt adopted in 1971; – Law No. 27 of 1994 on Arbitration in Civil and Commercial Matters, as amended. – Disputes may also be settled by means of arbitration before the	**Agreement between the Government of the Hashemite Kingdom of Jordan and the Government of the Arab Republic of Egypt on the Mutual Promotion and Protection of Investments** *Article 2(1)* – Promotion of Investments *Article 2(2)* – Fair & Equitable Treatment Standard and Full Protection & Security *Article 3(1)* – Most-Favoured-Nation Treatment *Article 4* – Protection against Expropriation	**Agreement between the Government of the Hashemite Kingdom of Jordan and the Government of the Arab Republic of Egypt on the Mutual Promotion and Protection of Investments** ***Article 6. Settlement of Dispute between the Investor and the Host State*** 1. Each Contracting party accepts to present each dispute of legal character arise between him and any of the other Contracting party nationals concerning investments exists in his territory to the International Center for Settlement of Investment Disputes, in order to settle it through conciliation and arbitration according to procedure. Provided for in the Convention on the Settlement of Investment Disputes between States and Nationals of Other States, opened for signature at Washington on 18 March 1965. 2. The nationals of any Contracting Party may present to the local

	Foreign experts' salaries are exempted from income tax if their stay in Egypt is shorter than one year. Projects are free to maintain foreign currency bank accounts. Projects are subject to a flat rate of 5 percent in customs duties on imported equipment and machinery.	Cairo Regional Center for International Commercial Arbitration.		judicial authorities of the other Contracting Party; the Host of the investment, any dispute with legal character arise between themselves and the other contracting party concerning the investment that exists on the territory of that Contracting Party. 3. If a national of any of the two Contracting Parties chose to file a case with any of the two bodies mentioned in paragraphs 1 and 2 of this Article it will be impossible for him to file the same with another body.
Ethiopia	**Proclamation No. 280/2002 Re-Enactment of the Investment Proclamation (July 2, 2002)** *Article 4* – Investment Objectives *Article 9* – Investment Incentives *Article 20* – Remittance of Funds for Investors and Foreign Employees *Article 21* – Investment Guarantees and Protections, including Protection against Expropriation & Nationalization and Right to Remit Compensation in Convertible Foreign Currency *Article 24* – One-Stop Shop Service *Article 25* – Transmission of Information on Investment *Article 36* – Employment of Expatriates	**Proclamation No. 280/2002 Re-Enactment of the Investment of Proclamation (July 2, 2002)** *Article 17. Right to Appeal* An investor who has a grievance against a decision of an appropriate investment organ may, within 30 days from receipt of the decision, appeal to the Federal Investment Board or to the concerned organ of a Regional Government, as may be appropriate.	**Agreement between the Government of the Federal Democratic Republic of Ethiopia and the Government of the Republic of the Sudan on the Reciprocal Promotion and Protection of Investment** *Article 2* – Promotion of Investments *Article 3(1)* – Assurance of Non-Interference with Foreign Investment *Article 3(2)* – Fair and Equitable Treatment Standard *Article 3(2)* – National Treatment Standard *Article 3(2)* – Most-Favoured-Nation Treatment Standard *Article 4* – Protection against Expropriation & Nationalization	**Agreement between the Government of the Federal Democratic Republic of Ethiopia and the Government of the Republic of the Sudan on the Reciprocal Promotion and Protection of Investments** *Article 9. Settlement of Disputes between a Contracting Party and an Investor of the Other Contracting Party* 1. Disputes which might arise between one of the contracting Parties and an Investor of the other Contracting Party concerning an investment of that Investor in the territory of the former Contracting Party shall, whenever possible, be settled amicably between the parties concerned.

2. If the dispute has not been settled within a period of six months from the date either party to the dispute requested amicable settlement, the dispute shall at the request of the Investor concerned be submitted for settlement to:

a) the competent court of the Contracting Party in the territory of which the investment has been made; or

b) the International Center for Settlement of Investment Disputes (ICSID) established pursuant to the Convention on the Settlement of Investment Disputes between States and Nationals of Other States, opened for signature, at Washington, on March 18, 1965, if both Contracting Parties are members of this Convention;

c) the International Center for Settlement of Investment Disputes under the Rules Governing Additional Facility for the Administration of Proceedings by the Secretariat of the Center (Additional Facility Rules) if one of the Contracting Parties is not a Contracting State of the

				Convention as mentioned in Paragraph 2(b) of this Article; d) an international ad hoc arbitral which, unless and otherwise agreed upon by the parties to the dispute, shall be established under the Arbitration Rules of the United Nations Commission on International Trade Law (UNCITRAL). 3. The arbitral awards shall be final and binding on both parties to the dispute and shall be executed according to the international laws of the Contracting Party. 4. Each Contracting Party hereby consents to submit investments disputes for resolution to the alternative dispute settlement mechanisms and shall be executed in accordance with the preceding paragraphs.
Ghana	**Act 478: Ghana Investment Promotion Centre Act (August 29, 1994)** ***Article*** *2* – Object of Act Is to Promote Investments ***Article*** *3* – Functions of the Centre ***Articles*** *23–26* – Entitlement to Incentives and Priority Areas ***Article*** *27* – Investment Guarantee of Transferability ***Article*** *28* – Protection against Expropriation & Nationalization	**Act 478: Ghana Investment Promotion Centre Act (August 29, 1994)** ***Article 29. Dispute Settlement Procedures*** (1) Where a dispute arises between an investor and the Government in respect of an enterprise, efforts shall be made through mutual discussion to reach an amicable settlement.	**Agreement between the Government of the Republic of India and the Government of the Republic of Ghana for the Reciprocal Promotion and Protection of Investments** ***Article*** *3(1)* – Promotion of Investments ***Article*** *3(2)* – Fair & Equitable Treatment Standard ***Article*** *4(1)* – National Treatment Standard	**Agreement between the Government of the Republic of India and the Government of the Republic of Ghana for the Reciprocal Promotion and Protection of Investments** ***Article 9. Settlement of Disputes between an Investor and a Contracting Party*** (1) Any dispute between an investor of one Contracting Party and the

Article 31 – Assistance to Investment Enterprises, Including Provision for the Centre to Act as Liaison to Government for Enterprise ***Article 32*** – Personal Remittances	(2) Ad dispute between an investor and the government in respect to an enterprise to which this Act applies which is not amicably settled through mutual discussions may be submitted at the option of the aggrieved party to arbitration: (a) in accordance with the rules of procedure for arbitration of the United Nations Commission of International Trade Law, or (b) in the case of a foreign investor, within the framework of a bilateral or multilateral agreement on investment protection to which the Government and the country of which the investor is a national are parties, or (c) in accordance with any other national or investment dispute agreed to by the parties. (3) Where in respect of a dispute, there is disagreement between the investor and the Government as to the method of dispute settlement to be adopted, the choice of the investor shall prevail.	***Article 4(1)*** – Most-Favoured-Nation Treatment Standard ***Article 5*** – Protection against Expropriation & Nationalization	other Contracting Party in relation to an investment of the former under this Agreement shall, as far as possible, be settled amicably through negotiations between the parties to the dispute. (2) Any such dispute which has not been amicably settled within a period of six months may, if both Parties agree, be submitted: (a) for resolution, in accordance with the law of the Contracting Party which has admitted the investment to that Contracting Party's competent judicial, arbitral or administrative bodies; or (b) to the International conciliation under the Conciliation Rules of the United Nations Commission on International Trade Law. (3) Should the Parties fail to agree on a settlement procedure provided under paragraph (2) of this Article or where a dispute is referred to conciliation but conciliation proceedings are terminated other than by signing of a settlement agreement, the dispute may be referred to Arbitration. The Arbitration procedure shall be as follows: (a) If the Contracting Party of the Investor and the other

Contracting Party are both parties to the Convention on the Settlement of Investment Disputes between States and Nationals of Other States, 1965 and the investor consents in writing to submit the dispute to the International Centre for the Settlement of Investment Disputes, such a dispute shall be referred to the Centre; or

(b) If both parties to the dispute so agree, under the Additional Facility for the Administration of Conciliation, Arbitration and Fact-Finding proceedings; or

(c) to an ad hoc arbitral tribunal by either party to the dispute in accordance with the Arbitration Rules of the United Nations Commission on International Trade Law, 1976, subject to the following modifications:

1. The appointing authority under Article 7 of the Rules shall be the President, the Vice-President or the next senior Judge of the

				International Court of Justice, who is not a national of either Contracting Party. 2. The parties shall appoint their respective arbitrators within two months. 3. The arbitral award shall be made in accordance with the provisions of this Agreement and shall be binding for the parties in dispute.
Guatemala	Foreign Investment Law (March 3, 1998) *Article 2* – Promotion of Investments *Article 3* – National Treatment Standard; Protection against Discrimination *Article 4 & 5* – Permission for Ownership by Foreign Investors *Article 6* – Protection against Expropriation & Nationalization *Article 7* – Guarantee of Free Trade *Article 8* – Access to Foreign Exchange and Transfers *Article 10* – Prohibition against Double Taxation	Foreign Investment Law (March 3, 1998) ***Article 11. Settlement of Disputes*** If permitted under an international treaty or agreement duly signed, approved, and ratified by the Guatemalan State, any investment-related disputes that may arise between a foreign investor and the Guatemalan State, its agencies, or other State entities may be submitted to international arbitration or other alternate dispute-settlement mechanisms, as applicable, in accordance with the provisions of said treaty or convention and with applicable domestic laws.	**Agreement between the Government of the Republic of Korea and the Government of the Republic of Guatemala for the Promotion and Protection of Investments** *Article 2(1)* – Promotion of Investment *Article 2(2)* – Fair & Equitable Treatment Standard and Full Protection & Security *Article 2(3)* – Assurance of Non-Interference with Foreign Investment *Article 3* – National Treatment Standard *Article 3* – Most-Favoured-Nation Treatment Standard *Article 5* – Protection against Expropriation	**Agreement between the Government of the Republic of Korea and the Government of the Republic of Guatemala for the Promotion and Protection of Investments** ***Article 8. Settlement of Investment Disputes between a Contracting Party and an Investor of the Other Contracting Party*** (1) Any dispute between either Contracting Party and the investor of the other Contracting Party including expropriation or nationalization of an investment shall, as far as possible, be settled by the disputing parties in an amicable way. (2) The local remedies under the laws and regulations of one Contracting party in the territory of which the investment has been made shall be available for the

				investors of the other Contracting Party on the basis of treatment no less favorable than that accorded to investments of its own investors or investors of any third State, whichever is more favorable to the investor. (3) If the dispute cannot be settled within six (6) months from the date on which the claim has been raised by either party, it shall be submitted upon request of the investor of the Contracting Party to the International Centre for Settlement of Investment Disputes (ICSID) established by the Convention on the Settlement of Investment Disputes between States and Nationals of Other States opened for signature in Washington on 18 March 1965, or ICSID additional facility. (4) The award made by ICSID shall be final and binding on the parties to the dispute. Each Contracting Party shall ensure the recognition and enforcement of the award.
Peru	**Legislative Decree No. 662 – Approving the Juridical Stability System for Foreign Investment (September 2, 1991)** *Article 1* – General Investment Promotion and Guarantees		**Agreement between Japan and the Republic of Peru for the Promotion, Protection, and Liberalization of Investment** *Article 3* – National Treatment Standard	**Agreement between Japan and the Republic of Peru for the Promotion, Protection and Liberalization of Investment** ***Article 18. Settlement of Investment Disputes between a Contracting***

Article 2 – National Treatment Standard and Non-Discrimination Provision *Article 3* – Automatic Authorization of Foreign Investment *Article 5* – Intellectual & Industrial Property Rights for Foreign Investors *Article 6* – Right to Import & Export *Article 7* – Right to Transfer *Article 8* – Right to Acquire Shares and Other Property Interests *Article 9* – Right to Utilize Foreign Exchange *Articles 10–18* – Provisions Related to Providing Stability for Foreign Investments *Article 31* – Abolishment of Laws Previously Restricting Foreign Investment	*Article 4* – Most-Favoured-Nation Treatment Standard *Article 5(1)* – International Minimum Standard of Treatment *Article 5(2)* – Fair & Equitable Treatment Standard and Full Protection & Security *Article 9* – Transparency *Article 13* – Protection against Expropriation	***Party and an Investor of the Other Contracting Party*** 1. For the purposes of this Article, an investment dispute is a dispute between a Contracting Party and an investor of the other contracting Party that has incurred loss or damage by reason of, or arising out of, an alleged breach of any obligation under this Agreement with respect to the investor of the other Contracting Party or its investments in the area of the former Contracting Party. 2. Nothing in this Article shall construed so as to prevent an investor who is a party to an investment dispute (hereinafter referred to in this Article as "disputing investor") from seeking administrative or judicial settlement within the Area of the Contracting Party that is a party to the investment dispute (hereinafter referred to in this Article as "disputing Party"). However, in the event that the disputing investor has submitted the investment dispute for resolution under one of the international conciliations or arbitrations referred to in paragraph 4, the same investment dispute shall not be submitted for

resolution under courts of justice, administrative tribunals or agencies or any other binding dispute settlement mechanism established under the national law.

3. An investment dispute shall, as far as possible, be settled amicably through consultation or negotiation between the disputing investor and the disputing Party (hereinafter referred to in this Article as "the disputing parties").
4. If the investment dispute cannot be settled through such consultation or negotiation within six months from the date on which the disputing investor requested for the consultation or negotiation in writing and if the disputing investor has not submitted the investment dispute for resolution under courts of justice, administrative tribunals or agencies or any other binding dispute settlement mechanism established under the national law, if any, the disputing investor may submit the investment dispute to one of the following international conciliation or arbitrations:
    (a) conciliation or arbitration in accordance with the

Convention on the Settlement of Investment Disputes between States and Nationals of Other States, done at Washington, March 18, 1965 (hereinafter referred to in this Article as "ICSI Convention"), so long as the ICSID Convention is in force between the Contracting Parties;

(b) conciliation or arbitration under the Additional Facility Rules of the International Centre for Settlement of Investment Disputes so long as the ICSID Convention is not in force between the Contracting Parties;

(c) arbitration under the Arbitration Rules of the United Nations Commission on International Trade law; and

(d) if agreed with the disputing Party, any arbitration in accordance with other arbitration rules.

5. The applicable arbitration rules shall govern the arbitration set forth in paragraph 4 except to the extent modified in this Article.

<table>
<tr>
<td>Nicaragua</td>
<td><u>Law for the Promotion of Foreign Investment (Law No. 344) (May 24, 2000)</u>
Overview from ProNicaragua.org
Law No. 344 provides: a) equal treatment of foreign and domestic investment; b) eliminates restrictions on the way in which foreign capital can enter the country, and c) recognizes the foreign investor's right to own and use property without limitation, and in the case of a declaration of eminent domain, to receive proper identification. The law makes no distinction between acquisition, merger, takeover, or green-field investment. There are no restrictions in Nicaragua on converting or transferring funds associated with investments. Remittances of investment capital, earnings, loan repayments and lease repayments are freely allowed through the private foreign exchange market operated by local financial institutions.
There is no pre-established minimum or maximum investing amount and 100% international ownership permitted. There is no discrimination against foreign investors, whether it be on total ownership of the company or as shareholders.
National loans are accessible through local banks, according to their terms of approval. The law provides property protection and security as well as equal treatment for foreign and local investors.</td>
<td><u>Mediation and Arbitration Law (Law No. 540)</u>
Overview from ProNicaragua.org
The Law governs two methods alternate to the judicial process (Mediation and Arbitration) to expeditiously solve any dispute resulting from contractual relations.
Can be used by both national and foreign investors, and by State of Nicaragua to resolve differences on property and non-property assets.
Applies both nationally and internationally, without detriment to the treaties, Conventions, covenant or any other instrument of International Law subscribed by Nicaragua.</td>
<td><u>Agreement between the Government of the United Kingdom of Great Britain and Northern Ireland and the Government of the Republic of Nicaragua for the Promotion and Protection of Investments</u>
Article 2(1) – Promotion of Investment
Article 3(1) – National Treatment Standard
Article 3(1) – Most-Favoured-Nation Treatment Standard
Article 5 – Protection against Expropriation</td>
<td><u>Agreement between the Government of the United Kingdom of Great Britain and Northern Ireland and the Government of the Republic of Nicaragua for the Promotion and Protection of Investments</u>
Article 8. Reference to International Centre for Settlement of Investment Disputes
(1) Each Contracting Party hereby consents to submit to the International Centre for the Settlement of Investment Disputes (hereinafter referred to as "the Centre") for settlement by conciliation or arbitration under the Convention on the Settlement of Investment Disputes between States and Nationals of Other States opened for signature at Washington on 18 March 1965 any legal dispute arising between that Contracting Party and a national or company of the other Contracting Party concerning an investment of the latter in the territory of the former.
(2) A company which is incorporated or constituted under the law in force in the territory of one Contracting Party and in which before such a dispute arises the majority of shares are owned by nationals or companies of the other Contracting Party shall in accordance with Article 25(2)(b)</td>
</tr>
</table>

of the Convention be treated for the purposes of that Convention as a company of the other Contracting Party.

(3) If any such dispute should arise and agreement cannot be reached within three months between the parties to this dispute through pursuit of local remedies or otherwise, then, if the national or company affected also consents in writing to submit the dispute to the Centre for settlement by conciliation or arbitration under the Convention, either party may institute proceedings by addressing a request to that effect to the Secretary-General of the Centre as provided in Article 28 and 36 of the Convention. In the event of disagreement as to whether conciliation or arbitration is the more appropriate procedure the national or company affected shall have the right to choose. The contracting Party which is a party to the dispute shall not raise as an objection at any stage of the proceedings or enforcement of an award the fact that the national or company which is the other party to the dispute has

received in pursuance of an insurance contract an indemnity in respect of some or all of his or its losses.

(4) Neither Contracting party shall pursue through the diplomatic channel any dispute referred to the Centre unless:

(a) the Secretary-General of the Centre, or a conciliation commission or an arbitral tribunal constituted by it, decides that the dispute is [[not within the jurisdiction of the Centre; or

(b) the other Contracting Party should fail to abide by or to comply with an award rendered by an arbitral tribunal.

APPENDIX IV

Table of Citations

CASES

Abdilla v. Malta, First Section Decision, App. No. 38244/03, Eur. Ct. H.R. (November 3, 2005).

Asylum Case (Columbia v. Peru), 1950 I.C.J. 266 (November 20).

Banco Nacional de Cuba v. Sabbatino, 376 U.S. 398, 458 (1964).

Barcelona Traction Light & Power Co., Ltd. (Belg. v. Spain) 1970 I.C.J. 3, 46–47 (February 5).

Biloune and Marine Drive Complex Ltd. v. Ghana Investments Centre and the Government of Ghana, Award on Jurisdiction and Liability (27 October 1989), 95 I.L.R. 183 (1993).

Cargill, Inc. v. United Mexican States, ICSID Case No. ARB(AF)/05/2, Award (September 18, 2009), http://www.italaw.com/sites/default/files/case-documents/ita0133_0.pdf.

Case of Claude-Reyes et al. v. Chile, Merits, Reparations and Costs, Judgment, Inter-Am. Ct. H.R. (ser. C) No. 151 (September 19, 2006).

Case of James & Others v. United Kingdom, 98 Eur. Ct. H.R. (ser. A) (February 21, 1986). Case of the S.S. Lotus, 1927 P.C.I.J. (ser. A) No. 10, at 18 (September 7).

Cha'are Shalom Ve Tsedek v. France [GC], App. No. 27417/95, 2000-VIII Eur. Ct. H.R.

Compania del Desarrollo de Santa Elena, S.A. v. Republic of Costa Rica, ICSID Case No. ARB/96/1 (February 17, 2000), 5 ICSID Rev. 169, 192 (2000).

Continental Casualty Company v. Argentine Republic, ICSID Case No. ARB/03/9, Award (September 5, 2008), http://www.italaw.com/sites/default/files/case-documents/ita0228.pdf.

Coplin v. United States, 6 Cl. Ct. 115, 127 (1984).

Corn Products Intl. v. United Mexican States, ICSID Case No. ARB(AF)/04/01, Decision on Responsibility (January 15, 2008), http://italaw.com/sites/default/files/case-documents/ita0244.pdf.
Dahlab v. Switzerland, 2001-V Eur. Ct. H.R. 447.
Daimler Financial Services AG v. Argentine Republic, ICSID Case No. ARB/05/1, Award (August 22, 2012), http://www.italaw.com/sites/default/files/case-documents/ita1082.pdf.
EDF International S.A v. Argentine Republic, ICSID Case No. ARB/03/23, Award (June 11, 2012), http://www.italaw.com/sites/default/files/case-documents/ita1069.pdf.
Farrugia v. Malta, Fourth Section Decision, App. No. 67557/20, Eur. Ct. H.R. (March 6, 2012).
Feldman v. United Mexican States, ICSID Case No. ARB (AF)/99/1, Award (December 16, 2002), 7 ICSID Rep. 341 (2005).
Fireman's Fund Insurance Co. v. United Mexican States, ICSID Case No. ARB (AF)/02/01, Award (July 17, 2006), 16 ICSID Rep. 523 (2012).
Fisheries Case (U.K. v. Norway), 1951 I.C.J. 116, 131 (December 18). Flores v. S. Peru Copper Corp., 414 F.3d 233, 248 (2d Cir. 2003).
Gemplus, S.A., SLP, S.A. and Gemplus Industrial, S.A. de C.V. v. United Mexican States, ICSID Case No. ARB(AF)/04/3 & ARB(AF)/04/4, Award (June 16, 2010), http://italaw.com/sites/default/files/case-documents/ita0357.pdf.
Government of Kuwait v. American Independent Oil Co ("Aminoil"), 66 ILR 518 (1982).
Holy Monasteries v. Greece, 301-A Eur. Ct. H.R. (ser. A) (1994).
International Thunderbird Gaming Corp. v. United Mexican States, NAFTA Ch. 11/UNCITRAL, Final Award (January 26, 2005), http://www.iisd.org/pdf/2006/itn_award.pdf.
J. Lautier Company Ltd. v. Malta, Decision, App. No. 37448/06 (December 2, 2008).
Karaduman v. Turkey, App. No. 16278/90, 74 Eur. Comm'n H.R. December & Rep. 93 (1993).
Kelo v. City of New London, 545 U.S. 469, 480 (2005).
Kiobel v. Royal Dutch Petroleum Co., 621 F.3d 111, 137 (2d Cir. 2010).
LG&E Energy Corp., LG&E Capital Corp. and LG&E International Inc. v. Argentine Republic, ICSID Case No. ARB/02/1, Award (July 25, 2007), http://italaw.com/sites/default/files/case-documents/ita0462.pdf.
Lozano v. Alvarez, 697 F.3d 41 (2d Cir. 2012).
Metalclad Corp. v. United Mexican States, ICSID Case No. ARB (AF)/97/1, Award (August 30, 2000), 5 ICSID Rep. 212 (2002).

Methanex Corp. v. United States of America, NAFTA Ch. 11/UNCITRAL, Final Award on Jurisdiction and Merits (August 3, 2005), 16 ICSID Rep. 40 (2012).
Methanex Corp. v. United States of America, NAFTA Ch. 11/UNCITRAL, Partial Award (August 3, 2005), 7 ICSID Rep. 239 (2012).
Methanex v. United States, Decision of the Tribunal on Petition from Third Persons to Intervene as "Amici Curiae" (January 15, 2001), http://www.iisd.org/pdf/methanex_tribunal_first_amicus_decision.pdf.
Methanex v. United States of America, Petitioner's Final Submission Regarding the Petition of the International Institute for Sustainable Development to the Arbitral Tribunal for Amicus Curiae Status (October 16, 2000), http://www.iisd.org/pdf/methanex_petition_oct162000.pdf.
Mondev International Ltd. v. United States of America, ICSID Case No. ARB (AF)/99/2, Award (October 11, 2002), 6 ICSID Rep. 192 (2004).
North Sea Continental Shelf Cases, 1969 I.C.J. 3 (February 20).
Pope & Talbot Inc. v. Government of Canada, Interim Award (June 26, 2000), 7 ICSID Rep. 69 (2005).
Revere Copper & Brass, Incorporated v. Overseas Private Investment Corporation (OPIC), Am. Arb. Ass'n (August 24, 1978), 17 I.L.M. 1321 (1978).
Robert Azinian et al. v. United Mexican States, ICSID Case No. ARB/AF/97/2, Award (November 1, 1999), 5 ICSID Rep. 272 (2002).
S.D. Myers Inc. v. Government of Canada, First Partial Award on Liability (November 13, 2000), 8 ICSID Rep. 18 (2005).
S.S. Wimbledon (U.K. v. Japan), 1923 P.C.I.J. (ser. A) No. 1 (August 17).
Sahin v. Turkey, 2005-XI Eur. Ct. H.R. 173.
Saipem S.p.A. v. The People's Republic of Bangladesh, ICSID Case No. ARB/05/07, Award (June 30, 2009), http://italaw.com/sites/default/files/case-documents/ita0734.pdf.
Salini Costruttori SpA and Italstrade SpA v. Morocco, ICSID Case No. ARB/00/4, Decision on Jurisdiction (July 23, 2001), 14 ICSID Rep. 306 (2010).
Sempra Energy International v. Argentine Republic, ICSID Case No. ARB/02/16, Decision on the Argentine Republic's Application for Annulment of the Award (June 29, 2010), http://www.italaw.com/sites/default/files/case-documents/ita0776.pdf.
Sporrong and Lonnroth v. Sweden, 52 Eur. Ct. H.R. (ser. A) (1982).
Tecnicas Medioambientales Tecmed S.A. v. United Mexican States, ICSID Case No. ARB (AF)/00/2, Award (May 29, 2003), 10 ICSID Rep. 134 (2006).
Tucker v. Alexandroff, 183 U.S. 424, 436 (1902).

United Mexican States v. Metalclad Corp., 2001 BCSC 664 (2001).

Waste Management, Inc. v. United Mexican States, ICSID Case No. ARB (AF)/00/3, Award (April 30, 2004), 11 ICSID Rep. 361 (2007).

MULTILATERAL TREATIES AND CONVENTIONS

African (Banjul) Charter on Human and People's Rights art. 14, June 27, 1981, 21 I.L.M. 58 (1982) (entered into force October 21, 1986).

Agreement among the Government of Japan, the Government of the Republic of Korea and the Government of the People's Republic of China for the Promotion, Facilitation and Protection of Investment, May 13, 2012, http://www.bilaterals.org/IMG/pdf/20120513001-3.pdf.

Agreement on Government Procurement, April 15, 1994, Marrakesh Agreement Establishing the World Trade Organization, Annex 4, http://www.wto.org/english/docs_e/legal_e/gpr-94_e.pdf (last visited April 1, 2013).

Agreement on Trade-Related Aspects of Intellectual Property Rights, April 15, 1994, Marrakesh Agreement Establishing the World Trade Organization, Annex 1C, 33 I.L.M. 1197 (1994).

American Convention on Human Rights, November 22, 1969, 1144 U.N.T.S. 123 (entered into force on July 18, 1978).

ASEAN Comprehensive Investment Agreement, February 26, 2009, http://www.boi.go.th/english/ASEAN/finalsign.pdf.

Convention on the Settlement of Investment Disputes between States and Nationals of Other States, March 18, 1965, 17 U.S.T. 1270, 575 U.N.T.S. 159.

Dominican Republic-Central America-United States Free Trade Agreement, August 5, 2004, http://www.ustr.gov/archive/Trade_Agreements/Regional/CAFTA/CAFTA-DR_Final_Texts/Section_Index.html.

European Convention for the Protection of Human Rights and Fundamental Freedoms, as amended by Protocols Nos. 11 & 14, November 4, 1950, 213 U.N.T.S. 222.

General Agreement on Tariffs and Trade, October 20, 1947, 55 U.N.T.S. 188, 262.

General Agreement on Trade in Services, April 15, 1994, Marrakesh Agreement Establishing the World Trade Organization, Annex 1B, 33 I.L.M. 1167 (1994).

North American Free Trade Agreement, U.S.-Can-Mex., December 17, 1992, 32 I.L.M.639 (1993).

Organization for Economic Cooperation and Development (OECD), The Multilateral Agreement on Investment: Draft Consolidated Text, DAFFE/

MAI(98)7/REV1 (April 22, 1998), http://www1.oecd.org/daf/mai/pdf/ng/ng987r1e.pdf.
Protocol No. 4 to the Convention for the Protection of Human Rights and Fundamental Freedoms, securing certain rights and freedoms other than those already included in the Convention and in the first Protocol thereto, September 16, 1963, Europ. T.S. No. 046.
Protocol No. 7 to the Convention for the Protection of Human Rights and Fundamental Freedoms, November 22, 1984, Europ. T.S. No. 117.
Protocol to the Convention for the Protection of Human Rights and Fundamental Freedoms, March 20, 1952, Europ. T. S. No. 009.
South African Development Community, *SADC Model Bilateral Investment Treaty Template with Commentary*, July 2012, http://www.iisd.org/itn/wp-content/uploads/2012/10/SADC-Model-BIT-Template-Final.pdf.
Statute of the International Court of Justice, June 26, 1945, 59 Stat. 1055.
Treaty Establishing the European Economic Community, March 25, 1957, 298 U.N.T.S. 3.
Vienna Convention on the Law of Treaties, May 23, 1969, 1155 U.N.T.S. 331.

BILATERAL INVESTMENT TREATIES

Agreement between the Government of Australia and the Government of the Argentine Republic on the Promotion and Protection of Investments, Aus.-Arg., August 23, 1995, http://investmentpolicyhub.unctad.org/Download/TreatyFile/72.
Australia-Singapore Free Trade Agreement, Aus.-Sin., February 17, 2003, http://www.dfat.gov.au/fta/safta/index.html.
Australia-Thailand Free Trade Agreement, Aus.-Tha., entered into force January 1, 2005, http://www.dfat.gov.au/fta/tafta/aus-thai_FTA_text.pdf.
Agreement between the Government of the Republic of Austria and the Government of the Republic of India for the Promotion and Protection of Investments, Ind.-Aust., December 18, 2000, http://investmentpolicyhub.unctad.org/Download/TreatyFile/192.
Agreement between Barbados and the Federal Republic of Germany, Ger.-Bar., December 2, 1994, available at http://investmentpolicyhub.unctad.org/Download/TreatyFile/283.
Agreement between the Belgium-Luxembourg Economic Union and the Republic of Colombia on the Reciprocal Promotion and Protection of Investments, Bel.-Col., February 4, 2009, http://investmentpolicyhub.unctad.org/Download/TreatyFile/342.

Agreement between the Government of Canada and the Government of the Republic of Armenia for the Promotion and Protection of Investments, Can.-Arm., May 8, 1997, http://investmentpolicyhub.unctad.org/Download/TreatyFile/131.

Agreement between the Government of Canada and the Government of Barbados for the Reciprocal Promotion and Protection of Investment, Can.-Bar., May 29, 1996, http://investmentpolicyhub.unctad.org/Download/TreatyFile/280

Agreement between the Government of Canada and the Government of the Republic of Costa Rica for the Promotion and Protection of Investments, Can.-C.R., March 18, 1998, http://investmentpolicyhub.unctad.org/Download/TreatyFile/601.

Agreement between the Government of Canada and the Government of the Kingdom of Thailand for the Promotion and Protection of Investments, Can.-Thai., January 17, 1997, http://investmentpolicyhub.unctad.org/Download/TreatyFile/637.

Agreement between the Government of Canada and the Government of the People's Republic of China for the Promotion and Reciprocal Protection of Investments, Can.-China, September 9, 2012, http://investmentpolicyhub.unctad.org/Download/TreatyFile/600.

Agreement between Canada and the Hashemite Kingdom of Jordan for the Promotion and Protection of Investments, Can.-Jord., June 28, 2009, http://investmentpolicyhub.unctad.org/Download/TreatyFile/617.

Agreement between Canada and the Republic of Peru for the Promotion and Protection of Investments, Can.-Peru, November 14, 2006, http://investmentpolicyhub.unctad.org/Download/TreatyFile/626.

Agreement between Canada and the Slovak Republic for the Promotion and Protection of Investments, Can.-Slo. July 20, 2010, http://investmentpolicyhub.unctad.org/Download/TreatyFile/634.

Agreement between the Government of Canada and the Government of Ukraine for the Promotion and Protection of Investments, Can.-Ukr., October 24, 1994, http://investmentpolicyhub.unctad.org/Download/TreatyFile/640.

Bilateral Agreement for the Promotion and Protection of Investments between the Government of the Republic of Colombia and the Government of the Republic of China, Colom.-Chi, November 22, 2008, http://investmentpolicyhub.unctad.org/Download/TreatyFile/720.

Agreement for the Promotion and Protection of Investments between the Republic of Colombia and the Republic of India, Colom.-Ind., November 10, 2009, http://investmentpolicyhub.unctad.org/Download/TreatyFile/796.

Agreement between Government of the Republic of Croatia and the Government of the Republic of Azerbaijan on the Promotion and Reciprocal Protection of Investments, Cro.-Azer., November 2, 2007, http://investmentpolicyhub.unctad.org/Download/TreatyFile/229.

Treaty between the Federal Republic of Germany and Antigua & Barbuda Concerning the Encouragement and Reciprocal Protection of Investments, Ger.-Ant., November 5, 1998, http://investmentpolicyhub.unctad.org/Download/TreatyFile/68.

Agreement between the Federal Republic of Germany and Benin Concerning the Promotion and Reciprocal Protection of Capital Investment, Ger.-Ben., June 28, 1978, http://investmentpolicyhub.unctad.org/Download/TreatyFile/441.

Agreement between the Federal Republic of Germany and the People's Republic of Bangladesh Concerning the Promotion and Reciprocal Protection of Investments, Ger.- Ban., May 8, 1981, http://investmentpolicyhub.unctad.org/Download/TreatyFile/264.

Treaty between the Federal Republic of Germany and the Co-operative Republic of Guyana Concerning the Encouragement and Reciprocal Protection of Investments, Ger.-Guy., December 6, 1989, http://investmentpolicyhub.unctad.org/Download/TreatyFile/1335.

Treaty between the Federal Republic of Germany and the Federal Democratic Republic of Ethiopia Concerning the Encouragement and Reciprocal Protection of Investments, Ger.-Eth., January 19, 2004, http://investmentpolicyhub.unctad.org/Download/TreatyFile/1164.

Treaty between the Federal Republic of Germany and the Federal Republic of Nigeria Concerning the Encouragement and Reciprocal Protection of Investments, Nig.-Ger., March 28, 2000, http://investmentpolicyhub.unctad.org/Download/TreatyFile/1382.

Agreement between the United Mexican States and the Federal Republic of Germany on the Promotion and Reciprocal Protection of Investments, Ger.-Mex., August 25, 1998, http://investmentpolicyhub.unctad.org/Download/TreatyFile/1371.

Agreement between the Federal Republic of Germany and the Republic of the Philippines for the Promotion and Reciprocal Protection of Investments, Ger.-Phi., April 18, 1997, http://investmentpolicyhub.unctad.org/Download/TreatyFile/1392.

Agreement between the Government of the Republic of Hungary and the Government of the Russian Federation for the Promotion and Reciprocal Protection of Investments, Hun.-Rus., March 6, 1995, http://investmentpolicyhub.unctad.org/Download/TreatyFile/1544.

Agreement between the Government of the Republic of France and the Government of the United Mexican States on the Reciprocal Promotion and Protection of Investments, Fra.-Mex., November 12, 1998, http://investmentpolicyhub.unctad.org/Download/TreatyFile/1253.

Agreement between Japan and the Democratic Socialist Republic of Sri Lanka Concerning the Promotion and Protection of Investment, Jap.-Sri., March 1, 1982, http://investmentpolicyhub.unctad.org/Download/TreatyFile/1735

Agreement between Japan and the Islamic Republic of Pakistan Concerning the Promotion and Protection of Investment, Jap.-Pak., March 10, 1998, http://investmentpolicyhub.unctad.org/Download/TreatyFile/1731.

Agreement between Japan and the Laos People's Democratic Republic for the Liberalisation, Promotion and Protection of Investment, Jap.-Laos, January 16, 2008, http://investmentpolicyhub.unctad.org/Download/TreatyFile/1729.

Agreement between Japan and the People's Republic of China Concerning the Encouragement and Reciprocal Protection of Investment, Jap.-Chi., August 27, 1988, http://investmentpolicyhub.unctad.org/Download/TreatyFile/747.

Agreement between Japan and the Republic of Colombia for the Liberalization, Promotion and Protection of Investments, Jap.-Col., September 12, 2011, http://investmentpolicyhub.unctad.org/Download/TreatyFile/797.

Agreement between the Government of Japan and the Government of the Independent State of Papua New Guinea for the Promotion and Protection of Investment, Jap.-Pap. New Guin., April 26, 2011, http://investmentpolicyhub.unctad.org/Download/TreatyFile/1732.

Agreement between Japan and the Republic of Iraq for the Promotion and Protection of Investments, Jap.-Iraq, June 7, 2012, http://investmentpolicyhub.unctad.org/Download/TreatyFile/1663.

Agreement between Japan and the Socialist Republic of Vietnam for the Liberalization, Promotion and Protection of Investment, Jap.-Viet., November 14, 2003, http://investmentpolicyhub.unctad.org/Download/TreatyFile/1738.

Agreement between the Government of the Republic of Korea and the Government of Japan for the Liberalisation, Promotion and Protection of Investment, Kor.-Jap., entered into force January 1, 2003, http://investmentpolicyhub.unctad.org/Download/TreatyFile/1727.

Republic of Korea-United States Free Trade Agreement, June 30, 2007, http://www.ustr.gov/trade-agreements/free-trade-agreements/korus-fta/final-text.

Agreement between the Lebanese Republic and the Federal Republic of Germany on the Promotion and Reciprocal Protection of Investments, Leb.-Ger., March 18, 1997, http://investmentpolicyhub.unctad.org/Download/TreatyFile/1358.

Agreement between the Government of New Zealand and the Government of the People's Republic of China on the Promotion and Protection of Investments, NZ-Chi., November 22, 1988, http://investmentpolicyhub.unctad.org/Download/TreatyFile/764.

Panama-United States Trade Promotion Agreement, June 28, 2007, http://www.ustr.gov/trade-agreements/free-trade-agreements/panama-tpa/final-text.

Agreement between the Government of the People's Republic of China and the Government of the State of Kuwait for the Promotion and Protection of Investments, Chi.-Kuw., November 23, 1985, http://investmentpolicyhub.unctad.org/Download/TreatyFile/752.

Free Trade Agreement between the Republic of China ("Taiwan") and the Republic of Panama, Tai.-Pan., March 26, 1992, http://www.sice.oas.org/Investment/BITSbyCountry/BITs/PAN_TW_s.pdf.

Agreement between the Government of the People's Republic of China and the Government of the Republic of Singapore on the Promotion and Protection of Investments, Chi.-Sing., November 21, 1985, http://investmentpolicyhub.unctad.org/Download/TreatyFile/776.

Agreement between the Government of the Slovak Republic and the Government of the Republic of Kenya for the Promotion and Reciprocal Protection of Investments, Slo.-Ken., December 14, 2011, http://investmentpolicyhub.unctad.org/Download/TreatyFile/1794.

Agreement on the Reciprocal Promotion and Protection of Investments between the Kingdom of Spain and the Federal Republic of Nigeria, Spa.-Nig., July 9, 2002, http://investmentpolicyhub.unctad.org/Download/TreatyFile/2107.

Agreement between the Kingdom of Spain and the Republic of Venezuela for the Promotion and Protection of Investments, Spa.-Ven., November 2, 1995, http://investmentpolicyhub.unctad.org/Download/TreatyFile/2289.

Agreement between the Swiss Confederation and the Republic of Indonesia Concerning the Reciprocal Protection of Investments, Switz.-Indo., February 6, 1974, http://investmentpolicyhub.unctad.org/Download/TreatyFile/1640.

Agreement between the Swiss Confederation and the United Mexican States on the Promotion and Reciprocal Protection of Investments, Mex.-Swi., July 10, 1995, http://investmentpolicyhub.unctad.org/Download/TreatyFile/2006.

Agreement between the Government of the Kingdom of Thailand and the Government of the Russian Federation on the Promotion and Reciprocal Protection of Investments, Rus.-Tha., October 17, 2002, http://investmentpolicyhub.unctad.org/Download/TreatyFile/2230.

Agreement between the Government of the Republic of Turkey and the Government of the United Republic of Tanzania Concerning the Reciprocal Promotion and Protection of Investments, Turk.-Tanz., March 11, 2011, http://investmentpolicyhub.unctad.org/Download/TreatyFile/2342

Agreement between the Government of the United Arab Emirates and the Government of the Republic of Azerbaijan on the Promotion and Reciprocal Protection of Investments, UAE-Aze., November 20, 2006, http://investmentpolicyhub.unctad.org/Download/TreatyFile/243.

Bilateral Agreement for the Promotion and Protection of Investments between the Government of the United Kingdom of Great Britain & Northern Ireland and the Republic of Colombia, U.K.-Col., March 17, 2010, http://investmentpolicyhub.unctad.org/Download/TreatyFile/805.

United States-Colombia Trade Promotion Agreement, November 22, 2006, available at http://www.ustr.gov/trade-agreements/free-trade-agreements/colombia-fta/final-text.

Treaty between the Government of the United States of America and the Government of the Republic of Nicaragua Concerning the Encouragement and Reciprocal Protection of Investment, USA-Nic., July 1, 1995, http://investmentpolicyhub.unctad.org/Download/TreatyFile/2106.

Treaty between the Government of the United States of America and the Government of the Republic of Rwanda Concerning the Encouragement and Reciprocal Protection of Investment, USA-Rwa., February 19, 2008, http://investmentpolicyhub.unctad.org/Download/TreatyFile/2241.

Treaty between the United States of America and the Oriental Republic of Uruguay Concerning the Encouragement and Reciprocal Protection of Investment, USA-Um., November 5, 2005, http://investmentpolicyhub.unctad.org/Download/TreatyFile/2380.

Treaty between the United States of America and the Republic of Mozambique Concerning the Encouragement and Reciprocal Protection of Investment, USA-Moz., December 1, 1998, http://investmentpolicyhub.unctad.org/Download/TreatyFile/2058.

UNITED NATIONS MATERIALS AND PUBLICATIONS

Charter of Economic Rights & Duties of States, G.A. Res. 3281, U.N. GAOR, 29th Sess., U.N. Doc. A/Res/29/3281 (1974).

Future Government of Palestine, G.A. Res. 181 (II), U.N. Doc. A/RES/181(II) (November 29, 1947).
Integrated Economic Development and Commercial Agreements, G.A. Res. 523, U.N. GAOR, 6th Sess., Supp. No. 20, at 20, U.N. Doc. A/2119 (1952).
International Covenant on Civil and Political Rights, G.A. Res. 2200, U.N. GAOR, 21st Sess., Supp. No. 16, at 56, U.N. Doc. A/6316 (1966).
International Law Commission, Articles on Responsibility of States for Internationally Wrongful Acts, with Commentaries, UN Doc. A/56/10 (2001), http://legal.un.org/ilc/texts/instruments/english/commentaries/9_6_2001.pdf.
Marrakesh Agreement Establishing the World Trade Organization, April 15, 1994, 1867 U.N.T.S. 154.
Permanent Sovereignty over Natural Resources, G.A. Res. 1803, U.N. GAOR, 17th Sess., Supp. No. 17, at 15, U.N. Doc. A/5217 (1962).
Permanent Sovereignty over Natural Resources, G.A. Res. 2158, UN GAOR, 21st Sess., Supp. No. 16, at 29, U.N. Doc. A/6518 (1966).
Permanent Sovereignty over Natural Resources of Developing Countries, G.A. Res. 3016, UN GAOR, 27th Sess., Supp. No. 30, at 48, U.N. Doc. A/8963 (1972).
Permanent Sovereignty over Natural Resources, G.A. Res. 3171, U.N. GAOR, 28th Sess., Supp. No. 30, at 52, U.N. Doc. A/9030 (1973).
Report of the Economic & Social Council, Alternative Approaches and Ways and Means within the United Nations System for Improving the Effective Enjoyment of Human Rights and Fundamental Freedoms: Respect for the right of everyone to own property alone as well as in association with others and its contribution to the economic and social development of Member States, October 27, 1988, U.N. Doc. A/43/739; GAOR, 43rd Sess. (1988).
Right to Exploit Freely Natural Wealth and Resources, G.A. Res. 626, U.N. GAOR, 7th Sess., Supp. No. 20, at 18, U.N. Doc. A/2361 (1952).
United Nations Conference on Environment & Development, Rio de Janeiro, Braz., June 3–14, 1992, Rio Declaration on Environment & Development, U.N. Doc.A/CONF.151/26/Rev. 1 (Vol. I), Annex I (August 12, 1992).
United Nations Conference on Trade & Development, Expropriation: UNCTAD Series on Issues in International Investment Agreements II, U.N. Doc. UNCTAD/DIAE/IA/2011/7, U.N. Sales No. E.12.II.D.7 (2011).
United Nations Conference on Trade & Development, November 6–8, 2002, Geneva, Switz., The Development Dimension of Foreign Direct Investment: Policies to Enhance the Role of FDI, in the National and International Context – Policy Issues to Consider (Note by UNCTAD Secretariat) 1, 3, U.N. Doc. TD/B/COM.2/EM.12/2 (September 23, 2002).

United Nations Conference on Trade & Development, Taking of Property, U.N. Doc. UNCTAD/ITE/IIT/15, U.N. Sales No. E.00.II.D.4 (2000).
United Nations Conference on Trade & Development, World Investment Report 2012, U.N. Doc. UNCTAD/WIR/2012, U.N. Sales No. E.12.II.D.3 (2012).
United Nations GAOR, 62nd Sess., 121st plen. mtg. at 4, U.N. Doc. A/62/PV.121 (September 11, 2008).
Universal Declaration of Human Rights, G.A. Res. 217 (III) A, U.N. Doc. A/RES/217(III) (December 10, 1948).
World Trade Organization, Ministerial Declaration of 14 November 2001 ¶ 22, WT/MIN(01)/DEC/1, 41 I.L.M. 746 (2002).

FOREIGN INVESTMENT PROTECTION STATUTES

Albania Law No. 7764 ("For Foreign Investments") (February 11, 1999), http://www.slas.info/legislazione_albanese/law%20_7764_1993_foreign_investments.php.
Investment Guarantees and Incentives & Its Executive Regulations: Investment Law No. 8 [Egypt] (1997), http://www.egypt-law.com/Investments_law.pdf.
Ethiopia: Proclamation No. 280/2002 Re-Enactment of the Investment Proclamation (July 2, 2002), http://www.wipo.int/edocs/lexdocs/laws/en/et/et013en.pdf.
Act 478: Ghana Investment Promotion Centre Act (August 29, 1994), http://www.intax-info.com/pdf/law_by_country/Ghana/Ghana%20Investment%20Promotion%20Centre%20Act%201994.pdf.
Law of Georgia on the Investment Activity Promotion & Guarantees (November 12, 1999), http://www.wipo.int/wipolex/en/text.jsp?file_id=243072.
Guatemala: Foreign Investment Law (March 3, 1998),
http://www.lexadin.nl/wlg/legis/nofr/oeur/arch/gua/investment_law.pdf
Law of the Republic of Kazakhstan On Investments (January 8, 2003), http://www.kazembassy.org.uk/img/001%20Law%20of%20the%20Republic%20of%20Kazakhstan%20on%20Investments(1).doc.
Law No. 8/2001 Regulating Direct Foreign Capital Investment in the State of Kuwait (April 17, 2001), http://www.kuwaitemb-australia.com/files/direct_investment.pdf.
Lao Law on Investment Promotion (July 8, 2009), http://thailand.nlambassade.org/binaries/content/assets/postenweb/t/thailand/nederlandse-ambassade-in-bangkok/import/producten_en_diensten/handel_en_investeren/zakendoen_in_laos/laotiaanse-investeringswet-2009.

Oman: The Foreign Capital Investment Law for the Organization and Encouragement of Industry (October 16, 1994), http://om.mofcom.gov.cn/table/wgtz.pdf.

Law of the People's Republic of China on Foreign-capital Enterprises (October 31, 2000), http://www.china.org.cn/english/features/investment/36754.htm.

Peru: Legislative Decree No. 662 – Approving the Juridical Stability System for Foreign Investment (September 2, 1991), http://www.lexadin.nl/wlg/legis/nofr/oeur/arch/per/D.L.%2520662tradrev.pdf.

Federal Law on Foreign Investment in the Russian Federation (July 9, 1999), 39 ILM 894 (2000).

Vietnam: Law on Investment (November 29, 2005), http://bit.ly/1uwQYsM (translation by Phillips Fox).

Nicaragua: Overview of Law for the Promotion of Foreign Investment (Law No. 344) (May 24, 2000), http://www.PROnicaragua.org.

OTHER AUTHORITIES

Government of Canada, Statement on Implementation of the North American Free Trade Agreement, CANADA GAZ. PART 1C(1) 147 (January 1, 1994).

Notes of Interpretation of Certain Chapter Eleven Provisions of the NAFTA Free Trade Commission (July 31, 2001), http://sice.oas.org/tpd/nafta/Commission/CH11understanding_e.asp

Office of U.S. Trade Rep., Exec. Office of the President, NAFTA Ch. 11 Trilateral Negotiating Draft Texts.

RESTATEMENT (THIRD) OF FOREIGN RELATIONS LAW § 712 cmt. e (1987).

World Bank, World Development Indicators: GDP growth (annual%), http://data.worldbank.org/indicator/NY.GDP.MKTP.KD.ZG?page=1 (last visited April 8, 2013).

Index

CPSIA information can be obtained at www.ICGtesting.com
Printed in the USA
LVOW04*2114050215

425921LV00002B/4/P

9 781107 081741